Steps in Analyzing a Transaction

STEP 1. Decide which accounts are involved.

STEP 2. Classify the accounts involved (asset, liability, owner's equity, revenue, expense).

STEP 3. Decide if the accounts are increased or decreased.

STEP 4. Write the transaction as a debit to one account (or accounts) and a credit to another account (or accounts).

STEP 5. Check to see if the equation is in balance after the transaction has been recorded.

Journalizing and Posting

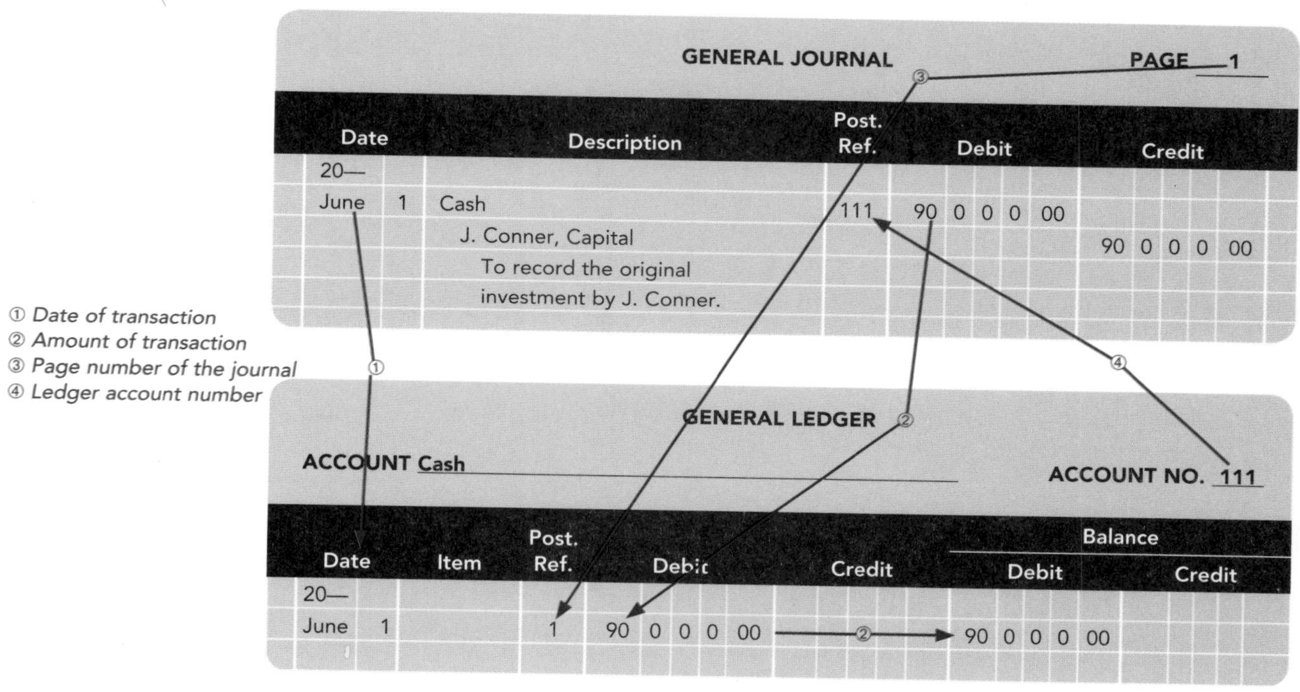

GENERAL JOURNAL — PAGE 1

Date		Description	Post. Ref.	Debit	Credit
20—					
June	1	Cash	111	90 0 0 0 00	
		J. Conner, Capital			90 0 0 0 00
		To record the original			
		investment by J. Conner.			

GENERAL LEDGER

ACCOUNT Cash — ACCOUNT NO. 111

Date		Item	Post. Ref.	Debit	Credit	Balance Debit	Balance Credit
20—							
June	1		1	90 0 0 0 00		90 0 0 0 00	

The Work Sheet

Account Name	Trial Balance Debit	Trial Balance Credit	Adjustments Debit	Adjustments Credit	Adjusted Trial Balance Debit	Adjusted Trial Balance Credit	Income Statement Debit	Income Statement Credit	Balance Sheet Debit	Balance Sheet Credit
	Assets →				Assets →				Assets	
		Liabilities →				Liabilities →				Liabilities
		Capital →				Capital →				Capital
	Drawing →				Drawing →				Drawing	
		Revenue →				Revenue →		Revenue		
	Expenses →				Expenses →		Expenses			

College Accounting

10e

1–12

Douglas J. McQuaig
Wenatchee Valley College, Emeritus

Patricia A. Bille
Highline Community College

Tracie L. Nobles, CPA
Austin Community College

Judy McQuaig Courshon, CPA
Contributing Editor

Australia • Brazil • Japan • Korea • Mexico • Singapore • Spain • United Kingdom • United States

College Accounting, 10th Edition

Douglas J. McQuaig, Patricia A. Bille, Tracie L. Nobles, Judy McQuaig Courshon, CPA

Vice President of Editorial, Business: Jack W. Calhoun

Editor-in-Chief: Rob Dewey

Executive Editor: Sharon Oblinger

Developmental Editor: Leslie Kauffman, LEAP Publishing Services, Inc.

Editorial Assistant: Julie Warwick

Associate Marketing Manager: Laura-Aurora Stopa

Marketing Coordinator: Heather Mooney

Senior Content Project Manager: Tim Bailey

Media Development Director: Rick Lindgren

Media Editor: Bryan England

Senior Frontlist Buyer, Manufacturing: Doug Wilke

Production Service: LEAP Publishing Services, Inc.

Compositor: Knowledgeworks Global Limited

Senior Art Director: Stacy Jenkins Shirley

Cover and Internal Designer: Craig Ramsdell

Cover Image: Alamy

Rights Acquisition Account Manager-Image: Deanna Ettinger

Photo Researcher: Raquel Sousa, Pre-PressPMG

Library of Congress Control Number: 2010921701
ISBN-13: 978-1-4390-3878-9
ISBN-10: 1-4390-3878-3

South-Western Cengage Learning
5191 Natorp Boulevard
Mason, OH 45040
USA

Cengage Learning products are represented in Canada by Nelson Education, Ltd.

For your course and learning solutions, visit **www.cengage.com**
Purchase any of our products at your local college store or at our preferred online store **www.CengageBrain.com**

Printed in the United States of America
1 2 3 4 5 6 7 13 12 11 10

Contents

About the Authors

This book is dedicated to the founding author, Douglas J. McQuaig.

Doug started this project in 1972 so he could give his students the best foundation to develop their accounting skills. He loved to teach and wanted his students to succeed and create new opportunities for themselves. Doug is an inspiration to us all, and his vision to have the best possible book for students to learn basic accounting skills continues to this day.

PATRICIA A. BILLE received her Associates of Arts from Olympic College and her Bachelor of Arts and Master of Education from the University of Washington. She has completed the first year of her doctorate at Capella University in distance learning design. Her accounting experience includes Norris Grain and Phelps Dodge Copper in Chicago as well as nonprofit organizations and small business accounting. Pat teaches accounting at Highline Community College, formerly in the classroom and now solely online. She developed and directed the Business Division's satellite-campus learning center. She coordinated the Accounting Department's cooperative education program and was instrumental in developing and implementing computer labs for the Business Division. Pat had the honor of representing the Accounting Department in South Africa and Namibia as part of Highline's long-time relationship with African educators in these countries. She has been persistent in supporting instructional development as well as serving on tenure review and peer review committees, helping to secure and grow an effective and dedicated diverse faculty. She has been a long-time member of Northwest Accounting Educators and has educational affiliations with the American Accounting Association and the Washington Society of CPAs. These affiliations have allowed her to attend and speak at a variety of state, regional, and national conferences and workshops, sharing her love of teaching and enthusiasm for accounting education. She has authored and co-authored two College Accounting textbooks as well as videos, practice sets, and a variety of accounting ancillaries. Pat and her husband Bruce enjoy traveling and spending time with their two beagles and their two young grandchildren.

TRACIE L. NOBLES, CPA, received her bachelor's and master's degrees in accounting from Texas A&M University. She has served as Department Chair of the Accounting, Business, Computer Information Systems, and Marketing/Management Department at Aims Community College, Greely, Colorado, and is currently an Associate Professor of Accounting at Austin Community College, Austin, Texas. Tracie has consulted on numerous other accounting and computerized accounting books. She has public accounting experience with Deloitte Tax LLP and Sample & Bailey, CPAs. She is a recipient of Aims Community College Excellence in Teaching Award and the NISOD Excellence Award. Tracie is a member of the Teachers of Accounting at Two-Year Colleges, the American Accounting Association, the American Institute of Certified Public Accountants, and the Texas Community College Teachers Association. She is currently serving on the board of directors and as webmaster of Teachers of Accounting at Two-Year Colleges, as member of the American Institute of Certified Public Accountants Pre-certification Education Executive Committee, and as Two-Year College Section Vice-Chair for the American Accounting Association. In addition, she is the current Accounting Section Co-chair for the Texas Community Colleges Teachers Association. In her spare time, Tracie enjoys camping and fishing with her husband, Trey, and spending time with her family and friends.

JUDY MCQUAIG COURSHON, CPA, MT, graduated from Western Washington University with a B.A. in Business Administration and Computer Science and then earned her Master of Taxation degree from the University of Denver. She has been practicing public accounting for the past 34 years with Deloitte Touche LLP, PricewaterhouseCoopers, and a local firm she founded in 1985. She is currently president and founder of Wellspring Group P.S., CPAs, which is an independent accounting firm that provides personalized financial management, consulting, and tax services to individuals and their families. Judy consulted on various editions of this book, most significantly on the ninth and tenth editions. She has taught accounting and uses these accounting skills every day in her accounting profession. Judy is a member of the American Society of CPAs and the Washington Society of CPAs and serves on numerous charitable gift planning and private foundation boards. Judy's interests outside the office include spending time with her family, participating in sports, and enjoying time at Chelan, Washington.

Best Wishes To You and Your Students,
Sharon Oblinger and the South-Western/Cengage Accounting Team

Preface

College Accounting is a course for the times. The practical concepts and skills students take away from the College Accounting course have the power to launch new careers and bright futures. Students of College Accounting have many different goals: to train for accounting careers; to develop skills that lend themselves to technical, managerial, and executive positions; or to go on and earn Accounting or Business degrees. *College Accounting, 10e* was written with the singular purpose of helping students reach these goals. And because achieving goals in today's fast-paced, competitive job market requires more than just basic accounting skills, *College Accounting, 10e* takes the study of accounting to the next level. The authors emphasize the importance of student experience with current accounting technology, business ethics, and correlate problem solving and communication skills to improve student marketability and post-classroom success. *College Accounting, 10e* is revised for optimum currency and relevance to today's modern business.

CONNECTING THE CLASSROOM TO THE REAL WORLD

To emphasize the significance of the College Accounting course as a launching pad to rewarding careers and continued college success, *College Accounting, 10e* has added new features designed to grab students' interest and relate their coursework to a real-world context.

WHY IT MATTERS

SOLID ROCK GYM, Phoenix, Arizona

Individuals and groups of all ages come to Solid Rock Gym for fun and fitness. Part of the appeal of Solid Rock Gym, whose services include several types of indoor rock-climbing experiences, is around-the-clock access with its all-day-and-night passes. Services include individual and group instruction, team development, fitness programs, and bouldering (climbing close to the bottom—no rope or hardware), top-roping (climbing while protected by a rope running through anchors above the intended route), or lead climbing (climbing while protected by a rope clipped to anchors as the climber ascends a route).

In Chapter 1, we learned that a company such as Solid Rock Gym would have a chart of accounts with many different kinds of accounts. Can you imagine the kinds of accounts that Solid Rock Gym might have? In this chapter, you will learn that the chart of accounts can be used as the starting point for recording transactions with T accounts and debits and credits.

Why It Matters

These chapter-opening vignettes introduce the concepts covered in the chapter in the context of a real-world small business.

Accounting in Your Future

This feature focuses on various real careers that your students could have. It emphasizes that solid accounting skills are necessary for employment in these types of jobs.

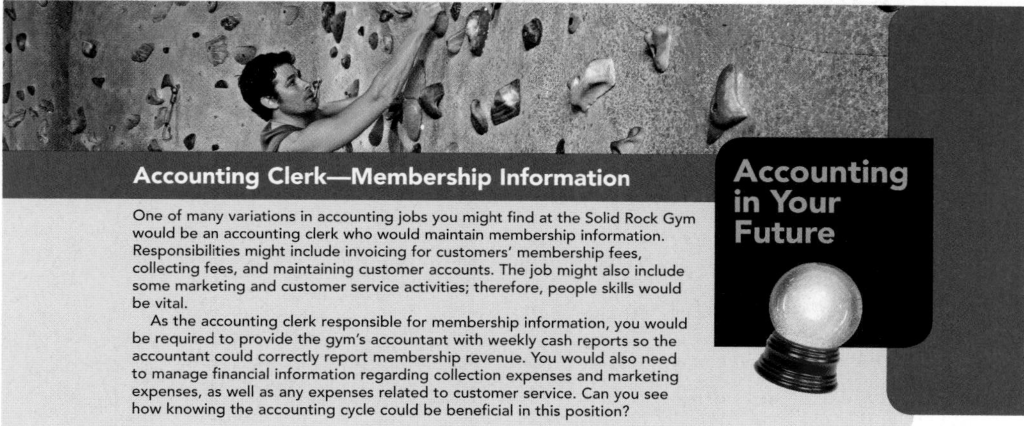
Accounting Clerk—Membership Information
One of many variations in accounting jobs you might find at the Solid Rock Gym would be an accounting clerk who would maintain membership information. Responsibilities might include invoicing for customers' membership fees, collecting fees, and maintaining customer accounts. The job might also include some marketing and customer service activities; therefore, people skills would be vital.
As the accounting clerk responsible for membership information, you would be required to provide the gym's accountant with weekly cash reports so the accountant could correctly report membership revenue. You would also need to manage financial information regarding collection expenses and marketing expenses, as well as any expenses related to customer service. Can you see how knowing the accounting cycle could be beneficial in this position?
Accounting in Your Future

You Make the Call

These boxed features encourage critical thinking and problem solving by placing the student into a realistic accounting dilemma. Each scenario is followed by a detailed, clearly explained solution.

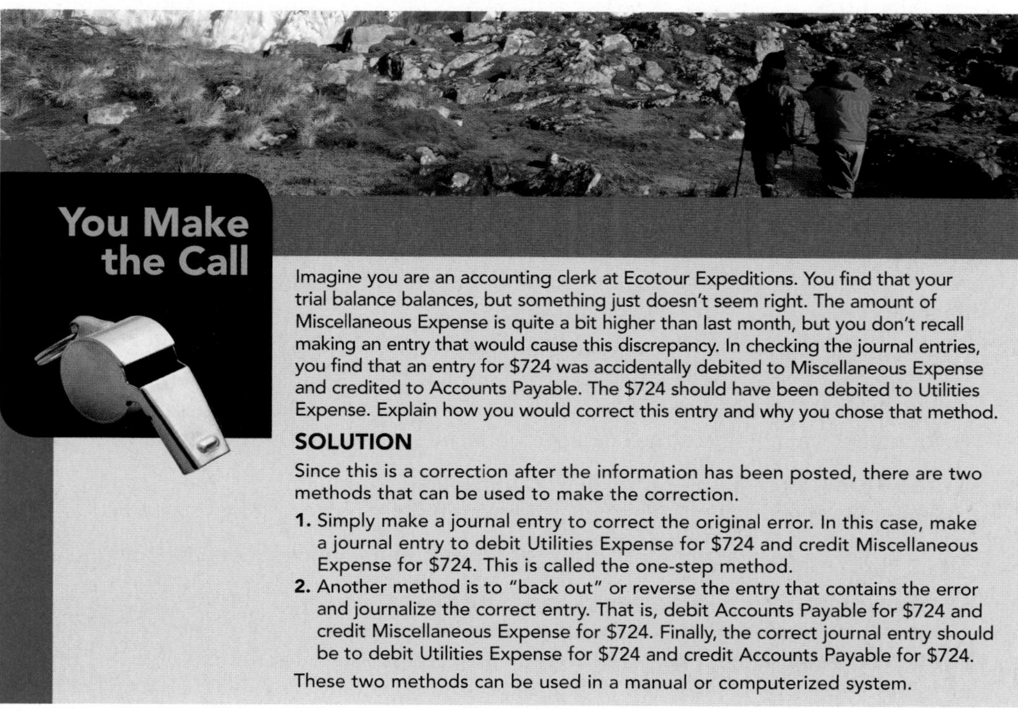
You Make the Call
Imagine you are an accounting clerk at Ecotour Expeditions. You find that your trial balance balances, but something just doesn't seem right. The amount of Miscellaneous Expense is quite a bit higher than last month, but you don't recall making an entry that would cause this discrepancy. In checking the journal entries, you find that an entry for $724 was accidentally debited to Miscellaneous Expense and credited to Accounts Payable. The $724 should have been debited to Utilities Expense. Explain how you would correct this entry and why you chose that method.
SOLUTION
Since this is a correction after the information has been posted, there are two methods that can be used to make the correction.
1. Simply make a journal entry to correct the original error. In this case, make a journal entry to debit Utilities Expense for $724 and credit Miscellaneous Expense for $724. This is called the one-step method.
2. Another method is to "back out" or reverse the entry that contains the error and journalize the correct entry. That is, debit Accounts Payable for $724 and credit Miscellaneous Expense for $724. Finally, the correct journal entry should be to debit Utilities Expense for $724 and credit Accounts Payable for $724.
These two methods can be used in a manual or computerized system.

Small Business Success

Students will find this motivating feature in several chapters throughout the text. Here, the authors emphasize how accounting knowledge and best practices ensure the success of a small business in a competitive environment.

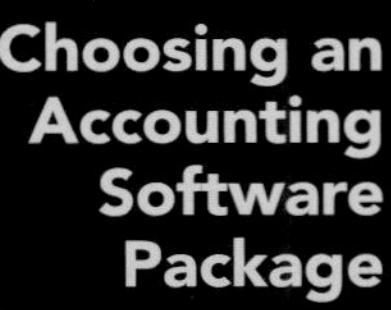

Choosing an accounting software package is an important decision for small businesses. There are two popular software packages designed for small businesses: Peachtree and QuickBooks™. When picking an accounting software package, it's important to consider the needs of the business such as:

- How many individuals will use the software?
- What tools are available?
- Can the software handle inventory?
- Is it easy to use?
- What is the cost of the program?

Both of the accounting software packages listed here will handle most basic small business accounting transactions. Each software program includes general ledger, subsidiary ledgers, and financial statements and also the ability to export data into Excel® or Word®. Most of the differences among the packages relate to appearance and how to enter transactions. For example, QuickBooks uses different "centers" such as vendors, customers, employees, company, and banking. Peachtree uses navigation bars that are located across the top of the screen.

Almost all local colleges offer courses that can teach you how to use either of these accounting software programs. It is highly recommended that all small business owners and accounting majors take at least one course in how to use accounting software, as the knowledge of accounting software is a skill needed for success in the business world.

PROVEN PEDAGOGY

College Accounting, 10e is built on the solid pedagogical foundation created by Douglas McQuaig and appreciated by instructors and students through nine editions. The careful pacing of new topics, consistent review, and thorough and meaningful assignments create the well-balanced presentation that has launched thousands of accounting students into successful careers.

- **Learning Objectives** appear at the beginning of each chapter to help students focus on key learning outcomes. They are then highlighted in the margin alongside the related text discussion. A learning objective number serves as a reference to the objectives in the chapter review, exercises, and problems.
- **Key Terms** appear in blue and are defined in the text and repeated in the glossary at the end of each chapter. In addition, page numbers are included for each glossary term, making it easy for students to refer to a term in the chapter. This consistent emphasis on accounting terminology as the language of business is found throughout the text.
- **Remember** margin notes provide learning hints or summaries, often alerting students to common procedural pitfalls to help them complete their work successfully.
- **FYI** margin notes provide practical tips or information about accounting and business.
- **Color-Coding of Documents and Reports** continues in the tenth edition of *College Accounting*. This tried and true visual system helps students recognize and remember key points. This use of color also helps students understand the flow of accounting data by clearly identifying the different documents and reports used in the accounting cycle. Students begin to visualize how accountants transform data into useful information.
    - Source documents, such as invoices, bank statements, tax forms, and other material that originates with outside sources, are shown in yellow, salmon, and beige.
    - Journals, ledgers, trial balances, work sheets, and other forms and schedules used as part of the internal accounting process are shown in green.
    - Financial statements, including balances sheets, income statements, statements of owner's equity, and statements of cash flows, are shown in blue.

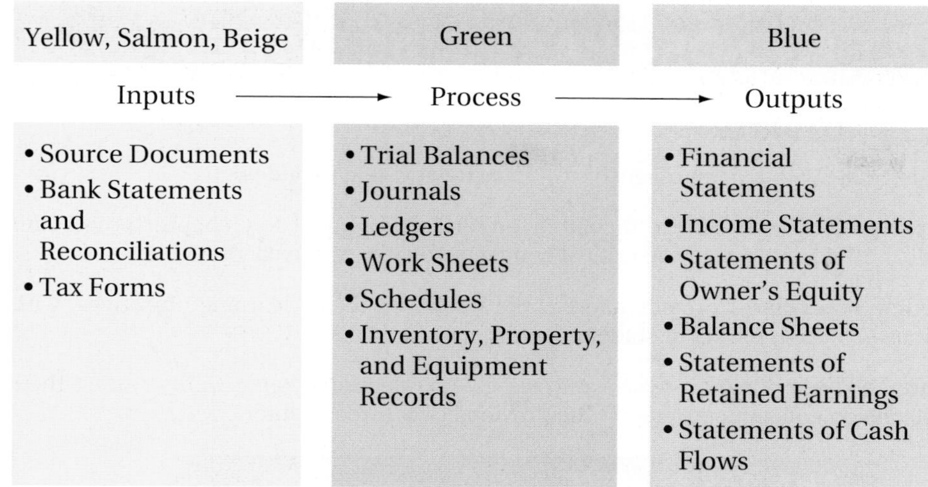

THOROUGHLY REVISED CHAPTERS

College Accounting, 10e has been thoroughly revised for clarity and relevance. Here is a list of the important revisions we have made in this edition based on customer feedback and reviews:

- **Introduction to Accounting** Added discussion of the SEC, IASB, and IFRS in the section on Accounting Standards. Updated the Accounting and Technology section to discuss the need for accounting and computer skills. Expanded the Career Opportunities in Accounting section to include forensic accounting and internal auditors, as well as a new figure showing salary ranges for various accounting positions.

- **Chapter 6: Bank Accounts and Cash Funds** Increased the coverage of internal control of cash.

- **Chapter 7: Employee Earnings and Deductions** Added more discussion and examples of independent contractors in the section on Employer/Employee Relationships. Added discussion of pre-tax deductions in the section on Deductions from Total Earnings. Updated all examples, figures, and end-of-chapter materials for 2009 tax rates.

- **Chapter 8: Employer Taxes, Payments, and Reports** Updated the discussion on electronic tax deposits and the depositing of FUTA taxes. Updated all figures to show 2009 tax forms; updated discussion of those forms accordingly. Added a new section on Payroll Fraud.

- **Chapter 9: Sales and Purchases** Divided this chapter into two main parts: recording sales and purchases transactions in the general journal, and recording sales and purchases transactions in special journals.

- **Chapter 10: Cash Receipts and Cash Payments** Divided this chapter into two main parts: recording cash receipts and cash payments transactions in the general journal, and recording cash receipts and cash payments transactions in special journals. Added a new section on recording cash receipts and cash payments using a computerized accounting system.

ROBUST END-OF-CHAPTER ACTIVITIES

Chapter Review

Each chapter ends with a comprehensive Chapter Review that includes:

- **Learning Objectives** are repeated for reinforcement of key chapter points and include a brief summary of the critical concepts covered in the chapter.
- **Practice Exercises** provide short exercises keyed to the learning objectives, with solutions provided, for aid in student comprehension and study.
- **Before a Test Check** review quizzes give students the opportunity to test their knowledge on concepts covered in the previous two–three chapters.

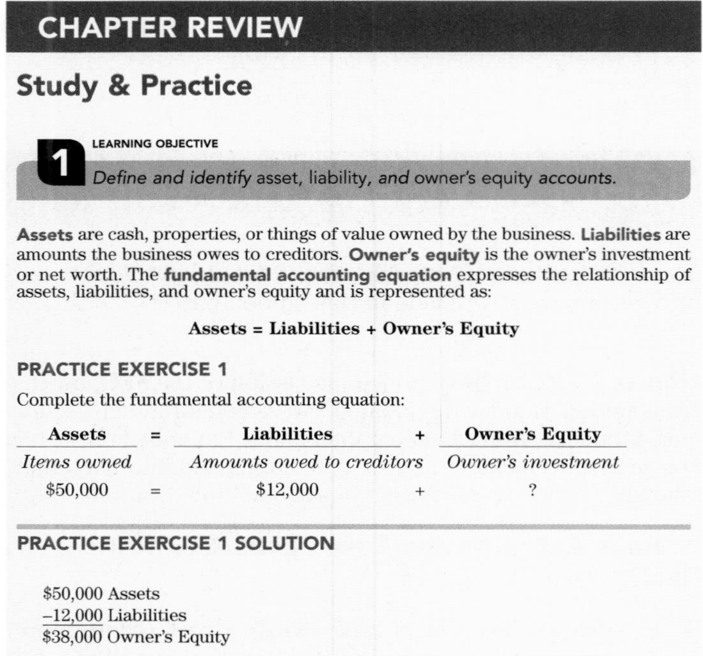
CHAPTER REVIEW

Study & Practice

LEARNING OBJECTIVE 1

Define and identify asset, liability, *and* owner's equity *accounts.*

Assets are cash, properties, or things of value owned by the business. **Liabilities** are amounts the business owes to creditors. **Owner's equity** is the owner's investment or net worth. The **fundamental accounting equation** expresses the relationship of assets, liabilities, and owner's equity and is represented as:

Assets = Liabilities + Owner's Equity

PRACTICE EXERCISE 1

Complete the fundamental accounting equation:

Assets	=	Liabilities	+	Owner's Equity
Items owned		*Amounts owed to creditors*		*Owner's investment*
$50,000	=	$12,000	+	?

PRACTICE EXERCISE 1 SOLUTION

$50,000 Assets
–12,000 Liabilities
$38,000 Owner's Equity

Glossary

Key terms with definitions are provided in an alphabetical glossary at the end of each chapter. Page references are provided for easy student reference.

Chapter Assignments

A variety of study and homework assignments are provided at the end of each chapter and include:

- **Discussion Questions** are found at the end of each chapter and can be used for class discussion or for individual practice.
- **Exercises** are provided in each chapter to help students learn to apply new concepts. Each exercise includes margin references to the appropriate learning objective and Chapter Review practice exercise.
- **Problems** are found in every chapter. For those problems designed for Excel, students have access to Excel templates on the student website. The General Ledger problems can be completed on any general ledger software you package with your students' textbook: Klooster & Allen, QuickBooks, or Peachtree. Each problem is designated with an Excel or GL icon to direct students to the correct application.

1,2,3 LO

PROBLEM 3-3B Following is the chart of accounts of Vance Rehab Clinic.

Assets
111 Cash
113 Accounts Receivable
117 Prepaid Insurance
124 Equipment

Liabilities
221 Accounts Payable

Owner's Equity
311 J. Vance, Capital
312 J. Vance, Drawing

Revenue
411 Professional Fees

Expenses
511 Salary Expense
512 Rent Expense
513 Laboratory Expense
514 Utilities Expense
515 Supplies Expense

Each chapter contains a minimum of four A and four B problems. The A and B problems are parallel in content and level of difficulty. They are arranged in order of difficulty, with Problems 1A and 1B in each chapter being the simplest and the last problem in each series being the most comprehensive. Check Figures appear alongside every A and B problem's instructions in the text.

Accounting Cycle Review Problems and **Comprehensive Review Problems** give students the opportunity to apply accounting procedures to help them understand the process they have just studied in a series of chapters (1–5) and (6–12). Accounting Cycle Review Problems A and B involve the full accounting cycle, one for Surf's Up! and the other for Wind Sailors, both sole proprietorship service businesses. The Comprehensive Review Problem following Chapter 12 involves the full accounting cycle for Fabulous Furnishings, a sole proprietorship merchandising business. Peachtree and QuickBooks data files are provided for these review problems.

- **Activities** at the end of each chapter hone students' problem-solving and communication skills.

ALL ABOUT YOU SPA

This continuous general ledger problem takes students through the accounting cycles of a service and merchandising business in this day spa simulation. It replicates the continuity and follow-through of real accounting operations, putting students in the "driver's seat" of a small business.

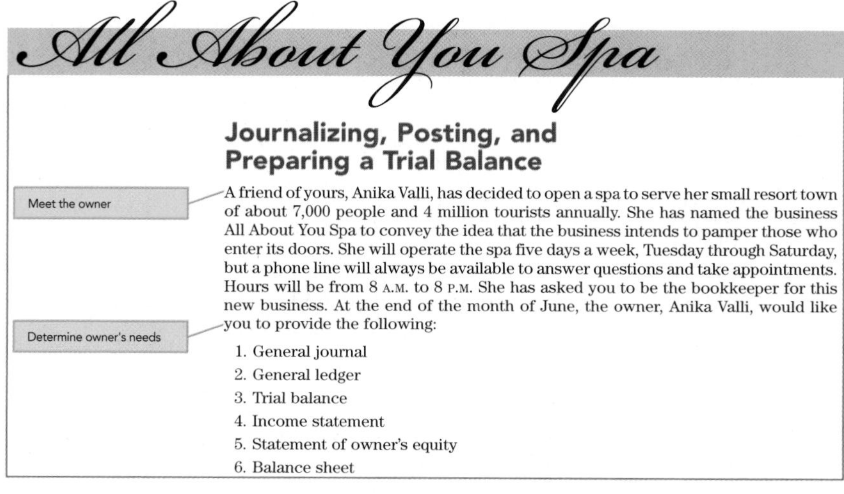
All About You Spa

Journalizing, Posting, and Preparing a Trial Balance

Meet the owner

A friend of yours, Anika Valli, has decided to open a spa to serve her small resort town of about 7,000 people and 4 million tourists annually. She has named the business All About You Spa to convey the idea that the business intends to pamper those who enter its doors. She will operate the spa five days a week, Tuesday through Saturday, but a phone line will always be available to answer questions and take appointments. Hours will be from 8 A.M. to 8 P.M. She has asked you to be the bookkeeper for this new business. At the end of the month of June, the owner, Anika Valli, would like you to provide the following:

Determine owner's needs

1. General journal
2. General ledger
3. Trial balance
4. Income statement
5. Statement of owner's equity
6. Balance sheet

CUSTOMIZABLE CHAPTER AND TECHNOLOGY COVERAGE

Individual teaching styles may call for unique approaches to College Accounting curricula. Through Cengage Learning's ***Make It Yours*** program, you can—simply, quickly, and affordably—create a quality College Accounting text that is tailored to your course.

Consider some of the following customization options:

- Build a College Accounting textbook with the content and chapter progression that *precisely* matches your course syllabus.
- Let us bind-in your syllabus, course notes, study guides, and working papers to create a convenient "all-in-one" solution for your students.
- Prepare your students for the *real world* of accounting by including practice sets or general ledger software and guides from Peachtree, QuickBooks Pro, and Klooster & Allen.
- Peruse our extensive Cover Gallery or create a personalized cover that reflects the uniqueness of your course.

Get Started!

Visit www.cengage.com/custom/makeityours/McQuaig to make your selections and provide details on anything else you would like to include.

INSTRUCTOR SUPPLEMENTS

McQuaig/Bille/Nobles' *College Accounting, 10e* provides you with the robust and flexible teaching supplements you need to launch your course efficiently and successfully semester after semester.

CengageNOW™ for *College Accounting, 10e*

CengageNOW offers you a flexible course management system that allows you to assign, grade, and assess your students' progress quickly and easily. End-of-chapter materials are available online, and your students can test their mastery of new concepts through pre- and post-tests. Students engage with multimedia study tools via personalized study plans that target the areas on which they need to focus. CengageNOW also allows you to identify course content as it relates to ACBSP, AICPA, and AACSB accreditation standards. Ideal for both your traditional lecture-based courses and distance learning, CengageNOW is compatible with both WebCT® and Blackboard®. For more information on CengageNOW, please visit www.cengage.com/tlc.

Instructor's Resource Manual with Solutions

This manual contains valuable resources to assist you with your course. You'll find Teaching Objectives, Key Points, and Lecture Outlines for every chapter as well as solutions for all questions, exercises, problems, and activities in the text.

Test Bank

Revised and verified to ensure accuracy, the test bank includes questions now clearly identified by Learning Objectives, level of difficulty, and AACSB standards to allow you greater guidance in developing assessments and evaluating student progress.

Instructor's Resource CD

This powerful tool contains the content from the instructor's resource manual as well as PowerPoint® lecture slides, solutions manual, solutions to Excel template problems, achievement tests, and ExamView® testing software.

Instructor Companion Site www.cengage.com/accounting/mcquaig

The companion site contains online versions of the instructor's resource manual, solutions manual, PowerPoint® lecture slides, Excel template solutions, and teaching transparency masters.

STUDENT SUPPLEMENTS THAT LAUNCH SUCCESSFUL STUDENTS

Preparing your students for the real world means giving them the confidence to tackle a variety of accounting challenges. Including Working Papers with Study Guides, Practice Sets, and General Ledger Software with your students' course materials will give them the practical skills and employability they deserve.

Working Papers with Study Guide, Chapters 1–12

The Working Papers with Study Guides are provided together in one convenient resource. The Study Guide portion reinforces learning with chapter outlines that are linked to chapter learning objectives. The Working Papers are tailored to the text's end-of-chapter assignments.

New General Ledger Practice Sets

Give your students hands-on practice tackling accounting challenges with our practice sets. These realistic simulations include a CD with both Klooster & Allen and Peachtree software along with the data files needed to complete the practice sets.

- **Trey's Fast Cleaning Service Practice Set** Put your students to work in this dynamic sole-proprietorship simulation. This practice set will thoroughly review the Accounting Cycle and accounting for cash. (Chapters 1–6)
- **Coolspring Furniture Practice Set** This practice set features a sole-proprietorship merchandising business that can be completed using the general journal alone or with special journals. This more advanced practice set also covers the topic of payroll. (Chapters 1–12)

General Ledger Software

Launching your students to the next level requires preparing them to use real-world software and applications. Real general ledger software is available for your course and will provide your students with current job skills.

- **Quickbooks Pro, 2009 and Peachtree, 2009** Clear step-by-step instructions and a continuing problem provide students with hands-on experience completing the accounting cycle with QuickBooks Pro 2009 and Peachtree 2009.
- **Klooster & Allen Integrated Accounting for Windows, 7e** Designed to duplicate the look, feel, and capabilities of commercial software packages, Klooster & Allen General Ledger Software is a best-selling, educational, general ledger package that introduces students to the world of computerized accounting. With an interface that is user-friendly, Klooster & Allen General Ledger Software ensures your students will adapt quickly to computerized accounting systems used in business today.

CengageNOW™ for *College Accounting, 10e*

CengageNOW allows students to test their mastery of new concepts through pre- and post-tests. Students engage with multimedia study tools via personalized study plans that target the areas on which they need to focus. Ideal for both traditional lecture-based courses and distance learning, CengageNOW is compatible with both WebCT® and Blackboard®. For more information on CengageNOW and how it will enhance your students' mastery of accounting, please visit www.cengage.com/tlc.

ACKNOWLEDGMENTS

We sincerely thank the editorial staff of South-Western/Cengage Learning for their continuous support. During the writing of the tenth edition, we consulted many users of the text throughout the country. Their constructive suggestions are reflected in the changes that we have made. Unfortunately, space does not permit mention of all those who have contributed to this volume. Those reviewers and advisors who have contributed to *College Accounting, 10e* through their reviews, focus group attendance, class testing, market feedback, and accuracy checking are as follows:

Ellen Benowitz, *Mercer County Community College*
Daniel Biddlecom, *Erie Community College—North Campus*
Jane C. Bloom, *Palm Beach Community College*
Anna Marie Boulware, *St. Charles Community College*
Gary R. Bower, *Community College of Rhode Island*
Leonor Cabrera, *Canada College*
Dan Carroll, *Miami University—Hamilton Campus*
Susan S. Davis, *Green River Community College*
Larry Dragosavac, *Edison Community College*
Charles D. Edwards, *Miami University—Hamilton Campus*
James Ellis, *Central Oregon Community College*
Steven Ernest, *Baton Rouge Community College*
John Fasler, *Centralia College*
Janice Feingold, *Moorpark College*
Irena Gallio, *Western Nevada College*
Marina Grau, *Houston Community College*
Toni R. Hartley, *Laurel Business Institute*
Scott Hays, *Central Oregon Community College*
Lora Hines, *John A. Logan College*
Patricia H. Holmes, *Des Moines Area Community College—Ankeny Campus*
James Hurst, *National College—Lexington*
Linda Jaeger, *Southeast Community College*
Jennifer Mack, *Eastern Oklahoma State College*
Josephine Mathias, *Mercer County Community College*
Ken Newton, *Cleveland State Community College*
Jon Nitschke, *Montana State University*
Rafael Pulmano, *College of Micronesia—FSM*
Aaron L. Reeves Jr., *St. Louis Community College at Forest Park*
Tom Schaffer, *Spencerian College*
Carolyn M. Seefer, *Diablo Valley College*
Ercan Sinmaz, *Houston Community College*
Linda L. Stevens, *Alamance Community College*
Leslie Thompson, *Hutchinson Community College*
Ski R. VanderLaan, *Delta College*
Richard O. Vogel, *Forrest Junior College*
Linda Whitten, *Skyline College*

As always, we would like to thank our families for their understanding and cooperation. Without their support, this text would never have been written. Pat Bille would like to express continued gratitude to Bruce Bille, Tracy Bille-Newkirk, and James Newkirk, CPA, for their encouragement and assistance; and to the memory of Ryan Bille and Wesley and Adeline Harris for their courage and inspiration. Tracie Nobles would like to thank her husband, Trey, for his love, support, and understanding. She would also like to express gratitude to the world's best cheerleaders: her parents, Kipp and Sylvia Miller; her sister, Michelle Miller; and a great friend, Wendy Wilson. Judy Courshon would like to thank her father, Doug McQuaig, for giving her the opportunity to be a part of this project. Also, for technical support, she would like to thank her brother, John McQuaig, CPA, CMC; her sister, Laurie McQuaig; and William Courshon and Caitlin Courshon for their writing and editing skills.

Douglas J. McQuaig
Patricia A. Bille
Tracie L. Nobles
Judy M. Courshon

Introduction to Accounting

WHY IT MATTERS

WHERE'S YOUR FUTURE?

In this book, you hold one of the keys to your future—knowledge of accounting and business! Throughout the pages of this text, you'll be introduced to individuals, just like yourself, who dreamed about working in, operating, or even owning a business. You will read about businesses such as a small cupcake business that has grown to international fame, an exotic catering business that brings food to far-reaching destinations, and an indoor rock-climbing business that caters to all ages. With all of these companies, one important skill stands out—the need to know and understand accounting!

So where's your future? It is in learning accounting, and this book is designed to help you succeed. As you go through this book, you will learn keys to understanding accounting, business success, and why the study of accounting matters. So let's get started working toward your future!

LEARNING OBJECTIVES

After you have completed this introduction to accounting, you will be able to do the following:

1. *Define accounting.*
2. *Explain the importance of accounting information.*
3. *Describe the various career opportunities in accounting.*
4. *Define ethics.*

ACCOUNTING LANGUAGE

Accountant *(p. 3)*
Accounting *(p. 2)*
Economic unit *(p. 3)*
Ethics *(p. 8)*
Financial Accounting Standards Board (FASB) *(p. 3)*
Generally accepted accounting principles (GAAP) *(p. 3)*
International Accounting Standards Board (IASB) *(p. 3)*
International Financial Reporting Standards (IFRS) *(p. 3)*
Paraprofessional accountants *(p. 6)*
Sarbanes-Oxley Act *(p. 8)*
Securities and Exchange Commission (SEC) *(p. 3)*
Transaction *(p. 2)*

Accounting is often called the language of business because, when confronted with events of a business nature, all people in society—owners, managers, creditors, employees, attorneys, engineers, and so forth—must use accounting terms and concepts to describe these events. Examples of accounting terms are *net*, *gross*, *yield*, *valuation*, *accrued*, *deferred*—the list could go on and on. So it is logical that anyone entering the business world should know enough of its "language" to communicate with others and to understand their communications.

As you acquire knowledge of accounting, you will gain an understanding of the way businesses operate and the reasoning involved in making business decisions. Even if you are not involved directly in accounting activities, you will certainly need to be sufficiently acquainted with the "language" to be able to understand the meaning of accounting information, how it is compiled, how it can be used, and its limitations.

You may be surprised to find that you are already familiar with many accounting terms. Recalling your personal business activities and relating them to your study of accounting will be very helpful to you. For example, when you purchased this textbook, you exchanged cash or a promise to pay cash for the book. As you will see, this exchange is an accounting event. You are going to recognize many activities and terms as you begin your study of accounting.

DEFINITION OF ACCOUNTING

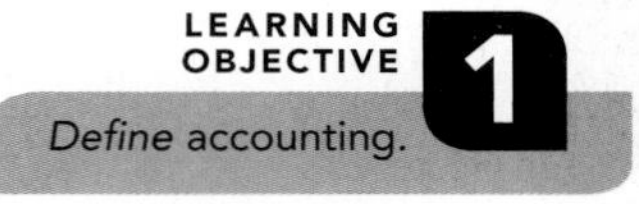

Accounting is the process of analyzing, classifying, recording, summarizing, and interpreting business transactions in financial or monetary terms. A business **transaction** is an event that has a direct effect on the operation of an economic unit, is expressed in terms of money, and is recorded. Examples of business transactions are buying or selling goods, renting a building, paying employees, and buying insurance.

The primary purpose of accounting is to provide the financial information needed for the efficient operation of an economic unit. The term **economic unit** includes not only business enterprises but also not-for-profit entities, such as government bodies, churches and synagogues, clubs, and public charities. Business enterprises or organizations may be called firms or companies.

Another important purpose of accounting is to provide useful information for decision making in the business enterprise. Similar to decisions that you have to make in your daily life, accounting helps businesses make decisions. For example, knowing whether or not there is enough cash to purchase new equipment or whether or not the business is making a profit requires knowledge of accounting.

All business entities require some type of accounting records. An **accountant** is a person who keeps the financial history of the transactions of an economic unit in written or computerized form.

Accounting Standards

Because it is important that all those who receive accounting reports be able to interpret them, a set of rules or guidelines for the accounting process has been developed. These guidelines or rules are known as **generally accepted accounting principles (GAAP)** and are developed by the **Financial Accounting Standards Board (FASB)**.

The FASB was created by the **Securities and Exchange Commission (SEC)** in 1973. The SEC is the agency responsible for regulating public companies that are traded on a U.S. stock exchange. The SEC relies on the FASB to create accounting standards. However, the ultimate responsibility for setting and enforcing accounting standards for public companies lies with the SEC.

With the globalization of the world economy, an international standard-setting board, the **International Accounting Standards Board (IASB)**, has been created to provide guidelines or rules on international accounting standards known as **International Financial Reporting Standards (IFRS)**. The IASB and FASB are currently working to combine GAAP and IFRS into one set of standards.

Bookkeeping and Accounting

There are distinctions between bookkeeping and accounting. The two processes are closely related, but there is no universally accepted line of separation. Generally, bookkeeping involves the systematic recording of business transactions in financial terms. Accounting functions at a higher level. An accountant sets up the system that a bookkeeper uses to record business transactions. An accountant may supervise the work of the bookkeeper and prepare financial statements and tax reports. Although the bookkeeper's work is more routine, it is hard to draw a line where the bookkeeper's work ends and the accountant's begins.

IMPORTANCE OF ACCOUNTING INFORMATION

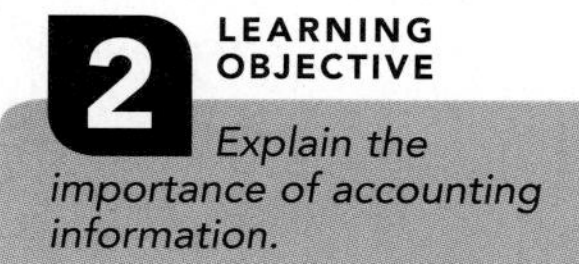

Anyone who aspires to a position of leadership in business or government needs knowledge of accounting. A study of accounting gives a person the necessary background and also gives him or her an understanding of the scope, functions, and policies of an organization. A person may not be doing the accounting work, but he or she will be continually dealing with accounting forms, language, and reports.

Users of Accounting Information

There are many users of accounting information, as outlined below.

Owners

Owners have invested their money or goods in a business organization. They desire information regarding the company's earnings, its prospects for future earnings, and its ability to pay its debts.

Managers

Managers and supervisors have to prepare financial reports, understand accounting data contained in reports and budgets, and express future plans in financial terms. People who have management jobs must know how accounting information is developed in order to evaluate performance in meeting goals.

Creditors

Creditors lend money or extend credit to the company for the purchase of goods and services. The company's creditors include suppliers, banks, and other lending institutions, such as loan companies. Creditors are interested in the firm's ability to pay its debts.

Government Agencies

Taxing authorities verify information submitted by companies concerning a variety of taxes, such as income taxes, sales taxes, and employment taxes. Public utilities, such as electric and gas companies, must provide financial information to regulatory agencies.

Accounting and Technology

Before the invention of computers, all business transactions were recorded by hand. Now computers perform routine recordkeeping operations and prepare financial reports. Computers are used today in all types of businesses, both large and small. All accounting positions now require that workers use computers, have knowledge of word processing and spreadsheet software, and possess an understanding of accounting software such as QuickBooks® or Peachtree®.

Even though virtually all businesses now use computers to do their accounting, the nature of accounting is the same. The computer is a powerful tool of the accountant. However, as a tool, the computer is only as useful as the ability of and understanding of accounting by the operator. The operator must be skilled to key the correct information into the computer program; otherwise, as the saying goes, "garbage in, garbage out."

CAREER OPPORTUNITIES IN ACCOUNTING

LEARNING OBJECTIVE 3

Describe the various career opportunities in accounting.

There are a number of career opportunities in accounting in every industry. To find job opportunities in accounting, all you need to do is browse Internet job sites or read the newspapers' classified advertisements. Although the jobs listed in these ads require varying amounts of education and experience, many of them are for positions as accounting and auditing clerks, general bookkeepers, or accountants. The Bureau of Labor Statistics *Occupational Outlook Handbook* estimates that employment is expected to grow faster than average for accountants, bookkeepers, clerks, and auditors. The number of accounting-related jobs is expected to grow by 12 percent between 2006 and 2016. The requirements and duties of these positions are discussed next. Figure 1 provides a listing of the average salaries for some of these various positions.

FIGURE 1
Salary ranges for various accounting positions

TITLE	SALARY RANGE
ACCOUNTING CLERK	\$27,250–\$36,000
– Accounts receivable/Accounts payable clerk	\$29,750–\$39,250[a]
	\$29,250–\$38,000[b]
	\$27,250–\$35,500[c]
– Inventory clerk	\$29,250–\$36,500[a]
	\$27,750–\$35,250[b]
– Payroll clerk	\$30,500–\$39,000[a]
	\$29,750–\$38,250[b]
	\$27,750–\$34,750[c]
BOOKKEEPER	\$31,750–\$40,750
PARAPROFESSIONAL ACCOUNTANT	\$37,000–\$51,000
ACCOUNTANT	
– Chief financial officer	\$94,250–\$384,000
– Controller	\$66,000–\$167,750
– Financial analyst (entry level)	\$39,500–\$49,500[a]
	\$38,000–\$45,500[b]
	\$35,000–\$42,750[c]
– Forensic accountant	\$58,500–\$92,750
– General accountant (entry level)	\$38,000–\$46,250[a]
	\$35,750–\$43,000[b]
	\$33,500–\$40,000[c]
– Internal auditor (entry level)	\$43,250–\$52,750[a]
	\$41,500–\$51,500[b]

[a]Large companies
[b]Midsize companies
[c]Small companies

Source: Robert Half International, *2009 Salary Guide—Accounting & Finance*, © 2009 Robert Half International.

Accounting Clerk/Technician

An accounting clerk/technician performs routine recording of financial information. The duties of accounting clerks vary with the size of the company. In small businesses, accounting clerks handle most of the recordkeeping functions. In large companies, clerks specialize in one part of the accounting system, such as payroll, accounts receivable, accounts payable, cash, inventory, or purchases. The minimum requirement for most accounting clerk positions is usually one term or semester of an accounting course. Experience in a related job and working in an office environment is also recommended, as is knowledge of word processing and spreadsheet software. Accounting clerks/technicians should also be detail-oriented and have good communication skills.

Auditing Clerk

Auditing clerks are an organization's financial recordkeepers. An auditing clerk's primary responsibility involves verifying transactions and records posted by other employees. Other responsibilities include maintaining and updating individual or groups of accounting records, checking documents to ensure they are mathematically correct, and correcting or noting errors for accountants or other workers to adjust. Most auditing clerks are required to have a high school degree at a minimum, while an associate's degree in business or accounting is required for some positions. Knowledge of word processing and spreadsheet software and experience in a related job are also recommended.

General Bookkeeper

Many small- and medium-sized companies employ one person to oversee their bookkeeping operations. This person is called a general or full-charge bookkeeper. The general bookkeeper supervises the work of accounting clerks. Requirements for this job vary with the size of the company and the complexity of the accounting system. The minimum requirement for most general bookkeeper jobs is one or two years of accounting education as well as experience as an accounting clerk. Many companies require a certificate in business or accounting and experience working with computers and accounting software.

Paraprofessional Accountant

To bridge a gap between the general bookkeeper and the professional accountant, many firms are hiring **paraprofessional accountants**. They are able to manage the duties of the general bookkeeper as well as many of the duties of a professional accountant under that accountant's supervision. Qualifications generally include a two-year degree in accounting and knowledge of accounting software, as well as appropriate prior experience.

Certifications Available

Several organizations offer certification for accounting and auditing clerks, bookkeepers, and paraprofessional accountants. The Certified Bookkeeper (CB) designation is awarded by the American Institute of Professional Bookkeepers (www.aipb.org) and certifies that an individual has the knowledge needed to carry out bookkeeping functions. For certification, candidates must have at least two years of bookkeeping experience, pass an examination, and adhere to a code of ethics. The Accreditation Council for Accountancy and Taxation (www.acatcredentials.org) offers an Accredited Business Accountant® (ABA) certification designed for individuals who work with small- to medium-sized businesses in the areas of financial accounting, tax, and ethics. For accreditation, candidates must pass a one-day, seven-hour exam.

Accountant

The term *accountant* describes a fairly broad range of jobs. The accountant may design and manage the entire accounting system for a business. The accountant may also prepare the financial statements and tax returns and perform audits. Many accountants enter the field with a four-year college degree in accounting; however, it is not unusual for accountants to start at entry-level positions and work their way up to management positions. Although accountants are employed in every kind of economic unit, they are classified into one of four categories: public accounting, managerial or private accounting, government and not-for-profit accounting, and internal auditing. We'll briefly look at these categories.

Public Accounting

Most public accountants are Certified Public Accountants (CPAs). To become a CPA, a person must have a bachelor's degree, complete 150 hours of college coursework (in most states), pass a rigorous examination, and complete a work-experience requirement. CPAs design accounting systems, prepare tax returns, provide financial advice about business operations, and audit financial statements. Many CPAs work for a public accounting firm such as Deloitte LLP or own their own small business. CPAs can also be employed by corporations in the private sector in finance positions such as chief financial officers (CFOs), controllers, or financial analysts.

A relatively new and upcoming career opportunity in public accounting is forensic accounting. Forensic accountants specialize in investigating business crimes such as fraud, embezzlement, and money laundering. Accountants in this area of

CHUCK SAVAGE/SURF/CORBIS

Accountants are employed in every kind of economic unit. Many start in entry-level positions and work their way up to management.

specialty require knowledge of accounting, law, and finance and work closely with law enforcement personnel. Individuals wishing to specialize in forensic accounting can apply for a Certified Fraud Examiner (CFE) certificate (www.acfe.com). Requirements for a CFE certificate include a minimum of a bachelor's degree and two years of professional experience in a field either directly or indirectly related to the detection or deterrence of fraud.

If you are interested in finding out more about becoming a CPA or other public accounting jobs, the American Institute of Certified Public Accountants (www.aicpa.org) has an excellent Web site that describes accounting degrees and job opportunities called Start Here, Go Places (www.startheregoplaces.com). The site includes study information, simulation games, scholarship and internship listings, profiles of successful CPAs, and career opportunities.

Managerial or Private Accounting

Most people who are accountants are employed by private business organizations. These accountants (not necessarily CPAs) manage the accounting system, prepare budgets, determine costs of products, and provide financial information for managers and owners. Accountants have many opportunities to advance into top management positions. The Certified Management Accountant (CMA) exam (www.imanet.org) has become an important partner to the CPA credentials.

Government and Not-for-Profit Accounting

Not-for-profit accounting is used for government agencies, hospitals, churches and synagogues, and schools. Accountants for these organizations prepare budgets and maintain records of revenues and expenses. Local, state, and federal government bodies employ vast numbers of people in accounting positions. For example, a top federal government employer in the area of accounting is the Internal Revenue Service (IRS).

Internal Auditing

Due to recent accounting regulations, the demand for internal auditors has increased. Internal auditors verify the effectiveness of an organization's accounting system and controls. They examine and ensure that the company's financial information is accurate and protected. Internal auditors also ensure that organizations are following government regulations and corporate policies.

ETHICS

LEARNING OBJECTIVE 4
Define ethics.

Ethics is a philosophy or code or system of morality—that is, how we conduct ourselves from day to day in a variety of situations requiring a decision, usually of a right or wrong nature. Ethics, as it relates to accounting, is the way accountants and other keepers of financial information conduct the business of accounting according to laws of the state and their own personal code or system of morality.

There are many books and textbooks available on ethics, as well as classes on the subject. All organizations provide a code of ethical conduct for their members. With mounting evidence of questionable ethics in business reported in print and portrayed through the visual media, it is apparent that understanding and learning about ethics is an important part of accounting.

Related to ethics, a recent change to the accounting profession is the **Sarbanes-Oxley Act**, commonly referred to as SOX. SOX was created as a response to various large-scale corporate accounting frauds such as Enron and WorldCom. The Sarbanes-Oxley Act established a wide range of new rules related to the audit environment and internal controls.

CHAPTER REVIEW

Study & Practice

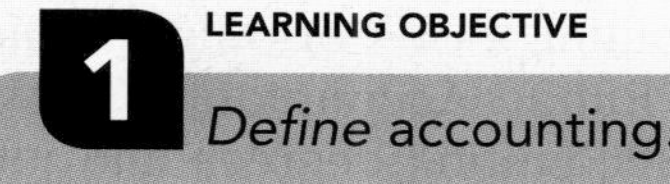

LEARNING OBJECTIVE 1
Define accounting.

Accounting is the process of analyzing, classifying, recording, summarizing, and interpreting business **transactions** in financial or monetary terms. It is also an information system and the language of business.

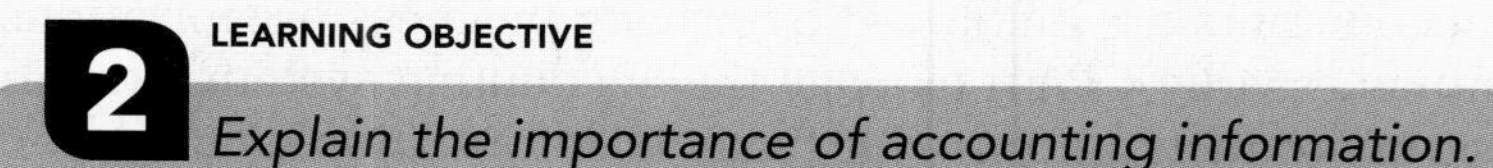

LEARNING OBJECTIVE 2
Explain the importance of accounting information.

A study of accounting gives a person the necessary background to understand the scope, functions, and policies of an organization.

3 LEARNING OBJECTIVE

Describe the various career opportunities in accounting.

Accounting and auditing clerks, bookkeepers, **paraprofessional accountants**, and **accountants** will find employment opportunities in several areas—in the public sector, the private sector, or not-for-profit organizations.

LEARNING OBJECTIVE

Define ethics.

Ethics is a code of morality—that is, how we respond to a variety of situations on a daily basis that require a decision, usually of a right or wrong nature. Ethics, as it relates to accounting, is the way accountants and other keepers of financial information conduct themselves according to laws of the state and their own personal code or system of morality.

Glossary

Accountant A person who keeps the financial history of the transactions of an economic unit in written form. *(p. 3)*

Accounting The process of analyzing, classifying, recording, summarizing, and interpreting business transactions in financial or monetary terms. *(p. 2)*

Economic unit Includes both business enterprises and not-for-profit entities. *(p. 3)*

Ethics A philosophy or code or system of morality—that is, how we conduct ourselves from day to day in a variety of situations requiring a decision, usually of a right or wrong nature. *(p. 8)*

Financial Accounting Standards Board (FASB) The organization created in 1973 by the SEC that creates GAAP. *(p. 3)*

Generally accepted accounting principles (GAAP) The rules or guidelines used for carrying out the accounting process. *(p. 3)*

International Accounting Standards Board (IASB) The international organization that provides standards or rules for international financial reporting. *(p. 3)*

International Financial Reporting Standards (IFRS) The rules or guidelines that guide international financial reporting. *(p. 3)*

Paraprofessional accountants Persons who are qualified in accounting to assume the duties of a general bookkeeper as well as some of those of a professional accountant under that accountant's supervision. *(p. 6)*

Sarbanes-Oxley Act A U.S. federal law enacted as a response to a number of major corporate and accounting scandals that establishes a wide range of rules related to the audit environment and internal controls. *(p. 8)*

Securities and Exchange Commission (SEC) The agency responsible for regulating public companies traded on a U.S. stock exchange. *(p. 3)*

Transaction An event directly affecting an economic entity that can be expressed in terms of money and that must be recorded in the accounting records. *(p. 2)*

PART 1

1 Asset, Liability, Owner's Equity, Revenue, and Expense Accounts

WHY IT MATTERS

EXTREME EVENTS CATERING, Memphis, Tennessee

Extreme Events Catering goes way beyond the day-to-day events of delivering food to a customer. Extreme Events Catering caters to clientele who prefer either food with unusual tastes or unusual dining locations.

While Extreme Events Catering is unusual in its mission, it must still account for changes in assets, liabilities, owner's equity, revenues, and expenses. Each financial change in business requires an entry in the company's accounting records.

Extreme Events Catering, like other businesses, has assets—for example, equipment, serving pieces, and vehicles. To buy these assets, the company either paid cash or created a liability by promising to pay for them later. The company also has expenses such as wages and rent. These are some of the costs of doing business as the company earns revenue or income by preparing and serving delicious dishes to special diners in unusual venues.

LEARNING OBJECTIVES

After you have completed this chapter, you will be able to do the following:

1. *Define and identify* asset, liability, *and* owner's equity *accounts.*
2. *Record a group of business transactions, in column form, involving changes in assets, liabilities, and owner's equity.*
3. *Define and identify* revenue *and* expense *accounts.*
4. *Record a group of business transactions, in column form, involving all five elements of the fundamental accounting equation.*

ACCOUNTING LANGUAGE

Accounts *(p. 14)*
Accounts Payable *(p. 15)*
Accounts Receivable *(p. 23)*
Assets *(p. 11)*
Business entity *(p. 11)*
Capital *(p. 11)*
Chart of accounts *(p. 19)*
Creditor *(p. 12)*
Double-entry accounting *(p. 17)*
Equity *(p. 11)*
Expenses *(p. 18)*
Fair market value *(p. 16)*
Fundamental accounting equation *(p. 12)*
Liabilities *(p. 12)*
Owner's equity *(p. 11)*
Revenues *(p. 18)*
Separate entity concept *(p. 14)*
Sole proprietorship *(p. 14)*
Withdrawal *(p. 26)*

As we stated in the Introduction, accounting is the process of analyzing, classifying, recording, summarizing, and interpreting business transactions. We now introduce the analyzing, classifying, and recording steps in the accounting process.

ASSETS, LIABILITIES, AND OWNER'S EQUITY

The Fundamental Accounting Equation

Assets are properties or things of value, such as cash, equipment, copyrights, buildings, and land, owned and controlled by an economic unit or business entity. By the term **business entity**, we mean that the business is an economic unit in itself, and the assets or properties of the business are completely separate from the owner's personal assets. However, the owner has a claim on the assets of the business and generally has a responsibility for its debts. **The owner's right, claim, or financial interest is expressed by the word equity in the business.** Another term that could be used is **capital**. Whenever you see the term **owner's equity**, it means the owner's right to or investment in the business.

1 LEARNING OBJECTIVE *Define and identify* asset, liability, *and* owner's equity *accounts.*

FYI Other terms for equity are *investment, net worth,* or *proprietorship.*

Assets	=	**Owner's Equity**
Properties or things of value owned by the business		Owner's *right* to or investment in the business

Suppose the total value of the assets is $80,000 and the business entity does not owe any amount against the assets. Then,

Assets	=	Owner's Equity
$80,000	=	$80,000

Or suppose the assets consist of a truck that costs $35,000. The owner has invested $12,000 for the truck, and the business entity has borrowed the remainder from the bank, which is a **creditor** (one to whom money is owed). This business transaction or event can be shown as follows:

Assets	=	Liabilities	+	Owner's Equity
Items owned		*Amounts owed to creditors*		*Owner's investment*
$35,000	=	$23,000	+	$12,000

We have now introduced a new classification, **liabilities**, which represent debts. They are the amounts that the business entity owes its creditors. The debts may originate because the business bought goods or services on credit, borrowed money, or otherwise created an obligation to pay. The creditors' claims to the assets have priority over the claims of the owner.

An equation expressing the relationship of assets, liabilities, and owner's equity is called the **fundamental accounting equation**:

Assets = Liabilities + Owner's Equity

We'll deal with this equation constantly from now on. If we know two parts of this equation, we can determine the third. Let's look at some examples.

Determine Assets

Millie Adair has $17,000 invested in her travel agency, and the agency owes creditors $5,000; that is, the agency has liabilities of $5,000. Then,

Assets	=	Liabilities	+	Owner's Equity
?	=	$5,000	+	$17,000

We can find the amount of the business's assets by adding the liabilities and the owner's equity:

$ 5,000 Liabilities
+17,000 Owner's Equity
$22,000 Assets

The completed equation now reads

Assets	=	Liabilities	+	Owner's Equity
$22,000	=	$5,000	+	$17,000

Determine Owner's Equity

Larry Roland owns a car repair shop. His business has assets of $40,000, and it owes creditors $16,000; that is, it has liabilities of $16,000. Then,

Assets	=	Liabilities	+	Owner's Equity
$40,000	=	$16,000	+	?

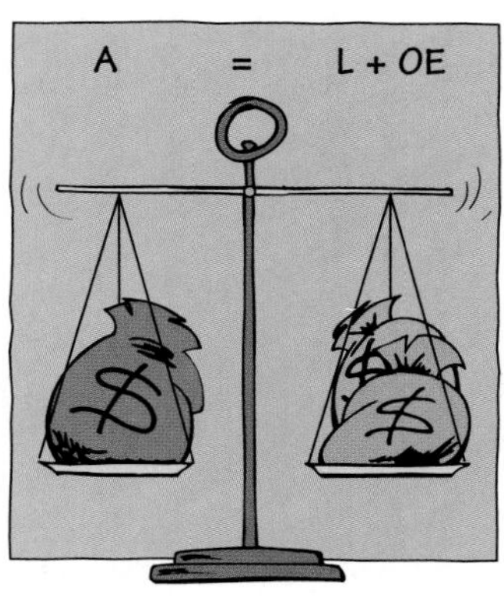

Like a balancing scale, the equation stays in balance by making equal or offsetting increases and decreases to one side or both sides.

We find the owner's equity by subtracting the liabilities from the assets:

$40,000 Assets
–16,000 Liabilities
$24,000 Owner's Equity

The completed equation now reads

Assets	=	Liabilities	+	Owner's Equity
$40,000	=	$16,000	+	$24,000

Determine Liabilities

Theo Viero's insurance agency has assets of $86,000; his investment (his equity) amounts to $46,000. Then,

Assets	=	Liabilities	+	Owner's Equity
$86,000	=	?	+	$46,000

To find the firm's total liabilities, we subtract the equity from the assets:

$86,000 Assets
–46,000 Owner's Equity
$40,000 Liabilities

The completed equation reads

Assets	=	Liabilities	+	Owner's Equity
$86,000	=	$40,000	+	$46,000

Recording Business Transactions

2 LEARNING OBJECTIVE

Record a group of business transactions, in column form, involving changes in assets, liabilities, and owner's equity.

As you know, business transactions are events that have a direct effect on the operations of an economic unit or enterprise and are expressed in terms of money. Each business transaction must be recorded in the accounting records. As business transactions are recorded, the amounts listed under the headings Assets, Liabilities, and Owner's Equity change. However, **the total of one side of the fundamental**

accounting equation must always equal the total of the other side. The categories under these three main headings are called **accounts**.

Let's look at a group of business transactions. These transactions are typical of those seen in a service or professional type of business. In these transactions, let's assume that J. Conner establishes her own business and calls it Conner's Whitewater Adventures. Conner's Whitewater Adventures is a **sole proprietorship**, or a one-owner business.

Transaction (a). Conner deposited $90,000 in a bank account in the name of the business. Conner deposits $90,000 cash in a separate bank account in the name of Conner's Whitewater Adventures. This separate bank account will help Conner keep her business investment separate from her personal funds. This is an example of the **separate entity concept**, according to which a business is treated as a separate economic or accounting entity. (See Figure 1.) The business is independent or stands by itself; it is separate from its owners, creditors, and customers.

FIGURE 1
Separate entity concept

The separate entity concept means that a business is separated from its owners, creditors, and customers. In other words, the assets, liabilities, and capital of a business entity are maintained separately from the individuals who may own it, be owed, or owe it.

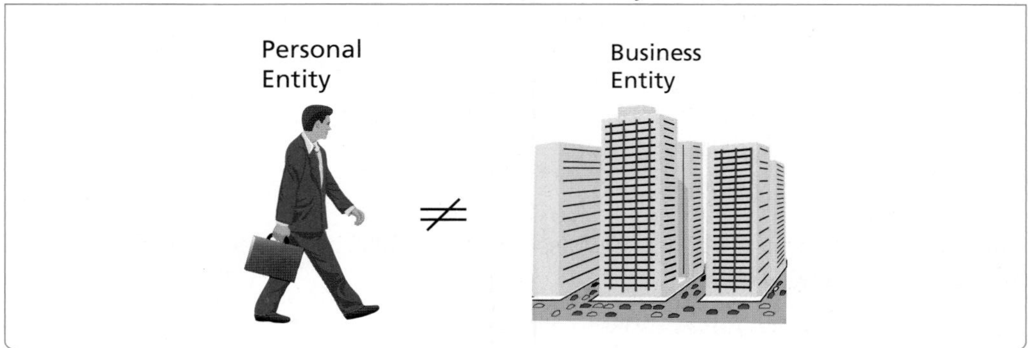

The Cash account consists of bank deposits and money on hand. The business now has $90,000 more in cash than before, and Conner's investment has also increased by $90,000. The account denoted by the owner's name followed by the word *Capital* records the amount of the owner's investment, or equity, in the business. The effect of this transaction on the fundamental accounting equation is as follows:

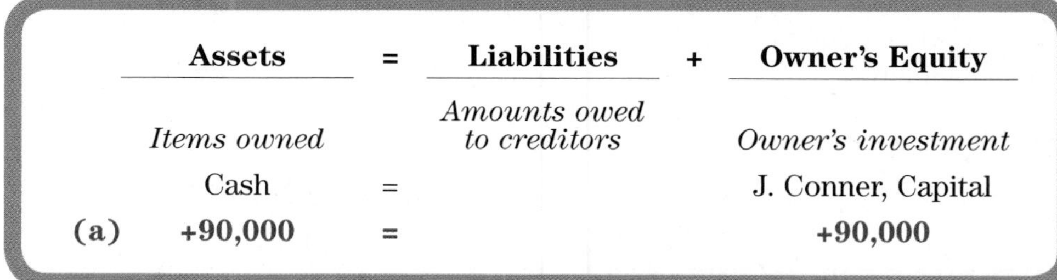

	Assets	=	Liabilities	+	Owner's Equity
	Items owned		*Amounts owed to creditors*		*Owner's investment*
	Cash	=			J. Conner, Capital
(a)	+90,000	=			+90,000

Besides cash, an investment may be in the form of goods, such as equipment. The word *Capital* used under Owner's Equity therefore does not always mean that cash was invested.

Transaction (b). Company bought equipment, paying cash, $38,000. Conner's first task is to get her company ready for business; to do that, she needs the proper equipment. Accordingly, Conner buys equipment costing $38,000 and pays cash. **It is important to note at this point that Conner does not invest any new money. She simply exchanges part of the business's cash for equipment.** Because equipment is a new type of property for the firm, a new account, Equipment, is created. Equipment is included under Assets. As a result of this transaction, the accounting equation changes:

	Assets			=	Liabilities	+	Owner's Equity
	Items owned				*Amounts owed to creditors*		*Owner's investment*
	Cash	+	Equipment	=			J. Conner, Capital
Initial Investment	90,000			=			90,000
(b)	**−38,000**	**+**	**38,000**				
New balances	52,000	+	38,000	=			90,000
	90,000				90,000		

Transaction (c). Company bought equipment on account from Signal Products, $4,320. Conner's Whitewater Adventures buys equipment costing $4,320 on credit from Signal Products.

The Equipment account shows an increase because the business owns $4,320 more in equipment. The term "on credit" means that Conner's Whitewater Adventures does not pay cash for the equipment but instead will owe the money to Signal Products to be paid in the future. This causes an increase in liabilities because the business now owes $4,320. The liability account **Accounts Payable** is used for short-term liabilities or charge accounts, usually due within 30 days. Because Conner's Whitewater Adventures owes money to Signal Products, Signal Products is called a creditor of Conner's Whitewater Adventures. (The company to which money is owed is called a creditor.) There is now a total of $94,320 on each side of the equals sign.

	Assets			=	Liabilities	+	Owner's Equity
	Items owned				*Amounts owed to creditors*		*Owner's investment*
	Cash	+	Equipment	=	Accounts Payable	+	J. Conner, Capital
Previous balances	52,000	+	38,000	=			90,000
(c)			**+4,320**		**+4,320**		
New balances	52,000	+	42,320	=	4,320	+	90,000
	94,320				94,320		

Observe that the recording of each transaction must yield an equation that is in balance. For example, transaction (b) resulted in a minus $38,000 and a plus $38,000 *on the same side*, with nothing recorded on the other side, and transaction (c) resulted in a $4,320 increase to both sides of the equation. It does not matter whether you change one side or both sides. **The important point is that whenever a transaction is properly recorded, the accounting equation remains in balance.**

Transaction (d). Company paid Signal Products, a creditor, on account, $2,000. Conner's Whitewater Adventures pays $2,000 to Signal Products, to be applied against the firm's liability of $4,320.

With this payment, cash is being reduced. At the same time, the firm *owes* less than before, so the transaction should be recorded as a reduction in liabilities.

	Assets			=	**Liabilities**	+	**Owner's Equity**
	Items owned				*Amounts owed to creditors*		*Owner's investment*
	Cash	+	Equipment	=	Accounts Payable	+	J. Conner, Capital
Previous balances	52,000	+	42,320	=	4,320	+	90,000
(d)	**−2,000**				**−2,000**		
New balances	50,000	+	42,320	=	2,320	+	90,000
	92,320				92,320		

Transaction (e). Owner invested equipment in the business. Conner invested her own computer equipment, having a **fair market value** of $5,200 in Conner's Whitewater Adventures. **Fair market value is the present worth of an asset.** It is the amount that would be received if the asset were sold on the open market. Additional investments may be in the form of equipment, cash, tools, or real estate.

	Assets			=	**Liabilities**	+	**Owner's Equity**
	Items owned				*Amounts owed to creditors*		*Owner's investment*
	Cash	+	Equipment	=	Accounts Payable	+	J. Conner, Capital
Previous balances	50,000	+	42,320	=	2,320	+	90,000
(e)			**+5,200**				**+5,200**
New balances	50,000	+	47,520	=	2,320	+	95,200
	97,520				97,520		

Accounting, as we said before, is the process of analyzing, classifying, recording, summarizing, and interpreting business transactions in terms of money. Look at the transactions thus far for Conner's Whitewater Adventures and see if you understand that we have gone through certain steps (in the form of questions). Let's illustrate these steps using transaction (e), owner invested equipment in the business.

STEP 1. What accounts are involved? Equipment and J. Conner, Capital are involved.

STEP 2. What are the classifications of the accounts involved? Equipment is an asset, and J. Conner, Capital is an owner's equity account.

STEP 3. Are the accounts increased or decreased? Equipment is increased because Conner's Whitewater Adventures has more equipment than before. J. Conner, Capital is increased because Conner has a greater investment than before.

STEP 4. Is the equation in balance after the transaction has been recorded? Yes.

We will stress this step-by-step process throughout the text. This example serves as an introduction to **double-entry accounting**. The "double" entry method is demonstrated by the fact that each transaction must be recorded in at least two accounts, keeping the accounting equation in balance.

Summary of Transactions

Let's summarize the business transactions of Conner's Whitewater Adventures in column form, identifying each transaction by a letter of the alphabet. To test your understanding of the recording procedure, describe the nature of the transactions that have taken place.

	Assets			=	**Liabilities**	+	**Owner's Equity**
	Items owned				*Amounts owed to creditors*		*Owner's investment*
	Cash	+	Equipment	=	Accounts Payable	+	J. Conner, Capital
Transaction (a)	+90,000						+90,000
Transaction (b)	−38,000		+38,000				
Balance	52,000	+	38,000	=			90,000
Transaction (c)			+4,320		+4,320		
Balance	52,000	+	42,320	=	4,320	+	90,000
Transaction (d)	−2,000				−2,000		
Balance	50,000	+	42,320	=	2,320	+	90,000
Transaction (e)			+5,200				+5,200
Balance	50,000	+	47,520	=	2,320	+	95,200
	97,520				97,520		

The following observations apply to all types of business transactions:

1. Every transaction is recorded as an increase and/or decrease in two or more accounts.
2. One side of the equation is always equal to the other side of the equation.

In this chapter we are using a column arrangement as a practical device to show how transactions are recorded. This arrangement is useful for showing increases and decreases in various accounts as a result of the transactions. We also show new balances after recording each transaction.

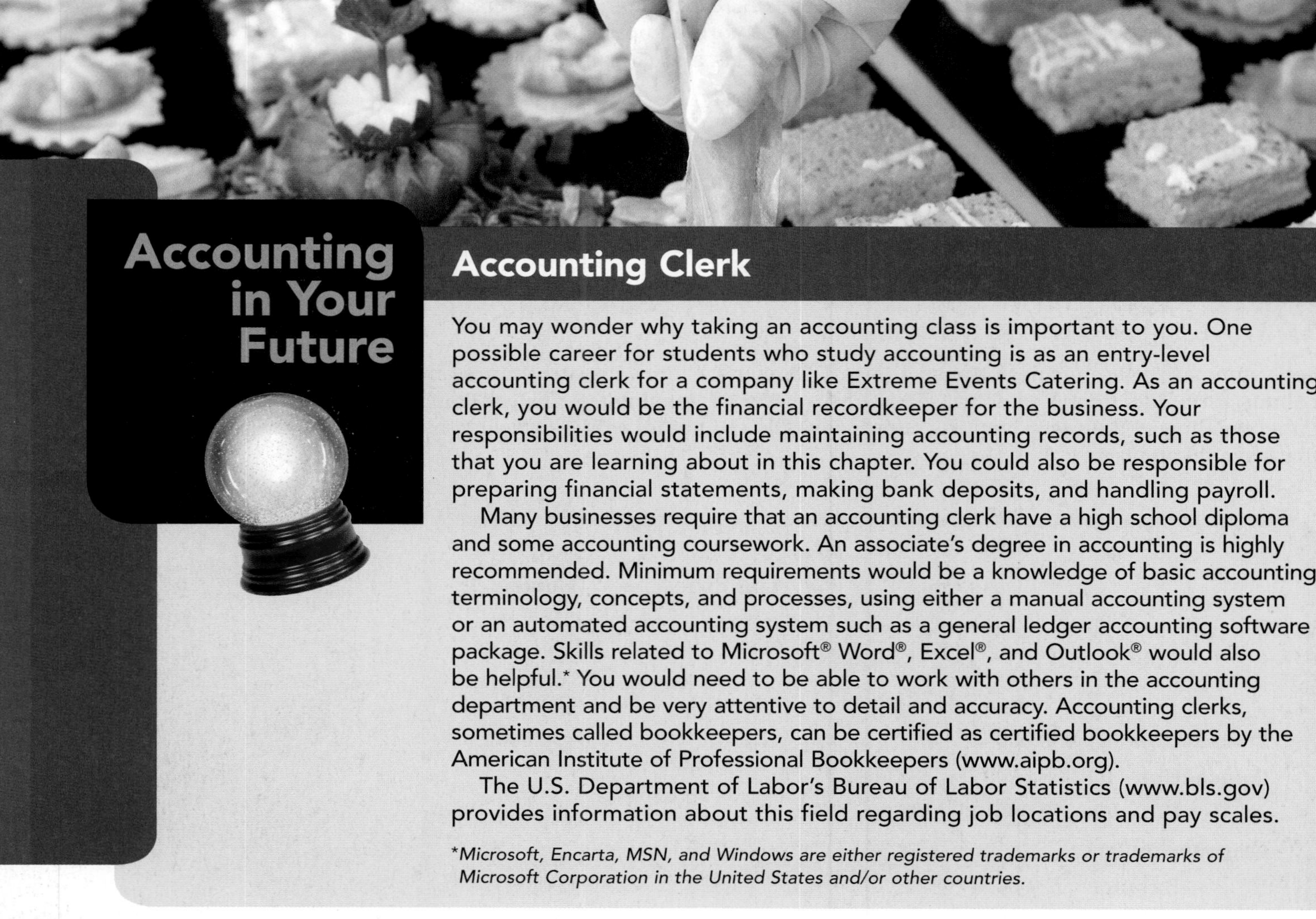

Accounting in Your Future

Accounting Clerk

You may wonder why taking an accounting class is important to you. One possible career for students who study accounting is as an entry-level accounting clerk for a company like Extreme Events Catering. As an accounting clerk, you would be the financial recordkeeper for the business. Your responsibilities would include maintaining accounting records, such as those that you are learning about in this chapter. You could also be responsible for preparing financial statements, making bank deposits, and handling payroll.

Many businesses require that an accounting clerk have a high school diploma and some accounting coursework. An associate's degree in accounting is highly recommended. Minimum requirements would be a knowledge of basic accounting terminology, concepts, and processes, using either a manual accounting system or an automated accounting system such as a general ledger accounting software package. Skills related to Microsoft® Word®, Excel®, and Outlook® would also be helpful.* You would need to be able to work with others in the accounting department and be very attentive to detail and accuracy. Accounting clerks, sometimes called bookkeepers, can be certified as certified bookkeepers by the American Institute of Professional Bookkeepers (www.aipb.org).

The U.S. Department of Labor's Bureau of Labor Statistics (www.bls.gov) provides information about this field regarding job locations and pay scales.

**Microsoft, Encarta, MSN, and Windows are either registered trademarks or trademarks of Microsoft Corporation in the United States and/or other countries.*

REVENUE AND EXPENSE ACCOUNTS

LEARNING OBJECTIVE 3
Define and identify revenue and expense accounts.

Revenues are the amounts earned by a business. Examples of revenues are fees earned for performing services, income from selling merchandise, rent income for the use of property, and interest income for lending money. Revenues may be in the form of cash or credit card receipts. Revenues may also result from credit sales to charge customers, in which case cash will be received at a later time.

Expenses are the costs that relate to earning revenue (or the costs of doing business). Examples of expenses are wages expense for labor performed, rent expense for the use of property, interest expense for the use of money, and advertising expense for the use of various media (for example, newspapers, radio, direct mail, and the Internet). Another example is supplies expense to include supplies used in the completion of a task performed by a service business, such as cleaning fluids used by a carpet cleaning company. Expenses may be paid in cash when incurred or at a later time. Expenses to be paid at a later time involve Accounts Payable.

Revenues and expenses directly affect owner's equity. **If a business earns revenue, an increase in owner's equity occurs. When a business incurs expenses, owner's equity decreases.** For the present, think of it this way: If the company makes money, the owner's equity is increased. If the company has to pay out money for the costs of doing business, then the owner's equity is decreased. Revenues and expenses fall under the umbrella of owner's equity: Revenue increases owner's equity; expenses decrease owner's equity. (See Figure 2.)

FIGURE 2
The umbrella of owner's equity

These temporary accounts fall under the umbrella of owner's equity, In Chapter 5, we will learn how temporary accounts are closed into the Capital account to determine net income or net loss as well as the increase or decrease to Capital.

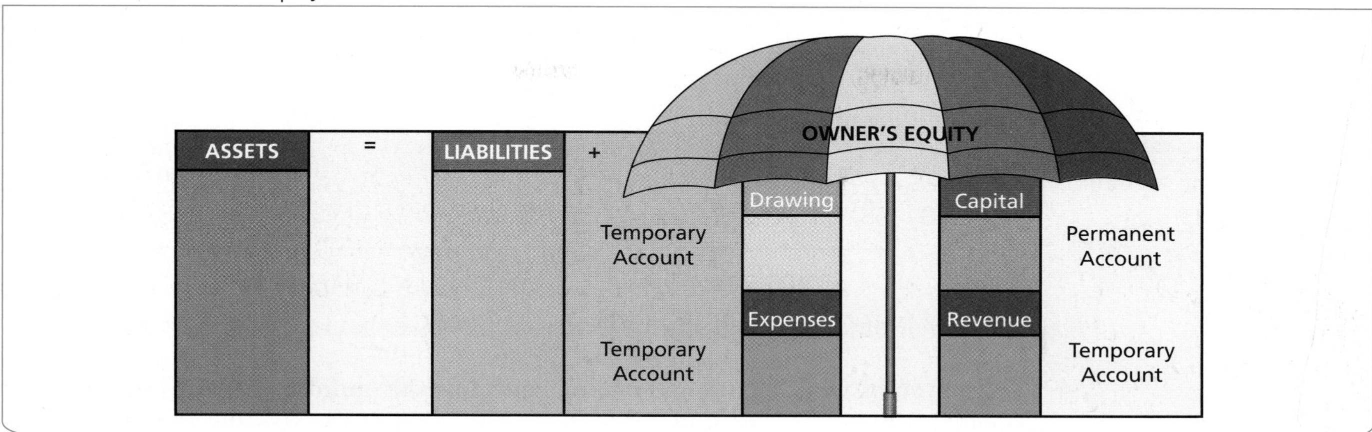

Chart of Accounts

The **chart of accounts** is the official list of accounts *tailor-made* for the business. All the company's transactions must be recorded using the official account titles.

We now present the chart of accounts for Conner's Whitewater Adventures. Some of the accounts are new to you, but they will be explained as we move along. When numbering account titles, the 100s are used for assets, the 200s are used for liabilities, the 300s are used for owner's equity accounts, the 400s are used for revenue accounts, and the 500s are used for expense accounts. You will encounter longer account numbers, but the first digit will usually be the same for any service business. In any case, use the exact account titles listed in the company's chart of accounts. Any changes must be approved by management.

FYI

When setting up and maintaining the chart of accounts on a computer, you may find that you must reserve the 500 accounts for cost accounts (used in a merchandising business). You may need to number expenses as 600s. Read the setup instructions in your software package.

CHART OF ACCOUNTS

Assets
111 Cash
113 Accounts Receivable
117 Prepaid Insurance
124 Equipment

Liabilities
221 Accounts Payable

Owner's Equity
311 J. Conner, Capital
312 J. Conner, Drawing

Revenue (increase in Owner's Equity)
411 Income from Tours

Expenses (decrease in Owner's Equity)
511 Wages Expense
512 Rent Expense
513 Supplies Expense
514 Advertising Expense
515 Utilities Expense

Recording Business Transactions

4 LEARNING OBJECTIVE

Record a group of business transactions, in column form, involving all five elements of the fundamental accounting equation.

Soon after the opening of Conner's Whitewater Adventures the first customers arrive, beginning a flow of revenue for the business. Let's examine more transactions of Conner's Whitewater Adventures for the first month of operations.

Transaction (f). Company sold whitewater rafting tours for cash, $8,000. Conner's Whitewater Adventures receives cash revenue of $8,000 in return for whitewater rafting tours performed for customers over two weeks. In other words, the company earns $8,000 for services performed for cash customers. Revenue has the effect of increasing owner's equity, but because the company wants to know how much revenue is earned, we set up a special column for revenue. The revenue account for Conner's Whitewater Adventures is called Income from Tours. The accounting equation is affected as follows (PB stands for previous balance, and NB stands for new balance).

	Assets			=	Liabilities	+	Owner's Equity		
	Cash	+	Equipment	=	Accounts Payable	+	J. Conner, Capital	+	Revenue
PB	50,000	+	47,520	=	2,320	+	95,200		
(f)	**+8,000**								**+8,000** (Income from Tours)
NB	58,000	+	47,520	=	2,320	+	95,200	+	8,000
	105,520				105,520				

Transaction (g). Company paid rent for the month, $1,250. Shortly after opening the business, Conner's Whitewater Adventures pays the month's rent of $1,250. Rent is payment for the privilege of occupying a building.

It seems logical that, if revenue is added to owner's equity, then expenses (the opposite of revenue) must be subtracted from owner's equity. To be consistent, a separate column is set up for expenses.

We want to have a running total of the amount of expenses to be subtracted from owner's equity. To keep up this running total, as each new expense is incurred (or happens), it must be added to the previous total.

	Assets			=	Liabilities	+	Owner's Equity				
	Cash	+	Equip.	=	Accounts Payable	+	J. Conner, Capital	+	Revenue	–	Expenses
PB	58,000	+	47,520	=	2,320	+	95,200	+	8,000		
(g)	**–1,250**										**+1,250** (Rent Expense)
NB	56,750	+	47,520	=	2,320	+	95,200	+	8,000	–	1,250
	104,270				104,270						

Because the time period represented by the rent payment is one month or less, we record the $1,250 as an expense. If the payment covered a period longer than one month, we would record the amount under an asset called Prepaid Rent.

Let's review the mental process for formulating the entry by asking:

STEP 1. What are the accounts involved? In this transaction, they are Cash and Rent Expense.

STEP 2. What are the classifications of the accounts involved? Cash is an asset, and Rent Expense is an expense and part of owner's equity.

STEP 3. Are the accounts increased or decreased? Cash is decreased because after the payment we have less cash than we had before. Rent Expense is increased. Thus there is a $1,250 reduction in total owner's equity.

STEP 4. Is the equation in balance after the transaction has been recorded?
Yes.

Transaction (h). Company bought supplies on credit, $675. Conner's Whitewater Adventures buys office supplies costing $675 on credit from Fineman Company. Computer paper, ink cartridges, invoice pads, pens and pencils, folders, filing cabinets, and 10-key calculators are considered to be supplies to be used up by Conner's Whitewater Adventures for clients and are recorded as an expense. For a service business, for tax purposes (IRS Notice 2001-76), supplies may be originally recorded as an expense rather than being added to an inventory account.

	Assets			= Liabilities +		Owner's Equity				
	Cash	+	Equip.	=	Accounts Payable	+	J. Conner, Capital	+ Revenue	–	Expenses
PB	56,750	+	47,520	=	2,320	+	95,200	+ 8,000	–	1,250
(h)					**+675**					**+675** (Supplies Expense)
NB	56,750	+	47,520	=	2,995	+	95,200	+ 8,000	–	1,925
	104,270				104,270					

Transaction (i). Company paid for insurance, $1,875. Conner's Whitewater Adventures paid $1,875 for a three-month liability insurance policy. At the time of payment, the company has not used up the insurance; thus, it is not yet an expense. As the insurance expires (is used), it will become an expense. **However, because it is paid in advance for a period longer than one month, it has value and is therefore recorded as Prepaid Insurance, an asset.**

	Assets			= Liabilities +		Owner's Equity			
	Cash	+ Equip. +	Ppd. Ins.	=	Accounts Payable	+	J. Conner, Capital	+ Revenue –	Expenses
PB	56,750	+ 47,520		=	2,995	+	95,200	+ 8,000 –	1,925
(i)	**–1,875**		**+1,875**						
NB	54,875	+ 47,520 +	1,875	=	2,995	+	95,200	+ 8,000 –	1,925
	104,270				104,270				

At the end of the year or accounting period, an adjustment will have to be made to take out the expired portion (that is, coverage for the months that have been used up) and record it as an expense. We discuss this adjustment in a later chapter.

Observe that each time a transaction is recorded, the total amount on one side of the equation **remains equal** to the total amount on the other side. As proof of this equality, look at the following computation:

Cash	$ 54,875	**Accounts Payable**	$ 2,995
Equipment	47,520	**J. Conner, Capital**	95,200
Prepaid Insurance	1,875	**Revenue**	8,000
		Expenses	–1,925
	$104,270		$104,270

Steps in Analyzing Transactions

Now that we have recorded transactions in all five classifications of accounts, let's pause to go through the steps we have followed:

STEP 1. Read the transaction to understand what is happening and how it affects the business. For example, the business has more revenue, or has more expenses, or has more cash, or owes less to creditors. Identify the accounts involved. Look for Cash first; you will quickly recognize if cash is coming in or going out.

STEP 2. Decide on the classifications of the accounts involved. For example, Equipment is something the business owns, and it's an asset; Accounts Payable is an amount the business owes, and it's a liability; Rent is an expense.

STEP 3. Decide whether the accounts are increased or decreased.

STEP 4. After recording the transaction, make sure the accounting equation is in balance.

Tools to Success—The U.S. Small Business Administration

Throughout the pages of this text, you will occasionally find a feature labeled Small Business Success. This feature is designed to provide insight into accounting issues surrounding small businesses. Some of you will probably own a small business when you graduate; maybe you are thinking of starting your own small bookkeeping firm. Or many of you will work in small businesses such as a local or regional accounting firm. These features contain information that is useful to small and large businesses and will be helpful if you are thinking about owning your own business.

The U.S. Small Business Administration Web site (www.sba.gov) is a great place to find information about managing, accounting for, and running a small business. Take a moment to go to the Web site and review the tools that are available to small businesses. Click on the Tools link, and you will find different series that deal with management, finances, and crime prevention.

You can also find audio and video podcasts on the Web site that provide information about business success. If you are interested in hearing about other successful small businesses, you can find a series on small business features. The series discusses various small businesses that have used the tools provided by the Small Business Administration and have grown to be successful and profitable entities.

Keep an eye out for the Small Business Success feature! It will add some insight into how businesses use the accounting information that you are learning in this course.

Transaction (j). Company received a bill for an expense, $620. Conner's Whitewater Adventures receives a bill from *The Times* for newspaper advertising, $620. **Conner's Whitewater Adventures has simply received the bill for advertising; it has not paid any cash.** Previously, we described an expense as money to be paid for the cost of doing business. An expense of $620 has now been incurred (or has taken place), and it should be recorded as an increase in expenses (Advertising Expense). Also, since the company owes $620 more than before and intends to pay at a later time, this amount should be recorded as an increase in Accounts Payable. Notice Cash is not used because the bill has not been paid.

	Assets					= Liabilities +		Owner's Equity				
	Cash	+	Equip.	+	Ppd. Ins.	=	Accounts Payable	+	J. Conner, Capital	+ Revenue	–	Expenses
PB	54,875	+	47,520	+	1,875	=	2,995	+	95,200	+ 8,000	–	1,925
(j)							**+620**					**+620** (Advertising Expense)
NB	54,875	+	47,520	+	1,875	=	3,615	+	95,200	+ 8,000	–	2,545
	104,270						104,270					

Transaction (k). Company sold services on account, $6,750. Conner's Whitewater Adventures signs a contract with Crystal River Lodge to provide rafting adventures for guests. Conner's Whitewater Adventures provides 27 one-day rafting tours and bills Crystal River Lodge for $6,750.

A company uses the **Accounts Receivable** account to record the amounts due from (legal claims against) charge customers. Since Conner's Whitewater Adventures' claim against Crystal River Lodge of $6,750 is promised to be paid, it is recorded in Accounts Receivable. Revenue is earned or recognized when the service is performed, even though the $6,750 has not been received in cash. We count the $6,750 as an increase in revenue and an increase in Accounts Receivable. Keep in mind that Accounts Receivable is an asset; or something that is owned. Conner's Whitewater Adventures owns a claim of $6,750 against Crystal River Lodge.

	Assets							= Liabilities +		Owner's Equity				
	Cash	+	Equip.	+	Ppd. Ins.	+	Accts. Rec.	=	Accounts Payable	+	J. Conner, Capital	+	Revenue	– Expenses
PB	54,875	+	47,520	+	1,875			=	3,615	+	95,200	+	8,000	– 2,545
(k)							**+6,750**						**+6,750** (Income from Tours)	
NB	54,875	+	47,520	+	1,875	+	6,750	=	3,615	+	95,200	+	14,750	– 2,545
	111,020								111,020					

When Crystal River Lodge pays the $6,750 bill in cash, Conner's Whitewater Adventures will record this transaction as an increase in Cash and a decrease in Accounts Receivable. At that time, Conner's Whitewater Adventures will *not* have to make an entry for the revenue, because the revenue was earned and recorded when the service was performed.

Transaction (l). Company paid creditor on account. Conner's Whitewater Adventures pays $1,500 to Signal Products, its creditor (the party to whom it owes money), as partial payment on account.

	Assets							=	Liabilities	+	Owner's Equity				
	Cash	+	Equip.	+	Ppd. Ins.	+	Accts. Rec.	=	Accounts Payable	+	J. Conner, Capital	+	Revenue	–	Expenses
PB	54,875	+	47,520	+	1,875	+	6,750	=	3,615	+	95,200	+	14,750	–	2,545
(l)	**–1,500**								**–1,500**						
NB	53,375	+	47,520	+	1,875	+	6,750	=	2,115	+	95,200	+	14,750	–	2,545
	109,520								109,520						

Transaction (m). Company paid an expense in cash, $225. Conner's Whitewater Adventures receives a bill from Solar Power, Inc. for $225. Because the bill was not previously recorded as a liability and is to be paid immediately, we record the amount directly as an expense.

	Assets							=	Liabilities	+	Owner's Equity				
	Cash	+	Equip.	+	Ppd. Ins.	+	Accts. Rec.	=	Accounts Payable	+	J. Conner, Capital	+	Revenue	–	Expenses
PB	53,375	+	47,520	+	1,875	+	6,750	=	2,115	+	95,200	+	14,750	–	2,545
(m)	**–225**														**+225** (Utilities Expense)
NB	53,150	+	47,520	+	1,875	+	6,750	=	2,115	+	95,200	+	14,750	–	2,770
	109,295								109,295						

Transaction (n). Company paid creditor on account, $620. Conner's Whitewater Adventures pays $620 to *The Times* for advertising. **Recall that this bill had previously been recorded as a liability in transaction (j).**

	Assets							=	Liabilities	+	Owner's Equity				
	Cash	+	Equip.	+	Ppd. Ins.	+	Accts. Rec.	=	Accounts Payable	+	J. Conner, Capital	+	Revenue	–	Expenses
PB	53,150	+	47,520	+	1,875	+	6,750	=	2,115	+	95,200	+	14,750	–	2,770
(n)	**–620**								**–620**						
NB	52,530	+	47,520	+	1,875	+	6,750	=	1,495	+	95,200	+	14,750	–	2,770
	108,675								108,675						

Transaction (o). Company paid an expense in cash, $2,360. Conner's Whitewater Adventures pays wages of a part-time employee, $2,360.

	Assets				= Liabilities +	Owner's Equity		
	Cash +	Equip. +	Ppd. Ins. +	Accts. Rec. =	Accounts Payable +	J. Conner, Capital	+ Revenue	– Expenses
PB	52,530 +	47,520 +	1,875 +	6,750 =	1,495 +	95,200	+ 14,750	– 2,770
(o)	**–2,360**							**+2,360** (Wages Expense)
NB	50,170 +	47,520 +	1,875 +	6,750 =	1,495 +	95,200	+ 14,750	– 5,130
	106,315				106,315			

Transaction (p). Company buys equipment on account for $3,780, making a cash down payment of $1,850 and charging $1,930. Conner's Whitewater Adventures buys additional equipment from Signal Products for $3,780, paying $1,850 down with the remaining $1,930 on account. Because buying an item *on account* is the same as buying it *on credit,* both terms are used to describe such transactions and involve Accounts Payable.

	Assets				= Liabilities +	Owner's Equity		
	Cash +	Equip. +	Ppd. Ins. +	Accts. Rec. =	Accounts Payable +	J. Conner, Capital	+ Revenue	– Expenses
PB	50,170 +	47,520 +	1,875 +	6,750 =	1,495 +	95,200	+ 14,750	– 5,130
(p)	**–1,850**	**+3,780**			**+1,930**			
NB	48,320 +	51,300 +	1,875 +	6,750 =	3,425 +	95,200	+ 14,750	– 5,130
	108,245				108,245			

Again, because the equipment is expected to last for years, Conner's Whitewater Adventures lists this $3,780 as an increase in the assets. Note that three accounts are involved in this transaction: Cash, because cash was paid out; Equipment, because the company has more equipment than before; and Accounts Payable, because the company owes more than before.

Transaction (q). Company receives cash on account from credit customer, $2,500. Conner's Whitewater Adventures receives $2,500 from Crystal River Lodge to apply against the amount billed in transaction (k). Crystal River Lodge now owes Conner's Whitewater Adventure less than it did, and so Conner's Whitewater Adventures deducts the $2,500 from Accounts Receivable. An exchange of assets has no effect on the totals of the equation.

	Assets				= Liabilities +	Owner's Equity		
	Cash +	Equip. +	Ppd. Ins. +	Accts. Rec. =	Accounts Payable +	J. Conner, Capital	+ Revenue	– Expenses
PB	48,320 +	51,300 +	1,875 +	6,750 =	3,425 +	95,200	+ 14,750	– 5,130
(q)	**+2,500**			**–2,500**				
NB	50,820 +	51,300 +	1,875 +	4,250 =	3,425 +	95,200	+ 14,750	– 5,130
	108,245				108,245			

Conner's Whitewater Adventures previously listed the amount as revenue [see transaction (k)], so it should definitely *not* be recorded as revenue again.

Transaction (r). **Company sells services for cash, $8,570.** Conner's Whitewater Adventures receives revenue from cash customers during the rest of the month, $8,570.

	Assets								= Liabilities +		Owner's Equity				
	Cash	+	Equip.	+	Ppd. Ins.	+	Accts. Rec.	=	Accounts Payable	+	J. Conner, Capital	+	Revenue	–	Expenses
PB	50,820	+	51,300	+	1,875	+	4,250	=	3,425	+	95,200	+	14,750	–	5,130
(r)	**+8,570**												**+8,570** (Income from Tours)		
NB	59,390	+	51,300	+	1,875	+	4,250	=	3,425	+	95,200	+	23,320	–	5,130
	116,815								116,815						

Transaction (s). **Owner makes a cash withdrawal, $3,500.** At the end of the month, Conner withdraws $3,500 in cash from the business for her personal living costs. A **withdrawal** may be considered the opposite of an investment in cash by the owner and is treated as a temporary decrease in owner's equity because it is made in anticipation of profits. Withdrawals are different from expenses. Expenses are paid to someone else for the cost of goods or services used in the business, whereas withdrawals are paid directly to the owner. A withdrawal may consist of cash or other assets.

Because the owner takes cash out of the business, there is a decrease of $3,500 in Cash. This also decreases owner's equity. We record $3,500 under J. Conner, Drawing.

	Assets								= Liabilities +		Owner's Equity						
	Cash	+	Equip.	+	Ppd. Ins.	+	Accts. Rec.	=	Accounts Payable	+	J. Conner, Capital	–	J. Conner, Drawing	+	Revenue	–	Expenses
PB	59,390	+	51,300	+	1,875	+	4,250	=	3,425	+	95,200			+	23,320	–	5,130
(s)	**–3,500**												**+3,500**				
NB	55,890	+	51,300	+	1,875	+	4,250	=	3,425	+	95,200	–	3,500	+	23,320	–	5,130
	113,315								113,315								

Summary of Transactions (f) Through (s)

Figure 3 summarizes business transactions (f) through (s) of Conner's Whitewater Adventures with the transactions identified by letter. To test your understanding of the recording procedure, describe the nature of the transactions.

Summary of transactions (f) through (s) **FIGURE 3**

	Assets				= Liabilities +	Owner's Equity			
	Cash	+ Equip.	+ Ppd. Ins.	+ Accts. Rec.	= Accounts Payable	+ J. Conner, Capital	– J. Conner, Drawing	+ Revenue	– Expenses
Bal.	50,000	47,520			2,320	95,200			
(f)	**+8,000**							**+8,000** (Income from Tours)	
Bal.	58,000	47,520			2,320	95,200		8,000	
(g)	**-1,250**								**+1,250** (Rent Exp.)
Bal.	56,750	47,520			2,320	95,200		8,000	1,250
(h)					**+675**				**+675** (Sup. Exp.)
Bal.	56,750	47,520			2,995	95,200		8,000	1,925
(i)	**–1,875**		**+1,875**						
Bal.	54,875	47,520	1,875		2,995	95,200		8,000	1,925
(j)					**+620**				**+620** (Adv. Exp.)
Bal.	54,875	47,520	1,875		3,615	95,200		8,000	2,545
(k)				**+6,750**				**+6,750** (Income from Tours)	
Bal.	54,875	47,520	1,875	6,750	3,615	95,200		14,750	2,545
(l)	**–1,500**				**–1,500**				
Bal.	53,375	47,520	1,875	6,750	2,115	95,200		14,750	2,545
(m)	**–225**								**+225** (Util. Exp.)
Bal.	53,150	47,520	1,875	6,750	2,115	95,200		14,750	2,770
(n)	**–620**				**–620**				
Bal.	52,530	47,520	1,875	6,750	1,495	95,200		14,750	2,770
(o)	**–2,360**								**+2,360** (Wages Exp.)
Bal.	50,170	47,520	1,875	6,750	1,495	95,200		14,750	5,130
(p)	**–1,850**	**+3,780**			**+1,930**				
Bal.	48,320	51,300	1,875	6,750	3,425	95,200		14,750	5,130
(q)	**+2,500**			**–2,500**					
Bal.	50,820	51,300	1,875	4,250	3,425	95,200		14,750	5,130
(r)	**+8,570**							**+8,570** (Income from Tours)	
Bal.	59,390	51,300	1,875	4,250	3,425	95,200		23,320	5,130
(s)	**–3,500**						**+3,500**		
Bal.	55,890	51,300	1,875	4,250	3,425	95,200	3,500	23,320	5,130

Left Side of Equals Sign:	
Cash	$ 55,890
Equipment	51,300
Prepaid Insurance	1,875
Accounts Receivable	4,250
	$113,315

Right Side of Equals Sign:	
Accounts Payable	$ 3,425
J. Conner, Capital	95,200
J. Conner, Drawing	–3,500
Revenue	23,320
Expenses	–5,130
	$113,315

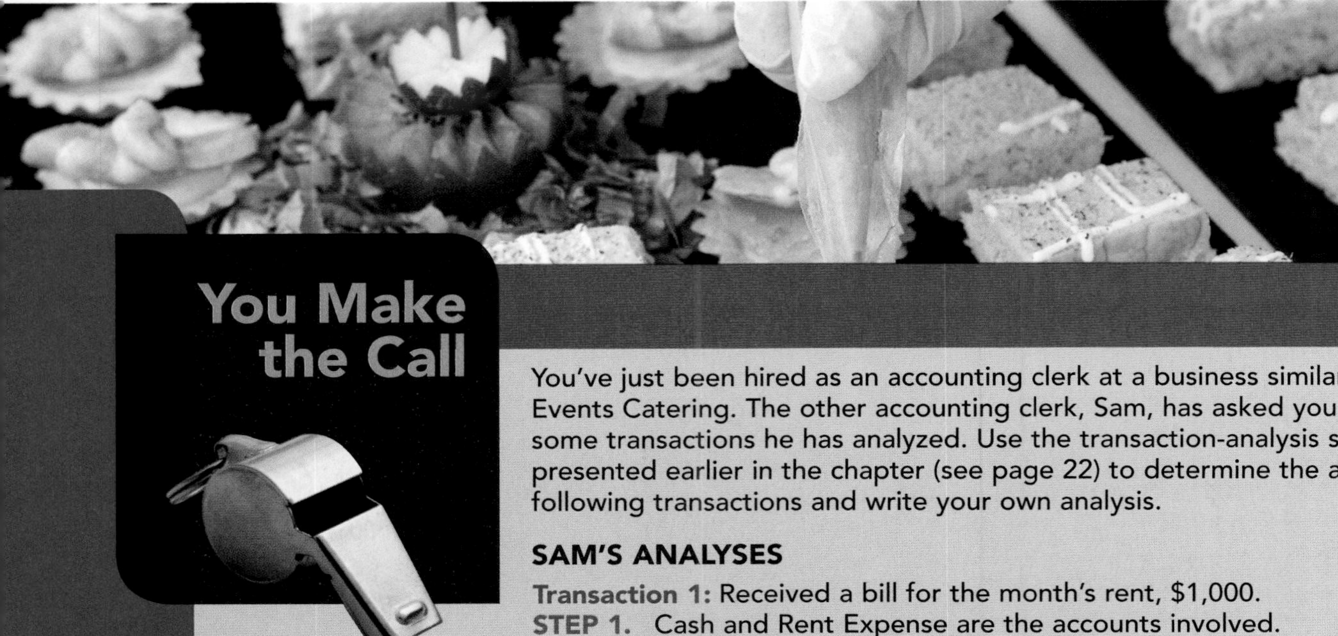

You Make the Call

You've just been hired as an accounting clerk at a business similar to Extreme Events Catering. The other accounting clerk, Sam, has asked you to check some transactions he has analyzed. Use the transaction-analysis steps presented earlier in the chapter (see page 22) to determine the accuracy of the following transactions and write your own analysis.

SAM'S ANALYSES

Transaction 1: Received a bill for the month's rent, $1,000.

STEP 1. Cash and Rent Expense are the accounts involved.
STEP 2. Cash is an asset, and Rent Expense is an expense.
STEP 3. Equipment is decreased, and Rent Expense is decreased.

Transaction 2: Bought equipment on account for $1,800.

STEP 1. Equipment and Accounts Receivable are the accounts involved.
STEP 2. Equipment is an asset, and Accounts Receivable is an asset.
STEP 3. Equipment is decreased, and Accounts Receivable is increased.

SOLUTION

Sam's analyses for both transactions are incorrect.

Transaction 1:

STEP 1. Accounts Payable and Rent Expense are the accounts involved.
STEP 2. The bill was received but not paid, therefore creating a liability. Cash is not involved because the business has not paid the monthly rent. Accounts Payable is a liability, and Rent Expense is an expense.
STEP 3. Accounts Payable is increased, and Rent Expense is increased. Remember, the bill was only received, not paid; therefore no cash is involved. Rent Expense increases, but its ultimate effect is a subtraction in the fundamental accounting equation.

Transaction 2:

STEP 1. Equipment and Accounts Payable are the accounts involved.
STEP 2. Accounts Payable is involved because the business owes money to the seller. Accounts Payable is the account used to manage short-term liabilities. Accounts Receivable is the account used to keep track of what customers owe us.
Equipment is an asset, and Accounts Payable is a liability.
STEP 3. Equipment is increased, and Accounts Payable is increased.

CHAPTER REVIEW

Study & Practice

LEARNING OBJECTIVE

Define and identify asset, liability, *and* owner's equity *accounts.*

Assets are cash, properties, or things of value owned by the business. **Liabilities** are amounts the business owes to creditors. **Owner's equity** is the owner's investment or net worth. The **fundamental accounting equation** expresses the relationship of assets, liabilities, and owner's equity and is represented as:

Assets = Liabilities + Owner's Equity

PRACTICE EXERCISE 1

Complete the fundamental accounting equation:

Assets	=	**Liabilities**	+	**Owner's Equity**
Items owned		*Amounts owed to creditors*		*Owner's investment*
$50,000	=	$12,000	+	?

PRACTICE EXERCISE 1 SOLUTION

$50,000 Assets
−12,000 Liabilities
$38,000 Owner's Equity

2 LEARNING OBJECTIVE

Record a group of business transactions, in column form, involving changes in assets, liabilities, and owner's equity.

The accounting equation is stated as assets equals liabilities plus owner's equity. Under the appropriate classification, a separate column is set up for each **account**. Transactions are recorded by listing amounts as either additions to or deductions from the various accounts. The equation must always remain in balance.

PRACTICE EXERCISE 2

Write the corresponding amounts for each transaction where you see question marks. Compute the balance to be sure the equation is in balance before proceeding to the next transaction.

	Assets			=	Liabilities	+	Owner's Equity
	Items owned				*Amounts owed to creditors*		*Owner's investment*
	Cash	+	Equipment	=	Accounts Payable	+	J. Lawson, Capital
Transaction (a)	+90,000						?
Transaction (b)	?		+53,000				
Balance	?	+	?	=			?
Transaction (c)			?		+9,000		
Balance	?	+	?	=	?	+	?
Transaction (d)	?				−4,000		
Balance	?	+	?	=	?	+	?
Transaction (e)			?				+5,200
Balance	?	+	?	=	?	+	?
		?				?	

PRACTICE EXERCISE 2 SOLUTION

	Assets			=	Liabilities	+	Owner's Equity
	Items owned				*Amounts owed to creditors*		*Owner's investment*
	Cash	+	Equipment	=	Accounts Payable	+	J. Lawson, Capital
Transaction (a)	+90,000						+90,000
Transaction (b)	−53,000		+53,000				
Balance	37,000	+	53,000	=			90,000
Transaction (c)			+9,000		+9,000		
Balance	37,000	+	62,000	=	9,000	+	90,000
Transaction (d)	−4,000				−4,000		
Balance	33,000	+	62,000	=	5,000	+	90,000
Transaction (e)			+5,200				+5,200
Balance	33,000	+	67,200	=	5,000	+	95,200
		100,200				100,200	

LEARNING OBJECTIVE

3 *Define and identify* revenue *and* expense *accounts.*

Revenues consist of amounts earned by a business, such as fees earned for performing services, income from selling merchandise, rent income for the use of property, or interest earned for lending money. **Expenses** are the costs of earning revenue—that is, of doing business—such as wages expense, rent expense, interest expense, and advertising expense.

CHAPTER REVIEW

PRACTICE EXERCISE 3

Identify the revenue and expense accounts from the following list of accounts. If the account is a revenue account, write R. If the account is an expense account, write E. If it is neither, leave blank.

___	Accounts Payable	___	Service Income
___	Rent Expense	___	Utilities Expense
___	J. Martin, Drawing	___	Professional Fees Earned
___	Wages Expense	___	Accounts Receivable

PRACTICE EXERCISE 3 SOLUTION

___	Accounts Payable	R	Service Income
E	Rent Expense	E	Utilities Expense
___	J. Martin, Drawing	R	Professional Fees Earned
E	Wages Expense	___	Accounts Receivable

LEARNING OBJECTIVE

4

Record a group of business transactions, in column form, involving all five elements of the fundamental accounting equation.

The accounting equation has been expanded and should appear as follows:

Assets = Liabilities + Owner's Equity (Capital) – Drawing + Revenue – Expenses

Accounts are classified and listed under each heading. Transactions are recorded by listing amounts as either additions to or deductions from the various accounts. The equation must always remain in balance.

PRACTICE EXERCISE 4

Record the following transactions in the grid provided below:

Transaction (a). Company bought equipment for $8,000 on account.
Transaction (b). Company sold services on account for $6,200.
Transaction (c). Customer paid $3,000 on account.
Transaction (d). Company owner invested personal computer system in the business, fair market value, $3,400 (Equipment).

	Assets			=	**Liabilities**	+	**Owner's Equity**			
	Cash +	Equipment +	Accounts Receivable	=	Accounts Payable	+	Capital –	Drawing +	Revenue –	Expenses
(a)										
(b)										
(c)										
(d)										

CHAPTER REVIEW

PRACTICE EXERCISE 4 SOLUTION

	Assets			=	Liabilities	+	Owner's Equity						
	Cash	+ Equipment	+ Accounts Receivable	=	Accounts Payable	+	Capital	–	Drawing	+	Revenue	–	Expenses
(a)		+8,000			+8,000								
(b)			+6,200								+6,200		
(c)	+3,000		–3,000										
(d)		+3,400					+3,400						
Bal.	3,000	+ 11,400	+ 3,200	=	8,000	+	3,400			+	6,200		
		17,600					17,600						

Glossary

Accounts The categories under the Assets, Liabilities, and Owner's Equity headings. *(p. 14)*

Accounts Payable A liability account used for short-term liabilities or charge accounts, usually due within 30 days. *(p. 15)*

Accounts Receivable An account used to record the amounts owed by (legal claims against) charge customers. (p. 23)

Assets Cash, properties, and other things of value owned by an economic unit or business entity. *(p. 11)*

Business entity A business enterprise, separate and distinct from the persons who supply the assets it uses. *(p. 11)*

Capital The owner's investment, or equity, in an enterprise. *(p. 11)*

Chart of accounts The official list of account titles to be used to record the transactions of a business. *(p. 19)*

Creditor One to whom money is owed. *(p. 12)*

Double-entry accounting The system by which each business transaction is recorded in at least two accounts and the accounting equation is kept in balance. *(p. 17)*

Equity The value of a right or claim to or financial interest in an asset or group of assets. *(p. 11)*

Expenses The costs that relate to earning revenue (the costs of doing business); examples are wages, rent, interest, and advertising. They may be paid in cash immediately or at a future time (Accounts Payable). (p. 18)

Fair market value The present worth of an asset or the amount that would be received if the asset were sold to an outsider on the open market. *(p. 16)*

Fundamental accounting equation (Assets = Liabilities + Owner's Equity) An equation expressing the relationship of assets, liabilities, and owner's equity. *(p. 12)*

Liabilities Debts or amounts owed to creditors. *(p. 12)*

Owner's equity The owner's right to or investment in the business. *(p. 11)*

Revenues The amounts a business earns; examples are fees earned for performing services, sales of merchandise, rent income, and interest income. They may be in the form of cash, credit card receipts, or accounts receivable (charge accounts). *(p. 18)*

Separate entity concept The concept by which a business is treated as a separate economic or accounting entity. The business stands by itself, separate from its owners, creditors, and customers. *(p. 14)*

Sole proprietorship A one-owner business. *(p. 14)*

Withdrawal The taking of cash or other assets out of a business by the owner for his or her own use. (This is also referred to as drawing.) A withdrawal is treated as a temporary decrease in owner's equity. *(p. 26)*

CHAPTER ASSIGNMENTS

Discussion Questions

1. Define *assets*, *liabilities*, *owner's equity*, *revenues*, and *expenses*.
2. Explain the separate entity concept.
3. How do Accounts Payable and Accounts Receivable differ?
4. Describe two ways to increase owner's equity and two ways to decrease owner's equity.
5. What is the effect on the fundamental accounting equation if supplies are purchased on account? How will the fundamental accounting equation change if supplies are purchased with cash? Explain how this purchase will or will not change the owner's equity.
6. When an owner withdraws cash or goods from the business, why is this considered an increase to the Drawing account and not an increase to the Wages Expense account?
7. Define *chart of accounts*, and identify the categories of accounts.
8. What account titles would you suggest for the chart of accounts for a city touring company owned by W. Sanders? List the accounts by account category and include an appropriate account number for each.

Exercises

LO 1

PRACTICE EXERCISE 1

EXERCISE 1-1 Complete the following equations:

a. Assets of $22,000 = Liabilities of $7,200 + Owner's Equity of $_____
b. Assets of $_____ – Liabilities of $18,000 = Owner's Equity of $22,000
c. Assets of $27,000 – Owner's Equity of $15,000 = Liabilities of $_____

LO 1

PRACTICE EXERCISE 1

EXERCISE 1-2 Determine the following amounts:

a. The amount of the liabilities of a business that has $60,800 in assets and in which the owner has $34,500 equity.
b. The equity of the owner of a tour bus that cost $57,000 who owes $21,800 on an installment loan payable to the bank.
c. The amount of the assets of a business that has $11,780 in liabilities and in which the owner has $28,500 equity.

LO 1

PRACTICE EXERCISE 1

EXERCISE 1-3 Dr. L. M. Patton is an ophthalmologist. As of December 31, Dr. Patton owned the following property that related to his professional practice, Patton Eye Clinic:

Cash, $2,995
Professional Equipment, $63,000
Office Equipment, $8,450

On the same date, he owed the following business creditors:

Munez Supply Company, $3,816
Martin Equipment Sales, $3,728

Compute the following amounts in the accounting equation:

Assets $______ = Liabilities $______ + Owner's Equity $______

PRACTICE EXERCISES 1,3

EXERCISE 1-4 Describe a business transaction that will do the following:

a. Increase an asset and increase a liability
b. Decrease an asset and decrease a liability
c. Decrease an asset and increase an expense
d. Increase an asset and increase owner's equity
e. Increase an asset and decrease an asset
f. Increase an asset and increase revenue

PRACTICE EXERCISE 2

EXERCISE 1-5 Describe a transaction that resulted in each of the following entries affecting the accounting equation.

	Assets					=	Liabilities	+	Owner's Equity
	Cash	+	Office Equipment	+	Professional Equipment	=	Accounts Payable	+	B. Lake, Capital
(a)	+18,200								+18,200
(b)	−1,375				+1,375				
Bal.	16,825			+	1,375	=			18,200
(c)			+640				+640		
Bal.	16,825	+	640	+	1,375	=	640	+	18,200
(d)	−2,200				+7,000		+4,800		
Bal.	14,625	+	640	+	8,375	=	5,440	+	18,200
(e)	−1,000						−1,000		
Bal.	13,625	+	640	+	8,375	=	4,440	+	18,200

PRACTICE EXERCISES 1,3

EXERCISE 1-6 Label each of the following accounts as an asset (A), liability (L), owner's equity (OE), revenue (R), or expense (E):

a. Office Supplies Expense
b. Professional Fees
c. Prepaid Insurance
d. R. Baker, Drawing
e. Accounts Payable
f. Service Income
g. R. Baker, Capital
h. Rent Expense
i. Accounts Receivable
j. Wages Expense

PRACTICE EXERCISES 2,4

EXERCISE 1-7 Describe a transaction that resulted in the following changes in accounts:

a. Rent Expense is increased by $1,050, and Cash is decreased by $1,050.
b. Advertising Expense is increased by $835, and Accounts Payable is increased by $835.
c. Accounts Receivable is increased by $372, and Service Income is increased by $372.
d. Cash is decreased by $410, and C. Tryon, Drawing, is increased by $410.
e. Equipment is increased by $1,850, Cash is decreased by $850, and Accounts Payable is increased by $1,000.
f. Cash is increased by $1,650, and Accounts Receivable is decreased by $1,650.

EXERCISE 1-8 Describe the transactions that are recorded in the following equation.

PRACTICE EXERCISES 2,4

	Assets			= Liabilities +	Owner's Equity			
	Cash	+ Accounts Receivable	+ Equipment	= Accounts Payable	+ J. Onyx, Capital	− J. Onyx, Drawing	+ Revenue	− Expenses
(a)	+25,000		+4,500		+29,500			
(b)	−1,250							+1,250 (Rent Expense)
Bal.	23,750		4,500		29,500			1,250
(c)		+2,000					+2,000 (Income from Services)	
Bal.	23,750	2,000	4,500		29,500		2,000	1,250
(d)	−3,700		+16,000	+12,300				
Bal.	20,050	2,000	20,500	12,300	29,500		2,000	1,250
(e)	−2,500					+2,500		
Bal.	17,550	2,000	20,500	12,300	29,500	2,500	2,000	1,250
		40,050				40,050		

Problem Set A

For additional help, see the demonstration problem at the beginning of each chapter in your Working Papers.

PROBLEM 1-1A On June 1 of this year, J. Larkin, Optometrist, established the Larkin Eye Clinic. The clinic's account names are presented below. Transactions completed during the month follow.

Assets		=	Liabilities	+	Owner's Equity			
Cash	+ Office Equipment	=	Accounts Payable	+	______, Capital	− ______, Drawing	+ Revenue	− Expenses

a. Larkin deposited $25,000 in a bank account in the name of the business.
b. Paid the office rent for the month, $950, Ck. No. 1001 (Rent Expense).
c. Bought supplies for cash, $357, Ck. No. 1002 (Supplies Expense).
d. Bought office equipment on account from NYC Office Equipment Store, $8,956.
e. Bought a computer from Warden's Office Outfitters, $1,636, paying $750 in cash and placing the balance on account, Ck. No. 1003.
f. Sold professional services for cash, $3,482 (Professional Fees).
g. Paid on account to Warden's Office Outfitters, a creditor, $900, Ck. No. 1004.
h. Received and paid the bill for utilities, $382, Ck. No. 1005 (Utilities Expense).
i. Paid the salary of the assistant, $1,050, Ck. No. 1006 (Salary Expense).
j. Sold professional services for cash, $3,295 (Professional Fees).
k. Larkin withdrew cash for personal use, $1,250, Ck. No. 1007 (J. Larkin, Drawing).

Check Figure Left side of equals sign total, $36,730

Required

1. In the equation, write the owner's name above the terms *Capital* and *Drawing*.
2. Record the transactions and the balance after each transaction. Identify the account affected when the transaction involves revenues or expenses.
3. Write the account totals from the left side of the equals sign and add them. Write the account totals from the right side of the equals sign and add them. If the two totals are not equal, first check the addition and subtraction. If you still cannot find the error, reanalyze each transaction.

LO 1,2,3,4

PROBLEM 1-2A On July 1 of this year, R. Green established the Green Rehab Clinic. The organization's account headings are presented below. Transactions completed during the month of July follow.

Assets			= Liabilities +	Owner's Equity			
Cash +	Office Equipment +	Professional Equipment =	Accounts Payable +	______, Capital −	______, Drawing +	Revenue −	Expenses

a. Green deposited $30,000 in a bank account in the name of the business.
b. Paid the office rent for the month, $1,800, Ck. No. 2001 (Rent Expense).
c. Bought supplies for cash, $362, Ck. No. 2002 (Supplies Expense).
d. Bought professional equipment on account from Rehab Equipment Company, $18,000 (Professional Equipment).
e. Bought office equipment from Hi-Tech Computers, $2,890, paying $890 in cash and placing the balance on account, Ck. No. 2003.
f. Sold professional services for cash, $4,600 (Professional Fees).
g. Paid on account to Rehab Equipment Company, a creditor, $700, Ck. No. 2004.
h. Received and paid the bill for utilities, $367, Ck. No. 2005 (Utilities Expense).
i. Paid the salary of the assistant, $1,150, Ck. No. 2006 (Salary Expense).
j. Sold professional services for cash, $3,868 (Professional Fees).
k. Green withdrew cash for personal use, $1,800, Ck. No. 2007 (R. Green, Drawing).

Check Figure Cash, $31,399

Required

1. In the equation, write the owner's name above the terms *Capital* and *Drawing*.
2. Record the transactions and the balance after each transaction. Identify the account affected when the transaction involves revenues or expenses.
3. Write the account totals from the left side of the equals sign and add them. Write the account totals from the right side of the equals sign and add them. If the two totals are not equal, first check the addition and subtraction. If you still cannot find the error, reanalyze each transaction.

LO 1,2,3,4

PROBLEM 1-3A S. Davis, a graphic artist, opened a studio for her professional practice on August 1. The account headings are presented below. Transactions completed during the month follow.

Assets				= Liabilities +	Owner's Equity			
Cash +	Prepaid Insurance +	Office Equipment +	Photo Equipment =	Accounts Payable +	______, Capital −	______, Drawing +	Revenue +	Expenses

a. Davis deposited $20,000 in a bank account in the name of the business.
b. Bought office equipment on account from Starkey Equipment Company, $4,120.
c. Davis invested her personal photographic equipment, $5,370. (Increase the account Photo Equipment and increase the account S. Davis, Capital.)

d. Paid the rent for the month, $1,500, Ck. No. 1000 (Rent Expense).
e. Bought supplies for cash, $215, Ck. No. 1001 (Supplies Expense).
f. Bought insurance for two years, $1,840, Ck. No. 1002.
g. Sold graphic services for cash, $3,616 (Professional Fees).
h. Paid the salary of the part-time assistant, $982, Ck. No. 1003 (Salary Expense).
i. Received and paid the bill for telephone service, $134, Ck. No. 1004 (Telephone Expense).
j. Paid cash for minor repairs to graphics equipment, $185, Ck. No. 1005 (Repair Expense).
k. Sold graphic services for cash, $3,693 (Professional Fees).
l. Paid on account to Starkey Equipment Company, a creditor, $650, Ck. No. 1006.
m. Davis withdrew cash for personal use, $1,800, Ck. No. 1007 (S. Davis, Drawing).

Required

1. In the equation, write the owner's name above the terms *Capital* and *Drawing*.
2. Record the transactions and the balance after each transaction. Identify the account affected when the transaction involves revenues or expenses.
3. Write the account totals from the left side of the equals sign and add them. Write the account totals from the right side of the equals sign and add them. If the two totals are not equal, first check the addition and subtraction. If you still cannot find the error, reanalyze each transaction.

Check Figure
Right side of equals sign total, $31,333

PROBLEM 1-4A On March 1 of this year, B. Gervais established Gervais Catering Service. The account headings are presented below. Transactions completed during the month follow.

Assets					= Liabilities +	Owner's Equity			
Cash +	Accounts Receivable +	Prepaid Insurance +	Truck +	Equipment =	Accounts Payable	+ ______, Capital –	______, Drawing +	Revenue –	Expenses

a. Gervais deposited $25,000 in a bank account in the name of the business.
b. Bought a truck from Kelly Motors for $26,329, paying $8,000 in cash and placing the balance on account, Ck. No. 500.
c. Bought catering equipment on account from Luigi's Equipment, $3,795.
d. Paid the rent for the month, $1,255, Ck. No. 501 (Rent Expense).
e. Bought insurance for the truck for one year, $400, Ck. No. 502.
f. Sold catering services for cash for the first half of the month, $3,012 (Catering Income).
g. Bought supplies for cash, $185, Ck. No. 503 (Supplies Expense).
h. Sold catering services on account, $4,307 (Catering Income).
i. Received and paid the heating bill, $248, Ck. No. 504 (Utilities Expense).
j. Received a bill from GC Gas and Lube for gas and oil for the truck, $128 (Gas and Oil Expense).
k. Sold catering services for cash for the remainder of the month, $2,649 (Catering Income).
l. Gervais withdrew cash for personal use, $1,550, Ck. No. 505 (B. Gervais, Drawing).
m. Paid the salary of the assistant, $1,150, Ck. No. 506 (Salary Expense).

Required

1. In the equation, write the owner's name above the terms *Capital* and *Drawing*.
2. Record the transactions and the balance after each transaction. Identify the account affected when the transaction involves revenues or expenses.
3. Write the account totals from the left side of the equals sign and add them. Write the account totals from the right side of the equals sign and add them. If the two totals are not equal, first check the addition and subtraction. If you still cannot find the error, reanalyze each transaction.

Check Figure
Cash, $17,873

Problem Set B

For additional help, see the demonstration problem at the beginning of each chapter in your Working Papers.

1,2,3,4 **LO**

PROBLEM 1-1B In July of this year, M. Wallace established a business called Wallace Realty. The account headings are presented below. Transactions completed during the month follow.

Assets		= Liabilities +	Owner's Equity			
Cash +	Office Equipment =	Accounts Payable	+ ______, Capital –	______, Drawing +	Revenue –	Expenses

a. Wallace deposited $24,000 in a bank account in the name of the business.
b. Paid the office rent for the current month, $650, Ck. No. 1000 (Rent Expense).
c. Bought office supplies for cash, $375, Ck. No. 1001 (Supplies Expense).
d. Bought office equipment on account from Dellos Computers, $6,300.
e. Received a bill from the *City Crier* for advertising, $455 (Advertising Expense).
f. Sold services for cash, $3,944 (Service Income).
g. Paid on account to Dellos Computers, a creditor, $1,500, Ck. No. 1002.
h. Received and paid the bill for utilities, $340, Ck. No. 1003 (Utilities Expense).
i. Paid on account to the *City Crier*, a creditor, $455, Ck. No. 1004.
j. Paid truck expenses, $435, Ck. No. 1005 (Truck Maintenance Expense).
k. Wallace withdrew cash for personal use, $1,500, Ck. No. 1006 (M. Wallace, Drawing).

Check Figure
Left side of equals sign total, $28,989

Required

1. In the equation, write the owner's name above the terms *Capital* and *Drawing*.
2. Record the transactions and the balance after each transaction. Identify the account affected when the transaction involves revenues or expenses.
3. Write the account totals from the left side of the equals sign and add them. Write the account totals from the right side of the equals sign and add them. If the two totals are not equal, first check the addition and subtraction. If you still cannot find the error, reanalyze each transaction.

1,2,3,4 **LO**

PROBLEM 1-2B In March, K. Haas, M.D., established the Haas Sports Injury Clinic. The clinic's account headings are presented below. Transactions completed during the month of March follow.

Assets		= Liabilities +	Owner's Equity			
Cash +	Office Equipment =	Accounts Payable	+ ______, Capital –	______, Drawing +	Revenue –	Expenses

a. Haas deposited $48,000 in a bank account in the name of the business.
b. Paid the rent for the month, $2,200, Ck. No. 1000 (Rent Expense).
c. Bought supplies for cash from Medco Co., $2,138.
d. Bought professional equipment on account from Med-Tech Company, $18,000.
e. Bought office equipment on account from Equipment Depot, $1,955.
f. Sold professional services for cash, $8,960 (Professional Fees).
g. Paid on account to Med-Tech Company, a creditor, $3,000, Ck. No. 1001.
h. Received and paid the bill for utilities, $472, Ck. No. 1002 (Utilities Expense).
i. Paid the salary of the assistant, $1,738, Ck. No. 1003 (Salary Expense).
j. Sold professional services for cash, $10,196 (Professional Fees).
k. Haas withdrew cash for personal use, $3,500, Ck. No. 1004 (K. Haas, Drawing).

Required

Check Figure
Cash, $54,108

1. In the equation, write the owner's name above the terms *Capital* and *Drawing.*
2. Record the transactions and the balance after each transaction. Identify the account affected when the transaction involves revenue, expenses, or a withdrawal.
3. Write the account totals from the left side of the equals sign and add them. Write the account totals from the right side of the equals sign and add them. If the two totals are not equal, first check the addition and subtraction. If you still cannot find the error, reanalyze each transaction.

LO 1,2,3,4

PROBLEM 1-3B P. Schwartz, Attorney at Law, opened his office on October 1. The account headings are presented below. Transactions completed during the month follow.

Assets				= Liabilities +	Owner's Equity			
	Prepaid	Office		Accounts	______,	______,		
Cash +	Insurance +	Equipment +	Library =	Payable	+ Capital −	Drawing +	Revenue −	Expenses

a. Schwartz deposited $25,000 in a bank account in the name of the business.
b. Bought office equipment on account from QuipCo, $9,670.
c. Schwartz invested his personal law library, which cost $2,800. (Increase the account Library and increase the account P. Schwartz, Capital.)
d. Paid the office rent for the month, $1,700, Ck. No. 2000 (Rent Expense).
e. Bought office supplies for cash, $418, Ck. No. 2001 (Supplies Expense).
f. Bought insurance for two years, $944, Ck. No. 2002.
g. Sold legal services for cash, $8,518 (Professional Fees).
h. Paid the salary of the part-time receptionist, $1,820, Ck. No. 2003 (Salary Expense).
i. Received and paid the telephone bill, $388, Ck. No. 2004 (Telephone Expense).
j. Received and paid the bill for utilities, $368, Ck. No. 2005 (Utilities Expense).
k. Sold legal services for cash, $9,260 (Professional Fees).
l. Paid on account to QuipCo, a creditor, $2,670, Ck. No. 2006.
m. Schwartz withdrew cash for personal use, $2,500, Ck. No. 2007 (P. Schwartz, Drawing).

Required

Check Figure
Right side of equals sign total, $45,384

1. In the equation, write the owner's name above the terms *Capital* and *Drawing.*
2. Record the transactions and the balance after each transaction. Identify the account affected when the transaction involves revenues or expenses.
3. Write the account totals from the left side of the equals sign and add them. Write the account totals from the right side of the equals sign and add them. If the two totals are not equal, first check the addition and subtraction. If you still cannot find the error, reanalyze each transaction.

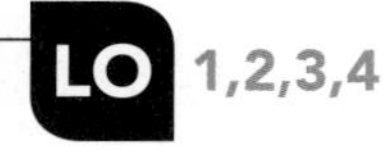

LO 1,2,3,4

PROBLEM 1-4B In March, T. Carter established Carter Delivery Service. The account headings are presented below. Transactions completed during the month of March follow.

Assets					= Liabilities +	Owner's Equity			
	Accounts	Prepaid			Accounts	______,	______,		
Cash +	Receivable +	Insurance +	Truck +	Equipment =	Payable	+ Capital −	Drawing +	Revenue −	Expenses

a. Carter deposited $25,000 in a bank account in the name of the business.
b. Bought a used business from Degroot Motors for $15,140, paying $5,140 in cash and placing the remainder on account.

c. Bought equipment on account from Flemming Company, $3,450.
d. Paid the rent for the month, $1,000, Ck. No. 3001 (Rent Expense).
e. Sold services for cash for the first half of the month, $6,927 (Service Income).
f. Bought supplies for cash, $301, Ck. No. 3002 (Supplies Expense).
g. Bought insurance for the truck for the year, $1,200, Ck. No. 3003.
h. Received and paid the bill for utilities, $349, Ck. No. 3004 (Utilities Expense).
i. Received a bill for gas and oil for the truck, $218 (Gas and Oil Expense).
j. Sold services on account, $3,603 (Service Income).
k. Sold services for cash for the remainder of the month, $4,612 (Service Income).
l. Paid wages to the employees, $3,958, Ck. Nos. 3005–3007 (Wages Expense).
m. Carter withdrew cash for personal use, $1,250, Ck. No. 3008 (T. Carter, Drawing).

Check Figure
Cash, $23,341

Required

1. In the equation, write the owner's name above the terms *Capital* and *Drawing*.
2. Record the transactions and the balance after each transaction. Identify the account affected when the transaction involves revenues or expenses.
3. Write the account totals from the left side of the equals sign and add them. Write the account totals from the right side of the equals sign and add them. If the two totals are not equal, first check the addition and subtraction. If you still cannot find the error, reanalyze each transaction.

ACTIVITIES

CONSIDER AND COMMUNICATE

A friend of yours wants to start her own pet sitting business. She already has a business license that is required in her city. She has had a personal checking account for years. You have told her that she also needs to open a separate account for her business needs, but she does not understand why she needs to have two separate accounts. Explain to her why she should have a business account separate from her personal account. Use some of the language of business you have learned in your text's Introduction and in this chapter.

CRITICAL THINKING

Please read the following memorandum and follow the instructions set forth.

MEMORANDUM

TO: Your Name
FROM: J. Perrault, Supervisor
DATE: July 31, 20—
SUBJECT: Calculations for Richter Co.

Please provide the following ASAP (as soon as possible).

1. The balance of cash in Richter Company's checkbook shows $13,364. I need to know if this ties to or matches the Cash account balance. I do know that total assets amount to $43,560, Office Equipment amounts to $3,896, and other noncash assets are Professional Equipment, $24,375 and Prepaid Insurance, $1,925.
2. D. Richter, the owner, wants to know the amount of his owner's equity. I pulled the outstanding bills, which amount to $7,942.
3. Please put the information in a memo addressed to me.
4. Thank you for your prompt response.

T Accounts, Debits and Credits, Trial Balance, and Financial Statements

2

WHY IT MATTERS

SOLID ROCK GYM, Phoenix, Arizona

Individuals and groups of all ages come to Solid Rock Gym for fun and fitness. Part of the appeal of Solid Rock Gym, whose services include several types of indoor rock-climbing experiences, is around-the-clock access with its all-day-and-night passes. Services include individual and group instruction, team development, fitness programs, and bouldering (climbing close to the bottom—no rope or hardware), top-roping (climbing while protected by a rope running through anchors above the intended route), or lead climbing (climbing while protected by a rope clipped to anchors as the climber ascends a route).

In Chapter 1, we learned that a company such as Solid Rock Gym would have a chart of accounts with many different kinds of accounts. Can you imagine the kinds of accounts that Solid Rock Gym might have? In this chapter, you will learn that the chart of accounts can be used as the starting point for recording transactions with T accounts and debits and credits.

LEARNING OBJECTIVES

After you have completed this chapter, you will be able to do the following:

1. *Determine balances of T accounts having entries recorded on both sides of the accounts.*
2. *Present the fundamental accounting equation using the T account form, and label the plus and minus sides.*
3. *Present the fundamental accounting equation using the T account form, and label the debit and credit sides.*
4. *Record directly in T accounts a group of business transactions involving changes in asset, liability, owner's equity, revenue, and expense accounts for a service business.*
5. *Prepare a trial balance.*
6. *Prepare (a) an income statement, (b) a statement of owner's equity, and (c) a balance sheet.*
7. *Recognize the effect of transpositions and slides on account balances.*

ACCOUNTING LANGUAGE

Balance sheet *(p. 58)*
Compound entry *(p. 53)*
Credit *(p. 45)*
Debit *(p. 45)*
Financial position *(p. 58)*
Financial statement *(p. 56)*
Footings *(p. 44)*
Income statement *(p. 56)*
Net income *(p. 56)*
Net loss *(p. 56)*
Normal balance *(p. 44)*
Report form *(p. 58)*
Slide *(p. 60)*
Statement of owner's equity *(p. 58)*
T account form *(p. 43)*
Transposition *(p. 60)*
Trial balance *(p. 55)*

In the previous chapter, we introduced the fundamental accounting equation as *Assets = Liabilities + Owner's Equity*. We also discussed the recording of transactions involving two other classifications of accounts: *Revenue* and *Expenses*. With the addition of Revenue and Expenses, the fundamental accounting equation was brought up to its full size of five account classifications: Assets, Liabilities, Owner's Equity, Revenue, and Expenses. There are only five classifications in accounting; so, whether you are dealing with a small, one-owner business or a large corporation, there will be these five major classifications of accounts only.

In this chapter, we will record the same transactions from Chapter 1 (see pages 14–27) in T account form and prove the equality of both sides of the fundamental accounting equation using a trial balance, which is discussed later in this chapter.

THE T ACCOUNT FORM

In Chapter 1, we recorded business transactions in a column arrangement. For example, the Cash account column in the books of Conner's Whitewater Adventures is as follows:

Cash Account Column

Transaction	(a)	90,000
Transaction	(b)	–38,000
Balance		52,000
Transaction	(d)	–2,000
Balance		50,000
Transaction	(f)	+8,000
Balance		58,000
Transaction	(g)	–1,250
Balance		56,750
Transaction	(i)	–1,875
Balance		54,875
Transaction	(l)	–1,500
Balance		53,375
Transaction	(m)	–225
Balance		53,150
Transaction	(n)	–620
Balance		52,530
Transaction	(o)	–2,360
Balance		50,170
Transaction	(p)	–1,850
Balance		48,320
Transaction	(q)	+2,500
Balance		50,820
Transaction	(r)	+8,570
Balance		59,390
Transaction	(s)	–3,500
		55,890

Cash

	+		–
(a)	90,000	(b)	38,000
(f)	8,000	(d)	2,000
(q)	2,500	(g)	1,250
(r)	8,570	(i)	1,875
		(l)	1,500
	109,070	(m)	225
		(n)	620
		(o)	2,360
		(p)	1,850
Footings		(s)	3,500
Balance →	**55,890**		**53,180**

As an introduction to the recording of transactions, the column arrangement had the following advantages:

1. **In the process of analyzing the transaction, you**
   a. Recognized the need to determine which accounts are involved.
   b. Determined the classification of the accounts involved.
   c. Decided whether the transaction resulted in an increase or a decrease in each of these accounts.
2. **You further realized that, after each transaction was recorded, the two sides of the fundamental accounting equation were in balance. In other words, the total of one side of the accounting equation equaled the total of the other side.**

Now, instead of recording transactions in a column for each account, we will use a **T account form** for each account, as shown in the Cash T account above. *The T account form has the advantage of providing two sides for each account; one side is used to record increases in the account, and the other side is used to record decreases.*

After we record a group of transactions in a T account, we add both sides and record the totals in small, pencil-written figures called **footings**. Next, we subtract one footing from the other to determine the balance of the account. For the Cash account, shown previously, the balance is $55,890 ($109,070 – $53,180).

We now record the balance on the side of the account having the larger footing, which, with a few minor exceptions, is the plus (+) side. The plus side of a T account is the side that represents the **normal balance** of that account. The normal balance may, however, fall on either the left or the right side of an account, depending on the type of account.

LEARNING OBJECTIVE 1

Determine balances of T accounts having entries recorded on both sides of the accounts.

How to Determine Balances of T Accounts

STEP 1. Add each side separately and record the totals (called footing).

STEP 2. Subtract the large footing number from the small footing number.

STEP 3. Record the balance on the large footing side.

To review, we presented the T account for Cash. Cash is classified as an asset, and all assets look like the following T account:

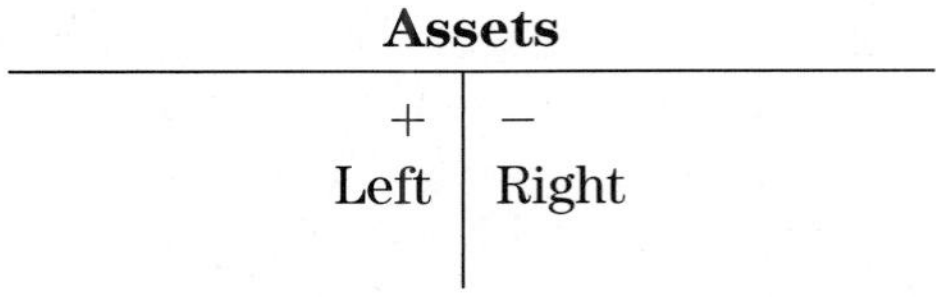

Assets	
+ Left	– Right

However, **not all classifications of accounts have the increase side on the left.**

Recall that we placed revenue and expenses under the umbrella of owner's equity. Revenue increases owner's equity, and expenses decrease owner's equity. The T accounts for this situation are as follows:

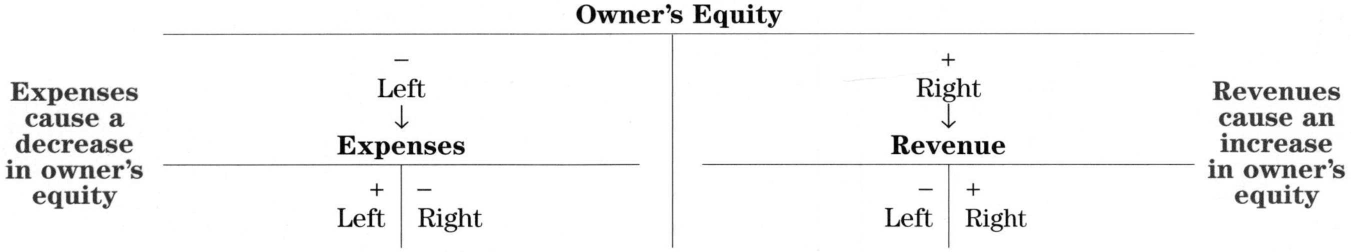

Owner's Equity

– Left	+ Right
↓	↓

Expenses cause a decrease in owner's equity

Expenses	
+ Left	– Right

Revenues cause an increase in owner's equity

Revenue	
– Left	+ Right

Increases in owner's equity are recorded on the right side of the account. Because revenue increases owner's equity, additions to revenue are also recorded on the right side.

Decreases in owner's equity are recorded on the left side of the account. Because expenses decrease owner's equity, additions to expenses are also recorded on the left side.

Using the five classifications of accounts, the fundamental accounting equation looks like this:

Assets = Liabilities + Owner's Equity

Owner's Equity = Capital – Drawing + Revenue – Expenses

Because revenue and expenses appear separately on the income statement, we will stretch out the equation to include them as separate headings, as shown here:

Assets = Liabilities + Owner's Equity + Revenue – Expenses

We can now restate the equation with the T account forms and plus and minus signs for each account classification:

Assets		=	Liabilities		+	Owner's Equity		+	Revenue		–	Expenses	
+ Left	– Right		– Left	+ Right		– Left	+ Right		– Left	+ Right		+ Left	– Right

Before we go on, let us point out the increase, or plus, side of each account classification. You can recognize these in the accounting equation using T accounts.

2 LEARNING OBJECTIVE *Present the fundamental accounting equation using the T account form, and label the plus and minus sides.*

Assets	The *left* side is the *increase* side.
Liabilities	The *right* side is the *increase* side.
Owner's Equity	The *right* side is the *increase* side.
Revenue	The *right* side is the *increase* side.
Expenses	The *left* side is the *increase* side.

Because revenue is an addition to owner's equity, the placement of the plus and minus signs is the same as for owner's equity. On the other hand, because expenses are treated as deductions from owner's equity, the placement of the plus and minus signs is reversed. We will use this form of the fundamental accounting equation throughout the remainder of the text.

Your accounting background up to this point has taught you to analyze business transactions to determine which accounts are involved and to recognize that each amount should be recorded as either an increase or a decrease in these accounts. Now the recording process becomes a simple matter of knowing which side of the T accounts should be used to record increases and which should be used to record decreases. **Generally, you will not be using the minus side of the revenue and expense accounts, since transactions involving revenue and expense accounts usually result in increases in these accounts.** An exception to this statement is where errors have been made and require correction. Let's now add the last element to the T account before we record the familiar Conner's Whitewater Adventures transactions.

THE T ACCOUNT FORM WITH DEBITS AND CREDITS

3 LEARNING OBJECTIVE *Present the fundamental accounting equation using the T account form, and label the debit and credit sides.*

The left side of a T account is called the **debit** side; the right side is called the **credit** side. The T accounts representing the accounting equation now contain both the signs and the words *Debit* and *Credit*. There are only five classifications of accounts. These classifications are contained in the fundamental accounting equation:

Assets		=	Liabilities		+	Owner's Equity		+	Revenue		–	Expenses	
+ Debit	– Credit		– Debit	+ Credit		– Debit	+ Credit		– Debit	+ Credit		+ Debit	– Credit

Before we begin recording transactions, notice the new T account following the Capital account, Drawing. Recall that the Capital account is increased when amounts are invested and decreased when amounts are taken out.

Capital	
– Debit	+ Credit Amounts invested

Remember

In the fundamental accounting equation, all accounts before the equal sign (assets) have the plus sign on the left side. Accounts after the equal sign (liabilities and capital) have the plus sign on the right side.

Since revenues increase capital, when the equation is expanded to include revenue and expenses the plus sign is on the right side, like the Capital account. Similarly, since expenses decrease capital, the plus sign is on the left side, like the Drawing account.

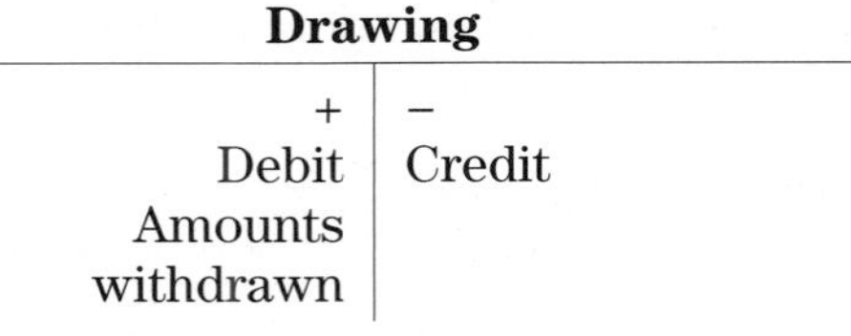

We reserve the minus or debit side of the Capital account for permanent withdrawals, those made when the owner decides to reduce the size of the business permanently or when a net loss forces such a reduction. This concept is best illustrated by showing the Drawing T account under the umbrella of the Capital T account.

Capital	
– Debit	+ Credit
Drawing (+ Debit | – Credit)	

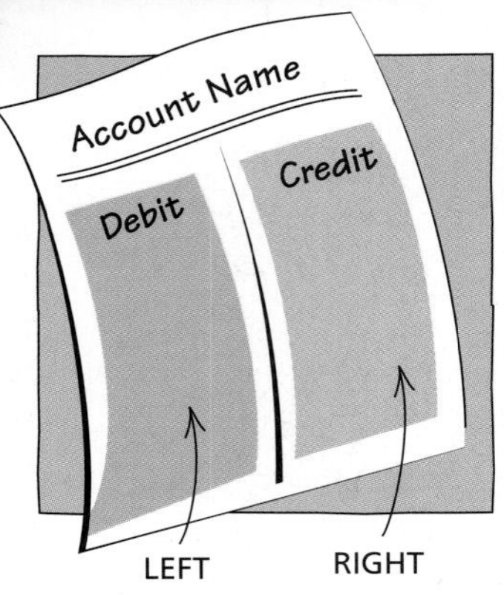

Debit is always the left side of the account, and credit is always the right side of the account. The + or –, however, changes with the type of account.

The following table summarizes debits and credits and how they are affected by increases and decreases. **The critical rule to remember is that the amount placed on the debit side of one or more accounts MUST equal the amount placed on the credit side of another account or accounts.**

Debits Signify		Credits Signify	
Increases in	Assets Drawing Expenses	Decreases in	Assets Drawing Expenses
Decreases in	Liabilities Capital Revenue	Increases in	Liabilities Capital Revenue

RECORDING BUSINESS TRANSACTIONS IN T ACCOUNTS

LEARNING OBJECTIVE 4

Record directly in T accounts a group of business transactions involving changes in asset, liability, owner's equity, revenue, and expense accounts for a service business.

Our task now is to learn how to record business transactions in the T account form. First, let's review the steps in analyzing a business transaction.

STEP 1. Decide which accounts are involved.

STEP 2. Classify the accounts involved (asset, liability, owner's equity, revenue, expense).

STEP 3. Decide if the accounts involved are increased or decreased.

STEP 4. Write the transaction as a debit to one account (or accounts) and a credit to another account (or accounts).

STEP 5. Check to see if the equation is in balance after the transaction has been recorded.

For example, let's analyze the first transaction of the Conner's Whitewater Adventures transactions using this five-step process. To formulate the entry, you must be able to visualize the fundamental accounting equation in the form of T accounts. With that in mind, the first transaction is as follows:

In transaction (a), Conner deposited $90,000 in a bank account in the name of the business. This transaction results in an increase to Cash with a debit and an increase in the Capital account with a credit.

STEP 1. Decide which accounts are involved. The two accounts involved are Cash and J. Conner, Capital.

STEP 2. Classify the accounts involved (asset, liability, owner's equity, revenue, expense). Cash is an asset and J. Conner, Capital, is an owner's equity account.

STEP 3. Decide if the accounts involved are increased or decreased. Cash is being deposited in the bank account, an increase to Cash. The owner has invested that cash in the business and has increased J. Conner, Capital.

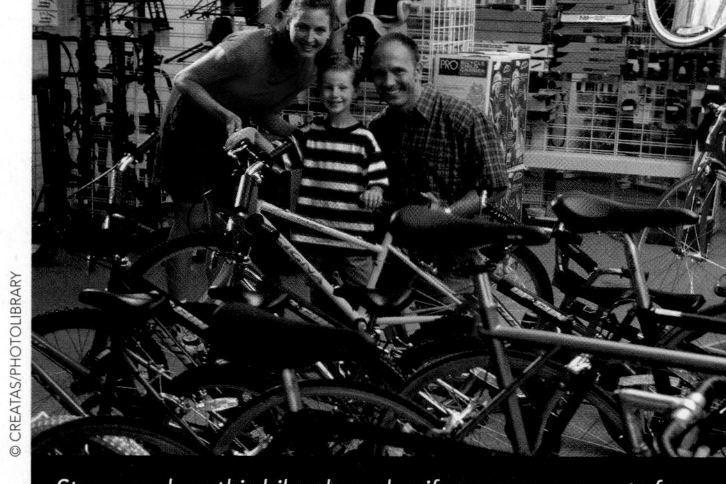

Stores such as this bike shop classify revenue accounts for each activity—sales, repairs, and rentals. They also classify expense accounts separately.

STEP 4. Write the transaction as a debit to one account (or accounts) and a credit to another account (or accounts). Since Cash is an asset and Cash is increased, Cash is debited. We now need an offsetting credit. J. Conner, Capital, is an owner's equity account and is increased. J. Conner, Capital, is credited.

STEP 5. Check to see if the equation is in balance. There is at least one account debited and at least one account credited, *and* the total amount(s) debited equals the total amount(s) credited. You now have a debit equal to a credit, a $90,000 debit to Cash and a $90,000 credit to J. Conner, Capital.

The resulting transaction in T account form follows:

Assets		=	Liabilities		+	Owner's Equity		+	Revenue		−	Expenses	
+	−		−	+		−	+		−	+		+	−
Debit	Credit		Debit	Credit		Debit	Credit		Debit	Credit		Debit	Credit

Cash	
+	−
Debit	Credit
(a) 90,000	

J. Conner, Capital	
−	+
Debit	Credit
	(a) 90,000

In transaction (b), Conner's Whitewater Adventures bought equipment, paying cash, $38,000. This transaction results in an increase to Equipment with a debit and a decrease to Cash with a credit.

Assets		=	Liabilities		+	Owner's Equity		+	Revenue		−	Expenses	
+	−		−	+		−	+		−	+		+	−
Debit	Credit		Debit	Credit		Debit	Credit		Debit	Credit		Debit	Credit

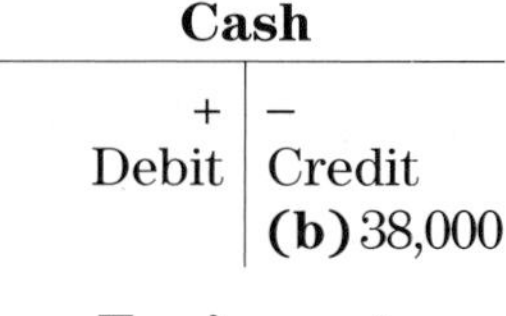

Cash	
+	−
Debit	Credit
	(b) 38,000

Equipment	
+	−
Debit	Credit
(b) 38,000	

Remember

When we describe the transactions of the business, notice that we say "Conner's Whitewater Adventure's paid or bought" and "J. Conner paid or bought." We do so because the business is treated as a separate economic entity—independent and separate from its owner.

In transaction (c), Conner's Whitewater Adventures bought equipment on account from Signal Products, $4,320. This transaction results in an increase to Equipment with a debit and an increase to Accounts Payable with a credit and is shown in T account form as follows:

Assets		=	Liabilities		+	Owner's Equity		+	Revenue		–	Expenses	
+	–		–	+		–	+		–	+		+	–
Debit	Credit		Debit	Credit		Debit	Credit		Debit	Credit		Debit	Credit

Equipment		Accounts Payable	
+	–	–	+
Debit	Credit	Debit	Credit
(c) 4,320			**(c)** 4,320

In transaction (d), Conner's Whitewater Adventures paid Signal Products, a creditor, $2,000. This transaction results in a decrease to Cash with a credit and a decrease to Accounts Payable with a debit.

Assets		=	Liabilities		+	Owner's Equity		+	Revenue		–	Expenses	
+	–		–	+		–	+		–	+		+	–
Debit	Credit		Debit	Credit		Debit	Credit		Debit	Credit		Debit	Credit

Cash		Accounts Payable	
+	–	–	+
Debit	Credit	Debit	Credit
	(d) 2,000	**(d)** 2,000	

In transaction (e), J. Conner invests her personal computer, with a fair market value of $5,200, in the business.

Assets		=	Liabilities		+	Owner's Equity		+	Revenue		–	Expenses	
+	–		–	+		–	+		–	+		+	–
Debit	Credit		Debit	Credit		Debit	Credit		Debit	Credit		Debit	Credit

Equipment		J. Conner, Capital	
+	–	–	+
Debit	Credit	Debit	Credit
(e) 5,200			**(e)** 5,200

Here is a restatement of the accounts after recording transactions (a) through (e). To test your understanding of the process, trace through the recording of each transaction and describe what happened in the transaction. Footings or subtotals (remember, always write the footings smaller than the entries and in pencil) are required to compute the balances of the accounts. The balances are written in the accounts on the side with the larger total.

Assets = **Liabilities** + **Owner's Equity** + **Revenue** − **Expenses**

Assets		=	Liabilities		+	Owner's Equity		+	Revenue		−	Expenses	
+	−		−	+		−	+		−	+		+	−
Debit	Credit		Debit	Credit		Debit	Credit		Debit	Credit		Debit	Credit

Cash

+ Debit	− Credit
(a) 90,000	(b) 38,000
	(d) 2,000
	40,000
Bal. 50,000	

Accounts Receivable

+ Debit	− Credit

Prepaid Insurance

+ Debit	− Credit

Equipment

+ Debit	− Credit
(b) 38,000	
(c) 4,320	
(e) 5,200	
Bal. 47,520	

Accounts Payable

− Debit	+ Credit
(d) 2,000	(c) 4,320
	Bal. 2,320

J. Conner, Capital

− Debit	+ Credit
	(a) 90,000
	(e) 5,200
	Bal. 95,200

J. Conner, Drawing

+ Debit	− Credit

Income from Tours

− Debit	+ Credit

Wages Expense

+ Debit	− Credit

Rent Expense

+ Debit	− Credit

Supplies Expense

+ Debit	− Credit

Advertising Expense

+ Debit	− Credit

Utilities Expense

+ Debit	− Credit

Let's pause to see if the debits are equal to the credits by listing the balances of the accounts:

	Accounts with Normal Balances on the Left or Debit Side:	Accounts with Normal Balances on the Right or Credit Side:
Account Name	**Assets Drawing Expenses**	**Liabilities Capital Revenue**
Cash	$50,000	
Equipment	47,520	
Accounts Payable		$ 2,320
J. Conner, Capital		95,200
	$97,520	$97,520

In transaction (f), Conner's Whitewater Adventures sold rafting tours for cash, $8,000. This transaction results in an increase to Cash with a debit and an increase to Income from Tours with a credit.

Remember

The normal balance of an account classification is on the plus side.

FYI

The T account is not only a learning tool; it will serve you well as a problem-solving device when you need to analyze a transaction, whether recording it manually or on a computer.

Assets		=	Liabilities		+	Owner's Equity		+	Revenue		−	Expenses	
+ Debit	− Credit		− Debit	+ Credit		− Debit	+ Credit		− Debit	+ Credit		+ Debit	− Credit

Cash	
+ Debit	− Credit
(f) 8,000	

Income from Tours	
− Debit	+ Credit
	(f) 8,000

In transaction (g), Conner's Whitewater Adventures paid rent for the month, $1,250. This transaction results in an increase to Rent Expense with a debit and a decrease to Cash with a credit.

Assets		=	Liabilities		+	Owner's Equity		+	Revenue		−	Expenses	
+ Debit	− Credit		− Debit	+ Credit		− Debit	+ Credit		− Debit	+ Credit		+ Debit	− Credit

Cash	
+ Debit	− Credit
	(g) 1,250

Rent Expense	
+ Debit	− Credit
(g) 1,250	

In transaction (h), Conner's Whitewater Adventures bought computer paper, ink cartridges, invoice pads, pens and pencils, folders, filing cabinets, and 10-key calculators on account. These items are considered to be supplies to be used up by Conner's Whitewater Adventures and are recorded as an expense for $675 on account from Fineman Company. This transaction results in an increase to Supplies Expense with a debit and an increase to Accounts Payable with a credit.

Assets		=	Liabilities		+	Owner's Equity		+	Revenue		−	Expenses	
+ Debit	− Credit		− Debit	+ Credit		− Debit	+ Credit		− Debit	+ Credit		+ Debit	− Credit

Accounts Payable	
− Debit	+ Credit
	(h) 675

Supplies Expense	
+ Debit	− Credit
(h) 675	

In transaction (i), Conner's Whitewater Adventures bought a three-month liability insurance policy, $1,875. This transaction results in an increase to Prepaid Insurance with a debit and a decrease to Cash with a credit.

Assets		=	Liabilities		+	Owner's Equity		+	Revenue		−	Expenses	
+ Debit	− Credit		− Debit	+ Credit		− Debit	+ Credit		− Debit	+ Credit		+ Debit	− Credit

Cash	
+ Debit	− Credit
	(i) 1,875

Prepaid Insurance	
+ Debit	− Credit
(i) 1,875	

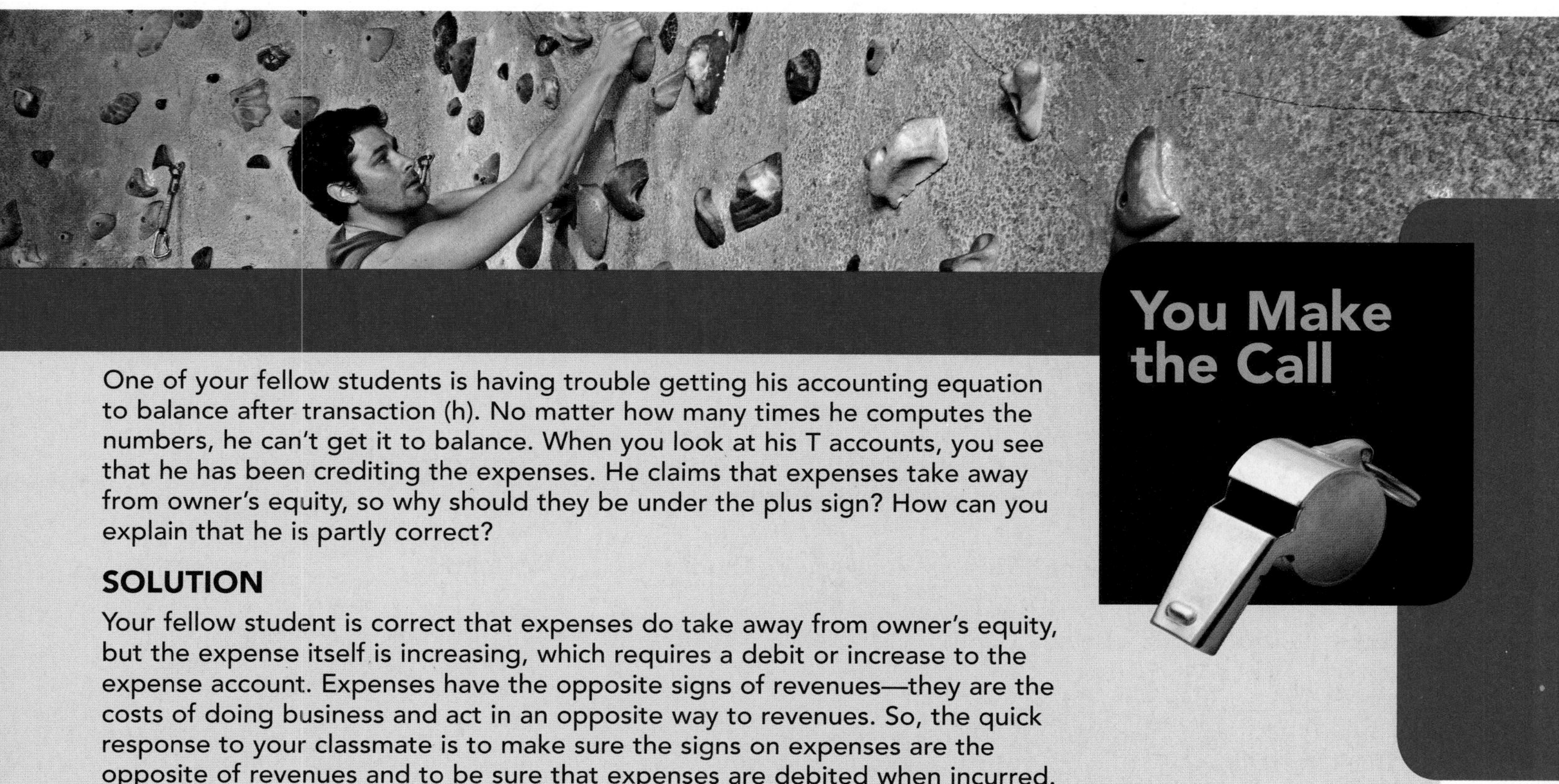

You Make the Call

One of your fellow students is having trouble getting his accounting equation to balance after transaction (h). No matter how many times he computes the numbers, he can't get it to balance. When you look at his T accounts, you see that he has been crediting the expenses. He claims that expenses take away from owner's equity, so why should they be under the plus sign? How can you explain that he is partly correct?

SOLUTION

Your fellow student is correct that expenses do take away from owner's equity, but the expense itself is increasing, which requires a debit or increase to the expense account. Expenses have the opposite signs of revenues—they are the costs of doing business and act in an opposite way to revenues. So, the quick response to your classmate is to make sure the signs on expenses are the opposite of revenues and to be sure that expenses are debited when incurred.

In transaction (j), Conner's Whitewater Adventures received a bill for newspaper advertising from *The Times*, $620. This results in an increase to Advertising Expense with a debit and an increase to Accounts Payable with a credit.

Assets		=	Liabilities		+	Owner's Equity		+	Revenue		−	Expenses	
+ Debit	− Credit		− Debit	+ Credit		− Debit	+ Credit		− Debit	+ Credit		+ Debit	− Credit

Accounts Payable	
− Debit	+ Credit
	(j) 620

Advertising Expense	
+ Debit	− Credit
(j) 620	

In transaction (k), Conner's Whitewater Adventures signs a contract with Crystal River Lodge to provide rafting adventures for guests. Conner's Whitewater Adventures provides 27 one-day rafting tours and bills Crystal River Lodge for $6,750. This results in an increase to Accounts Receivable with a debit and an increase to Income from Tours with a credit.

Assets		=	Liabilities		+	Owner's Equity		+	Revenue		−	Expenses	
+ Debit	− Credit		− Debit	+ Credit		− Debit	+ Credit		− Debit	+ Credit		+ Debit	− Credit

Accounts Receivable	
+ Debit	− Credit
(k) 6,750	

Income from Tours	
− Debit	+ Credit
	(k) 6,750

In transaction (l), Conner's Whitewater Adventures pays on account to Signal Products, $1,500. This transaction results in a decrease to Accounts Payable with a debit and a decrease to Cash with a credit.

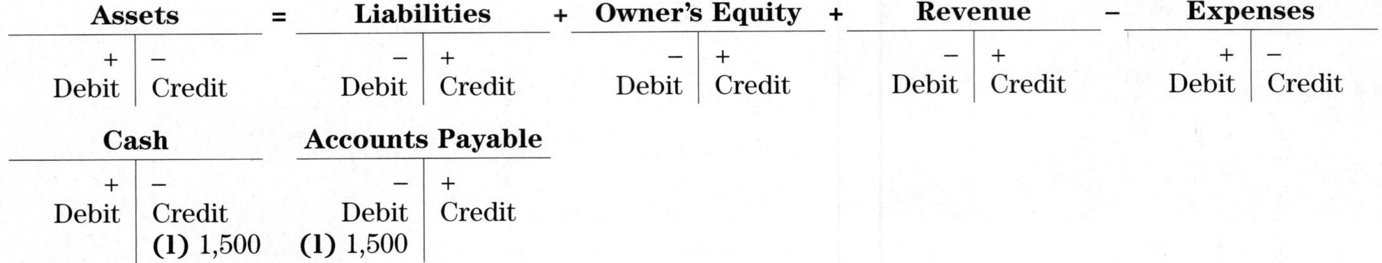

In transaction (m), Conner's Whitewater Adventures received and paid Solar Power, Inc. for the electric bill, $225. The result of this transaction is an increase to Utilities Expense with a debit and a decrease to Cash with a credit.

Assets		=	Liabilities		+	Owner's Equity		+	Revenue		–	Expenses	
+ Debit	– Credit		– Debit	+ Credit		– Debit	+ Credit		– Debit	+ Credit		+ Debit	– Credit

Cash		Utilities Expense	
+ Debit	– Credit	+ Debit	– Credit
	(m) 225	(m) 225	

In transaction (n), Conner's Whitewater Adventures paid on account to *The Times*, $620. This transaction results in a decrease to Accounts Payable with a debit and a decrease to Cash with a credit. **Recall that this bill had previously been recorded as a liability in transaction (j).**

Assets		=	Liabilities		+	Owner's Equity		+	Revenue		–	Expenses	
+ Debit	– Credit		– Debit	+ Credit		– Debit	+ Credit		– Debit	+ Credit		+ Debit	– Credit

Cash		Accounts Payable	
+ Debit	– Credit	– Debit	+ Credit
	(n) 620	(n) 620	

In transaction (o), Conner's Whitewater Adventures paid the wages of a part-time employee, $2,360. This transaction results in an increase to Wages Expense with a debit and a decrease to Cash with a credit.

Assets		=	Liabilities		+	Owner's Equity		+	Revenue		–	Expenses	
+ Debit	– Credit		– Debit	+ Credit		– Debit	+ Credit		– Debit	+ Credit		+ Debit	– Credit

Cash		Wages Expense	
+ Debit	– Credit	+ Debit	– Credit
	(o) 2,360	(o) 2,360	

In transaction (p), Conner's Whitewater Adventures bought additional equipment from Signal Products, $3,780, paying $1,850 in cash and placing the balance on account. This transaction results in an increase to Equipment with a debit, an increase to Accounts Payable with a credit, and a decrease to Cash with a credit. This is called a **compound entry**; that is, more than one debit or more than one credit is recorded.

Assets = Liabilities + Owner's Equity + Revenue − Expenses

Assets		Liabilities		Owner's Equity		Revenue		Expenses	
+	−	−	+	−	+	−	+	+	−
Debit	Credit	Debit	Credit	Debit	Credit	Debit	Credit	Debit	Credit

Cash		Accounts Payable	
+	−	−	+
Debit	Credit	Debit	Credit
	(p) 1,850		(p) 1,930

Equipment	
+	−
Debit	Credit
(p) 3,780	

In transaction (q), Conner's Whitewater Adventures received $2,500 cash from Crystal River Lodge to apply against the amount billed in transaction (k). This transaction results in an increase to Cash with a debit and a decrease to Accounts Receivable with a credit.

Assets = Liabilities + Owner's Equity + Revenue − Expenses

Assets		Liabilities		Owner's Equity		Revenue		Expenses	
+	−	−	+	−	+	−	+	+	−
Debit	Credit	Debit	Credit	Debit	Credit	Debit	Credit	Debit	Credit

Cash	
+	−
Debit	Credit
(q) 2,500	

Accounts Receivable	
+	−
Debit	Credit
	(q) 2,500

In transaction (r), Conner's Whitewater Adventures sold tours for cash, $8,570. This transaction results in an increase to Cash with a debit and an increase to Income from Tours with a credit.

Assets = Liabilities + Owner's Equity + Revenue − Expenses

Assets		Liabilities		Owner's Equity		Revenue		Expenses	
+	−	−	+	−	+	−	+	+	−
Debit	Credit	Debit	Credit	Debit	Credit	Debit	Credit	Debit	Credit

Cash		Income from Tours	
+	−	−	+
Debit	Credit	Debit	Credit
(r) 8,570			(r) 8,570

In transaction (s), J. Conner withdrew cash for her personal use, $3,500. This transaction increases J. Conner, Drawing with a debit and decreases Cash with a credit.

Assets		=	Liabilities		+	Owner's Equity		+	Revenue		−	Expenses	
+ Debit	− Credit		− Debit	+ Credit		− Debit	+ Credit		− Debit	+ Credit		+ Debit	− Credit

Cash	
+ Debit	− Credit
	(s) 3,500

J. Conner, Drawing	
+ Debit	− Credit
(s) 3,500	

The Drawing account is used to record any withdrawals by the owner from the business for his or her living expenses. The owner hopes that the withdrawals will be offset by net income which will cause the Capital account to be increased. If, instead, the withdrawals are more than net income, the Capital account will be decreased.

Summary of Transactions

FYI Traditionally, accountants use the abbreviations Dr. for Debit and Cr. for Credit.

The following T accounts provide a summary of all transactions for Conner's Whitewater Adventures. Footings are shown in color. You will notice that the balance of each account is normally on the plus side. Note that, in recording expenses, you normally place the entries only on the plus, or debit, side. Also, in recording revenue, you normally place the entries only on the plus, or credit, side.

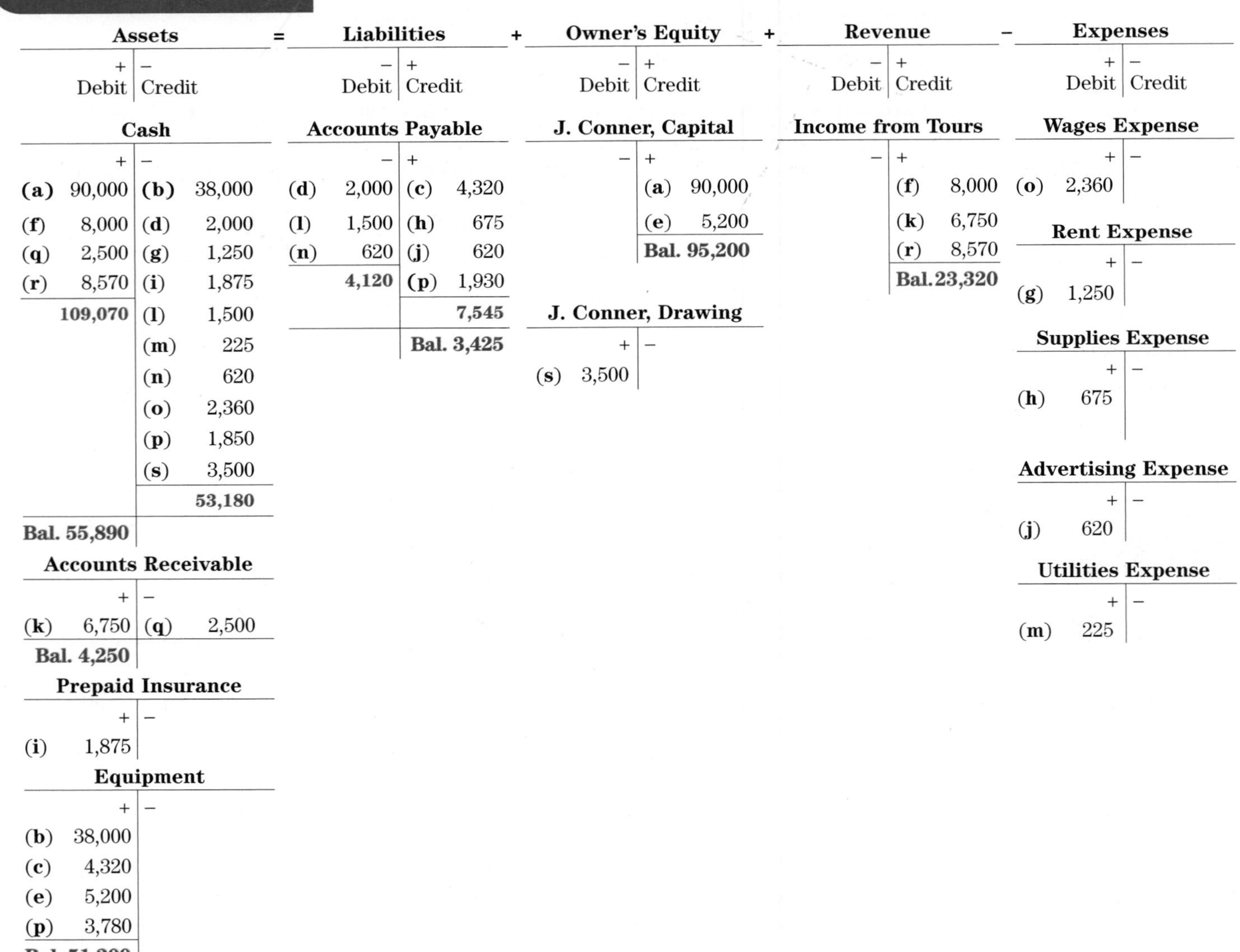

Assets = Liabilities + Owner's Equity + Revenue − Expenses
+ Debit | − Credit
− Debit | + Credit
− Debit | + Credit
− Debit | + Credit
+ Debit | − Credit
Cash
(a) 90,000 | (b) 38,000
(f) 8,000 | (d) 2,000
(q) 2,500 | (g) 1,250
(r) 8,570 | (i) 1,875
109,070 | (l) 1,500
(m) 225
(n) 620
(o) 2,360
(p) 1,850
(s) 3,500
53,180
Bal. 55,890
Accounts Receivable
(k) 6,750 | (q) 2,500
Bal. 4,250
Prepaid Insurance
(i) 1,875
Equipment
(b) 38,000
(c) 4,320
(e) 5,200
(p) 3,780
Bal. 51,300
Accounts Payable
(d) 2,000 | (c) 4,320
(l) 1,500 | (h) 675
(n) 620 | (j) 620
4,120 | (p) 1,930
7,545
Bal. 3,425
J. Conner, Capital
(a) 90,000
(e) 5,200
Bal. 95,200
J. Conner, Drawing
(s) 3,500
Income from Tours
(f) 8,000
(k) 6,750
(r) 8,570
Bal. 23,320
Wages Expense
(o) 2,360
Rent Expense
(g) 1,250
Supplies Expense
(h) 675
Advertising Expense
(j) 620
Utilities Expense
(m) 225

FIGURE 1

Accounting memory tool

A memory tool that helps some students to memorize debits and credits in T accounts is the equation A + D + E = L + C + R. All accounts on the left side of the equation have normal debit balances and all accounts on the right side have normal credit balances. You can make up a memorable sentence or use this one—All Drippy Eels Love Cucumbers and Radishes. Picture an eel dripping with water devouring cucumbers and radishes.

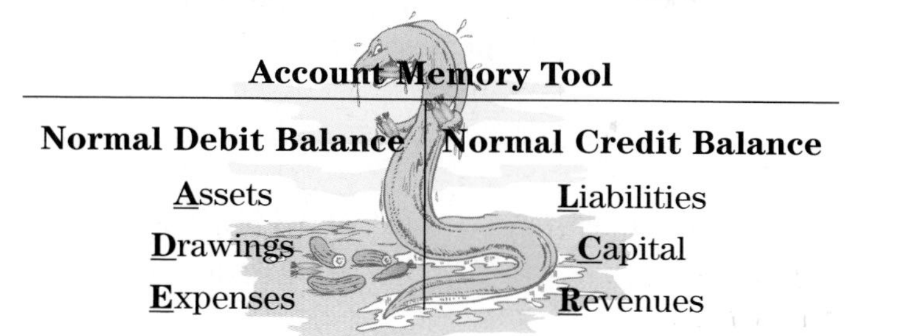

Account Memory Tool
Normal Debit Balance
Normal Credit Balance
Assets
Drawings
Expenses
Liabilities
Capital
Revenues

THE TRIAL BALANCE

5 LEARNING OBJECTIVE

Prepare a trial balance.

After recording the transactions in the T accounts, you can now prepare a trial balance by simply recording the balances of the T accounts in two columns. The **trial balance** is a listing of account balances in two columns—one labeled Debit and one labeled Credit—to prove that the total of all the debit balances equals the total of all the credit balances. A trial balance is not considered a financial statement; it is, as the name implies, a trial run by the accountant to prove that the total of the debit balances equals the total of the credit balances. This is evidence of the equality of the two sides of the fundamental accounting equation. The accountant must prove that the accounts are in balance before preparing the company's financial statements.

In preparing a trial balance, shown in Figure 2, record the accounts with balances in the same order as they are listed in the chart of accounts.

- Assets
- Liabilities
- Owner's Equity
- Revenue
- Expenses

FIGURE 2

Trial balance

Conner's Whitewater Adventures
Trial Balance
June 30, 20—

Column headings identify information in each column

Account Name	Debit	Credit
Cash	55,890	
Accounts Receivable	4,250	
Prepaid Insurance	1,875	
Equipment	51,300	
Accounts Payable		3,425
J. Conner, Capital		95,200
J. Conner, Drawing	3,500	
Income from Tours		23,320
Wages Expense	2,360	
Rent Expense	1,250	
Supplies Expense	675	
Advertising Expense	620	
Utilities Expense	225	
	121,945	121,945

Accounts listed in order of the chart of accounts

Dollar signs not used on a trial balance

Single underline beneath figures to be added

Double underline beneath column totals

The normal balance of each account is on its plus side. Remember that when there is more than one entry in an account, we record the totals in footings and subtract one footing from the other to determine the balance. **Record this balance on the side of the account with the larger footing.** (Here we record the Drawing account balance in the debit column because it has a debit balance. We do not deduct Drawing from the Capital account when we prepare the trial balance.) The following table indicates where each of the account balances would normally be shown in a trial balance.

	TRIAL BALANCE	
Account Titles	**Left or Debit Balances**	**Right or Credit Balances**
Assets	Assets	
Liabilities		Liabilities
Capital		Capital
Drawing	Drawing	
Revenue		Revenue
Expenses	Expenses	
Totals	X,XXX	X,XXX

MAJOR FINANCIAL STATEMENTS

Earlier we listed summarizing as one of the five basic tasks of the accounting process. To accomplish this task, accountants use financial statements. A **financial statement** is a report prepared by accountants to summarize the financial affairs of a business for managers and others, both inside and outside the business.

Note that the headings of all financial statements require three lines:

1. Name of the company (or owner, if there is no company name)
2. Title of the financial statement
3. Period of time covered by the financial statement, or its date

Remember

The three-line heading of a financial statement answers the questions Who? What? and When?

Also, note that dollar signs are placed at the head of each column and with each total. Single lines are used to show that the figures above are being added or subtracted. Lines should be drawn across the entire column. A double line is drawn under the final total in a column.

The financial statements are all interconnected. The income statement must be prepared first, followed by the statement of owner's equity, and then the balance sheet.

The Income Statement

LEARNING OBJECTIVE 6a

Prepare an income statement.

The **income statement** shows total revenue minus total expenses, which yields the net income or net loss. The income statement reports the results of business transactions involving revenue and expense accounts—in other words, how the business has performed—over a period of time, usually a month or a year. When total revenue exceeds total expenses over the period, the result is **net income**, or profit. If the total revenue is less than the total expenses, the result is a **net loss**.

FYI

The income statement is sometimes called the *statement of income and expenses* or *profit and loss statement*.

The income statement in Figure 3 shows the results of the first month of operations for Conner's Whitewater Adventures.

For convenience, the individual expense amounts are recorded in the first amount column. Thus, the total expenses ($5,130) may be subtracted directly from the total revenue ($23,320).

Where to locate a business expansion is an important business decision. The decision to expand a business—as well as other operating decisions—is made from financial statements such as an income statement.

The income statement covers a period of time, whereas the balance sheet has only one date: the end of the financial period. On the income statement, the revenue for June, less the expenses for June, shows the results of operations—a net income of $18,190. To the accountant, the term *net income* means "clear" income, or profit after all expenses have been deducted. Expenses are usually listed in the same order as in the chart of accounts. Revenue and expense amounts are taken directly from the trial balance. If total expenses were greater than the revenue, then a net loss would be recorded.

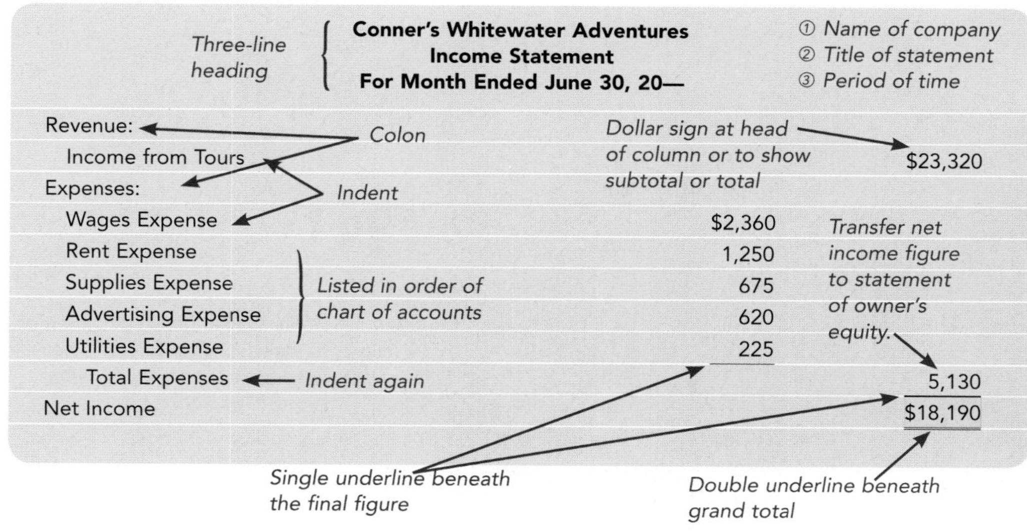

Conner's Whitewater Adventures
Income Statement
For Month Ended June 30, 20—

Revenue:		
Income from Tours		$23,320
Expenses:		
Wages Expense	$2,360	
Rent Expense	1,250	
Supplies Expense	675	
Advertising Expense	620	
Utilities Expense	225	
Total Expenses		5,130
Net Income		$18,190

FIGURE 3
Income statement

FYI

Compare the third line of the income statement heading with the third line of the balance sheet heading shown in Figure 5. Notice that the lines are different—the income statement covers a period of time and the balance sheet has only one date: the end of the financial period.

The Statement of Owner's Equity

LEARNING OBJECTIVE **6b**

Prepare a statement of owner's equity.

In the previous chapter, we said that revenue and expenses are connected with owner's equity through the financial statements. Now let's demonstrate this by a statement of owner's equity, shown in Figure 4, which the accountant prepares after he or she has determined the net income or net loss on the income statement.

The **statement of owner's equity** shows how—and why—the owner's equity, or Capital account, has changed over a stated period of time (in this case, the month of June). Notice the third line in the heading of Figure 4. It shows that the statement of owner's equity covers the same period of time as the income statement.

Now look at the body of the statement. The first line shows the zero balance in the Capital account at the beginning of the month. The beginning balance is zero because this is a new business. All new businesses will start with a zero beginning balance in the Capital account. An investment of $95,200 was made by J. Conner: total investment, $95,200. Two items have affected owner's equity during the month: A net income of $18,190 was earned, and the owner withdrew $3,500. To perform the calculations, move to the left-hand column and add the total investments and the net income ($95,200 + $18,190 = $113,390). Then subtract the withdrawals from the subtotal ($113,390 – $3,500 = $109,890). The difference ($109,890) represents an increase in capital. This difference is placed in the right-hand column to be added directly to the beginning capital. The final figure is the ending amount in the owner's Capital account.

Remember

The income statement is prepared first, so that the net income can be recorded on the statement of owner's equity. The statement of owner's equity is prepared second, so that the ending amount of capital can be recorded on the balance sheet, which is prepared last. Here's another memory tool for recalling the order of statement preparation: Izzy Swung Off Every Branch (Income, Statement of Owner's Equity, Balance Sheet).

The Balance Sheet

After preparing the statement of owner's equity, we prepare a balance sheet. The **balance sheet** shows the **financial position**, or the condition of a business's assets offset by claims against them *as of one particular date*. It summarizes the balances of the asset, liability, and owner's equity accounts on a given date (usually the end of a month or year). The balance sheet is, thus, like a snapshot—a picture of the financial condition of the business at that particular date.

The ending capital balance on the balance sheet is taken from the statement of owner's equity. Note that the accounts appear in the same order as in the chart of accounts.

In the **report form** of the balance sheet, the elements in the accounting equation are presented one on top of the other. A balance sheet prepared on June 30 for Conner's Whitewater Adventures in report form would look like Figure 5.

FIGURE 4

Statement of owner's equity

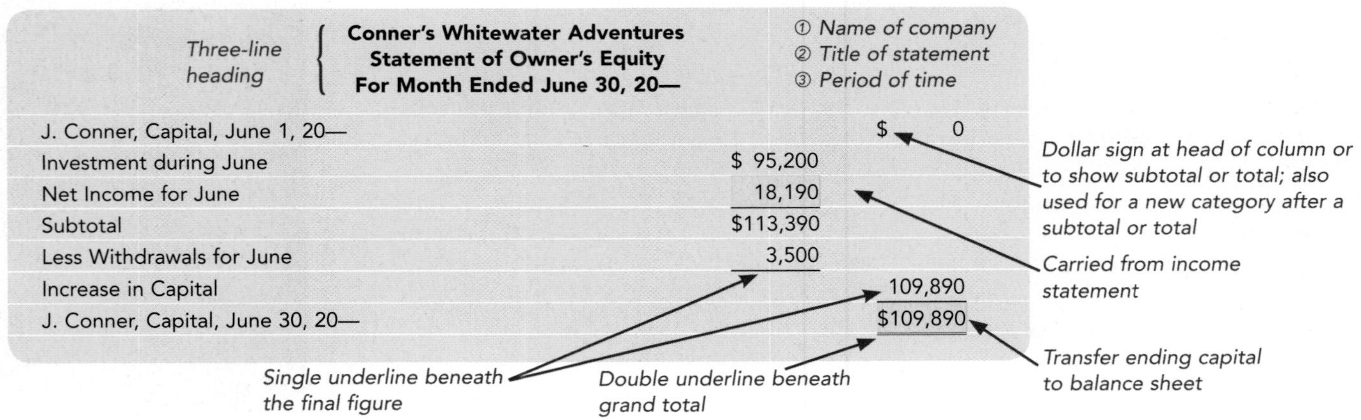

Conner's Whitewater Adventures
Statement of Owner's Equity
For Month Ended June 30, 20—

J. Conner, Capital, June 1, 20—		$ 0
Investment during June	$ 95,200	
Net Income for June	18,190	
Subtotal	$113,390	
Less Withdrawals for June	3,500	
Increase in Capital		109,890
J. Conner, Capital, June 30, 20—		$109,890

Conner's Whitewater Adventures
Balance Sheet
June 30, 20—

Assets		
Cash	$55,890	
Accounts Receivable	4,250	
Prepaid Insurance	1,875	
Equipment	51,300	
Total Assets		$113,315
Liabilities		
Accounts Payable		$ 3,425
Owner's Equity		
J. Conner, Capital		109,890
Total Liabilities and Owner's Equity		$ 113,315

Carried from statement of owner's equity (note pointing to J. Conner, Capital, 109,890)

FIGURE 5
Balance sheet

ERRORS EXPOSED BY THE TRIAL BALANCE

If the debit and credit columns in a trial balance are not equal, then it is evident that we have made an error. Possible mistakes include the following:

- Making errors in arithmetic, such as errors in adding the trial balance columns or in finding the balances of the accounts.
- Recording only half an entry, such as a debit without a corresponding credit, or vice versa.
- Recording both halves of the entry on the same side, such as two debits rather than a debit and a credit.
- Recording one or more amounts incorrectly.

Accounting Clerk—Membership Information

Accounting in Your Future

One of many variations in accounting jobs you might find at the Solid Rock Gym would be an accounting clerk who would maintain membership information. Responsibilities might include invoicing for customers' membership fees, collecting fees, and maintaining customer accounts. The job might also include some marketing and customer service activities; therefore, people skills would be vital.

As the accounting clerk responsible for membership information, you would be required to provide the gym's accountant with weekly cash reports so the accountant could correctly report membership revenue. You would also need to manage financial information regarding collection expenses and marketing expenses, as well as any expenses related to customer service. Can you see how knowing the accounting cycle could be beneficial in this position?

FYI

Even if debits equal credits, this does not necessarily mean that there were no errors in the recording of the transactions. For example, a transaction may have been forgotten, it may have been included twice, or it may have been written for an incorrect amount.

Although using a computer greatly reduces the occurrence of addition and subtraction errors, it does not prevent the occurrence of other kinds of errors, such as recording transactions incorrectly.

Procedure for Locating Errors

Suppose that you are in a business situation where you have recorded transactions for a month in the account books, and the accounts do not balance. To save yourself time, you need to have a definite procedure for tracking down the errors. The best method is to do everything in reverse, as follows:

- Look at the pattern of balances to see if a normal balance was placed in the wrong column on the trial balance.
- Re-add the trial balance columns.
- Check the transferring of the figures from the accounts to the trial balance.
- Verify the footings and balances of the accounts.

As an added precaution, form the habit of verifying all addition and subtraction as you go along. You can thus correct many mistakes *before* the time comes to prepare a trial balance.

When the trial balance totals do not balance, the difference might indicate that you forgot to record half of an entry in the accounts. For example, if the difference in the trial balance totals is $20, you may have recorded $20 on the debit side of one account without recording $20 on the credit side of another account.

Another possibility is to divide the difference by 2; this may provide a clue that you accidentally recorded half an entry twice. For example, if the difference in the trial balance is $600, you may have recorded $300 on the debit side of one account and an additional $300 on the debit side of another account. Look for a transaction that involved $300 and then see if you have recorded both a debit and a credit. By knowing which transactions to check, you can save a lot of time.

Transpositions and Slides

LEARNING OBJECTIVE 7

Recognize the effect of transpositions and slides on account balances.

If the difference is evenly divisible by 9, the discrepancy may be either a transposition or a slide. A **transposition** means that the digits have been transposed, or switched around, when the numbers were copied from one place to another. For example, one transposition of digits in 916 can be written as 619:

Correct Number	Number Copied	Difference	Difference Divided by 9
916	619	297	297 ÷ 9 = 33

A **slide** is an error in placing the decimal point; in other words, a slide in the decimal point. For example, $27,000 could be inadvertently written as $2,700:

Correct Number	Number Copied	Difference	Difference Divided by 9
27,000	2,700	24,300	24,300 ÷ 9 = 2,700

Or the error may be a combination of a transposition and a slide, as when $450 is written as $54:

Correct Number	Number Copied	Difference	Difference Divided by 9
450	54	396	396 ÷ 9 = 44

Again, the difference is evenly divisible by 9 (with no remainder).

CHAPTER REVIEW

Study & Practice

LEARNING OBJECTIVE 1

Determine balances of T accounts having entries recorded on both sides of the accounts.

To determine balances of T accounts, add the amounts listed on each side of the T account. The totals are called **footings**. To get the account balance, subtract the total of the smaller side from the total of the larger side. Record the account balance on the larger side.

PRACTICE EXERCISE 1

Using the T accounts presented below, determine the balances.

Cash

	+ Debit		− Credit
(a)	90,000	(b)	38,000
		(f)	1,200

Accounts Payable

	− Debit		+ Credit
(d)	1,500	(c)	4,500

J. Jay, Capital

	− Debit		+ Credit
		(a)	90,000
		(e)	5,000

Equipment

	+ Debit		−
(b)	38,000	(d)	1,500
(c)	4,500		
(e)	5,000		

J. Jay, Drawing

	+ Debit		− Credit
(f)	1,200		

PRACTICE EXERCISE 1 SOLUTION

Cash

	+ Debit		− Credit
(a)	90,000	(b)	38,000
		(f)	1,200
			39,200
Bal.	50,800		

Accounts Payable

	− Debit		+ Credit
(d)	1,500	(c)	4,500
		Bal.	3,000

J. Jay, Capital

	− Debit		+ Credit
		(a)	90,000
		(e)	5,000
		Bal.	95,000

Equipment

	+ Debit		−
(b)	38,000	(d)	1,500
(c)	4,500		
(e)	5,000		
	47,500		
Bal.	46,000		

J. Jay, Drawing

	+ Debit		− Credit
(f)	1,200		

LEARNING OBJECTIVE

Present the fundamental accounting equation using the T account form, and label the plus and minus sides.

The fundamental accounting equation can be restated in **T account form** using plus and minus sides. The following table summarizes the rules:

Assets	The *left* side is the *increase* side.
Liabilities	The *right* side is the *increase* side.
Owner's Equity	The *right* side is the *increase* side.
Revenue	The *right* side is the *increase* side.
Expenses	The *left* side is the *increase* side.

PRACTICE EXERCISE 2

Using the fundamental accounting equation in T account form, label each side with plus and minus.

PRACTICE EXERCISE 2 SOLUTION

Assets		=	Liabilities		+	Owner's Equity		+	Revenue		–	Expenses	
+	–		–	+		–	+		–	+		+	–
Left	Right		Left	Right		Left	Right		Left	Right		Left	Right

LEARNING OBJECTIVE

Present the fundamental accounting equation using the T account form, and label the debit and credit sides.

Each account category in the fundamental accounting equation has a debit and credit. The left side of a T account, regardless of the account category, is called the **debit** side. The right side is called the **credit** side. A debit or credit could signify either an increase or a decrease—it depends on the account category. The following table summarizes these rules:

Debits Signify		Credits Signify	
Increases in	Assets Drawing Expenses	Decreases in	Assets Drawing Expenses
Decreases in	Liabilities Capital Revenue	Increases in	Liabilities Capital Revenue

PRACTICE EXERCISE 3

Using the fundamental accounting equation in T account form, label each side as debit and credit.

CHAPTER REVIEW

PRACTICE EXERCISE 3 SOLUTION

Assets		=	Liabilities		+	Owner's Equity		+	Revenue		–	Expenses	
+	–		–	+		–	+		–	+		+	–
Left Debit	Right Credit		Left Debit	Right Credit		Left Debit	Right Credit		Left Debit	Right Credit		Left Debit	Right Credit

LEARNING OBJECTIVE

4 *Record directly in T accounts a group of business transactions involving changes in asset, liability, owner's equity, revenue, and expense accounts for a service business.*

Transactions can be recorded directly into the T accounts. When analyzing a business transaction, follow these steps:

STEP 1. Decide which accounts are involved.

STEP 2. Classify the accounts involved (asset, liability, owner's equity, revenue, expense).

STEP 3. Decide if the accounts involved are increased or decreased.

STEP 4. Write the transaction as a debit to one account (or accounts) and a credit to another account (or accounts).

STEP 5. Check to see if the equation is in balance after the transaction has been recorded.

PRACTICE EXERCISE 4

Record the following transactions directly into the appropriate T accounts.

a. J. Molson deposited $90,000 in the name of the business.
b. Bought equipment for cash, $38,000.
c. Bought equipment on account, $4,320.
d. Paid $2,000 on account.
e. J. Molson invested his personal equipment, valued at $5,200, in the business.
f. J. Molson withdrew $1,200 from the business for personal use.

PRACTICE EXERCISE 4 SOLUTION

Assets		=	Liabilities		+	Owner's Equity		+	Revenue		–	Expenses	
+	–		–	+		–	+		–	+		+	–
Debit	Credit		Debit	Credit		Debit	Credit		Debit	Credit		Debit	Credit

Cash

+ Debit	– Credit
(a) 90,000	**(b)** 38,000
	(d) 2,000
	(f) 1,200
	41,200
Bal. 48,800	

Accounts Payable

– Debit	+ Credit
(d) 2,000	**(c)** 4,320
	Bal. 2,320

J. Molson, Capital

– Debit	+ Credit
	(a) 90,000
	(e) 5,200
	Bal. 95,200

Equipment

+ Debit	– Credit
(b) 38,000	
(c) 4,320	
(e) 5,200	
Bal. 47,520	

J. Molson, Drawing

+ Debit	– Credit
(f) 1,200	

LEARNING OBJECTIVE

5 *Prepare a trial balance.*

A **trial balance** is a list of all account balances in two columns—one labeled Debit and one labeled Credit. The trial balance shows that both sides of the accounting equation are equal. The heading consists of the company name, the title of the form (trial balance), and the date.

PRACTICE EXERCISE 5

Using the following account balances, prepare a trial balance for Collins's Backpack Adventures as of July 31, 20—.

Accounts Receivable	4,150	J. Collins, Capital	95,400
Equipment	51,500	Income from Treks	23,220
Cash	55,990	Accounts Payable	3,325
Prepaid Insurance	1,675	J. Collins, Drawing	3,400
Wages Expense	2,460	Rent Expense	1,350
Supplies Expense	575	Advertising Expense	520
Utilities Expense	325		

PRACTICE EXERCISE 5 SOLUTION

Collins's Backpack Adventures
Trial Balance
July 31, 20—

Account Name	Debit	Credit
Cash	55,990	
Accounts Receivable	4,150	
Prepaid Insurance	1,675	
Equipment	51,500	
Accounts Payable		3,325
J. Collins, Capital		95,400
J. Collins, Drawing	3,400	
Income from Treks		23,220
Wages Expense	2,460	
Rent Expense	1,350	
Supplies Expense	575	
Advertising Expense	520	
Utilities Expense	325	
	121,945	121,945

LEARNING OBJECTIVE

6 *Prepare (a) an income statement, (b) a statement of owner's equity, and (c) a balance sheet.*

(a) An **income statement** shows the results of operations of a business for a period of time. It includes revenue and expense accounts and reports either a **net income** or a **net loss**. (b) A **statement of owner's equity** shows the activity in the owner's equity, or Capital account, for a period of time. It includes the balance in the Capital account at the beginning of the period plus any additional investments and any increase or decrease in capital as the result of a net income (or a net loss) minus any withdrawals. (c) A **balance sheet** shows the financial condition of a business at a particular date in time. It summarizes the balances of the asset, liability, and owner's equity accounts on a given date.

PRACTICE EXERCISE 6

Use the trial balance in Practice Exercise 5 to prepare (a) an income statement, (b) a statement of owner's equity, and (c) a balance sheet. Assume Collins's Backpack Adventures started business on July 1, 20—.

PRACTICE EXERCISE 6 SOLUTION

(a)

Collins's Backpack Adventures
Income Statement
For Month Ended July 31, 20—

Revenue:		
Income from Treks		$23,220
Expenses:		
Wages Expense	$2,460	
Rent Expense	1,350	
Supplies Expense	575	
Advertising Expense	520	
Utilities Expense	325	
Total Expenses		5,230
Net Income		$17,990

(b)

Collins's Backpack Adventures
Statement of Owner's Equity
For Month Ended July 31, 20—

J. Collins, Capital, July 1, 20—		$ 0
Investments during July	$ 95,400	
Net Income for July	17,990	
Subtotal	$113,390	
Less Withdrawals for July	3,400	
Increase in Capital		109,990
J. Collins, Capital, July 31, 20—		$109,990

(c)

Collins's Backpack Adventures Balance Sheet July 31, 20—		
Assets		
Cash	$55,990	
Accounts Receivable	4,150	
Prepaid Insurance	1,675	
Equipment	51,500	
Total Assets		$ 113,315
Liabilities		
Accounts Payable		$ 3,325
Owner's Equity		
J. Collins, Capital		109,990
Total Liabilities and Owner's Equity		$ 113,315

LEARNING OBJECTIVE

7 *Recognize the effect of transpositions and slides on account balances.*

Transpositions and slides account for many trial balance errors. The clue is whether the difference in account balances or trial balance totals is evenly divisible by 9.

a. A **transposition** occurs when digits are switched around, such as 541 written as 415.

b. A **slide** is an error in placing the decimal point; in other words, a *slide* in the decimal point. For example, $35,000 could be inadvertently written as $3,500.

c. An error in a trial balance may be a combination of a transposition and a slide, as when $230 is written as $32.

PRACTICE EXERCISE 7

Identify the following errors as transpositions or slides, and indicate the amount of the difference and whether it is divisible by 9.

a. The amount of supplies bought totaled $341, but it was written as $431.

b. Equipment was purchased for $3,500, but it was written as $35,000.

c. An error was made in the trial balance because $35 was written as $530.

PRACTICE EXERCISE 7 SOLUTION

a. Transposition: The difference is $90 and can be evenly divided by 9.

Correct Number	Number Copied	Difference	Difference Divided by 9
$341	$431	$90	$90 ÷ 9 = $10

b. Slide: The difference is $31,500 and can be evenly divided by 9.

Correct Number	Number Copied	Difference	Difference Divided by 9
$3,500	$35,000	$31,500	$31,500 ÷ 9 = $3,500

c. Transposition and slide: The difference is $495 and can be evenly divided by 9.

Correct Number	Number Copied	Difference	Difference Divided by 9
$35	$530	$495	$495 ÷ 9 = $55

Glossary

Balance sheet A financial statement showing the financial position of an organization on a given date, such as June 30 or December 31. The balance sheet lists the balances in the asset, liability, and owner's equity accounts. *(p. 58)*

Compound entry A transaction that requires more than one debit or more than one credit to be recorded. *(p. 53)*

Credit The right side of a T account; to credit is to record an amount on the right side of a T account. Credits represent increases in liability, capital, or revenue accounts and decreases in asset, drawing, or expense accounts. *(p. 45)*

Debit The left side of a T account; to debit is to record an amount on the left side of a T account. Debits represent increases in asset, drawing, or expense accounts and decreases in liability, capital, or revenue accounts. *(p. 45)*

Financial position The resources or assets owned by an organization at a point in time, offset by the claims against those resources and owner's equity; shown on a balance sheet. *(p. 58)*

Financial statement A report prepared by accountants that summarizes the financial affairs of a business. *(p. 56)*

Footings The totals of each side of a T account, recorded in small, pencil-written figures. *(p. 44)*

Income statement A financial statement showing the results of business transactions involving revenue and expense accounts over a period of time. *(p. 56)*

Net income The result when total revenue exceeds total expenses over a period of time. *(p. 56)*

Net loss The result when total expenses exceed total revenue over a period of time. *(p. 56)*

Normal balance The plus side of a T account. *(p. 44)*

Report form The form of the balance sheet in which assets are placed at the top and liabilities and owner's equity are placed below. *(p. 58)*

Slide An error in placing the decimal point in a number. *(p. 60)*

Statement of owner's equity A financial statement showing the activity in the owner's equity, or Capital account, over the financial period. *(p. 58)*

T account form A form of account shaped like the letter T in which increases and decreases in the account may be recorded. One side of the T is for entries on the debit or left side. The other side of the T is for entries on the credit or right side. *(p. 43)*

Transposition An error that involves interchanging, or switching around, digits during the recording of a number. *(p. 60)*

Trial balance A list of all account balances to prove that the total of all the debit balances equals the total of all the credit balances. *(p. 55)*

CHAPTER ASSIGNMENTS

Discussion Questions

1. Explain how a trial balance and a balance sheet differ.
2. Explain why the term *debit* doesn't always mean "increase" and why the term *credit* doesn't always mean "decrease."
3. What are footings in accounting?
4. How are the three financial statements shown in this chapter connected?
5. What is a compound entry?
6. List two reasons why the debits and credits in the trial balance might not balance.
7. Give an example of a slide and an example of a transposition. Explain how you might decide whether an error is a slide or a transposition.
8. What do we mean when we say that revenue and expense accounts are under the "umbrella" of owner's equity?

Exercises

2,3 

PRACTICE EXERCISES 2,3

EXERCISE 2-1 On a sheet of paper, draw the fundamental accounting equation with T accounts under each of the five account classifications, with plus and minus signs and debit and credit on the appropriate sides of each account. Under each of the five classifications, draw T accounts, again with the correct plus and minus signs and debit and credit, for each of the following accounts of Barlow Engine Repair.

- Cash
- Accounts Receivable
- Equipment
- Accounts Payable
- D. Barlow, Capital
- D. Barlow, Drawing
- Income from Repairs
- Wages Expense
- Rent Expense
- Supplies Expense
- Utilities Expense
- Miscellaneous Expense

2,3 

PRACTICE EXERCISES 2,3

EXERCISE 2-2 List the classification of each of the following accounts as A (asset), L (liability), OE (owner's equity), R (revenue), or E (expense). Write Debit or Credit to indicate the increase side, the decrease side, and the normal balance side.

Account	Classification	Increase Side	Decrease Side	Normal Balance Side
0. Cash	A	Debit	Credit	Debit
1. Wages Expense				
2. Equipment				
3. L. Cross, Capital				
4. Service Revenue				
5. L. Cross, Drawing				
6. Accounts Receivable				
7. Rent Expense				
8. Fees Earned				
9. Accounts Payable				

2,3,4 

PRACTICE EXERCISE 4

EXERCISE 2-3 R. Dalberg operates Dalberg's Tours. The company has the following chart of accounts:

Assets
Cash
Accounts Receivable
Prepaid Insurance
Display Equipment
Van
Office Equipment

Liabilities
Accounts Payable

Owner's Equity
R. Dalberg, Capital
R. Dalberg, Drawing

Revenue
Income from Tours

Expenses
Wages Expense
Gas Expense
Supplies Expense
Advertising Expense
Utilities Expense

CHAPTER ASSIGNMENTS

Using the chart of accounts, record the following transactions in pairs of T accounts. Give the T account to be debited first and the account to be credited to the right. Show debit and credit and plus and minus signs. (Example: Received and paid the bill for the month's rent, $480.)

Rent Expense	
+	−
Debit	Credit
480	

Cash	
+	−
Debit	Credit
	480

a. Received and paid the electric bill, $175.
b. Bought supplies on account, $135.
c. Paid for insurance for one year, $580.
d. Made a payment on account to a creditor, $65.
e. Received and paid the telephone bill, $186.
f. Sold services on account, $1,375.
g. Received and paid the gasoline bill for the van, $130.
h. Received cash on account from customers, $1,458.
i. Dalberg withdrew cash for personal use, $700.

PRACTICE EXERCISE 4

EXERCISE 2-4 During the first month of operation, Lorens's Expeditions recorded the following transactions. Describe what has happened in each of the transactions (a) through (k).

Cash	
(a) 3,200	(b) 525
(k) 1,125	(c) 98
	(e) 75
	(g) 1,050
	(i) 92
	(j) 345

Accounts Receivable	
(h) 615	

Equipment	
(f) 3,510	
(g) 2,050	

Accounts Payable	
	(d) 280
	(g) 1,000

D. L. Lorens, Capital	
	(a) 3,200
	(f) 3,510

D. L. Lorens, Drawing	
(j) 345	

Income from Tours	
	(h) 615
	(k) 1,125

Rent Expense	
(b) 525	

Supplies Expense	
(d) 280	

Advertising Expense	
(c) 98	

Utilities Expense	
(i) 92	

Miscellaneous Expense	
(e) 75	

PRACTICE EXERCISE 5

EXERCISE 2-5 Business Services, owned by T. Morris, hired a new bookkeeper who is not entirely familiar with the process of preparing a trial balance. All the accounts have normal balances. Find the errors, and prepare a corrected trial balance for December 31 of this year.

Business Services
Trial Balance
December 31, 20—

Account Name	Debit	Credit
Accounts Receivable		7,700
Cash	3,200	
Accounts Payable		8,700
Equipment	26,000	
T. Morris, Capital		24,800
T. Morris, Drawing		1,900
Prepaid Insurance		1,300
Income from Services		33,000
Wages Expense	17,500	
Rent Expense		3,700
Supplies Expense	1,800	
Utilities Expense	3,400	
	51,900	81,100

5,6 LO

PRACTICE EXERCISES 5,6

EXERCISE 2-6 During the first month of operations, Landish Modeling Agency recorded transactions in T account form. Foot and balance the accounts; then prepare a trial balance, an income statement, a statement of owner's equity, and a balance sheet dated March 31, 20—.

Cash

(a)	8,200	(b)	350
(c)	8,400	(d)	1,600
(i)	7,580	(f)	175
		(g)	3,400
		(h)	2,200

Accounts Receivable

(e)	2,600		

Office Furniture

(b)	350		

Office Equipment

(k)	2,800		

Accounts Payable

		(k)	2,800
		(j)	82

R. Landish, Capital

		(a)	8,200

R. Landish, Drawing

(h)	2,200		

Modeling Fees

		(c)	8,400
		(e)	2,600
		(i)	7,580

Salary Expense

(g)	3,400		

Rent Expense

(d)	1,600		

Supplies Expense

(j)	82		

Utilities Expense

(f)	175		

7 LO

PRACTICE EXERCISE 7

EXERCISE 2-7 The following errors were made in journalizing transactions. In each case, calculate the amount of the error and indicate whether the debit or the credit column of the trial balance will be understated or overstated.

	Amount of Difference	Debit or Credit Column of Trial Balance Understated or Overstated
0. Example: A $149 debit to Accounts Receivable was not recorded.	$149	Debit column understated
a. A $42 debit to Supplies Expense was recorded as $420.		
b. A $155 debit to Accounts Receivable was recorded twice.		
c. A $179 debit to Prepaid Insurance was not recorded.		
d. A $65 credit to Cash was not recorded.		
e. A $190 debit to Equipment was recorded twice.		
f. A $57 debit to Utilities Expense was recorded as $75.		

7

PRACTICE EXERCISE 7

EXERCISE 2-8 Would the following errors cause the trial balance to have equal or unequal totals? As a result of the errors, which accounts are overstated (by how much) or understated (by how much)?

a. A purchase of office equipment for $380 was recorded as a debit to Office Equipment for $38 and a credit to Cash for $38.
b. A payment of $280 to a creditor was debited to Accounts Receivable and credited to Cash for $280 each.
c. A purchase of supplies for $245 was recorded as a debit to Equipment for $245 and a credit to Cash for $245.
d. A payment of $76 to a creditor was recorded as a debit to Accounts Payable for $76 and a credit to Cash for $67.

Problem Set A

For additional help, see the demonstration problem at the beginning of each chapter in your Working Papers.

1,2,3,4

PROBLEM 2-1A During December of this year, G. Elden established Ginny's Gym. The following asset, liability, and owner's equity accounts are included in the chart of accounts:

Cash
Exercise Equipment
Store Equipment
Office Equipment
Accounts Payable
G. Elden, Capital
Income from Services
Supplies Expense

During December, the following transactions occurred:

a. Elden deposited $35,000 in a bank account in the name of the business.
b. Bought exercise equipment for cash, $8,150, Ck. No. 1001.
c. Bought supplies on account from Hazel Company, $105.
d. Bought a display rack (Store Equipment) on account from Cyber Core, $790.
e. Bought office equipment on account from Office Aids, $185.
f. Elden invested her exercise equipment with a fair market value of $1,200 in the business.
g. Made a payment to Cyber Core, a creditor, $200, Ck. No. 1002.
h. Sold services for the month of December for cash, $800.

Check Figure
Balance of Cash, $27,450

Required

1. Write the account classifications (Assets, Liabilities, Owner's Equity, Revenue, Expense) in the fundamental accounting equation, as well as the plus and minus signs and Debit and Credit.
2. Write the account names on the T accounts under the classifications, place the plus and minus signs for each T account, and label the debit and credit sides of the T accounts.
3. Record the amounts in the proper positions in the T accounts. Write the letter next to each entry to identify the transaction.
4. Foot and balance the accounts.

1,2,3,4,5 

PROBLEM 2-2A B. Kelso established Computer Wizards during November of this year. The accountant prepared the following chart of accounts:

Assets
Cash
Computer Software
Office Equipment
Neon Sign

Liabilities
Accounts Payable

Owner's Equity
B. Kelso, Capital
B. Kelso, Drawing

Revenue
Income from Services

Expenses
Wages Expense
Rent Expense
Supplies Expense
Advertising Expense
Utilities Expense
Miscellaneous Expense

The following transactions occurred during the month:

a. Kelso deposited $45,000 in a bank account in the name of the business.
b. Paid the rent for the current month, $1,800, Ck. No. 2001.
c. Bought office desks and filing cabinets for cash, $790, Ck. No. 2002.
d. Bought a computer and printer (Office Equipment) from Cyber Center for use in the business, $2,700, paying $1,700 in cash and placing the balance on account, Ck. No. 2003.
e. Bought a neon sign on account from Signage Co., $1,350.
f. Kelso invested her personal computer software with a fair market value of $600 in the business.
g. Received a bill from *Country News* for newspaper advertising, $365.
h. Sold services for cash, $1,245.
i. Received and paid the electric bill, $345, Ck. No. 2004.
j. Paid on account to *Country News*, a creditor, $285, Ck. No. 2005.
k. Sold services for cash, $1,450.
l. Paid wages to an employee, $925, Ck. No. 2006.
m. Received and paid the bill for the city business license, $75, Ck. No. 2007 (Miscellaneous Expense).
n. Kelso withdrew cash for personal use, $850, Ck. No. 2008.
o. Bought printer paper and letterhead stationery on account from Office Aids, $115.

Check Figure
Trial balance total, $50,840

Required

1. Record the owner's name in the Capital and Drawing T accounts.
2. Correctly place the plus and minus signs for each T account, and label the debit and credit sides of the accounts.
3. Record the transactions in T accounts. Write the letter of each entry to identify the transaction.
4. Foot the T accounts and show the balances.
5. Prepare a trial balance, with a three-line heading, dated November 30, 20—.

PROBLEM 2-3A R. Morgis, a speech therapist, opened a clinic in the name of Morgis Clinic. Her accountant prepared the following chart of accounts:

Assets
Cash
Accounts Receivable
Office Equipment
Office Furniture

Liabilities
Accounts Payable

Owner's Equity
R. Morgis, Capital
R. Morgis, Drawing

Revenue
Professional Fees

Expenses
Salary Expense
Rent Expense
Utilities Expense
Miscellaneous Expense

The following transactions occurred during June of this year:

a. Morgis deposited $40,000 in a bank account in the name of the business.
b. Bought waiting room chairs and tables (Office Furniture) on account, $1,330.
c. Bought a fax/copier/scanner combination (Office Equipment) from Max's Equipment for $595, paying $200 in cash and placing the balance on account, Ck. No. 1001.
d. Bought an intercom system (Office Equipment) on account from Regan Office Supply, $375.
e. Received and paid the telephone bill, $155, Ck. No. 1002.
f. Sold professional services on account, $1,484.
g. Received and paid the electric bill, $190, Ck. No. 1003.
h. Received and paid the bill for the state speech therapy convention, $450, Ck. No. 1004 (Miscellaneous Expense).
i. Sold professional services for cash, $2,575.
j. Paid on account to Regan Office Supply, a creditor, $300, Ck. No. 1005.
k. Paid the rent for the current month, $940, Ck. No. 1006.
l. Paid salary of the receptionist, $880, Ck. No. 1007.
m. R. Morgis withdrew cash for personal use, $800, Ck. No. 1008.
n. Received $885 on account from patients who were previously billed.

Required

1. Record the owner's name in the Capital and Drawing T accounts.
2. Correctly place the plus and minus signs for each T account, and label the debit and credit sides of the accounts.
3. Record the transactions in the T accounts. Write the letter of each entry to identify the transaction.
4. Foot the T accounts and show the balances.
5. Prepare a trial balance as of June 30, 20—.
6. Prepare an income statement for June 30, 20—.
7. Prepare a statement of owner's equity for June 30, 20—.
8. Prepare a balance sheet as of June 30, 20—.

Check Figure
Net Income, $1,444

PROBLEM 2-4A On May 1, B. Bangle opened Self-Wash Laundry. His accountant listed the following chart of accounts:

Cash
Prepaid Insurance
Equipment
Furniture and Fixtures
Accounts Payable
B. Bangle, Capital
B. Bangle, Drawing

Laundry Revenue
Wages Expense
Rent Expense
Supplies Expense
Utilities Expense
Miscellaneous Expense

The following transactions were completed during May:

a. Bangle deposited $35,000 in a bank account in the name of the business.
b. Bought chairs and tables (Furniture and Fixtures) paying cash, $1,870, Ck. No. 1000.
c. Bought supplies on account from Barnes Supply Company, $225.
d. Paid the rent for the current month, $875, Ck. No. 1001.
e. Bought washing machines and dryers from Lara Equipment Company, $12,500, paying $3,600 in cash and placing the balance on account, Ck. No. 1002.
f. Sold services for cash for the first half of the month, $1,925.
g. Bought insurance for one year, $1,560, Ck. No. 1003.
h. Paid on account to Lara Equipment Company, a creditor, $1,800, Ck. No. 1004.
i. Received and paid electric bill, $285, Ck. No. 1005.
j. Sold services for cash for the second half of the month, $1,835.
k. Paid wages to an employee, $940, Ck. No. 1006.
l. Bangle withdrew cash for his personal use, $800, Ck. No. 1007.
m. Paid on account to Barnes Supply Company, a creditor, $225, Ck. No. 1008.
n. Received and paid bill from the county for sidewalk repair assessment, $280, Ck. No. 1009 (Miscellaneous Expense).

Check Figure
Trial balance total, $45,860

Required

1. Record the owner's name in the Capital and Drawing T accounts.
2. Correctly place the plus and minus signs for each T account, and label the debit and credit sides of the accounts.
3. Record the transactions in the T accounts. Write the letter of each entry to identify the transaction.
4. Foot the T accounts and show the balances.
5. Prepare a trial balance as of May 31, 20—.
6. Prepare an income statement for May 31, 20—.
7. Prepare a statement of owner's equity for May 31, 20—.
8. Prepare a balance sheet as of May 31, 20—.

Problem Set B

For additional help, see the demonstration problem at the beginning of each chapter in your Working Papers.

PROBLEM 2-1B During February of this year, R. Willard established Willard Shoe Hospital. The following asset, liability, and owner's equity accounts are included in the chart of accounts:

Cash
Shop Equipment
Store Equipment
Office Equipment
Accounts Payable
R. Willard, Capital
Income from Services
Supplies Expense

The following transactions occurred during the month of February:

a. Willard deposited $25,000 cash in a bank account in the name of the business.
b. Bought shop equipment for cash, $1,525, Ck. No. 1000.
c. Bought supplies on account from Milland Company, $325.
d. Bought store shelving on account from Inger Hardware, $750.
e. Bought office equipment from Shara's Office Supply, $625, paying $225 in cash and placing the balance on account, Ck. No. 1001.
f. Paid on account to Inger Hardware, a creditor, $750, Ck. No. 1002
g. Willard invested his personal leather working tools with a fair market value of $800 in the business.
h. Sold services for the month of February for cash, $250.

CHAPTER ASSIGNMENTS

Required

1. Write the account classifications (Assets, Liabilities, Owner's Equity, Revenue, Expense) in the fundamental accounting equation, as well as the plus and minus signs and Debit and Credit.
2. Write the account names on the T accounts under the classifications, place the plus and minus signs for each T account, and label the debit and credit sides of the T accounts.
3. Record the amounts in the proper positions in the T accounts. Write the letter next to each entry to identify the transaction.
4. Foot and balance the accounts.

Check Figure
Cash balance, $22,750

PROBLEM 2-2B J. Carrie established Carrie Photo Tours during June of this year. The accountant prepared the following chart of accounts:

LO 1,2,3,4,5

Assets
Cash
Computer Software
Office Equipment
Neon Sign

Liabilities
Accounts Payable

Owner's Equity
J. Carrie, Capital
J. Carrie, Drawing

Revenue
Income from Services

Expenses
Wages Expense
Rent Expense
Supplies Expense
Advertising Expense
Utilities Expense
Miscellaneous Expense

The following transactions occurred during the month of June:

a. Carrie deposited $30,000 cash in a bank account in the name of the business.
b. Bought office equipment for cash, $1,850, Ck. No. 1001.
c. Bought computer software from Morey's Computer Center, $640, paying $350 in cash and placing the balance on account, Ck. No. 1002.
d. Paid current month's rent, $950, Ck. No. 1003 (Rent Expense).
e. Sold services for cash, $1,575 (Income from Services).
f. Bought a neon sign from The Sign Company, $1,335, paying $435 in cash and placing the balance on account, Ck. No. 1004.
g. Received bill from *The Gossiper* for advertising, $445 (Advertising Expense).
h. Bought supplies on account from City Supply, $460.
i. Received and paid the electric bill, $380, Ck. No. 1005.
j. Paid on account to *The Gossiper*, a creditor, $245, Ck. No. 1006.
k. Sold services for cash, $3,474.
l. Paid wages to an employee, $930, Ck. No. 1007.
m. Carrie invested his personal computer (Office Equipment) with a fair market value of $1,000 in the business.
n. Carrie withdrew cash for personal use, $800, Ck. No. 1008.
o. Received and paid the bill for city business license, $75, Ck. No. 1009 (Miscellaneous Expense).

Required

1. Record the owner's name in the Capital and Drawing T accounts.
2. Correctly place the plus and minus signs for each T account, and label the debit and credit sides of the accounts.
3. Record the transactions in the T accounts. Write the letter of each entry to identify the transaction.
4. Foot the T accounts and show the balances.
5. Prepare a trial balance, with a three-line heading, dated June 30, 20—.

Check Figure
Trial balance total, $37,899

PROBLEM 2-3B D. Julia, a physical therapist, opened Julia's Clinic. His accountant provided the following chart of accounts:

Assets
Cash
Accounts Receivable
Office Equipment
Office Furniture

Liabilities
Accounts Payable

Owner's Equity
D. Julia, Capital
D. Julia, Drawing

Revenue
Professional Fees

Expenses
Salary Expense
Rent Expense
Utilities Expense
Miscellaneous Expense

The following transactions occurred during July of this year:

a. Julia deposited $35,000 in a bank account in the name of the business.
b. Bought filing cabinets (Office Equipment) on account from Muller Office Supply, $560.
c. Paid cash for chairs and carpeting (Office Furniture) for the waiting room, $835, Ck. No. 1000.
d. Bought a photocopier from Rob's Office Equipment, $650, paying $250 in cash and placing the balance on account, Ck. No. 1001.
e. Received and paid the telephone bill, which included installation charges, $185, Ck. No. 1002.
f. Sold professional services on account, $2,255.
g. Received and paid the bill for the state physical therapy convention, $445, Ck. No. 1003 (Miscellaneous Expense).
h. Received and paid the electric bill, $335, Ck. No. 1004.
i. Received cash on account from credit customers, $1,940.
j. Paid on account to Muller Office Supply, a creditor, $250, Ck. No. 1005.
k. Paid the office rent for the current month, $1,245, Ck. No. 1006.
l. Sold professional services for cash, $1,950.
m. Paid the salary of the receptionist, $960, Ck. No. 1007.
n. Julia withdrew cash for personal use, $1,200, Ck. No. 1008.

Check Figure
Net Income, $1,035

Required

1. Record the owner's name in the Capital and Drawing T accounts.
2. Correctly place the plus and minus signs for each T account, and label the debit and credit sides of the accounts.
3. Record the transactions in the T accounts. Write the letter of each entry to identify the transaction.
4. Foot the T accounts and show the balances.
5. Prepare a trial balance as of July 31, 20—.
6. Prepare an income statement for July 31, 20—.
7. Prepare a statement of owner's equity for July 31, 20—.
8. Prepare a balance sheet as of July 31, 20—.

1,2,4,5,6 LO

PROBLEM 2-4B On July 1, K. Resser opened Resser's Quick Clean. Resser's accountant listed the following chart of accounts:

Cash
Prepaid Insurance
Equipment
Furniture and Fixtures
Accounts Payable
K. Resser, Capital
K. Resser, Drawing
Laundry Revenue
Wages Expense
Rent Expense
Supplies Expense
Utilities Expense
Miscellaneous Expense

The following transactions were completed during July:

a. Resser deposited $25,000 in a bank account in the name of the business.
b. Bought tables and chairs (Furniture and Fixtures) for cash, $725, Ck. No. 1200.
c. Paid the rent for the current month, $1,750, Ck. No. 1201.
d. Bought washers and dryers from Ferber Equipment, $15,700, paying $4,000 in cash and placing the balance on account, Ck. No. 1202.
e. Bought supplies on account from Wiggins's Distributors, $535.
f. Sold services for cash, $1,742.
g. Bought insurance for one year, $1,375, Ck. No. 1203.
h. Paid on account to Ferber Equipment, a creditor, $700, Ck. No. 1204.
i. Received and paid the electric bill, $438, Ck. No. 1205.
j. Paid on account to Wiggins's Distributors, a creditor, $315, Ck. No. 1206.
k. Sold services to customers for cash for the second half of the month, $1,820.
l. Received and paid the bill for the business license, $75, Ck. No. 1207 (Miscellaneous Expense).
m. Paid wages to an employee, $1,200, Ck. No. 1208.
n. Resser withdrew cash for personal use, $700, Ck. No. 1209.

Required

Check Figure
Net Loss, $(436)

1. Record the owner's name in the Capital and Drawing T accounts.
2. Correctly place the plus and minus signs for each T account, and label the debit and credit sides of the accounts.
3. Record the transactions in the T accounts. Write the letter of each entry to identify the transaction.
4. Foot the T accounts and show the balances.
5. Prepare a trial balance as of July 31, 20—.
6. Prepare an income statement for July 31, 20—.
7. Prepare a statement of owner's equity for July 31, 20—.
8. Prepare a balance sheet as of July 31, 20—.

ACTIVITIES

CONSIDER AND COMMUNICATE

A fellow accounting student has difficulty understanding how the fundamental accounting equation stays in balance when a compound entry with one debit and two credits is recorded. Consider, for example, that a business bought equipment for $7,000, paid $3,000 in cash, and placed the remainder on account.

This means that there are two credits and one debit—one debit and one credit on the left side of the equation and the other credit on the right side of the equation. Explain to your fellow student how the equation stays in balance.

WHAT'S WRONG WITH THIS PICTURE?

A new bookkeeper can't find the errors that are causing the company's month-end trial balance to be out of balance. The bookkeeper is too shy to ask for help at the office, so she takes the financial records home and asks her uncle, a retired bookkeeper, to help her locate the errors. Even with the help of her uncle, she is still out of balance and is now too embarrassed to return to the office and ask for help. What is wrong with this practice, if anything?

3 The General Journal and the General Ledger

WHY IT MATTERS

ECOTOUR EXPEDITIONS, INC., Jamestown, Rhode Island

You probably have never imagined the possibility of being an accountant who could have a direct impact on improving global ecosystems. Accountants who work for Ecotour Expeditions, Inc., might manage accounting details for guest air travel and accommodations, tour guide compensation, expedition revenue, and a variety of other expenses. Not only would you need to know debits and credits within the accounting cycle, but you would have to become familiar with many countries and their languages and currencies. Supplies Expense might include reusable water bottles and malaria nets. Prepaid Insurance might include trip insurance for cancellations or delays due to weather or other problems.

In this chapter, you will journalize and post transactions and prepare a trial balance to see if debits equal credits. You'll need these skills to understand how to record accounting transactions similar to those you might find if you worked for Ecotour Expeditions, Inc.

LEARNING OBJECTIVES

After you have completed this chapter, you will be able to do the following:

1. *Record a group of transactions pertaining to a service business in a two-column general journal.*
2. *Post entries from a two-column general journal to general ledger accounts.*
3. *Prepare a trial balance from the ledger accounts.*
4. *Correct entries using the manual ruling method.*
5. *Correct entries using the manual or computerized correcting entry method.*

ACCOUNTING LANGUAGE

Account numbers *(p. 88)*
Cost principle *(p. 83)*
Cross-reference *(p. 89)*
General ledger *(p. 88)*
Journal *(p. 79)*
Journalizing *(p. 80)*
Ledger account *(p. 88)*
Posting *(p. 88)*
Source documents *(p. 80)*
Two-column general journal *(p. 80)*

In Chapter 2, we learned how to use T accounts as a tool for practicing debits and credits. We also used the trial balance as a means of making sure the debits equal the credits. In this chapter, we will further formalize our accounting procedures by presenting the general journal and the posting procedure.

Recall that *recording* is a step in the definition of accounting. Here we introduce the journal as the official record of business transactions. We have recorded business transactions as debits and credits to T accounts because, in the process of formulating debits and credits for business transactions, it's easier to visualize these debits and credits as the plus and minus sides of the T accounts involved. **Formulating the appropriate transaction debits and credits is the most important element in the accounting process.** It represents the very basic foundation of accounting, and all the structure represented by financial statements and other reports is entirely dependent upon it. After determining the debits and credits, the accountant records the transactions in a journal and a ledger.

The initial steps in the accounting process are:

STEP 1. Record business transactions in a journal.

STEP 2. Post entries to accounts in the ledger.

STEP 3. Prepare a trial balance.

In this chapter, we present the general journal and the posting procedure.

THE GENERAL JOURNAL

We have seen that an accountant must keep a record of each transaction. In Chapter 2, we recorded the transactions directly in T accounts; however, only part of the transaction would be listed in each T account. A **journal** is a book in which business transactions are recorded as they happen. In the journal, both the debits and the

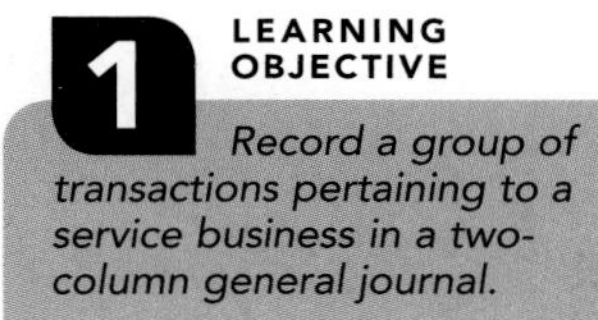

Record a group of transactions pertaining to a service business in a two-column general journal.

credits of the entire transaction are recorded in one place. Actually, the journal is a diary for the business, in which you record in day-by-day or chronological order all the events involving financial affairs. A journal is called a *book of original entry*. In other words, a transaction is always recorded first in the journal. The process of recording a business transaction in the journal is called **journalizing**. The information about transactions comes from business papers, such as checks, invoices, receipts, letters, and memos. These **source documents** furnish proof (objective evidence) that a transaction has taken place, and they should be identified in the journal entry whenever possible. The basic form of journal is the **two-column general journal**. The term *two-column* refers to the two columns used for debit and credit amounts.

As an example of journalizing business transactions, let's use the transactions for Conner's Whitewater Adventures. The pages of the journal are numbered in consecutive order. This is the first page, so we write a 1 in the space for the page number. Also, we must write the date of each transaction. Let's begin with the first entry.

Transaction (a). June 1: J. Conner deposited $90,000 in a bank account in the name of Conner's Whitewater Adventures. First, we will show the complete journal entry.

GENERAL JOURNAL — PAGE 1

Date		Description	Post. Ref.	Debit	Credit
20—					
June	1	Cash		90 0 0 0 00	
		J. Conner, Capital			90 0 0 0 00
		To record the original			
		investment by J. Conner.			

The same elements will be found whether handwriting the entries or journalizing them in an accounting software package. To explain the entry, we break it down line by line. At the top of the page, we record the page number where indicated. On the first line, we record the year in the left part of the Date column. On the second line, we record the month in the left part of the Date column and the day of the month in the right part of the Date column. We don't have to repeat the year and month until we start a new page, or until the year or month changes. (Because our illustrations are separated, however, the month may be repeated to eliminate confusion.)

GENERAL JOURNAL — PAGE 1 (*Page number*)

Date		Description	Post. Ref.	Debit	Credit
20—		*Date*			
June	1				

Decide which accounts should be debited and credited. We do this by analyzing the transactions as we did in Chapter 2.

STEP 1. Decide which accounts are involved.

STEP 2. Classify the accounts involved (asset, liability, owner's equity, revenue, expense).

STEP 3. Decide if the accounts involved are increased or decreased.

STEP 4. Write the transactions as a debit to one account (or accounts) and a credit to another account (or accounts).

STEP 5. Check to see if the equation is in balance.

Cash is involved in our example. Cash is an asset because it falls within the definition of "things owned." Cash is increased, and the increase side of Cash is the left or debit side. So we debit Cash $90,000.

J. Conner, Capital, is involved. J. Conner, Capital, is an owner's equity account because it represents the owner's investment. J. Conner, Capital, is increased, and the increase side of Capital is the right or credit side. So we credit J. Conner, Capital, $90,000. Let's show these entries by referring to our reliable fundamental accounting equation with the accompanying T accounts:

Assets		=	**Liabilities**		+	**Owner's Equity**		+	**Revenue**		–	**Expenses**	
+	–		–	+		–	+		–	+		+	–
Debit	Credit		Debit	Credit		Debit	Credit		Debit	Credit		Debit	Credit

Cash	
+	–
90,000	

J. Conner, Capital	
–	+
	90,000

You perform this process mentally. If the transaction is more complicated, draw the T accounts on paper. Using T accounts is the accountant's way of drawing a picture of the transaction. You must get into the T account habit; it will be a great help to you in the future.

Always record the debit part of the entry first. Enter the account title—in this case, Cash—in the Description column. Record the amount—$90,000—in the Debit amount column.

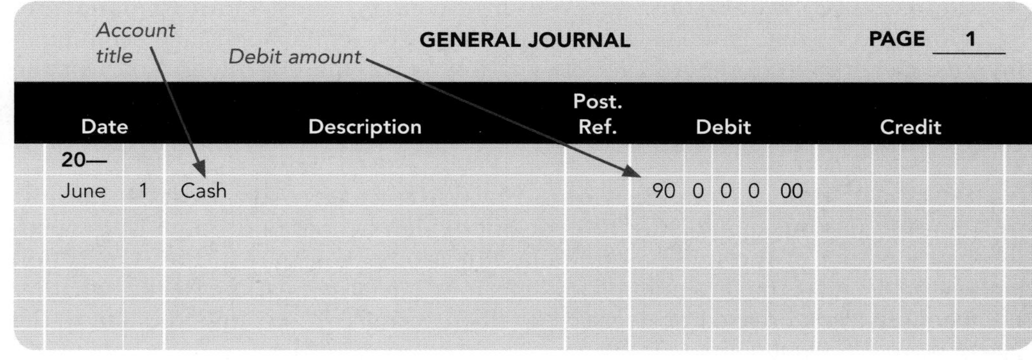

Next, record the credit part of the entry. Enter the account title—in this case, J. Conner, Capital—on the line below the debit in the Description column, indented about one-half inch. On the same line, enter the amount—$90,000—in the Credit column.

FYI

Customarily, accountants don't abbreviate account titles. If you are keying accounts into an accounting software program, you will probably only have to key the first few letters before the program will recognize the account. Or, you may only have to key in an account number.

GENERAL JOURNAL PAGE 1

Date		Description	Post. Ref.	Debit	Credit
20—					
June	1	Cash		90 0 0 0 00	
		J. Conner, Capital			90 0 0 0 00

Indent the account title that is credited

FYI

In accounting software, there is also space for a brief explanation.

You should now write a brief explanation, in which you should refer to source documents, giving such information as check numbers, receipt numbers, or invoice numbers. You may also list names of charge customers or creditors, or terms of payment. Enter the explanation below the credit entry, indented an additional one-half inch.

GENERAL JOURNAL PAGE 1

Date		Description	Post. Ref.	Debit	Credit
20—					
June	1	Cash		90 0 0 0 00	
		J. Conner, Capital			90 0 0 0 00
		To record the original			
		investment by J. Conner.			

Indent again for the explanation

Remember

As in a trial balance, there are no dollar signs in journal entries.

For an entry in the general journal to be complete, it must contain (1) the date, (2) a debit entry, (3) a credit entry, and (4) an explanation. To anyone thoroughly familiar with the accounts, the explanation may seem quite obvious. Nevertheless, record the explanation as a required, integral part of the entry. To make the journal entries easier to read, leave one blank line between each transaction in your homework.

Transaction (b). June 2: Conner's Whitewater Adventures bought equipment, paying cash, $38,000. Decide which accounts are involved. Next, determine which of the five possible classifications each part of the transaction applies to. Visualize the plus and minus signs for each classification. Decide whether the accounts are increased or decreased. When you use T accounts to analyze the transaction, the results are as follows:

Equipment	
+	−
Debit	Credit
38,000	

Cash	
+	−
Debit	Credit
	38,000

Now journalize this analysis below the first transaction. Record the day of the month in the Date column. Remember, you do not have to record the month and year again until the month or year changes or you use a new journal page.

GENERAL JOURNAL PAGE 1

Date		Description	Post. Ref.	Debit	Credit
20—					
June	1	Cash		90 0 0 0 00	
		J. Conner, Capital			90 0 0 0 00
		To record the original			
		investment by J. Conner.			
	2	Equipment		38 0 0 0 00	
		Cash			38 0 0 0 00
		Bought equipment for cash.			

Skip a line between entries in homework

Transaction (c). June 3: Conner's Whitewater Adventures bought equipment on account from Signal Products, $4,320. Again, start with the T accounts.

Equipment	
+	−
Debit	Credit
4,320	

Accounts Payable	
−	+
Debit	Credit
	4,320

After skipping a line in the journal, record the day of the month and then the entry. In journalizing a transaction involving Accounts Payable, always state the name of the creditor in the explanation. Similarly, in journalizing a transaction involving Accounts Receivable, always state the name of the customer who charged the amount in the explanation.

GENERAL JOURNAL PAGE 1

Date		Description	Post. Ref.	Debit	Credit
	3	Equipment		4 3 2 0 00	
		Accounts Payable			4 3 2 0 00
		Bought equipment on account			
		from Signal Products.			

Remember

In trying to figure out how a transaction should be recorded, first decide on the accounts involved. Then classify the accounts as A, L, OE, R, or E. Next, ask yourself whether the accounts are increased or decreased, and think of the related accounts with their plus and minus sides. Now the debits and credits of the transaction will fall into place.

When a business buys an asset, the asset should be recorded at the actual cost (the agreed amount of a transaction). This is called the **cost principle**. For example, suppose that the $4,320 that Conner's Whitewater Adventures paid for the equipment from Signal Products was a bargain price, as Signal Products had been asking $7,500 for the equipment. Conner's Whitewater Adventures *should record the cost of the equipment as the actual amount paid in the transaction that occurred*, which is $4,320. This is true even though the fair market value may indeed be $7,500.

Transaction (d). June 4: Conner's Whitewater Adventures paid Signal Products, a creditor, on account, $2,000. Picture the T accounts like this:

Cash	
+	−
Debit	Credit
	2,000

Accounts Payable	
−	+
Debit	Credit
2,000	

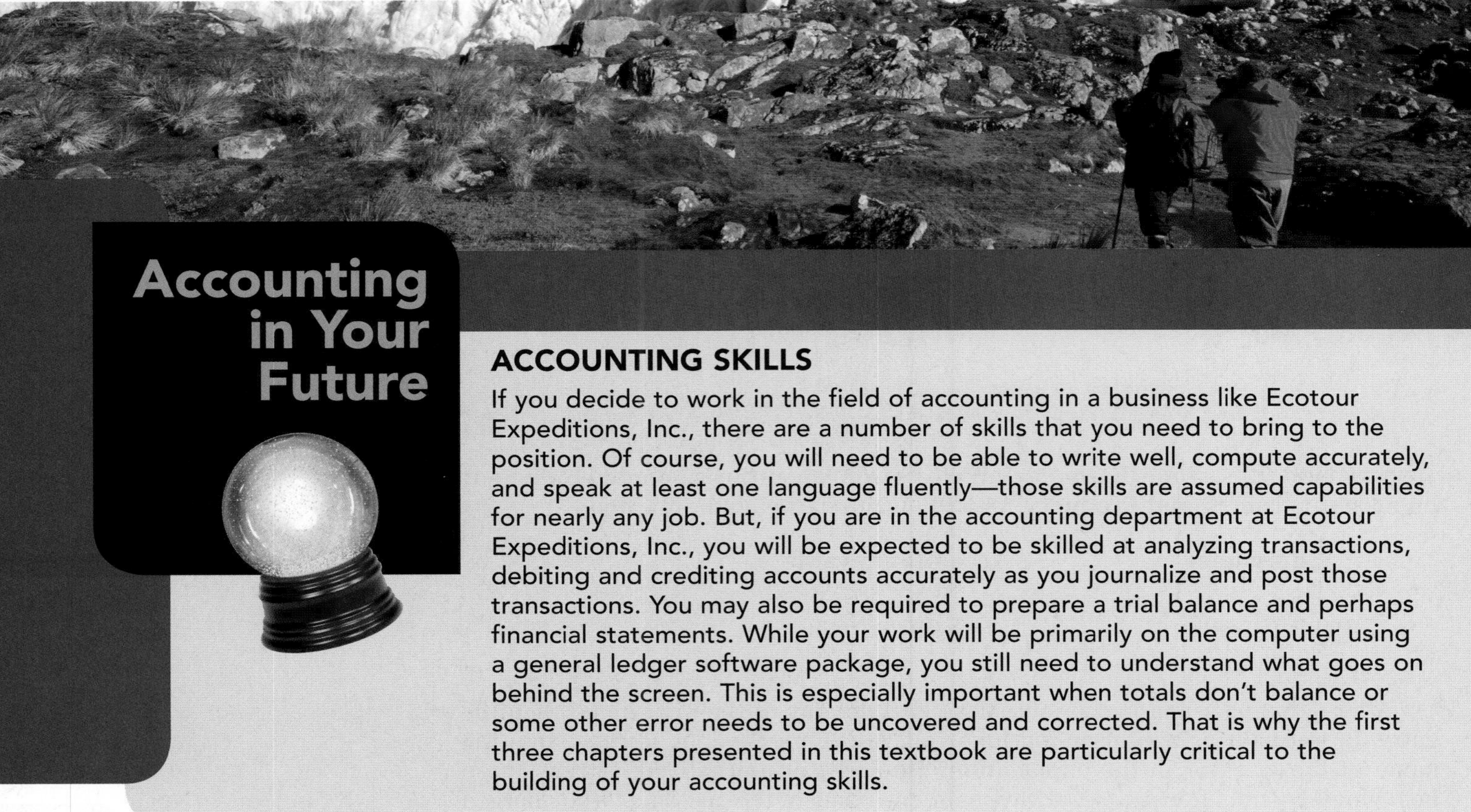

Accounting in Your Future

ACCOUNTING SKILLS

If you decide to work in the field of accounting in a business like Ecotour Expeditions, Inc., there are a number of skills that you need to bring to the position. Of course, you will need to be able to write well, compute accurately, and speak at least one language fluently—those skills are assumed capabilities for nearly any job. But, if you are in the accounting department at Ecotour Expeditions, Inc., you will be expected to be skilled at analyzing transactions, debiting and crediting accounts accurately as you journalize and post those transactions. You may also be required to prepare a trial balance and perhaps financial statements. While your work will be primarily on the computer using a general ledger software package, you still need to understand what goes on behind the screen. This is especially important when totals don't balance or some other error needs to be uncovered and corrected. That is why the first three chapters presented in this textbook are particularly critical to the building of your accounting skills.

Remember

Get in the T account habit. Picture the T accounts in your mind, or draw T accounts on paper with their plus and minus signs. The T account habit is a must.

In this case, we see that cash is decreasing, so we record it on the minus side. We now have a credit to Cash and have completed half of the entry. Next, we recognize that Accounts Payable is involved. We ask ourselves, "Do we owe more or less as a result of this transaction?" The answer is "less," so we record it on the minus, or debit, side of the account.

GENERAL JOURNAL PAGE 1

Date		Description	Post. Ref.	Debit	Credit
	4	Accounts Payable		2,000.00	
		Cash			2,000.00
		Paid Signal Products on account.			

Now let's list the transactions for June for Conner's Whitewater Adventures with the date of each transaction. The journal entries are illustrated in Figures 1, 2, and 3.

June 1 J. Conner invests $90,000 cash in her new business.

2 Buys equipment costing $38,000, paying cash.

June 3 Buys equipment costing $4,320 on credit from Signal Products.
4 Pays $2,000 to Signal Products to be applied against the firm's liability of $4,320.
4 J. Conner invests her personal equipment valued at $5,200 in her new business.
7 Receives cash revenue, $8,000.
8 Pays rent for the month, $1,250.
10 Buys supplies on account from Fineman Company, $675.

FIGURE 1
Journal entries for Conner's Whitewater Adventures, June 1–10

GENERAL JOURNAL PAGE 1

Date		Description	Post. Ref.	Debit	Credit
20—					
June	1	Cash		90 0 0 0 00	
		J. Conner, Capital			90 0 0 0 00
		To record the original			
		investment by J. Conner.			
	2	Equipment		38 0 0 0 00	
		Cash			38 0 0 0 00
		Bought equipment for cash.			
	3	Equipment		4 3 2 0 00	
		Accounts Payable			4 3 2 0 00
		Bought equipment on account			
		from Signal Products.			
	4	Accounts Payable		2 0 0 0 00	
		Cash			2 0 0 0 00
		Paid Signal Products on			
		account.			
	4	Equipment		5 2 0 0 00	
		J. Conner, Capital			5 2 0 0 00
		To record the investment			
		by J. Conner in Conner's			
		Whitewater Adventures.			
	7	Cash		8 0 0 0 00	
		Income from Tours			8 0 0 0 00
		Cash revenue.			
	8	Rent Expense		1 2 5 0 00	
		Cash			1 2 5 0 00
		For month ended June 30.			
	10	Supplies Expense		6 7 5 00	
		Accounts Payable			6 7 5 00
		Bought supplies on account			
		from Fineman Company.			

FIGURE 2
Journal entries for Conner's Whitewater Adventures, June 10–24

GENERAL JOURNAL PAGE 2

Date		Description	Post. Ref.	Debit	Credit
20—					
June	10	Prepaid Insurance		1,875.00	
		Cash			1,875.00
		Premium for three-month			
		liability insurance policy.			
	14	Advertising Expense		620.00	
		Accounts Payable			620.00
		Received bill from			
		advertising with *The Times*.			
	15	Accounts Receivable		6,750.00	
		Income from Tours			6,750.00
		Billed Crystal River Lodge			
		for services performed.			
	15	Accounts Payable		1,500.00	
		Cash			1,500.00
		Paid Signal Products on			
		account.			
	18	Utilities Expense		225.00	
		Cash			225.00
		Paid Solar Power, Inc., for			
		utilities bill.			
	20	Accounts Payable		620.00	
		Cash			620.00
		Paid *The Times* in full.			
	24	Wages Expense		2,360.00	
		Cash			2,360.00
		Paid wages of part-time			
		employee.			

Remember

You must enter the year and the month at the top of every page in the journal.

Remember

Six types of information must be entered in the general journal for each transaction: the date, the title of the account to be debited, the amount of the debit, the title of the account to be credited, the amount of the credit, and the explanation.

June 10 Pays for three-month liability insurance policy, $1,875.

14 Receives bill for newspaper advertising from *The Times*, $620.

15 Conner's Whitewater Adventures signs a contract with Crystal River Lodge to provide rafting adventures for guests. Conner's Whitewater Adventures provides 27 one-day rafting tours and bills Crystal River Lodge for $6,750.

15 Pays $1,500 to Signal Products as a partial payment on account.

18 Receives and pays bill for utilities from Solar Power, Inc., $225.

20 Pays *The Times* for advertising, $620 in full. (This bill has been previously recorded.)

24 Pays wages of part-time employee, $2,360.

26 Buys additional equipment costing $3,780 from Signal Products, paying $1,850 down with the remaining $1,930 on account.

GENERAL JOURNAL				PAGE 3
Date	**Description**	**Post. Ref.**	**Debit**	**Credit**
20—				
June 26	Equipment		3,780.00	
	Cash			1,850.00
	Accounts Payable			1,930.00
	Bought equipment on account			
	from Signal Products.			
30	Cash		2,500.00	
	Accounts Receivable			2,500.00
	Received from Crystal River Lodge			
	to apply on account.			
30	Cash		8,570.00	
	Income from Tours			8,570.00
	Cash revenue.			
30	J. Conner, Drawing		3,500.00	
	Cash			3,500.00
	Withdrawal for personal use.			

FIGURE 3
Journal entries for Conner's Whitewater Adventures, June 26–30

Remember

Every business transaction requires at least one debit and at least one credit. In a general journal, the debit part of the entry is recorded first. The credit part of the entry is recorded next, followed by a brief explanation of the transaction.

June 30 Receives $2,500 from Crystal River Lodge to apply on amount previously billed.

30 Receives cash revenue, $8,570.

30 J. Conner withdraws cash for personal use, $3,500.

POSTING TO THE GENERAL LEDGER

You can see that the journal is the *book of original entry.* Each transaction must first be recorded in the journal in full. However, it is difficult to determine the balance

The journal is like a diary of the business's financial changes written in chronological or date order.
=
DIARY
Diary of the business
The ledger is like sorted laundry—grouped information about each account is summarized in one place.
=
A = L + OE + R − E

FYI

Notice the space in the account numbers between 117 and 124. Generally, the account numbers from 120 to 129 are reserved for assets that have a length of life of more than one year, such as equipment, buildings, and land. Such space lets you add accounts in any part of the chart of accounts.

of any one account, such as Cash, from the general journal entries. So the **ledger account** has been devised to give us a complete record of the transactions recorded in each individual account. The **general ledger** contains all the accounts. It may be a loose-leaf binder so that you can add or remove pages or printouts from your accounting software program. The process of transferring information from the journal to the ledger accounts is called **posting**.

The Chart of Accounts

The accounts in the ledger are arranged according to the chart of accounts, which **is the official list of the ledger accounts in which transactions of a business are recorded.** Assets are listed first, liabilities second, owner's equity third, revenue fourth, and expenses fifth. The chart of accounts for Conner's Whitewater Adventures is as follows:

CHART OF ACCOUNTS

Assets (100–199)
111 Cash
113 Accounts Receivable
117 Prepaid Insurance
124 Equipment

Liabilities (200–299)
221 Accounts Payable

Owner's Equity (300–399)
311 J. Conner, Capital
312 J. Conner, Drawing

Revenue (400–499)
411 Income from Tours

Expenses (500–599)
511 Wages Expense
512 Rent Expense
513 Supplies Expense
514 Advertising Expense
515 Utilities Expense

Remember

In recording transactions for a business in the journal, one must use the exact account titles as listed in the company's chart of accounts.

Notice that the arrangement of the chart of accounts consists of the balance sheet accounts followed by the income statement accounts. The numbers preceding the account titles are the **account numbers**. The digits in the account numbers also indicate account *classifications*. For most companies, assets start with 1, liabilities with 2, owner's equity with 3, revenue with 4, and expenses with 5. The second and third digits indicate the positions of the individual accounts within their respective classifications.

While charts of accounts vary from business to business, the beginning numbers for assets, liabilities, owner's equity, revenues, and expenses are standard for a service business. Some account numbers are much longer than three digits.

For merchandising businesses selling goods (versus services), expenses will start with a 6 because accounts starting with a 5 are reserved for accounts related to the cost of the goods being sold.

Most accounting programs, such as QuickBooks and Peachtree, include a standard chart of accounts set up for many different types of businesses.

The Ledger Account Form (Running Balance Format)

We have been looking at accounts in the simple T account form primarily because T accounts illustrate situations so well. The debit and credit sides are specifically labeled, making the T account form a good way to picture account activity. However, determining the balance of an account using the T account form is difficult. You must add both columns and subtract the smaller total from the larger. To overcome this disadvantage, accountants generally use the four-column account form with Balance columns in the general ledger. Let's look at the Cash account of Conner's Whitewater Adventures in four-column form (Figure 4) compared with the T account form. *Leave the Post. Ref. column blank for now.*

GENERAL LEDGER

ACCOUNT Cash ACCOUNT NO. 111

Date		Item	Post. Ref.	Debit	Credit	Balance Debit	Balance Credit
20—							
June	1			90 0 0 0 00		90 0 0 0 00	
	2				38 0 0 0 00	52 0 0 0 00	
	4				2 0 0 0 00	50 0 0 0 00	
	7			8 0 0 0 00		58 0 0 0 00	
	8				1 2 5 0 00	56 7 5 0 00	
	10				1 8 7 5 00	54 8 7 5 00	
	15				1 5 0 0 00	53 3 7 5 00	
	18				2 2 5 00	53 1 5 0 00	
	20				6 2 0 00	52 5 3 0 00	
	24				2 3 6 0 00	50 1 7 0 00	
	26				1 8 5 0 00	48 3 2 0 00	
	30			2 5 0 0 00		50 8 2 0 00	
	30			8 5 7 0 00		59 3 9 0 00	
	30				3 5 0 0 00	55 8 9 0 00	

Transaction amount *Running balance*

FIGURE 4

General ledger for Conner's Whitewater Adventures

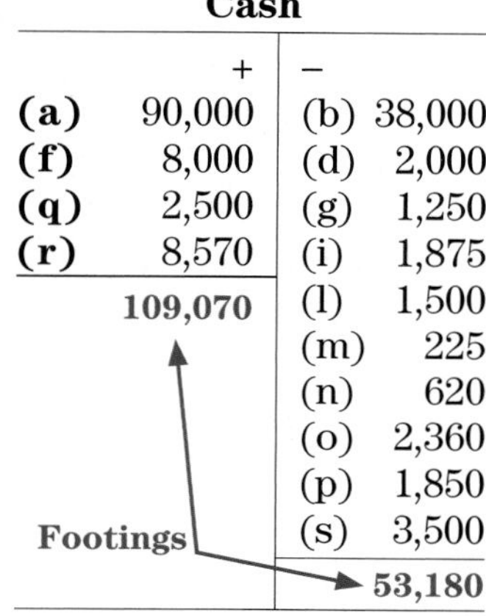

Cash
+ | −
(a) 90,000 | (b) 38,000
(f) 8,000 | (d) 2,000
(q) 2,500 | (g) 1,250
(r) 8,570 | (i) 1,875
109,070 | (l) 1,500
(m) 225
(n) 620
(o) 2,360
(p) 1,850
Footings | (s) 3,500
53,180
Balance → 55,890

Note the calculation of the running balance. In the abbreviated form, it looks like this:

Remember

To analyze transactions, accountants use T accounts to draw pictures of the transactions. As transactions become more complicated, this is a "must."

GENERAL LEDGER

ACCOUNT Cash ACCOUNT NO. 111

Date		Item	Post. Ref.	Debit	Credit	Balance Debit	Balance Credit
20—							
June	1			90 0 0 0 00		90 0 0 0 00	
	2				38 0 0 0 00	52 0 0 0 00	
	4				2 0 0 0 00	50 0 0 0 00	

90,000
− 38,000
52,000
− 2,000
50,000

The Posting Process

2 LEARNING OBJECTIVE

Post entries from a two-column general journal to general ledger accounts.

In the posting process, you must transfer the following information from the journal to the ledger accounts: the *date of the transaction*, the *debit and credit amounts*, and the *page number* of the journal. Post each account separately, using the following steps. Post the debit part of the entry first.

STEP 1. Write the date of the transaction in the account's Date column.

STEP 2. Write the amount of the transaction in the Debit or Credit column, and enter the new balance in the Balance columns under Debit or Credit.

STEP 3. Write the page number of the journal in the Post. Ref. column of the ledger account. (This is a **cross-reference**; it tells where the amount came from.)

STEP 4. Record the ledger account number in the Post. Ref. column of the journal. (This is also a cross-reference; it tells where the amount was posted.)

Entering the account number in the Post. Ref. column of the journal should be the last step. It acts as a verification of the three preceding steps.

FIGURE 5

Posting from the general journal to the general ledger—debit entry (Transaction 1)

① Date of transaction
② Amount of transaction
③ Page number of the journal
④ Ledger account number

GENERAL JOURNAL PAGE 1

Date		Description	Post. Ref.	Debit	Credit
20—					
June	1	Cash	111	90 0 0 0 00	
		J. Conner, Capital			90 0 0 0 00
		To record the original			
		investment by J. Conner.			

GENERAL LEDGER

ACCOUNT Cash ACCOUNT NO. 111

Date		Item	Post. Ref.	Debit	Credit	Balance Debit	Balance Credit
20—							
June	1		1	90 0 0 0 00		90 0 0 0 00	

The first transaction for Conner's Whitewater Adventures is illustrated in Figure 5. Let's look first at the debit part of the entry.

Next we post the credit part of the entry, as shown in Figure 6.

The accountant normally uses the Item column only at the end of a financial period. The words that may appear in this column are *balance*, *closing*, *adjusting*, and *reversing*. We will explain the use of these terms later.

Incidentally, some accountants use running balance-type ledger account forms that have only one balance column. However, we have used the two-balance-column arrangement to show clearly the appropriate balance of an account. For example, in Figure 5, Cash has a $90,000 balance recorded in the Debit column (normal balance). In Figure 6, J. Conner, Capital, has a $90,000 balance recorded in the Credit column (normal balance).

FIGURE 6

Posting from the general journal to the general ledger—credit entry (Transaction 1)

① Date of transaction
② Amount of transaction
③ Page number of the journal
④ Ledger account number

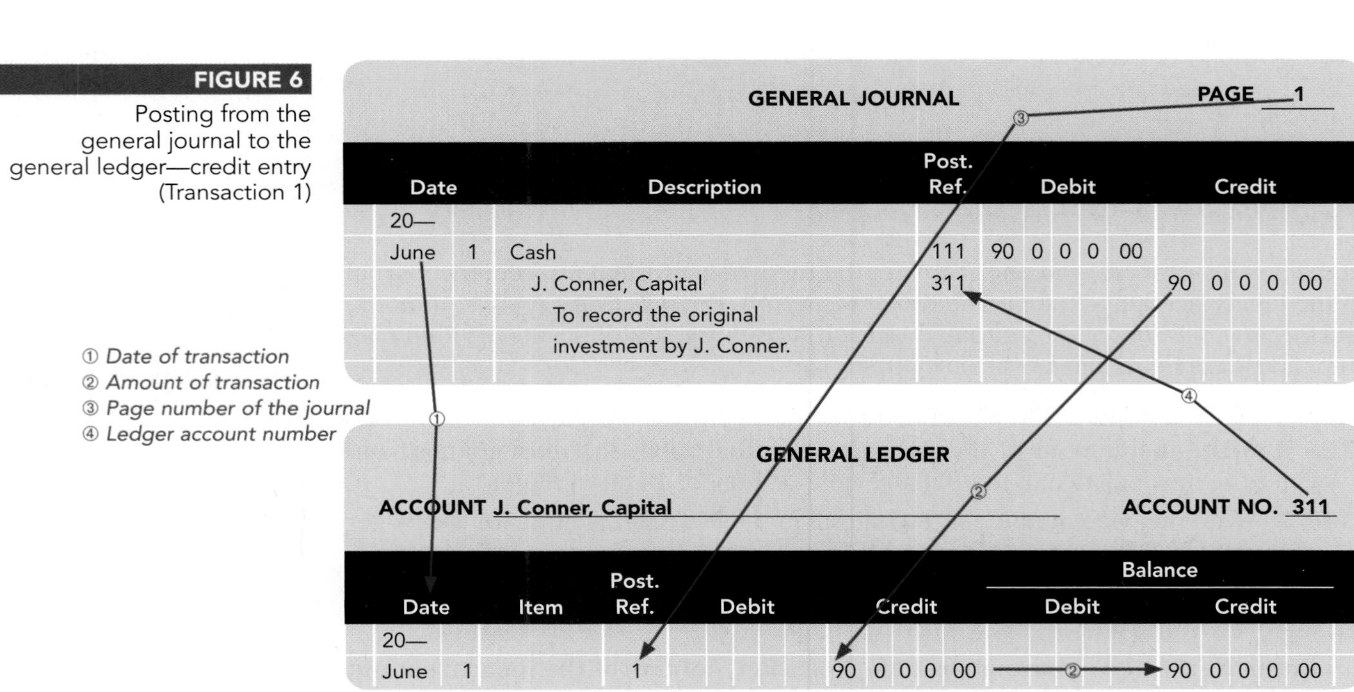
GENERAL JOURNAL PAGE 1

Date		Description	Post. Ref.	Debit	Credit
20—					
June	1	Cash	111	90 0 0 0 00	
		J. Conner, Capital	311		90 0 0 0 00
		To record the original			
		investment by J. Conner.			

GENERAL LEDGER

ACCOUNT J. Conner, Capital ACCOUNT NO. 311

Date		Item	Post. Ref.	Debit	Credit	Balance Debit	Balance Credit
20—							
June	1		1		90 0 0 0 00		90 0 0 0 00

In the recording of the second transaction, shown in Figure 7, see if you can identify in order the four steps in the posting process.

FIGURE 7
Posting from the general journal to the general ledger (Transaction 2)

GENERAL JOURNAL PAGE 1

Date		Description	Post. Ref.	Debit	Credit
	2	Equipment	124	38 0 0 0 00	
		Cash	111		38 0 0 0 00
		Bought equipment for cash.			

GENERAL LEDGER

ACCOUNT Cash ACCOUNT NO. 111

Date		Item	Post. Ref.	Debit	Credit	Balance Debit	Balance Credit
20—							
June	1		1	90 0 0 0 00		90 0 0 0 00	
	2		1		38 0 0 0 00	52 0 0 0 00	

ACCOUNT Equipment ACCOUNT NO. 124

Date		Item	Post. Ref.	Debit	Credit	Balance Debit	Balance Credit
20—							
June	2		1	38 0 0 0 00		38 0 0 0 00	

Remember

Do not record account numbers in the Post. Ref. column of the journal until the amounts have been posted to the ledger accounts as either debits or credits. When posting with accounting software, the amounts from each transaction are automatically posted to the appropriate general ledger accounts.

Remember

Posting is simply transferring or copying exactly the same date and the debits and credits listed in the journal entry from the journal to the ledger.

Now let's look at the journal entries for the first month of operation for Conner's Whitewater Adventures. As you can see in Figure 8, the Post. Ref. column has been filled in, because the posting has been completed.

If the temporary balance of an account happens to be zero, insert long dashes through both the Debit Balance and the Credit Balance columns. We'll use another business, the Becker Company, in this example. Its Accounts Receivable ledger account follows. Notice that the zero balance on October 29 is represented by long dashes in the Debit and Credit columns.

GENERAL LEDGER

ACCOUNT Accounts Receivable ACCOUNT NO. 113

Date		Item	Post. Ref.	Debit	Credit	Balance Debit	Balance Credit
20—							
Oct.	7		96	1 5 0 00		1 5 0 00	
	19		97	2 4 8 00		3 9 8 00	
	21		97		1 5 0 00	2 4 8 00	
	29		98		2 4 8 00	———	———
	31		98	1 8 2 00		1 8 2 00	

FIGURE 8

Journal entries for Conner's Whitewater Adventures (first month of operation)

GENERAL JOURNAL PAGE 1

Date		Description	Post. Ref.	Debit	Credit
20—					
June	1	Cash	111	90,000.00	
		J. Conner, Capital	311		90,000.00
		To record the original			
		investment by J. Conner.			
	2	Equipment	124	38,000.00	
		Cash	111		38,000.00
		Bought equipment for cash.			
	3	Equipment	124	4,320.00	
		Accounts Payable	221		4,320.00
		Bought equipment on			
		account from Signal			
		Products.			
	4	Accounts Payable	221	2,000.00	
		Cash	111		2,000.00
		Paid Signal Products on			
		account.			
	4	Equipment	124	5,200.00	
		J. Conner, Capital	311		5,200.00
		To record the investment			
		by J. Conner in Conner's			
		Whitewater Adventures.			
	7	Cash	111	8,000.00	
		Income from Tours	411		8,000.00
		Cash revenue.			
	8	Rent Expense	512	1,250.00	
		Cash	111		1,250.00
		For month ended June 30.			
	10	Supplies Expense	513	675.00	
		Accounts Payable	221		675.00
		Bought supplies on account			
		from Fineman Company.			

GENERAL JOURNAL PAGE 2

Date		Description	Post. Ref.	Debit	Credit
20—					
June	10	Prepaid Insurance	117	1,875.00	
		Cash	111		1,875.00
		Premium for three-month			
		liability insurance policy.			
	14	Advertising Expense	514	620.00	
		Accounts Payable	221		620.00
		Received bill from			
		advertising with *The Times*.			

FIGURE 8
(Concluded)

Date		Description	Post. Ref.	Debit	Credit
	15	Accounts Receivable	113	6,750.00	
		Income from Tours	411		6,750.00
		Billed Crystal River Lodge			
		for services performed.			
	15	Accounts Payable	221	1,500.00	
		Cash	111		1,500.00
		Paid Signal Products on			
		account.			
	18	Utilities Expense	515	225.00	
		Cash	111		225.00
		Paid Solar Power, Inc.,			
		for utilities bill.			
	20	Accounts Payable	221	620.00	
		Cash	111		620.00
		Paid *The Times* in full.			
	24	Wages Expense	511	2,360.00	
		Cash	111		2,360.00
		Paid wages of part-time			
		employee.			

GENERAL JOURNAL PAGE 3

Date		Description	Post. Ref.	Debit	Credit
20—					
June	26	Equipment	124	3,780.00	
		Cash	111		1,850.00
		Accounts Payable	221		1,930.00
		Bought equipment on			
		account from Signal			
		Products.			
	30	Cash	111	2,500.00	
		Accounts Receivable	113		2,500.00
		Received from Crystal			
		River Lodge to apply on			
		account.			
	30	Cash	111	8,570.00	
		Income from Tours	411		8,570.00
		Cash revenue.			
	30	J. Conner, Drawing	312	3,500.00	
		Cash	111		3,500.00
		Withdrawal for personal use.			

Although Figure 8 contains a written version of the journal entries, journal entries prepared in computerized accounting programs are very similar. Computerized accounting programs still require you to record the journal entries as we have demonstrated, including the journal explanations. The ledger accounts and entries for Conner's Whitewater Adventures are shown in Figure 9.

FIGURE 9

General ledger for Conner's Whitewater Adventures (first month of operation)

GENERAL LEDGER

ACCOUNT Cash **ACCOUNT NO.** 111

Date		Item	Post. Ref.	Debit	Credit	Balance Debit	Balance Credit
20—							
June	1		1	90,000.00		90,000.00	
	2		1		38,000.00	52,000.00	
	4		1		2,000.00	50,000.00	
	7		1	8,000.00		58,000.00	
	8		1		1,250.00	56,750.00	
	10		2		1,875.00	54,875.00	
	15		2		1,500.00	53,375.00	
	18		2		225.00	53,150.00	
	20		2		620.00	52,530.00	
	24		2		2,360.00	50,170.00	
	26		3		1,850.00	48,320.00	
	30		3	2,500.00		50,820.00	
	30		3	8,570.00		59,390.00	
	30		3		3,500.00	55,890.00	

ACCOUNT Accounts Receivable **ACCOUNT NO.** 113

Date		Item	Post. Ref.	Debit	Credit	Balance Debit	Balance Credit
20—							
June	15		2	6,750.00		6,750.00	
	30		3		2,500.00	4,250.00	

ACCOUNT Prepaid Insurance **ACCOUNT NO.** 117

Date		Item	Post. Ref.	Debit	Credit	Balance Debit	Balance Credit
20—							
June	10		2	1,875.00		1,875.00	

ACCOUNT Equipment **ACCOUNT NO.** 124

Date		Item	Post. Ref.	Debit	Credit	Balance Debit	Balance Credit
20—							
June	2		1	38,000.00		38,000.00	
	3		1	4,320.00		42,320.00	
	4		1	5,200.00		47,520.00	
	26		3	3,780.00		51,300.00	

FIGURE 9
(Continued)

ACCOUNT Accounts Payable ACCOUNT NO. 221

Date		Item	Post. Ref.	Debit	Credit	Balance Debit	Balance Credit
20—							
June	3		1		4,320.00		4,320.00
	4		1	2,000.00			2,320.00
	10		1		675.00		2,995.00
	14		2		620.00		3,615.00
	15		2	1,500.00			2,115.00
	20		2	620.00			1,495.00
	26		3		1,930.00		3,425.00

ACCOUNT J. Conner, Capital ACCOUNT NO. 311

Date		Item	Post. Ref.	Debit	Credit	Balance Debit	Balance Credit
20—							
June	1		1		90,000.00		90,000.00
	4		1		5,200.00		95,200.00

ACCOUNT J. Conner, Drawing ACCOUNT NO. 312

Date		Item	Post. Ref.	Debit	Credit	Balance Debit	Balance Credit
20—							
June	30		3	3,500.00		3,500.00	

ACCOUNT Income from Tours ACCOUNT NO. 411

Date		Item	Post. Ref.	Debit	Credit	Balance Debit	Balance Credit
20—							
June	7		1		8,000.00		8,000.00
	15		2		6,750.00		14,750.00
	30		3		8,570.00		23,320.00

ACCOUNT Wages Expense ACCOUNT NO. 511

Date		Item	Post. Ref.	Debit	Credit	Balance Debit	Balance Credit
20—							
June	24		2	2,360.00		2,360.00	

FIGURE 9
(Concluded)

ACCOUNT Rent Expense ACCOUNT NO. 512

Date		Item	Post. Ref.	Debit	Credit	Balance Debit	Balance Credit
20—							
June	8		1	1 2 5 0 00		1 2 5 0 00	

ACCOUNT Supplies Expense ACCOUNT NO. 513

Date		Item	Post. Ref.	Debit	Credit	Balance Debit	Balance Credit
20—							
June	10		1	6 7 5 00		6 7 5 00	

ACCOUNT Advertising Expense ACCOUNT NO. 514

Date		Item	Post. Ref.	Debit	Credit	Balance Debit	Balance Credit
20—							
June	14		2	6 2 0 00		6 2 0 00	

ACCOUNT Utilities Expense ACCOUNT NO. 515

Date		Item	Post. Ref.	Debit	Credit	Balance Debit	Balance Credit
20—							
June	18		2	2 2 5 00		2 2 5 00	

Preparation of the Trial Balance

LEARNING OBJECTIVE 3

Prepare a trial balance from the ledger accounts.

The trial balance is simply a list of the ledger accounts that have balances. A trial balance is presented in Figure 10.

Remember that the trial balance proves only that the total ledger debit balances equal the total ledger credit balances. Even when the debit and credit balances are equal, other types of errors may slip through—for example,

1. Posting the correct debit or credit amounts to the incorrect account.
2. Neglecting to journalize or post an entire transaction.

FIGURE 10

Trial balance for Conner's Whitewater Adventures

Conner's Whitewater Adventures
Trial Balance
June 30, 20—

Account Name	Debit	Credit
Cash	55,890	
Accounts Receivable	4,250	
Prepaid Insurance	1,875	
Equipment	51,300	
Accounts Payable		3,425
J. Conner, Capital		95,200
J. Conner, Drawing	3,500	
Income from Tours		23,320
Wages Expense	2,360	
Rent Expense	1,250	
Supplies Expense	675	
Advertising Expense	620	
Utilities Expense	225	
	121,945	121,945

Steps in the Accounting Process

So far, you have learned the first three steps in the accounting process.

STEP 1. Record the transactions of a business in a journal (book of original entry or the day-by-day record of the transactions of a firm). An entry should be based on some source document or evidence that a transaction has occurred, such as an invoice, a receipt, or a check.

STEP 2. Post entries to the accounts in the ledger. Transfer the amounts from the journal to the Debit or Credit columns of the specified accounts in the ledger. Use a cross-reference system. Accounts are organized in the ledger according to the account numbers assigned to them in the chart of accounts.

STEP 3. Prepare a trial balance. Record the balances of the ledger accounts in the appropriate column, Debit or Credit, of the trial balance form. Prove that the total of the debit balances equals the total of the credit balances.

Source Document

A source document can be an invoice, a receipt, a check, or so forth. We now add an important detail in the recording of a journal entry. This detail consists of listing the related source document number, which is used as a reference for the proof of a transaction. Figure 11 is an example of a source document followed by the journal entry (Figure 12) and ledger accounts (Figure 13). Note how the explanation differs from the one we showed earlier.

Using the source document, the journal entry is recorded in the journal (Figure 12). Note how the explanation includes important information from the source document.

The journal entry is then posted to the ledger (Figure 13).

FIGURE 11
Source document

INVOICE

FINEMAN COMPANY No. 4-962

220 East Ames Street, Denver CO 80012
Sold By: 203 Date: 6/10/20—
Name: Conner's Whitewater Adventures
Address: 1701 East Delaware Street
Colorado Springs, CO 80902
Terms: Net 30 days

Quantity	Description	Unit Price		Amount	
10 bx	Invoice forms	12	00	120	00
5 bx	Ink cartridges	32	00	160	00
3 bx	8 x 11 copy paper	20	00	60	00
2	File cabinets, 2-drawer	32	00	64	00
4 bx	3-tab folders	12	00	48	00
3	10-key electric calculators	24	00	72	00
5 bx	12-count black ink pens	12	00	60	00
5 bx	10-count mechanical pencils	10	00	50	00
	SUBTOTAL			634	00
	SALES TAX			41	00
	SHIPPING—free			0	00
	TOTAL			675	00

FIGURE 12
Journal entry related to source document

GENERAL JOURNAL **PAGE 1**

Date		Description	Post. Ref.	Debit	Credit
June	10	Supplies Expense	513	675 00	
		Accounts Payable	221		675 00
		Bought supplies on account			
		from Fineman Company,			
		Invoice No. 4-962.			

FIGURE 13
Ledger posting

ACCOUNT Accounts Payable **ACCOUNT NO. 221**

Previous postings

Date		Item	Post. Ref.	Debit	Credit	Balance Debit	Balance Credit
20—							
June	3		1		4,320 00		4,320 00
	4		1	2,000 00			2,320 00
	10		1		675 00		2,995 00

ACCOUNT Supplies Expense **ACCOUNT NO. 513**

Date		Item	Post. Ref.	Debit	Credit	Balance Debit	Balance Credit
20—							
June	10		1	675 00		675 00	

Paperwork—Why It's Worth Keeping Track Of!

As you analyze transactions for a business, you may have noticed that each transaction must be evidenced by a source document. Source documents, or the paperwork for transactions, is very important to all businesses. This is because all accounting transactions are developed from source documents. So what are some examples of source documents? Bills from vendors, checks from customers, deposit slips, credit card receipts, bank statements, and customer invoices are all example of source documents.

Many times businesses will use an accounting software program to create source documents that can be printed for the businesses' or customers' records. Source documents should include the name and address of the business, as well as the date, amount, and description of the transaction. The documents should also include any customer information. The detail provided on the source documents will help the accountant record the transactions.

Source documents are also needed to substantiate the transactions should the business be audited. Internal and external auditors will review the paperwork when determining if the transactions recorded by the business are accurate. The Internal Revenue Service (IRS) will also require the business to provide proof of transactions for income and deductions shown on the entity's tax return.

Is it necessary for the business to keep source documents forever? Well, that depends on what the source document is and who you talk to! Many accountants agree on the following guidelines:

Source Document	Time Period
Support for your tax return	3 years
Related to assets purchased, such as a business vehicle or computer	Keep until you sell or dispose
Documents such as accounts receivable or accounts payable ledgers, bank statements, canceled checks, and invoices	7 years
Items such as loan documents, tax returns, and financial statements	Indefinitely

Source documents are an important part of the accounting cycle. Take a moment to make sure that you are comfortable with the information provided on the documents and also that you are familiar with the most common documents used in accounting, such as invoices, deposit slips, receipts, and bills from vendors. As you go through the chapters of the textbook, you will be introduced to many types of source documents. Be sure to review them—there is important information included on these documents!

CORRECTION OF ERRORS—MANUAL AND COMPUTERIZED

Errors are occasionally made in recording journal entries and posting to the ledger accounts whether recording them manually or on a computer. Never erase them, because it might look as if you were trying to hide something. The method for correcting errors depends on how and when the errors were made. There are two manual methods for correcting errors; they are

1. The ruling method.
2. The correcting entry method.

Manual Ruling Method

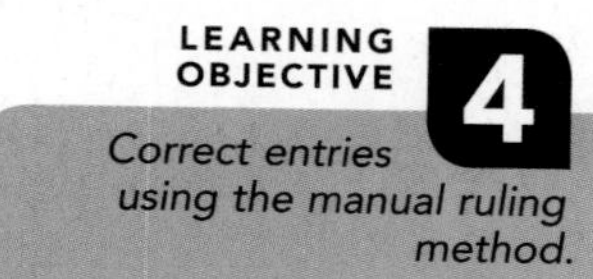

Correct entries using the manual ruling method.

You can use the manual ruling method to correct an error in the journal before posting or to correct an error in the ledger after an entry has been posted.

Manually Correcting Errors Before Posting Has Taken Place

When an error has been made in recording an account title in a journal entry, draw a line through the incorrect account title in the journal entry, and write the correct account title immediately above it. Include your initials with the correction. For example, an entry to record payment of $1,500 rent was incorrectly debited to Salary Expense.

GENERAL JOURNAL — PAGE 1

Date		Description	Post. Ref.	Debit	Credit
20—		*Rent Expense*			
Mar.	1	~~Salary Expense~~ *DJM*		1 5 0 0 00	
		Cash			1 5 0 0 00
		Paid rent for the month.			

When an error has been made in recording an amount, draw a line through the incorrect amount in the journal entry, and write the correct amount immediately above it. For example, an entry for a $120 payment for office supplies was recorded as $210. Include your initials with the correction.

GENERAL JOURNAL — PAGE 1

Date		Description	Post. Ref.	Debit	Credit
20—				*DJM* 1 2 0 00	
Apr.	6	Supplies Expense		~~2 1 0~~ 00	*DJM* 1 2 0 00
		Cash			~~2 1 0~~ 00
		Bought office supplies.			

Manually Correcting Errors After Posting Has Taken Place

When an entry was journalized correctly but one of the amounts was posted incorrectly, correct the error by drawing a single line through the amount and recording the correct amount above it. For example, an entry to record cash received for professional fees was correctly journalized as $400. However, it was posted as a debit to Cash for $400 and a credit to Professional Fees for $4,000. In the Professional Fees account, draw a line through $4,000 and insert $400 either above or next to the incorrect amount. Change the running balance of the account and initial the corrections.

ACCOUNT Professional Fees — ACCOUNT NO. 411

Date	Item	Post. Ref.	Debit	Credit	Balance Debit	Balance Credit
				DJM 4 0 0 00		*DJM* 25 6 0 0 00
6		94		~~4 0 0 0 00~~		~~29 2 0 0~~ 00

FYI

Use a ruler to draw a line through an error when completing manual corrections.

Correcting Entry Method—Manual or Computerized

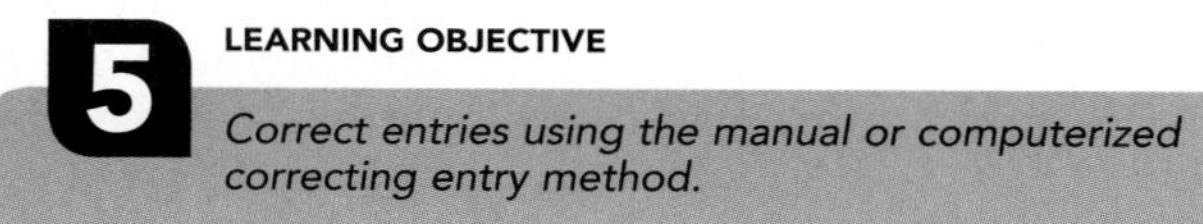

LEARNING OBJECTIVE 5

Correct entries using the manual or computerized correcting entry method.

©KUMZA, 2009. USED LICENSE FROM STUTTERSTOCK.COM

Whether you are preparing accounting records manually or on computer, accuracy is of primary importance. Rapid and accurate ten-key calculator and computer keyboard skills are a must for the accountant or bookkeeper.

You should use the correcting entry method when incorrectly journalized amounts have been posted. There are two correcting entry methods; they are

1. *One-step method.* Simply make one entry that undoes the error and provides the correct account.
2. *Two-step method.* The first step reverses the error made by the original entry. The second step includes the correct entry.

The correcting entry should *always* include an explanation. For example, on January 9, a $620 payment for advertising was incorrectly journalized and posted as a debit to Miscellaneous Expense for $620 and a credit to Cash for $620. The error was discovered and corrected on January 27 as follows using the one-step method:

GENERAL JOURNAL PAGE 1

Date		Description	Post. Ref.	Debit	Credit
20—					
Jan.	27	Advertising Expense		620.00	
		Miscellaneous Expense			620.00
		To correct error of			
		January 9 in which a			
		payment for Advertising			
		Expense was debited to			
		Miscellaneous Expense.			

Following the two-step method, if the original entry was recorded as a debit to Miscellaneous Expense and a credit to Cash, then reverse this entry by debiting Cash and crediting Miscellaneous Expense, and then record the correct entry.

GENERAL JOURNAL PAGE 1

Date		Description	Post. Ref.	Debit	Credit
20—					
Jan.	27	Cash		620.00	
		Miscellaneous Expense			620.00
		To reverse out an			
		incorrect entry recorded			
		January 9.			
	27	Advertising Expense		620.00	
		Cash			620.00
		To correct error of			
		January 9 in which a			
		payment for Advertising			
		Expense was debited to			
		Miscellaneous Expense.			

Correcting Errors on the Computer

Again, never delete an error; most commercial accounting programs will not allow deletion because if you could delete an entry, it would destroy the audit trail that tracks the life of each transaction. The procedure (as previously discussed) is to make a correcting entry with a brief and appropriate explanation followed by posting.

After the correcting entry has been journalized, the accounts are posted as for any other entry. After posting, the account balances should be correct.

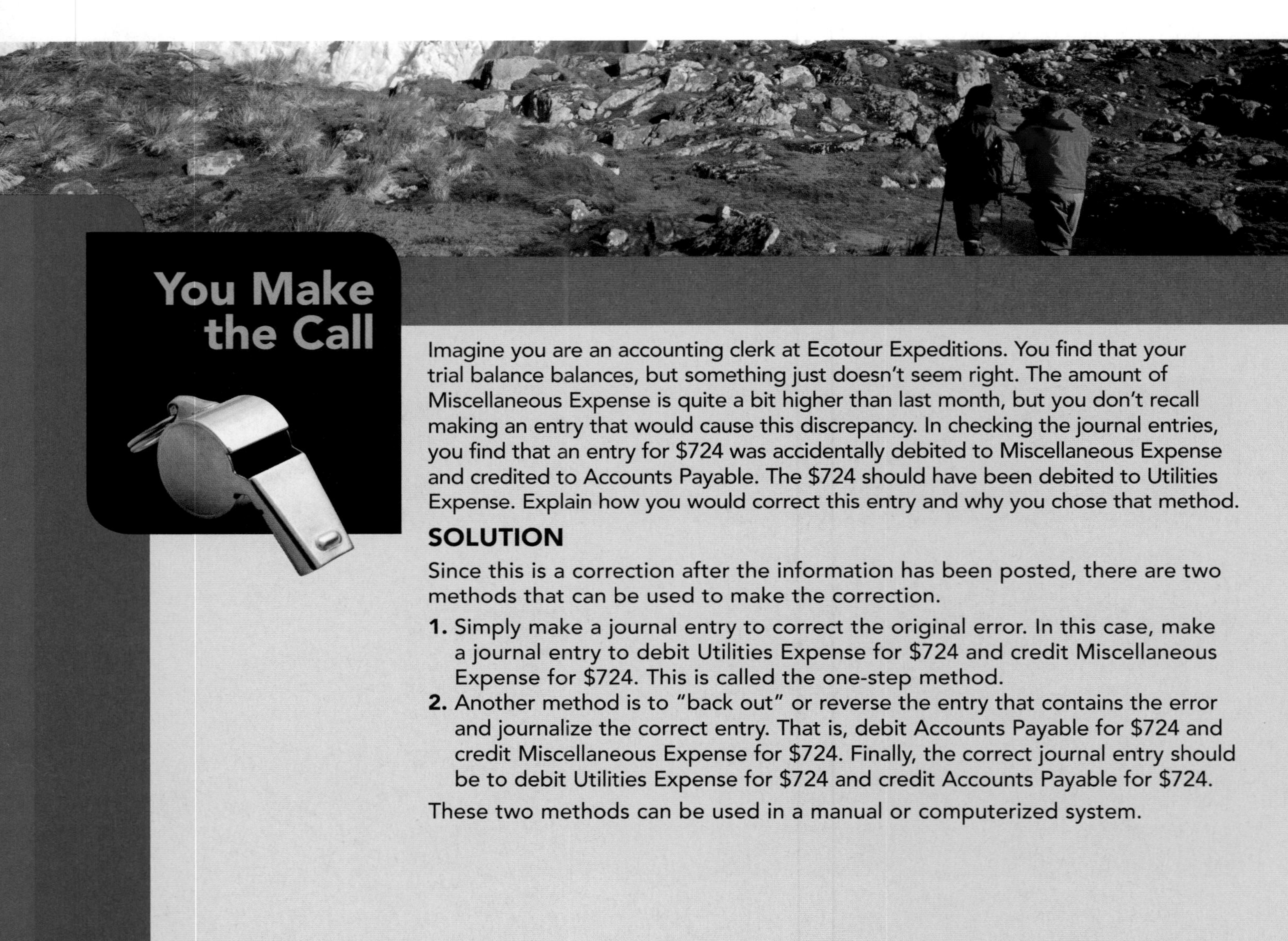

You Make the Call

Imagine you are an accounting clerk at Ecotour Expeditions. You find that your trial balance balances, but something just doesn't seem right. The amount of Miscellaneous Expense is quite a bit higher than last month, but you don't recall making an entry that would cause this discrepancy. In checking the journal entries, you find that an entry for $724 was accidentally debited to Miscellaneous Expense and credited to Accounts Payable. The $724 should have been debited to Utilities Expense. Explain how you would correct this entry and why you chose that method.

SOLUTION

Since this is a correction after the information has been posted, there are two methods that can be used to make the correction.

1. Simply make a journal entry to correct the original error. In this case, make a journal entry to debit Utilities Expense for $724 and credit Miscellaneous Expense for $724. This is called the one-step method.
2. Another method is to "back out" or reverse the entry that contains the error and journalize the correct entry. That is, debit Accounts Payable for $724 and credit Miscellaneous Expense for $724. Finally, the correct journal entry should be to debit Utilities Expense for $724 and credit Accounts Payable for $724.

These two methods can be used in a manual or computerized system.

CHAPTER REVIEW

Study & Practice

LEARNING OBJECTIVE 1

Record a group of transactions pertaining to a service business in a two-column general journal.

Based on **source documents**, the transactions are analyzed to determine the accounts involved and whether the accounts are debited or credited. For each transaction, total debits must equal total credits. The **journal** is a book of original entry in which a day-by-day record of business transactions is maintained. The parts of a journal entry consist of the transaction date, the title of the account(s) debited, the title of the account(s) credited, the amounts recorded in the Debit and Credit columns, and an explanation.

PRACTICE EXERCISE 1

Journalize the following transactions for the month of June:

June 1 J. Jonah deposited $35,000 in the bank in the name of the business (Jonah Company).
2 The business purchased $8,000 in equipment, paying $2,000 in cash and placing the remainder on account.
4 The business purchased supplies for cash, $250.
10 The business received cash revenue, $3,250.
20 The business paid the monthly rent, $1,800.
24 J. Jonah withdrew $500 for personal use.

PRACTICE EXERCISE 1 SOLUTION

GENERAL JOURNAL PAGE 1

Date		Description	Post. Ref.	Debit	Credit
20—					
June	1	Cash		35,000.00	
		J. Jonah, Capital			35,000.00
		Jonah invested cash.			
	2	Equipment		8,000.00	
		Cash			2,000.00
		Accounts Payable			6,000.00
		Purchased equipment.			
	4	Supplies Expense		250.00	
		Cash			250.00
		Purchased supplies.			
	10	Cash		3,250.00	
		Income from Services			3,250.00
		Cash revenue.			
	20	Rent Expense		1,800.00	
		Cash			1,800.00
		Paid the monthly rent.			
	24	J. Jonah, Drawing		500.00	
		Cash			500.00
		Withdrawal for personal use.			

LEARNING OBJECTIVE

2 *Post entries from a two-column general journal to general ledger accounts.*

The **general ledger** is a book that contains all the accounts, arranged according to the chart of accounts. **Posting** is the process of transferring information from the journal to the **ledger accounts**. The posting process consists of four steps:

STEP 1. Write the date of the transaction in the account's Date column.

STEP 2. Write the amount of the transaction in the Debit or Credit column, and enter the new balance in the Balance columns under Debit or Credit.

STEP 3. Write the page number of the journal in the Post. Ref. column of the ledger account.

STEP 4. Record the ledger account number in the Post. Ref. column of the journal.

PRACTICE EXERCISE 2

Post the journal entries from Practice Exercise 1 to the following general ledger accounts:

Assets
111 Cash
124 Equipment

Liabilities
221 Accounts Payable

Owner's Equity
311 J. Jonah, Capital
312 J. Jonah, Drawing

Revenue
411 Income from Services

Expenses
512 Rent Expense
513 Supplies Expense

PRACTICE EXERCISE 2 SOLUTION

GENERAL LEDGER

ACCOUNT Cash ACCOUNT NO. 111

Date		Item	Post. Ref.	Debit	Credit	Balance Debit	Balance Credit
20—							
June	1		1	35,000.00		35,000.00	
	2		1		2,000.00	33,000.00	
	4		1		250.00	32,750.00	
	10		1	3,250.00		36,000.00	
	20		1		1,800.00	34,200.00	
	24		1		500.00	33,700.00	

ACCOUNT Equipment ACCOUNT NO. 124

Date		Item	Post. Ref.	Debit	Credit	Balance Debit	Balance Credit
20—							
June	2		1	8,000.00		8,000.00	

CHAPTER REVIEW

ACCOUNT Accounts Payable ACCOUNT NO. 221

Date		Item	Post. Ref.	Debit	Credit	Balance Debit	Balance Credit
20—							
June	2		1		6 0 0 0 00		6 0 0 0 00

ACCOUNT J. Jonah, Capital ACCOUNT NO. 311

Date		Item	Post. Ref.	Debit	Credit	Balance Debit	Balance Credit
20—							
June	1		1		35 0 0 0 00		35 0 0 0 00

ACCOUNT J. Jonah, Drawing ACCOUNT NO. 312

Date		Item	Post. Ref.	Debit	Credit	Balance Debit	Balance Credit
20—							
June	24		1	5 0 0 00		5 0 0 00	

ACCOUNT Income from Services ACCOUNT NO. 411

Date		Item	Post. Ref.	Debit	Credit	Balance Debit	Balance Credit
20—							
June	10		1		3 2 5 0 00		3 2 5 0 00

ACCOUNT Rent Expense ACCOUNT NO. 512

Date		Item	Post. Ref.	Debit	Credit	Balance Debit	Balance Credit
20—							
June	20		1	1 8 0 0 00		1 8 0 0 00	

ACCOUNT Supplies Expense ACCOUNT NO. 513

Date		Item	Post. Ref.	Debit	Credit	Balance Debit	Balance Credit
20—							
June	4		1	2 5 0 00		2 5 0 00	

LEARNING OBJECTIVE

Prepare a trial balance from the ledger accounts.

The trial balance consists of a listing of account balances in two columns, one labeled Debit and one labeled Credit. The balances come from the ledger accounts.

PRACTICE EXERCISE 3

Prepare a trial balance from the ledger accounts in Practice Exercise 2.

PRACTICE EXERCISE 3 SOLUTION

Jonah Company
Trial Balance
June 30, 20—

Account Name	Debit	Credit
Cash	33,700	
Equipment	8,000	
Accounts Payable		6,000
J. Jonah, Capital		35,000
J. Jonah, Drawing	500	
Income from Services		3,250
Rent Expense	1,800	
Supplies Expense	250	
	44,250	44,250

LEARNING OBJECTIVE

Correct entries using the manual ruling method.

The manual ruling method can be used if an error is discovered before or after an entry has been posted. Draw a line through the incorrect account title or amount, and write the correct account title or amount immediately above. Include your initials with the correction.

PRACTICE EXERCISE 4

Show the manual correction for the following error: On March 1, an entry to record a payment of $950 rent was incorrectly debited to Wages Expense.

PRACTICE EXERCISE 4 SOLUTION

GENERAL JOURNAL PAGE 1

Date		Description	Post. Ref.	Debit	Credit
20—		*Rent Expense*			
Mar.	1	~~Wages Expense~~ *DJM*		950.00	
		Cash			950.00
		Paid rent for the month.			

CHAPTER REVIEW

LEARNING OBJECTIVE

5 *Correct entries using the manual or computerized correcting entry method.*

This method is used if an error is discovered after an incorrectly journalized entry has been posted. If the error consists of the wrong account(s), an entry is made to cancel out or reverse the incorrect account(s) and insert the correct account(s). The correcting entry should *always* include an explanation.

PRACTICE EXERCISE 5

On July 9, a $380 payment for Supplies Expense was incorrectly journalized and posted as a debit to Utilities Expense for $380 and a credit to Cash for $380. Provide the correcting entry, following the one-step method.

PRACTICE EXERCISE 5 SOLUTION

GENERAL JOURNAL PAGE 1

Date		Description	Post. Ref.	Debit	Credit
20—					
July	9	Supplies Expense		380 00	
		Utilities Expense			380 00
		To correct error of July 9			
		in which a payment for			
		Supplies Expense was			
		debited to Utilities Expense.			

Before a Test Check: Chapters 1–3

PART I: MULTIPLE-CHOICE QUESTIONS

____ **1.** Which of the following is not considered an account?
a. Cash
b. Prepaid Insurance
c. Equipment
d. Assets
e. Accounts Receivable

____ **2.** In which of the following transactions would an expense be recorded?
a. Received a bill for advertising.
b. Paid on an account payable for the utility bill.
c. Received and paid a bill for repairs.
d. All of these should be recorded as an expense.
e. Only a and c should be recorded as an expense.

____ **3.** The ending capital balance appears on which of the following statements?
a. Statement of owner's equity
b. Balance sheet
c. Income statement
d. Statement of owner's equity and balance sheet
e. Statement of owner's equity and income statement

____ **4.** On a statement of owner's equity, if beginning capital is $42,000 and there are an additional investment of $5,000, a net loss of $9,000, and owner withdrawals of $15,000, the ending capital amount would be
a. $70,000.
b. $23,000.
c. $40,000.
d. $54,000.
e. none of these.

____ **5.** If a $26 cash purchase of supplies is recorded as a $62 debit to Supplies Expense and a $62 credit to Cash, the result will be that
a. the trial balance will be in balance.
b. the Supplies Expense account will be overstated.
c. the Cash account will be understated.
d. Supplies Expense will be overstated and Cash will be understated.
e. all of these will be true.

____ **6.** A person who wanted to know the balance of an account would look in
a. the ledger.
b. the chart of accounts.
c. the journal.
d. the source documents.
e. none of these.

PART II: THE ACCOUNTING CYCLE

Journalizing, Posting, Trial Balance, and Financial Statements

The accounts and their balances, as of December 1 of this year, for Antec Services are as follows:

111 Cash	$18,900	411 Service Income	$39,600
113 Accounts Receivable	6,300		
116 Prepaid Insurance	1,230	511 Wages Expense	10,450
124 Equipment	31,200	512 Utilities Expense	2,760
		513 Rent Expense	12,620
221 Accounts Payable	6,340	514 Supplies Expense	870
311 J. Dunn, Capital	49,590		
312 J. Dunn, Drawing	11,200		

Check Figure
Net Income, $21,153

Required

1. Journalize the following December transactions in general journal form on journal page 31.

Dec.	1	Sold services for cash, $9,500.
	4	Received and paid the bill for the rent for December, $1,000, Ck. No. 2331.
	11	Received $1,750 on account from customers, Cash Receipt Nos. 1430–1438.
	19	Sold services on account, $2,075, Sales Inv. No. 2591.
	22	Received and paid the bill for utilities, $255, Ck. No. 2332.
	23	Bought supplies on account from Office Works, $292, Inv. No. 2606.
	31	Paid the wages for the month, $1,775, Ck. No. 2333.
	31	Dunn withdrew $1,500 for personal use, Ck. No. 2334.

2. Label T accounts with the above account names.
3. Correctly place the plus and minus signs under all T accounts, and label the debit and credit sides of each T account.
4. Post the entries to the T accounts by date, and foot and balance the accounts.

5. Prepare a trial balance as of December 31.
6. Prepare an income statement for the year ended December 31.
7. Prepare a statement of owner's equity for the year ended December 31.
8. Prepare a balance sheet as of December 31.

ANSWERS: PART I

1. d; **2.** e; **3.** d; **4.** b; **5.** e; **6.** a

ANSWERS: PART II

1.

GENERAL JOURNAL PAGE 31

Date		Description	Post. Ref.	Debit	Credit
20—					
Dec.	1	Cash	111	9 5 0 0 00	
		Service Income	411		9 5 0 0 00
		Sold services for cash.			
	4	Rent Expense	513	1 0 0 0 00	
		Cash	111		1 0 0 0 00
		Ck. No. 2331.			
	11	Cash	111	1 7 5 0 00	
		Accounts Receivable	113		1 7 5 0 00
		Cash on account from customers,			
		Cash Receipt Nos. 1430–1438.			
	19	Accounts Receivable	113	2 0 7 5 00	
		Service Income	411		2 0 7 5 00
		Sales Inv. No. 2591.			
	22	Utilities Expense	512	2 5 5 00	
		Cash	111		2 5 5 00
		Ck. No. 2332.			
	23	Supplies Expense	514	2 9 2 00	
		Accounts Payable	221		2 9 2 00
		Office Works, Inv. No. 2606.			
	31	Wages Expense	511	1 7 7 5 00	
		Cash	111		1 7 7 5 00
		Paid month's wages, Ck. No. 2333.			
	31	J. Dunn, Drawing	312	1 5 0 0 00	
		Cash	111		1 5 0 0 00
		Ck. No. 2334.			

CHAPTER REVIEW

2., 3., and 4.

Assets = Liabilities + Owner's Equity + Revenue − Expenses

Assets		Liabilities		Owner's Equity		Revenue		Expenses	
+	−	−	+	−	+	−	+	+	−
Debit	Credit	Debit	Credit	Debit	Credit	Debit	Credit	Debit	Credit

Cash 111

	+ Debit		− Credit
Bal.	18,900	12/4	1,000
12/1	9,500	12/22	255
12/11	1,750	12/31	1,775
	30,150	12/31	1,500
			4,530
Bal.	**25,620**		

Accounts Receivable 113

	+ Debit		− Credit
Bal.	6,300	12/11	1,750
12/19	2,075		
	8,375		
Bal.	**6,625**		

Prepaid Insurance 116

	+ Debit		− Credit
Bal.	**1,230**		

Equipment 124

	+ Debit		− Credit
Bal.	**31,200**		

Accounts Payable 221

− Debit		+ Credit
	Bal.	6,340
	12/23	292
	Bal.	**6,632**

J. Dunn, Capital 311

− Debit		+ Credit
	Bal.	**49,590**

J. Dunn, Drawing 312

	+ Debit	− Credit
Bal.	11,200	
12/31	1,500	
Bal.	**12,700**	

Service Income 411

− Debit		+ Credit
	Bal.	39,600
	12/1	9,500
	12/19	2,075
	Bal.	**51,175**

Wages Expense 511

	+ Debit	− Credit
Bal.	10,450	
12/31	1,775	
Bal.	**12,225**	

Utilities Expense 512

	+ Debit	− Credit
Bal.	2,760	
12/22	255	
Bal.	**3,015**	

Rent Expense 513

	+ Debit	− Credit
Bal.	12,620	
12/4	1,000	
Bal.	**13,620**	

Supplies Expense 514

	+ Debit	− Credit
Bal.	870	
12/23	292	
Bal.	**1,162**	

5.

Antec Services Trial Balance December 31, 20—		
Account Name	**Debit**	**Credit**
Cash	25,620	
Accounts Receivable	6,625	
Prepaid Insurance	1,230	
Equipment	31,200	
Accounts Payable		6,632
J. Dunn, Capital		49,590
J. Dunn, Drawing	12,700	
Service Income		51,175
Wages Expense	12,225	
Utilities Expense	3,015	
Rent Expense	13,620	
Supplies Expense	1,162	
	107,397	107,397

6.

Antec Services Income Statement For Year Ended December 31, 20—		
Revenue:		
Service Income		$51,175
Expenses:		
Wages Expense	$12,225	
Utilities Expense	3,015	
Rent Expense	13,620	
Supplies Expense	1,162	
Total Expenses		30,022
Net Income		$21,153

7.

Antec Services Statement of Owner's Equity For Year Ended December 31, 20—		
J. Dunn, Capital, January 1, 20—		$49,590
Investments during Year	$ 0	
Net Income for Year	21,153	
Subtotal	$21,153	
Less Withdrawals for Year	12,700	
Increase in Capital		8,453
J. Dunn, Capital, December 31, 20—		$58,043

8.

Antec Services Balance Sheet December 31, 20—		
Assets		
Cash	$25,620	
Accounts Receivable	6,625	
Prepaid Insurance	1,230	
Equipment	31,200	
Total Assets		$64,675
Liabilities		
Accounts Payable		$ 6,632
Owner's Equity		
J. Dunn, Capital		58,043
Total Liabilities and Owner's Equity		$64,675

Glossary

Account numbers The numbers assigned to accounts according to the chart of accounts. *(p. 88)*

Cost principle The principle that a purchased asset should be recorded at its actual cost. *(p. 83)*

Cross-reference The ledger account number in the Post. Ref. column of the journal and the journal page number in the Post. Ref. column of the ledger account. *(p. 89)*

General ledger A book or file containing the activity (by accounts), either manual or computerized, of a business. *(p. 88)*

Journal The book in which a person makes the original record of a business transaction; commonly referred to as a *book of original entry. (p. 79)*

Journalizing The process of recording a business transaction in a journal. *(p. 80)*

Ledger account A complete record of the transactions recorded in an individual account. *(p. 88)*

Posting The process of transferring figures from the journal to the ledger accounts. *(p. 88)*

Source documents Business papers, such as checks, invoices, receipts, letters, and memos, that furnish proof that a transaction has taken place. *(p. 80)*

Two-column general journal A general journal in which there are two amount columns, one used for debit amounts and one used for credit amounts. *(p. 80)*

CHAPTER ASSIGNMENTS

Discussion Questions

1. Why is the journal called a book of original entry?
2. How does the journal differ from the ledger?
3. What is the purpose of providing a ledger account for each account?
4. List by account classification the order of the accounts in the general ledger.
5. Arrange the following steps in the posting process in correct order:
   a. Write the ledger account number in the Post. Ref. column of the journal.
   b. Write the amount of the transaction.
   c. Write the date of the transaction.
   d. Write the page number of the journal in the Post. Ref. column of the ledger account.
6. What does cross-referencing mean in the posting process?

7. Why is a source document important?
8. What is the first number for each of the following accounts in a chart of accounts listed by account number?
   a. Professional Fees
   b. Utilities Expense
   c. J. R. Watson, Capital
   d. Accounts Receivable
   e. Accounts Payable

Exercises

PRACTICE EXERCISE 1

EXERCISE 3-1 In the following two-column journal, the capital letters represent where parts of a journal entry appear. Write the numbers 1 through 8 on a piece of paper. After each number, match the capital letter where these items appear with the number of the item.

GENERAL JOURNAL PAGE 1

Date		Description	Post. Ref.	Debit	Credit
G					
H	I	J	O	M	
		K	P		N
		L			

1. Year
2. Month
3. Explanation
4. Title of account debited
5. Ledger account number of account credited
6. Amount of debit
7. Day of the month
8. Title of account credited

PRACTICE EXERCISE 1

EXERCISE 3-2 Decor Services completed the following transactions. Journalize the transactions in general journal form, including brief explanations.

Oct. 7 Received cash on account from Ron Hoyt, a customer, Inv. No. 312, $790.
15 Paid on account to Modern Ideas, a creditor, $275, Ck. No. 2242.
20 B. Bunge, the owner, withdrew cash for personal use, $780, Ck. No. 2243.
23 Bought store supplies for $92 and office supplies for $83 on account from Wegner Office Supply, Inv. No. 1040.
29 B. Bunge, the owner, invested $4,500 cash and $2,500 of her personal equipment.

PRACTICE EXERCISE 1

EXERCISE 3-3 Montoya Tutoring Service completed the following transactions. Journalize the transactions in general journal form, including brief explanations.

Mar. 1 Bought equipment for $5,798 from Teaching Suppliers, paying $3,798 in cash and placing the balance on account, Ck. No. 3230.
10 Paid the wages for the first week of March, $1,536, Ck. No. 3231.
15 Sold services for cash to Mason District, $1,481, Sales Inv. 121.
26 Sold services on account to Tempe School, $1,400, Sales Inv. 122.
31 Paid on account to Teaching Suppliers, $725, Ck. No. 3232.

PRACTICE EXERCISE 2

EXERCISE 3-4 The following May journal entries all involved cash.

Increases to Cash—Debits		Decreases to Cash—Credits	
5/1	8,500	5/3	840
5/9	1,748	5/8	952
5/16	4,600	5/12	2,100
5/23	890	5/25	3,842
5/30	5,900		

Post the amounts to the ledger account for Cash, Account No. 111. Assume that all transactions appeared on page 6 of the general journal.

PRACTICE EXERCISE 2

EXERCISE 3-5 Arrange the following steps in the posting process in correct order:

a. The amount of the balance of the ledger account is recorded in the Debit Balance or Credit Balance column.
b. The amount of the transaction is recorded in the Debit or Credit column of the ledger account.
c. The ledger account number is recorded in the Post. Ref. column of the journal.
d. The date of the transaction is recorded in the Date column of the ledger account.
e. The page number of the journal is recorded in the Post. Ref. column of the ledger account.

PRACTICE EXERCISE 3

EXERCISE 3-6 The bookkeeper for Nevado Company has prepared the following trial balance.

Nevado Company
Trial Balance
June 30, 20—

Account Name	Debit	Credit
Cash		2,500
Accounts Receivable	8,300	
Prepaid Insurance	650	
Equipment	15,300	
Accounts Payable		2,700
M. Nevado, Capital		12,500
M. Nevado, Drawing	4,890	
Professional Fees		17,540
Supplies Expense	600	
Rent Expense	500	
Miscellaneous Expense	1,800	
	32,040	35,240

The bookkeeper has asked for your help. In examining the company's journal and ledger, you discover the following errors. Use this information to construct a corrected trial balance.

a. The debits to the Cash account total $8,000, and the credits total $3,300.
b. A $500 payment to a creditor was entered in the journal correctly but was not posted to the Accounts Payable account.

c. The first two numbers in the balance of the Accounts Receivable account were transposed in copying the balance from the ledger to the trial balance.
d. The $1,500 amount withdrawn by the owner for personal use was debited to Miscellaneous Expense by mistake—it was correctly credited to Cash.

LO 4,5

PRACTICES EXERCISES 4,5

EXERCISE 3-7 Determine the effect of the following errors on a company's total revenue, total expenses, and net income. Indicate the effect by writing O for "Overstated (too much)"; U for "Understated (too little)"; or NA for "Not Affected."

Transactions	Total Revenue	Total Expenses	Net Income
Example: A check for $325 was written to pay on account. The accountant debited Rent Expense for $325 and credited Cash for $325.	NA	O	U
a. $420 was received on account from customers. The accountant debited Cash for $420 and credited Professional Fees for $420.			
b. The owner withdrew $1,200 for personal use. The accountant debited Wages Expense for $1,200 and credited Cash for $1,200.			
c. A check was written for $1,250 to pay the rent. The accountant debited Rent Expense for $1,520 and credited Cash for $1,520.			
d. $1,800 was received on account from customers. The accountant debited Cash for $1,800 and credited the Capital account for $1,800.			
e. A check was written for $225 to pay the phone bill received and recorded earlier in the month. The accountant debited Phone Expense for $225 and credited Cash for $225.			

PRACTICE EXERCISES 4,5

EXERCISE 3-8 Journalize correcting entries for each of the following errors and include a brief explanation.

a. A cash purchase of office equipment for $680 was journalized as a cash purchase of store equipment for $680. (Use the ruling method; assume the entry has not been posted.)
b. An entry for a $180 payment for office supplies was journalized as $810. (Use the ruling method; assume the entry has not been posted.)
c. A $620 payment for repairs was journalized and posted as a debit to Equipment instead of a debit to Repair Expense. (Use the correcting entry method to journalize the correction.)
d. A $750 bill for vehicle insurance was received and immediately paid. It was journalized and posted as $660. (Use the correcting entry method to journalize the correction.)

Problem Set A

For additional help, see the demonstration problem at the beginning of each chapter in your Working Papers.

1 LO

PROBLEM 3-1A The chart of accounts of the Barnes School is shown here, followed by the transactions that took place during October of this year:

Assets
111 Cash
113 Accounts Receivable
115 Prepaid Insurance
124 Equipment
127 Furniture

Liabilities
221 Accounts Payable

Owner's Equity
311 R. Barnes, Capital
312 R. Barnes, Drawing

Revenue
411 Tuition Income

Expenses
511 Salary Expense
512 Rent Expense
513 Gas and Oil Expense
514 Advertising Expense
515 Repair Expense
516 Telephone Expense
517 Utilities Expense
529 Miscellaneous Expense

Oct.	1	Bought liability insurance for one year, $1,850, Ck. No. 1527.
	3	Received a bill for advertising from *Business Summary*, $415.
	4	Paid the rent for the current month, $1,870, Ck. No. 1528.
	7	Received a bill for equipment repair from Fix-It Service, $318, Inv. No. 436.
	10	Received and deposited tuition from students, $6,375.
	11	Received and paid the telephone bill, $312, Ck. No. 1529.
	15	Bought desks and chairs from The Oak Center, $1,980, paying $980 in cash and placing the balance on account, Ck. No. 1530.
	18	Paid on account to *Business Summary*, a creditor, $415, Ck. No. 1531.
	21	R. Barnes withdrew $1,000 for personal use, Ck. No. 1532.
	24	Received a bill for gas and oil from Wagner Oil Company, $225, Inv. No. 682.
	25	Received and deposited tuition from students, $6,380.
	27	Paid the salary of the part-time office assistant, $1,150, Ck. No. 1533.
	28	Bought a photocopier on account from Gorst Office Machines, $1,950, Inv. No. 417.
	29	Received $950 tuition from a student who had charged the tuition on account last month.
	30	Received and paid the bill for utilities, $623, Ck. No. 1534.
	31	Paid for flower arrangements for front office, $87, Ck. No. 1535.
	31	R. Barnes invested his personal computer and printer, with a fair market value of $1,549, in the business.

Check Figure
Equipment increased by $3,499 in October

Required
Record these transactions in the general journal, including a brief explanation for each entry. Number the journal pages 31 and 32.

2,3 LO

PROBLEM 3-2A The journal entries for August, Carley's Car Care's second month of business, have been journalized in the general journal in your Working Papers. The balances of the accounts as of July 31 have been recorded in the general ledger in your Working Papers. Notice the word *Balance* in the Item column, the check mark in the Post. Ref. column, and that the amount is in the Balance column only. This indicates a balance brought forward from a prior page or month.

CHAPTER ASSIGNMENTS

Required

Check Figure
Net Income, $10,534

1. Write the owner's name, M. Carley, in the Capital and Drawing accounts.
2. Post the general journal entries to the general ledger accounts.
3. Prepare a trial balance as of August 31, 20—.
4. Prepare an income statement for the two months ended August 31, 20—.
5. Prepare a statement of owner's equity for the two months ended August 31, 20—.
6. Prepare a balance sheet as of August 31, 20—.

LO 1,2,3

PROBLEM 3-3A Following is the chart of accounts of the C. Lucern Clinic.

Assets
111 Cash
113 Accounts Receivable
117 Prepaid Insurance
124 Equipment

Liabilities
221 Accounts Payable

Owner's Equity
311 C. Lucern, Capital
312 C. Lucern, Drawing

Revenue
411 Professional Fees

Expenses
511 Salary Expense
512 Rent Expense
513 Laboratory Expense
514 Utilities Expense
515 Supplies Expense

Dr. Lucern completed the following transactions during July:

July 1 Bought laboratory equipment on account from Laser Surgical Supply Company, $3,660, paying $1,660 in cash and placing the remainder on account, Ck. No. 1730.
3 Paid the office rent for the current month, $1,300, Ck. No. 1731.
5 Received cash on account from patients, $360.
6 Bought supplies on account from McRae Supply Company, $315, Inv. No. 3455.
7 Received and paid the bill for laboratory services, $1,380, Ck. No. 1732.
8 Bought insurance for one year, $2,650, Ck. No. 1733.
12 Performed medical services for patients on account, $5,886.
15 Performed medical services for patients for cash, $4,793.
16 The equipment purchased on July 1 was found to be broken. Dr. Lucern returned the damaged part and received a reduction in his bill, $518, Inv. No. 3162, Credit Memo No. 141. (Credit Equipment.)
18 Paid the salary of the part-time nurse, $2,100, Ck. No. 1734.
24 Received and paid the telephone bill for the month, $624, Ck. No. 1735.
28 Performed medical services for patients on account, $7,381.
29 Dr. Lucern withdrew cash for his personal use, $2,000, Ck. No. 1736.

Required

Check Figure
Trial balance total, $62,679

1. Journalize the transactions for July in the general journal, beginning on page 21.
2. Write the name of the owner next to the Capital and Drawing accounts in the general ledger. The balances of the accounts as of June 30 have been recorded in the general ledger in your Working Papers. Notice the word *Balance* in the Item column, the check mark in the Post. Ref. column, and that the amount is in the Balance column only. This indicates a balance brought forward from a prior page or month.
3. Post the entries to the general ledger accounts.
4. Prepare a trial balance.

1,2,3 LO

PROBLEM 3-4A Lara's Landscaping Service has the following chart of accounts:

Assets
111 Cash
113 Accounts Receivable
117 Prepaid Insurance
124 Equipment

Liabilities
221 Accounts Payable

Owner's Equity
311 J. Lara, Capital
312 J. Lara, Drawing

Revenue
411 Landscaping Income

Expenses
511 Salary Expense
512 Rent Expense
513 Gas and Oil Expense
514 Utilities Expense
515 Supplies Expense

The following transactions were completed by Lara's Landscaping Service:

Mar.	1	Lara deposited $35,000 in a bank account in the name of the business.
	4	Lara invested his personal landscaping equipment, with a fair market value of $1,325, in the business.
	6	Bought a used trailer on account from Tow Sales, $915, Inv. No. 314.
	7	Paid the rent for the current month, $950, Ck. No. 1000.
	9	Bought a used backhoe from Digger's Equipment, $5,300, paying $3,000 in cash and placing the balance on account, Inv. 4166, Ck. No. 1001.
	10	Bought liability insurance for one year, $1,800, Ck. No. 1002.
	13	Sold landscaping services on account to Fredkey's, $3,895, Inv. No. 100.
	14	Bought supplies on account from Office Requip, $380, Inv. No. 5172.
	15	Sold landscaping services on account to C. Endel, $2,832, Inv. No. 101.
	17	Received and paid the bill from Commercial Services for gas and oil for the equipment, $180, Ck. No. 1003.
	19	Sold landscaping services for cash to Riston Company, $1,864, Inv. No. 102.
	22	Paid on account to Tow Sales, a creditor, $500, Inv. No. 314, Ck. No. 1004.
	24	Received on account from Fredkey's, a customer, $800, Inv. No. 100.
	28	Sold landscaping services on account to Stevens, Inc., $1,830, Inv. No. 103.
	29	Received and paid the telephone bill, $260, Ck. No. 1005.
	30	Paid the salary of the employee, $1,850, Ck. No. 1006.
	31	Lara withdrew cash for his personal use, $1,500, Ck. No. 1007.

Check Figure
Trial balance total, $49,841

Required

1. Journalize the transactions in the general journal, beginning on page 1. Write a brief explanation for each entry.
2. Write the name of the owner on the Capital and Drawing accounts.
3. Post the journal entries to the general ledger accounts.
4. Prepare a trial balance dated March 31, 20—.

Problem Set B

For additional help, see the demonstration problem at the beginning of each chapter in your Working Papers.

1 LO

PROBLEM 3-1B The chart of accounts of Ethan Academy is shown here, followed by the transactions that took place during December of this year:

CHAPTER ASSIGNMENTS

Assets
111 Cash
113 Accounts Receivable
115 Prepaid Insurance
124 Equipment
127 Furniture

Liabilities
221 Accounts Payable

Owner's Equity
311 R. Ethan, Capital
312 R. Ethan, Drawing

Revenue
411 Tuition Income

Expenses
511 Salary Expense
512 Rent Expense
513 Gas and Oil Expense
514 Advertising Expense
515 Repair Expense
516 Telephone Expense
517 Utilities Expense
518 Supplies Expense
529 Miscellaneous Expense

Dec. 1 Bought liability insurance for one year, $2,260, Ck. No. 1627.
11 Received a bill for advertising from the *City News*, $415, Statement No. 4267.
12 Paid the rent for the current month, $1,850, Ck. No. 1628.
13 Received a bill for equipment repair from Electronic Services, $345, Inv. No. 547.
16 Received and deposited tuition from students, $5,850.
17 Received and paid the telephone bill, $305, Ck. No. 1629.
18 Bought desks and chairs from School Furniture, $1,625, paying $625 in cash and placing the balance on account, Ck. No. 1630.
20 Paid on account to the *City News*, a creditor, $415, Statement No. 4267, Ck. No. 1631.
21 R. Ethan withdrew $1,000 for personal use, Ck. No. 1632.
26 Received a bill for gas and oil from Discount Oil Company, $210, Inv. No. 591.
27 Received and deposited tuition from students, $6,045.
31 Paid the salary of the office assistant, $1,375, Ck. No. 1633.
31 Bought a fax machine on account from EquipCo, $118, Inv. No. 529.
31 Received $1,150 tuition from a student who had charged the tuition on account last month.
31 Received and paid the bill for utilities, $470, Ck. No. 1634.
31 R. Ethan invested her personal computer and printer, with a fair market value of $1,150, in the business.
31 Bought supplies, $295, Ck. No. 1635.

Required
Record these transactions in the general journal, including a brief explanation for each entry. Number the journal pages 31 and 32.

Check Figure
Equipment increased by $1,268 in December

2,3

PROBLEM 3-2B The journal entries for May, Kiddy Day Care's second month of business, have been journalized in the general journal in your Working Papers. The balances of the accounts as of April 30 have been recorded in the general ledger in your Working Papers. Notice the word *Balance* in the Item column, the check mark in the Post. Ref. column, and that the amount is in the Balance column only. This indicates a balance brought forward from a prior page or month.

Required
1. Write the owner's name, R. Ramirez, in the Capital and Drawing accounts.
2. Post the general journal entries to the general ledger accounts.
3. Prepare a trial balance as of May 31, 20—.
4. Prepare an income statement for the two months ended May 31, 20—.
5. Prepare a statement of owner's equity for the two months ended May 31, 20—.
6. Prepare a balance sheet as of May 31, 20—.

Check Figure
Net Income, $11,726

PROBLEM 3-3B Following is the chart of accounts of Vance Rehab Clinic.

Assets
111 Cash
113 Accounts Receivable
117 Prepaid Insurance
124 Equipment

Liabilities
221 Accounts Payable

Owner's Equity
311 J. Vance, Capital
312 J. Vance, Drawing

Revenue
411 Professional Fees

Expenses
511 Salary Expense
512 Rent Expense
513 Laboratory Expense
514 Utilities Expense
515 Supplies Expense

Vance completed the following transactions during July:

July	1	Bought laboratory equipment on account from Sage Surgical Supply Company, $6,520, paying $1,520 in cash and placing the remainder on account, Inv. No. 2071, Ck. No. 1930.
	3	Paid the office rent for the current month, $1,550, Ck. No. 1931.
	5	Received cash on account from patients, $3,045.
	6	Bought supplies on account from Allround Supply, $320, Inv. No. 3455.
	9	Received and paid the bill for laboratory services, $1,484, Ck. No. 1932.
	10	Bought insurance for one year, $2,600, Ck. No. 1933.
	12	Performed rehab services for patients on account, $5,185.
	14	Performed rehab services for patients for cash, $5,050.
	18	Part of the equipment purchased on July 1 was found to be broken. Vance returned the damaged part and received a reduction in her bill, $410, Inv. No. 2071, Credit Memo No. 218. (Credit Equipment.)
	20	Paid the salary of the part-time nurse, $2,200, Ck. No. 1934.
	22	Received and paid the telephone bill for the month, $380, Ck. No. 1935.
	24	Performed rehab services for patients on account, $4,235.
	30	Vance withdrew cash for her personal use, $2,000, Ck. No. 1936.

Check Figure
Trial balance total, $46,028

Required

1. Journalize the transactions for July in the general journal, beginning on page 21.
2. Write the name of the owner next to the Capital and Drawing accounts in the general ledger. The balances of the accounts as of June 30 have been recorded in the general ledger in your Working Papers. Notice the word *Balance* in the Item column, the check mark in the Post. Ref. column, and that the amount is in the Balance column only. This indicates a balance brought forward from a prior page or month.
3. Post the entries to the general ledger accounts.
4. Prepare a trial balance.

1,2,3 LO

PROBLEM 3-4B Leander's Landscaping Service maintains the following chart of accounts.

Assets
111 Cash
113 Accounts Receivable
117 Prepaid Insurance
124 Equipment

Liabilities
221 Accounts Payable

Owner's Equity
311 O. Leander, Capital
312 O. Leander, Drawing

Revenue
411 Landscaping Income

Expenses
511 Salary Expense
512 Rent Expense
513 Gas and Oil Expense
514 Utilities Expense
515 Supplies Expense

The following transactions were completed by Leander:

Apr.	1	Leander deposited $30,000 in a bank account in the name of the business.
	4	Leander invested his personal landscaping equipment, with a fair market value of $1,750, in the business.
	6	Bought a used trailer on account from Used Mart, $1,450, Inv. No. 415.
	7	Paid the rent for the current month, $925, Ck. No. 100.
	9	Bought a used bulldozer from Dray's Equipment, $5,100, paying $2,100 in cash and placing the balance on account, Inv. No. 3255, Ck. No. 101.
	10	Bought liability insurance for one year, $2,800, Ck. No. 102.
	13	Sold landscaping services on account to Fulton Homes, $4,595, Inv. No. 100.
	14	Bought supplies on account from Perry's Supply, $427, Inv. No. 4281.
	15	Sold landscaping services on account to D. D. Mau Inc., $3,997, Inv. No. 101.
	17	Received and paid the bill from Pumpers for gas and oil for the equipment, $227, Ck. No. 103.
	19	Sold landscaping services for cash to Cliff's House, $1,437, Inv. No. 102.
	22	Paid on account to Used Mart, a creditor, $450, Inv. No. 415, Ck. No. 104.
	24	Received on account from Fulton Homes, a customer, $800, Inv. No. 100.
	28	Sold landscaping services on account to H. Ron, $1,785, Inv. No. 103.
	29	Received and paid the telephone bill, $321, Ck. No. 105.
	30	Paid the salary of the employee, $1,836, Ck. No. 106.
	30	Leander withdrew cash for his personal use, $1,500, Ck. No. 107.

Required

1. Journalize the transactions in the general journal, beginning on page 1. Write a brief explanation for each entry.
2. Write the name of the owner on the Capital and Drawing accounts.
3. Post the journal entries to the general ledger accounts.
4. Prepare a trial balance dated April 30, 20—.

Check Figure
Trial balance total, $47,991

ACTIVITIES

CONSIDER AND COMMUNICATE

You are the new bookkeeper in a small business. The bookkeeper whose job you are taking is training you on the business's manual system. As he journalizes, he writes the account number in the Post. Ref. column because he thinks it's easier. Then, when he posts, he won't have to be bothered writing the account numbers. How would you explain why he should *not* write the account number in the Post. Ref. column immediately and should instead enter the account number after he has posted the amount to the ledger?

CRITICAL THINKING

You work as an accounting clerk. You have received the following information supplied by a client, S. Winston, from the client's bank statement, the client's tax returns, and a variety of other July documents. The client wants you to prepare an income statement, a statement of owner's equity, and a balance sheet for the month of July for Winston Company.

Income from Services	$ 9,570	Utilities Expense	$ 388
Beginning Capital	50,000	Drawing	2,500
Cash	24,940	Supplies Expense	635
Truck	?	Equipment	16,148
Accounts Payable	?	Total Liabilities and Owner's Equity	56,838
Rent Expense	1,200		
Wages Expense	4,200		

All About You Spa

Journalizing, Posting, and Preparing a Trial Balance

Meet the owner

A friend of yours, Anika Valli, has decided to open a spa to serve her small resort town of about 7,000 people and 4 million tourists annually. She has named the business All About You Spa to convey the idea that the business intends to pamper those who enter its doors. She will operate the spa five days a week, Tuesday through Saturday, but a phone line will always be available to answer questions and take appointments. Hours will be from 8 A.M. to 8 P.M. She has asked you to be the bookkeeper for this new business. At the end of the month of June, the owner, Anika Valli, would like you to provide the following:

Determine owner's needs

1. General journal
2. General ledger
3. Trial balance
4. Income statement
5. Statement of owner's equity
6. Balance sheet

Gather information and make assessment

She has kept a checkbook and a file folder with summary evidence of June's spa activity: a check register, a summary report of charges by customers for services provided, all receipts that were issued, and a summary of charges made by All About You Spa. Most of the income from services is received in cash and as charges to credit cards. No checks are accepted, except from approved clients (primarily conference planners and other organizations that book packages as prizes for attendees or gifts for employees, speakers, or other people they want to thank with a spa service or package of services). Anika deposits cash receipts on the 7th, 14th, 21st, and last day of each month.

The first page in the file folder contains the following chart of accounts.

CHART OF ACCOUNTS FOR ALL ABOUT YOU SPA

Assets
111 Cash
113 Accounts Receivable
117 Prepaid Insurance
124 Spa Equipment
128 Office Equipment

Liabilities
211 Accounts Payable

Owner's Equity
311 A. Valli, Capital
312 A. Valli, Drawing

Revenue
411 Income from Services

Expenses
511 Wages Expense
512 Rent Expense
513 Office Supplies Expense
514 Spa Supplies Expense
515 Laundry Expense
516 Advertising Expense
517 Utilities Expense
530 Miscellaneous Expense

Clipped to the front of the file folder is a brochure listing the services of All About You Spa. Part of the brochure is shown on the following page.

WHERE TO START
Open the data file and save it under a new name that identifies it as containing your work.

1. Install and open Klooster and Allen's General Ledger Software, Version 7.0.
2. Click on the ***Open*** toolbar button, and select the file entitled ***All_About_You_Spa_Ch03.IA7***.
3. Enter your name when prompted and click ***OK***.
4. You will be asked if you want to open on-screen instructions and check figures. If you select "No" at this time, you may pull the information up at any time by clicking on the ***Info.*** toolbar button.

CONTINUING CASE

All About You Spa Services

Massages			
Type	*Time*	*Description*	*Price*
Deep-Tissue Destresser	90 min.	Vigorous, prescriptive	$90.00
Herbal Body Sea Wrap	90 min.	Gentle, cleansing	$90.00
Aromatherapy Healing Experience	90 min.	Gentle, relaxing	$90.00
Healing Stones Experience	90 min.	Healing, relaxing	$90.00
Post-Workout Massage	90 min.	Invigorating, prescriptive	$90.00
Exfoliating Ginger and Sea Salt Scrub	90 min.	Cleansing, invigorating	$90.00
Custom Massage	60 min.	Highlights problem areas	$60.00
Other Spa Experiences			
Type	*Time*	*Description*	*Price*
Reflexology Points Experience	60 min.	Problem areas, relaxing	$60.00
Reiki Healing Experience	60 min.	Full body, relaxing	$60.00
All About You Women's Facial	60 min.	Relaxing, individualized	$60.00
All About You Men's Facial	60 min.	Relaxing, individualized	$60.00
All About You Pedicure	60 min.	Beautifying, relaxing	$60.00
Day of Beauty	Full day or Half day	Let us help you select a memorable combination of services.	
Body Analysis and Consultation	60 min.	Informative, prescriptive	$60.00
All About You Makeup Consultation	60 min.	Beautifying, individualized	$60.00
Packages and Gift Certificates			
Type	*Time*	*Description*	*Price*
Package of three 90-minute services	270 min.	Mix and match to your needs.	$250.00
Package of two 90-minute services	180 min.	Select your favorite duo.	$160.00
Package of three 60-minute services	180 min.	Mix and match to your needs.	$160.00
Package of two 60-minute services	120 min.	Select your favorite duo.	$110.00
Gift certificates available at any price		Reward employees, friends, or relatives.	

5. Click on the ***Save As*** toolbar button. When the Save As window appears, select the folder in which you wish to save your data files (if not already selected). In the File Name box, key ***All_About_You_Spa_Ch03_Your_Name.IA7*** (for example, All_About_You_Spa_Ch03_John_Doe.IA7) to identify the file containing your work. Click on the ***Save*** button.

6. Key the journal entries for June. The chart of accounts for All About You Spa has already been set up in the data file, but there are no beginning balances since this is a new business. Click on the ***Journal*** toolbar button and key the journal entries for the month of June in the General Journal, following these steps:

WHAT TO DO FIRST
Enter June's transactions from documents and/or input forms.

a. Key the date of each transaction in the Date column.
b. Enter check numbers and invoice numbers, as appropriate, in the Refer. column (this is optional).
c. In the Account column, key the account number, key the account name (must be exact), or select from the Chart of Accounts list (click on the ***Chart of Accounts*** button that is activated when the Account field is selected) of the account to be debited.
d. Tab to the Debit column and enter the amount to be debited (omit commas).
e. Tab to the next line and enter the account to be credited in the Account column.
f. Tab to the Credit column and enter the amount to be credited.
g. When you have entered all debit and credit parts of an entry, click on the ***Post*** button (or press Enter on your keypad).

The basis of your entries will be the following documents:

Checkbook Entries
(Deposits made and checks written)

Check No.	Date	Explanation	√	Deposits	Check Amount
	6/1	Invested cash in business.		15,000.00	
1011	6/3	Bought 6-month liability insurance policy.			960.00
1012	6/3	Bought spa equipment for $4,235.00, putting $2,000.00 cash down.			2,000.00
1013	6/3	Paid June rent.			1,650.00
1014	6/5	Bought office supplies.			248.00
1015	6/5	Purchased flowers and balloons for grand opening (Misc. Exp.).			112.00
1016	6/7	Paid first week's wages.			1,847.50
	6/7	Deposited first week's cash revenue.		2,630.00	
1017	6/11	Paid on account payable for spa equipment (June 3).			873.00
	6/14	Deposited second week's cash revenue.		3,703.00	
1018	6/14	Paid second week's wages.			1,847.50
1019	6/18	Paid on account payable for spa equipment (June 3).			1,200.00
	6/21	Deposited third week's cash revenue.		4,758.00	
1020	6/21	Paid third week's wages.			1,847.50
1021	6/25	Paid on account payable for spa equipment (June 3).			73.00
1022	6/28	Paid fourth week's wages.			1,847.50
1023	6/28	Paid month's laundry bill.			84.00
	6/30	Deposited end of month's cash revenue.		5,992.00	
1024	6/30	A. Valli withdrew $1,850 for personal use.			1,850.00
1025	6/30	Paid June telephone bill.			225.00
1026	6/30	Paid June power and water bill.			248.00

Other documents that also require journal entries:

Receipt: 6/1
A. Valli, owner of All About You Spa, invested her personal spa equipment valued at $3,158.00.

June Accounts Payable Charges Summary Report	
6/3 Bought spa supplies on account from Spa Supplies, Inv. No. 804	$492.00
6/5 Bought office equipment on account from Office Equipment, Inv. No. 3415	$318.00
6/5 Bought advertising pamphlets on account from Adco, Inv. No. 512	$397.00
6/5 Bought office equipment on account from Office Equipment, Co. Inv. No. 3445	$832.00
6/5 Bought office supplies on account from Office Staples, Inv. No. 522	$120.00

June Sales to Customers on Account Summary Report	
6/7	$325.00
6/14	$486.00
6/21	$344.00
6/30	$109.00

7. Display the journal entries. Click on the ***Reports*** toolbar button. Click on ***Journals*** and ***General Journal*** to choose a report to display. Click on ***Include All Journal Entries*** and the ***OK*** button to display a General Journal report. To print the report, click on the ***Print*** button.
8. Review your entries and make corrections to them, if necessary. In the General Journal window, click on the entry to be corrected, key the correction(s), and click on the ***Post*** button (or press Enter). If you need to add an additional line to an entry, select the entry and then click on the ***Insert*** button. If you wish to delete an entry, select any portion of it, and click on the ***Delete*** button. If an entry was omitted, key it on the next available lines. The software will automatically put the entry in its proper date order when you post.
9. Display the Trial Balance report. Click on the ***Reports*** toolbar button. Click on ***Ledger Reports*** and ***Trial Balance*** to choose a report to display. Be sure the Run Date is set to June 30. Click ***OK*** to display the report. To print the report, click on the ***Print*** button at the bottom of the report window.

WHAT TO DO AT THE END OF THE MONTH
Month-end wrap-up.

10. Display the income statement. Click on the ***Reports*** toolbar button. Click on ***Financial Statements*** and select ***Income Statement*** to choose the report to display. To print the report, click on the ***Print*** button.
11. Display the statement of owner's equity. Click on the ***Reports*** toolbar button. Click on ***Financial Statements*** and select ***Statement of Owner's Equity*** to choose the report to display. To print the report, click on the ***Print*** button.

Check Figures
9. Trial balance total, $38,753
10. Net income, $7,381
11. A. Valli, Capital, ending balance, $23,689
12. Total assets, $25,937

12. Display the balance sheet. Click on the ***Reports*** toolbar button. Click on ***Financial Statements*** and select ***Balance Sheet*** to choose the report to display. To print the report, click on the ***Print*** button.
13. Click on the ***Save*** toolbar button to save your data file.
14. Click on the ***Check*** toolbar button to check your solution against the answer key. If there are errors, go back to Steps 7 and 8.

Note: The trial balance and financial statements are unadjusted. In the next chapter, you will learn that certain accounts need to be adjusted. These adjustments will change some of the figures in these reports.

Adjusting Entries and the Work Sheet

4

WHY IT MATTERS

RIDE THE DUCKS OF SEATTLE, Seattle, Washington

Ride the Ducks of Seattle seems an unlikely name for a thriving business—but, it actually is! The year-round Seattle tour company employs vehicles that can be doing a road tour one minute and plying the waters of Elliott Bay the next. One of Ride the Ducks' employees is a bookkeeper who also serves as a reservationist, tour vehicle cleaner, and computer specialist. In addition to recording and posting journal entries each month, he makes adjusting entries for such accounts as insurance, wages, and depreciation of the Ducks (tour bus/tour boat) at the end of each fiscal period. The method used to depreciate such an asset would most likely require the advice of a professional, such as a CPA (Certified Public Accountant). So, the next time you see a Duck, remember that it cannot operate without the skills of a bookkeeper/accountant.

LEARNING OBJECTIVES

After you have completed this chapter, you will be able to do the following:

1. *Define* fiscal period *and* fiscal year.
2. *List the classifications of the accounts that occupy each column of a ten-column work sheet.*
3. *Complete a work sheet for a service enterprise, involving adjustments for expired insurance, depreciation, and accrued wages.*
4. *Prepare an income statement, a statement of owner's equity, and a balance sheet for a service business directly from the work sheet.*
5. *Journalize and post the adjusting entries.*
6. *Prepare (a) an income statement involving more than one revenue account and a net loss, (b) a statement of owner's equity with an additional investment and either a net income or a net loss, (c) a balance sheet for a business having more than one accumulated depreciation account, and (d) a balance sheet containing the statement of owner's equity information.*

ACCOUNTING LANGUAGE

Accounting cycle *(p. 129)*
Accrual *(p. 136)*
Accrued wages *(p. 136)*
Adjusting entries *(p. 145)*
Adjustments *(p. 131)*
Book value (carrying value) *(p. 134)*
Contra account *(p. 134)*
Depreciation *(p. 133)*
Fiscal period *(p. 128)*
Fiscal year *(p. 128)*
Matching principle *(p. 147)*
Mixed accounts *(p. 138)*
Straight-line depreciation *(p. 133)*
Work sheet *(p. 129)*

Remember

Accounting steps:
Analyzing: *Which accounts are involved?*
Classifying: *assets, liabilities, owner's equity, revenue, and expenses*
Recording: *journalizing*
Summarizing: *financial statements*
Interpreting: *drawing conclusions*

As part of the *summarizing* step in the definition of accounting, we now introduce the work sheet and the financial statements. Now that you are familiar with the classifying and recording phases of accounting for a service business, let's look at the remaining steps in the accounting process.

FISCAL PERIOD

LEARNING OBJECTIVE 1
Define fiscal period *and* fiscal year.

A **fiscal period** is any period of time covering a complete accounting cycle. A **fiscal year** is a fiscal period consisting of twelve consecutive months. It does not have to coincide with the calendar year. If a business has seasonal peaks, it is a good idea to complete the accounting operations at the end of the most active season. At that time, management wants to know the results of the year and where the business stands financially. The fiscal year of a resort that operates during the summer may be from October 1 of one year to September 30 of the next year. The government has a fiscal year from October 1 of one year to September 30 of the following year. Department stores often use a fiscal period from February 1 of one year to January 31 of the next year.

THE ACCOUNTING CYCLE

The **accounting cycle** represents the sequence of steps in the accounting process completed during the fiscal period. Figure 1 shows how we introduce these steps on a chapter-by-chapter basis. This outline brings you up to date on what we have accomplished so far and how each chapter fits into the steps in the accounting cycle.

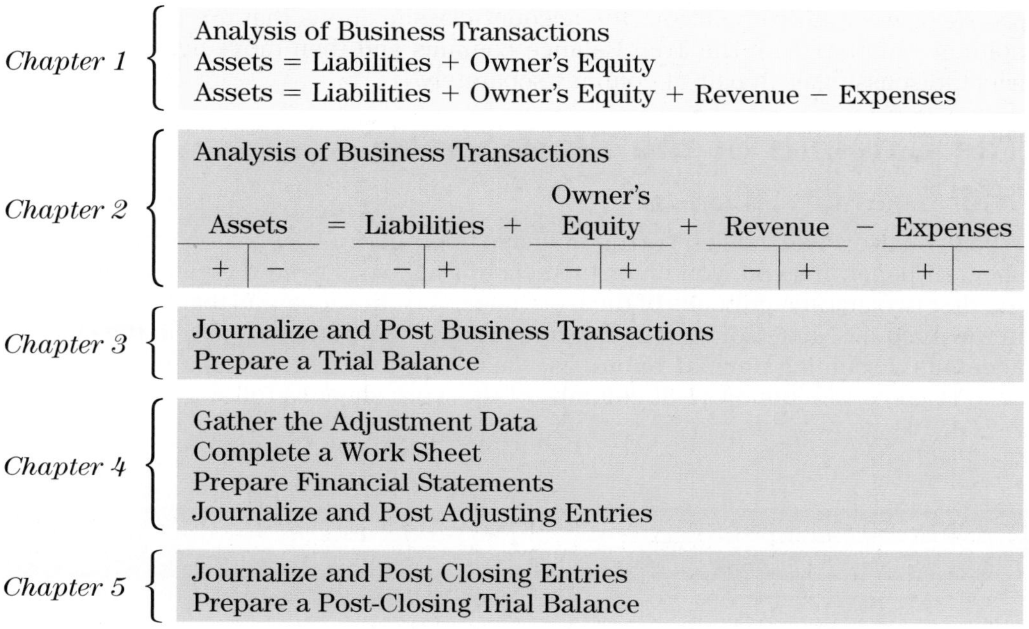

Chapter 1
Analysis of Business Transactions
Assets = Liabilities + Owner's Equity
Assets = Liabilities + Owner's Equity + Revenue − Expenses
Chapter 2
Analysis of Business Transactions
Assets = Liabilities + Owner's Equity + Revenue − Expenses
+ | − − | + − | + − | + + | −
Chapter 3
Journalize and Post Business Transactions
Prepare a Trial Balance
Chapter 4
Gather the Adjustment Data
Complete a Work Sheet
Prepare Financial Statements
Journalize and Post Adjusting Entries
Chapter 5
Journalize and Post Closing Entries
Prepare a Post-Closing Trial Balance

FIGURE 1
The accounting cycle by chapter

THE WORK SHEET

The **work sheet** is a working paper used by accountants to record necessary adjustments and provide up-to-date account balances needed to prepare the financial statements. **The work sheet is a tool that accountants use to help in preparing the financial statements.** As a tool, the work sheet serves as a central place for bringing together the information needed to record the adjustments. With up-to-date account balances, the accountant can then prepare the financial statements.

First, we present the work sheet form so that you can see the big picture. Next, we describe and show examples of adjustments. Finally, we show how the adjustments are entered on the work sheet and how the work sheet is completed.

We will use a ten-column work sheet—so called because two amount columns are provided for each of the work sheet's five major sections. Work sheets are most often prepared by using a spreadsheet program such as Microsoft Excel®. We will explain the function of each of these sections, again basing our discussion on the accounting activities of Conner's Whitewater Adventures. But first we need to fill in the heading, which consists of three lines: (1) the name of the company, (2) the title of the working paper, and (3) the period of time covered.

FYI

The use of computerized accounting software can eliminate the preparation of the work sheet, which can be prepared manually or electronically. It does not, however, eliminate the journalizing and posting of the adjusting entries.

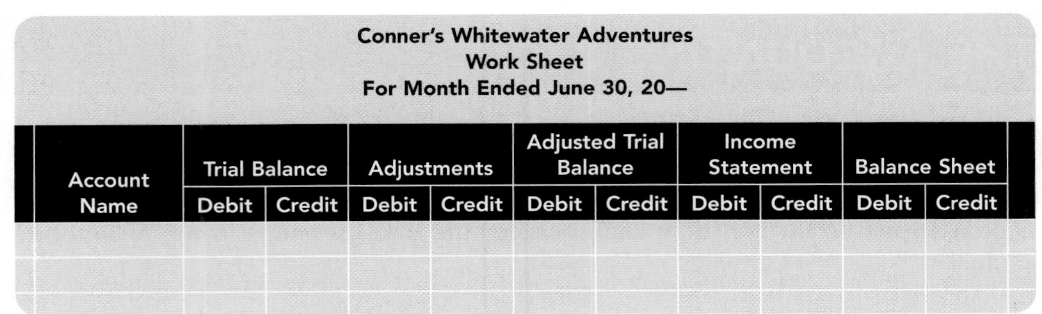

Conner's Whitewater Adventures
Work Sheet
For Month Ended June 30, 20—

Account Name	Trial Balance		Adjustments		Adjusted Trial Balance		Income Statement		Balance Sheet	
	Debit	Credit	Debit	Credit	Debit	Credit	Debit	Credit	Debit	Credit

Next, we want to point out the account classifications that are placed in each column. We start with the Trial Balance columns and then move across the work sheet, discussing each pair of columns separately.

The Columns of the Work Sheet

Trial Balance Columns

LEARNING OBJECTIVE 2

List the classifications of the accounts that occupy each column of a ten-column work sheet.

When you use a work sheet, you do not have to prepare a trial balance on a separate sheet of paper. Instead, you enter the account balances from the general ledger in the first two amount columns of the work sheet. List the accounts that have balances in the Account Name column in the same order in which they appear in the chart of accounts. Assuming **normal balances,** the account classifications are listed in the Trial Balance Debit and Credit columns of the work sheet as follows:

Account Name	Trial Balance		Adjustments		Adjusted Trial Balance		Income Statement		Balance Sheet	
	Debit	Credit	Debit	Credit	Debit	Credit	Debit	Credit	Debit	Credit
	Assets →				Assets					
		Liabilities →				Liabilities				
		Capital →				Capital				
	Drawing →				Drawing					
		Revenue →				Revenue				
	Expenses →				Expenses					

Remember

You have already prepared a trial balance. Record the normal balances in the Trial Balance Debit or Credit column. The normal balance is the + side of any account.

As we move along in this chapter, we will discuss the adjustments. The Adjusted Trial Balance columns contain the same account classifications as the Trial Balance columns. **The Adjusted Trial Balance columns are merely extensions of the Trial Balance columns, plus or minus any adjustment amounts.** If an adjustment is required, the amounts are carried from the Trial Balance columns through the Adjustments columns and into the Adjusted Trial Balance columns.

Income Statement Columns

An income statement contains the revenues minus the expenses. Revenue accounts have credit balances, so they are recorded in the Income Statement Credit column. Expense accounts have debit balances, so they are recorded in the Income Statement Debit column.

Account Name	Trial Balance		Adjustments		Adjusted Trial Balance		Income Statement		Balance Sheet	
	Debit	Credit	Debit	Credit	Debit	Credit	Debit	Credit	Debit	Credit
	Assets →				Assets					
		Liabilities →				Liabilities				
		Capital →				Capital				
	Drawing →				Drawing					
		Revenue →				Revenue →		Revenue		
	Expenses →				Expenses →		Expenses			

Balance Sheet Columns

As you recall, the balance sheet is a statement showing assets, liabilities, and owner's equity. Asset accounts have debit balances, so they are recorded in the Balance Sheet Debit column. Liability accounts have credit balances, so they are recorded in the Balance Sheet Credit column. The Capital account has a credit balance, so it is recorded in the Balance Sheet Credit column. Because the Drawing account is a deduction from Capital, it has a debit balance and is recorded in the Balance Sheet Debit column (the opposite column from that in which Capital is recorded).

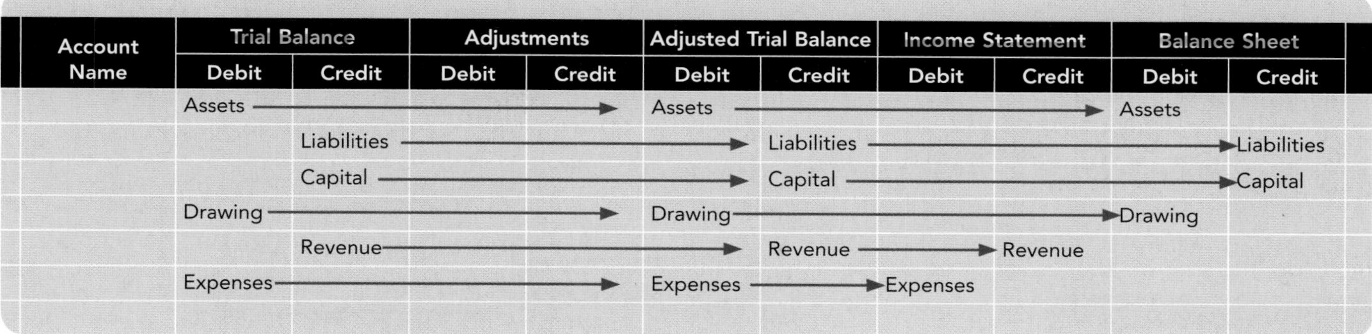

Account Name	Trial Balance		Adjustments		Adjusted Trial Balance		Income Statement		Balance Sheet	
	Debit	Credit	Debit	Credit	Debit	Credit	Debit	Credit	Debit	Credit
	Assets →				Assets →				Assets	
		Liabilities →				Liabilities →				Liabilities
		Capital →				Capital →				Capital
	Drawing →				Drawing →				Drawing	
		Revenue →				Revenue →		Revenue		
	Expenses →				Expenses →		Expenses			

ADJUSTMENTS

3 LEARNING OBJECTIVE

Complete a work sheet for a service enterprise, involving adjustments for expired insurance, depreciation, and accrued wages.

Adjustments are a way of updating the ledger accounts. They may be considered *internal transactions*. They have not been recorded in the accounts up to this time because no outside party has been involved. Adjustments are determined after the trial balance has been prepared. Adjustments fine-tune the accounts to present a more accurate concept of the accounts.

Only a few accounts are adjusted. To describe the reasons for making adjustments, let's return to Conner's Whitewater Adventures. First, we select the accounts that require adjustments. Next, we show the adjustments recorded in T accounts so you can see the effect on the accounts. **However, bear in mind that the adjustments are first recorded on the work sheet when using a manual accounting system.** When using general ledger software, adjustments are recorded in the general journal. The adjustments are made at the end of the company's accounting period—in the case of Conner's Whitewater Adventures, June 30.

Choosing an Accounting Software Package

SMALL BUSINESS SUCCESS

Choosing an accounting software package is an important decision for small businesses. There are two popular software packages designed for small businesses: Peachtree and QuickBooks™. When picking an accounting software package, it's important to consider the needs of the business such as:

- How many individuals will use the software?
- What tools are available?
- Can the software handle inventory?
- Is it easy to use?
- What is the cost of the program?

Both of the accounting software packages listed here will handle most basic small business accounting transactions. Each software program includes general ledger, subsidiary ledgers, and financial statements and also the ability to export data into Excel® or Word®. Most of the differences among the packages relate to appearance and how to enter transactions. For example, QuickBooks uses different "centers" such as vendors, customers, employees, company, and banking. Peachtree uses navigation bars that are located across the top of the screen.

Almost all local colleges offer courses that can teach you how to use either of these accounting software programs. It is highly recommended that all small business owners and accounting majors take at least one course in how to use accounting software, as the knowledge of accounting software is a skill needed for success in the business world.

Remember

When using a manual accounting system, adjustments are recorded on the work sheet first. They will be journalized and posted later in the accounting cycle. When using a general ledger software package, adjustments are entered directly into the general journal.

Without adjustments, the financial statements would be out of focus.

Prepaid Insurance

The $1,875 balance in Prepaid Insurance represents the premium paid in advance for a three-month liability insurance policy. One month of the three months of premium has now expired, which amounts to $625.

$$\$1{,}875 \text{ premium} \div 3 \text{ months} = \$625 \text{ per month}$$

In the adjustment, Conner's Whitewater Adventures deducts the expired or used portion from Prepaid Insurance and adds it to Insurance Expense.

	Prepaid Insurance		Insurance Expense	
	+	−	+	−
(Old)	Balance 1,875	**Adjusting 625**	**Adjusting 625**	
(New)	Balance 1,250			

The new balance of Prepaid Insurance, $1,250 ($1,875 − $625), represents the cost of insurance that remains paid in advance and should therefore appear in the Balance Sheet Debit column. The $625 amount in Insurance Expense represents the cost of insurance that has expired and should therefore appear in the Income Statement Debit column.

Remember

For the adjustment of insurance, you are given the amount used (expired). So, in the adjusting entry, take the amount used directly out of Prepaid Insurance and put it into Insurance Expense.

Depreciation of Equipment

We have recorded durable items, such as appliances and fixtures, under Equipment because they will last longer than one year. The benefits of these assets will eventually be used up (the assets will either wear out or become obsolete). Therefore, we should systematically spread out the cost of these assets over their useful lives. That is, we allocate the cost of the equipment as an expense *over its estimated useful life* and call this **depreciation** because such equipment loses its usefulness. A part of this depreciation expense is allotted to each fiscal period. In the case of Conner's Whitewater Adventures, the Equipment account has a balance of $51,300. Suppose we estimate that the equipment will have a useful life of seven years, with a trade-in (salvage) value of $8,292 at the end of that time. Using **straight-line depreciation**, we can allocate the cost of an asset, less any trade-in value, evenly over the useful life of the asset. Depreciation for one month is figured like this:

STEP 1. Subtract the trade-in (salvage) value from the cost to get the full depreciation.

$51,300 − $8,292 = $43,008 full depreciation

STEP 2. Divide the full depreciation by the number of years in the asset's useful life to get the depreciation for one year.

$43,008 full depreciation ÷ 7 years = $6,144 per year

STEP 3. Divide the depreciation for one year by 12 to get the depreciation for one month.

$6,144 per year ÷ 12 months = $512 per month

FYI

There are several methods of depreciation for assets. Straight-line depreciation is shown here—equal amounts of estimated loss of usefulness are taken each year. There are also accelerated methods that assign larger amounts to expense in the early years of the life of an asset.

When depreciation is recorded, we do not subtract it directly from the asset account. In asset accounts, such as Equipment or Building, we must keep the original cost recorded in the account. Consequently, the amount of depreciation has to be recorded in another account; that account is Accumulated Depreciation. If you were to incorrectly record depreciation by crediting the asset account, the balance of your asset account will eventually reach zero, which is not correct. You still have the equipment and need to maintain the original cost in the account; therefore, the credit should be to the contra asset account, Accumulated Depreciation.

Always record the adjusting entry for depreciation as a debit to Depreciation Expense (an income statement item) and a credit to Accumulated Depreciation (a balance sheet item), which increases both accounts. The adjustment in T account form would appear as follows:

Accumulated Depreciation, Equipment, is contrary to, or a deduction from, Equipment, so we call it a **contra account**. To show the accounts under their proper headings, let's look at the fundamental accounting equation. Brackets indicate that Accumulated Depreciation, Equipment, is a deduction from the Equipment account. Note that the plus and minus signs are opposite.

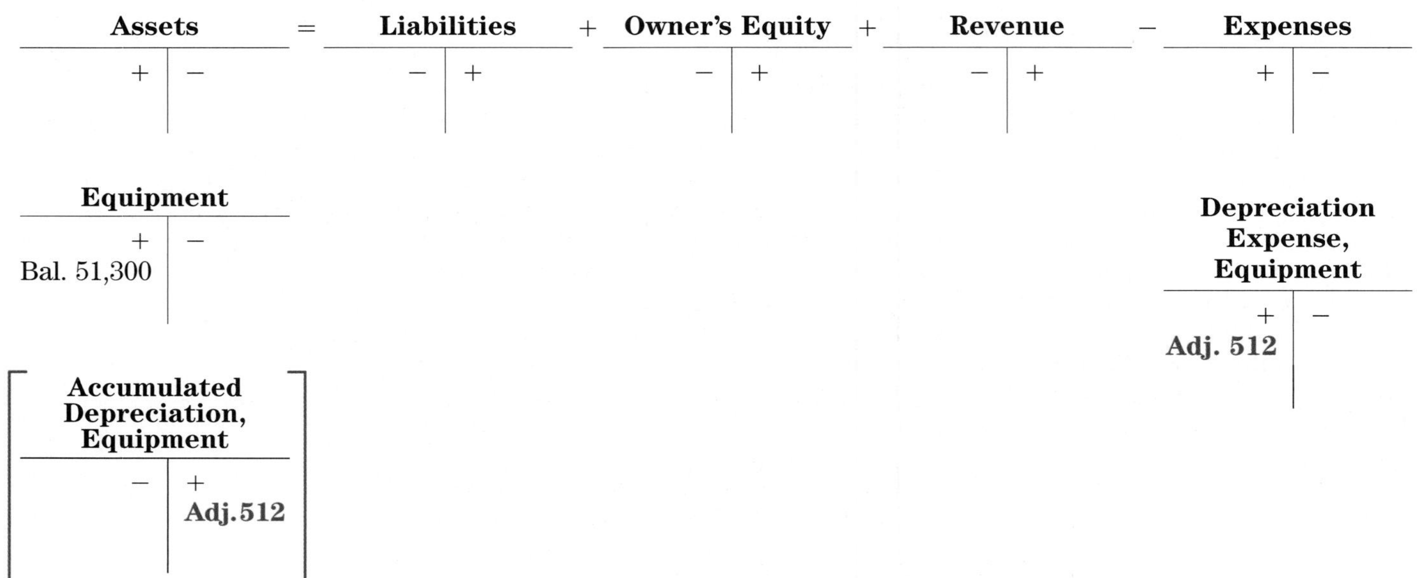

On the work sheet, Equipment (an asset) appears in the Balance Sheet Debit column. Accumulated Depreciation (a deduction from an asset) appears in the opposite column, which is the Balance Sheet Credit column.

Accumulated Depreciation, Equipment, as the title implies, is the total depreciation that the company has taken since the original purchase of the asset. Rather than crediting the Equipment account, Conner's Whitewater Adventures keeps track of the total depreciation taken since it first acquired the asset in a separate account. The maximum depreciation it could take would be the cost of the equipment, \$51,300, less the trade-in value of \$8,292. So, for the first year, Accumulated Depreciation, Equipment, will increase at the rate of \$512 per month, assuming that no additional equipment has been purchased. For example, at the end of the second month, Accumulated Depreciation, Equipment, will amount to \$1,024 (\$512 + \$512).

On the balance sheet, the balance of Accumulated Depreciation is deducted from the balance of the related asset account as illustrated on the following partial balance sheet for Conner's Whitewater Adventures. The net amount shown, \$50,788, is referred to as the book value of the asset. Thus, **book value** (or **carrying value**) is the cost of an asset minus its accumulated depreciation (\$51,300 − \$512).

FYI

If we had a Building account, the adjusting entry would be a debit to Depreciation Expense, Building, and a credit to Accumulated Depreciation, Building. Building and Accumulated Depreciation, Building, would be listed separately on the balance sheet.

If we had a Land account, it would have no adjusting entry. Land supposedly lasts forever, so it is not depreciated.

Conner's Whitewater Adventures
Partial Balance Sheet
June 30, 20—

Assets		
Equipment	$51,300	
Less Accumulated Depreciation	512	$50,788

Wages Expense

The end of the fiscal period and the end of the employees' payroll period rarely fall on the same day. A diagram of the situation looks like this:

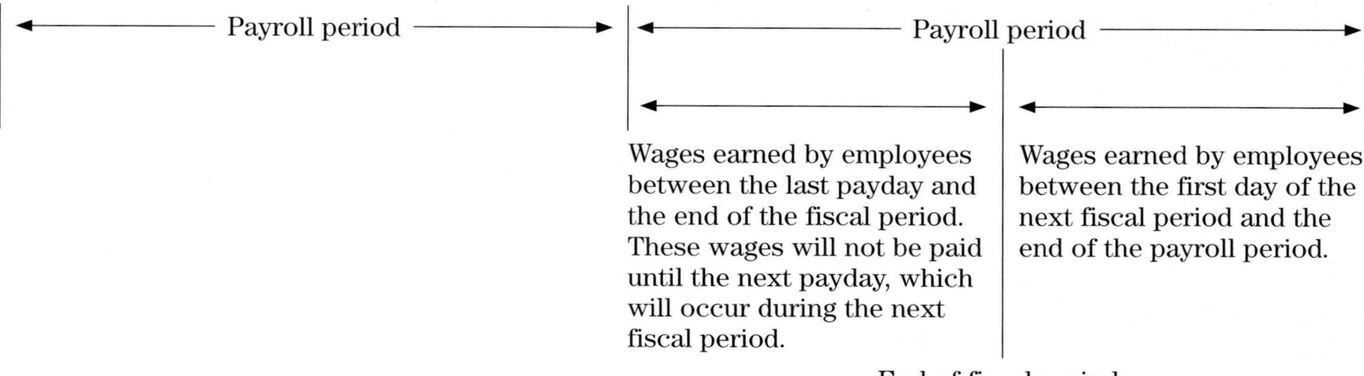
Payroll period
Payroll period
Wages earned by employees between the last payday and the end of the fiscal period. These wages will not be paid until the next payday, which will occur during the next fiscal period.
Wages earned by employees between the first day of the next fiscal period and the end of the payroll period.
End of fiscal period

Since the last day of the fiscal period falls in the middle of the payroll period, we have to split up the wages earned in that payroll period between the fiscal period just ended and the next fiscal period. We will use another company for this example.

Assume that Brown Company pays its employees $400 per day and that payday falls on Friday. The employees work a five-day week. When employees pick up their paychecks on Friday, the amount of the checks includes their wages for that day and for the preceding four days. Suppose that the last day of the fiscal period falls on Wednesday, December 31. The following diagram illustrates this situation.

End of Fiscal Period

Mon	Tue	Wed	Thur	Dec. 26 Fri	Dec. 29 Mon	Dec. 30 Tue	Dec. 31 Wed	Jan. 1 Thur	Jan. 2 Fri
$400	$400	$400	$400	$400	$400	$400	$400	$400	$400
Payroll period					Payroll period				
				Payday $2,000					Payday $2,000
					$1,200			$800	

December						
S	M	T	W	R	F	S
	1	2	3	4	(5)	6
7	8	9	10	11	(12)	13
14	15	16	17	18	(19)	20
21	22	23	24	25	(26)	27
28	29	30	31			

Paydays (circled: 5, 12, 19, 26)

Remember

If the end of the fiscal period (or end of the fiscal year) occurs during the middle of a payroll period, Wages Expense must be adjusted to bring it up to date. In the adjusting entry, add the amount employees have earned between the end of the last payroll period and the end of the fiscal period.

To have the Wages Expense account show an accurate balance for the fiscal period, you need to add $1,200 for the cost of labor between the last payday, December 26, and the end of the year, December 31 ($400 for December 29; $400 for December 30; $400 for December 31). Because the $1,200 will not be paid at this time but is owed to the employees as of December 31, you also need to add $1,200 to Wages Payable, a liability account, because the company owes this amount to employees.

Wages Expense

		+	−
(Old)	Balance	104,000	
	Adj.	**1,200**	
(New)	Balance	105,200	

Wages Payable

−	+	
	Adj.	**1,200**

Remember

In the adjusting entry for accrued wages, increase both the Wages Expense and the Wages Payable accounts.

Returning to our illustration of Conner's Whitewater Adventures, the amount of wages that has been paid so far for the month of June is $2,360. However, the last payday was June 24. Between June 24 and the end of the month, Conner's Whitewater Adventures has determined that it owes an additional $472 in wages to its employees.

Accountants refer to this extra amount that has not been recorded at the end of the month as **accrued wages**. In accounting terms, **accrual** means recognition of an expense or a revenue that has been incurred (expense) or earned (revenue) but has not yet been recorded.

Wages Expense

		+	−
(Old)	Balance	2,360	
	Adj.	**472**	
(New)	Balance	2,832	

Wages Payable

−	+	
	Adj.	**472**

Placement of Accounts on the Work Sheet

We have to enter the adjustments on the work sheet, but before doing so, let's briefly discuss the Drawing and Accumulated Depreciation accounts, as well as net income, and their effect on the work sheet.

Capital and Drawing Account Balances

The Drawing account is a contra account (contrary to Capital). In the statement of owner's equity, Drawing is deducted from Capital. To show one account as a deduction from another, the plus and minus signs are switched around. The T accounts look like this:

J. Conner, Capital

−	+
Debit	Credit Balance

J. Conner, Drawing

+	−
Debit Balance	Credit

The normal balance for the Capital account is recorded in the Credit columns of the Trial Balance, the Adjusted Trial Balance, and the Balance Sheet sections. The normal balance for the Drawing account is recorded in the Debit columns of the Trial Balance, the Adjusted Trial Balance, and the Balance Sheet sections.

Equipment and Accumulated Depreciation, Equipment, Account Balances

The Accumulated Depreciation, Equipment, account is a contra account (contrary to Equipment). On the balance sheet, Accumulated Depreciation, Equipment, is deducted from Equipment. The T accounts look like this:

Equipment	
+ Debit Balance	– Credit

Accumulated Depreciation, Equipment	
– Debit	+ Credit Balance

The normal balance for the Equipment account is recorded in the Debit columns of the Trial Balance, the Adjusted Trial Balance, and the Balance Sheet sections. The normal balance for the Accumulated Depreciation, Equipment, account is recorded in the Credit columns of the Trial Balance, the Adjusted Trial Balance, and the Balance Sheet sections.

Net Income

Net income (or net loss) is the difference between revenue and expenses. It is used to balance the Income Statement columns; since revenue is normally larger than expenses, the balancing amount must be added to the expense side. Net income (or net loss) is also used to balance the Balance Sheet columns. On the statement of owner's equity, you add net income to the owner's beginning Capital balance. Since the Capital balance is located in the Balance Sheet Credit column, net income must also be added to that side. The following diagram shows these relationships.

Account Name	Trial Balance		Adjustments		Adjusted Trial Balance		Income Statement		Balance Sheet	
	Debit	Credit	Debit	Credit	Debit	Credit	Debit	Credit	Debit	Credit
	A + Draw. + E	Accum. Depr. + L + Cap. + R			A + Draw. + E	Accum. Depr. + L + Cap. + R	E	R	A + Draw.	Accum. Depr. + L + Cap.
Net Income							NI			NI

On the other hand, if expenses are larger than revenue, the result is a net loss. You must add net loss to the revenue side to balance the Income Statement columns. Also, because a net loss is deducted from the owner's beginning Capital balance, you must include net loss in the debit side of the Balance Sheet columns, thereby balancing these columns. To show this, let's look at the Income Statement and Balance Sheet columns diagrammed here.

Remember

A net income amount is entered in the Income Statement Debit column and the Balance Sheet Credit column (same side as the increase side of Capital). A net loss is entered in the Income Statement Credit column and the Balance Sheet Debit column (same side as the decrease side of Capital).

Account Name	Income Statement		Balance Sheet	
	Debit	Credit	Debit	Credit
	E	R	A + Draw.	Accum. Depr. + L + Cap.
Net Loss		NL	NL	

Mixed Accounts

At this point, take special notice of the fact that each **adjusting entry contains an income statement account (revenue or expense) and a balance sheet account (asset, contra asset, or liability).** Accountants refer to these accounts as **mixed accounts**—accounts with balances that are partly income statement amounts and partly balance sheet amounts. The income statement and balance sheet accounts involved are separate accounts having a part of their name in common, like Prepaid Insurance and Insurance Expense. Prepaid Insurance is recorded as $1,875 in the Trial Balance columns but is apportioned as $625 in Insurance Expense in the Income Statement columns and $1,250 in Prepaid Insurance in the Balance Sheet columns. In other words, portions of these trial balance amounts are recorded in each section.

In the previous examples, we used T accounts to explain how to handle adjustments. T accounts help organize any type of accounting entry into debits and credits. But now it is time to record the adjustments on the work sheet. To help you remember which classifications of accounts appear in each column of the work sheet, we will label the columns with letters specifying each classification of accounts; for example, A for assets, L for liabilities, etc., as shown in Figure 2.

Steps in the Completion of the Work Sheet

A completed work sheet is shown in Figure 3. Before we complete the work sheet, let's list the recommended steps to follow.

STEP 1. Complete the Trial Balance columns, total, and rule (single underline before double underlining totals).

STEP 2. Complete the Adjustments columns, total, and rule.

STEP 3. Complete the Adjusted Trial Balance columns, total, and rule.

STEP 4. Record balances in the Income Statement and Balance Sheet columns and total each column.

STEP 5. Record net income or net loss in the Income Statement columns by subtracting the smaller side from the larger side and adding the difference to the smaller side, total, and rule.

STEP 6. Record net income or net loss in the Balance Sheet columns by subtracting the smaller side from the larger side and adding the difference to the smaller side (the amount should be the same as the difference between the Income Statement column totals—if not, there is an error), total, and rule.

The steps assume the work sheet is prepared manually. The work sheet can also be prepared using a computer spreadsheet program, such as Microsoft Excel®. Whether the work sheet is prepared manually or on a computer, the columns must be completed, totaled, and ruled. An Excel version of the work sheet is shown in Figure 4 on page 142.

FIGURE 2 Partial work sheet for Conner's Whitewater Adventures

Conner's Whitewater Adventures Work Sheet For Month Ended June 30, 20—				
	Trial Balance		Adjustments	
	Debit	Credit	Debit	Credit
Account Name	*A + Draw. + E*	*Accum. Depr. + L + Cap. + R*		
Cash	55,890.00			
Accounts Receivable	4,250.00			
Prepaid Insurance	1,875.00			(a) 625.00
Equipment	51,300.00			
Accounts Payable		3,425.00		
J. Conner, Capital		95,200.00		
J. Conner, Drawing	3,500.00			
Income from Tours		23,320.00		
Wages Expense	2,360.00		(c) 472.00	
Rent Expense	1,250.00			
Supplies Expense	675.00			
Advertising Expense	620.00			
Utilities Expense	225.00			
	121,945.00	121,945.00		
Insurance Expense			(a) 625.00	
Depreciation Expense, Equipment			(b) 512.00	
Accumulated Depreciation, Equipment				(b) 512.00
Wages Payable				(c) 472.00
			1,609.00	1,609.00

Step 1: Trial Balance Columns

Note that the trial balance in Figure 2 is the same trial balance presented earlier for Conner's Whitewater Adventures. You will be able to follow the completion of the entire work sheet for Conner's Whitewater Adventures in Figure 3.

Remember

The Trial Balance columns are exactly the same as they are listed in the Trial Balance presented in Chapter 3.

Step 2: Adjustments Columns

When we enter the adjustments, we identify them as (a), (b), (c), to indicate the relationships between the debit and credit sides and the sequence of the individual adjusting entries (see Figures 2 and 3).

Note that Insurance Expense; Depreciation Expense, Equipment; Accumulated Depreciation, Equipment; and Wages Payable did not appear in the trial balance because there were no balances in the accounts at that time. We wrote them below the Trial Balance totals to complete the work sheet.

Here is a brief review of the adjustments:

a. To record the $625 cost of insurance expired during June.
b. To record $512 depreciation for the month of June.
c. To record $472 of accrued wages owed at the end of June.

Now let's look at the work sheet shown in Figure 5 on pages 144 and 145. To reinforce the idea of adjusting entries, see the brief explanation of each adjustment at the right of the work sheet. Again, the completed work sheet is shown in Figure 3.

FIGURE 3
Work sheet with steps of completion explained for Conner's Whitewater Adventures

Conner's Whitewater Adventures
Work Sheet
For Month Ended June 30, 20—

Account Name	Trial Balance Debit (A + Draw. + E)	Trial Balance Credit (Accum. Depr. + L + Cap. + R)	Adjustments Debit	Adjustments Credit
Cash	55,890.00			
Accounts Receivable	4,250.00			
Prepaid Insurance	1,875.00			(a) 625.00
Equipment	51,300.00			
Accounts Payable		3,425.00		
J. Conner, Capital		95,200.00		
J. Conner, Drawing	3,500.00			
Income from Tours		23,320.00		
Wages Expense	2,360.00		(c) 472.00	
Rent Expense	1,250.00			
Supplies Expense	675.00			
Advertising Expense	620.00			
Utilities Expense	225.00			
	121,945.00	121,945.00		
Insurance Expense	Step 1		(a) 625.00	
Depr. Expense, Equipment			(b) 512.00	
Accum. Depr., Equipment				(b) 512.00
Wages Payable				(c) 472.00
			1,609.00	1,609.00
Net Income			Step 2	

(a) Insurance expired, $625
(b) Depr. of equip., $512
(c) Accrued wages, $472

Step 1
In the Account Name column, list the accounts that have balances. Enter the account balances in the Trial Balance columns. Total and rule the columns.

Step 2
Enter the adjustments, labeling each adjustment as (a), (b), (c), and so on. Total and rule the columns.

Adjusted Trial Balance		Income Statement		Balance Sheet	
Debit	Credit	Debit	Credit	Debit	Credit
A + Draw. + E	*Accum. Depr. + L + Cap. + R*	*E*	*R*	*A + Draw.*	*Accum. Depr. + L + Cap.*
55 8 9 0 00				55 8 9 0 00	
4 2 5 0 00				4 2 5 0 00	
1 2 5 0 00				1 2 5 0 00	
51 3 0 0 00				51 3 0 0 00	
	3 4 2 5 00				3 4 2 5 00
	95 2 0 0 00				95 2 0 0 00
3 5 0 0 00				3 5 0 0 00	
	23 3 2 0 00		23 3 2 0 00		
2 8 3 2 00		2 8 3 2 00			
1 2 5 0 00		1 2 5 0 00			
6 7 5 00		6 7 5 00			
6 2 0 00		6 2 0 00			
2 2 5 00		2 2 5 00			
6 2 5 00		6 2 5 00			
5 1 2 00		5 1 2 00			
	5 1 2 00				5 1 2 00
	4 7 2 00				4 7 2 00
122 9 2 9 00	122 9 2 9 00	6 7 3 9 00	23 3 2 0 00	116 1 9 0 00	99 6 0 9 00
		16 5 8 1 00			16 5 8 1 00
Step 3		23 3 2 0 00	23 3 2 0 00	116 1 9 0 00	116 1 9 0 00
		Steps 4, 5, 6			

Step 3
Carry amounts across from the Trial Balance columns plus or minus any amounts appearing in the Adjustments columns. Total and rule the columns.

Step 4
From the top of the Adjusted Trial Balance columns, go down line by line carrying each amount over to the Income Statement or Balance Sheet columns. Total the columns.

Step 5
Write Net Income or Net Loss in the Account Name column and the amount in the appropriate Income Statement column. Total and rule the columns.

Step 6
Enter the net income or loss amount in the appropriate Balance Sheet column. Total, balance, and rule the columns.

FIGURE 4 Work sheet for Conner's Whitewater Adventures—Excel version

	A	B	C	D	E	F	G	H	I	J	K
1	Conner's Whitewater Adventures										
2	Work Sheet										
3	For Month Ended June 30, 20—										
4											
5		TRIAL BALANCE		ADJUSTMENTS		ADJUSTED TRIAL BALANCE		INCOME STATEMENT		BALANCE SHEET	
6	ACCOUNT NAME	DEBIT	CREDIT	DEBIT	CREDIT	DEBIT	CREDIT	DEBIT	CREDIT	DEBIT	CREDIT
7			*Accum. Depr.*				*Accum. Depr.*				*Accum. Depr.*
8		*A* + *Draw.* + *E*	+ *L* + *Cap.* + *R*			*A* + *Draw.* + *E*	+ *L* + *Cap.* + *R*	*E*	*R*	*A* + *Draw.*	+ *L* + *Cap.*
9	Cash	55,890.00				55,890.00				55,890.00	
10	Accounts Receivable	4,250.00				4,250.00				4,250.00	
11	Prepaid Insurance	1,875.00			*(a)* 625.00	1,250.00				1,250.00	
12	Equipment	51,300.00				51,300.00				51,300.00	
13	Accounts Payable		3,425.00				3,425.00				3,425.00
14	J. Conner, Capital		95,200.00				95,200.00				95,200.00
15	J. Conner, Drawing	3,500.00				3,500.00				3,500.00	
16	Income from Tours		23,320.00				23,320.00		23,320.00		
17	Wages Expense	2,360.00		*(c)* 472.00		2,832.00		2,832.00			
18	Rent Expense	1,250.00				1,250.00		1,250.00			
19	Supplies Expense	675.00				675.00		675.00			
20	Advertising Expense	620.00				620.00		620.00			
21	Utilities Expense	225.00				225.00		225.00			
22		121,945.00	121,945.00								
23	Insurance Expense			*(a)* 625.00		625.00		625.00			
24	Depr. Exp., Equip.			*(b)* 512.00		512.00		512.00			
25	Accum. Depr., Equip.				*(b)* 512.00		512.00				512.00
26	Wages Payable				*(c)* 472.00		472.00				472.00
27				1,609.00	1,609.00	122,929.00	122,929.00	6,739.00	23,320.00	116,190.00	99,609.00
28	Net Income							16,581.00			16,581.00
29								23,320.00	23,320.00	116,190.00	116,190.00
30											
31											

Sheet1 Sheet2 Sheet3

In this chapter, the business is in its first accounting period; therefore, Accumulated Depreciation, Equipment had no balance until the end of the fiscal period adjustments, which meant it was not in the trial balance prior to adjustments. After the first fiscal period, Accumulated Depreciation will always have a balance until the related asset is sold or disposed of and will be listed in the Trial Balance columns immediately below the appropriate asset.

Again, we emphasize that the work sheet is strictly a tool used to gather all the up-to-date information needed to prepare the financial statements. **The adjustments are always recorded in the work sheet first.**

Remember

After the first fiscal period, Accumulated Depreciation will have a balance, so it will be listed immediately below the asset being depreciated (which in this example is Equipment). Consequently, Accumulated Depreciation will not appear at the bottom of next month's work sheet.

Step 3: Adjusted Trial Balance Columns

Once the Adjustments columns are totaled and ruled, extend each Trial Balance amount, plus or minus any adjustment from the Adjustments columns, to the Adjusted Trial Balance columns as shown in Figure 3.

Step 4: Income Statement and Balance Sheet Columns

Extend the balances in the Adjusted Trial Balance columns to either the Income Statement or the Balance Sheet columns (see Figure 3).

Step 5: Net Income or Net Loss—Income Statement Columns

Total each of the two Income Statement columns. Subtract the smaller side from the larger side, write the difference under the smaller Income Statement column total, and total and rule as shown in Figure 3.

If there is a net income, the credit side of the Income Statement columns will be larger than the debit side—more revenue than expenses. In this case, write Net Income in the Account Name column on the same line as the difference you calculated. If there is a net loss, the debit side of the Income Statement columns will be larger than the credit side—more expenses than revenue. In this case, write Net Loss in the Account Name column on the same line as the difference you calculated.

Remember

Insurance is adjusted by adding the amount expired to Insurance Expense while deducting the same amount from Prepaid Insurance.

Depreciation is added to both Depreciation Expense and Accumulated Depreciation.

Accrued wages are added to both Wages Expense and Wages Payable.

Step 6: Net Income or Net Loss—Balance Sheet Columns

Total the two Balance Sheet columns. Subtract the smaller side from the larger side, write the difference under the smaller Balance Sheet column total (the amount should equal the difference between the Income Statement column totals—if not, there is an error), and total and rule as shown in Figure 3.

Finding Errors in the Income Statement and Balance Sheet Columns

As you have seen, the amount of the net income or net loss must be recorded in both an Income Statement column and a Balance Sheet column. Suppose that, after the net income is added to the Balance Sheet Credit column, the Balance Sheet columns are not equal. To find the error, follow this procedure:

STEP 1. Check to see that the amount of the net income or loss is recorded in the correct columns. For example, net income is placed in the Income Statement Debit column and the Balance Sheet Credit column.

STEP 2. Verify the addition of all the columns.

STEP 3. Look to see if the appropriate amounts have been recorded in the Income Statement and Balance Sheet columns. For example, asset amounts should be listed in the Balance Sheet Debit column, expense amounts should be listed in the Income Statement Debit column, and so forth.

STEP 4. Verify, by adding or subtracting across each line, that the amounts carried over from the Trial Balance columns through the Adjustments columns into the Adjusted Trial Balance columns are correct.

FIGURE 5

Work sheet with explanations of adjustments for Conner's Whitewater Adventures

Conner's Whitewater Adventures
Work Sheet
For Month Ended June 30, 20—

Account Name	Trial Balance Debit (A + Draw. + E)	Trial Balance Credit (Accum. Depr. + L + Cap. + R)	Adjustments Debit	Adjustments Credit
Cash	55 8 9 0 00			
Accounts Receivable	4 2 5 0 00			
Prepaid Insurance	1 8 7 5 00			(a) 6 2 5 00
Equipment	51 3 0 0 00			
Accounts Payable		3 4 2 5 00		
J. Conner, Capital		95 2 0 0 00		
J. Conner, Drawing	3 5 0 0 00			
Income from Tours		23 3 2 0 00		
Wages Expense	2 3 6 0 00		(c) 4 7 2 00	
Rent Expense	1 2 5 0 00			
Supplies Expense	6 7 5 00			
Advertising Expense	6 2 0 00			
Utilities Expense	2 2 5 00			
	121 9 4 5 00	121 9 4 5 00		
Insurance Expense	Step 1		(a) 6 2 5 00	
Depr. Expense, Equipment			(b) 5 1 2 00	
Accum. Depr., Equipment				(b) 5 1 2 00
Wages Payable				(c) 4 7 2 00
			1 6 0 9 00	1 6 0 9 00
(a) Insurance expired, $625			Step 2	
(b) Depr. of equip., $512				
(c) Accrued wages, $472				

STEP 5. Verify that the correct amounts of the revenue and expense accounts are transferred to the Income Statement columns.

STEP 6. Verify that the correct amounts of assets, liabilities, and owner's equity accounts are transferred to the Balance Sheet columns.

Generally, one of these steps will expose the error.

Completion of the Financial Statements

LEARNING OBJECTIVE 4

Prepare an income statement, a statement of owner's equity, and a balance sheet for a service business directly from the work sheet.

As we stated, the purpose of the work sheet is to help the accountant prepare the financial statements. Since we have completed the work sheet for Conner's Whitewater Adventures, we can now prepare the income statement, the statement of owner's equity, and the balance sheet by taking the figures directly from the work sheet. These statements are shown in Figure 6 on page 146.

Note that you record Accumulated Depreciation, Equipment, in the asset section of the balance sheet as a direct deduction from Equipment. As we have said, accountants refer to this as a contra account because it is contrary to its companion asset account. The difference, $50,788, is called the book value or carrying value because it represents the cost of the asset after Accumulated Depreciation has been deducted.

Adjusted Trial Balance		
Debit A + Draw. + E	Credit Accum. Depr. + L + Cap. + R	
55,890.00		No adjustment, so carry over amount directly
4,250.00		
1,250.00		Adjustment involved, subtract $625.00 (expired) from $1,875.00
51,300.00		No adjustment, so carry over amount directly
	3,425.00	
	95,200.00	
3,500.00		
	23,320.00	
2,832.00		Adjustment involved, add $472.00 (accrued) to $2,360.00
1,250.00		No adjustment, so carry over amount directly
675.00		
620.00		
225.00		
		This line is blank because of the trial balance total
625.00		Adjustment involved, carry $625.00 over to the same column
512.00		Adjustment involved, carry $512.00 over to the same column
	512.00	Adjustment involved, carry $512.00 over to the same column
	472.00	Adjustment involved, carry $472.00 over to the same column
122,929.00	122,929.00	

Step 3

When preparing the statement of owner's equity, always remember to check the beginning balance of Capital against the balance shown in the Capital account in the general ledger. An additional investment may have been made during the fiscal period, and you need to record any such additional investment in the statement of owner's equity.

JOURNALIZING ADJUSTING ENTRIES

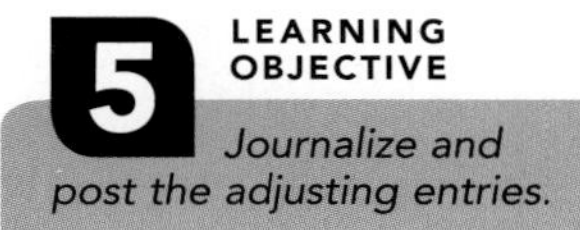

5
LEARNING OBJECTIVE
Journalize and post the adjusting entries.

To change the balance of a ledger account, you need a journal entry as evidence of the change. So far, we have been listing adjustments only in the Adjustments columns of the work sheet. The work sheet is not a journal, so we must journalize **adjusting entries** to update the ledger accounts. **Take the information for these entries directly from the Adjustments columns of the work sheet, debiting and crediting exactly the same accounts and amounts in the journal entries.**

In the Description column of the general journal, write "Adjusting Entries" before you begin making these entries. This eliminates the need to write an explanation for each entry. The adjusting entries for Conner's Whitewater Adventures are shown in Figure 7 on page 147.

FIGURE 6
Financial statements for Conner's Whitewater Adventures

Remember

The columns shown on the financial statements do not represent Debit or Credit. Each column simply shows account balances. Amounts in these columns are either added or subtracted.

Remember

Ruling columns correctly is very important. There should be a single rule below a column to be added or subtracted and double rules below the totals.

Conner's Whitewater Adventures
Income Statement
For Month Ended June 30, 20—

Revenue:		
Income from Tours		$23,320
Expenses:		
Wages Expense	$2,832	
Rent Expense	1,250	
Supplies Expense	675	
Advertising Expense	620	
Utilities Expense	225	
Insurance Expense	625	
Depreciation Expense, Equipment	512	
Total Expenses		6,739
Net Income		$16,581

Conner's Whitewater Adventures
Statement of Owner's Equity
For Month Ended June 30, 20—

J. Conner, Capital, June 1, 20—		$ 0
Investment during June	$ 95,200	
Net Income for June	16,581	
Subtotal	$111,781	
Less Withdrawals for June	3,500	
Increase in Capital		108,281
J. Conner, Capital, June 30, 20—		$108,281

Conner's Whitewater Adventures
Balance Sheet
June 30, 20—

Assets		
Cash		$ 55,890
Accounts Receivable		4,250
Prepaid Insurance		1,250
Equipment	$51,300	
Less Accumulated Depreciation	512	50,788
Total Assets		$112,178
Liabilities		
Accounts Payable	$ 3,425	
Wages Payable	472	
Total Liabilities		$ 3,897
Owner's Equity		
J. Conner, Capital		108,281
Total Liabilities and Owner's Equity		$112,178

GENERAL JOURNAL — PAGE 4

Date		Description	Post. Ref.	Debit	Credit
20—		Adjusting Entries			
June	30	Insurance Expense	516	625 00	
		Prepaid Insurance	117		625 00
	30	Depr. Expense, Equipment	517	512 00	
		Accum. Depr., Equipment	125		512 00
	30	Wages Expense	511	472 00	
		Wages Payable	222		472 00

FIGURE 7

Adjusting entries for Conner's Whitewater Adventures

Remember

Each adjusting entry consists of an income statement account and a balance sheet account.

When you post the adjusting entries to the ledger accounts, write the abbreviation "Adj." in the Item column of the ledger account. The adjusting entry for Prepaid Insurance is posted as follows:

ACCOUNT Prepaid Insurance — ACCOUNT NO. 117

Date		Item	Post. Ref.	Debit	Credit	Balance Debit	Balance Credit
20—							
June	10		2	1875 00		1875 00	
	30	Adj.	4		625 00	1250 00	

ACCOUNT Insurance Expense — ACCOUNT NO. 516

Date		Item	Post. Ref.	Debit	Credit	Balance Debit	Balance Credit
20—							
June	30	Adj.	4		625 00		625 00

In the adjusted accounts for Conner's Whitewater Adventures, notice that the intent is to make sure that the expenses recorded match up or compare with the revenues for the same period of time. In other words, for the month of June, we record all the revenues for June and all the expenses for June. Thus the revenues and expenses for the same time period are matched. This is called the **matching principle**.

FYI

Many businesses produce monthly financial statements. Adjustments must be made every time a financial statement is produced.

Accounting Treatment for the Cost of Supplies

In Chapter 1, when Conner's Whitewater Adventures bought supplies, the amount paid was recorded as an expense. Generally, most service businesses expense supplies when they buy them. An alternative to expensing supplies is to record the cost as an asset (debit to Supplies, credit to Cash). At the end of the accounting period, an inventory is taken to determine the amount of supplies used in operations. The debit would be to Supplies Expense for the amount of supplies used during the accounting period, and the credit would be to Supplies (an asset account). The ending balance in Supplies (asset account) would be the supplies on hand at the end of the accounting period.

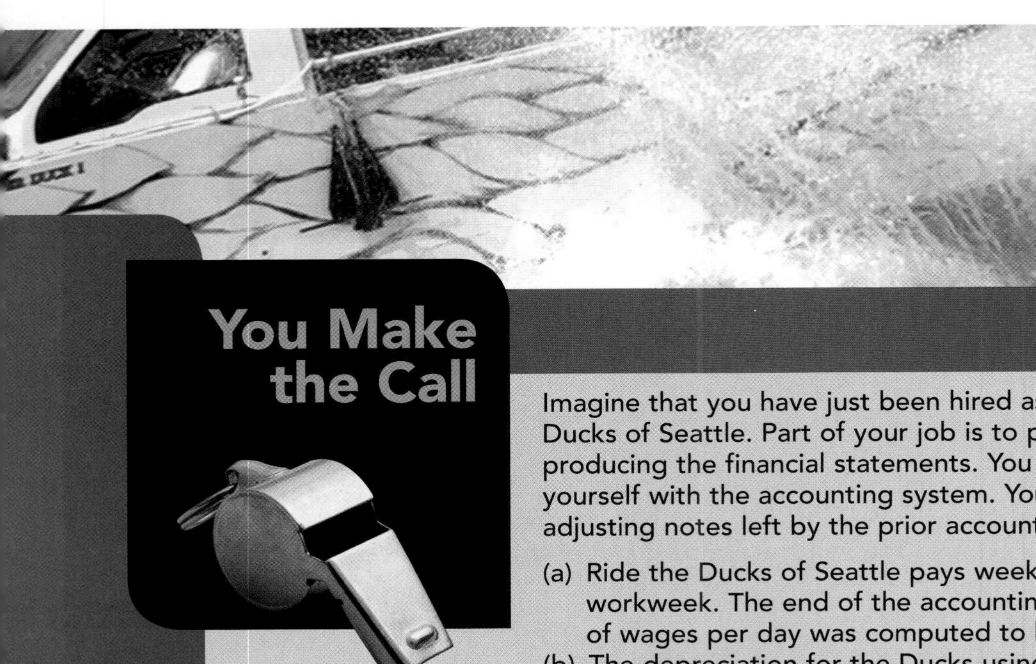

You Make the Call

Imagine that you have just been hired as an accounting clerk for Ride the Ducks of Seattle. Part of your job is to prepare adjusting entries prior to producing the financial statements. You have spent the week familiarizing yourself with the accounting system. You find the following preliminary adjusting notes left by the prior accounting clerk.

(a) Ride the Ducks of Seattle pays weekly salaries of $606.65 for a five-day workweek. The end of the accounting period is on a Thursday. The amount of wages per day was computed to be $121.33.

(b) The depreciation for the Ducks using the straight-line method is $33,392.86 per year and $2,782.74 per month. (The Ducks cost $275,000, with an estimated useful life of 7 years and a trade-in value of $41,250 at the end of that time.)

(c) The balance of the Prepaid Insurance account is $2,480, which covers one year. The amount of the adjusting entry for Insurance Expense for this one-month period is $206.67.

As the new accounting clerk, it is your job to review these figures for accuracy and then record the appropriate adjusting entries in the general journal.

SOLUTION

(a) $606.65 ÷ 5 = $121.33
$121.33 × 4 days = $485.32 adjustment amount

(b) 1. $275,000 − $41,250 = $233,750 full depreciation
2. $233,750 full depreciation ÷ 7 years = $33,392.86 per year
3. $33,392.86 per year ÷ 12 months = $2,782.74 per month

(c) $2,480 per year ÷ 12 months = $206.67 per month

GENERAL JOURNAL PAGE 6

Date	Description	Post. Ref.	Debit	Credit
	Adjusting Entries			
(a)	Wages Expense		485.32	
	Wages Payable			485.32
(b)	Depreciation Expense, Equipment		2,782.74	
	Accumulated Depreciation, Equipment			2,782.74
(c)	Insurance Expense		206.67	
	Prepaid Insurance			206.67

If supplies are a major cost to a business and expensing the supplies when they are purchased would distort the income statement, then recording the cost as an asset and adjusting accordingly would be the preferable method of accounting for supplies. **We will continue expensing supplies in this text when they are purchased.**

Income Statement Involving More than One Revenue Account and a Net Loss

6a LEARNING OBJECTIVE

Prepare an income statement involving more than one revenue account and a net loss.

When an organization has more than one distinct source of revenue, a separate revenue account is set up for each source. See, for example, the income statement of Harris Miniature Golf presented in Figure 8. Also note that expenses are greater than revenues, resulting in a net loss.

FIGURE 8

Income statement for Harris Miniature Golf

Harris Miniature Golf
Income Statement
For Month Ended September 30, 20—

Revenue:		
Admissions Fees	$2,624	
Concession Fees	1,512	
Total Revenue		$ 4,136
Expenses:		
Wages Expense	$3,123	
Advertising Expense	1,317	
Rent Expense	1,900	
Miscellaneous Expense	128	
Total Expenses		6,468
Net Loss		$(2,332)

Statement of Owner's Equity with an Additional Investment and a Net Income

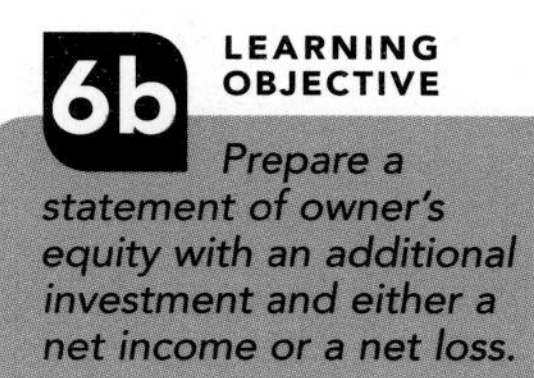

6b
LEARNING OBJECTIVE
Prepare a statement of owner's equity with an additional investment and either a net income or a net loss.

Any additional investment by the owner during the period covered by the financial statements should be shown on the statement of owner's equity, since such a statement should show everything that has affected the Capital account from the *beginning* until the *end* of the period covered by the financial statements. For example, in Figure 9, assume that the following information is true for L. A. Grand Company, which has a net income:

Balance of L. A. Grand, Capital, on April 1	$86,000
Additional investment by L. A. Grand on April 12	8,000
Net income for the month (from income statement)	6,200
Total withdrawals for the month	4,000

The additional investment may be in the form of cash. Or the investment may be in the form of other assets, such as tools, equipment, and similar items. In the case of investments of assets other than cash, the assets should be recorded at their fair market value. Fair market value is the present worth of an asset, or the amount that would be received if the asset were sold to an outsider on the open market. Fair market value may differ greatly from the amount the owner originally paid for the asset.

FIGURE 9

Statement of owner's equity for L. A. Grand Company

L. A. Grand Company Statement of Owner's Equity For Month Ended April 30, 20—		
L. A. Grand, Capital, April 1, 20—		$86,000
Investment during April	$ 8,000	
Net Income for April	6,200	
Subtotal	$14,200	
Less Withdrawals for April	4,000	
Increase in Capital		10,200
L. A. Grand, Capital, April 30, 20—		$96,200

FYI

The information normally shown on the statement of owner's equity is sometimes included as part of the owner's equity section of the balance sheet in computerized general ledger systems.

Statement of Owner's Equity with an Additional Investment and a Net Loss

Assume the following for J. D. Ross Company, which has a net loss:

J. D. Ross, Capital, on Oct. 1	$75,000
Additional investment by J. D. Ross on Oct. 25	10,000
Net loss for the month (from income statement)	1,500
Total withdrawals for the month	5,100

The statement of owner's equity in Figure 10 shows this information.

FIGURE 10

Statement of owner's equity for J. D. Ross Company

J. D. Ross Company Statement of Owner's Equity For Month Ended October 31, 20—		
J. D. Ross, Capital, October 1, 20—		$75,000
Investment during October	$10,000	
Net Loss for October	1,500	
Subtotal	$ 8,500	
Less Withdrawals for October	5,100	
Increase in Capital		3,400
J. D. Ross, Capital, October 31, 20—		$78,400

LEARNING OBJECTIVE 6c

Prepare a balance sheet for a business having more than one accumulated depreciation account.

Businesses with More than One Depreciation Expense Account and More than One Accumulated Depreciation Account

Figures 11 and 12 show the income statement and the balance sheet for Molen Veterinary Clinic. In Figure 12, note that the company has two assets subject to depreciation: Building and Equipment. In the financial statements, Depreciation Expense and Accumulated Depreciation must be listed for each asset.

LEARNING OBJECTIVE 6d

Prepare a balance sheet containing the statement of owner's equity information.

Balance Sheet with Statement of Owner's Equity Included

The information normally shown in the statement of owner's equity is sometimes included as part of the owner's equity section of the balance sheet, as shown in Figure 13.

Molen Veterinary Clinic
Income Statement
For Month Ended December 31, 20—

Revenue:		
Professional Fees	$332,300	
Boarding Fees	65,270	
Total Revenue		$397,570
Expenses:		
Salary Expense	$250,000	
Depreciation Expense, Building	19,450	
Depreciation Expense, Equipment	11,500	
Supplies Expense	11,380	
Insurance Expense	2,240	
Miscellaneous Expense	4,420	
Total Expenses		298,990
Net Income		$ 98,580

FIGURE 11
Income statement for Molen Veterinary Clinic

Molen Veterinary Clinic
Balance Sheet
December 31, 20—

Assets		
Cash		$ 21,320
Land		15,200
Building	$349,100	
Less Accumulated Depreciation	112,200	236,900
Equipment	$124,800	
Less Accumulated Depreciation	87,600	37,200
Total Assets		$310,620
Liabilities		
Accounts Payable		$ 7,400
Owner's Equity		
R. N. Molen, Capital		303,220
Total Liabilities and Owner's Equity		$310,620

FIGURE 12
Balance sheet for Molen Veterinary Clinic

Conner's Whitewater Adventures
Balance Sheet
June 30, 20—

Assets		
Cash		$ 55,890
Accounts Receivable		4,250
Prepaid Insurance		1,250
Equipment	$ 51,300	
Less Accumulated Depreciation	512	50,788
Total Assets		$112,178
Liabilities		
Accounts Payable	$ 3,425	
Wages Payable	472	
Total Liabilities		$ 3,897
Owner's Equity		
J. Conner, Capital, June 1, 20—		$ 0
Investment during June	$ 95,200	
Net Income for June	16,581	
Subtotal	$111,781	
Less Withdrawals for June	3,500	
Increase in Capital		108,281
J. Conner, Capital, June 30, 20—		$108,281
Total Liabilities and Owner's Equity		$112,178

FIGURE 13
Balance sheet for Conner's Whitewater Adventures

FYI

Computerized accounting programs frequently do not produce a separate statement of owner's equity.

CHAPTER REVIEW

Study & Practice

LEARNING OBJECTIVE 1

Define fiscal period *and* fiscal year.

A **fiscal period** is any period of time covering a complete accounting cycle. A **fiscal year** consists of twelve consecutive months.

PRACTICE EXERCISE 1

Which of the following would be considered a fiscal year?

(a) July 1, 20— to June 30, 20—
(b) October 1, 20— to August 31, 20—
(c) April 1, 20— to January 31, 20—
(d) January 1, 20— to December 31, 20—

PRACTICE EXERCISE 1 SOLUTION

(a) and (d)

LEARNING OBJECTIVE 2

List the classifications of the accounts that occupy each column of a ten-column work sheet.

Trial Balance Debit	Assets + Drawing + Expenses
Trial Balance Credit	Accum. Depr. + Liabilities + Capital + Revenue
Adjusted Trial Balance Debit	Assets + Drawing + Expenses
Adjusted Trial Balance Credit	Accum. Depr. + Liabilities + Capital + Revenue
Income Statement Debit	Expenses
Income Statement Credit	Revenue
Balance Sheet Debit	Assets + Drawing
Balance Sheet Credit	Accum. Depr. + Liabilities + Capital

PRACTICE EXERCISE 2

Using a ten-column work sheet, list the classifications of accounts that are found in each column, with the exception of the Adjustments columns (Trial Balance, Adjusted Trial Balance, Income Statement, and Balance Sheet).

PRACTICE EXERCISE 2 SOLUTION

Account Name	Trial Balance		Adjustments		Adjusted Trial Balance		Income Statement		Balance Sheet	
	Debit	Credit	Debit	Credit	Debit	Credit	Debit	Credit	Debit	Credit
	Assets	Accum. Depr.			Assets	Accum. Depr.			Assets	Accum. Depr.
	Drawing	Liabilities			Drawing	Liabilities			Drawing	Liabilities
	Expenses	Capital			Expenses	Capital	Expenses			Capital
		Revenue				Revenue		Revenue		

3 LEARNING OBJECTIVE

Complete a work sheet for a service enterprise, involving adjustments for expired insurance, depreciation, and accrued wages.

Adjustment for expired insurance: debit Insurance Expense and credit Prepaid Insurance.
Adjustment for **depreciation**: debit Depreciation Expense and credit Accumulated Depreciation.
Adjustment for accrued wages: debit Wages Expense and credit Wages Payable.

PRACTICE EXERCISE 3

Complete the work sheet on page 154 for Fun and Games for the month of September.

Adjustment information:

(a) Insurance expired during September, $175
(b) Depreciation of equipment for the month of September, $540
(c) Accrued wages owed at the end of September, $260

PRACTICE EXERCISE 3 SOLUTION

See the completed work sheet on page 155.

4 LEARNING OBJECTIVE

Prepare an income statement, a statement of owner's equity, and a balance sheet for a service business directly from the work sheet.

Prepare the income statement directly from the amounts listed in the Income Statement Debit and Credit columns. The net income should equal the net income previously determined on the **work sheet**. For the statement of owner's equity, use the amount of the beginning capital listed in the Balance Sheet Credit column after checking the general ledger for any additional investment(s), the amount of the net income from the Balance Sheet Credit column, and the amount of Drawing from the Balance Sheet Debit column. Prepare the balance sheet directly from the amounts listed in the Balance Sheet Debit and Credit columns (except Drawing and Capital).

Fun and Games
Work Sheet
For Month Ended September 30, 20—

Account Name	Trial Balance		Adjustments		Adjusted Trial Balance		Income Statement		Balance Sheet	
	Debit	Credit	Debit	Credit	Debit	Credit	Debit	Credit	Debit	Credit
Cash	24,900.00									
Accounts Receivable	5,750.00									
Prepaid Insurance	2,100.00									
Equipment	36,000.00									
Accum. Depr., Equip.		540.00								
Accounts Payable		3,985.00								
J. Jay, Capital		54,075.00								
J. Jay, Drawing	5,000.00									
Income from Services		21,000.00								
Wages Expense	2,670.00									
Rent Expense	1,950.00									
Supplies Expense	500.00									
Advertising Expense	450.00									
Utilities Expense	280.00									
	79,600.00	79,600.00								
Insurance Expense										
Depr. Exp., Equip.										
Wages Payable										
Net Income										

Fun and Games
Work Sheet
For Month Ended September 30, 20—

Account Name	Trial Balance		Adjustments		Adjusted Trial Balance		Income Statement		Balance Sheet	
	Debit	Credit	Debit	Credit	Debit	Credit	Debit	Credit	Debit	Credit
Cash	24,900.00				24,900.00				24,900.00	
Accounts Receivable	5,750.00				5,750.00				5,750.00	
Prepaid Insurance	2,100.00			*(a)* 175.00	1,925.00				1,925.00	
Equipment	36,000.00				36,000.00				36,000.00	
Accum. Depr., Equip.		540.00		*(b)* 540.00		1,080.00				1,080.00
Accounts Payable		3,985.00				3,985.00				3,985.00
J. Jay, Capital		54,075.00				54,075.00				54,075.00
J. Jay, Drawing	5,000.00				5,000.00				5,000.00	
Income from Services		21,000.00				21,000.00		21,000.00		
Wages Expense	2,670.00		*(c)* 260.00		2,930.00		2,930.00			
Rent Expense	1,950.00				1,950.00		1,950.00			
Supplies Expense	500.00				500.00		500.00			
Advertising Expense	450.00				450.00		450.00			
Utilities Expense	280.00				280.00		280.00			
	79,600.00	79,600.00								
Insurance Expense			*(a)* 175.00		175.00		175.00			
Depr. Exp., Equip.			*(b)* 540.00		540.00		540.00			
Wages Payable				*(c)* 260.00		260.00				260.00
			975.00	975.00	80,400.00	80,400.00	6,825.00	21,000.00	73,575.00	59,400.00
Net Income							14,175.00			14,175.00
							21,000.00	21,000.00	73,575.00	73,575.00

PRACTICE EXERCISE 4

Prepare an income statement, a statement of owner's equity, and a balance sheet for Fun and Games using the information from Practice Exercise 3.

PRACTICE EXERCISE 4 SOLUTION

Fun and Games
Income Statement
For Month Ended September 30, 20—

Revenue:		
Income from Services		$21,000
Expenses:		
Wages Expense	$2,930	
Rent Expense	1,950	
Supplies Expense	500	
Advertising Expense	450	
Utilities Expense	280	
Insurance Expense	175	
Depreciation Expense, Equipment	540	
Total Expenses		6,825
Net Income		$14,175

Fun and Games
Statement of Owner's Equity
For Month Ended September 30, 20—

J. Jay, Capital, September 1, 20—		$54,075
Investment during September	$ 0	
Net Income for September	14,175	
Subtotal	$14,175	
Less Withdrawals for September	5,000	
Increase in Capital		9,175
J. Jay, Capital, September 30, 20—		$63,250

Fun and Games
Balance Sheet
September 30, 20—

Assets		
Cash		$24,900
Accounts Receivable		5,750
Prepaid Insurance		1,925
Equipment	$36,000	
Less Accumulated Depreciation	1,080	34,920
Total Assets		$67,495
Liabilities		
Accounts Payable	$ 3,985	
Wages Payable	260	
Total Liabilities		$ 4,245
Owner's Equity		
J. Jay, Capital		63,250
Total Liabilities and Owner's Equity		$67,495

CHAPTER REVIEW

5 LEARNING OBJECTIVE

Journalize and post the adjusting entries.

Adjustments are a way of updating the ledger accounts. They are determined after the trial balance has been prepared. To change the balance of the ledger accounts, **adjusting entries** are needed in the general journal as evidence of the changes. The information for these entries are taken directly from the Adjustments columns of the work sheet, debiting and crediting exactly the same accounts and amounts in the journal entries. Therefore, each adjusting entry consists of an income statement account and a balance sheet account. When the adjusting entries are posted to the ledger accounts, the abbreviation "Adj." is written in the Item column of the ledger account.

PRACTICE EXERCISE 5

Journalize and post the adjusting entries for Fun and Games from Practice Exercise 3.

PRACTICE EXERCISE 5 SOLUTION

GENERAL JOURNAL PAGE 4

Date		Description	Post. Ref.	Debit	Credit
20—		Adjusting Entries			
Sept.	30	Insurance Expense	516	175 00	
		Prepaid Insurance	117		175 00
	30	Depr. Expense, Equipment	517	540 00	
		Accum. Depr., Equipment	125		540 00
	30	Wages Expense	511	260 00	
		Wages Payable	222		260 00

ACCOUNT Prepaid Insurance **ACCOUNT NO.** 117

Date		Item	Post. Ref.	Debit	Credit	Balance Debit	Balance Credit
20—							
Sept.	*15*		*2*	*2 100 00*		*2 100 00*	
	30	Adj.	4		175 00	1 925 00	

ACCOUNT Accumulated Depreciation, Equipment **ACCOUNT NO.** 125

Date		Item	Post. Ref.	Debit	Credit	Balance Debit	Balance Credit
20—							
		Bal.	*2*		*540 00*		*540 00*
Sept.	30	Adj.	4		540 00		1 080 00

CHAPTER REVIEW

ACCOUNT Wages Payable **ACCOUNT NO.** 222

Date		Item	Post. Ref.	Debit	Credit	Balance Debit	Balance Credit
20—							
Sept.	30	Adj.	4		260.00		260.00

ACCOUNT Wages Expense **ACCOUNT NO.** 511

Date		Item	Post. Ref.	Debit	Credit	Balance Debit	Balance Credit
20—							
Sept.	15		2	2,670.00		2,670.00	
	30	Adj.	4	260.00		2,930.00	

ACCOUNT Insurance Expense **ACCOUNT NO.** 516

Date		Item	Post. Ref.	Debit	Credit	Balance Debit	Balance Credit
20—							
Sept.	30	Adj.	4	175.00		175.00	

ACCOUNT Depreciation Expense, Equipment **ACCOUNT NO.** 517

Date		Item	Post. Ref.	Debit	Credit	Balance Debit	Balance Credit
20—							
Sept.	30	Adj.	4	540.00		540.00	

LEARNING OBJECTIVE 6

Prepare (a) an income statement involving more than one revenue account and a net loss, (b) a statement of owner's equity with an additional investment and either a net income or a net loss, (c) a balance sheet for a business having more than one accumulated depreciation account, and (d) a balance sheet containing the statement of owner's equity information.

(a) An income statement containing more than one revenue account requires an additional line for each type of revenue, followed by a total amount of revenue.

(b) A statement of owner's equity involving an additional investment requires a line for each additional investment beneath the beginning capital amount, followed by a total amount of investment.

(c) Businesses that have more than one type of asset that is subject to depreciation must show a separate account for each on the balance sheet.

(d) A balance sheet sometimes contains in the owner's equity section the information normally placed in a separate statement of owner's equity. The section would contain the beginning capital, plus the amount of net income (or minus the net loss), minus total withdrawals. The result is the same amount that would be calculated in a separate statement of owner's equity—the ending capital.

PRACTICE EXERCISE 6a

Using the following information, prepare an income statement for the month of September for The Swim Shack.

Depreciation Expense, Equipment	$ 525
Income from Concessions	4,000
Income from Services	1,500
Insurance Expense	200
Rent Expense	1,950
Utilities Expense	890
Wages Expense	3,580

PRACTICE EXERCISE 6a SOLUTION

The Swim Shack
Income Statement
For Month Ended September 30, 20—

Revenue:		
Income from Concessions	$4,000	
Income from Services	1,500	
Total Revenue		$ 5,500
Expenses:		
Wages Expense	$3,580	
Rent Expense	1,950	
Utilities Expense	890	
Insurance Expense	200	
Depreciation Expense, Equipment	525	
Total Expenses		7,145
Net Loss		$(1,645)

PRACTICE EXERCISE 6b

Using the following information, prepare a statement of owner's equity for the month of July for Stanley's Computers and Electronics.

P. Stanley, Capital, on July 1	$205,077
Additional investment by P. Stanley on July 21	15,500
Net loss for the month (from income statement)	1,850
Total withdrawals for the month	3,500

PRACTICE EXERCISE 6b SOLUTION

Stanley's Computers and Electronics
Statement of Owner's Equity
For Month Ended July 31, 20—

P. Stanley, Capital, July 1, 20—		$205,077
Investment during July	$15,500	
Net Loss for July	1,850	
Subtotal	$13,650	
Less Withdrawals for July	3,500	
Increase in Capital		10,150
P. Stanley, Capital, July 31, 20—		$215,227

CHAPTER REVIEW

PRACTICE EXERCISE 6c

Using the following information, prepare a year-end balance sheet for Moreland Clinic as of December 31.

Accounts Payable	$ 7,380
Accumulated Depreciation, Building	112,200
Accumulated Depreciation, Equipment	87,600
Building	339,100
Cash	31,520
Equipment	114,800
Land	25,000
W. Moreland, Capital	303,240

PRACTICE EXERCISE 6c SOLUTION

Moreland Clinic
Balance Sheet
December 31, 20—

Assets		
Cash		$ 31,520
Land		25,000
Building	$339,100	
Less Accumulated Depreciation	112,200	226,900
Equipment	$114,800	
Less Accumulated Depreciation	87,600	27,200
Total Assets		$310,620
Liabilities		
Accounts Payable		$ 7,380
Owner's Equity		
W. Moreland, Capital		303,240
Total Liabilities and Owner's Equity		$310,620

PRACTICE EXERCISE 6d

Complete a balance sheet at the end of July for Stanley's Computers and Electronics by (a) using the following information for the Assets and Liabilities sections, and (b) including the information from the statement of owner's equity you created in Practice Exercise 6b for the Owner's Equity section.

Accounts Payable	$ 4,030
Accounts Receivable	4,725
Accumulated Depreciation, Building	1,420
Accumulated Depreciation, Equipment	600
Building	119,700
Cash	47,270
Equipment	48,500
Prepaid Insurance	1,500
Wages Payable	418

CHAPTER REVIEW

PRACTICE EXERCISE 6d SOLUTION

Stanley's Computers and Electronics
Balance Sheet
July 31, 20—

Assets		
Cash		$ 47,270
Accounts Receivable		4,725
Prepaid Insurance		1,500
Building	$119,700	
Less Accumulated Depreciation	1,420	118,280
Equipment	$ 48,500	
Less Accumulated Depreciation	600	47,900
Total Assets		$219,675
Liabilities		
Accounts Payable	$ 4,030	
Wages Payable	418	
Total Liabilities		$ 4,448
Owner's Equity		
P. Stanley, Capital, July 1, 20—		$205,077
Investment during July	$ 15,500	
Net Loss for July	1,850	
Subtotal	$ 13,650	
Less Withdrawals for July	3,500	
Increase in Capital		10,150
P. Stanley, Capital, July 31, 20—		$215,227
Total Liabilities and Owner's Equity		$219,675

Glossary

Accounting cycle The sequence of steps in the accounting process completed during the fiscal period. *(p. 129)*

Accrual Recognition of an expense or a revenue that has been incurred or earned but has not yet been recorded. *(p. 136)*

Accrued wages Unpaid wages owed to employees for the time between the end of the last pay period and the end of the fiscal period. *(p. 136)*

Adjusting entries Entries that bring the books up to date at the end of the fiscal period. *(p. 145)*

Adjustments Internal transactions that bring ledger accounts up to date, as a planned part of the accounting procedure. They are first recorded in the Adjustments columns of the work sheet when using a manual accounting system. *(p. 131)*

Book value or carrying value The cost of an asset minus the accumulated depreciation. *(p. 134)*

Contra account An account that is contrary to, or a deduction from, another account; for example, Accumulated Depreciation, Equipment is listed as a deduction from Equipment. *(p. 134)*

Depreciation An expense based on the expectation that an asset will gradually decline in usefulness due to time, wear and tear, or obsolescence; the cost of the asset is therefore spread out over its estimated useful life. A part of depreciation expense is apportioned to each fiscal period. *(p. 133)*

Fiscal period Any period of time covering a complete accounting cycle, generally consisting of twelve consecutive months. *(p. 128)*

Fiscal year A fiscal period consisting of twelve consecutive months. *(p. 128)*

Matching principle The principle that the revenue for one time period is matched up with the related expenses for the same time period. *(p. 147)*

Mixed accounts Certain accounts that appear on the trial balance with balances that are partly income statement amounts and partly balance sheet amounts—for example, Prepaid Insurance and Insurance Expense. *(p. 138)*

Straight-line depreciation A means of calculating depreciation in which the cost of an asset, less any trade-in value, is allocated evenly over the useful life of the asset. *(p. 133)*

Work sheet A working paper used by accountants to record necessary adjustments and provide up-to-date account balances needed to prepare the financial statements. *(p. 129)*

CHAPTER ASSIGNMENTS

Discussion Questions

1. What is the purpose of a work sheet in a manual system?
2. What is the purpose of adjusting entries?
3. What is a mixed account? A contra account? Give an example of each.
4. In which column of the work sheet—Income Statement (IS) or Balance Sheet (BS)—would the adjusted balances of the following accounts appear?

Account	IS or BS?	Account	IS or BS?
a. Prepaid Insurance	BS	e. Accumulated Depreciation, Equipment	BS
b. Wages Expense	IS	f. J. Karl, Drawing	BS
c. Wages Payable	BS	g. Insurance Expense	IS
d. Income from Services	IS	h. Depreciation Expense, Equipment	IS

5. Why is it necessary to make an adjustment if wages for work performed for the pay period Monday through Friday are paid on Friday and the accounting period ends on a Wednesday?
6. Define depreciation as it relates to a van you bought for your business.
7. Define an internal transaction and provide an example.
8. Why is it necessary to journalize and post adjusting entries?

Exercises

PRACTICE EXERCISE 2

EXERCISE 4-1 List the following classifications of accounts in all the columns in which they appear on the work sheet, with the exception of the Adjustments columns. (Example: Assets.)

Assets	Capital
Accumulated Depreciation (with previous balance)	Drawing
	Revenue
Liabilities	Expenses

Write Net Income in the appropriate columns.

Account Name	Trial Balance		Adjustments		Adjusted Trial Balance		Income Statement		Balance Sheet	
	Debit	Credit	Debit	Credit	Debit	Credit	Debit	Credit	Debit	Credit
	Assets				Assets				Assets	
Net Income										

EXERCISE 4-2 Classify each of the accounts listed below as assets (A), liabilities (L), owner's equity (OE), revenue (R), or expenses (E). Indicate the normal debit or credit balance of each account. Indicate whether each account will appear in the Income Statement columns (IS) or the Balance Sheet columns (BS) of the work sheet. Item 0 is given as an example.

PRACTICE EXERCISE 2

Account	Classification	Normal Balance	IS or BS Columns
0. Example: Wages Expense	E	Debit	IS
a. Prepaid Insurance			
b. Accounts Payable			
c. Wages Payable			
d. T. Bristol, Capital			
e. Accumulated Depreciation, Building			
f. T. Bristol, Drawing			
g. Rental Income			
h. Equipment			
i. Depreciation Expense, Equipment			
j. Supplies Expense			

EXERCISE 4-3 Place a check mark next to any account(s) requiring adjustment. Explain why those accounts must be adjusted.

✓	Account Name (in trial balance order)	Reason for Adjusting This Account
	a. Cash	
	b. Prepaid Insurance	
	c. Equipment	
	d. Accumulated Depreciation, Equipment	
	e. Wages Payable	
	f. R. Wesley, Capital	
	g. R. Wesley, Drawing	
	h. Wages Expense	

LO 3

EXERCISE 4-4 A partial work sheet for Marge's Place is on page 164. Prepare the following adjustments on this work sheet for the month ended June 30, 20—.

PRACTICE EXERCISE 3

a. Expired or used-up insurance, $450.
b. Depreciation expense on equipment, $750 (remember to credit the Accumulated Depreciation account for equipment, not Equipment).
c. Wages accrued or earned since the last payday, $380 (owed and to be paid on the next payday).

Marge's Place
Work Sheet
For Month Ended June 30, 20—

Account Name	Trial Balance		Adjustments	
	Debit	Credit	Debit	Credit
Cash	4,620.00			
Prepaid Insurance	1,800.00			
Equipment	4,880.00			
Accumulated Depreciation, Equipment		1,350.00		
Accounts Payable		2,539.00		
M. Benson, Capital		4,544.00		
M. Benson, Drawing	2,000.00			
Income from Services		6,937.00		
Rent Expense	1,086.00			
Supplies Expense	256.00			
Wages Expense	660.00			
Miscellaneous Expense	68.00			
	15,370.00	15,370.00		

PRACTICE EXERCISE 3

EXERCISE 4-5 Complete the work sheet for Ramey Company, dated December 31, 20—, through the adjusted trial balance using the following adjustment information:

a. Expired or used-up insurance, $460.
b. Depreciation expense on equipment, $870 (remember to credit the Accumulated Depreciation account for equipment, not Equipment).
c. Wages accrued or earned since the last payday, $120 (owed and to be paid on the next payday).

Ramey Company
Work Sheet
For Year Ended December 31, 20—

Account Name	Trial Balance		Adjustments		Adjusted Trial Balance	
	Debit	Credit	Debit	Credit	Debit	Credit
Cash	5,620.00					
Prepaid Insurance	1,200.00					
Equipment	4,678.00					
Accumulated Depr., Equip.		1,556.00				
Accounts Payable		1,875.00				
S. Ramey, Capital		6,026.00				
S. Ramey, Drawing	1,700.00					
Service Fees		5,836.00				
Rent Expense	965.00					
Supplies Expense	267.00					
Wages Expense	765.00					
Miscellaneous Expense	98.00					
	15,293.00	15,293.00				

PRACTICE EXERCISE 5

EXERCISE 4-6 Journalize the three adjusting entries from the partial work sheet below for Brady Company for the month ended May 31. (*Hint:* Use what you know about opening new accounts for adjusting entries.)

Brady Company
Work Sheet
For Month Ended May 31, 20—

Account Name	Income Statement Debit	Income Statement Credit	Balance Sheet Debit	Balance Sheet Credit
Cash			5731 00	
Prepaid Insurance			841 00	
Equipment			4832 00	
Accumulated Depreciation, Equipment				1720 00
Accounts Payable				1085 00
S. Brady, Capital				6800 00
S. Brady, Drawing			2150 00	
Professional Fees		9673 00		
Salary Expense	3787 00			
Rent Expense	1200 00			
Supplies Expense	284 00			
Miscellaneous Expense	134 00			
Insurance Expense	285 00			
Depreciation Expense, Equipment	364 00			
Salaries Payable				330 00
	6054 00	9673 00	13554 00	9935 00
Net Income	3619 00			3619 00
	9673 00	9673 00	13554 00	13554 00

PRACTICE EXERCISE 5

EXERCISE 4-7 Journalize the adjustments for Newkirk Company as of August 31.

Newkirk Company
Work Sheet
For Month Ended August 31, 20—

Account Name	Trial Balance Debit	Trial Balance Credit	Adjustments Debit	Adjustments Credit
Cash	3871 00			
Prepaid Insurance	3973 00			(a) 365 00
Equipment	3678 00			
Accumulated Depreciation, Equipment		645 00		(b) 206 00
Accounts Payable		1843 00		
J. Newkirk, Capital		10752 00		
J. Newkirk, Drawing	3000 00			
Service Fees		5683 00		
Rent Expense	1795 00			
Supplies Expense	663 00			
Wages Expense	1865 00		(c) 268 00	
Miscellaneous Expense	78 00			
	18923 00	18923 00		
Insurance Expense			(a) 365 00	
Depreciation Expense, Equipment			(b) 206 00	
Wages Payable				(c) 268 00
			839 00	839 00

CHAPTER ASSIGNMENTS

PRACTICE EXERCISE 5

EXERCISE 4-8 Journalize the following adjusting entries that were included on the work sheet for the month ended December 31. Assume the financial statements have been prepared.

Dec. 31 Salaries for three days are unpaid at December 31, $2,700. Salaries are $4,500 for a five-day week.

31 Insurance was bought on September 1 for $3,600 for 12 months' coverage. Four months' coverage has expired, $1,200.

31 Depreciation for the month on equipment, $50, based on an asset costing $3,200 with a trade-in value of $200 and an estimated life of 5 years.

Problem Set A

For additional help, see the demonstration problem at the beginning of each chapter in your Working Papers.

PROBLEM 4-1A The trial balance of Morgan's Insurance Agency as of September 30, after the firm has completed its first month of operations, is as follows:

Morgan's Insurance Company
Trial Balance
September 30, 20—

Account Name	Debit	Credit
Cash	3,337	
Accounts Receivable	1,428	
Prepaid Insurance	775	
Office Equipment	5,146	
Accounts Payable		1,367
S. Morgan, Capital		9,528
S. Morgan, Drawing	1,000	
Commissions Earned		2,843
Rent Expense	885	
Supplies Expense	487	
Travel Expense	388	
Utilities Expense	227	
Miscellaneous Expense	65	
	13,738	13,738

Check Figure
Net Loss, $259

Required

1. Record the amounts in the Trial Balance columns of the work sheet.
2. Complete the work sheet by making the following adjustments and lettering each adjustment:
   a. Expired or used-up insurance, $300.
   b. Depreciation expense on office equipment, $750.

PROBLEM 4-2A The completed work sheet for Chelsey Decorators for the month of March is in your Working Papers.

Check Figure
Total Assets, $14,471

Required

1. Prepare an income statement.
2. Prepare a statement of owner's equity. Assume no additional investments were made in March.
3. Prepare a balance sheet.
4. Journalize the adjusting entries.

LO 3,5

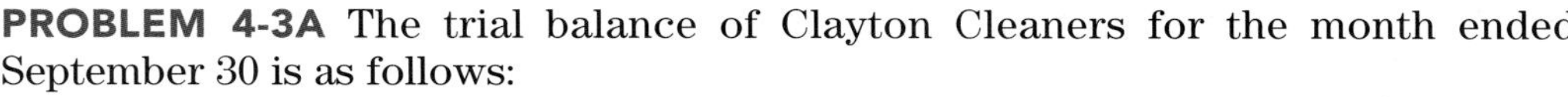

PROBLEM 4-3A The trial balance of Clayton Cleaners for the month ended September 30 is as follows:

Clayton Cleaners
Trial Balance
September 30, 20—

Account Name	Debit	Credit
Cash	2,589	
Prepaid Insurance	1,136	
Equipment	21,752	
Accumulated Depreciation, Equipment		14,357
Accounts Payable		2,647
K. Clayton, Capital		28,169
K. Clayton, Drawing	21,359	
Income from Services		40,850
Wages Expense	23,983	
Rent Expense	11,673	
Utilities Expense	1,254	
Supplies Expense	652	
Telephone Expense	1,144	
Miscellaneous Expense	481	
	86,023	86,023

Data for the adjustments are as follows:

a. Expired or used-up insurance, $800.
b. Depreciation expense on equipment, $2,700.
c. Wages accrued or earned since the last payday, $585 (owed and to be paid on the next payday).

Required

1. Complete a work sheet.
2. Journalize the adjusting entries.

Check Figure
Net Loss, $2,422

LO 3,4,5,6

PROBLEM 4-4A The trial balance for Game Time on July 31 is as follows:

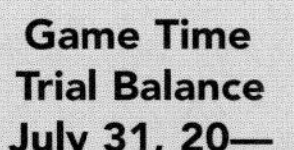

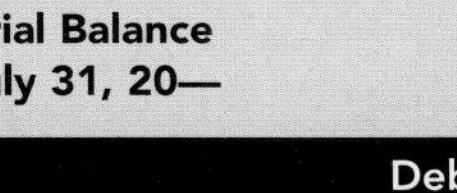

Game Time
Trial Balance
July 31, 20—

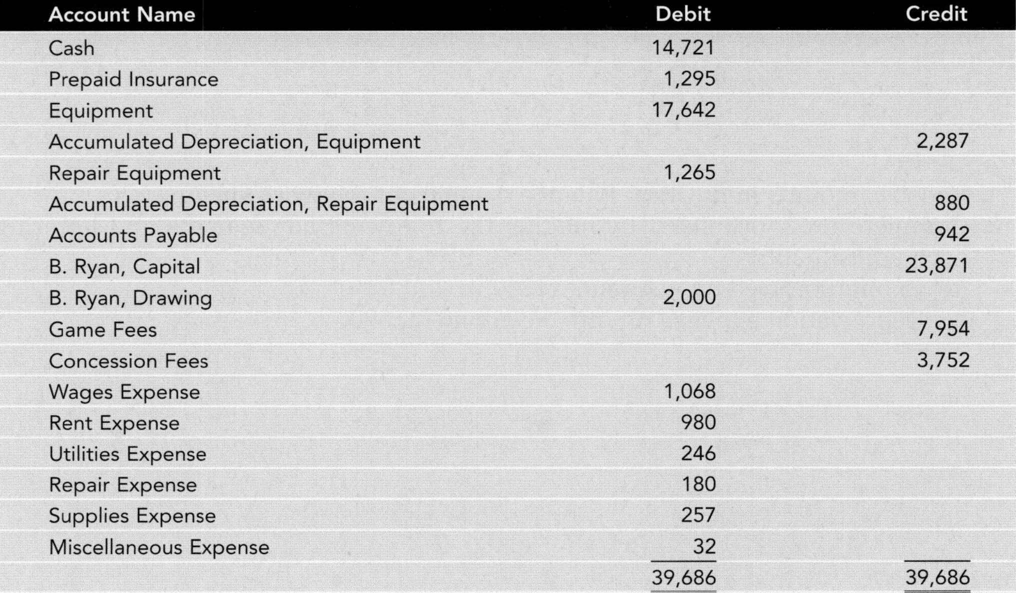

Account Name	Debit	Credit
Cash	14,721	
Prepaid Insurance	1,295	
Equipment	17,642	
Accumulated Depreciation, Equipment		2,287
Repair Equipment	1,265	
Accumulated Depreciation, Repair Equipment		880
Accounts Payable		942
B. Ryan, Capital		23,871
B. Ryan, Drawing	2,000	
Game Fees		7,954
Concession Fees		3,752
Wages Expense	1,068	
Rent Expense	980	
Utilities Expense	246	
Repair Expense	180	
Supplies Expense	257	
Miscellaneous Expense	32	
	39,686	39,686

Data for month-end adjustments are as follows:

a. Expired or used-up insurance, $480.
b. Depreciation expense on equipment, $850.
c. Depreciation expense on repair equipment, $120.
d. Wages accrued or earned since the last payday, $525 (owed and to be paid on the next payday).

Check Figure
Net Income, $6,968

Required

1. Complete a work sheet for the month.
2. Prepare an income statement, a statement of owner's equity, and a balance sheet. Assume that no additional investments were made during July.
3. Journalize the adjusting entries.

Problem Set B

For additional help, see the demonstration problem at the beginning of each chapter in your Working Papers.

PROBLEM 4-1B The trial balance for Mason's Insurance Agency as of August 31, after the firm has completed its first month of operations, is as follows:

Mason's Insurance Company
Trial Balance
August 31, 20—

Account Name	Debit	Credit
Cash	3,527	
Accounts Receivable	1,219	
Prepaid Insurance	1,362	
Office Equipment	3,939	
Accounts Payable		2,071
C. Mason, Capital		9,020
C. Mason, Drawing	1,900	
Commissions Earned		3,520
Rent Expense	1,695	
Supplies Expense	492	
Travel Expense	225	
Utilities Expense	198	
Miscellaneous Expense	54	
	14,611	14,611

Check Figure
Net Loss, $304

Required

1. Record amounts in the Trial Balance columns of the work sheet.
2. Complete the work sheet by making the following adjustments and lettering each adjustment:
   a. Expired or used-up insurance, $260.
   b. Depreciation expense on office equipment, $900.

PROBLEM 4-2B The completed work sheet for Juarez Design for the month of March is in your Working Papers.

Check Figure
Total Assets, $21,817

Required

1. Prepare an income statement.
2. Prepare a statement of owner's equity. Assume that no additional investments were made in March.
3. Prepare a balance sheet.
4. Journalize the adjusting entries.

PROBLEM 4-3B The trial balance of The New Decors for the month ended September 30 is as follows:

The New Decors
Trial Balance
September 30, 20—

Account Name	Debit	Credit
Cash	4,378	
Prepaid Insurance	1,345	
Equipment	30,978	
Accumulated Depreciation, Equipment		15,235
Accounts Payable		3,751
R. Becker, Capital		44,208
R. Becker, Drawing	20,445	
Income from Services		44,791
Wages Expense	29,761	
Rent Expense	15,932	
Supplies Expense	1,864	
Utilities Expense	1,573	
Telephone Expense	1,271	
Miscellaneous Expense	438	
	107,985	107,985

Data for the adjustments are as follows:

a. Expired or used-up insurance, $425.
b. Depreciation expense on equipment, $2,750.
c. Wages accrued or earned since the last payday, $475 (owed and to be paid on the next payday).

Check Figure
Net Loss, $9,698

Required

1. Complete a work sheet.
2. Journalize the adjusting entries.

PROBLEM 4-4B The trial balance for Harris Pitch and Putt on June 30 is as follows:

Harris Pitch and Putt
Trial Balance
June 30, 20—

Account Name	Debit	Credit
Cash	5,532	
Prepaid Insurance	1,284	
Equipment	21,687	
Accumulated Depreciation, Equipment		1,478
Repair Equipment	5,289	
Accumulated Depreciation, Repair Equipment		1,285
Accounts Payable		860
W. Harris, Capital		23,110
W. Harris, Drawing	2,565	
Golf Fees		11,487
Concession Fees		3,763
Wages Expense	3,163	
Rent Expense	1,350	
Utilities Expense	457	
Repair Expense	171	
Supplies Expense	246	
Miscellaneous Expense	239	
	41,983	41,983

Data for month-end adjustments are as follows:

a. Expired or used-up insurance, $380.
b. Depreciation expense on equipment, $1,950.
c. Depreciation expense on repair equipment, $1,650.
d. Wages accrued or earned since the last payday, $585 (owed and to be paid on the next payday).

Check Figure
Net Income, $5,059

Required

1. Complete a work sheet for the month.
2. Prepare an income statement, a statement of owner's equity, and a balance sheet. Assume that no additional investments were made during June.
3. Journalize the adjusting entries.

ACTIVITIES

CONSIDER AND COMMUNICATE

You are the bookkeeper for a small but thriving business. You have asked the owner for the information you need in order to make adjusting entries for depreciation, insurance, and wages. He says he's really busy, and what you've done so far is "close enough." Explain the need for adjusting entries and how they can affect his balance sheet and the "bottom line" on the income statement.

A QUESTION OF ETHICS

Your client is preparing financial statements to show the bank. You know that he has incurred a refrigeration repair expense during the month, but you see no such expense on the books. When you question the client, he tells you that he has not paid the $1,255 bill yet. Your client is on the accrual basis of accounting. He does not want the refrigeration repair expense on the books as of the end of the month because he wants his profits to look good for the bank. Is your client behaving ethically by suggesting that the refrigeration repair expense should not be booked until the $1,255 is paid? Are you behaving ethically if you go along with the client's request? What principle is involved here?

CRITICAL THINKING

Your supervisor just finished a work sheet for the month of June, but all the columns except the following were destroyed by a spilled latte. You have been asked to journalize the adjusting entries using the surviving partial work sheet.

	Income Statement		Balance Sheet	
Account Name	Debit	Credit	Debit	Credit
Cash			8,476.00	
Accounts Receivable			1,486.00	
Equipment			12,367.00	
Accumulated Depreciation, Equipment				3,610.00
Accounts Payable				2,813.00
G. Kramer, Capital				11,707.00
G. Kramer, Drawing			1,100.00	
Income from Services		11,216.00		
Rent Expense	1,400.00			
Supplies Expense	1,110.00			
Wages Expense	2,467.00			
Insurance Expense	210.00			
Depreciation Expense, Equipment	750.00			
Wages Payable				620.00
	5,937.00	11,216.00	24,029.00	18,750.00
Net Income	5,279.00			5,279.00
	11,216.00	11,216.00	24,029.00	24,029.00

All About You Spa

Adjustments

Although you printed the trial balance and financial statements to get an idea of how All About You Spa is doing, some accounts are not accurate. You need to make adjusting entries to provide a clearer picture of how the spa is doing.

Month-end adjusting entries

HOW TO COMPUTE THE ADJUSTMENTS

Compute the adjustment amounts for the month of June, using the following information:

Adjustment (a): Liability insurance for six months was purchased during the first days of the month. That protection for one month has been used or expended (Insurance Expense), and the asset (Prepaid Insurance) is not worth what the balance sheet says. Therefore, since All About You Spa paid $960 for a six-month policy and one month of the coverage has been used, $160 of that policy is no longer an asset and represents an expense to the company. How was the figure $160 computed?

Adjustments (b) and (c): Spa equipment and office equipment have depreciated. That means that they have been in use for a month and have, for accounting purposes, lost some usefulness. This is an estimate, of course, which allows us to expense the depreciation and, in effect, lowers the book value (value on the books) of both types of equipment.

(b): The owner, Anika Valli, invested spa equipment totaling $7,393 in the business ($3,158 of her own spa equipment, plus $4,235 of new spa equipment purchased). The spa equipment will be depreciated using the straight-line method. The spa equipment is estimated to have a trade-in or salvage value of $3,500 and is expected to last five years. Therefore, the spa equipment is estimated to have depreciated $64.88 for the month of June. How was the figure $64.88 computed? Remember, you want to compute the depreciation for one month, not one year.

(c): Anika Valli purchased office equipment totaling $1,150. The office equipment will be depreciated using the straight-line method. The office equipment is estimated to have a salvage (trade-in) value of $550 and is expected to last five years. Therefore, the office equipment is estimated to have depreciated $10 for the month of June. How was the figure $10 computed? Remember, you want to compute the depreciation for one month, not one year.

Adjustment (d): All About You Spa owes one day of wages to its employees. The month's total wages paid in June amounted to $7,390. The employees worked 21 days, but were paid for only 20 days because the payday for the last day worked is in the next pay period. Therefore, the spa owes them one day's pay ($369.50), which also needs to be expensed. How was the figure $369.50 computed?

WHAT TO DO WITH THE ADJUSTMENT AMOUNTS

Follow these steps to enter the adjusting entries in your general ledger software.

1. If you are completing a work sheet (separately on paper or spreadsheet software), enter the adjusting entries and complete the work sheet by extending totals to the Adjusted Trial Balance columns and those totals to either the Income Statement or Balance Sheet columns. Total and compute the adjusted net income or net loss.

2. Open the file entitled ***All_About_You_Spa_Ch04.IA7***. Enter your name when prompted and click ***OK***. Select "Yes" or "No" as desired when asked if you want to open on-screen instructions and check figures.
3. Click on the ***Save As*** toolbar button. When the Save As window appears, select the folder in which you wish to save your data files (if not already selected). In the File Name box, key ***All_About_You_Ch04_Your_Name.IA7*** (for example, All_About_You_Spa_Ch04_John_Doe.IA7) to identify the file containing your work. Click on the ***Save*** button.
4. You need to add six new accounts to the Chart of Accounts. Click on the ***Accts.*** toolbar button. On the next available line, key "125" in the Account column and "Accum. Depr., Spa Equip." in the Account Title column. (Note that abbreviation is necessary because there is a limited number of characters allowed per account title.) Click on the ***Add Account*** button. The new account will be inserted in account number order in the Chart of Accounts. Follow the same procedure for the remaining five accounts to be entered:

   129 Accum. Depr., Office Eq.
   212 Wages Payable
   518 Insurance Expense
   519 Depr. Exp., Spa Equip.
   520 Depr. Exp., Office Eq.

   If you make a mistake and need to go back and change an account title, click on the title, key the change, and click on the ***Change*** button (The Add Account button becomes activated as a Change button when an existing account is selected). If you enter a wrong account number, the account will need to be deleted and re-entered. Select the account and click on the ***Delete*** button (but note that an account with an existing balance may not be deleted).
5. Click on the ***Journal*** toolbar button and key the adjusting journal entries in the General Journal. Follow these steps for each entry:
   (a) Key the date, June 30, in the Date column.
   (b) Enter a reference of "Adj.Ent." in the Refer. column (this is required for generating the Adjusting Journal Entries report later).
   (c) Enter the debit and credit parts of the entry as you learned to do in Chapter 3.
6. Display the adjusting journal entries. Click on the ***Reports*** toolbar button. Click on ***Journals*** and ***General Journal*** to choose a report to display. Click on ***Customize Journal Report***. In the Reference drop-down list, choose "Adj. Ent." and then click the ***OK*** button to display the Adjusting Journal Entries report. To print the report, click on the ***Print*** button.
7. Review your entries and make corrections to them, if necessary. In the General Journal window, click on the entry to correct, key the correction(s), and click on the ***Post*** button (or press **Enter**).
8. Display the Trial Balance report. Click on the ***Reports*** toolbar button. Click on ***Ledger Reports*** and select ***Trial Balance*** to choose the report to display. Be sure the run date is set to June 30. To print the report, click on the ***Print*** button at the bottom of the report window.
9. Display the income statement. Click on the ***Reports*** toolbar button. Click on ***Financial Statements*** and select ***Income Statement*** to choose the report to display. To print the report, click on the ***Print*** button.
10. Display the statement of owner's equity. Click on the ***Reports*** toolbar button. Click on ***Financial Statements*** and select ***Statement of Owner's Equity*** to choose the report to display. To print the report, click on the ***Print*** button.
11. Display the balance sheet. Click on the ***Reports*** toolbar button. Click on ***Financial Statements*** and select ***Balance Sheet*** to choose the report to display. To print the report, click on the ***Print*** button.
12. Compare the statements before adjustments (that you generated for All About You Spa in Chapter 3) with the statements after adjustments. What do you find?

Check Figures
8. Adjusted trial balance total, $39,197.38
9. Net income, $6,776.62
10. A. Valli, Capital, ending balance, $23,084.62
11. Total assets, $25,702.12

5 Closing Entries and the Post-Closing Trial Balance

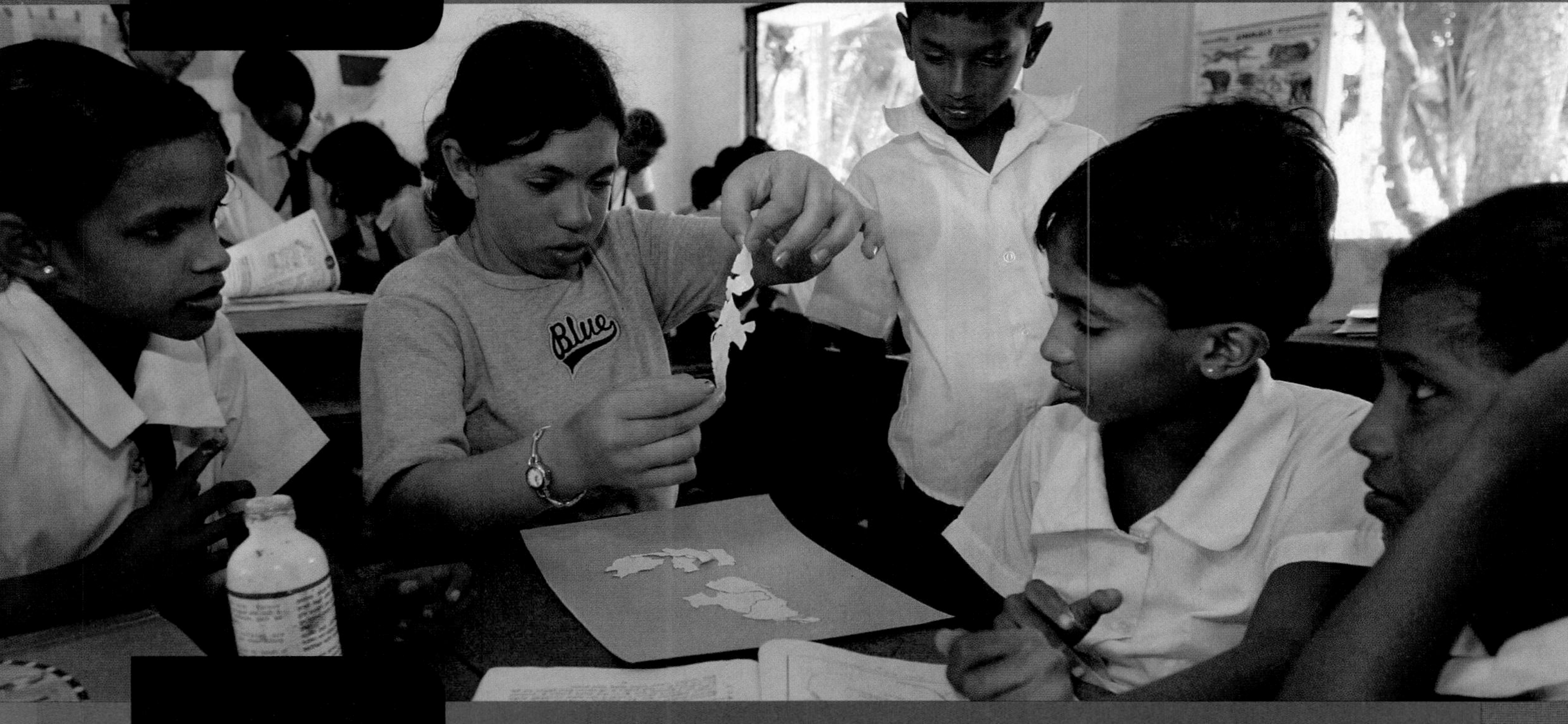

WHY IT MATTERS

REAL GAP EXPERIENCE, Tunbridge Wells, Kent (UK)

Rather than going directly to college, some students take time off to travel abroad, learn new skills, or volunteer. This period is known as a "gap year." Real Gap Experience provides hundreds of gap year traveling opportunities in over 45 countries around the world. The company offers everything from volunteering to build houses in Guatemala to a paid teaching job in China to a year-long, around-the-world trip.

What does this have to do with accounting, and why is it important? Every company needs to keep a record of its financial activities so that financial statements can be presented and used for decision making. Real Gap Experience's accounting records are most likely computerized, but the company's employees will still make adjustments if they are using the accrual basis of accounting. They will also need to prepare the accounting records for the next year of business. This process is known as the closing process, which you will learn about in this chapter.

LEARNING OBJECTIVES

After you have completed this chapter, you will be able to do the following:

1. *List the steps in the accounting cycle.*
2. *Journalize and post closing entries for a service enterprise.*
3. *Prepare a post-closing trial balance.*
4. *Define the following methods of accounting: cash basis and accrual basis.*
5. *Prepare interim statements.*

ACCOUNTING LANGUAGE

Accrual basis of accounting *(p. 187)*
Cash basis of accounting *(p. 187)*
Closing entries *(p. 178)*
Income Summary account *(p. 179)*
Interim statements *(p. 187)*
Nominal (temporary-equity) accounts *(p. 184)*
Post-closing trial balance *(p. 186)*
Real (permanent) accounts *(p. 184)*

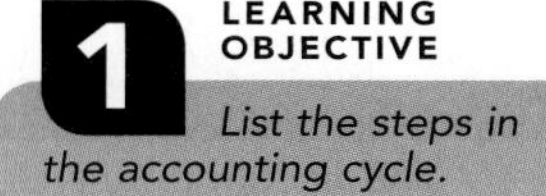

1 LEARNING OBJECTIVE *List the steps in the accounting cycle.*

Let's review the steps in the accounting cycle for an entire fiscal period. Remember that a fiscal period is generally twelve consecutive months, but it can also consist of other time frames like three months or six months.

STEP 1. Analyze source documents and record business transactions in a journal.
STEP 2. Post journal entries to the accounts in the ledger.
STEP 3. Prepare a trial balance.
STEP 4. Gather adjustment data and record the adjusting entries on a work sheet.
STEP 5. Complete the work sheet.
STEP 6. Prepare financial statements from the data on the work sheet.
STEP 7. Journalize and post the adjusting entries from the data on the work sheet.
STEP 8. Journalize and post the closing entries.
STEP 9. Prepare a post-closing trial balance.

This chapter explains the procedure for completing the final steps: journalizing and posting the closing entries and preparing the post-closing trial balance.

Adjusting entries, closing entries, and a post-closing trial balance are prepared at the end of a fiscal period. The number of months in a fiscal period varies. To introduce you to these final steps in the accounting cycle, we assume here that the fiscal period for Conner's Whitewater Adventures is one month. We make this assumption so that we can thoroughly cover the material and give you a chance to practice its application. The entire accounting cycle is outlined in Figure 1.

CLOSING ENTRIES

To help you understand the reason for the closing entries, let's take a look at a version of the fundamental accounting equation:

Assets = Liabilities + Capital + Revenue − Expenses − Drawing

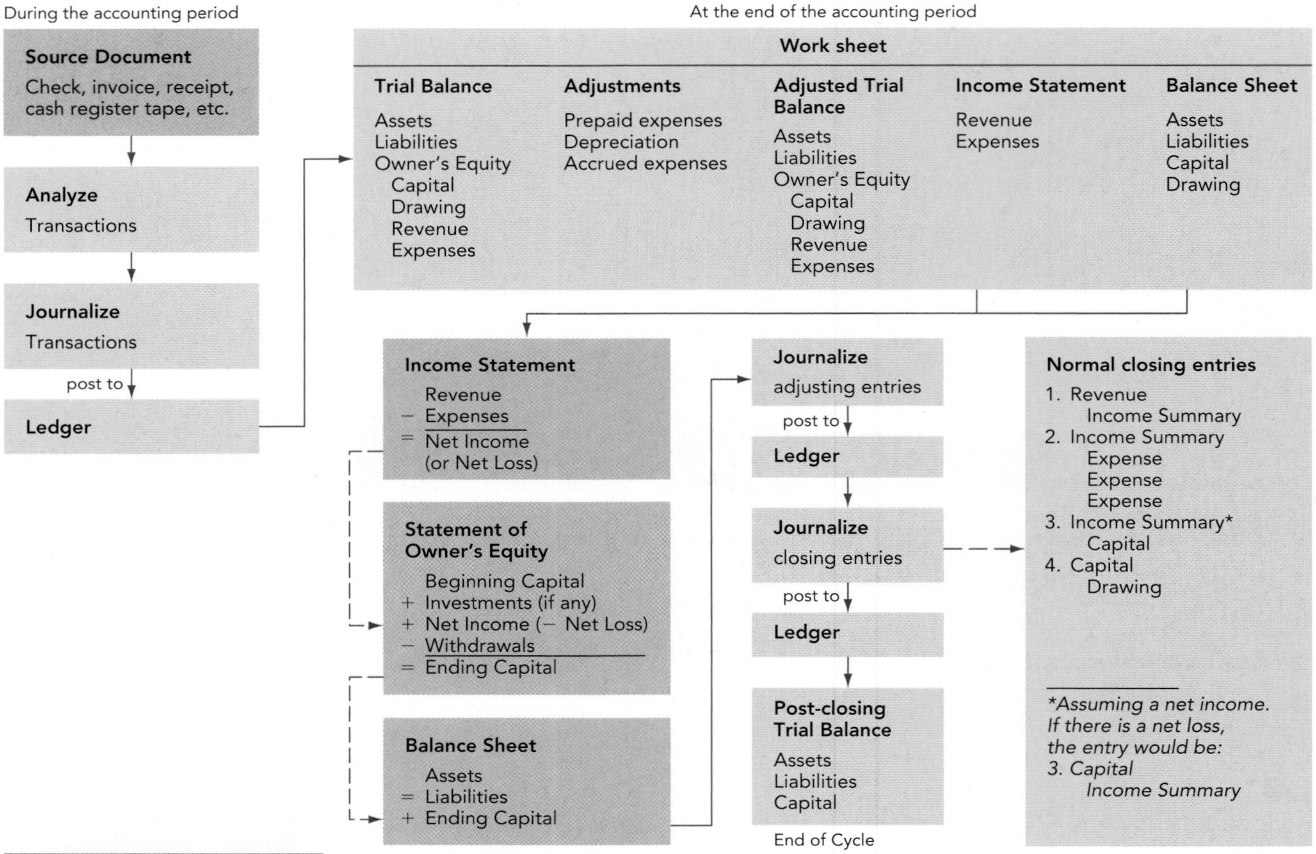

During the accounting period

Source Document
Check, invoice, receipt, cash register tape, etc.

Analyze
Transactions

Journalize
Transactions

post to

Ledger

At the end of the accounting period

Work sheet

Trial Balance	Adjustments	Adjusted Trial Balance	Income Statement	Balance Sheet
Assets	Prepaid expenses	Assets	Revenue	Assets
Liabilities	Depreciation	Liabilities	Expenses	Liabilities
Owner's Equity	Accrued expenses	Owner's Equity		Capital
Capital		Capital		Drawing
Drawing		Drawing		
Revenue		Revenue		
Expenses		Expenses		

Income Statement
Revenue
− Expenses
= Net Income
(or Net Loss)

Statement of Owner's Equity
Beginning Capital
+ Investments (if any)
+ Net Income (− Net Loss)
− Withdrawals
= Ending Capital

Balance Sheet
Assets
= Liabilities
+ Ending Capital

Journalize
adjusting entries

post to

Ledger

Journalize
closing entries

post to

Ledger

Post-closing Trial Balance
Assets
Liabilities
Capital

End of Cycle

Normal closing entries
1. Revenue
    Income Summary
2. Income Summary
    Expense
    Expense
    Expense
3. Income Summary*
    Capital
4. Capital
    Drawing

**Assuming a net income. If there is a net loss, the entry would be:*
3. Capital
Income Summary

FIGURE 1
The accounting cycle

We know that the income statement, as stated in the third line of its heading, covers a period of time. The income statement consists of revenue minus expenses for this period of time only. So, when the next fiscal period begins, we should start with zero balances. We start over again each period.

Closing entries empty or zero out temporary owner's equity accounts and prepare the accounts for the new accounting period—much like when you empty the information from your tax folders one year so that the folders can be filled with the new year's revenue and expense receipts.

Purpose of Closing Entries

This brings us to the *purpose* of the **closing entries**, which is to close (or zero) the temporary-equity or nominal accounts (revenue, expense, and Drawing accounts). We do this because their balances apply to only one fiscal period. Closing entries are made after the last adjusting entry and after the financial statements have been prepared. With the coming of the next fiscal period, we want to start from zero, recording revenue and expenses for the new fiscal period. The closing entries also update the owner's Capital account.

Accountants also refer to closing the accounts as *clearing the accounts*. For income tax purposes, this is certainly understandable. No one wants to pay income tax more than once on the same income, and the Internal Revenue Service doesn't allow you to count an expense more than once. So now we have this:

$$\text{Assets} = \text{Liabilities} + \text{Capital} + \underset{}{\overset{\text{(closed)}}{\cancel{\text{Revenue}}}} - \overset{\text{(closed)}}{\cancel{\text{Expenses}}} - \overset{\text{(closed)}}{\cancel{\text{Drawing}}}$$

The assets, liabilities, and owner's Capital accounts remain open. The balance sheet gives the present balances of these accounts. The accountant carries the asset, liability, and Capital account balances over to the next fiscal period.

Procedure for Closing

2 LEARNING OBJECTIVE

Journalize and post closing entries for a service enterprise.

The procedure for closing is simply to balance off the account; in other words, to make the balance *equal to zero*. This meets our objective, which is to start from zero in the next fiscal period. Let's illustrate this first with T accounts. Suppose an account to be closed has a debit balance of $870. To make the balance equal to zero, we *credit* the account for $870.

Debit		Credit	
Balance	870	Closing	870

Remember

The matching principle is why we close revenue, expense, and Drawing accounts.

Now suppose an account to be closed has a credit balance of $1,400. To make the balance equal to zero, we *debit* the account for $1,400.

Debit		Credit	
Closing	1,400	Balance	1,400

Remember, every entry must have at least one debit and one credit. So, to record the other half of the closing entry, we bring into existence the **Income Summary account**. The Income Summary account does not have plus and minus signs, just debit and credit.

There are four steps in the closing procedure:

STEP 1. Close the revenue account(s) into Income Summary.

STEP 2. Close the expense accounts into Income Summary.

STEP 3. Close the Income Summary account into the Capital account, transferring the net income or net loss to the Capital account.

STEP 4. Close the Drawing account into the Capital account.

To illustrate, we return to Conner's Whitewater Adventures. For the purpose of the illustration, assume that Conner's Whitewater Adventures' fiscal period consists of one month. We have the following T account balances in the revenue and expense accounts after the adjustments have been posted.

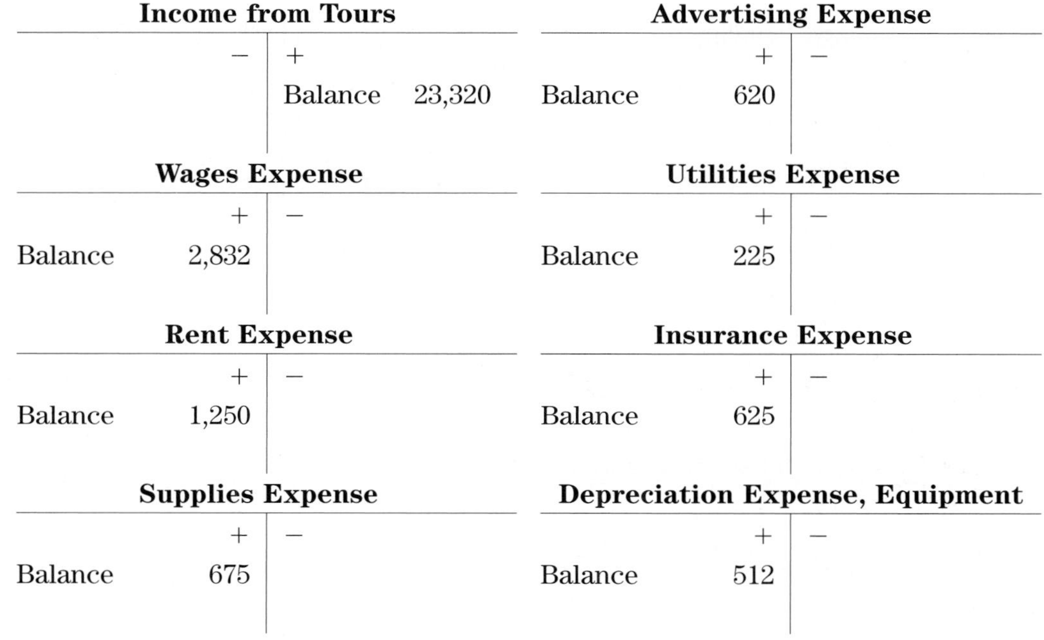

Income from Tours

−		+	
		Balance	23,320

Advertising Expense

+		−
Balance	620	

Wages Expense

+		−
Balance	2,832	

Utilities Expense

+		−
Balance	225	

Rent Expense

+		−
Balance	1,250	

Insurance Expense

+		−
Balance	625	

Supplies Expense

+		−
Balance	675	

Depreciation Expense, Equipment

+		−
Balance	512	

STEP 1. Close the revenue account(s) into Income Summary.

In order to make the balance of Income from Tours equal to zero, we *balance it off,* or debit it, in the amount of $23,320. Because we need an offsetting credit, we credit Income Summary for the same amount. Notice that there are no signs in Income Summary, only Debit and Credit like the other accounts.

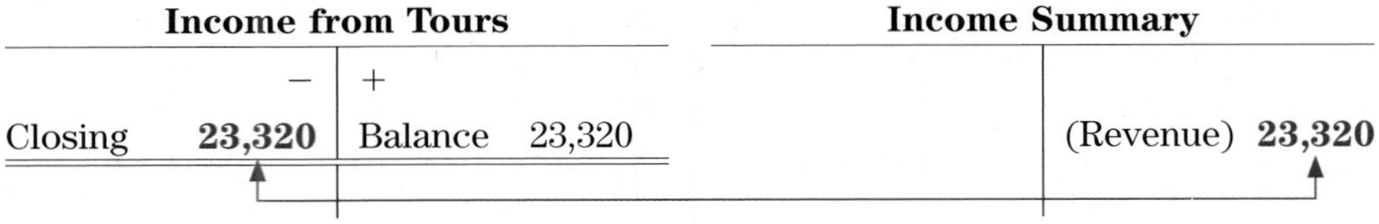

Income from Tours

	−	+	
Closing	**23,320**	Balance	23,320

Income Summary

		(Revenue)	**23,320**

The balance of Income from Tours is transferred to Income Summary.

STEP 2. Close the expense accounts into Income Summary.

To make the balances of the expense accounts equal to zero, we need to balance them off, or credit them. Again the T accounts are useful for formulating this journal entry.

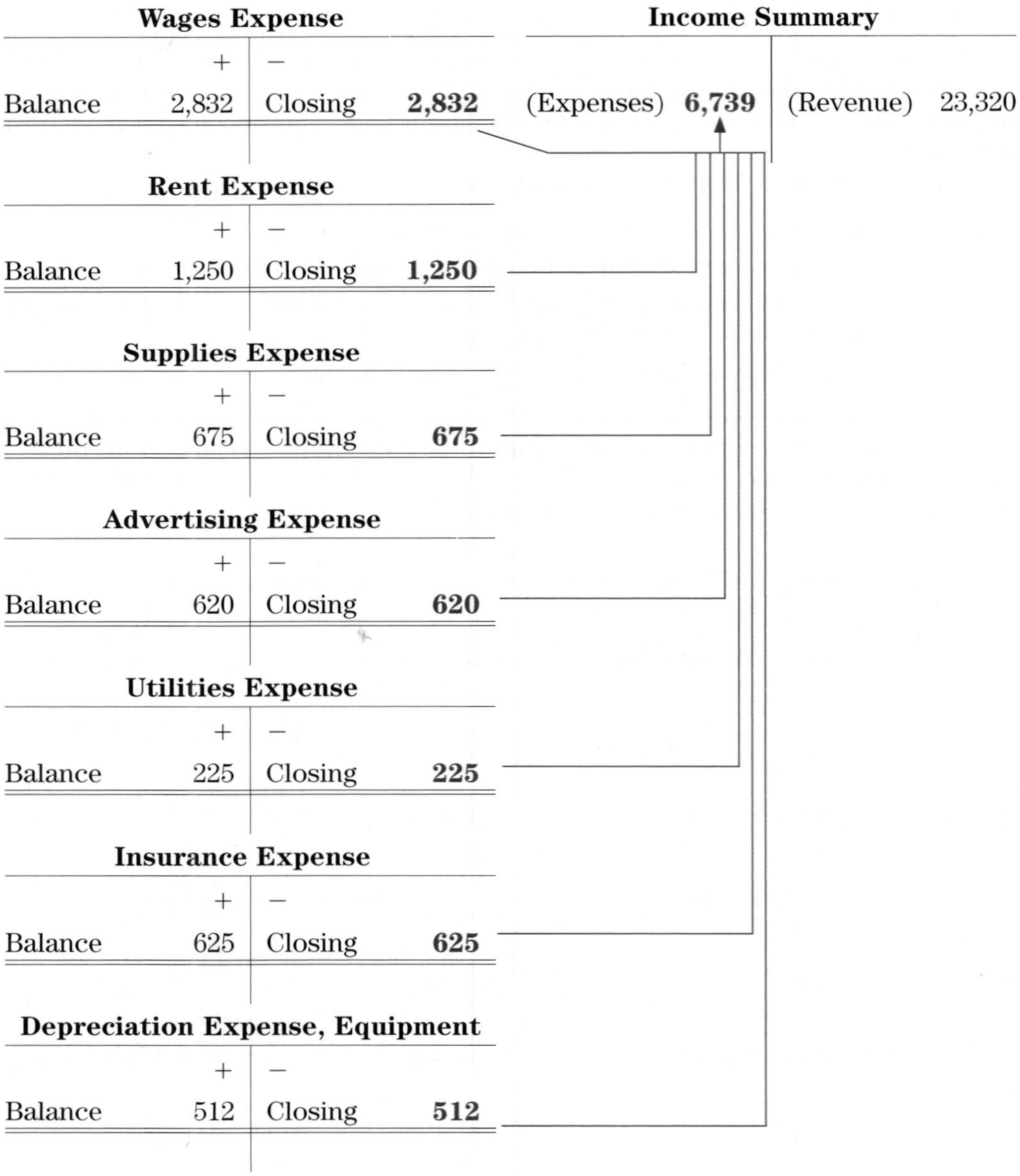

Wages Expense

	+	−	
Balance	2,832	Closing	**2,832**

Income Summary

(Expenses)	**6,739**	(Revenue)	23,320

Rent Expense

	+	−	
Balance	1,250	Closing	**1,250**

Supplies Expense

	+	−	
Balance	675	Closing	**675**

Advertising Expense

	+	−	
Balance	620	Closing	**620**

Utilities Expense

	+	−	
Balance	225	Closing	**225**

Insurance Expense

	+	−	
Balance	625	Closing	**625**

Depreciation Expense, Equipment

	+	−	
Balance	512	Closing	**512**

STEP 3. Close the Income Summary account into the Capital account, transferring the net income or loss to the Capital account.

Recall that we created Income Summary so that we could have a debit and a credit in each closing entry. Now that it has done its job, we close it out. We use the same procedure as before, in that we make the balance equal to zero, or balance off the account. We transfer, or close, the balance of the Income Summary account into the Capital account, as shown in the T accounts and in Figure 2.

Income Summary			
(Expenses)	6,739	(Revenue)	23,320
Closing	**16,581**		

J. Conner, Capital			
	−	+	
		Balance	95,200
		(Net Inc.)	**16,581**

FIGURE 2
Closing entries for Conner's Whitewater Adventures

GENERAL JOURNAL PAGE 4

	Date	Description	Post. Ref.	Debit	Credit
		Closing Entries			
Step 1	30	Income from Tours		23 3 2 0 00	
		Income Summary			23 3 2 0 00
Step 2	30	Income Summary		6 7 3 9 00	
		Wages Expense			2 8 3 2 00
		Rent Expense			1 2 5 0 00
		Supplies Expense			6 7 5 00
		Advertising Expense			6 2 0 00
		Utilities Expense			2 2 5 00
		Insurance Expense			6 2 5 00
		Depreciation Expense, Equipment			5 1 2 00
Step 3	30	Income Summary		16 5 8 1 00	
		J. Conner, Capital			16 5 8 1 00

Income Summary is always closed into the Capital account by the amount of the net income (revenue minus expenses) or the net loss. Comparing net income or net loss on the work sheet with the closing entry for Income Summary can serve as a checkpoint or verification for you.

Net income is added (credited) to the Capital account because, as shown in the statement of owner's equity, net income is treated as an addition. Net loss, on the other hand, is subtracted from (debited to) the Capital account, because net loss is treated as a deduction in the statement of owner's equity. Here's how to close Income Summary for J. Doe Company (net loss of $600):

Income Summary			
(Expenses)	3,000	(Revenue)	**2,400**
		Closing	**600**

J. Doe, Capital			
	−	+	
(Net Loss)	**600**	Balance	42,000

The entry to close Income Summary into J. Doe's Capital account would look like the following.

GENERAL JOURNAL PAGE 3

Date		Description	Post. Ref.	Debit	Credit
		Closing Entries			
	31	J. Doe, Capital		600 00	
		Income Summary			600 00

STEP 4. Close the Drawing account into the Capital account.

Let's return to the example of Conner's Whitewater Adventures. The Drawing account applies to only one fiscal period, so it too must be closed. Drawing is not an expense because it did not help the business generate revenue. **And because Drawing is not an expense, it cannot affect net income or net loss.** It appears in the statement of owner's equity as a deduction from the Capital account, so it is closed directly into the Capital account. We balance off the Drawing account, or make its balance equal to zero. The balance of Drawing is transferred to the Capital account.

J. Conner, Drawing

+	−
Balance **3,500**	Closing **3,500**

J. Conner, Capital

−	+
(Drawing) **3,500**	Balance 95,200
	(Net Inc.) 16,581

The journal entries in the closing procedure are shown in Figure 3.

FIGURE 3
Closing entries for Conner's Whitewater Adventures

GENERAL JOURNAL PAGE 4

	Date	Description	Post. Ref.	Debit	Credit
		Closing Entries			
Step 1	30	Income from Tours	411	23,320 00	
		Income Summary	313		23,320 00
Step 2	30	Income Summary	313	6,739 00	
		Wages Expense	511		2,832 00
		Rent Expense	512		1,250 00
		Supplies Expense	513		675 00
		Advertising Expense	514		620 00
		Utilities Expense	515		225 00
		Insurance Expense	516		625 00
		Depreciation Expense, Equipment	517		512 00
Step 3	30	Income Summary	313	16,581 00	
		J. Conner, Capital	311		16,581 00
Step 4	30	J. Conner, Capital	311	3,500 00	
		J. Conner, Drawing	312		3,500 00

FYI

As a memory tool for the sequence of steps in the closing procedure, use the letters of the closing elements, **REID:** Revenue, Expenses, Income Summary, Drawing.

These closing entries show that Conner's Whitewater Adventures has net income of \$16,581, the owner has withdrawn \$3,500 for personal expenses, and \$13,081 (\$16,581 − \$3,500) has been retained in the business, thereby increasing capital.

Making closing entries using accounting software is frequently an instantaneous procedure. Be sure that all financial statements required have been printed and saved prior to closing, since the closing procedure causes zero balances in the temporary owner's equity accounts. The operator selects the command/function to close the accounting period, and the revenue and expense accounts are automatically closed. The Drawing account may need to be closed with a journal entry. The net income (or loss) is sent to the Capital account. The bad news is that any errors made prior to closing are included. Always make a backup copy of your file prior to closing in case you have made a mistake and need to backtrack to correct an error.

Closing Entries Taken Directly from the Work Sheet

You can gather the information for the closing entries either directly from the ledger accounts or from the work sheet. Since the Income Statement columns of the work sheet consist entirely of revenues and expenses, you can pick up the figures for three of the four closing entries from these columns. Figure 4 shows a partial work sheet for Conner's Whitewater Adventures.

You may plan the closing entries by balancing off all the figures that appear in the Income Statement columns. For example, in the Income Statement Credit column, there is a credit for \$23,320 (Income from Tours), so we debit that account for \$23,320 and credit Income Summary for \$23,320.

FIGURE 4
Partial work sheet for Conner's Whitewater Adventures

Account Name	Trial Balance Debit	Trial Balance Credit	Adjustments Debit	Adjustments Credit	Income Statement Debit	Income Statement Credit
Cash	55 8 9 0 00					
Accounts Receivable	4 2 5 0 00					
Prepaid Insurance	1 8 7 5 00			(a) 6 2 5 00		
Equipment	51 3 0 0 00					
Accounts Payable		3 4 2 5 00				
J. Conner, Capital		95 2 0 0 00				
J. Conner, Drawing	3 5 0 0 00					
Income from Tours		23 3 2 0 00				23 3 2 0 00
Wages Expense	2 3 6 0 00		(c) 4 7 2 00		2 8 3 2 00	
Rent Expense	1 2 5 0 00				1 2 5 0 00	
Supplies Expense	6 7 5 00				6 7 5 00	
Advertising Expense	6 2 0 00				6 2 0 00	
Utilities Expense	2 2 5 00				2 2 5 00	
	121 9 4 5 00	121 9 4 5 00				
Insurance Expense			(a) 6 2 5 00		6 2 5	
Depr. Exp., Equip.			(b) 5 1 2 00		5 1 2 00	
Accum. Depr., Equip.				(b) 5 1 2 00		
Wages Payable				(c) 4 7 2 00		
			1 6 0 9 00	1 6 0 9 00	6 7 3 9 00	23 3 2 0 00
Net Income					16 5 8 1 00	
					23 3 2 0 00	23 3 2 0 00

There are debits for $2,832, $1,250, $675, $620, $225, $625, and $512 (expense accounts). So now we *credit* these accounts for the same amounts, and we debit Income Summary for their total ($6,739).

Next, we close Income Summary into Capital, using the net income figure already shown on the work sheet in Figure 4.

We do, of course, have to get the last closing entry from the Balance Sheet columns to close Drawing.

Incidentally, accountants call the accounts that are to be closed (such as revenue, expenses, Income Summary, and Drawing) **nominal (temporary-equity) accounts**. These accounts are temporary in that their balances apply to only one fiscal period. The *equity* aspect pertains because these accounts all come under the umbrella of owner's equity.

Remember

The temporary-equity accounts (revenue, expenses, and Drawing) are closed out because they apply to only one fiscal period.

On the other hand, accountants call the accounts that remain open (such as assets, liabilities, and Capital) **real (permanent) accounts**. These accounts have balances that will be carried over to the next fiscal period. They are *permanent* because as long as the company exists, there will be balances in these accounts.

Posting the Closing Entries

In the Item column of the ledger account, we write the word *Closing*. To show that the balance of an account is zero, we draw a line through both the Debit Balance and the Credit Balance columns.

After we have posted the closing entries, the Capital, Drawing, Income Summary, revenue, and expense accounts of Conner's Whitewater Adventures appear as follows:

GENERAL LEDGER

ACCOUNT J. Conner, Capital — ACCOUNT NO. 311

Date		Item	Post. Ref.	Debit	Credit	Balance Debit	Balance Credit
20—							
June	1		1		90 0 0 0 00		90 0 0 0 00
	4		1		5 2 0 0 00		95 2 0 0 00
	30	Closing	4		16 5 8 1 00		111 7 8 1 00
	30	Closing	4	3 5 0 0 00			108 2 8 1 00

ACCOUNT J. Conner, Drawing — ACCOUNT NO. 312

Date		Item	Post. Ref.	Debit	Credit	Balance Debit	Balance Credit
20—							
June	30		3	3 5 0 0 00		3 5 0 0 00	
	30	Closing	4		3 5 0 0 00	—	—

ACCOUNT Income Summary — ACCOUNT NO. 313

Date		Item	Post. Ref.	Debit	Credit	Balance Debit	Balance Credit
20—							
June	30	Closing	4		23 3 2 0 00		23 3 2 0 00
	30	Closing	4	6 7 3 9 00			16 5 8 1 00
	30	Closing	4	16 5 8 1 00		—	—

ACCOUNT **Income from Tours** ACCOUNT NO. **411**

Date		Item	Post. Ref.	Debit	Credit	Balance Debit	Balance Credit
20—							
June	7		1		8 0 0 0 00		8 0 0 0 00
	15		2		6 7 5 0 00		14 7 5 0 00
	30		3		8 5 7 0 00		23 3 2 0 00
	30	Closing	4	23 3 2 0 00		—	—

ACCOUNT **Wages Expense** ACCOUNT NO. **511**

Date		Item	Post. Ref.	Debit	Credit	Balance Debit	Balance Credit
20—							
June	24		2	2 3 6 0 00		2 3 6 0 00	
	30	Adj.	4	4 7 2 00		2 8 3 2 00	
	30	Closing	4		2 8 3 2 00	—	—

ACCOUNT **Rent Expense** ACCOUNT NO. **512**

Date		Item	Post. Ref.	Debit	Credit	Balance Debit	Balance Credit
20—							
June	8		1	1 2 5 0 00		1 2 5 0 00	
	30	Closing	4		1 2 5 0 00	—	—

ACCOUNT **Supplies Expense** ACCOUNT NO. **513**

Date		Item	Post. Ref.	Debit	Credit	Balance Debit	Balance Credit
20—							
June	10		1	6 7 5 00		6 7 5 00	
	30	Closing	4		6 7 5 00	—	—

ACCOUNT **Advertising Expense** ACCOUNT NO. **514**

Date		Item	Post. Ref.	Debit	Credit	Balance Debit	Balance Credit
20—							
June	14		2	6 2 0 00		6 2 0 00	
	30	Closing	4		6 2 0 00	—	—

ACCOUNT Utilities Expense **ACCOUNT NO.** 515

Date		Item	Post. Ref.	Debit	Credit	Balance Debit	Balance Credit
20—							
June	18		2	2 2 5 00		2 2 5 00	
	30	Closing	4		2 2 5 00	—	—

ACCOUNT Insurance Expense **ACCOUNT NO.** 516

Date		Item	Post. Ref.	Debit	Credit	Balance Debit	Balance Credit
20—							
June	30	Adj.	4	6 2 5 00		6 2 5 00	
	30	Closing	4		6 2 5 00	—	—

ACCOUNT Depreciation Expense, Equipment **ACCOUNT NO.** 517

Date		Item	Post. Ref.	Debit	Credit	Balance Debit	Balance Credit
20—							
June	30	Adj.	4	5 1 2 00		5 1 2 00	
	30	Closing	4		5 1 2 00	—	—

THE POST-CLOSING TRIAL BALANCE

LEARNING OBJECTIVE 3

Prepare a post-closing trial balance.

After posting the closing entries and before going on to the next fiscal period, verify the balances of the accounts that remain open. To do so, prepare a **post-closing trial balance**, using the final balance figures from the ledger accounts. The purpose of the post-closing trial balance is to make sure that the debit balances equal the credit balances.

Note that the accounts listed in the post-closing trial balance (assets, liabilities, and Capital) are the *real* or *permanent accounts* (see Figure 5). The accountant carries forward the balances of the permanent accounts from one fiscal period to another.

FIGURE 5

Post-closing trial balance for Conner's Whitewater Adventures

Conner's Whitewater Adventures
Post-Closing Trial Balance
June 30, 20—

Account Name	Debit	Credit
Cash	55,890	
Accounts Receivable	4,250	
Prepaid Insurance	1,250	
Equipment	51,300	
Accumulated Depreciation, Equipment		512
Accounts Payable		3,425
Wages Payable		472
J. Conner, Capital		108,281
	112,690	112,690

Contrast this to the handling of *nominal* or *temporary-equity accounts* (revenue, expenses, Income Summary, and Drawing), which are closed at the end of each fiscal period.

If the total debits and total credits of the post-closing trial balance are not equal, here's a recommended procedure for tracking down the error.

1. Re-add the trial balance columns.
2. Check to see that the figures were correctly transferred from the ledger accounts to the post-closing trial balance.
3. Verify the posting of the adjusting entries and the recording of the new balances.
4. Make sure that the closing entries have been posted and that all revenue, expense, Income Summary, and Drawing accounts have zero balances.

THE BASES OF ACCOUNTING: CASH AND ACCRUAL

4 LEARNING OBJECTIVE

Define the following methods of accounting: cash basis and accrual basis.

The basis of accounting that a company chooses has a direct effect on the company's net income and the company's income tax. The business must use the same basis of accounting from year to year, and the basis of accounting must clearly reflect the net income of the business.

Under the **cash basis of accounting**, revenue is recorded when it is received in cash, and generally expenses are recorded when they are paid in cash. If the expenditures have an economic life of more than one year (for example, equipment purchases and insurance), then the cost of these items must be prorated or spread out over their useful lives. Many small businesses' and individuals' personal income taxes are recorded on the cash basis.

Under the **accrual basis of accounting**, revenue is recorded when it is earned, and expenses are recorded when they are incurred (when they occur or the bill is received). For example, in the sale of goods, revenue is counted by the seller when the buyer accepts delivery of the goods. Expenses are recorded by the seller of the goods when the costs are incurred. This is called the matching principle, since revenue in one fiscal period is matched up with expenses incurred in the same period. If your business produces, purchases, or sells merchandise, the business must keep an inventory and use the accrual method for sales and purchases of merchandise.

Most businesses will use the same method of accounting for their financial statements and income tax reporting. According to the Internal Revenue Service, businesses with average annual gross receipts of $5 million or less may be allowed to use the cash method rather than the accrual method, which is more complicated and time consuming. However, there are some important exceptions to this general rule. A business may also use a combination of cash and accrual bases of accounting, called the *hybrid method*. Selecting a basis of accounting can often be complicated and confusing. IRS Publication 538, Accounting Periods and Methods, provides information that makes this decision less confusing. Publication 538 is available on the IRS Web site at www.irs.gov.

INTERIM STATEMENTS

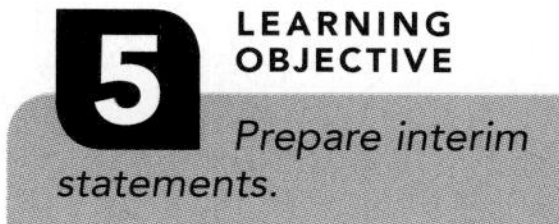

The owner of a business understandably does not want to wait until the end of the twelve-month fiscal period to determine whether the company is making a profit or a loss. Instead, most owners want financial statements at the end of each month. Financial statements prepared during the fiscal year, for periods of less than twelve months, are called **interim statements**. (They are given this name because they are

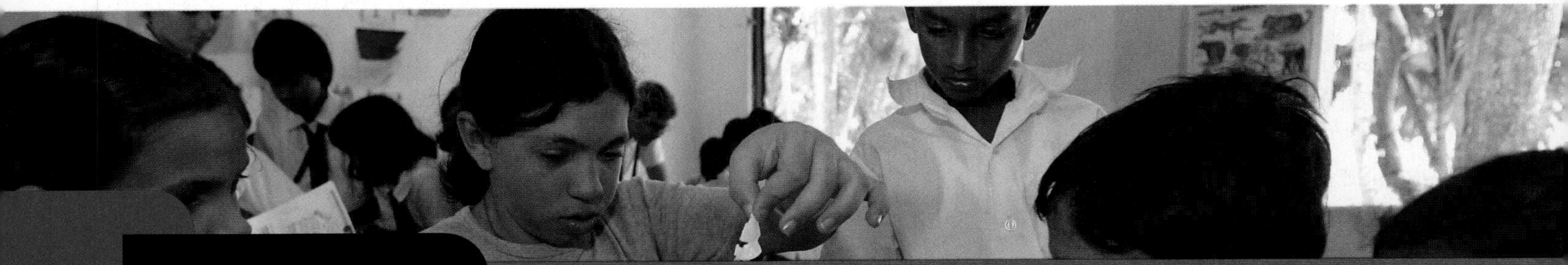

You Make the Call

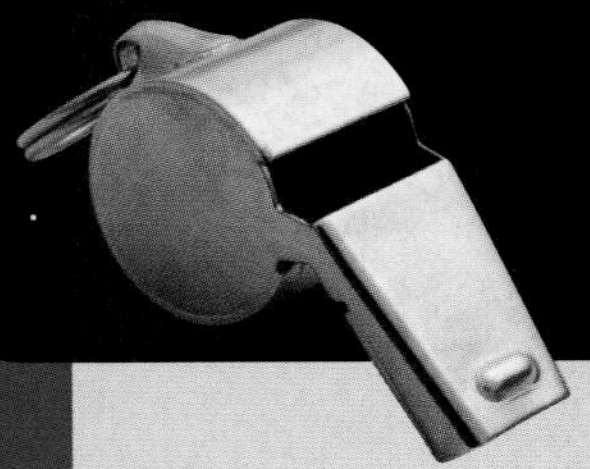

Using the information you know about the cash basis versus the accrual basis, review the four types of businesses listed below. First, consider the type of accounting transactions the following businesses might make. Second, suggest whether the cash basis or the accrual basis would be a logical fit for the business.

1. An investment advisory firm owned by outside investors with $12 million in annual gross receipts
2. A crane sales company with $1 million in annual gross receipts
3. A travel agency with $2 million in annual gross receipts
4. A tractor sales company with $6 million in annual gross receipts

SOLUTION

The travel agency would probably be on the cash basis because it has less than $5 million in annual gross receipts. However, the investment advisory firm would likely be on the accrual basis because its annual gross receipts exceed $5 million. The crane sales company and the tractor sales company would also use the accrual basis since both companies have inventory.

prepared within the fiscal period.) For example, a business may prepare the income statement, the statement of owner's equity, and the balance sheet *monthly.* These statements provide up-to-date information about the results and status of operations. For example, a company might have the following interim statements:

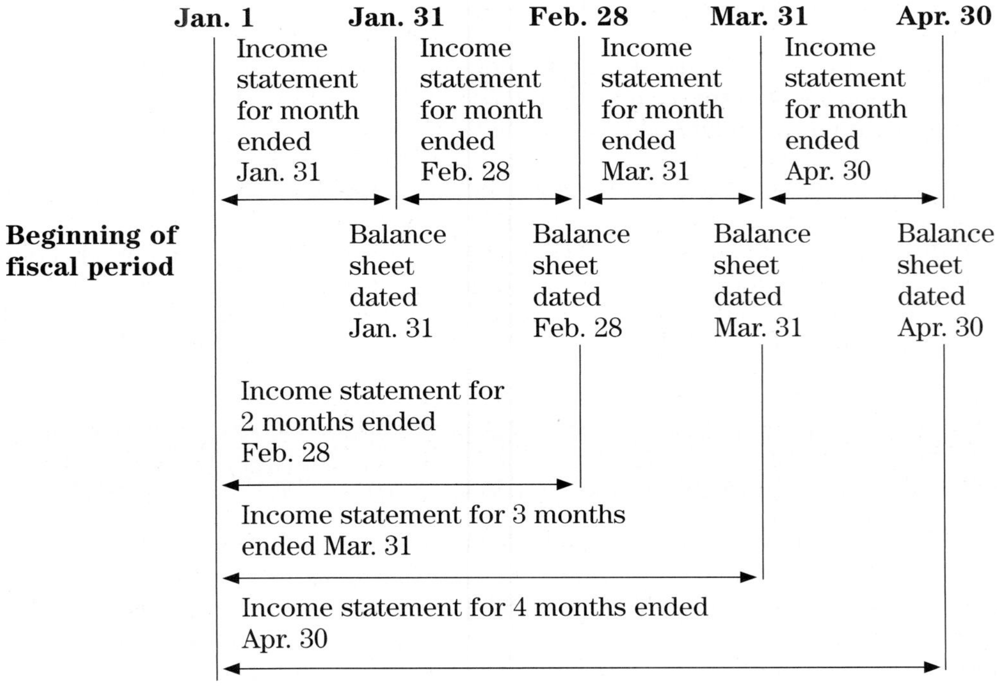

Do I Need an Accountant?

If you are not taking this class because you want to be an accountant or bookkeeper, you might be taking this class because you plan on owning and operating a small business. Many new small business owners take on the responsibilities of being the accountant for their business. However, at some point your business will begin to grow, and you might need to consider hiring an accountant to manage your accounting books so that your time is free to run the business.

An accountant can help you in many areas of your small business, such as:

- What should my business structure be—sole proprietorship, partnership, S corporation, or corporation?
- What software should I use for my accounting?
- How do I handle the payroll for employees?
- What are my requirements for filing taxes?
- What expenses are deductible for tax purposes?
- How do I prepare financial statements when applying for a loan?

So, how do you find an accountant? The best way is by referrals. Ask other businesses in your industry for references or visit your local Certified Public Accounting Society Web site (www.aicpa.org/yellow/ypascpa.htm) for more recommendations.

In this case, the accountant would prepare a work sheet at the end of each month. Next, based on these work sheets, he or she would prepare the financial statements. However, the remaining steps—journalizing the adjusting and closing entries and preparing the post-closing trial balance—would be performed only at the end of the year.

CHAPTER REVIEW

Study & Practice

LEARNING OBJECTIVE

List the steps in the accounting cycle.

STEP 1. Analyze source documents and record business transactions in a journal.
STEP 2. Post journal entries to the accounts in the ledger.
STEP 3. Prepare a trial balance.
STEP 4. Gather adjustment data and record the adjusting entries on a work sheet.
STEP 5. Complete the work sheet.
STEP 6. Prepare financial statements from the data on the work sheet.
STEP 7. Journalize and post the adjusting entries from the data on the work sheet.
STEP 8. Journalize and post the **closing entries**.
STEP 9. Prepare a post-closing trial balance.

PRACTICE EXERCISE 1

Match the steps of the accounting cycle to their corresponding number.

____ **1.** Step 1
____ **2.** Step 2
____ **3.** Step 3
____ **4.** Step 4
____ **5.** Step 5
____ **6.** Step 6
____ **7.** Step 7
____ **8.** Step 8
____ **9.** Step 9

a. Journalize and post the closing entries.
b. Prepare a trial balance.
c. Analyze source documents and record business transactions in a journal.
d. Prepare a post-closing trial balance.
e. Prepare financial statements from the data on the work sheet.
f. Post journal entries to the accounts in the ledger.
g. Complete the work sheet.
h. Journalize and post the adjusting entries from the data on the work sheet.
i. Gather adjustment data and record the adjusting entries on a work sheet.

PRACTICE EXERCISE 1 SOLUTION

1. c; **2.** f; **3.** b; **4.** i; **5.** g; **6.** e; **7.** h; **8.** a; **9.** d

LEARNING OBJECTIVE

Journalize and post closing entries for a service enterprise.

The four steps in the closing procedure are as follows:

STEP 1. Close the revenue account(s) into Income Summary.
STEP 2. Close the expense accounts into Income Summary.
STEP 3. Close the **Income Summary account** into the Capital account, transferring the net income or net loss to the Capital account.
STEP 4. Close the Drawing account into the Capital account.

PRACTICE EXERCISE 2

The following is a work sheet for the month of June for Larson Floral:

Larson Floral
Work Sheet
For the Month Ended June 30, 20—

Account Name	Trial Balance		Adjustments		Adjusted Trial Balance		Income Statement		Balance Sheet	
	Debit	Credit	Debit	Credit	Debit	Credit	Debit	Credit	Debit	Credit
Cash	14,935.00				14,935.00				14,935.00	
Accounts Receivable	500.00				500.00				500.00	
Prepaid Insurance	350.00			(a) 30.00	320.00				320.00	
Delivery Van	28,275.00				28,275.00				28,275.00	
Accum. Depr., Delivery Van		510.00		(b) 300.00		810.00				810.00
Accounts Payable		750.00				750.00				750.00
E. Larson, Capital		37,435.00				37,435.00				37,435.00
E. Larson, Drawing	1,500.00				1,500.00				1,500.00	
Income from Services		12,170.00				12,170.00		12,170.00		
Wages Expense	3,300.00		(c) 300.00		3,600.00		3,600.00			
Rent Expense	775.00				775.00		775.00			
Supplies Expense	710.00				710.00		710.00			
Advertising Expense	270.00				270.00		270.00			
Utilities Expense	250.00				250.00		250.00			
	50,865.00	50,865.00								
Insurance Expense			(a) 30.00		30.00		30.00			
Depr. Exp., Delivery Van			(b) 300.00		300.00		300.00			
Wages Payable				(c) 300.00		300.00				300.00
			630.00	630.00	51,465.00	51,465.00	5,935.00	12,170.00	45,530.00	39,295.00
Net Income							6,235.00			6,235.00
							12,170.00	12,170.00	45,530.00	45,530.00

CHAPTER REVIEW

Using information from the work sheet and assuming the fiscal period is the month of June, journalize the four closing entries for Larson Floral.

PRACTICE EXERCISE 2 SOLUTION

GENERAL JOURNAL PAGE 4

Date		Description	Post. Ref.	Debit	Credit
20—		Closing Entries			
June	30	Income from Services		12,170.00	
		Income Summary			12,170.00
	30	Income Summary		5,935.00	
		Wages Expense			3,600.00
		Rent Expense			775.00
		Supplies Expense			710.00
		Advertising Expense			270.00
		Utilities Expense			250.00
		Insurance Expense			30.00
		Depreciation Expense, Delivery Van			300.00
	30	Income Summary		6,235.00	
		E. Larson, Capital			6,235.00
	30	E. Larson, Capital		1,500.00	
		E. Larson, Drawing			1,500.00

LEARNING OBJECTIVE

3 *Prepare a post-closing trial balance.*

A **post-closing trial balance** consists of the final balances of the accounts remaining open. It is the final proof that the debit balances equal the credit balances before the posting for the new fiscal period begins.

PRACTICE EXERCISE 3

Using the information from the work sheet in Practice Exercise 2, prepare a post-closing trial balance for Larson Floral.

PRACTICE EXERCISE 3 SOLUTION

Larson Floral
Post-Closing Trial Balance
June 30, 20—

Account Name	Debit	Credit
Cash	14,935	
Accounts Receivable	500	
Prepaid Insurance	320	
Delivery Van	28,275	
Accumulated Depreciation, Delivery Van		810
Accounts Payable		750
Wages Payable		300
E. Larson, Capital		42,170
	44,030	44,030

LEARNING OBJECTIVE 4

Define the following methods of accounting: cash basis and accrual basis.

Under the **cash basis of accounting**, revenue is recorded when it is received in cash, and expenses are generally recorded when they are paid in cash. Under the **accrual basis of accounting**, revenue is recorded when earned, even if cash is received at a later date, and expenses are recorded when incurred, even if cash is to be paid at a later date.

PRACTICE EXERCISE 4

Considering the following events, determine which month the revenue or expenses would be recorded using the accounting method specified.

a. Crane Company uses the *accrual basis of accounting*. Crane prepays cash in June for insurance that covers the following month, July, only.
b. Loggins & Rogers Tax Services uses the *cash basis of accounting*. Loggins & Rogers receives cash from customers in January for services to be performed in March.
c. Red Tractor Supplies Company uses the *accrual basis of accounting*. Red Tractor Supplies makes a sale to a customer in September but does not expect payment until November.
d. Norton Company uses the *cash basis of accounting*. Norton prepays cash in February for insurance that covers the following month, March, only.

PRACTICE EXERCISE 4 SOLUTION

a. July
b. January
c. September
d. February

LEARNING OBJECTIVE 5

Prepare interim statements.

Interim statements consist of year-to-date income statements, statements of owner's equity, and balance sheets as of various dates during the fiscal period.

PRACTICE EXERCISE 5

Assume that Larson Floral's fiscal period does not end on June 30 but rather December 31. Using the information from the work sheet from Practice Exercise 2, complete an interim balance sheet for the month of June for Larson Floral.

PRACTICE EXERCISE 5 SOLUTION

Larson Floral Balance Sheet June 30, 20—		
Assets		
Cash		$14,935
Accounts Receivable		500
Prepaid Insurance		320
Delivery Van	$28,275	
Less Accumulated Depreciation	810	27,465
Total Assets		$43,220
Liabilities		
Accounts Payable	$ 750	
Wages Payable	300	
Total Liabilities		$ 1,050
Owner's Equity		
E. Larson, Capital		42,170
Total Liabilities and Owner's Equity		$43,220

Before a Test Check: Chapters 4–5

PART I: MULTIPLE-CHOICE QUESTIONS

____ **1.** The net income appears on all of the following statements except
a. the statement of owner's equity.
b. the balance sheet.
c. the income statement.
d. all of these.
e. none of these.

____ **2.** Which of the following entries records the withdrawal of cash for personal use by Dolan, the owner of a business firm?
a. Debit Cash and credit Drawing.
b. Debit Salary Expense and credit Cash.
c. Debit Cash and credit Salary Expense.
d. Debit Drawing and credit Cash.
e. None of these.

____ **3.** Which of the following errors, considered individually, would cause the trial balance totals to be unequal?
a. A payment of $52 for supplies was posted as a debit of $52 to Supplies Expense and a credit of $25 to Cash.
b. A payment of $625 to a creditor was posted as a debit of $625 to Accounts Payable and a debit of $625 to Cash.
c. Cash received from customers on account was posted as a debit of $380 to Cash and a credit of $38 to Accounts Receivable.
d. All of these.
e. None of these.

____ **4.** The balance in the Prepaid Insurance account before adjustment at the end of the year is $600. This represents six months' insurance paid on November 1. No adjusting entry was made on November 30. The adjusting entry required on December 31 is

CHAPTER REVIEW

a. debit Insurance Expense, $200; credit Prepaid Insurance, $200.
b. debit Prepaid Insurance, $100; credit Insurance Expense, $100.
c. debit Prepaid Insurance, $600; credit Insurance Expense, $600.
d. debit Insurance Expense, $600; credit Prepaid Insurance, $600.
e. none of these.

____ **5.** If an accountant fails to make an adjusting entry to record expired insurance at the end of a fiscal period, the omission will cause
a. total expenses to be understated.
b. total revenue to be understated.
c. total assets to be understated.
d. all of these.
e. none of these.

____ **6.** Farmer Company bought equipment on January 2 of this year for $9,000. At the time of purchase, the equipment was estimated to have a useful life of eight years and a trade-in value of $1,000 at the end of eight years. Using the straight-line method, the amount of depreciation for the first year is
a. $900.
b. $1,000.
c. $800.
d. $950.
e. none of these.

____ **7.** If expenses are greater than revenue, the Income Summary account will be closed by a debit to
a. Cash and a credit to Income Summary.
b. Income Summary and a credit to Cash.
c. Capital and a credit to Income Summary.
d. Income Summary and a credit to Capital.
e. none of these.

____ **8.** In preparing closing entries, it is helpful to refer to which of the following columns of the work sheet first?
a. The Balance Sheet columns
b. The Adjusted Trial Balance columns
c. The Income Statement columns
d. Both the Adjusted Trial Balance and the Income Statement columns
e. None of these

PART II: PRACTICAL APPLICATION

On December 31, the ledger accounts of Kristopher's Upholstery Shop have the following balances after all adjusting entries have been posted.

Cash	$ 1,200
Equipment	15,400
Accumulated Depreciation, Equipment	1,100
Accounts Payable	300
K. Payton, Capital	16,500
K. Payton, Drawing	16,400
Income Summary	
Income from Services	35,900
Wages Expense	11,500
Rent Expense	2,400
Supplies Expense	4,100
Utilities Expense	1,000
Depreciation Expense, Equipment	500
Miscellaneous Expense	900

Required
Journalize the four closing entries in the proper order.

PART III: MATCHING QUESTIONS

____ **1.** Creditor
____ **2.** Business entity
____ **3.** Fundamental accounting equation
____ **4.** Income statement
____ **5.** Owner's equity
____ **6.** Accounts Receivable
____ **7.** Net loss
____ **8.** Ledger
____ **9.** Credit
____ **10.** Compound entry
____ **11.** Trial balance
____ **12.** Journalizing
____ **13.** Posting
____ **14.** Cross-reference
____ **15.** Journal
____ **16.** Work sheet
____ **17.** Book value
____ **18.** Depreciation
____ **19.** Accounting cycle
____ **20.** Fiscal year
____ **21.** Contra account
____ **22.** Mixed accounts
____ **23.** Temporary-equity accounts
____ **24.** Real accounts
____ **25.** Debit

a. The book of original entry
b. One to whom money is owed
c. Accounts that are partly income statement and partly balance sheet accounts
d. Assets – Liabilities
e. A listing of the ending balances of all ledger accounts that proves the equality of total debits and total credits
f. The process of recording transactions in a journal
g. The left side of a T account
h. A business enterprise, separate and distinct from the person who owns its assets
i. The process of transferring accounts and amounts from the journal to the ledger
j. An account that is deducted from another account
k. Amounts owed by charge customers
l. Balance sheet accounts
m. Assets = Liabilities + Owner's Equity
n. A bookkeeping device for referring from journal to ledger or ledger to journal
o. The right side of a T account
p. Allocation of the cost of a plant asset over its estimated life
q. Financial statement that shows the net results of operations
r. Accounts that belong to only one fiscal period and are closed out at the end of each fiscal period
s. A transaction that has two or more debits and/or credits
t. Paper or spreadsheet used to record adjustments and provide balances to prepare financial statements
u. Excess of total expenses over total revenues
v. A period of twelve consecutive months
w. A book containing all the accounts of a business
x. The cost of an asset minus its accumulated depreciation
y. Steps in the accounting process, completed during the fiscal period

ANSWERS: PART I

1. b; **2.** d; **3.** d; **4.** a; **5.** a; **6.** b; **7.** c; **8.** c

ANSWERS: PART II

GENERAL JOURNAL PAGE 4

Date		Description	Post. Ref.	Debit	Credit
20—		Closing Entries			
Dec.	31	Income from Services		35 9 0 0 00	
		Income Summary			35 9 0 0 00
	31	Income Summary		20 4 0 0 00	
		Wages Expense			11 5 0 0 00
		Rent Expense			2 4 0 0 00
		Supplies Expense			4 1 0 0 00
		Utilities Expense			1 0 0 0 00
		Depreciation Expense, Equipment			5 0 0 00
		Miscellaneous Expense			9 0 0 00
	31	Income Summary		15 5 0 0 00	
		K. Payton, Capital			15 5 0 0 00
	31	K. Payton, Capital		16 4 0 0 00	
		K. Payton, Drawing			16 4 0 0 00

ANSWERS: PART III

1. b; **2.** h; **3.** m; **4.** q; **5.** d; **6.** k; **7.** u; **8.** w; **9.** o; **10.** s; **11.** e; **12.** f; **13.** i; **14.** n; **15.** a; **16.** t; **17.** x; **18.** p; **19.** y; **20.** v; **21.** j; **22.** c; **23.** r; **24.** l; **25.** g

Glossary

Accrual basis of accounting An accounting method under which revenue is recorded when it is earned, regardless of when it is received, and expenses are recorded when they are incurred, regardless of when they are paid. *(p. 187)*

Cash basis of accounting An accounting method under which revenue is recorded only when it is received in cash. Most expenses are recorded only when they are paid in cash. *(p. 187)*

Closing entries Entries made at the end of a fiscal period to close off the revenue, expense, and Drawing accounts—that is, to make the balances of the temporary-equity accounts equal to zero. Closing is also called *clearing the accounts. (p. 178)*

Income Summary account An account brought into existence in order to have a debit and credit in each closing entry. The revenue and expense account balances are transferred to this account to allow calculations of net income or net loss. *(p. 179)*

Interim statements Financial statements prepared during the fiscal year, covering a period of time of less than twelve months. *(p. 187)*

Nominal (temporary-equity) accounts Accounts that apply to only one fiscal period and that are to be closed at the end of that fiscal period, such as revenue, expense, Income Summary, and Drawing accounts. This category may also be described as all accounts except assets, liabilities, and the Capital account. *(p. 184)*

Post-closing trial balance The listing of the final balances of the real accounts at the end of the fiscal period. *(p. 186)*

Real (permanent) accounts The accounts that remain open (assets, liabilities, and the Capital account in owner's equity) and that have balances that will be carried over to the next fiscal period. *(p. 184)*

CHAPTER ASSIGNMENTS

Discussion Questions

1. Number in order the following steps in the accounting cycle.
   a. Prepare a trial balance.
   b. Post journal entries to the accounts in the ledger.
   c. Journalize and post the adjusting entries from the data on the work sheet.
   d. Analyze source documents and record business transactions in a journal.
   e. Prepare financial statements from the data on the work sheet.
   f. Gather adjustment data and record the adjusting entries on a work sheet.
   g. Journalize and post the closing entries.
   h. Prepare a post-closing trial balance.
   i. Complete the work sheet.
2. List the steps in the closing procedure in the correct order.
3. What is the purpose of closing entries? Consider the consequence of forgetting to make closing entries.
4. What happens if you do not print, save, and back up your financial statements before the closing entries occur?
5. What are real accounts? What are nominal accounts? Give examples of each.
6. What is the purpose of the Income Summary account, and how does it relate to the revenue and expense accounts?
7. What is the purpose of the post-closing trial balance? What is the difference between a trial balance and a post-closing trial balance?
8. Write the third closing entry to transfer the net income or net loss to the P. Hernandez, Capital account, assuming the following:
   a. A net income of $3,842 during the first quarter (Jan.–Mar.)
   b. A net loss of $1,781 during the second quarter (Apr.–Jun.)

Exercises

PRACTICE EXERCISE 2

EXERCISE 5-1 Classify the following accounts as real (permanent) or nominal (temporary), and indicate with an X whether the account is closed. Also, indicate the financial statement in which each account will appear. The Building account is given as an example.

Account Title	Real	Nominal	Closed		Income Statement	Balance Sheet
			Yes	No		
0. Example: Building	X			X		X
a. Prepaid Insurance	X			X		X
b. Accounts Payable	X			X		X
c. Wages Payable	X			X		X
d. Services Revenue		X	X		X	
e. Rent Expense		X	X		X	
f. Supplies Expense		X	X		X	
g. Accum. Depr., Equipment	X			X		X

EXERCISE 5-2 Number the closing entries as steps 1 through 4. Journalize the following closing entries.

PRACTICE EXERCISE 2

Assets		=	Liabilities		+	Owner's Equity		+	Revenue		−	Expenses	
Dr. +	Cr. −		Dr. −	Cr. +		Dr. −	Cr. +		Dr. −	Cr. +		Dr. +	Cr. −

Cash

Dr.	Cr.
Bal. 8,500	

Wages Payable

Dr.	Cr.
	(a) 210

J. Cortez, Capital

Dr.	Cr.
605	Bal. 24,000
400	
	Bal. 22,995

Professional Fees

Dr.	Cr.
3,850	Bal. 3,850

Wages Expense

Dr.	Cr.
Bal. 2,900	
(a) 210	
Bal. 3,110	3,110

Prepaid Insurance

Dr.	Cr.
Bal. 990	(c) 460
Bal. 530	

J. Cortez, Drawing

Dr.	Cr.
Bal. 400	400

Insurance Expense

Dr.	Cr.
(c) 460	460

Equipment

Dr.	Cr.
Bal. 18,125	

Income Summary

Dr.	Cr.
4,455	3,850
	605

Depr. Expense, Equipment

Dr.	Cr.
(b) 750	750

Accum. Depr., Equipment

Dr.	Cr.
	Bal. 3,200
	(b) 750
	Bal. 3,950

Misc. Expense

Dr.	Cr.
Bal. 135	135

EXERCISE 5-3 As of December 31, the end of the current year, the ledger of Harris Company contained the following account balances after adjustment. All accounts have normal balances. Journalize the closing entries.

PRACTICE EXERCISE 2

Cash	$ 8,440	C. Harris, Drawing	$1,498
Equipment	11,586	Professional Fees	7,075
Accumulated Depreciation, Equipment	2,587	Wages Expense	1,268
		Rent Expense	1,090
Accounts Payable	1,674	Depreciation Expense, Equipment	1,143
Wages Payable	658		
C. Harris, Capital	13,376	Miscellaneous Expense	345

EXERCISE 5-4 The Income Statement columns of the work sheet of Dunn Company for the fiscal year ended June 30 follow. During the year, K. Dunn withdrew $4,000. Journalize the closing entries.

PRACTICE EXERCISE 2

Account Name	Income Statement Debit	Income Statement Credit
Service Revenue		6 797 00
Rental Revenue		3 576 00
Rent Expense	2 800 00	
Wages Expense	1 854 00	
Utilities Expense	465 00	
Miscellaneous Expense	59 00	
	5 178 00	10 373 00
Net Income	5 195 00	
	10 373 00	10 373 00

2 

PRACTICE EXERCISE 2

EXERCISE 5-5 The Income Statement columns of the work sheet of Cederblom Company for the fiscal year ended December 31 follow. During the year, S. Cederblom withdrew $17,000. Journalize the closing entries.

Account Name	Income Statement Debit	Income Statement Credit
Service Revenue		41 740 00
Rental Revenue		22 000 00
Wages Expense	48 520 00	
Utilities Expense	7 130 00	
Miscellaneous Expense	2 200 00	
	57 850 00	63 740 00
Net Income	5 890 00	
	63 740 00	63 740 00

2 

PRACTICE EXERCISE 2

EXERCISE 5-6 After all revenue and expenses have been closed at the end of the fiscal period ended December 31, Income Summary has a debit of $45,550 and a credit of $36,520. On the same date, D. Mau, Drawing, has a debit balance of $12,000, and D. Mau, Capital, had a beginning credit balance of $63,410.

a. Journalize the entries to close the remaining temporary accounts.
b. What is the new balance of D. Mau, Capital, after closing the remaining temporary accounts? Show your calculations.

5 

PRACTICE EXERCISE 5

EXERCISE 5-7 Indicate with an X whether each of the following would appear on the income statement, statement of owner's equity, or balance sheet. An item may appear on more than one statement. The first item is provided as an example.

CHAPTER ASSIGNMENTS

Item	Income Statement	Statement of Owner's Equity	Balance Sheet
0. Example: The total liabilities of the business at the end of the year.			X
a. The amount of the owner's Capital balance at the end of the year.			
b. The amount of depreciation expense on equipment during the year.			
c. The amount of the company's net income for the year.			
d. The book value of the equipment.			
e. Total insurance expired during the year.			
f. Total accounts receivable at the end of the year.			
g. Total withdrawals by the owner.			
h. The cost of utilities used during the year.			
i. The amount of the owner's Capital balance at the beginning of the year.			

5

PRACTICE EXERCISE 5

EXERCISE 5-8 Prepare a statement of owner's equity for The Lindal Clinic for the year ended December 31. P. Lindal's capital amount on January 1 was $124,000, and there was an additional investment of $7,000 on May 12 and withdrawals of $31,500 for the year. Net income for the year was $20,418.

Problem Set A

For additional help, see the demonstration problem at the beginning of each chapter in your Working Papers.

2

PROBLEM 5-1A After the accountant posted the adjusting entries for B. Lyon, Designer, the work sheet contained the following account balances on May 31:

Account Name	Adjusted Trial Balance Debit (A + Draw. + E)	Adjusted Trial Balance Credit (Accum. Deprec. + L + C + R)
Cash	2,318.00	
Accounts Receivable	1,408.00	
Prepaid Insurance	987.00	
Office Equipment	5,790.00	
Accumulated Depreciation, Office Equipment		1,372.00
Accounts Payable		880.00
B. Lyon, Capital		7,520.00
B. Lyon, Drawing	1,550.00	
Commissions Earned		4,679.00
Rent Expense	995.00	
Supplies Expense	575.00	
Depreciation Expense, Office Equipment	462.00	
Utilities Expense	269.00	
Miscellaneous Expense	97.00	
	14,451.00	14,451.00

CHAPTER ASSIGNMENTS

Check Figure
Net Income, $2,281

Required

1. Write the owner's name on the Capital and Drawing T accounts found in the Working Papers.
2. Record the account balances in the T accounts for owner's equity, revenue, and expenses.
3. Journalize the closing entries with the four steps in correct order. Number the closing entries 1 through 4.
4. Post the closing entries to the T accounts right after you journalize each one to see the effect of the closing entries. Number the closing entries 1 through 4.

2 LO

PROBLEM 5-2A The partial work sheet for Ho Consulting for the month of May follows.

Account Name	Income Statement Debit *E*	Income Statement Credit *R*	Balance Sheet Debit *A + Draw.*	Balance Sheet Credit *Accum. Depr. + L + C*
Cash			5919 00	
Prepaid Insurance			1123 00	
Equipment			5731 00	
Accumulated Depreciation, Equipment				1444 00
Accounts Payable				1841 00
G. Ho, Capital				4302 00
G. Ho, Drawing			2400 00	
Consulting Revenue		13060 00		
Rent Expense	2200 00			
Wages Expense	1828 00			
Supplies Expense	422 00			
Miscellaneous Expense	230 00			
Insurance Expense	325 00			
Depreciation Expense, Equipment	835 00			
Wages Payable				366 00
	5840 00	13060 00	15173 00	7953 00
Net Income	7220 00			7220 00
	13060 00	13060 00	15173 00	15173 00

Check Figure
Debit to Income Summary, second entry, $5,840

Required

1. Write the owner's name on the Capital and Drawing T accounts found in the Working Papers.
2. Record the account balances in the T accounts for owner's equity, revenue, and expenses.
3. Journalize the closing entries with the four steps in correct order. Number the closing entries 1 through 4.
4. Post the closing entries to the T accounts right after you journalize each one to see the effect of the closing entries. Number the closing entries 1 through 4.

1,2,3 LO

PROBLEM 5-3A The completed work sheet for Valerie Insurance Agency as of December 31 is presented in your Working Papers, along with the general ledger as of December 31 before adjustments.

Required

1. Write the name of the owner, M. Valerie, in the Capital and Drawing accounts.
2. Write the balances from the unadjusted trial balance in the general ledger.
3. Journalize and post the adjusting entries.
4. Journalize and post the closing entries in the correct order.
5. Prepare a post-closing trial balance.

Check Figure
Post-closing trial balance total, $9,930

LO 1,2,3

PROBLEM 5-4A The account balances of Bryan Company as of June 30, the end of the current fiscal year, are as follows:

Account Name	Trial Balance Debit	Trial Balance Credit
Cash	5,491.00	
Accounts Receivable	624.00	
Prepaid Insurance	1,280.00	
Equipment	6,497.00	
Accumulated Depreciation, Equipment		2,672.00
Van	10,989.00	
Accumulated Depreciation, Van		4,368.00
Accounts Payable		1,036.00
B. Bryan, Capital		18,583.00
B. Bryan, Drawing	18,000.00	
Fees Earned		38,417.00
Salary Expense	18,600.00	
Advertising Expense	1,887.00	
Supplies Expense	397.00	
Van Operating Expense	462.00	
Utilities Expense	685.00	
Miscellaneous Expense	164.00	
	65,076.00	65,076.00

Required

1. Complete the work sheet. Data for the adjustments are as follows:
   a. Expired or used up insurance, $495
   b. Depreciation expense on equipment, $670.
   c. Depreciation expense on the van, $1,190.
   d. Salary accrued (earned) since the last payday, $540 (owed and to be paid on the next payday).
2. Prepare an income statement.
3. Prepare a statement of owner's equity; assume there was an additional investment of $2,000 on June 10.
4. Prepare a balance sheet.
5. Journalize the adjusting entries.
6. Journalize the closing entries with the four steps in the correct sequence.

Check Figure
Net Income, $13,327

Problem Set B

For additional help, see the demonstration problem at the beginning of each chapter in your Working Papers.

LO 2

PROBLEM 5-1B After the accountant posted the adjusting entries for M. Wally, Designer, the work sheet contained the following account balances on May 31:

Account Name	Adjusted Trial Balance Debit (A + Draw. + E)	Adjusted Trial Balance Credit (Accum. Deprec. + L + C + R)
Cash	2,429.00	
Accounts Receivable	886.00	
Prepaid Insurance	1,460.00	
Office Equipment	4,672.00	
Accumulated Depreciation, Office Equipment		1,170.00
Accounts Payable		943.00
M. Wally, Capital		6,221.00
M. Wally, Drawing	1,600.00	
Commissions Earned		4,997.00
Rent Expense	990.00	
Supplies Expense	480.00	
Depreciation Expense, Office Equipment	420.00	
Utilities Expense	286.00	
Miscellaneous Expense	108.00	
	13,331.00	13,331.00

Check Figure
Net Income, $2,713

Required

1. Write the owner's name on the Capital and Drawing T accounts found in the Working Papers.
2. Record the account balances in the T accounts for owner's equity, revenue, and expenses.
3. Journalize the closing entries with the four steps in correct order. Number the closing entries 1 through 4.
4. Post the closing entries to the T accounts right after you journalize each one to see the effect of the closing entries. Number the closing entries 1 through 4.

2 

PROBLEM 5-2B The partial work sheet for Emil Consulting for the month of June is as follows.

Account Name	Income Statement Debit (E)	Income Statement Credit (R)	Balance Sheet Debit (A + Draw.)	Balance Sheet Credit (Accum. Depr. + L + C)
Cash			6,104.00	
Prepaid Insurance			1,344.00	
Equipment			6,751.00	
Accumulated Depreciation, Equipment				4,212.00
Accounts Payable				1,356.00
W. Emil, Capital				5,367.00
W. Emil, Drawing			1,700.00	
Consulting Fees		9,546.00		
Rent Expense	1,800.00			
Wages Expense	1,533.00			
Miscellaneous Expense	168.00			
Supplies Expense	365.00			
Insurance Expense	364.00			
Depreciation Expense, Equipment	700.00			
Wages Payable				348.00
	4,930.00	9,546.00	15,899.00	11,283.00
Net Income	4,616.00			4,616.00
	9,546.00	9,546.00	15,899.00	15,899.00

Required

1. Write the owner's name on the Capital and Drawing T accounts found in the Working Papers.
2. Record the account balances in the T accounts for owner's equity, revenue, and expenses.
3. Journalize the closing entries with the four steps in correct order. Number the closing entries 1 through 4.
4. Post the closing entries to the T accounts right after you journalize each one to see the effect of the closing entries. Number closing entries 1 through 4.

Check Figure
Debit to Income Summary, second entry, $4,930

LO 1,2,3

PROBLEM 5-3B The completed work sheet for Oliver Tour Company as of December 31 is presented in your Working Papers, along with the general ledger as of December 31 before adjustments.

Required

1. Write the name of the owner, S. Oliver, in the Capital and Drawing accounts.
2. Write the balances from the unadjusted trial balance in the general ledger.
3. Journalize and post the adjusting entries.
4. Journalize and post the closing entries in the correct order.
5. Prepare a post-closing trial balance.

Check Figure
Post-closing trial balance total, $8,869

LO 1,2,3

PROBLEM 5-4B The account balances of Miss Beverly's Tutoring Service as of June 30, the end of the current fiscal year, are as follows.

	Trial Balance	
Account Name	Debit	Credit
Cash	6 4 9 1 00	
Accounts Receivable	6 2 4 00	
Prepaid Insurance	1 2 8 0 00	
Equipment	5 4 9 7 00	
Accumulated Depreciation, Equipment		2 4 7 2 00
Van	13 6 7 4 00	
Accumulated Depreciation, Van		4 1 6 8 00
Accounts Payable		1 4 3 6 00
B. Morrow, Capital		14 8 4 8 00
B. Morrow, Drawing	18 0 0 0 00	
Fees Earned		43 6 8 0 00
Salary Expense	16 0 0 0 00	
Advertising Expense	2 2 0 0 00	
Van Operating Expense	7 0 5 00	
Supplies Expense	5 2 7 00	
Utilities Expense	1 2 4 8 00	
Miscellaneous Expense	3 5 8 00	
	66 6 0 4 00	66 6 0 4 00

Required

1. Complete the work sheet. Data for the adjustments are as follows:
   a. Expired or used up insurance, $470.
   b. Depreciation expense on equipment, $948.
   c. Depreciation expense on the van, $1,490.
   d. Salary accrued (earned) since the last payday, $574 (owed and to be paid on the next payday).

Check Figure
Net income, $19,160

CHAPTER ASSIGNMENTS

2. Prepare an income statement.
3. Prepare a statement of owner's equity; assume there was an additional investment of $3,000 on June 10.
4. Prepare a balance sheet.
5. Journalize the adjusting entries.
6. Journalize the closing entries with the four steps in the proper sequence.

Accounting Cycle Review Problem A

This problem is designed to enable you to apply the knowledge you have acquired in the preceding chapters. In accounting, the ultimate test is being able to handle data in real-life situations. This problem will give you valuable experience.

CHART OF ACCOUNTS

Assets
111 Cash
112 Accounts Receivable
114 Prepaid Insurance
121 Land
122 Building
123 Accumulated Depreciation, Building
124 Pool/Slide Facility
125 Accumulated Depreciation, Pool/Slide Facility
126 Pool Furniture
127 Accumulated Depreciation, Pool Furniture

Liabilities
221 Accounts Payable
222 Wages Payable
223 Mortgage Payable

Owner's Equity
311 L. Lacy, Capital
312 L. Lacy, Drawing
313 Income Summary

Revenue
411 Income from Services
412 Income from Concessions

Expenses
511 Pool Maintenance Expense
512 Wages Expense
513 Advertising Expense
514 Utilities Expense
515 Interest Expense
517 Insurance Expense
518 Depreciation Expense, Building
519 Depreciation Expense, Pool/Slide Facility
520 Depreciation Expense, Pool Furniture
522 Miscellaneous Expense

You are to record transactions in a two-column general journal. Assume that the fiscal period is one month. You will then be able to complete all the steps in the accounting cycle.

When you are analyzing the transactions, think them through by visualizing the T accounts or by writing them down on scratch paper. For unfamiliar types of transactions, specific instructions for recording them are included. However, reason them out for yourself as well. Check off each transaction as it is recorded.

July 1 Lacy deposited $150,000 in a bank account for the purpose of buying Surf's Up! The business is a recreation area offering three large waterslides (called "tubes"), one children's slide, an inner tube run, and a looping extreme slide.

2 Bought Surf's Up! in its entirety for a total price of $540,800. The assets include pool furniture, $3,800; the pool/slide facility (includes filter system, pools, pump, and slides), $148,800; building, $96,200; and land, $292,000. Paid $120,000 down and signed a mortgage note for the remainder. (Debit the assets, and credit Cash and Mortgage Payable.)

2 Received and paid the bill for a one-year premium for insurance, $12,240.

2 Bought 125 inner tubes from Worn Tires for $1,225, paying $500 down, with the remainder due in 20 days. (Debit Pool/Slide Facility.)

3 Signed a contract with a video game company to lease space for video games and to provide a food concession. The rental income agreed upon is 10 percent of the revenues generated from the machines and food, with the estimated monthly rental income paid in advance. Received cash payment for July, $250. (Debit Cash and credit Concessions Income.)

July 5 Received bills totaling $1,320 for the grand opening/Fourth of July party. The bill from Party Rentals for the promotional handouts, balloons, decorations, and prizes was $620, and the newspaper advertising bills from the *City Star* were $700. (These expenses should all be considered advertising expense.)

6 Signed a one-year contract for the pool maintenance with All-Around Maintenance and paid the maintenance fee for July of $800.

6 Paid cash for employee picnic food and beverages, $128. (Debit Miscellaneous Expense.)

7 Received $12,086 in cash as income for the use of the facilities.

9 Bought parts for the filter system on account from Arlen's Pool Supply, $646. (Debit Pool Maintenance Expense.)

14 Received $10,445 in cash as income for the use of the facilities.

15 Paid wages to employees for the period ended July 14, $8,460.

16 Paid cash as partial payment on account for promotional expenses recorded on July 5, $1,150.

16 Lacy withdrew cash for personal use, $2,500.

17 Bought additional pool furniture from Pool Suppliers for $2,100; payment due in 30 days.

18 Paid cash to seamstress for alterations and repairs to the character costumes, $248. (Debit Miscellaneous Expense.)

21 Received $10,330 in cash as income for the use of the facilities.

21 Paid cash to Worn Tires as partial payment on account, $600.

23 Received a $225 reduction of our account from Pool Suppliers for lawn chairs received in damaged condition.

25 Received and paid telephone bill, $292.

29 Paid wages for the period July 15 through 28 of $8,227.

31 Received $11,870 in cash as income for the use of the facilities.

31 Paid cash to Arlen's Pool Supply to apply on account, $360.

31 Received and paid water bill, $684.

31 Paid cash as an installment payment on the mortgage, $3,890. Of this amount, $1,910 represents a reduction in the principal, and the remainder is interest. (Debit Mortgage Payable, debit Interest Expense, and credit Cash.)

31 Received and paid electric bill, $824.

31 Bought additional inner tubes from Worn Tires for $480, paying $100 down, with the remainder due in 30 days.

31 Lacy withdrew cash for personal use, $2,200.

31 Sales for the video and food concessions amounted to $4,840, and 10 percent of $4,840 equals $484. Since you have already recorded $250 as concessions income, record the additional $234 revenue due from the concessionaire (cash was not received).

Required

1. Journalize the transactions, starting on page 1 of the general journal.
2. Post the transactions to the ledger accounts.
3. Prepare a trial balance in the first two columns of the work sheet.

Check Figures
Trial balance total, $616,941; net income, $18,391; post-closing trial balance total, $587,612

4. Complete the work sheet. Data for the adjustments are as follows:
   a. Insurance expired during the month, $1,020.
   b. Depreciation of building for the month, $480.
   c. Depreciation of pool/slide facility for the month, $675.
   d. Depreciation of pool furniture for the month, $120.
   e. Wages accrued at July 31, $920.
5. Prepare the income statement.
6. Prepare the statement of owner's equity.
7. Prepare the balance sheet.
8. Journalize adjusting entries.
9. Post adjusting entries to the ledger accounts.
10. Journalize closing entries.
11. Post closing entries to the ledger accounts.
12. Prepare a post-closing trial balance.

Accounting Cycle Review Problem B

This problem is designed to enable you to apply the knowledge you have acquired in the preceding chapters. In accounting, the ultimate test is being able to handle data in real-life situations. This problem will give you valuable experience.

CHART OF ACCOUNTS

Assets
111 Cash
112 Accounts Receivable
114 Prepaid Insurance
121 Land
125 Pool Structure
126 Accumulated Depreciation, Pool Structure
127 Fan System
128 Accumulated Depreciation, Fan System
129 Sailboats
130 Accumulated Depreciation, Sailboats

Liabilities
221 Accounts Payable
222 Wages Payable
223 Mortgage Payable

Owner's Equity
311 R. Arden, Capital
312 R. Arden, Drawing
313 Income Summary

Revenue
411 Income from Services
412 Income from Concessions

Expenses
511 Sailboat Rental Expense
512 Wages Expense
513 Advertising Expense
514 Utilities Expense
515 Interest Expense
516 Insurance Expense
517 Depreciation Expense, Pool Structure
518 Depreciation Expense, Fan System
519 Depreciation Expense, Sailboats
522 Miscellaneous Expense

You are to record transactions in a two-column general journal. Assume that the fiscal period is one month. You will then be able to complete all the steps in the accounting cycle.

When you are analyzing the transactions, think them through by visualizing the T accounts or by writing them down on scratch paper. For unfamiliar types of transactions, specific instructions for recording them are included. However, reason them out for yourself as well. Check off each transaction as it is recorded.

June 1 Arden deposited $85,000 in a bank account for the purpose of buying Wind Sailors, a business offering the use of small sailboats to the public at a large indoor pool with a fan system that provides wind.

2 Bought Wind Sailors in its entirety for a total price of $216,100. The assets include sailboats, $25,800; fan system, $13,300; pool structure, $140,000; and land, $37,000. Paid $60,000 down, and signed a mortgage note for the remainder. (Debit each asset and credit Cash and Mortgage Payable.)

3 Received and paid bill for newspaper advertising, $350.

June 3 Received and paid bill for a one-year premium for insurance, $12,000.

3 Bought additional boats from Larkin Manufacturing Co. for $7,200, paying $3,200 down, with the remainder due in 30 days.

3 Signed a contract with a vending machine service to lease space for vending machines. The rental income agreed upon is 10 percent of the sales generated from the machines, with the estimated total rental income payable in advance. Received estimated cash payment for June, $150. (Debit Cash and credit Concessions Income.)

3 Received bill from Quick Printing for promotional handouts, $460 (Advertising Expense).

3 Signed a contract for leasing sailboats from K. Erdmon Boat Co. and paid rental fee for June, $700.

5 Paid cash for miscellaneous expenses, $96.

8 Received $2,855 in cash as income for the use of the boats.

9 Bought an addition for the fan system on account from Stark Pool Supply, $745.

15 Paid wages to employees for the period ended June 14, $3,900.

16 Paid on account for promotional handouts already recorded on June 3, $460.

16 Arden withdrew cash for personal use, $1,200.

16 Bought additional sails from Canvas Products, Inc., $850; payment due in 30 days. (Debit Sailboats.)

16 Received $4,850 in cash as income for the use of the boats.

19 Paid cash for miscellaneous expenses, $40.

20 Paid cash to Larkin Manufacturing Co. as part payment on account, $1,300.

22 Received $8,260 in cash for the use of the boats (Income from Services).

23 Received a reduction in the outstanding bill from Larkin Manufacturing Co. for a boat received in damaged condition, $380. (Debit Accounts Payable, credit Sailboats.)

24 Received and paid telephone bill, $284.

29 Paid wages for period June 15 through 28, $4,973.

30 Paid cash to Stark Pool Supply to apply on account, $475.

30 Received and paid electric bill, $345.

30 Paid cash as an installment payment on the mortgage, $1,848. Of this amount, $497 represents a reduction in the principal, and the remainder is interest. (Debit Mortgage Payable, debit Interest Expense, and credit Cash.)

30 Received and paid water bill, $590.

30 Bought additional boats from Ranger and Son for $5,320, paying $1,550 down, with the remainder due in 30 days.

30 Arden withdrew cash for personal use, $1,500.

30 Received $5,902 in cash as income for the use of the boats.

30 Sales from vending machines for the month amounted to $1,780. Ten percent of $1,780 equals $178. Since you have already recorded $150 as concessions income, list the additional $28 revenue earned from the vending machine operator. (Cash was not received.)

Check Figures
Trial balance total, $269,858; net income, $5,291; post-closing trial balance total, $253,069

Required

1. Journalize the transactions, starting on page 1 of the general journal.
2. Post the transactions to the ledger accounts.
3. Prepare a trial balance in the first two columns of the work sheet.
4. Complete the work sheet. Data for the adjustments are as follows:
   a. Insurance expired during the month, $1,000.
   b. Depreciation of pool structure for the month, $715.
   c. Depreciation of fan system for the month, $260.
   d. Depreciation of sailboats for the month, $900.
   e. Wages accrued at June 30, $790.
5. Prepare the income statement.
6. Prepare the statement of owner's equity.
7. Prepare the balance sheet.
8. Journalize adjusting entries.
9. Post adjusting entries to the ledger accounts.
10. Journalize closing entries.
11. Post closing entries to the ledger accounts.
12. Prepare a post-closing trial balance.

ACTIVITIES

CONSIDER AND COMMUNICATE

Your uncle owns a small sole proprietorship. He does his own bookkeeping, although he didn't finish the chapter on closing entries before he opened his business. He mentions to you that closing entries look like they take a long time. He wonders why he should bother to do them, because all he really looks at is the checkbook anyway. What would you say to convince him that closing entries are necessary?

CRITICAL THINKING

Following is the post-closing trial balance submitted to you by the bookkeeper. Assume that the debit total ($41,048) is correct.

a. Analyze the work and prepare a response to what you have reviewed.
b. Journalize the closing entries.
c. What is the net income or net loss?
d. Is there an increase or a decrease in Capital?
e. What would be the ending amount of Capital?
f. What is the new balance of the post-closing trial balance?

Tafoya Consulting Company
Post-Closing Trial Balance
December 31, 20—

Account Name	Debit	Credit
Cash	3,412	
Accounts Receivable	1,693	
Prepaid Insurance	2,147	
Accounts Payable		
C. Tafoya, Capital		13,818
C. Tafoya, Drawing	6,360	
Consulting Fees		25,603
Wages Expense	11,994	
Rent Expense	9,600	
Advertising Expense	2,582	
Supplies Expense	914	
Insurance Expense	1,610	
Miscellaneous Expense	736	
	41,048	41,048

A QUESTION OF ETHICS

You are preparing a post-closing trial balance for the company where you work, but it doesn't balance. You are tired, and besides, you don't think they pay you for this kind of hassle and extra time. You decide to increase the balance of an asset account to make the totals balance. Discuss this action and whether it is ethical or illegal.

WHAT'S WRONG WITH THIS PICTURE?

The bookkeeper has completed a work sheet and has journalized and posted the closing entries, but he forgot to journalize and post the adjusting entries from the work sheet. What are the effects of these actions and omissions? How would these actions and omissions affect the accounting records and the resulting financial statements?

All About You Spa

Closing Entries

Before the month-end closing entries

What to do *before* you perform the closing entries:

1. Open the file entitled ***All_About_You_Spa_Ch05.IA7***. Enter your name when prompted and click ***OK***. Select "Yes" or "No" as desired when asked if you want to open on-screen instructions and check figures.
2. Click on the ***Save As*** toolbar button. When the Save As window appears, select the folder in which you wish to save your data files (if not already selected). In the File Name box, key ***All_About_You_Ch05_Your_Name.IA7*** (for example, All_About_You_Spa_Ch05_John_Doe.IA7) to identify the file containing your work. Click on the ***Save*** button.
3. If you did not print out and keep the adjusted trial balance and financial statements you generated for Chapter 4, generate and print them out now. Click on the ***Reports*** toolbar button, then click on ***Ledger Reports*** and select ***Trial Balance*** to generate the Trial Balance report. Click on the ***Reports*** toolbar button, then in turn click on ***Income Statement, Statement of Owner's Equity,*** and ***Balance Sheet*** to generate each of these financial statements. To print these reports, click on the ***Print*** button at the bottom of the report window.
4. You will need a new account, Income Summary, to complete the closing process. This account has been added as Account No. 313.

Month-end closing entries

What to do to *close* (or zero out) the temporary owner's equity accounts (revenue(s), expenses, Income Summary, and Drawing), a process that transfers the net income into or deducts the net loss and the withdrawals from the Capital account. In addition, the closing process prepares the records for the new fiscal period:

5. Generate closing entries. Select ***Generate Closing Journal Entries*** from the ***Options*** menu. When the dialog box appears, click ***Yes*** to confirm that you wish the computer to generate the closing journal entries. The entries will display in a preview window. Click on the ***Post*** button to post the closing journal entries to the general journal.
6. Display the closing journal entries. Click on the ***Reports*** toolbar button. Click on ***Journals*** and ***General Journal*** to choose the report to display. Click on ***Customize Journal Report***. In the Reference drop-down list, choose "Clo.Ent." and then click the ***OK*** button to display the Closing Journal Entries report. To print the report, click on the ***Print*** button.

Check Figures
6. Closing Journal Entries report total, $38,544
7. Post closing trial balance total, $25,777
8. Net income from post-closing income statement, $0

After the month-end closing entries

What to do *after* the closing entries:

7. Display and print a post-closing trial balance. Post means "after," so you are printing a trial balance after closing. Click on the ***Reports*** toolbar button. Click on ***Ledger Reports*** and ***Trial Balance*** to choose the report to display. To print the report, click on the ***Print*** button at the bottom of the report window.
8. Display and print financial statements. Click on the ***Reports*** toolbar button, then in turn click on ***Income Statement, Statement of Owner's Equity,*** and ***Balance Sheet*** to generate each of these financial statements. To print these reports, click on the ***Print*** button at the bottom of the report window.
9. Compare the pre- and post-closing trial balance and financial statements. Notice that the post-closing trial balance is shorter and excludes the Drawing, revenue, and expense accounts, which now have zero balances after the closing process.

Likewise, the Drawing, revenue, and expense accounts no longer appear in any of the financial statements. Indeed, an income statement generated after closing will show no data whatsoever. The income statement accounts are ready to begin accumulating data for the next accounting period.

10. If you have not already done so, click on the ***Save*** toolbar button to save your data file.

11. Click on the ***Check*** toolbar button to check your solution against the answer key.

6 Bank Accounts and Cash Funds

WHY IT MATTERS

FEELEY & DRISCOLL, Boston, Massachusetts

Based in Boston, Massachusetts, Feeley & Driscoll is a full-service consulting and forensic accounting firm. Its services range from determining contract damages to fraud examination. Its forensic accountants are experts at finding even the cleverest trails of fraudulent financial data and then providing the hard numbers needed to prove a case of fraud. The forensic accountants look beyond the numbers to analyze and reveal all relevant aspects of the situation.

Feeley & Driscoll has extensive experience in information technology for consulting audits and assessments. It also delivers complete data analysis of electronic business records and files, including e-mails, financial spreadsheets, hard drives, tape backups, and more.

In this chapter, you will learn about the importance of managing bank accounts and cash funds, which is key to a company's internal control and its avoidance of fraudulent financial practices.

LEARNING OBJECTIVES

After you have completed this chapter, you will be able to do the following:

1. *Describe the procedure for depositing checks.*
2. *Reconcile a bank statement.*
3. *Record the required journal entries from the bank reconciliation.*
4. *Record journal entries to establish and reimburse a Petty Cash Fund.*
5. *Complete petty cash vouchers and petty cash payments records.*
6. *Record the journal entries to establish a Change Fund.*
7. *Record journal entries for transactions involving Cash Short and Over.*

ACCOUNTING LANGUAGE

ABA number *(p. 215)*
ATMs (automated teller machines) *(p. 217)*
Bank reconciliation *(p. 222)*
Bank statement *(p. 219)*
Blank endorsement *(p. 218)*
Canceled checks *(p. 221)*
Cash funds *(p. 214)*
Change Fund *(p. 233)*
Collections *(p. 222)*
Denominations *(p. 231)*
Deposit in transit *(p. 222)*
Deposit slips *(p. 215)*
Drawer *(p. 218)*
Electronic Funds Transfer (EFT) *(p. 217)*
Endorsement *(p. 217)*
Errors *(p. 223)*
Interest income *(p. 222)*
Internal control *(p. 213)*
Ledger balance of cash *(p. 222)*
MICR *(p. 216)*
NSF (not sufficient funds) check *(p. 222)*
Outstanding checks *(p. 222)*
Payee *(p. 218)*
Petty Cash Fund *(p. 230)*
Petty cash payments record *(p. 232)*
Petty cash voucher *(p. 231)*
Promissory note *(p. 224)*
Qualified endorsement *(p. 218)*
Restrictive endorsement *(p. 218)*
Service charge *(p. 222)*
Signature card *(p. 215)*

A very important aspect of any financial accounting system, either for an individual or for a business enterprise, is the accurate and efficient management of assets. The handling of assets in a manner that will prevent employees from stealing cash funds is known as **internal control**. Internal control is the system of policies and procedures that is designed to:

1. Protect assets against fraud and waste
2. Provide for accurate accounting data
3. Promote efficient operation
4. Encourage adherence to management policies

When we talk about cash, we mean currency, coins, checks, money orders, traveler's checks, and bank drafts or bank cashier's checks. Personal checks are accepted conditionally—that is, based on the condition that they are valid. In other words, we consider checks to be good until they are otherwise proven not to be good.

Managing cash is an important aspect of business. All embezzlement starts with an employee(s) failing to follow internal control procedures. Following are some simple internal control guidelines for better management of cash receipts and payments:

Cash receipts

- Maintain separation between cash handling and cash recording.
- Designate someone other than the bookkeeper to open mail.
- Make a record of cash received.
- Endorse checks immediately upon receipt with the stamp, "For Deposit Only."
- Deposit cash daily.
- Journalize cash receipts as soon as possible, preferably by someone different than the person who first received the cash.
- Post cash receipts to the Accounts Receivable account as soon as possible.

Cash payments

- Make sure that all cash payments are made by check (with the exception of petty cash).
- Make certain that all checks are prenumbered.
- Keep check supplies under lock.
- Assign someone different than the signer of the checks to prepare the checks.
- Appoint someone other than the person preparing checks to prepare the bank reconciliations.
- Keep petty cash under lock with access limited to one person other than the bookkeeper.

When cash register drawers are involved, additional security is involved. Cashiers must have their register drawer totals verified by a designated employee, manager, or owner when their shifts end. Later, we will see how the bank deposit amount is determined considering the cash in the till at the start of business.

Internal control of cash is a critical activity in any business. Divide the cash activities among several people to deter mishandling.

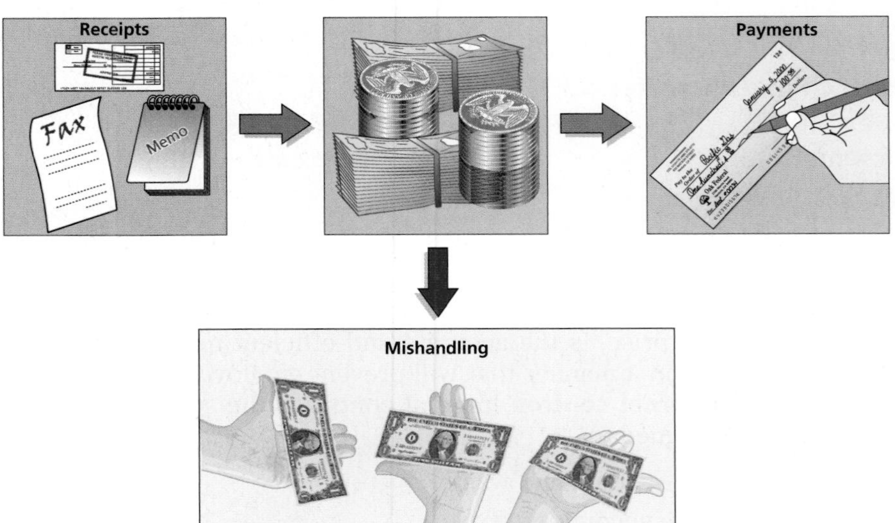

In this chapter, besides discussing bank accounts, we are going to talk about **cash funds**—Petty Cash Funds and Change Funds—which are separately held reserves of cash set aside for specific purposes.

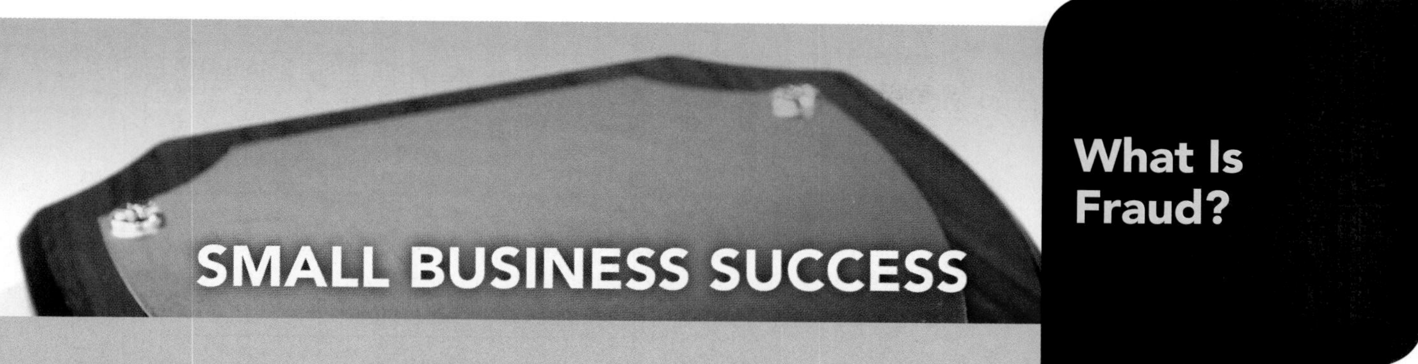

What Is Fraud?

Fraud is defined as an intentional misrepresentation of the truth. In its most recent 2008 Report to the Nation, the Association of Certified Fraud Examiners (ACFE) estimated that "small businesses are especially vulnerable to occupational fraud. The median loss suffered by organizations with fewer than 100 employees was $200,000." The ACFE is an organization that provides anti-fraud training and education (www.acfe.com).

A common type of fraud that occurs in small businesses involves theft of assets by employees. Theft of assets involves stealing of cash, supplies, inventory, and so forth. Employees will go to such extent as to create fake employees who receive payroll and falsify invoices for payment.

The ACFE suggests several strategies to prevent fraud in small business, such as promoting honesty in the workplace and removing the opportunity to commit fraud by maintaining internal controls on accounting records. In addition, companies should be especially careful when hiring employees and always conduct background checks.

USING A CHECKING ACCOUNT

Although you may be familiar with the process of opening a checking account, making deposits, and writing checks, let's review these and other procedures associated with opening and maintaining a business checking account. We will discuss signature cards, deposit slips, automated teller machines, Electronic Funds Transfer, night deposits, and endorsements.

Signature Card

When Melinda B. Roland founded Roland's Delivery Services, she opened a checking account in the name of the business. When she opened the account, she filled out a **signature card** for the bank's files. Because Roland gave her assistant Sheila R. Bayes the right to sign checks too, the assistant also signed the card. The signature card gives the bank a copy of the official signatures of any persons authorized to sign checks. The bank can use it to verify the signatures on any checks of Roland's Delivery Services presented for payment. This card helps the bank detect forgeries. Each banking entity has its own signature card. Figure 1 shows a typical signature card.

FYI

As a means of preventing employee theft, many companies require more than one signature on checks over a certain dollar amount.

Deposit Slips

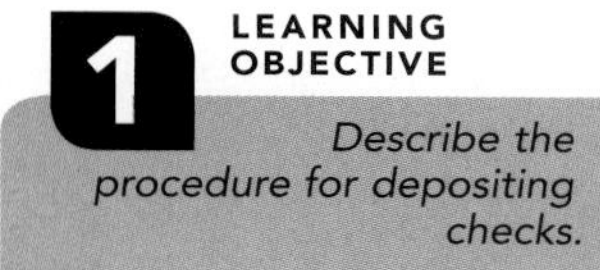

Describe the procedure for depositing checks.

The bank provides printed **deposit slips** on which customers record the amount of coins and currency they are depositing and list each individual check being deposited. A typical deposit slip is shown in Figure 2.

Each check should be listed according to its American Bankers Association (ABA) transit number. The **ABA number** is the small series of numbers located in the upper right corner of a check. The first part of the number indicates the city or state in which the bank is located and the specific bank on which the check is drawn. The second part of the number indicates the Federal Reserve District in

FIGURE 1

Signature card for Roland's Delivery Services

Title **Roland's Delivery Services**

Account number 5008-3007

In consideration of the acceptance by COMPASS BANK of my/our account of the type indicated below, I/we agree to be bound by such rules and regulations and/or such schedules of interest, fees and charges applicable to such account as may now or hereafter be adopted by and in effect at said Bank, and also by the provisions printed hereon. It is understood that the acceptance by said Bank of my/our account is subject to the receipt by said Bank of satisfactory credit information.

(1) Sign Here *Melinda B. Roland*

(2) Sign Here *Sheila R. Bayes*

Address	City	State	Zip
951 Bay Road	San Diego	California	92109

☑ CHECKING ☐ MULTIPLE MATURITY ☐ CASH MANAGER

☐ SAVINGS ☐ GUARANTEED INTEREST (Multiple Maturity) ☐ SAFE DEPOSIT ☐ OTHER ______

IF THIS IS A JOINT ACCOUNT, BOTH OWNERS MUST SIGN ABOVE

Each of the signers guarantees the genuineness of the signature of the other. Each signer also agrees with the other and the Bank that deposits now or hereafter made to this account may be withdrawn in whole or part by either or survivor, and that each may endorse for deposit to this account any instrument payable to the order of either or both. Provisions respecting this agreement shall be modified only upon receipt by the Bank of written notice, signed by both.

FIGURE 2

Deposit slip for Roland's Delivery Services

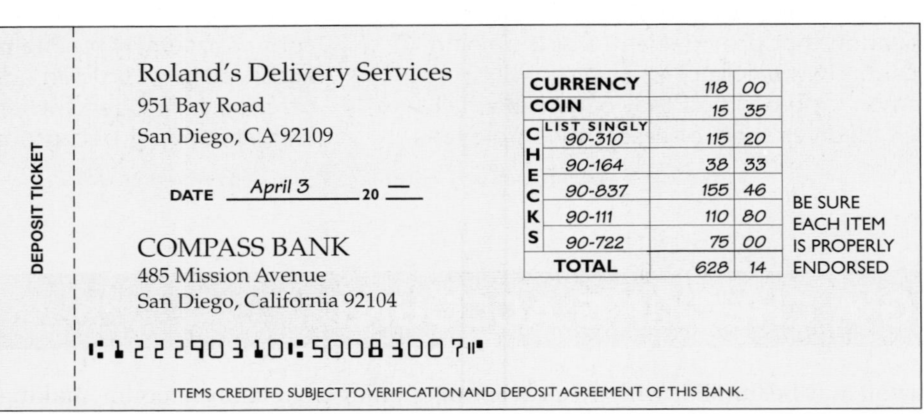

DEPOSIT TICKET

Roland's Delivery Services
951 Bay Road
San Diego, CA 92109

DATE April 3 20 —

COMPASS BANK
485 Mission Avenue
San Diego, California 92104

CURRENCY	118	00
COIN	15	35
CHECKS (LIST SINGLY) 90-310	115	20
90-164	38	33
90-837	155	46
90-111	110	80
90-722	75	00
TOTAL	628	14

BE SURE EACH ITEM IS PROPERLY ENDORSED

⑆1222903101⑆50083007⑈

ITEMS CREDITED SUBJECT TO VERIFICATION AND DEPOSIT AGREEMENT OF THIS BANK.

which the check is cleared and the routing number used by the Federal Reserve Bank. For example,

$$\frac{90\text{-}310}{1222}$$

FYI

The 12 in the last part of the ABA number represents the Twelfth Federal Reserve District, and the 22 represents the routing number used by the Federal Reserve Bank.

The 90 identifies the city or state, and the 310 indicates the specific bank within that area (see Figures 3 and 5).

For a business account, the depositor fills out the deposit slip in duplicate, giving the original to the bank teller and keeping the copy. (This procedure may vary from bank to bank.)

The bank prints the amount of each deposited check on the lower right side of the check in a distinctive script called **MICR**, which stands for *magnetic ink character recognition*. The routing number (as well as the depositor's number) used by the Federal Reserve Bank was printed on the lower left side of the blank check before it was sent to the account holder. The electronic equipment used to process the checks is able to rapidly read the script identifying the bank on which the check is drawn and the amount of the check.

A federal law called The Check Clearing for the 21st Century Act (or Check 21 Act) enacted in 2004 allows banks that receive a check from a depositor to create a two-sided digital version of the original check, called a *substitute* check. This substitute check eliminates the need to handle a paper check through the banking system. One of the several effects of the Check 21 Act is that consumers will no longer be able to require a bank to return to them their original cancelled checks with their monthly statement. Another side effect of the law is that it is now legal for anyone to use a computer scanner to capture images of checks and deposit them electronically, a process known as *remote deposit.* The Federal Reserve's Web site (www.federalreserve.gov/pubs/check21/consumer_guide.htm) provides more information about the Check 21 Act.

Automated Teller Machines

Deposits, withdrawals, and transfers can be made at all hours at banks with **ATMs (automated teller machines)**. Each depositor uses a plastic card that contains a code number and has a personal identification number (PIN). The amount to be deposited, withdrawn, or transferred is keyed in by the depositor. To make a deposit, the customer inserts an envelope containing cash and/or checks and, if required, a copy of the deposit slip into the ATM. To make a withdrawal, the customer requests an amount, the ATM dispenses it, and the customer removes the cash. In addition to deposits and withdrawals, a customer may transfer amounts from one account to another (for example, from savings to checking) as well as check the balance of their accounts.

Electronic Funds Transfer

A transfer of funds initiated through an electronic terminal, such as a telephone, computer, or magnetic tape, is an **Electronic Funds Transfer (EFT)**. There is no paper document, such as a check or deposit slip, starting the transaction. The monthly bank statement will list the EFT deposits and payments. Examples of EFTs include an ATM transaction, a wire transfer in or out of an account, electronic bill paying, and payments to the IRS for income and payroll taxes.

Night Deposits

Most banks provide night depositories so that businesses and individuals can make deposits after regular hours. These are secured chutes into which a business's representative can insert a bag of cash and checks, knowing that the day's receipts will be safe until the bank opens in the morning.

Endorsements

The bank does not accept for deposit a check made out to a business until someone from the business has endorsed the check by signature or by stamp. The endorsement should appear on the back of the left end of a check, as it does in Figure 3. The **endorsement** (1) transfers title to the money and (2) authorizes the payment of

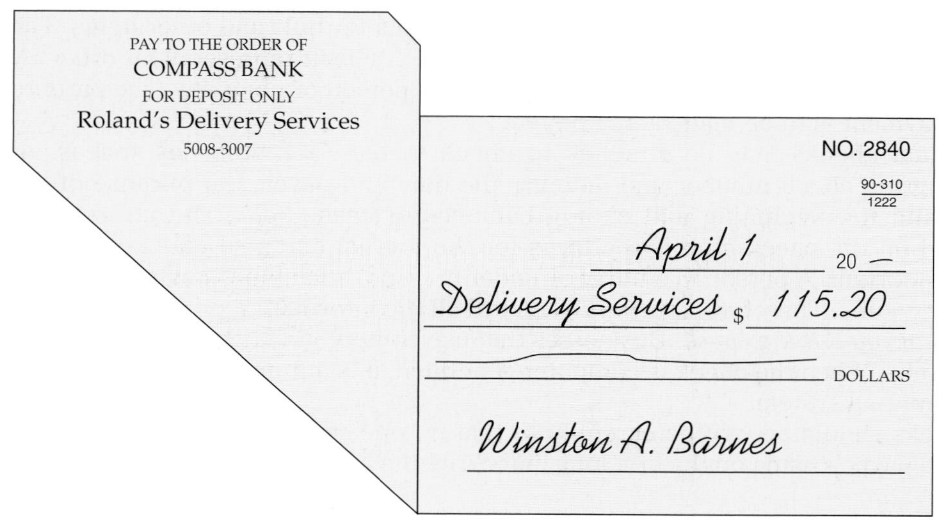

FIGURE 3
Endorsement for Roland's Delivery Services

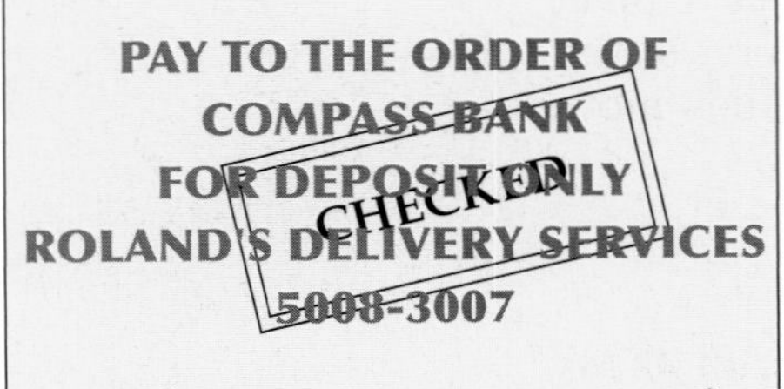

Restrictive Endorsement (with rubber stamp)

Melinda B. Roland

Blank Endorsement

Pay to the order of
M. E. Ransom
without recourse
Melinda B. Roland

Qualified Endorsement

FIGURE 4
Types of endorsements

the check. In other words, if the check is not good (does not have sufficient funds), then the bank, in order to protect itself, will deduct the amount of the check from the depositor's account.

Restrictive Endorsement

All checks made payable to Roland's Delivery Services are endorsed by stamping on the back of the checks "Pay to the Order of Compass Bank, For Deposit Only, Roland's Delivery Services." This is called a **restrictive endorsement** (see Figure 4) because it restricts or limits any further transfer of the check. This endorsement also forces the deposit of the check, because the endorsement is not valid for any other purpose.

Blank Endorsement

When the party to whom a check is made payable (the payee) endorses the check by signing only her or his name on the back of the check, this is known as a **blank endorsement** (Figure 4). With a blank endorsement, there are no restrictions attached.

Qualified Endorsement

A third type of endorsement is a **qualified endorsement** (see Figure 4), which generally includes the phrase "Pay to the order of," followed by the name of the person to whom the check is being transferred, and then followed by the phrase "without recourse." Such an endorsement frees the endorser from future liability in case the drawer of the check does not have sufficient funds to cover the check.

WRITING CHECKS

Most people generally use a check to make payments for bills and other items. The party who writes the check is called the **drawer**. A check represents an order by the drawer, directing the bank to pay a designated person or company. The party to whom payment is to be made is the **payee**.

Manual checks may be attached to check stubs. Each stub has spaces for recording the check number and amount, the date and payee, the purpose of the check, and the beginning and ending balances of cash. *Note:* The information recorded on the check stub is the basis for the journal entry, so check stubs are vitally important. A person in a hurry or under pressure sometimes neglects to fill in the check stubs. Therefore, it is best to record all the information on the check stub *before making out the check.* Businesses that use computerized checks do not need check stubs. When the check is computer generated, it is automatically entered into the accounting system.

Checks should be written carefully so that no one can successfully alter them. Write the payee's name on the first long line. Write the amount of the check in figures

Payee

NO. 1980 $ 367.00
DATE October 14 20 —
TO R. L. Michaels Co.
FOR Advertising

	DOLLARS	CENTS
BAL. BRO'T. FOR'D.	13,215	36
AMT. DEPOSITED		
" "		
TOTAL		
AMT. THIS CHECK	367	00
BAL. CAR'D. FOR'D.	12,848	36

Roland's Delivery Services
951 Bay Road
San Diego, California 92109

No. 1980
90-310/1222

October 14 20 —

PAY TO THE ORDER OF R. L. Michaels Company $ 367.00

Three hundred sixty-seven and 00/100 DOLLARS

COMPASS BANK
485 Mission Avenue
San Diego, California 92104

Melinda B. Roland

⑆122290310⑆ 50083007 ⑈ 1980 000036700

Drawer

FIGURE 5
Manual check with accompanying stub for Roland's Delivery Services

close to the dollar sign, then write the amount in words at the extreme left of the line provided for this information. Write cents as a fraction of 100. For example, write $727.50 as "Seven hundred twenty-seven and 50/100," or $89.00 as "Eighty-nine and 00/100." Legally, if there is a discrepancy between the amount in figures and the written amount, the written amount prevails. However, generally, the bank gets in touch with the drawer and asks what the correct amount should be.

Finally, the drawer's signature on the face of the check should match that on the signature card on file at the drawer's bank.

Figure 5 is a manual check, with the accompanying stub, drawn on the account of Roland's Delivery Services. A description of the script appears in Figure 6.

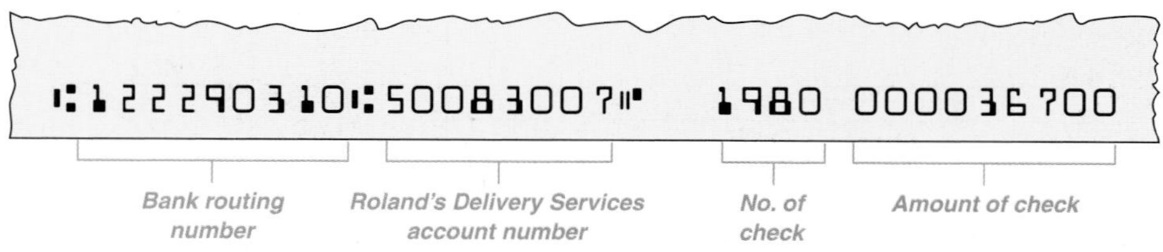

FIGURE 6
Description of the script from Ck. No. 1980 in Figure 5

BANK STATEMENTS

The bank prepares the **bank statement**, which is created from the bank's viewpoint. Keep in mind that, to the bank, a customer's account is a liability and, therefore, has a credit balance. Once a month, the bank sends each of its customers the following information with the bank statement:

- The balance at the beginning of the month
- Additions in the form of deposits and credit memos
- Deductions in the form of checks and debit memos
- Electronic transactions
- The final balance at the end of the month

A bank statement for Roland's Delivery Services is shown in Figure 7. The following legend of symbols is listed on the bottom of the statement:

CM (credit memo) Increases in or credits to the account, such as notes or accounts left with the bank for collection and interest income earned.

COMPASS BANK
485 Mission Avenue
San Diego, CA 92104

STATEMENT OF ACCOUNT

Roland's Delivery Services
951 Bay Road
San Diego, CA 92109

ACCOUNT NUMBER
5008-3007
STATEMENT DATE
September 30, 20— - October 31, 20—
TAX ID NUMBER
83-5249862

SUMMARY	
Balance Last Statement	$10,403.57
Amount of Checks and Debits	$37,947.06
Number of Checks	69
Amount of Deposits and Credits	$44,793.10
Number of Deposits	21
Balance This Statement	$17,249.61

CHECKS/ OTHER DEBITS

CHECKS

CHECK NUMBER	DATE POSTED	AMOUNT	CHECK NUMBER	DATE POSTED	AMOUNT
1952	10-01	55.00	1988	10-17	65.22
1953	10-01	210.40	1989	10-17	465.30
1954	10-01	440.00	1990	10-18	560.00
1955	10-02	146.80	1991	10-19	114.57
1956	10-02	186.25	1992	10-19	24.90
1957	10-02	651.75	1993	10-19	135.36
1958	10-03	742.20	1994	10-20	118.36
1984	10-14	564.55	2018	10-30	120.75
1985	10-15	617.00	2019	10-30	843.54
1986	10-16	60.64	2020	10-31	743.20
1987	10-16	481.85	2021	10-31	123.92

OTHER DEBITS DESCRIPTION	DATE POSTED	AMOUNT
DM NSF check from B. R. Rumson	10-15	283.00
DM Automated Teller Trans. 092349 customer M3272348 at terminal 30962—cash	10-16	100.00
DM Service charge	10-31	19.50

DEPOSITS/ OTHER CREDITS

DEPOSITS

DATE POSTED	AMOUNT	DATE POSTED	AMOUNT
10-01	832.00	10-17	973.22
10-02	1,567.20	10-18	836.79
10-03	451.63	10-21	438.49
10-04	790.46	10-22	1,217.25
10-07	1,048.15	10-23	814.15
10-08	1,399.00	10-26	377.82
10-14	872.25	10-28	559.47
10-15	760.42	10-29	713.14
10-16	636.34	10-30	854.32

OTHER CREDITS DESCRIPTION	DATE POSTED	AMOUNT
CM Note collected, principal $1,000, interest $10	10-29	1,010.00

PLEASE EXAMINE THIS STATEMENT CAREFULLY. REPORT ANY POSSIBLE ERRORS WITHIN 10 DAYS.

CODE SYMBOLS

CM Credit Memo **OD Overdraft**
DM Debit Memo **EC Error Correction**

FIGURE 7 Bank statement for Roland's Delivery Services

DM (debit memo) Decreases in or debits to the account, such as NSF checks (discussed later in this chapter) and service charges. Service charges are based on the number of items processed and the average account balance. Special charges may also be levied against the account for collections and other services performed, including check printing.

OD (overdraft) The withdrawal of more than the cash balance in the account, resulting in a negative balance.

EC (error correction) Corrections of errors made by the bank, such as encoding mistakes.

Remember

Debit memos represent deductions from and credit memos represent additions to a bank account.

The bank statement is a valuable aid to efficiency and accuracy because it provides a double record of the Cash account. If a business entity deposits all cash receipts in the bank and makes all payments by check, then the bank is keeping an independent record of the business's cash. You might think that the two balances—the business's and the bank's—should be equal, but this is unlikely. Some transactions may have been recorded in the business's account before being entered in the bank's records. In addition, there are unavoidable delays (by either the business or the bank) in recording transactions. Ordinarily, there is a delay of one or more days between the date on which a check is written and the date when it is presented to the bank for payment. Also, banks may not record deposits until the following business day. During this time lag, deposits made or checks written are recorded in the business's check register, but they are not yet listed on the bank statement.

The bank mails statements to its depositors each month either physically or via the Internet. The **canceled checks** (checks that have been paid or cleared by the bank) are listed on the bank statement. They are called *canceled checks* because they are canceled by a stamp on the back, indicating that they have been paid. Debit or credit memos are generally described on the bank statement.

Recording Deposits or Withdrawals

Each business entity keeps its accounts from its *own* point of view. As far as the bank is concerned, each customer's deposits are liabilities, in that the bank owes the customer the amount of the deposits. Using T accounts, it looks like this:

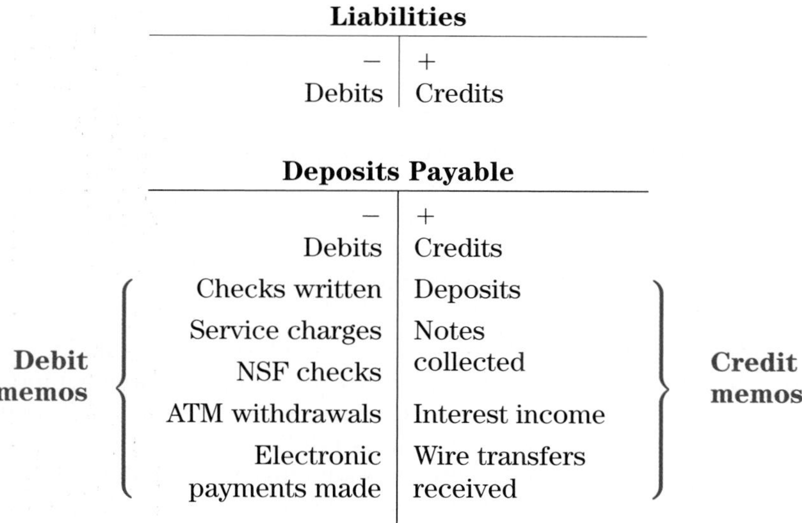

When the bank receives a cash deposit from a customer, the bank credits Deposits Payable, because it owes more to its customer. When the bank cashes a check (pays out) for a customer, the bank debits Deposits Payable, because it owes less to its customer.

The customer, on the other hand, uses the account titled Cash, or Cash in Bank, or simply the name of the bank. Deposits are recorded as debits and withdrawals are recorded as credits in the account. On a bank reconciliation, the balance of the account is listed as the **ledger balance of cash** before reconciliation with the bank statement.

Need for Reconciling Bank Balance and Ledger Balance

LEARNING OBJECTIVE 2

Reconcile a bank statement.

Since the bank statement balance and the ledger balance of cash are not always equal, a business prepares a **bank reconciliation** to uncover the reasons for the difference between the two balances and to correct any errors that may have been made by either the bank or the business. This makes it possible to arrive at the same balance in each account, which is called the *adjusted balance*, or *true balance*, of the Cash account.

Because identity theft and white-collar crimes are potential problems for a business, another purpose of the bank reconciliation is to make sure all of the amounts paid out from the account are proper disbursements for the business. As stated earlier, it is a mark of good internal control to have the bank reconciliation prepared by someone other than the check signer (if someone other than the business owner is signing checks). The person performing the bank reconciliation will be making sure (a) the dollar amount of each check has not been altered, (b) all of the charges, checks, and electronic transfers belong to the company, and (c) deposits are made in a timely way.

FYI

When a bank agrees to accept payments on behalf of a customer, the fee the bank charges does not necessarily mean that the bank will follow up on collection of a payment or notify the customer that the payment is late.

There are a variety of reasons for differences between the bank statement balance and the customer's cash balance. Here are some of the more common ones:

Deposit in transit A deposit made after the bank statement was issued. The depositor has already added the amount to the Cash account in his or her books, but the deposit has not been recorded by the bank (this is also called a *late deposit*).

Outstanding checks Checks that have been written by the company but not yet received for payment by the time the bank sends out its statement. The company employee, when preparing the checks, deducted the amounts from the Cash account in the company's books, which explains the difference.

Collections Money collected by the bank for the customer. When the bank acts as a collection point for its customers by accepting payments on their behalf, it adds the proceeds to the customer's bank account and sends a credit memorandum to notify the customer of the transaction or includes it on the next bank statement.

Interest income Interest earned for keeping cash in the bank account. Some checking accounts are interest bearing or earning. The depositor will not learn how much interest the bank has credited to the bank account until the bank statement is received.

NSF (not sufficient funds) check A deposited check that the bank cannot process because the check writer's account does not contain enough money. When a bank customer deposits a check, it is recorded as cash on the customer's books. Occasionally, however, a check is not paid (bounces). When the bank notifies the customer of this, the customer must make a deduction from the Cash account. Simultaneously, the depositor records an increase in accounts receivable because the client's debt to the depositor remains unpaid. An NSF check may also be called a *dishonored check*.

Service charge A bank charge for services rendered: For handling checks, for collecting money, for receiving payment of notes turned over to it by the customer for collection, for check printing, and for other such services. The bank immediately deducts the fee from the balance of the bank account and identifies the charges on the bank statement.

Errors Mistakes made by the customer or the bank. In spite of internal controls and systems designed to double-check to prevent errors, sometimes either the customer or the bank makes a mistake. Often these errors do not become evident until the bank reconciliation is performed.

Steps in Reconciling the Bank Statement

Follow these steps to reconcile a bank statement:

STEP 1. Canceled checks

a. Compare the amount of each canceled check with the bank statement and note any differences. The amount of the machine-readable characters should appear at the lower right-hand corner of the check, which should match the amount written on the check and the bank statements.

b. In the checkbook beside the check number, list the date of the bank statement. In some cases, a bank may not pay a check until one or two months after it was written. If a question arises as to whether or not you have paid a particular bill, you can look at the checkbook. Then you can refer directly to the bank statement to pick up the accompanying canceled check as proof of payment.

STEP 2. Deposits

a. Compare the deposits in transit (not recorded by the bank at the time of the statement) listed on last month's bank reconciliation with the deposits shown on the bank statement. All of last month's deposits in transit should be listed on this month's bank statement. If they are not, notify the bank immediately.

b. Compare the remaining deposits listed on this month's bank statement with deposits written in the company's accounting records. Consider any deposits not shown on the bank statement as deposits in transit.

STEP 3. Outstanding checks

a. Arrange the canceled checks in order by check number.

b. Look over the list of outstanding checks left over from last month's bank reconciliation, and note the checks that have now been returned or cleared.

c. For each canceled check, compare the amount recorded in MICR numbers at the lower right-hand corner of the check with the amount recorded in the checkbook. Next, compare the canceled check with the numerical listing in the statement. Use a check mark (✓) to indicate that the check has been paid and that the amount is correct. Any payments that have not been marked off, including the outstanding checks from last month's bank reconciliation, are the present outstanding checks.

d. Review the endorsements on the backs of the checks to verify that money has been sent to the correct payee.

STEP 4. Bank memoranda Trace the credit memos and debit memos to the journal. If the memos have not been recorded, make separate entries for them.

For businesses that have computerized check registers, the bank reconciliation can also be done on the computer. The procedures are similar as there is still the need to compare canceled checks, compare deposits, identify outstanding checks and deposits, and record adjustments.

Examples of Bank Reconciliations

Let's go through the reconciliation process for two businesses, W. Carson Company and Roland's Delivery Services.

W. Carson Company

The bank statement of W. Carson Company indicates a balance of $6,446 as of March 31. The balance of the Cash account in Carson's ledger as of that date is $4,650. Carson's accountant has taken the following steps:

STEP 1. Verified that canceled checks were recorded correctly on the bank statement.

STEP 2. Noted that the deposit made on March 31 was not recorded on the bank statement, $2,174.

STEP 3. Noted outstanding checks: no. 920, $1,695; no. 975, $325; no. 976, $1,279.

STEP 4. Noted credit memo: Note collected by the bank from T. Landon, $700, not recorded in the journal. Noted debit memo: Collection charge and service charge not recorded in the journal, $29.

The note received from T. Landon is called a promissory note. A **promissory note** is a written promise to pay a definite amount at a definite future time. Let's assume that W. Carson Company received the 60-day non-interest-bearing note from T. Landon for services performed. In recording the transaction, Carson's accountant debited Notes Receivable and credited Income from Services. (The account Notes Receivable is similar to Accounts Receivable. However, Accounts Receivable is reserved for customer charge accounts, with payments usually due in 30 days.) Next, W. Carson Company turned the note over to its bank for collection.

The bank will use a credit memo form to notify W. Carson Company that the note has been collected and that the company's bank account has been increased by the amount of the note. Based on the credit memo, Carson's accountant will make a journal entry debiting Cash and crediting Notes Receivable.

Think of the bank reconciliation in terms of the following:

1. Bring the bank statement balance up to date by recording the activities or transactions that we knew about but the bank did not know about when it prepared the statement (deposits in transit and outstanding checks as shown in our checkbook, for example).
2. Bring the balance of the Cash account up to date by recording the activities of transactions that the bank knew about but we did not know about until we received the statement (bank fees, NSF checks, notes collected, checks cleared, interest income, debit memos and credit memos as shown on the bank statement, for example).

Figure 8 shows W. Carson Company's bank reconciliation. The items in the reconciliation that require journal entries are shown in color.

FIGURE 8

Bank reconciliation for W. Carson Company

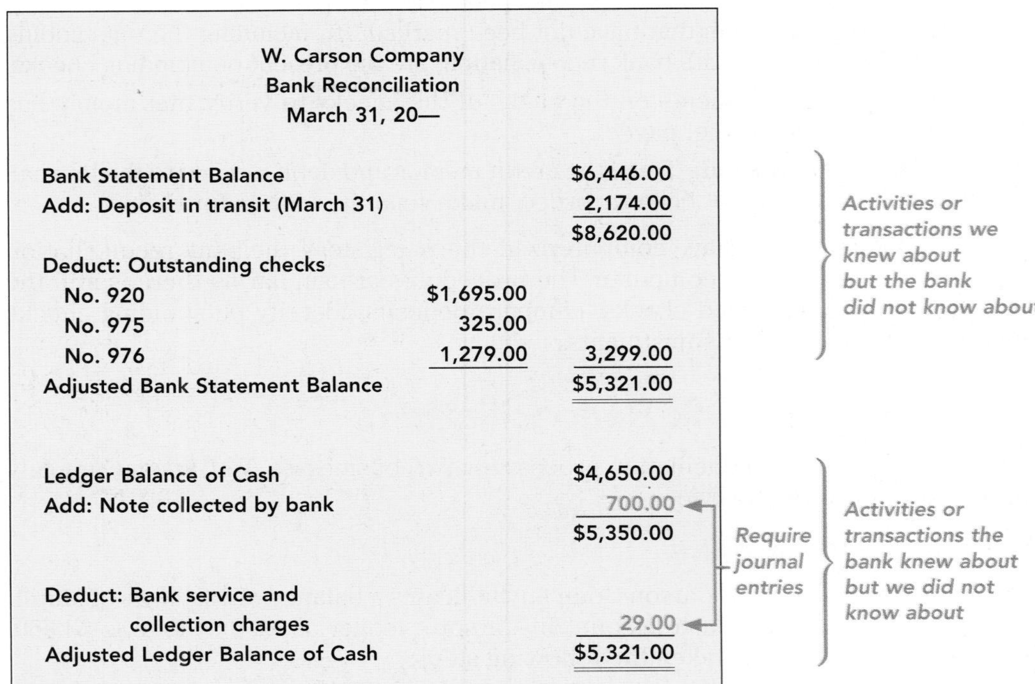

W. Carson Company
Bank Reconciliation
March 31, 20—

Bank Statement Balance		$6,446.00
Add: Deposit in transit (March 31)		2,174.00
		$8,620.00
Deduct: Outstanding checks		
No. 920	$1,695.00	
No. 975	325.00	
No. 976	1,279.00	3,299.00
Adjusted Bank Statement Balance		$5,321.00
Ledger Balance of Cash		$4,650.00
Add: Note collected by bank		700.00
		$5,350.00
Deduct: Bank service and collection charges		29.00
Adjusted Ledger Balance of Cash		$5,321.00

Activities or transactions we knew about but the bank did not know about
Require journal entries
Activities or transactions the bank knew about but we did not know about

You Make the Call

Assume that you manage a service business that has three employees: a bookkeeper, an office manager, and a salesperson. You are so busy growing your business that you have turned over all bookkeeping and cash activities to the bookkeeper, including check-writing and signing privileges, bank reconciliation, and data entry. Your time has been so limited that you have not looked at any reports or reviewed any bank statements. Today is payday and, to your utter surprise, you are informed that there is not enough cash to make this week's payroll. When you look at the last three bank statements and compare the deposits to your cash receipts and cash payments journal, you see that things are not matching up, leading you to the conclusion that embezzlement (theft) of cash has taken place. Thinking back to how you assigned duties for your employees, what could you have done differently to have prevented this disaster?

SOLUTION

There should have been a better segregation of duties to prevent this occurrence. First of all, the bookkeeper should never have been assigned all cash activities, especially check-writing and signing privileges. Checks should have been written and signed by you or the office manager only. The checks should also be mailed by you and no other employee in the business. The office manager should have the responsibility of opening and endorsing each check by stamping on the back of the check "For Deposit Only." This restricts or limits any further transfer of the check and also forces the deposit of the check, because the endorsement is not valid for any other purpose. The bank reconciliation should also be done by the office manager rather than the bookkeeper, with the completed statements reviewed by you. The bookkeeper's primary responsibilities should be to make journal entries for cash received for the general ledger as well as for the Accounts Receivable and Accounts Payable accounts.

3 LEARNING OBJECTIVE

Record the required journal entries from the bank reconciliation.

Note that the journal entries are based on the items used to adjust the ledger balance of Cash. These items represent the transactions that the bank has knowledge of but the business does not. According to the bank reconciliation, the true balance of Cash is $5,321, which is the balance we wish to show on the business's books. We can't change the balance of an account unless we first make a journal entry and then post the entry to the accounts involved. **Consequently, we have to make journal entries for items in the Ledger Balance of Cash section of the bank reconciliation.** The additions are debited to the Cash account, and the deductions are credited to the Cash account. W. Carson Company records the entries in its general journal:

GENERAL JOURNAL PAGE ____

Date		Description	Post. Ref.	Debit	Credit
20—					
Mar.	31	Cash		700 00	
		Notes Receivable			700 00
		Non-interest-bearing note signed by T. Landon was collected by the bank.			
	31	Miscellaneous Expense		29 00	
		Cash			29 00
		Service charge and collection charge levied by bank.			

Here bank service and collection charges are recorded in Miscellaneous Expense because the amounts are relatively small. Some accountants may use a separate expense account, such as Bank Charge Expense. After the entries have been posted, the T account for Cash looks like this:

Cash

Balance	4,650	Mar. 31	29
Mar. 31	700		
Bal.	**5,321**		

Note that the balance in the T account is now equal to both the adjusted bank statement balance and the adjusted ledger balance of cash.

Form of Bank Reconciliation

Now that you have seen an example of a bank reconciliation, let's look at the standard form of a bank reconciliation for an imaginary company.

Bank Statement Balance (last figure on the statement)		$4,000
Add:		
Deposits in transit (deposits made after the bank statement was issued and already added to the ledger balance of Cash)	$300	
Bank errors (that understate balance)	20	320
		$4,320
Deduct:		
Outstanding checks and transfers (they have already been deducted from the Cash account)	$960	
Bank errors (that overstate balance)	40	1,000
Adjusted Bank Statement Balance (the true balance of Cash)		$3,320

Ledger Balance of Cash (the latest balance of the Cash account if it has been posted up to date; otherwise take the beginning balance of Cash, plus cash receipts, minus cash payments)		$2,850
Add:		
Credit memos (additions by the bank not recorded in the Cash account, such as collections of notes)	$500	
Book errors (that understate balance)	40	540
		$3,390
Deduct:		
Debit memos (deductions by the bank not recorded in the Cash account, such as service charges or collection charges and NSF checks)	$ 20	
Book errors (that overstate balance)	50	70
Adjusted Ledger Balance of Cash (the true balance of Cash)		$3,320

Roland's Delivery Services

The bank statement of Roland's Delivery Services shows a final balance of $17,249.61 as of October 31 (see Figure 7). The present balance of the Cash account in the ledger, after Roland's Delivery Services' accountant has posted from the journal, is $16,296.11. The accountant took the following steps:

STEP 1. Verified that canceled checks were recorded correctly on the bank statement.

STEP 2. Discovered that a deposit of $1,012 made on October 31 was not recorded on the bank statement.

STEP 3. Noted outstanding checks: no. 1951, $687; no. 2022, $185; no. 2023, $367; no. 2024, $110.

STEP 4. Noted that a credit memo for a note collected by the bank from Lawson and Richards, $1,000 principal plus $10 interest, was not recorded in the journal. Found that check no. 2002 for $745, payable to Sanders, Inc., on account, was recorded in the journal as $754. (The correct amount is $745.) Noted that a debit memo for a collection charge and service charge of $19.50 was not recorded in the journal. Noted that a debit memo for an NSF check for $283 from B. R. Rumson was not recorded. Noted that a $100 personal withdrawal by Melinda B. Roland, the owner, using an ATM, was not recorded.

Remember

When you are reconciling a bank statement, always double-check for any outstanding checks or deposits from previous statements that have been carried forward. Also double-check for any bank service charges.

Look at Figure 9 to see how each step relates to the bank reconciliation.

The accountant makes journal entries for the items indicated in Figure 9 to change the balance of the Cash account from its present balance of $16,296.11 to the true balance of $16,912.61. Again, those items that require journal entries are highlighted in Figure 9 and shown in Figure 10.

Interest Income is classified as a revenue account. It represents the amount received on the promissory note that is over and above the face value of the note.

As for the NSF check, upon being notified by the bank, Roland's Delivery Services calls its customer (B. R. Rumson). Rumson can now take steps to cover the check. Review Roland's Delivery Services' transaction with B. R. Rumson. In return for services provided, Roland's Delivery Services received Rumson's check for $283. At that time, Roland's Delivery Services' accountant recorded the transaction as a debit to Cash for $283 and a credit to Income from Services for $283. Then the bank, through its debit memorandum, notified Roland's Delivery Services about Rumson's NSF check. To avoid overdrawing its own bank account, Roland's Delivery Services makes an entry crediting Cash (to correct its earlier debit to Cash) and debiting Accounts Receivable (to put the amount into Accounts Receivable). Since B. R. Rumson owes the money, it is logical to add the amount to Accounts Receivable.

FIGURE 9

Bank reconciliation for Roland's Delivery Services

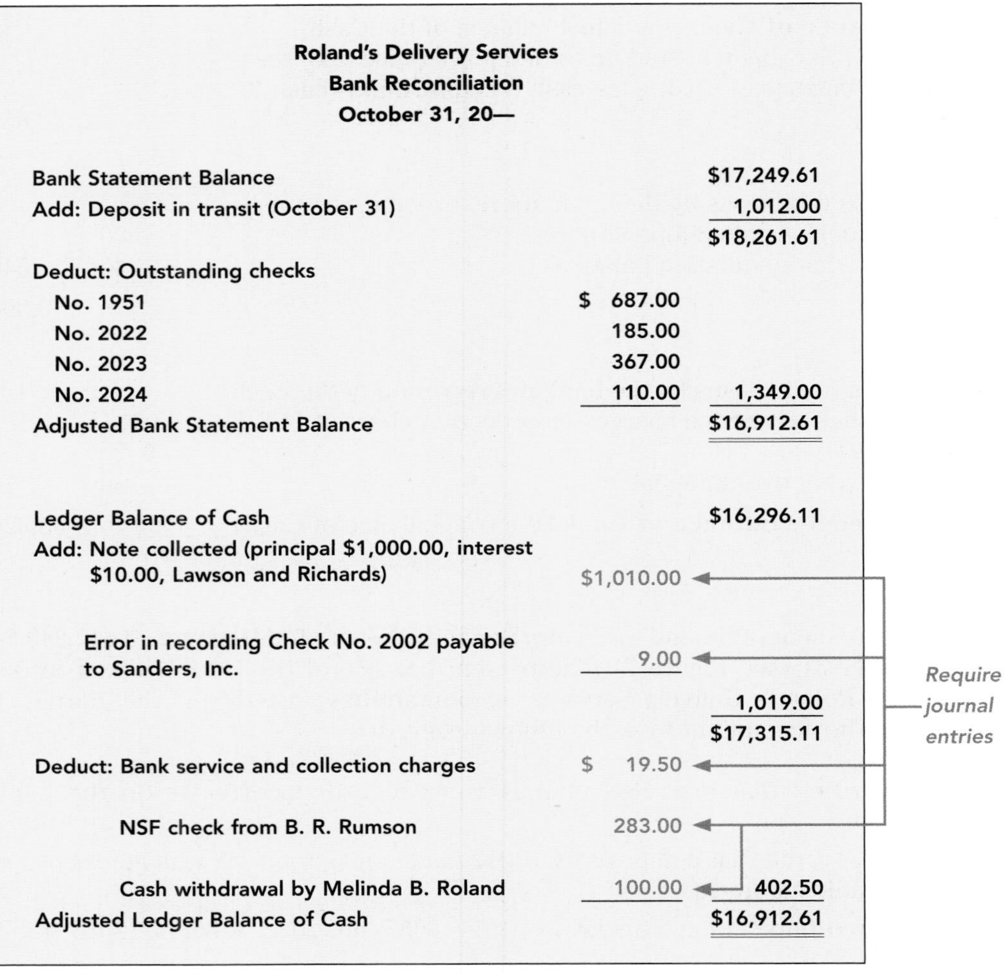

Roland's Delivery Services
Bank Reconciliation
October 31, 20—

Bank Statement Balance		$17,249.61
Add: Deposit in transit (October 31)		1,012.00
		$18,261.61
Deduct: Outstanding checks		
No. 1951	$ 687.00	
No. 2022	185.00	
No. 2023	367.00	
No. 2024	110.00	1,349.00
Adjusted Bank Statement Balance		$16,912.61
Ledger Balance of Cash		$16,296.11
Add: Note collected (principal $1,000.00, interest $10.00, Lawson and Richards)	$1,010.00	
Error in recording Check No. 2002 payable to Sanders, Inc.	9.00	
		1,019.00
		$17,315.11
Deduct: Bank service and collection charges	$ 19.50	
NSF check from B. R. Rumson	283.00	
Cash withdrawal by Melinda B. Roland	100.00	402.50
Adjusted Ledger Balance of Cash		$16,912.61

FIGURE 10

Journal entries for Roland's Delivery Services

GENERAL JOURNAL **PAGE** ______

Date		Description	Post. Ref.	Debit	Credit
20—					
Oct.	31	Cash		1 0 1 0 00	
		Notes Receivable			1 0 0 0 00
		Interest Income			1 0 00
		Bank collected note signed			
		by Lawson and Richards.			
	31	Cash		9 00	
		Accounts Payable			9 00
		Error in recording Ck. No.			
		2002 payable to Sanders, Inc.			
	31	Miscellaneous Expense		1 9 50	
		Cash			1 9 50
		Bank service charge and			
		collection charge.			
	31	Accounts Receivable		2 8 3 00	
		Cash			2 8 3 00
		NSF check received from			
		B. R. Rumson.			
	31	M. B. Roland, Drawing		1 0 0 00	
		Cash			1 0 0 00
		Withdrawal for personal use.			

THIS FORM IS PROVIDED TO HELP YOU BALANCE YOUR BANK STATEMENT

CHECKS OUTSTANDING—NOT CHARGED TO ACCOUNT

NO.	$	
1951	687	00
2022	185	00
2023	367	00
2024	110	00
TOTAL	$ 1,349	00

BEFORE YOU START

PLEASE BE SURE YOU HAVE ENTERED IN YOUR CHECKBOOK ALL AUTOMATIC TRANSACTIONS SHOWN ON THE FRONT OF YOUR STATEMENT.

YOU SHOULD HAVE ADDED IF ANY OCCURRED:

1. Loan advances.
2. Credit memos.
3. Other automatic deposits.

YOU SHOULD HAVE SUBTRACTED IF ANY OCCURRED:

1. Automatic loan payments.
2. Automatic savings transfers.
3. Service charges.
4. Debit memos.
5. Other automatic deductions and payments.

BANK BALANCE SHOWN ON THIS STATEMENT	$ 17,249.61
ADD	
DEPOSITS NOT SHOWN ON THIS STATEMENT *(IF ANY)*	$ 1,012.00
TOTAL	$ 18,261.61
SUBTRACT	
CHECKS OUTSTANDING	$ 1,349.00
BALANCE	$ 16,912.61

SHOULD AGREE WITH YOUR CHECKBOOK BALANCE AFTER DEDUCTING SERVICE CHARGE (IF ANY) SHOWN ON THIS STATEMENT.

Please examine immediately and report if incorrect. If no reply is received within 10 days, the account will be considered correct.

FIGURE 11
Bank form for Roland's Delivery Services

A bank reconciliation form is ordinarily printed on the back of the bank statement. The adjusted balance of the ledger balance of cash has already been determined. Consequently, the bank form is provided only for calculating the adjusted bank statement balance of the bank reconciliation. The bank form for Roland's Delivery Services is shown in Figure 11 above.

THE PETTY CASH FUND

Day after day, businesses are confronted with transactions requiring small immediate payments, such as paying for delivery charges, birthday cards, or pizza for after-hours workers. If the business had to make all payments by check, the time consumed would be frustrating and the whole process would be unduly expensive. For many businesses, the cost of writing each check is more than $10; this includes the cost

Forensic Accountant

If the super detective Sherlock Holmes was around today and needed to investigate corporate financial crimes, he would need to rely on not only his detective skills but also his accounting knowledge. The combination of accounting and detective skills is what makes accountants such good investigators in today's financial world. Many public accountants specialize in forensic accounting—investigating and interpreting white-collar crimes such as securities fraud and embezzlement, bankruptcies and contract disputes, as well as other complex and possibly criminal financial transactions such as money laundering. Forensic accountants combine their knowledge of accounting and finance with law and investigative techniques to determine whether an activity is illegal. Many forensic accountants work closely with law enforcement personnel and lawyers during investigations and often appear as expert witnesses during trials.

Increased focus on and numbers of financial crimes such as embezzlement, bribery, and securities fraud will increase the demand for forensic accountants. Computer technology has made these crimes easier to commit, and they are on the rise. At the same time, the development of new computer software and electronic surveillance technology has made tracking down financial criminals easier, thus increasing the ease and likelihood of discovery. As success rates of investigations grow, demand for forensic accountants will increase. In 2009, *U.S. News & World Report* listed forensic accounting as one of the eight most secure career tracks in America, while *SmartMoney* Magazine counted forensic accounting as one of its "ten hottest jobs" with salary amounts in six figures.

The Association of Certified Fraud Examiners offers the Certified Fraud Examiner (CFE) designation for forensic or public accountants involved in fraud prevention, detection, deterrence, and investigation. To obtain the designation, individuals must have a bachelor's degree, two years of relevant experience, pass a four-part exam, and abide by a code of ethics. Therefore, if you take the additional steps of securing your CPA status as well as education leading to you becoming a CFE, you can feed your taste for detective work while still enjoying your life as an accountant!

of an employee's time for writing and reconciling the check. Suppose you buy five stamps from an employee for $2.20, and you want to reimburse her. To write a check would not be practical. It only makes sense to pay in cash, using the **Petty Cash Fund**. *Petty* means "small," so the business sets a maximum amount that can be paid immediately out of petty cash. Payments that exceed this maximum must be processed by regular check through the journal.

LEARNING OBJECTIVE **4**

Record journal entries to establish and reimburse a Petty Cash Fund.

Establishing the Petty Cash Fund

After the business has set the maximum amount of a payment from petty cash, the next step is to estimate how much cash will be needed during a given period of time, such as a month. It is also important to consider the element of security when keeping cash in the office. If the risk is great, the amount kept in the fund should be small. Roland's Delivery Services decides to establish a Petty Cash Fund of $100 and put it under the control of the assistant. Accordingly, Roland's Delivery Services' accountant writes a check, cashes it at the bank, and records this transaction in the journal as follows:

GENERAL JOURNAL PAGE ____

Date		Description	Post. Ref.	Debit	Credit
20—					
Sept.	1	Petty Cash Fund		1 0 0 00	
		Cash			1 0 0 00
		Established a Petty Cash Fund,			
		Ck. No. 1880.			

T accounts for the entry look like this:

Petty Cash Fund	
+	–
100	

Cash	
+	–
	100

Because the Petty Cash Fund is an asset account, it is listed on the balance sheet immediately below Cash.

Once the fund has been created, it is not debited again unless the original amount is not large enough to handle the necessary transactions. In that case, the accountant has to increase the Petty Cash Fund—perhaps from $100 to $200. **But, if no change is made in the size of the fund, Petty Cash Fund is debited only once.**

Remember

If no change is made in the size of the fund, the Petty Cash Fund account is debited only once, and this happens when the fund is first established.

The check is written to the assistant, "Sheila R. Bayes, Petty Cash Fund." She converts it into convenient **denominations**, which are varieties of coins and currency, such as quarters and dimes and $1 and $5 bills. Then the assistant puts the money in a locked drawer and will not pay anything larger than $20 (or whatever is the agreed-upon amount) out of petty cash.

Payments from the Petty Cash Fund

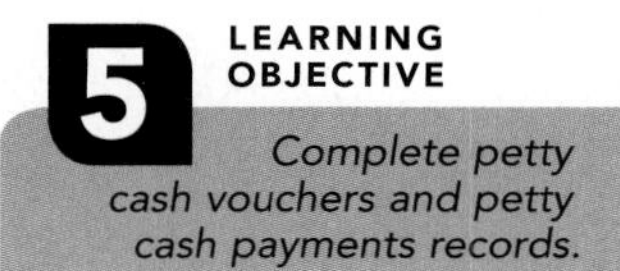

5
LEARNING OBJECTIVE
Complete petty cash vouchers and petty cash payments records.

The assistant is designated as the only person who can make payments from the Petty Cash Fund. In case of her illness, another employee should be named as stand-in. A **petty cash voucher** must be used to account for every payment from the fund. The voucher constitutes a receipt signed by the person who authorized the payment and by the person who received payment as well as the purpose of the payment. Thus, even for small payments of $20 or less, there would have to be collusion between the payee and the assistant for any theft to occur. Figure 12 shows an example of a petty cash voucher.

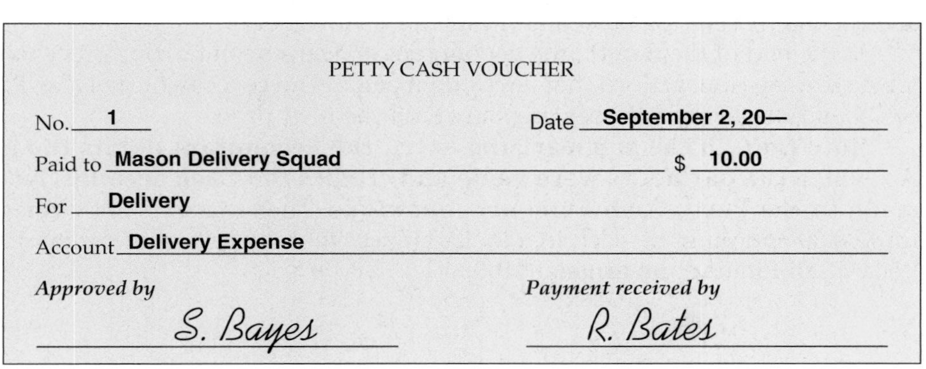
PETTY CASH VOUCHER

No. 1 Date September 2, 20—

Paid to Mason Delivery Squad $ 10.00

For Delivery

Account Delivery Expense

Approved by S. Bayes *Payment received by* R. Bates

FIGURE 12
Petty cash voucher

Remember

The petty cash payments record is not a journal; it is simply used as a basis for compiling information for the journal entry. Remember, to change an account, we have to make a journal entry.

Petty Cash Payments Record

Some businesses prefer to have a written record on one sheet of paper, so they keep a **petty cash payments record**. In a petty cash payments record, petty cash vouchers and the accounts that are to be charged are listed as well as the purpose of the expenditure. Special columns for frequent types of expenditures are included in the Distribution of Payments section. The petty cash payments record is not a journal.

Roland's Delivery Services made the following payments from its Petty Cash Fund during September:

Sept. 2 Paid $10 for flowers for the front counter to Mason Delivery Squad, voucher no. 1.
3 Bought pencils and pens, $8.59, voucher no. 2.
5 Bought local newspapers for article related to Roland's Delivery Services, $2.50, voucher no. 3.
7 Paid postage on incoming packages, $3.70, voucher no. 4.
10 Melinda B. Roland, the owner, withdrew $10 for personal use, voucher no. 5.
14 Reimbursed employee for stamps, $2.20, voucher no. 6.
21 Bought stick-on tabs, $4.10, voucher no. 7.
22 Paid $14 for gift for retiring employee, voucher no. 8.
26 Paid for mailing packages, $3.60, voucher no. 9.
27 Paid $9 for Girl Scout cookies, voucher no. 10.
29 Bought memo pads, $4.40, voucher no. 11.
29 Paid for making duplicate keys, $8.20, voucher no. 12.
30 Paid $8 to have parking area swept, voucher no. 13.
30 Paid for trash removal, $5, voucher no. 14.

Figure 13 on pages 234 and 235 shows how these payments are recorded.

Reimbursement of the Petty Cash Fund

To bring the fund back up to the original amount when it is nearly exhausted (for instance, at the end of the month), the accountant reimburses the fund for expenditures made. Consequently, the Petty Cash Fund may be considered a revolving fund. If the amount initially put in the Petty Cash Fund is $100 and at the end of the month only $6.71 is left, the accountant puts $93.29 in the fund as a reimbursement, thereby bringing the fund back up to $100 to start the new month.

Bear in mind that the petty cash payments record is only a supplementary record for gathering information. A less formal way of compiling the information concerning petty cash payments might consist of collecting one month's petty cash vouchers, then sorting them by accounts, such as Office Supplies Expense, Delivery Expense, and the like. Then run a calculator tape for each account.

At the end of the month, the accountant makes a summarizing entry to officially journalize the transactions that have taken place. The general journal and T accounts of Roland's Delivery Services are shown on the next page.

Note that, in the summarizing entry, the accountant debits the accounts for which the payments were made and credits the Cash account. No entry is made to the Petty Cash Fund account alone. Then the assistant cashes a check for $93.29 and puts the cash in a locked place, thereby restoring the amount in the Petty Cash Fund to the original $100.

GENERAL JOURNAL PAGE ____

Date		Description	Post. Ref.	Debit	Credit
20—					
Sept.	30	Office Supplies Expense		17 09	
		Maintenance Expense		21 20	
		Miscellaneous Expense		45 00	
		M. B. Roland, Drawing		10 00	
		Cash			93 29
		Reimbursed the Petty Cash			
		Fund, Ck. No. 1950.			

Cash	
+	−
	93.29

M. B. Roland, Drawing	
+	−
10.00	

Office Supplies Expense	
+	−
17.09	

Maintenance Expense	
+	−
21.20	

Miscellaneous Expense	
+	−
45.00	

THE CHANGE FUND

Anyone who has tried to pay for a small item with a $20 bill knows that any business that carries out numerous cash transactions needs a **Change Fund**.

Establishing the Change Fund

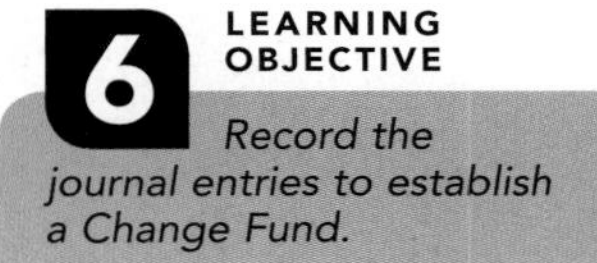

Record the journal entries to establish a Change Fund.

Before setting up a Change Fund, you have to decide two things: (1) how much money needs to be in the fund, and (2) what denominations of bills and coins are needed. Like the Petty Cash Fund, **the Change Fund is debited only once: when it is established.** It is left at the initial figure unless the person in charge decides to make it larger. The Change Fund account, like the Petty Cash Fund account, is an asset. It is recorded in the balance sheet immediately below Cash. If the Petty Cash Fund account is larger than the Change Fund account, it precedes the Change Fund.

The owner of Roland's Delivery Services, Melinda B. Roland, decides to establish a Change Fund; she decides this at the same time she sets up the company's Petty Cash Fund. The entries for the two transactions look like this:

FIGURE 13
Petty cash payments record for Roland's Delivery Services

Petty Cash Payments Record
Month of September 20—

Date		Vou. No.	Explanation		Payments	Office Supplies Expense
Sept.	1		Establish fund, Ck. No. 1880, $100			
	2	1	Mason Delivery Squad		10 00	
	3	2	Pencils and pens		8 59	8 59
	5	3	Local newspapers		2 50	
	7	4	Postage on incoming packages		3 70	
	10	5	Melinda B. Roland		10 00	
	14	6	Reimburse employee for stamps		2 20	
	21	7	Stick-on tabs		4 10	4 10
	22	8	Gift for retiring employee		14 00	
	26	9	Postage for mailings		3 60	
	27	10	Girl Scout cookies		9 00	
	29	11	Memo pads		4 40	4 40
	29	12	Making duplicate keys		8 20	
	30	13	Sweeping of parking area		8 00	
	30	14	Trash removal		5 00	
	30		Totals		93 29	17 09
			Balance in Fund	$ 6.71		
			Reimburse fund, Ck. No. 1950	93.29		
			Total	$100.00		

GENERAL JOURNAL PAGE ______

Date		Description	Post. Ref.	Debit	Credit
20—					
Sept.	1	Petty Cash Fund		100 00	
		Cash			100 00
		Established a Petty Cash Fund,			
		Ck. No. 1880.			
	1	Change Fund		150 00	
		Cash			150 00
		Established a Change Fund,			
		Ck. No. 1881.			

The T accounts for establishing the Change Fund are as follows:

Change Fund	
+	−
150	

Cash	
+	−
	150

Roland cashes a check for $150 and gets the money in several denominations. She is now prepared to make change for any normal business transactions.

Depositing Cash

At the end of each business day, Roland's Delivery Services' accountant deposits the cash taken in during the day but holds back the amount of the Change Fund, being

PAGE 1

Distribution of Payments			
Maintenance Expense	Miscellaneous Expense	Other Accounts: Account	Other Accounts: Amount
	10.00		
	2.50		
	3.70		
		M. B. Roland, Drawing	10.00
	2.20		
	14.00		
	3.60		
	9.00		
8.20			
8.00			
5.00			
21.20	45.00		10.00

sure that it is in convenient denominations. Let's say that on September 1, Roland's Delivery Services had $1,575 on hand at the end of the day.

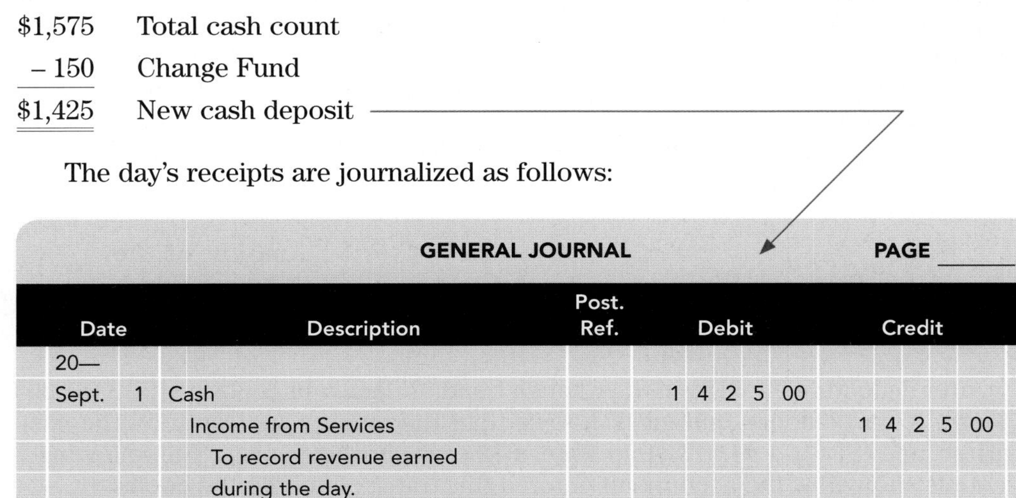

$1,575	Total cash count
– 150	Change Fund
$1,425	New cash deposit

The day's receipts are journalized as follows:

GENERAL JOURNAL PAGE ____

Date		Description	Post. Ref.	Debit	Credit
20—					
Sept.	1	Cash		1,425.00	
		Income from Services			1,425.00
		To record revenue earned			
		during the day.			

The T accounts look like this:

Cash	
+	–
1,425	

Income from Services	
–	+
	1,425

The amount of the cash deposit is the total cash count less the amount of the Change Fund. This should be equal to the income earned.

On September 9, the cash count is $1,672. So the accountant deposits $1,522 ($1,672 – $150). Roland's Delivery Services' accountant makes the following entry to record the day's receipts:

GENERAL JOURNAL — PAGE ____

Date		Description	Post. Ref.	Debit	Credit
20—					
Sept.	9	Cash		1 5 2 2 00	
		Income from Services			1 5 2 2 00
		To record revenue earned			
		during the day.			

Some businesses label the Cash account *Cash in Bank* and label the Change Fund *Cash on Hand*.

CASH SHORT AND OVER

LEARNING OBJECTIVE 7

Record journal entries for transactions involving Cash Short and Over.

There is an inherent danger in making change: Human beings make mistakes, especially when there are many customers to be waited on or when the business is temporarily short-handed. Because mistakes do happen, accounting records must be set up to cope with the situation. One reason that a business uses a cash register is to detect mistakes in handling cash. **If, after removing the Change Fund, the day's receipts are less than the register reading, then a cash shortage exists. Conversely, when the day's receipts are greater than the register reading, a cash overage exists.** Both shortages and overages are recorded in the same account, which is called Cash Short and Over. Shortages are considered an expense of operating a business, and therefore shortages are recorded on the debit side of the account. Overages are treated as another form of revenue, and therefore overages are recorded on the credit side of the account.

FYI

The Cash Short and Over account may also be used to handle shortages and overages in the Petty Cash Fund.

Let's say that on September 14, Roland's Delivery Services is faced with the following situation:

Cash Register Tape	Cash Count	Amount of the Change Fund
$1,515	$1,663	$150

After deducting the $150 in the Change Fund, Roland will deposit $1,513 ($1,663 – $150). Note that this amount is $2 less than the amount indicated by the cash register tape ($1,515 – $1,513); therefore, a $2 cash shortage exists. The following T accounts show how the accountant entered this transaction into the books:

Cash (+)	Cash (–)	Income from Services (–)	Income from Services (+)	Cash Short and Over (Dr.)	Cash Short and Over (Cr.)
1,513			1,515	2	

FYI

Like the Income Summary account, which has no normal balance, the Cash Short and Over account has no signs.

The next day, September 15, the pendulum happens to swing in the other direction:

Cash Register Tape	Cash Count	Amount of the Change Fund
$1,578	$1,732	$150

The amount to be deposited is $1,582 ($1,732 – $150). This figure is $4 greater than the $1,578 in income from services indicated by the cash register tape. Thus, there is a $4 cash overage ($1,582 – $1,578). The analysis of this transaction is shown in the following T accounts:

Cash		Income from Services		Cash Short and Over	
+	–	–	+		
1,582			1,578		4

Roland's Delivery Services' revenue for September 14 and 15 is recorded in the general journal as follows:

GENERAL JOURNAL PAGE ______

Date		Description	Post. Ref.	Debit	Credit
20—					
Sept.	14	Cash		1 5 1 3 00	
		Cash Short and Over		2 00	
		Income from Services			1 5 1 5 00
		To record revenue earned for the day			
		involving a cash shortage of $2.00.			
	15	Cash		1 5 8 2 00	
		Income from Services			1 5 7 8 00
		Cash Short and Over			4 00
		To record revenue earned for the day			
		involving a cash overage of $4.00.			

As far as errors are concerned, one would think that shortages would be offset by overages. However, customers receiving change are more likely to report shortages than overages. **Consequently, the business usually experiences a greater number of shortages.** A business may set a tolerance level for the cashiers. If the shortages consistently exceed the level of tolerance, either fraud is being committed or somebody is making entirely too many careless mistakes.

Now let's summarize our discussion of the Cash Short and Over account by drawing the following conclusions from the illustration:

1. At the close of the business day, the business deposits the difference between the amount in the cash drawer and the amount in the Change Fund.
2. The business records the amount shown on the cash register tape as its income from services.
3. If the amount of the cash deposit disagrees with the record of receipts, Cash Short and Over makes up the difference. In the first situation just described, there was a shortage of $2, and so there was a debit to Cash Short and Over. In the second situation, there was an overage of $4, and so there was a credit to

Cash Short and Over. It is apparent that, as a result of these transactions, the account looks like this:

Cash Short and Over

Shortage		Overage	
	2		4

Throughout any fiscal period, the accountant must continually record shortages and overages in the Cash Short and Over account. Let's say that Roland's Delivery Services' final balance is $18 on the debit side. Roland's Delivery Services winds up with a net shortage of $18.

At the end of the fiscal period, **if the account has a debit balance or net shortage, the accountant classifies it as an expense and credits Cash Short and Over and debits Miscellaneous Expense, so that the amount is put in the income statement under Miscellaneous Expense.** The T account would look like this:

Cash Short and Over

Shortage		Overage	
	2		4
	4		1
	3		1
	7		2
	5		1
	2		2
	3		1
	4		
Bal.	**18**		

Conversely, **if the account has a credit balance or net overage, the accountant classifies it as a revenue account and debits Cash Short and Over and credits Miscellaneous Income, so that the amount is put in the income statement under Miscellaneous Income.** This is an exception to the policy of recording accounts under their exact account title in financial statements. Rather than attaching plus and minus signs to the Cash Short and Over account immediately, we wait until we find out its final balance, then make a journal entry to send the balance to the correct account classification.

CHAPTER REVIEW

Study & Practice

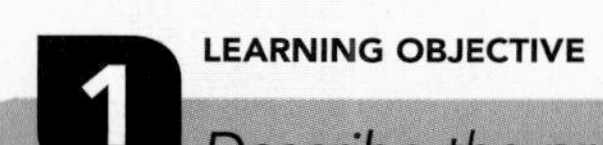

LEARNING OBJECTIVE 1

Describe the procedure for depositing checks.

The procedure for depositing checks consists of first endorsing each check and then completing a **deposit slip**. On the deposit slip, record the date, the amount of currency to be deposited, the amount and **ABA number** of each check, and the total amount to be deposited. The checks to be deposited should accompany the deposit slip.

PRACTICE EXERCISE 1

What are the three types of endorsements and how are they different from each other?

PRACTICE EXERCISE 1 SOLUTION

1. *Restrictive endorsement* – An endorsement, such as "Pay to the order of (name of bank), for deposit only," that restricts or limits any further negotiation of a check. It forces the check's deposit, because the endorsement is not valid for any other purpose.
2. *Blank endorsement* – An endorsement in which the holder (payee) of a check simply signs his or her name on the back of the check. There are no restrictions attached.
3. *Qualified endorsement* – An endorsement in which the holder (payee) of a check avoids future liability, in case the drawer of the check does not have sufficient funds to cover the check, by adding the words "Pay to the order of" and "without recourse" to the endorsement on the back of the check.

LEARNING OBJECTIVE

Reconcile a bank statement.

The standard form for a **bank reconciliation** is as follows:

Bank Statement Balance

Add:
Deposits in transit
Bank errors that understate the **bank statement** balance

Deduct:
Outstanding checks or electronic transfers
Bank errors that overstate the bank statement balance

Adjusted Bank Statement Balance
Ledger Balance of Cash

Add:
Notes collected
Interest income earned
Checkbook errors that understate the ledger balance of cash
Bank credit memos

Deduct:
Bank service charges
Checkbook errors that overstate the ledger balance of cash
NSF checks
Bank debit memos

Adjusted Ledger Balance of Cash

PRACTICE EXERCISE 2

The bank statement of M. C. Johnson Company indicates a balance of $7,428 as of July 31. The balance of the Cash account in Johnson's ledger as of that date is $6,872. Johnson's accountant has taken the following steps:

STEP 1. Verified that canceled checks were recorded correctly on the bank statement.

STEP 2. Noted that the deposit made on July 31 was not recorded on the bank statement, $2,071.

CHAPTER REVIEW

STEP 3. Noted outstanding checks: no. 1066, $1,075; no. 1099, $462; no. 1100, $605.

STEP 4. Noted credit memo: Note collected by the bank from L. Stewart, $500, not recorded in the journal. Noted debit memo: Collection charge and service charge not recorded in the journal, $15.

Based on the information above, prepare a bank reconciliation for M. C. Johnson Company.

PRACTICE EXERCISE 2 SOLUTION

M. C. Johnson Company
Bank Reconciliation
July 31, 20—

Bank Statement Balance		$7,428.00
Add: Deposit in transit (July 31)		2,071.00
		$9,499.00
Deduct: Outstanding checks		
No. 1066	$1,075.00	
No. 1099	462.00	
No. 1100	605.00	2,142.00
Adjusted Bank Statement Balance		$7,357.00
Ledger Balance of Cash		$6,872.00
Add: Note collected by bank		500.00
		$7,372.00
Deduct: Bank service and collection charges		15.00
Adjusted Ledger Balance of Cash		$7,357.00

LEARNING OBJECTIVE

Record the required journal entries from the bank reconciliation.

Journal entries for the Ledger Balance of Cash section are required. The entry for notes and interest collected is a debit to Cash and credits to Notes Receivable and Interest Income. The entry for a bank service charge is a debit to Miscellaneous Expense and a credit to Cash. The entry for an NSF check is a debit to Accounts Receivable and a credit to Cash.

PRACTICE EXERCISE 3

Prepare the necessary journal entries from the bank reconciliation in Practice Exercise 2 for M. C. Johnson Company.

PRACTICE EXERCISE 3 SOLUTION

GENERAL JOURNAL PAGE ______

Date		Description	Post. Ref.	Debit	Credit
20—					
July	31	Cash		500.00	
		Notes Receivable			500.00
		Non-interest-bearing note			
		signed by L. Stewart was			
		collected by the bank.			
	31	Miscellaneous Expense		15.00	
		Cash			15.00
		Service charge and collection			
		charge levied by bank.			

LEARNING OBJECTIVE **4**

Record journal entries to establish and reimburse a Petty Cash Fund.

The entry to establish a **Petty Cash Fund** is a debit to Petty Cash Fund and a credit to Cash. The entry to reimburse the Petty Cash Fund consists of debits to the items for which payments from the Petty Cash Fund were made and one credit to Cash for the total payments.

PRACTICE EXERCISE 4

A Petty Cash Fund of $100 was established on October 1. At the end of the month, the following accounts were charged for expenditures from the Petty Cash Fund: Office Supplies Expense, $13.75; Delivery Expense, $15.00; Miscellaneous Expense, $36.00; B. Thomas, Drawing, $25.00. Record the journal entries for the establishment and reimbursement of the Petty Cash Fund.

PRACTICE EXERCISE 4 SOLUTION

GENERAL JOURNAL PAGE ______

Date		Description	Post. Ref.	Debit	Credit
20—					
Oct.	1	Petty Cash Fund		100.00	
		Cash			100.00
		Established a Petty Cash Fund.			
	31	Office Supplies Expense		13.75	
		Delivery Expense		15.00	
		Miscellaneous Expense		36.00	
		B. Thomas, Drawing		25.00	
		Cash			89.75
		Reimbursed the Petty Cash Fund.			

LEARNING OBJECTIVE

5 Complete petty cash vouchers and petty cash payments records.

A **petty cash voucher** is made out for each payment from the Petty Cash Fund. In the **petty cash payments record**, each voucher is listed and a notation is made concerning the accounts involved; also, an explanation of why the money was paid out is recorded. The petty cash payments record is used as a source of information for making the journal entry to reimburse the Petty Cash Fund.

PRACTICE EXERCISE 5

Answer True (T) or False (F) for the following statements:

_______ **1.** A petty cash voucher must be used to account for every payment from the Petty Cash Fund.

_______ **2.** A petty cash voucher constitutes a receipt signed by the person who authorized the payment and by the person who received payment.

_______ **3.** The petty cash payments record is a type of journal.

_______ **4.** The petty cash payments record is used as a basis for compiling information for the journal entry to reimburse the Petty Cash Fund.

PRACTICE EXERCISE 5 SOLUTION

1. T
2. T
3. F
4. T

LEARNING OBJECTIVE

6 Record the journal entries to establish a Change Fund.

The entry to establish the **Change Fund** is a debit to Change Fund and a credit to Cash.

PRACTICE EXERCISE 6

Journalize the entry to establish a Change Fund amounting to $150 on July 1.

PRACTICE EXERCISE 6 SOLUTION

GENERAL JOURNAL PAGE ______

Date		Description	Post. Ref.	Debit	Credit
20—					
July	1	Change Fund		150.00	
		Cash			150.00
		Established a Change Fund.			

LEARNING OBJECTIVE

Record journal entries for transactions involving Cash Short and Over.

The Cash Short and Over account provides a way to keep a record of errors in making change. A debit balance in Cash Short and Over denotes a shortage, which is listed as Miscellaneous Expense; the entry is a debit to Miscellaneous Expense and a credit to Cash Short and Over. A credit balance in Cash Short and Over denotes an overage, which becomes Miscellaneous Income; the entry is a debit to Cash Short and Over and a credit to Miscellaneous Income.

PRACTICE EXERCISE 7

Journalize the entries to account for two bank deposits on June 29 and June 30. The amount of the Change Fund is $100.

a. On June 29, the cash register tape showed $950.86 in income from sales. The amount in the cash drawer was $1,051.86.
b. On June 30, the cash register tape showed $1,327.44 in income from sales. The amount in the cash drawer was $1,426.12.

PRACTICE EXERCISE 7 SOLUTION

GENERAL JOURNAL PAGE ____

Date		Description	Post. Ref.	Debit	Credit
20—					
June	29	Cash		951.86	
		Income from Sales			950.86
		Cash Short and Over			1.00
		To record revenue earned for the day involving a cash overage of $1.00.			
	30	Cash		1,326.12	
		Cash Short and Over		1.32	
		Income from Sales			1,327.44
		To record revenue earned for the day involving a cash shortage of $1.32.			

Glossary

ABA number The number assigned by the American Bankers Association to a given bank. The first part of the number denotes the city or state in which the bank is located and the specific bank on which the check is drawn. The second part of the number indicates the Federal Reserve District in which the check is cleared and the routing number used by the Federal Reserve Bank. *(p. 215)*

ATMs (automated teller machines) Machines that enable depositors to make deposits, withdrawals, and transfers using a coded plastic card. *(p. 217)*

Bank reconciliation A process by which an accountant determines whether and why there is a difference between the balance shown on the bank statement and the balance of the Cash account in the business's general ledger. The object is to determine the adjusted (or true) balance of the Cash account. *(p. 222)*

Bank statement A periodic statement that a bank sends to the drawer/depositor of a checking account listing deposits received and checks paid by the bank, debit and credit memos, electronic transactions, and beginning and ending balances. *(p. 219)*

Blank endorsement An endorsement in which the holder (payee) of a check simply signs her or his name on the back of the check. There are no restrictions attached. *(p. 218)*

Canceled checks Checks issued by the depositor that have been paid (cleared) by the bank and listed on the bank statement. They are called canceled checks because they are canceled by a stamp or perforation, indicating that they have been paid. *(p. 221)*

Cash funds Separately held reserves of cash set aside for specific purposes. *(p. 214)*

Change Fund A cash fund used by a business to make change for customers who pay cash for goods or services. *(p. 233)*

Collections Payments collected by the bank and added to the customer's bank account in the form of a credit memorandum. *(p. 222)*

Denominations Varieties of coins and currency, such as quarters, dimes, and nickels and $1 and $5 bills and so on. *(p. 231)*

Deposit in transit A deposit not recorded on the bank statement because the deposit was made between the time of the bank's closing date for compiling items for its statement and the time the statement is received by the depositor; also known as a *late deposit. (p. 222)*

Deposit slips Printed forms provided by a bank on which customers can list all items being deposited; also known as *deposit tickets. (p. 215)*

Drawer The party who writes the check. *(p. 218)*

Electronic Funds Transfer (EFT) A transfer of funds initiated through an electronic terminal, such as a telephone, computer, or magnetic tape. *(p. 217)*

Endorsement The process by which the payee transfers ownership of the check to a bank or another party. A check must be endorsed when deposited in a bank, because the bank must have legal title to it in order to collect payment from the drawer of the check (the person or firm who wrote the check). In case the check cannot be collected, the endorser guarantees all subsequent holders (*exception:* an endorsement "without recourse"). *(p. 217)*

Errors Mistakes made by the customer or bank. *(p. 223)*

Interest income The amount earned from lending money to another person or business. *(p. 222)*

Internal control Plans and procedures built into the accounting system with the following objectives: (1) to protect assets against fraud and waste, (2) to provide accurate accounting data, (3) to promote efficient operation, and (4) to encourage adherence to management policies. *(p. 213)*

Ledger balance of cash The balance of the Cash account in the general ledger before it is reconciled with the bank statement. *(p. 222)*

MICR Magnetic ink character recognition; the characters the bank uses to print the number of the depositor's account and the bank's number at the bottom of checks and deposit slips. The bank also prints the amount of the check in MICR when the check is deposited. A number written in these characters can be read by electronic equipment used by banks in clearing checks. *(p. 216)*

NSF (not sufficient funds) check Check drawn against an account in which there are *not sufficient funds* and returned by the payee's bank to the drawer's bank because of nonpayment; also known as a *dishonored check. (p. 222)*

Outstanding checks Checks that have been written by the drawer and deducted on his or her records but have not reached the bank for payment and are not deducted from the bank balance by the time the bank issues its statement. *(p. 222)*

Payee The person to whom a check is payable. *(p. 218)*

Petty Cash Fund A cash fund used to make small, immediate cash payments. *(p. 230)*

Petty cash payments record A record indicating the amount of each petty cash voucher, the accounts to which it should be charged, and the purpose of the expenditure. *(p. 232)*

Petty cash voucher A form stating who requested cash from the Petty Cash Fund, signed by (1) the person in charge of the fund and (2) the person who received the cash, and indicating the purpose of the petty cash payment. *(p. 231)*

Promissory note A written promise to pay a definite sum at a definite future time. *(p. 224)*

Qualified endorsement An endorsement in which the holder (payee) of a check avoids future liability, in case the drawer of the check does not have sufficient funds to cover the check, by adding the words "Pay to the order of" and "without recourse" to the endorsement on the back of the check. *(p. 218)*

Restrictive endorsement An endorsement, such as "Pay to the order of (name of bank), for deposit only," that restricts or limits any further negotiation of a check. It forces the check's deposit, because the endorsement is not valid for any other purpose. *(p. 218)*

Service charge The fee the bank charges for handling checks, collections, and other items. It is in the form of a debit memorandum. *(p. 222)*

Signature card The form a depositor signs to give the bank a copy of the official signatures of any persons authorized to sign checks. The bank can use it to verify the depositors' signatures on checks. *(p. 215)*

CHAPTER ASSIGNMENTS

Discussion Questions

1. Why does a bank keep a signature card on file for your account(s)?
2. What is the purpose of endorsing a check?
3. Why is there generally a difference between the balance in the Cash account on the company's books and the balance on the bank statement?
4. Indicate whether the following items in a bank reconciliation should be (1) added to the Cash account balance, (2) deducted from the Cash account balance, (3) added to the bank statement balance, or (4) deducted from the bank statement balance.
   a. NSF check
   b. Deposit in transit
   c. Outstanding check
   d. Bank error charging the business's account with another company's check
   e. Bank service charge
5. Why is it necessary to make general journal entries for the ledger balance side of the bank reconciliation?
6. a. Why would a business use a Petty Cash Fund?
   b. Describe the entry needed to establish a $50 Petty Cash Fund and an entry to reimburse the fund.
7. a. What does a debit balance in Cash Short and Over mean?
   b. Where does a debit balance in Cash Short and Over appear in the financial statements?
   c. What does a credit balance in Cash Short and Over mean?
   d. Where does a credit balance in Cash Short and Over appear in the financial statements?

Exercises

EXERCISE 6-1 Fill in the missing amounts for the following bank reconciliation:

LO 2

PRACTICE EXERCISE 2

Bank Reconciliation
March 31, 20—

Bank Statement Balance		$3,764.00
Add: Deposit in transit		(a)
		$4,031.00
Deduct: Outstanding checks		
No. 211	$212.00	
No. 225	(b)	
No. 228	318.00	850.00
Adjusted Bank Statement Balance		(c)
Ledger Balance of Cash		$2,837.00
Add: Note collected by bank		430.00
		(d)
Deduct: Bank service and collection charges	(e)	
NSF check from customer	74.00	86.00
Adjusted Ledger Balance of Cash		(f)

CHAPTER ASSIGNMENTS

PRACTICE EXERCISE 3

EXERCISE 6-2 The Ledger Balance of Cash section of the bank reconciliation for Lasha Company for July 31 follows.

Ledger Balance of Cash		$6,360.00
Add: Note collected (principal $700.00, interest $17.50, signed by D. Dansky)	$717.50	
Error in recording Ck. No. 2225 payable to Denton Company (recorded check for $12 too much)	12.00	729.50
		$7,089.50
Deduct: NSF check from J. Kenyon	$ 95.00	
Bank service and collection charges	29.00	124.00
Adjusted Ledger Balance of Cash		$6,965.50

Journalize the entries required to bring the general ledger up to date as of July of this year.

PRACTICE EXERCISE 2

EXERCISE 6-3 When the bank statement is received on December 3, it shows a balance, before reconciliation, of $3,600 as of November 30. After reconciliation, the adjusted balance is $2,500. If there was one deposit in transit amounting to $1,500, what was the total of the outstanding checks, assuming that there were no other adjustments to be made to the bank statement?

PRACTICE EXERCISE 2

EXERCISE 6-4 Place a check mark in the column that indicates the location of each item that would be found on a bank reconciliation. Assume that the checks written by the company are written correctly.

Item	Add to Bank Statement Balance	Subtract from Bank Statement Balance	Add to Ledger Balance of Cash	Subtract from Ledger Balance of Cash
a. A check-printing charge				
b. An outstanding check				
c. A deposit for $197 listed incorrectly on the bank statement as $179				
d. A collection charge the bank made for a note it collected for its depositor				
e. A check written for $41.73 and recorded incorrectly in the checkbook as $41.37				
f. A deposit in transit				
g. An NSF check received from a customer				
h. A check written for $82.40 and recorded incorrectly in the checkbook as $820.40				

PRACTICE EXERCISE 2

EXERCISE 6-5 Hosung Company's Cash account shows a balance of $801.65 as of August 31 of this year. The balance on the bank statement on that date is $1,383. Checks for $260.50, $425.10, and $331 are outstanding. The bank statement shows a check issued by another depositor for $237.25 (in other words, the bank made an error and charged Hosung Company for a check written by another company). The bank statement also shows an NSF check for $180 received from one of Hosung's customers. Service charges for the month were $18. What is the adjusted ledger balance of cash as of August 31?

LO 4

PRACTICE EXERCISE 4

EXERCISE 6-6 Record entries in general journal form to record the following:

a. Established a Petty Cash Fund, $100. Issued Ck. No. 857.
b. Reimbursed the Petty Cash Fund for expenditures of $98: Store Supplies Expense, $38; Office Supplies Expense, $21; Miscellaneous Expense, $39. Issued Ck. No. 889.
c. Increased the amount of the fund by an additional $50. Issued Ck. No. 891.
d. Reimbursed the Petty Cash Fund for expenditures of $96.58: Store Supplies Expense, $41.68; Delivery Expense, $35; Miscellaneous Expense, $19.90. Issued Ck. No. 936.

PRACTICE EXERCISE 7

EXERCISE 6-7 At the end of the day, the cash register tape lists $881.40 as total income from services. Cash on hand consists of $18.25 in coins, $433.60 in currency, $100 in traveler's checks, and $427 in customers' checks. The amount of the Change Fund is $100. In general journal form, record the entry to record the day's cash revenue.

PRACTICE EXERCISES 6,7

EXERCISE 6-8

a. Describe the entries that have been posted to the following accounts after the Change Fund was established.

Change Fund

Debit	Credit
200	

Sales

Debit	Credit
	Jan. 3 1,520
	4 1,421
	6 1,665

Cash

Debit	Credit
Jan. 3 1,522	
4 1,418	
6 1,664	

Cash Short and Over

Debit	Credit
Jan. 4 3	Jan. 3 2
6 1	

b. How will the balance of Cash Short and Over be reported on the income statement?

Problem Set A

For additional help, see the demonstration problem at the beginning of each chapter in your Working Papers.

PROBLEM 6-1A Arthur's Men's Shop deposits all receipts in the bank each evening and makes all payments by check. On November 30 its ledger balance of cash is

$2,375.05. The bank statement balance of cash as of November 30 is $2,784.77. Use the following information to reconcile the bank statement:

a. The reconciliation for October, the previous month, showed three checks outstanding on October 31: no. 1417 for $95, no. 1420 for $125.87, and no. 1422 for $136. Checks no. 1417 and 1422 were returned with the November bank statement; however, check no. 1420 was not returned.
b. Checks no. 1500 for $155, no. 1517 for $132, no. 1518 for $218, and no. 1519 for $128.85 were written during November and have not been returned by the bank.
c. A deposit of $945 was placed in the night depository on November 30 and did not appear on the bank statement.
d. The canceled checks were compared with the entries in the checkbook, and it was observed that check no. 1487, for $89, was written correctly, payable to M. A. Golden, the owner, for personal use, but was recorded in the checkbook as $98.
e. Included in the bank statement was a bank debit memo for service charges, $29.
f. A bank credit memo was also enclosed for the collection of a note signed by C. G. Tolson, $615, including $600 principal and $15 interest.

Check Figure
Adjusted ledger balance of cash, $2,970.05

Required

1. Prepare a bank reconciliation as of November 30, assuming that the debit and credit memos have not been recorded.
2. Record the necessary entries in general journal form.

PROBLEM 6-2A On May 1 of this year, Ellsworth and Company established a Petty Cash Fund. The following petty cash transactions took place during the month:

May	1	Cashed check no. 956 for $150 to establish a Petty Cash Fund, and put the $150 in a locked drawer in the office.
	3	Bought postage stamps, $8.80, voucher no. 1 (Miscellaneous Expense).
	4	Issued voucher no. 2 for taxi fare, $12 (Miscellaneous Expense).
	6	Issued voucher no. 3 for delivery charges on outgoing parts, $15.
	9	B. Ellsworth, the owner, withdrew $25 for personal use, voucher no. 4.
	13	Paid $8.29 for postage, voucher no. 5 (Miscellaneous Expense).
	19	Bought pens for office, $6, voucher no. 6.
	23	Paid $3.59 for a box of staples, voucher no. 7.
	28	Paid $15 for window cleaning service, voucher no. 8 (Miscellaneous Expense).
	29	Paid $2 for pencils for office, voucher no. 9.
	31	Issued for cash check no. 1098 for $95.68 to reimburse Petty Cash Fund.

Check Figure
Office Supplies Expense, $11.59

Required

1. Journalize the entry establishing the Petty Cash Fund in the general journal.
2. Record the disbursements of petty cash in the petty cash payments record.
3. Journalize the summarizing entry to reimburse the Petty Cash Fund.

PROBLEM 6-3A Ellie Harrod, owner of Harrod's Dry Cleaners, makes bank deposits in the night depository at the close of each business day. The following information for the last four days of July is available.

	July			
	28	29	30	31
Cash register tape	$895.20	$ 977.40	$884.50	$1,027.25
Cash count	993.50	1,075.80	986.60	1,124.40

CHAPTER ASSIGNMENTS

Required

In general journal form, record the cash deposit for each day, assuming that there is a $100 Change Fund.

Check Figure
Cash Short and Over, July 31, $2.85 cash shortage

PROBLEM 6-4A On August 31, Baginski and Company receives its bank statement (shown below). The company deposits its receipts in the bank and makes all payments by check. The debit memo for $95 is for an NSF check written by L. Pitts. Check no. 925 for $47, payable to Jardin Company (a creditor), was recorded in the checkbook and journal as $74.

LO 2,3

GL

The ledger balance of cash as of August 31 is $1,563. Outstanding checks as of August 31 are: no. 928, $150; no. 929, $292. The accountant notes that the deposit of August 31 for $599 did not appear on the bank statement.

Required

1. Prepare a bank reconciliation as of August 31, assuming that the debit memos have not been recorded.
2. Record the necessary journal entries.
3. Complete the bank form to determine the adjusted balance of cash.

Check Figure
Adjusted ledger balance of cash, $1,480

PEABODY NATIONAL BANK

STATEMENT OF ACCOUNT	**Baginski and Company** **416 Seneca Avenue** **Kansas City, Missouri 64102**	ACCOUNT NO. **152-655-217** STATEMENT DATE **August 1–31, 20—**

SUMMARY		
	Balance Last Statement	$961.00
	Amount of Checks and Debits	$2,289.00
	Number of Checks	11
	Amount of Deposits and Credits	$2,651.00
	Number of Deposits	7
	Balance This Statement	$1,323.00

CHECKS/ OTHER DEBITS

CHECKS	CHECK NUMBER	DATE POSTED	AMOUNT	CHECK NUMBER	DATE POSTED	AMOUNT
	917	8-04	172.00	923	8-09	621.00
	918	8-04	76.00	924	8-17	37.00
	919	8-05	146.00	925	8-17	47.00
	920	8-07	206.00	926	8-23	454.00
	921	8-07	139.00	927	8-28	94.00
	922	8-07	200.00			

OTHER DEBITS	DESCRIPTION	DATE POSTED	AMOUNT
	DM NSF check	8-31	95.00
	DM Service charge	8-31	15.00

DEPOSITS/ OTHER CREDITS

DEPOSITS	DATE POSTED	AMOUNT	DATE POSTED	AMOUNT
	8-02	326.00	8-18	419.00
	8-05	412.00	8-24	398.00
	8-09	437.00	8-28	291.00
	8-14	368.00		

PLEASE EXAMINE THIS STATEMENT CAREFULLY. REPORT ANY POSSIBLE ERRORS WITHIN 10 DAYS.

CODE SYMBOLS

CM Credit Memo DM Debit Memo OD Overdraft EC Error Correction

Problem Set B

For additional help, see the demonstration problem at the beginning of each chapter in your Working Papers.

2,3 

PROBLEM 6-1B Merkle Company deposits all receipts in the bank each evening and makes all payments by check. On November 30 its ledger balance of cash is $3,219.72. The bank statement balance of cash as of November 30 is $3,490.72. You are given the following information with which to reconcile the bank statement:

a. A deposit of $525.30 was placed in the night depository on November 30 and did not appear on the bank statement.
b. The reconciliation for October, the previous month, showed three checks outstanding on October 31: no. 728 for $80.20, no. 731 for $129, and no. 732 for $145.34. Checks no. 728 and 731 were returned with the November bank statement; however, check no. 732 was not returned.
c. Checks no. 743 for $42, no. 744 for $16.20, no. 745 for $119, and no. 746 for $35.26 were written during November but were not returned by the bank.
d. A $150 personal withdrawal by C. R. Merkle, the owner, using an ATM, was not recorded.
e. Included in the bank statement was a bank debit memo for service charges, $19.
f. A bank credit memo was also enclosed for the collection of a note signed by O. L. Leland, $607.50, including $600 principal and $7.50 interest

Check Figure
Adjusted ledger balance of cash, $3,658.22

Required

1. Prepare a bank reconciliation as of November 30, assuming that the debit and credit memos have not been recorded.
2. Record the necessary entries in general journal form.

4,5 

PROBLEM 6-2B On March 1 of this year, Stowe Company established a Petty Cash Fund, and the following petty cash transactions took place during the month:

Mar.	1	Cashed check no. 314 for $100 to establish a Petty Cash Fund, and put the $100 in a locked drawer in the office.
	4	Issued voucher no. 1 for taxi fare, $7.60 (Miscellaneous Expense).
	7	Issued voucher no. 2 for memo pads, $6.50 (Office Supplies Expense).
	9	Paid $21.50 for an advertisement in a college basketball program, voucher no. 3.
	16	Bought postage stamps, $8.80, voucher no. 4 (Miscellaneous Expense).
	20	Paid $10 to have snow removed from office front sidewalk, voucher no. 5 (Miscellaneous Expense).
	25	Issued voucher no. 6 for delivery charge, $12.
	28	R. C. Stowe, the owner, withdrew $20 for personal use, voucher no. 7.
	29	Paid $4.20 for postage, voucher no. 8 (Miscellaneous Expense).
	30	Paid $5.90 for delivery charge, voucher no. 9.
	31	Issued for cash check no. 372 for $96.50 to reimburse Petty Cash Fund.

Check Figure
Office Supplies Expense, $6.50

Required

1. Journalize the entry establishing the Petty Cash Fund in the general journal.
2. Record the disbursements of petty cash in the petty cash payments record.
3. Journalize the summarizing entry to reimburse the Petty Cash Fund.

PROBLEM 6-3B Roberta Felino, owner of Roberta's Beauty Salon, makes bank deposits in the night depository at the close of each business day. The following information for the first four days of April is available.

	April			
	1	2	3	4
Cash register tape	$386.75	$582.65	$586.65	$623.25
Cash count	485.50	685.75	685.75	726.15

Required

In general journal form, record the cash deposit for each day, assuming that there is a $100 Change Fund.

Check Figure
Cash Short and Over, April 3, $0.90 cash shortage

PROBLEM 6-4B On August 2, Northern Motel receives its bank statement (shown below). The company deposits its receipts in the bank and makes all payments by check. The debit memo for $37 is for an NSF check written by T. R. Royce. Check no.

STANTON NATIONAL BANK

STATEMENT OF ACCOUNT	Northern Motel 423 E. Long Avenue Rockford, IL 61104	ACCOUNT NO. 750-135-772 STATEMENT DATE July 1–31, 20—

SUMMARY		
	Balance Last Statement	$1,153.80
	Amount of Checks and Debits	$2,105.91
	Number of Checks	14
	Amount of Deposits and Credits	$2,528.17
	Number of Deposits	7
	Balance This Statement	$1,576.06

CHECKS/OTHER DEBITS

CHECKS	CHECK NUMBER	DATE POSTED	AMOUNT	CHECK NUMBER	DATE POSTED	AMOUNT
	1617	7-03	75.50	1624	7-08	120.00
	1618	7-03	164.00	1625	7-09	429.60
	1619	7-03	124.20	1626	7-12	37.40
	1620	7-05	137.20	1627	7-14	38.49
	1621	7-06	236.25	1628	7-22	182.71
	1622	7-06	159.89	1629	7-25	96.87
	1623	7-08	244.50	1630	7-26	19.20

OTHER DEBITS	DESCRIPTION	DATE POSTED	AMOUNT
	DM NSF check	7-22	37.00
	DM Service charge	7-31	23.00

DEPOSITS/OTHER CREDITS

DEPOSITS	DATE POSTED	AMOUNT	DATE POSTED	AMOUNT
	7-03	491.50	7-15	291.76
	7-06	415.72	7-18	142.90
	7-09	439.16	7-28	368.93
	7-11	378.20		

PLEASE EXAMINE THIS STATEMENT CAREFULLY. REPORT ANY POSSIBLE ERRORS WITHIN 10 DAYS.

CODE SYMBOLS

CM Credit Memo DM Debit Memo OD Overdraft EC Error Correction

CHAPTER ASSIGNMENTS

Check Figure
Adjusted ledger balance of cash, $1,831.30

1617 for $75.50, payable to Mitchel Company (a creditor), was incorrectly recorded in the checkbook and journal as $57.50.

The ledger balance of Cash as of July 31 is $1,909.30. Outstanding checks as of July 31 are: no. 1631, $118.20; no. 1632, $78.20; no. 1633, $178.36. The accountant notes that the July 31 deposit of $630 did not appear on the bank statement.

Required

1. Prepare a bank reconciliation as of July 31, assuming that the debit memos have not been recorded.
2. Record the necessary journal entries.
3. Complete the bank form to determine the adjusted balance of cash.

ACTIVITIES

CONSIDER AND COMMUNICATE

As the new bookkeeper at a small business, you find the Petty Cash Fund is accessed by several people, usually without anyone leaving any written explanation of what the money was used for. The amount of cash does not match the recorded amount of the fund. Explain how the Petty Cash Fund operation can be made more efficient in order to maintain an accurate accounting of how the money is used.

WHAT'S WRONG WITH THIS PICTURE?

You work as a cashier in a service business. Some days you are short of cash at the end of the day, and some days you have more cash than the cash register tape says was earned. You are embarrassed when your cash is short and don't want the owner to know, so you use your own money to make up the difference. On days when you are over, you keep the difference to help pay back what you paid to cover your shortages. What do you think of this practice and why?

Employee Earnings and Deductions

7

WHY IT MATTERS

RECREATIONAL EQUIPMENT INC. (REI), Sumner, Washington

Attracting and retaining the best employees are crucial to operating a business. Employees will join a company based upon opportunities for advancement, training, and company culture as well as the salary and benefits provided.

One business that is often listed in *Fortune* magazine's "100 Best Companies to Work For" is Recreational Equipment Inc. (REI). REI is committed to inspire, educate, and outfit its customers for a lifetime of outdoor adventure. REI offers competitive salaries as well as benefits, including paid sabbaticals, an onsite fitness center, health-care coverage, telecommuting, and a compressed workweek.

The accounting department at REI is responsible for determining salaries or wages and benefits for employees, calculating payroll deductions for taxes and other expenses, and ensuring that company payrolls are processed in a timely and accurate manner. In this chapter, you will learn how companies like REI complete the payroll records for their employees.

LEARNING OBJECTIVES

After you have completed this chapter, you will be able to do the following:

1. *Understand the role of income tax laws that affect payroll deductions and contributions.*
2. *Calculate total earnings based on an hourly, salary, piece-rate, or commission basis.*
3. *Determine deductions from gross pay, such as federal income tax withheld, Social Security tax, and Medicare tax, to calculate net pay.*
4. *Complete a payroll register.*
5. *Journalize the payroll entry from a payroll register.*
6. *Maintain employees' individual earnings records.*

ACCOUNTING LANGUAGE

Calendar year *(p. 263)*
Current Tax Payment Act *(p. 256)*
Employee *(p. 255)*
Employee's individual earnings record *(p. 270)*
Employee's Withholding Allowance Certificate (Form W-4) *(p. 260)*
Exemption *(p. 260)*
Fair Labor Standards Act *(p. 255)*
FICA taxes *(p. 261)*
Gross pay *(p. 254)*
Independent contractor *(p. 255)*
Medicare taxes *(p. 263)*
Net pay *(p. 254)*
Payroll bank account *(p. 269)*
Payroll register *(p. 264)*
Pre-tax deductions *(p. 259)*
Social Security Act of 1935 *(p. 256)*
Social Security taxes *(p. 263)*
Taxable earnings *(p. 260)*
Wage-bracket tax tables *(p. 261)*
Withholding allowance *(p. 260)*
Workers' compensation laws *(p. 257)*

Until now, we have been recording employees' earnings as a debit to Salary or Wages Expense and a credit to Cash, but we have really been talking only about **gross pay**—the total amount of an employee's pay before deductions. We have not mentioned the various deductions that we all know are taken out of our gross pay before we get to the **net pay**, or take-home pay. In this chapter, we will talk about types of deductions and how to enter them in the payroll records, and about journal entries to record the payroll and pay the employees.

OBJECTIVES OF PAYROLL RECORDS AND ACCOUNTING

There are two primary reasons to maintain accurate payroll records. First, we must collect the data necessary to compute the compensation for each employee for each payroll period.

Second, we must provide the information needed to complete the various government reports—federal and state—required of all employers. All business enterprises, both large and small, are required by law to withhold certain amounts from employees' pay for taxes, to make payments to government agencies by specific deadlines, and to submit reports on official forms. Because governments impose penalties if the requirements are not met, employers are vitally concerned with payroll accounting.

The employer is required to keep records of the following information:

1. **Personal data on employee** Name, address, Social Security number, date of birth
2. **Data on wage payments** Dates and amounts of payments, and payroll periods
3. **Amount of taxable wages paid** Dates and amount earned year to date for the calendar year involved
4. **Amount of tax withheld from each employee's earnings by pay period**

Many companies use software, such as Excel or Quickbooks, or outside payroll services, such as ADP or Paychex, to assist with their payroll accounting.

EMPLOYER/EMPLOYEE RELATIONSHIPS

Payroll accounting is concerned with employees and their compensation, withholdings, records, reports, and taxes. There is an important distinction between an employee and an independent contractor. An **employee** is one who is under the direction and control of the employer, such as a salesperson, administrative assistant, vice president, controller, and so on. An **independent contractor** is engaged for a definite job or service and may choose his or her own means of doing the work. Payments made to independent contractors are in the form of fees or charges. Independent contractors submit bills or invoices for the work they do. The payment is not subject to any withholding or payroll taxes by the person or firm paying that invoice. Such taxes are the responsibility of the independent contractor. Businesses are required to give an independent contractor an IRS Form 1099-MISC for the year if the fees paid exceed $600. If the worker is classified as an independent contractor and should be an employee, the IRS will impose substantial penalties on the employer. The IRS has published guidelines to determine the classification of workers. For more information, go to www.irs.gov.

FYI

Examples of independent contractors include a plumber, a lawyer, or a CPA that offers his or her services to the public.

LAWS AFFECTING EMPLOYEES' PAY DEDUCTIONS

Both federal and state laws require the employer to act as a collecting agent and deduct specified amounts from employees' gross earnings. The employer sends the withholdings to the appropriate government agencies, along with reports substantiating the figures. Let's look at some of the more important laws that pertain to employees' pay.

1 LEARNING OBJECTIVE

Understand the role of income tax laws that affect payroll deductions and contributions.

Fair Labor Standards Act

The **Fair Labor Standards Act** of 1938 is referred to as "the Act" or "FLSA." The Act provides for minimum standards for both wages and overtime. Included in the Act are also provisions related to child labor and equal pay for equal work. In addition, the Act exempts specified employees or groups of employees from the application of certain of its provisions. Details of the Act may be read at www.opm.gov.

Federal Income Tax Withholding

The **Current Tax Payment Act**, passed in 1943, requires employers not only to withhold the tax and then pay it to the U.S. Treasury but also to keep records of the names and addresses of persons employed, their earnings and withholdings, and the amounts and dates of payment. The employer has to submit reports to the Internal Revenue Service on a quarterly basis (Form 941) and to the employee on an annual basis (W-2 form). We will discuss these reports and the related deposits in Chapter 8.

FICA Taxes (Employees' Share)

The **Social Security Act of 1935** began as an attempt to provide retired workers with benefits based upon their work history. Several amendments have added benefits for spouses and minor children of retired workers, disability insurance, increasing the age when benefits may be collected, Medicare, and supplemental security income.

Currently, FICA consists of Social Security and Medicare. At the writing of this text, employees contribute 6.2 percent (0.062) on the first $106,800 earned in a calendar year for Social Security. Employees contribute 1.45 percent (0.0145) on all earnings in a calendar year with no limit for Medicare. Throughout this chapter, we will use these percentages and earnings limitations for our calculations.

LAWS AFFECTING EMPLOYER'S PAYROLL TAX CONTRIBUTIONS (PAYROLL TAX EXPENSE)

Certain payroll taxes, based on the total wages paid to employees, are levied on the employer. Let's look at some of the more important laws that pertain to the pay of employees.

FICA Taxes (Employer's Share)

The employer has to match the amount of FICA taxes withheld from the employees' wages, and the employer's share is recorded under Payroll Tax Expense. Every three months the employer has to submit reports to the U.S. Treasury, recording the information on Form 941, the same form that is used to report the income tax withheld. The employer's payment to the Internal Revenue Service consists of (1) the employee's share of the FICA taxes, (2) the employer's matching portion of the FICA taxes, and (3) the employee's income tax withheld. We will talk about this in detail in Chapter 8.

State Unemployment Taxes (SUTA)

Each state is responsible for paying its own unemployment compensation benefits. The revenue provided by state unemployment taxes is used exclusively for this purpose. However, there is considerable variation among the states concerning the tax rates and the amount of taxable income. **This tax is paid by employers only.** Most states, under a State Unemployment Tax Act, charge their employers a percentage of the first $7,000 based on the taxable income stipulated in the Federal Unemployment Tax Act. In this text, we will use 5.4 percent (0.054) of the first $7,000. States require employers to file reports on a quarterly, or three-month, basis. Included in these reports are a listing of employees' names, Social Security numbers, amounts of wages paid to each employee, and computations of unemployment taxes.

Federal Unemployment Tax Act (FUTA)

The purpose of the Federal Unemployment Tax Act is to provide financial support for the maintenance of government-run employment offices throughout the country. **FUTA taxes are paid by employers only**. Generally this includes all employers except nonprofit schools and charities.

The federal unemployment tax is based on the total earnings of each employee during the calendar year. For the examples and problems in this text, we will use the current federal unemployment tax rate of 0.8 percent (0.008) of the first $7,000 of earnings of each employee during the calendar year. Reports to the federal government (Form 940) must be submitted annually. We will discuss these reports in Chapter 8.

Workers' Compensation Laws

Workers' compensation laws protect employees and their dependents against losses due to death or injury incurred on the job. Most states require employers either to contribute to a state compensation insurance fund or to buy similar insurance from a private insurance company. The employer ordinarily pays the cost of the insurance premiums. The premium rates vary according to the degree of danger inherent in each job category and the employer's number of accidents. The employer has to keep records of job descriptions and classifications as well as claims of insured persons.

The following table presents a summary of the various payroll taxes and who is responsible for each.

Employee Pays	Employer Pays
Federal income tax withholding (based on income tax rates) FICA taxes – Social Security (6.2% of earnings up to $106,800) – Medicare (1.45% of all earnings)	FICA taxes – Social Security (6.2% of earnings up to $106,800.) – Medicare (1.45% of all earnings) Federal and state unemployment taxes Workers' compensation

HOW EMPLOYEES GET PAID

Employees may be paid salaries or wages, depending on the type of work and the period of time covered. Money paid to a person for managerial or administrative services is usually called a salary, and the time period covered is generally a month or a year. Money paid for either skilled or unskilled labor is usually called wages, and the time period covered is hours or weeks. Wages may also be paid on a piece-work basis (or per-unit basis, such as number of boxes of strawberries picked). A company may also supplement an employee's salary or wage by other benefits such as commissions, bonuses, cost-of-living adjustments, and profit-sharing plans. As a rule, employees are paid by check or by direct deposit to their bank account. However, their compensation may also include amounts for items such as personal use of company automobiles, athletic club dues, or holiday gift cards. When the compensation is in these forms, you must determine the fair value of the property or service given in payment for an employee's labor. See Publication 15-B, Employer's Tax Guide to Fringe Benefits, located on the IRS's Web site at www.irs.gov, for more information on what fringe benefits are taxable and how to value them.

Calculating Total Earnings

LEARNING OBJECTIVE **2**

Calculate total earnings based on an hourly, salary, piece-rate, or commission basis.

When compensation is based on the amount of time worked, the accountant must have a record of the number of hours worked by each employee. When there are only a few employees, this can be accomplished by means of a time book. When there are many employees, time clocks or other electronic time-keeping systems are used.

Employees may be paid weekly, biweekly, semimonthly, or monthly. Biweekly is every two weeks. Semimonthly is twice a month.

Wages

Consider Mark Anderson, who works for Green Sales Company. His regular rate of pay is $22.95 per hour. The company pays time-and-a-half for hours worked in excess of 40 per week. In addition, it pays him double time for any work he does on Sundays and holidays. Anderson has a ½-hour lunch break during an 8½-hour day. He is not paid for the lunch break nor is he paid for minutes before 8:00 A.M. or after 4:30 P.M. unless hours of overtime are authorized in advance. His time card for the week is shown in Figure 1.

Anderson's gross wages can be computed by one of two methods. The first method works like this:

40 hours at straight time	40 × $22.95 per hour =	$ 918.00
2 hours overtime on Thursday ($22.95 × 1.5 = $34.43)	2 × $34.43 per hour =	68.86
1 hour overtime on Friday	1 × $34.43 per hour =	34.43
3 hours overtime on Saturday	3 × $34.43 per hour =	103.29
Total hours and gross wages	46	$1,124.58

FYI

Minimum wages are set by Congress or state legislature—whichever is higher. Originally, in 1938, the minimum wage was $0.25 per hour.

The second method of calculating gross wages is often used when it is necessary to identify or track overtime premium.

46 hours at straight time	46 × $22.95 per hour =	$1,055.70
Overtime premium:		
6 hours overtime ($22.95 × 0.5 = $11.48)	6 × $11.48 per hour =	68.88
Total hours and gross wages	52	$1,124.58

Salaries

Employees who are paid a regular salary may also be entitled to extra pay for overtime. It is necessary to figure out their regular hourly rate of pay before you can determine their overtime rate. Consider Madeline Huan, who receives a salary of $4,350 per month. She is entitled to overtime pay for all hours worked in excess of 40 during a week at time-and-a-half her regular hourly rate. This past week she worked 44 hours, so we calculate her gross pay as follows:

$4,350 per month × 12 months	=	$52,200 per year
$52,200 per year ÷ 52 weeks	=	$1,003.85 per week
$1,003.85 per week ÷ 40 hours	=	$25.10 per regular hour
$25.10 per regular hour × 1.5	=	$37.65 per overtime hour

Earnings for 44 hours:		
40 hours at straight time (as calculated above)	=	$1,003.85
4 hours overtime	(4 × $37.65) =	150.60
Total gross earnings		$1,154.45

A shortcut to determine the hourly rate is to divide the annual salary by 2,080 (the standard work hours in a year). In this case, the calculation would be ($4,350 × 12) ÷ 2,080 = $25.10.

TIME CARD

Name: Anderson, Mark
Week ended: Oct. 7, 20—

Day	In	Out	In	Out	Hours Worked	
					Regular	Overtime
Mon	7:57	12:00	12:20	4:32	8	
Tue	7:56	12:06	12:36	4:37	8	
Wed	7:57	12:02	12:31	4:31	8	
Thu	8:00	12:11	12:40	6:32	8	2
Fri	8:00	12:03	12:33	5:33	8	1
Sat	7:59	11:02				3
Sun						

FIGURE 1
Time card for Mark Anderson

Piece-Rate

Workers under the piece-rate system are paid at the rate of so much per unit of production. For example, John Joseph, a strawberry picker, is paid $3 for each box of strawberries picked. If he picks 24 boxes during the day, his total earnings are 24 × $3 = $72.

Commissions

Some salespersons are paid on a purely commission basis. However, a more common arrangement is a salary plus a commission or bonus. Assume that Lora Brown receives an annual salary of $44,000. Her employer agrees to pay her a 5 percent commission on all sales during the year in excess of $200,000. Her sales for the year total $445,000. Her commission is $12,250 [($445,000 – $200,000) × 0.05]. Therefore, her total earnings are $56,250 ($44,000 + $12,250).

DEDUCTIONS FROM TOTAL EARNINGS

LEARNING OBJECTIVE 3
Determine deductions from gross pay, such as federal income tax withheld, Social Security tax, and Medicare tax, to calculate net pay.

Anyone who has ever earned a paycheck has encountered some of the many types of deductions. Total earnings minus deductions equal net pay. The most common deductions are for

1. Federal income tax withholding
2. State income tax withholding
3. FICA taxes (Social Security and Medicare), employee's share
4. Union dues
5. Medical insurance premiums and medical expenses under a flexible spending plan
6. Contributions to a charitable organization, such as United Way
7. Repayment of personal loans from the company
8. Savings through the company 401(k) plan
9. Dependent care expenses under a flexible spending plan (subject to a $5,000 limit)

Medical insurance premiums, medical expenses, and dependent care expenses under a flexible spending plan and 401(k) deductions are usually **pre-tax deductions**. If a deduction is pre-tax, the employee does not have to pay income tax on the amount withheld for federal income tax and sometimes FICA taxes. For example, if Lynn

Workers paid by the piece-rate system are paid according to how much they produce. Here, the number of boxes of strawberries picked determines the worker's total compensation.

Langseth has a weekly salary of $4,000 and the company deducts $200 for medical premiums paid for Lynn's dependents, her payroll subject to income tax is $3,800, not $4,000. If Lynn also contributes $100 to charity, her payroll subject to income tax is still $3,800 as the charitable deduction is not a pre-tax deduction.

Employees' Federal Income Tax Withholding

Employers are required not only to withhold employees' taxes and then pay them to the U.S. Treasury but also to keep records of the names and addresses of persons employed, their **taxable earnings** (the earnings subject to tax) and withholdings, and the amounts and dates of payment.

The amount of federal income tax withheld from an employee's earnings depends on the amount of his or her total earnings, marital status, and number of withholding allowances claimed. A **withholding allowance** is an amount of an individual's earnings that is exempt from income taxes (nontaxable). An employee is entitled to one personal allowance for the taxpayer, one for his or her spouse, and one for each dependent. An **exemption** is an amount of an employee's annual earnings not subject to income tax. Each employee has to fill out an **Employee's Withholding Allowance Certificate (Form W-4)**, shown in Figure 2. The employer retains this form as authorization to withhold money for the employee's federal income tax.

FYI

Federal tax rates change frequently, but the procedure stays the same. We will use the tax table given in this chapter for all computations.

Publication 15 (Circular E), Employer's Tax Guide, and Publication 15-T

Publication 15 (Circular E) contains the rules for depositing federal income, Social Security, and Medicare taxes, while Publication 15-T contains the withholding tables for these taxes. They are regularly updated to reflect changes in tax laws and withholding rates. Publication 15 also describes filing requirements for official

Form **W-4** Department of the Treasury Internal Revenue Service

Employee's Withholding Allowance Certificate

▶ Whether you are entitled to claim a certain number of allowances or exemption from withholding is subject to review by the IRS. Your employer may be required to send a copy of this form to the IRS.

OMB No. 1545-0074 **20XX**

1 Type or print your first name and middle initial. **Mark E.** Last name **Anderson** 2 Your social security number **543 24 1680**

Home address (number and street or rural route) **1104 Rosewood Street**

3 ☐ Single ☒ Married ☐ Married, but withhold at higher Single rate.
Note. If married, but legally separated, or spouse is a nonresident alien, check the "Single" box.

City or town, state, and ZIP code **Bangor, Maine 04401**

4 **If your last name differs from that shown on your social security card, check here. You must call 1-800-772-1213 for a new card.** ▶ ☐

5 Total number of allowances you are claiming (from line **H** above **or** from the applicable worksheet on page 2) 5 1
6 Additional amount, if any, you want withheld from each paycheck . . . . 6 $
7 I claim exemption from withholding for 20XX, and I certify that I meet **both** of the following conditions for exemption.
- Last year I had a right to a refund of **all** federal income tax withheld because I had **no** tax liability **and**
- This year I expect a refund of **all** federal income tax withheld because I expect to have **no** tax liability.

If you meet both conditions, write "Exempt" here . . . . ▶ 7

Under penalties of perjury, I declare that I have examined this certificate and to the best of my knowledge and belief, it is true, correct, and complete.
Employee's signature (Form is not valid unless you sign it.) ▶ *Mark E. Anderson* **Date** ▶ *January 2, 20XX*

8 Employer's name and address (Employer: Complete lines 8 and 10 only if sending to the IRS.) 9 Office code (optional) 10 Employer identification number (EIN)

For Privacy Act and Paperwork Reduction Act Notice, see page 2. Cat. No. 10220Q Form **W-4** (20XX)

FIGURE 2
Employee's Withholding Allowance Certificate (Form W-4) for Mark Anderson

employer reports. Both Publication 15 (Circular E) and Publication 15-T are provided free of charge by the Internal Revenue Service and are available on the Internet at www.irs.gov. Accountants responsible for preparation of payroll registers and forms should be familiar with the contents of these publications.

The **wage-bracket tax tables** cover monthly, semimonthly, biweekly, weekly, and daily payroll periods. The tables are also subdivided on the basis of marital status. To determine the federal income tax withheld, perform the following steps:

STEP 1. Locate the wage bracket in the first two columns of the table.

STEP 2. Find the column for the number of allowances claimed and read down this column until you get to the appropriate wage-bracket line.

A portion of the weekly federal income tax withholding table for married persons is reproduced in Figure 3 on pages 262–263.

Assume that Mark Anderson, who claims one allowance as of the October 7 payroll, has gross wages of $1,124.58 for the week. As $1,124.58 falls in the $1,120–$1,130 bracket, you can see from the table that $104 should be withheld.

Note the headings of the bracket columns: "At least" and "But less than." A strict interpretation of the $1,120–$1,130 bracket really means $1,120–$1,129.99. Therefore, if Anderson's salary were $1,130, it would fall into the $1,130–$1,140 bracket.

Employees' State Income Tax Withholding

Many states that levy state income taxes also furnish employers with withholding tables. Other states use a fixed percentage of the federal income tax withholding as the amount to be withheld for state taxes. In our illustration, we assume that the amount of each employee's state income tax deduction is 20 percent (0.20) of that employee's federal income tax deduction.

Employees' FICA Taxes Withholding (Social Security and Medicare)

The Federal Insurance Contributions Act provides for retirement pensions after a worker reaches age 62, disability benefits for any worker who becomes disabled (and for her or his dependents), and a health insurance program after age 65 (Medicare). Both the employee and the employer must pay **FICA taxes**, which are commonly

MARRIED Persons—**WEEKLY** Payroll Period

(For Wages Paid Through December 2009)

If the wages are–		And the number of withholding allowances claimed is—										
At least	But less than	0	1	2	3	4	5	6	7	8	9	10
		The amount of income tax to be withheld is—										
$0	**$310**	$0	$0	$0	$0	$0	$0	$0	$0	$0	$0	$0
310	**320**	1	0	0	0	0	0	0	0	0	0	0
320	**330**	2	0	0	0	0	0	0	0	0	0	0
330	**340**	3	0	0	0	0	0	0	0	0	0	0
340	**350**	4	0	0	0	0	0	0	0	0	0	0
350	**360**	5	0	0	0	0	0	0	0	0	0	0
360	**370**	6	0	0	0	0	0	0	0	0	0	0
370	**380**	7	0	0	0	0	0	0	0	0	0	0
380	**390**	8	1	0	0	0	0	0	0	0	0	0
390	**400**	9	2	0	0	0	0	0	0	0	0	0
400	**410**	10	3	0	0	0	0	0	0	0	0	0
410	**420**	11	4	0	0	0	0	0	0	0	0	0
420	**430**	12	5	0	0	0	0	0	0	0	0	0
430	**440**	13	6	0	0	0	0	0	0	0	0	0
440	**450**	14	7	0	0	0	0	0	0	0	0	0
450	**460**	15	8	1	0	0	0	0	0	0	0	0
460	**470**	16	9	2	0	0	0	0	0	0	0	0
470	**480**	17	10	3	0	0	0	0	0	0	0	0
480	**490**	19	11	4	0	0	0	0	0	0	0	0
490	**500**	20	12	5	0	0	0	0	0	0	0	0
500	**510**	22	13	6	0	0	0	0	0	0	0	0
510	**520**	23	14	7	0	0	0	0	0	0	0	0
520	**530**	25	15	8	1	0	0	0	0	0	0	0
530	**540**	26	16	9	2	0	0	0	0	0	0	0
540	**550**	28	17	10	3	0	0	0	0	0	0	0
550	**560**	29	19	11	4	0	0	0	0	0	0	0
560	**570**	31	20	12	5	0	0	0	0	0	0	0
570	**580**	32	22	13	6	0	0	0	0	0	0	0
580	**590**	34	23	14	7	0	0	0	0	0	0	0
590	**600**	35	25	15	8	1	0	0	0	0	0	0
600	**610**	37	26	16	9	2	0	0	0	0	0	0
610	**620**	38	28	17	10	3	0	0	0	0	0	0
620	**630**	40	29	19	11	4	0	0	0	0	0	0
630	**640**	41	31	20	12	5	0	0	0	0	0	0
640	**650**	43	32	22	13	6	0	0	0	0	0	0
650	**660**	44	34	23	14	7	0	0	0	0	0	0
660	**670**	46	35	25	15	8	1	0	0	0	0	0
670	**680**	47	37	26	16	9	2	0	0	0	0	0
680	**690**	49	38	28	17	10	3	0	0	0	0	0
690	**700**	50	40	29	19	11	4	0	0	0	0	0
700	**710**	52	41	31	20	12	5	0	0	0	0	0
710	**720**	53	43	32	22	13	6	0	0	0	0	0
720	**730**	55	44	34	23	14	7	0	0	0	0	0
730	**740**	56	46	35	25	15	8	1	0	0	0	0
740	**750**	58	47	37	26	16	9	2	0	0	0	0
750	**760**	59	49	38	28	17	10	3	0	0	0	0
760	**770**	61	50	40	29	19	11	4	0	0	0	0
770	**780**	62	52	41	31	20	12	5	0	0	0	0
780	**790**	64	53	43	32	22	13	6	0	0	0	0
790	**800**	65	55	44	34	23	14	7	0	0	0	0
800	**810**	67	56	46	35	25	15	8	1	0	0	0
810	**820**	68	58	47	37	26	16	9	2	0	0	0
820	**830**	70	59	49	38	28	17	10	3	0	0	0
830	**840**	71	61	50	40	29	19	11	4	0	0	0
840	**850**	73	62	52	41	31	20	12	5	0	0	0
850	**860**	74	64	53	43	32	22	13	6	0	0	0
860	**870**	76	65	55	44	34	23	14	7	0	0	0
870	**880**	77	67	56	46	35	25	15	8	1	0	0
880	**890**	79	68	58	47	37	26	16	9	2	0	0
890	**900**	80	70	59	49	38	28	17	10	3	0	0
900	**910**	82	71	61	50	40	29	19	11	4	0	0
910	**920**	83	73	62	52	41	31	20	12	5	0	0
920	**930**	85	74	64	53	43	32	22	13	6	0	0
930	**940**	86	76	65	55	44	34	23	14	7	0	0
940	**950**	88	77	67	56	46	35	25	15	8	1	0
950	**960**	89	79	68	58	47	37	26	16	9	2	0
960	**970**	91	80	70	59	49	38	28	17	10	3	0
970	**980**	92	82	71	61	50	40	29	19	11	4	0
980	**990**	94	83	73	62	52	41	31	20	12	5	0
990	**1,000**	95	85	74	64	53	43	32	22	13	6	0
1,000	**1,010**	97	86	76	65	55	44	34	23	14	7	0
1,010	**1,020**	98	88	77	67	56	46	35	25	15	8	1
1,020	**1,030**	100	89	79	68	58	47	37	26	16	9	2
1,030	**1,040**	101	91	80	70	59	49	38	28	17	10	3
1,040	**1,050**	103	92	82	71	61	50	40	29	19	11	4

FIGURE 3 2009 federal income tax withholding table for married persons (weekly payroll period)

MARRIED Persons—**WEEKLY** Payroll Period
(For Wages Paid Through December 2009)

If the wages are–		And the number of withholding allowances claimed is—										
At least	But less than	0	1	2	3	4	5	6	7	8	9	10
		The amount of income tax to be withheld is—										
$1,050	**$1,060**	$104	$94	$83	$73	$62	$52	$41	$31	$20	$12	$5
1,060	**1,070**	106	95	85	74	64	53	43	32	22	13	6
1,070	**1,080**	107	97	86	76	65	55	44	34	23	14	7
1,080	**1,090**	109	98	88	77	67	56	46	35	25	15	8
1,090	**1,100**	110	100	89	79	68	58	47	37	26	16	9
1,100	**1,110**	112	101	91	80	70	59	49	38	28	17	10
1,110	**1,120**	113	103	92	82	71	61	50	40	29	19	11
1,120	**1,130**	115	104	94	83	73	62	52	41	31	20	12
1,130	**1,140**	116	106	95	85	74	64	53	43	32	22	13
1,140	**1,150**	118	107	97	86	76	65	55	44	34	23	14
1,150	**1,160**	119	109	98	88	77	67	56	46	35	25	15
1,160	**1,170**	121	110	100	89	79	68	58	47	37	26	16
1,170	**1,180**	122	112	101	91	80	70	59	49	38	28	17
1,180	**1,190**	124	113	103	92	82	71	61	50	40	29	19
1,190	**1,200**	125	115	104	94	83	73	62	52	41	31	20
1,200	**1,210**	127	116	106	95	85	74	64	53	43	32	22
1,210	**1,220**	128	118	107	97	86	76	65	55	44	34	23
1,220	**1,230**	130	119	109	98	88	77	67	56	46	35	25
1,230	**1,240**	131	121	110	100	89	79	68	58	47	37	26
1,240	**1,250**	133	122	112	101	91	80	70	59	49	38	28
1,250	**1,260**	134	124	113	103	92	82	71	61	50	40	29
1,260	**1,270**	136	125	115	104	94	83	73	62	52	41	31
1,270	**1,280**	137	127	116	106	95	85	74	64	53	43	32
1,280	**1,290**	139	128	118	107	97	86	76	65	55	44	34
1,290	**1,300**	140	130	119	109	98	88	77	67	56	46	35
1,300	**1,310**	142	131	121	110	100	89	79	68	58	47	37
1,310	**1,320**	143	133	122	112	101	91	80	70	59	49	38
1,320	**1,330**	145	134	124	113	103	92	82	71	61	50	40
1,330	**1,340**	146	136	125	115	104	94	83	73	62	52	41
1,340	**1,350**	148	137	127	116	106	95	85	74	64	53	43
1,350	**1,360**	149	139	128	118	107	97	86	76	65	55	44
1,360	**1,370**	151	140	130	119	109	98	88	77	67	56	46
1,370	**1,380**	152	142	131	121	110	100	89	79	68	58	47
1,380	**1,390**	154	143	133	122	112	101	91	80	70	59	49
1,390	**1,400**	155	145	134	124	113	103	92	82	71	61	50
$1,400 and over		Use Table 1(b) for a **MARRIED person** on page 5. Also see the instructions on page 3.										

FIGURE 3
(Concluded)

referred to as **Social Security taxes** and **Medicare taxes**. The employer withholds FICA taxes from employees' wages and pays them to the U.S. Treasury.

FICA tax rates apply to the gross earnings of an employee during the **calendar year** (January 1 through December 31). After an employee has paid Social Security tax on the maximum taxable earnings, the employer stops deducting Social Security tax until the next calendar year begins. Congress has frequently changed the schedule of rates and taxable incomes.

In this text, we assume a Social Security rate of 6.2 percent (0.062) of the first $106,800 for each employee and a Medicare rate of 1.45 percent (0.0145) of all earnings for each employee. Both tax rates apply to earnings during the calendar year. (Tables for Social Security and Medicare tax withholdings are available in the Internal Revenue Service Publication 15-T.)

Let's return to Mark Anderson, who had gross wages of $1,124.58 for the week ending October 7. Suppose that his total accumulated gross wages earned this year prior to this payroll period are $44,960. Anderson's total gross wages including this payroll period were $46,084.58 ($44,960 + $1,124.58). Since the Social Security tax applies to the first $106,800 and the Medicare tax applies to all earnings, Anderson's earnings are subject to both taxes. For Anderson's Social Security tax, multiply $1,124.58 by 6.2 percent ($1,124.58 × 0.062 = $69.72). For Anderson's Medicare tax, multiply $1,124.58 by 1.45 percent ($1,124.58 × 0.0145 = $16.31).

Here's another example. At the beginning of the pay period, Grace Wallace had cumulative earnings of $103,900, which is $2,900 less than $106,800. During this pay period, she earned $3,010.35, which is greater than $2,900. Thus, she must pay Social Security tax of $179.80 ($2,900 × 0.062) on $2,900. However, because

FYI

At one time, Social Security and Medicare were not separated for tax computation and there was a limit on Medicare taxable earnings. Now ALL earnings are taxable for Medicare.

Payroll Department

The payroll department is an important part of the accounting and finance functions at companies such as REI. Payroll personnel are responsible for ensuring that all company employees receive compensation and benefits critical to maintaining a productive and motivated workforce. The payroll department at REI works closely with the Information Technology, Human Resources, and other departments to ensure that the company's payroll is accurate, up-to-date, and serving the company's current business objectives. For these reasons, it is important to understand how payroll is determined, whether you are directly responsible for processing payroll or you are employed in any other business department.

the Medicare tax applies to all earnings, she is not exempt from any Medicare tax. Her Medicare tax is \$43.65 (\$3,010.35 × 0.0145). Since Grace's cumulative earnings after this pay period are now over \$106,800, any remaining pay will not be subject to Social Security tax.

PAYROLL REGISTER

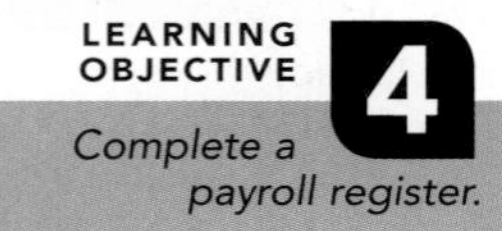

The **payroll register** is a manual or computerized schedule prepared for each payroll period listing the earnings, deductions, and net pay for each employee. In Figure 4 (shown on pages 266–267) we see a payroll register using Excel. It shows the data for each employee on a separate line. This would be suitable for a firm, like Green Sales Company, that has a small number of employees.

First, we'll show the entire payroll register; then, we'll break it down and explain it column by column. The number at the foot of each column refers to the related text description.

The payroll period shown in Figure 4 covers October 1 through October 7. The first part consists of employees' names, hours worked, beginning cumulative earnings, and taxable earnings.

(1) **Total Hours**—Taken from employees' time records (manual or computerized).

(2) **Beginning Cumulative Earnings**—The amount each employee has earned between January 1 and September 30 (the last day of the previous payroll period). It is taken from each employee's individual earnings record. (See Figure 7, pages 270–271.)

(3) **Regular Earnings**—Earnings for hours worked up to and including 40. In other words, the first 40 hours multiplied by each employee's regular hourly rate.

(4) **Overtime Earnings**—Hours in excess of 40 (relative to a 40-hour week) worked by each employee, multiplied by that employee's overtime rate.

(5) **Total Earnings**—Regular earnings plus overtime earnings.

(6) **Ending Cumulative Earnings**—Beginning Cumulative Earnings plus Total Earnings.

(7) **Taxable Earnings**—The amount of earnings subject to taxation, **not the tax itself.** We will use these columns later to figure the amount of each tax. In other words, **Taxable Earnings is the base on which to figure the tax. Taxable Earnings multiplied by the tax rate equals the amount of the tax.**

(7A) **Unemployment Taxable Earnings—**In our illustration, we are using a maximum of $7,000 for unemployment tax liability on the employer for each employee. This column represents the previously untaxed portion remaining of the $7,000 for the individual employees. **Unemployment tax is paid only by the employer in most states. An unemployment tax may be paid both to the state and to the federal government.** Actually, states may use different maximum earnings and different rates than does the federal government. However, many states use $7,000, which at the time of this writing is the amount used by the federal government. There are three possibilities for Unemployment Taxable Earnings, as follows:

a. **Employee's cumulative earnings including this pay period have not reached $7,000.** When an employee's cumulative earnings so far during the calendar year (since January 1) are less than $7,000, we record the total earnings for the payroll period in the Unemployment Taxable Earnings column. For example, Anna Bodell's cumulative earnings before this week were $5,987. Bodell's cumulative earnings after this week are $6,731.20 ($5,987 + $744.20). Because Bodell's cumulative earnings are still less than $7,000 (after the current check of $744.20), her entire $744.20 in wages earned during this pay period is listed in the Unemployment Taxable Earnings column.

b. **Employee's cumulative earnings were less than $7,000 before this week and are more than $7,000 after this week.** Look at the line for David Dorn and notice that his cumulative earnings before this week were $6,786. Dorn's new cumulative earnings (ending) are $7,702 ($6,786 + $916), putting him over the $7,000 maximum. Therefore, to bring Dorn up to the $7,000 limit, $214 ($7,000 – $6,786) of his earnings for the week are taxable. After this week, none of Dorn's earnings for the remainder of this calendar year will be taxable for unemployment.

c. **Employee's cumulative earnings before this week were more than $7,000.** After an employee's earnings top $7,000 during the calendar year, record a zero or a dash in the Unemployment Taxable Earnings column to indicate that the column has not been forgotten or overlooked. For example, Mark Anderson's total earnings before the payroll period ended October 7 (beginning) were $44,960 (as shown in his individual earnings record in Figure 7 on pages 270–271). Since he had previously earned more than $7,000 this year, we record a zero in the Unemployment Taxable Earnings column.

(7B) **Social Security Taxable Earnings**—The first $106,800 for each employee. We assume a Social Security tax rate of 6.2 percent of the first $106,800 paid to each employee during the calendar year.

a. **Employee's cumulative earnings including this pay period have not reached $106,800.** When an employee's cumulative earnings so far during the year are less than $106,800, we record the total earnings for the payroll period in the Social Security Taxable Earnings column. For example, Anna Bodell's cumulative earnings so far this year amount to $6,731.20. Because Bodell's total earnings are less than $106,800, the entire $744.20 of wages earned during this pay period is listed in the Social Security Taxable Earnings column. Note that this is true of all the employees except Grace Wallace.

Remember

Taxable earnings are the base on which to figure the tax, not the tax itself.

Remember

Unemployment taxable earnings are used for calculating the amount of the unemployment tax, which is paid by the employer only.

FYI

Social Security and Medicare taxes are recorded separately in the payroll register because there is no limit on Medicare as there is on Social Security.

	A	B	C	D	E	F	G	H	
1				EARNINGS					
2			BEGINNING				ENDING		
3		TOTAL	CUMULATIVE				CUMULATIVE		
4	NAME	HOURS	EARNINGS	REGULAR	OVERTIME	TOTAL	EARNINGS	UNEMPLOYMENT	
5	Anderson, Mark	46	44,960.00	918.00	206.58	1,124.58	46,084.58	0.00	
6	Bodell, Anna	45	5,987.00	626.20	118.00	744.20	6,731.20	744.20	
7	Dorn, David	49	6,786.00	686.00	230.00	916.00	7,702.00	214.00	
8	Fields, Sarah	40	38,462.00	1,084.50	0.00	1,084.50	39,546.50	0.00	
9	Graham, Jason	40	68,600.00	1,798.45	0.00	1,798.45	70,398.45	0.00	
10	Lee, Jeremy	40	68,500.00	1,895.58	0.00	1,895.58	70,395.58	0.00	
11	Mankowitz, Hanna	55	37,850.00	1,264.30	580.00	1,844.30	39,694.30	0.00	
12	Olsen, Barbara	40	45,820.00	1,487.20	0.00	1,487.20	47,307.20	0.00	
13	Parker, William	44	46,430.00	1,581.58	194.70	1,776.28	48,206.28	0.00	
14	Raman, Soma	45	54,867.00	1,674.16	275.00	1,949.16	56,816.16	0.00	
15	Tabor, Annette	40	42,740.00	1,168.83	0.00	1,168.83	43,908.83	0.00	
16	Wallace, Grace	40	103,900.00	3,010.35	0.00	3,010.35	106,910.35	0.00	
17			564,902.00	17,195.15	1,604.28	18,799.43	583,701.43	958.20	
18		*(1)*	*(2)*	*(3)*	*(4)*	*(5)*	*(6)*	*(7A)*	
19									

17,195.15 + 1,604.28 = 18,799.43

564,902.00 + 18,799.43 = 583,701.43

FIGURE 4
Payroll register for Green Sales Company

b. **Employee's cumulative earnings were less than $106,800 before this week and are more than $106,800 after this week.** The line for Grace Wallace shows her cumulative earnings before the payroll period ended October 7 were $103,900. However, the cumulative earnings including those of this payroll period total $106,910.35, which is greater than the $106,800 limit. That means only $2,900 ($106,800 – $103,900) of her current pay period earnings is recorded in the Social Security Taxable Earnings column. After an employee's earnings top $106,800 during the calendar year, record a zero or dash to indicate that the column has not been forgotten or overlooked. (Use the same procedure as for the Unemployment Taxable Earnings column.)

(7C) Medicare Taxable Earnings—All earnings for this period. We have assumed a Medicare tax rate of 1.45 percent (0.0145) on all earnings that are paid to each employee during the calendar year. Therefore, all earnings for this period are taxable and are recorded in the Medicare Taxable Earnings column.

(8) Deductions—Amounts taken away (withheld) from total earnings.

(8A) Federal Income Tax Deductions—The amount of the federal income tax deduction for each employee can be located directly on the wage-bracket tables or calculated on a percentage basis. We assumed the employees are married and have one withholding allowance.

(8B) State Income Tax Deductions—States that impose income taxes also provide wage-bracket tables. The state tax deduction for each employee can be located directly in the appropriate table. As stated previously, we are assuming a rate of 20 percent of the federal income tax.

Remember
Taxable earnings multiplied by the tax rate equals the tax.

(8C) Social Security Tax Deductions—For each employee's Social Security tax deduction, we first go to the Social Security Taxable Earnings column and note the amount subject to tax. Next, we multiply the Social Security taxable earnings by 6.2 percent (0.062). For example, Bodell's taxable earnings are $744.20, and her Social Security tax deduction is $46.14 ($744.20 × 0.062).

(8D) Medicare Tax Deductions—For each employee's Medicare tax deduction, we go to the Medicare Taxable Earnings column and note the amount subject to tax. Next, we multiply the Medicare taxable earnings by 1.45 percent. For example, Bodell's taxable earnings are $744.20, and her Medicare tax deduction is $10.79 ($744.20 × 0.0145).

GREEN SALES COMPANY
PAYROLL REGISTER FOR WEEK ENDED October 7, 20—

I	J	K	L	M	N	O	P	Q
(7) TAXABLE EARNINGS		(8) DEDUCTIONS						
SOCIAL SECURITY	MEDICARE	FEDERAL INCOME TAX	STATE INCOME TAX	SOCIAL SECURITY TAX	MEDICARE TAX	OTHER DEDUCTIONS		TOTAL
1,124.58	1,124.58	104.00	20.80	69.72	16.31		0.00	210.83
744.20	744.20	47.00	9.40	46.14	10.79	UW	35.00	148.33
916.00	916.00	73.00	14.60	56.79	13.28	UW	25.00	182.67
1,084.50	1,084.50	98.00	19.60	67.24	15.73	UW	10.00	210.57
1,798.45	1,798.45	232.77	46.55	111.50	26.08		0.00	416.90
1,895.58	1,895.58	257.05	51.41	117.53	27.49	AR	20.00	473.48
1,844.30	1,844.30	244.23	48.85	114.35	26.74		0.00	434.17
1,487.20	1,487.20	158.75	31.75	92.21	21.56		0.00	304.27
1,776.28	1,776.28	227.22	45.44	110.13	25.76		0.00	408.55
1,949.16	1,949.16	270.44	54.09	120.85	28.26	AR	30.00	503.64
1,168.83	1,168.83	110.00	22.00	72.47	16.95	UW	25.00	246.42
2,900.00	3,010.35	555.78	111.16	179.80	43.65	UW	100.00	990.39
18,689.08	18,799.43	2,378.24	475.65	1,158.73	272.60		245.00	4,530.22
(7B)	(7C)	(8A)	(8B)	(8C)	(8D)		(8E)	(8F)

2,378.24 + 475.65 + 1,158.73 + 272.60 + 245.00 = 4,530.22

PAGE 56

R	S	T	U
(9) PAYMENTS		(10) EXPENSE ACCOUNT DEBITED	
NET AMOUNT	CK. NO.	SALES WAGES EXPENSE	OFFICE WAGES EXPENSE
913.75	832	1,124.58	
595.87	833	744.20	
733.33	834	916.00	
873.93	835		1,084.50
1,381.55	836	1,798.45	
1,422.10	837		1,895.58
1,410.13	838	1,844.30	
1,182.93	839		1,487.20
1,367.73	840	1,776.28	
1,445.52	841	1,949.16	
922.41	842	1,168.83	
2,019.96	843		3,010.35
14,269.21		11,321.80	7,477.63
(9A)	(9B)	(10A)	(10B)

4,530.22 + 14,269.21 = 18,799.43

11,321.80 + 7,477.63 = 18,799.43

FIGURE 4
(Concluded)

(8E) Other Deductions—Employees' voluntary withholdings. In our illustration, UW represents the United Way, and AR stands for Accounts Receivable (employee pays off a loan with the company). For example, Jeremy Lee paid $20 on his loan with the company.

(8F) Total Deductions—The combined total of each employee's deductions for taxes and other. For example, Bodell's total deduction is $148.33 ($47.00 + $9.40 + $46.14 + $10.79 + $35.00).

(9) Payments—The amount of each employee's payroll check (net pay or take-home pay).

(9A) Net Amount—Each employee's Total Earnings minus Total Deductions. For example, Bodell's net amount is $595.87 ($744.20 – $148.33).

(9B) Ck. No.—The number of each employee's payroll check.

(10) Expense Account Debited—Columns used for distributing each amount into the appropriate wages expense account. Green Sales Company uses Sales Wages Expense and Office Wages Expense. The sum of these two columns equals the total earnings.

(10A) Sales Wages Expense—Amounts earned by employees involved in sales activities.

(10B) Office Wages Expense—Amounts earned by employees involved in office activities.

THE PAYROLL ENTRY

LEARNING OBJECTIVE 5

Journalize the payroll entry from a payroll register.

Because the payroll register summarizes the payroll data for the period, it is used as the basis for recording the payroll in the ledger accounts. Since the payroll register does not have the status of a journal, a journal entry is necessary. Figure 5 shows the entry in general journal form.

Note that the accountant records the total cost to the company for services of employees as debits to the Wages Expense accounts.

Also note that the total Social Security tax deductions ($1,158.73) and the total Medicare tax deductions ($272.60) are combined to become FICA Taxes Payable of $1,431.33 ($1,158.73 + $272.60). The two tax deductions are combined into the one liability account because they are paid together at the same time. Social Security and Medicare taxes are recorded separately in the payroll register because they must be listed separately on each employee's W-2 form (Wage and Tax Statement).

Remember

The totals from the payroll register are the amounts used in the payroll entry.

Social Security (6.2%, limited to $106,800)	+	Medicare (1.45%, unlimited)	=	FICA Taxes Payable

To pay the employees from the company's regular checking account, the accountant now makes the journal entry shown at the top of the next page.

FIGURE 5

Payroll journal entry for Green Sales Company

GENERAL JOURNAL PAGE 31

Date		Description	Post. Ref.	Debit	Credit
20—					
Oct.	7	Sales Wages Expense		11,321.80	
		Office Wages Expense		7,477.63	
		Employees' Federal Income			
		Tax Payable			2,378.24
		FICA Taxes Payable			1,431.33
		Employees' State Income Tax			
		Payable			475.65
		Employees' United Way Payable			195.00
		Accounts Receivable			50.00
		Wages Payable			14,269.21
		Payroll register for the week			
		ended October 7, 20—.			

$1,158.73 + $272.60

Date		Description	Post. Ref.	Debit	Credit
Oct.	8	Wages Payable		14 2 6 9 21	
		Cash—M. Anderson			9 1 3 75
		Cash—A. Bodell			5 9 5 87
		Cash—D. Dorn			7 3 3 33
		Cash—S. Fields			8 7 3 93
		Cash—J. Graham			1 3 8 1 55
		Cash—J. Lee			1 4 2 2 10
		Cash—H. Mankowitz			1 4 1 0 13
		Cash—B. Olson			1 1 8 2 93
		Cash—W. Parker			1 3 6 7 73
		Cash—S. Raman			1 4 4 5 52
		Cash—A. Tabor			9 2 2 41
		Cash—G. Wallace			2 0 1 9 96

FIGURE 5
(Concluded)

Remember

The amount shown as Wages Payable is the employees' take-home pay.

Special Payroll Bank Account—An Alternative

A firm with a large number of employees would probably open a special **payroll bank account** with its bank. One check drawn on the regular bank account is made payable to the special payroll account for the amount of the total net pay for a payroll period. All payroll checks for the period are then written on the special payroll account. To record this, the accountant makes the following journal entry. In this book, assume the entry to debit Cash—Payroll Bank Account and to credit Cash has already been made.

FYI

A company with a small number of employees would probably use its regular bank account to issue a check to each employee.

GENERAL JOURNAL PAGE 31

Date		Description	Post. Ref.	Debit	Credit
Oct.	8	Wages Payable		14 2 6 9 21	
		Cash—Payroll Bank Account			14 2 6 9 21
		Paid wages for week ended			
		October 7.			

Paycheck

All the data needed to make out a payroll check are available in the payroll register. Mark Anderson's paycheck is shown in Figure 6.

FYI

With the use of the special payroll bank account, if employees delay cashing their paychecks, then the checks do not have to be listed on the bank reconciliation of the firm's regular bank account. Balances of Employees' United Way Payable and other employee deductions are paid out of the firm's regular bank account.

EMPLOYEE	TOTAL HOURS	O.T. HOURS	REG. PAY	O.T. PREM. PAY	GROSS PAY	FED INC. TAX	STATE INC. TAX	SOCIAL SECURITY TAX	MEDICARE TAX	OTHER	TOTAL DED.	NET PAY
Mark Anderson	46	6	918.00	206.58	1,124.58	104.00	20.80	69.72	16.31	—	210.83	913.75

Payroll Account
Green Sales Company
610 First Avenue
Bangor, Maine 04401

CENTRAL NATIONAL BANK

98-461
252

October 8 20 — No. 832

PAY TO THE ORDER OF Mark Anderson $ 913.75

Nine hundred thirteen and 75/100 DOLLARS

Eileen Green

⑆252⑈0461⑆

FIGURE 6
Paycheck for Mark Anderson

EMPLOYEE'S INDIVIDUAL EARNINGS RECORD

NAME	Mark E. Anderson			EMPLOYEE NO.	55
ADDRESS	1104 Rosewood Street			SOC. SEC. NO.	543-24-1680
MALE	Bangor, Maine 04401			PAY RATE	$22.95
MALE	X	FEMALE		EQUIVALENT HOURLY RATE	$22.95
MARRIED	X	SINGLE		DATE TERMINATED	
PHONE NO.	207-555-2256	DATE OF BIRTH	9/17/72	CLASSIFICATION FOR WORKERS' COMPENSATION INSURANCE	Sales floor

	A	B	C	D	E	F	G	H	I	J
1			HOURS WORKED		EARNINGS				DEDUCTIONS	
2										
3	PERIOD	DATE						ENDING CUMULATIVE	FEDERAL INCOME	STATE INCOME
4	ENDED	PAID	REGULAR	OVERTIME	REGULAR	OVERTIME	TOTAL	EARNINGS	TAX	TAX
5	9/2	9/3	40	8	918.00	275.44	1,193.44	40,771.55	115.00	23.00
6	9/9	9/10	40	2	918.00	68.86	986.86	41,758.41	83.00	16.60
7	9/16	9/17	40	2	918.00	68.86	986.86	42,745.27	83.00	16.60
8	9/23	9/24	40	5	918.00	172.15	1,090.15	43,835.42	100.00	20.00
9	9/30	10/1	40	6	918.00	206.58	1,124.58	44,960.00	104.00	20.80
10	10/7	10/8	40	6	918.00	206.58	1,124.58	46,084.58	104.00	20.80
11										

FIGURE 7

Employee's individual earnings record for Mark Anderson

Employees' Individual Earnings Records

LEARNING OBJECTIVE 6

Maintain employees' individual earnings records.

To comply with government regulations, a firm has to keep current data on each employee's accumulated earnings, deductions, and net pay. The information contained in the payroll register is recorded each payday in each **employee's individual earnings record**. Figure 7 shows a portion of the earnings record for Mark Anderson.

CHAPTER REVIEW

Study & Practice

LEARNING OBJECTIVE 1

Understand the role of income tax laws that affect payroll deductions and contributions.

Employees and employers involved in the computation and paying of employees for their work must understand the laws, know the percentages and limits involved, and when and to whom to submit the funds deducted from employees and contributed by employees. The federal income tax withholding tables are provided by the IRS in Publication 15-T. FICA payroll taxes are currently 6.2 percent (0.062) on the first $106,800 of wages for Social Security and 1.45 percent (0.0145) on all wages for Medicare.

DATE EMPLOYED 2/1/--
NO. OF EXEMPTIONS 1
PER HOUR X PER DAY
PER WEEK PER MONTH

K	L	M	N	O	P	Q
DEDUCTIONS					PAID	
		OTHER				
SOCIAL SECURITY TAX	MEDICARE TAX	CODE	AMOUNT	TOTAL	NET AMOUNT	CK. NO.
73.99	17.30	UW	5.00	234.29	959.15	771
61.19	14.31	UW	0.00	175.10	811.76	783
61.19	14.31	UW	5.00	180.10	806.76	795
67.59	15.81	UW	0.00	203.40	886.75	807
69.72	16.31	UW	5.00	215.83	908.75	819
69.72	16.31	UW	0.00	210.83	913.75	832

FIGURE 7
(Concluded)

PRACTICE EXERCISE 1

Sally Quinn earns an annual salary of $150,000. How much does she pay in FICA payroll taxes this year?

PRACTICE EXERCISE 1 SOLUTION

Social Security taxes (limited to first $106,800)	$106,800 × 0.062 =	$6,621.60
Medicare taxes	$150,000 × 0.0145 =	2,175.00
Total FICA taxes		$8,796.60

LEARNING OBJECTIVE 2

Calculate total earnings based on an hourly, salary, piece-rate, or commission basis.

Earnings calculated on an *hourly basis* equal the hourly rate multiplied by the number of hours worked. If an employee is paid on a *salary basis* and is entitled to extra pay for overtime, the overtime rate is the annual salary divided by 52 (weeks) divided by 40 (normal hours per week). Earnings calculated on a *piece-rate basis* equals the total number of products produced multiplied by the rate per unit of product. Earnings calculated on a *commission basis* equal the total number of units sold or the price of units sold multiplied by the commission rate.

PRACTICE EXERCISE 2

Soma Raman worked 45 hours for the week ended November 7. His hourly rate is $41.85. Determine his gross wages if he is paid time-and-a-half for all overtime hours.

PRACTICE EXERCISE 2 SOLUTION

40 hours at straight time	40 × $41.85 per hour =	$1,674.00
5 hours overtime ($41.85 × 1.5 = $62.78)	5 × $62.78 per hour =	313.90
Total hours and gross wages	45	$1,987.90

3 LEARNING OBJECTIVE

Determine deductions from gross pay, such as federal income tax withheld, Social Security tax, and Medicare tax, to calculate net pay.

Starting with **gross pay**, an employee's pay is reduced for federal and state income tax withholding, **FICA taxes** (**Social Security** and **Medicare taxes**), and other items such as retirement savings through a 401(k) plan, medical reimbursement plans, etc., to arrive at **net pay**.

PRACTICE EXERCISE 3

Using Figure 3 on pages 262–263, calculate the federal income tax withholding for an employee who is married, paid weekly, and whose wages are $1,360 with one withholding allowance. Then calculate the Social Security tax and Medicare tax for the employee, assuming the employee has cumulative earnings of less than $106,800 for the calendar year to date.

PRACTICE EXERCISE 3 SOLUTION

According to Figure 3, $140 should be withheld for an employee who is married, paid weekly, and whose wages are $1,360 with one withholding allowance. Social Security and Medicare taxes would be computed as follows:

$1,360 × 0.062 = $84.32 Social Security tax
$1,360 × 0.0145 = $19.72 Medicare tax

LEARNING OBJECTIVE

Complete a payroll register.

To complete the **payroll register**, list the employees' names, hours worked, and beginning cumulative earnings. Add the total earnings to the beginning cumulative earnings to get ending cumulative earnings. The Unemployment Taxable Earnings column is used for the first $7,000 of each employee's earnings for FUTA and SUTA. The Social Security Taxable Earnings column is used for the first $106,800 paid to each employee during the **calendar year**. The Medicare Taxable Earnings column is used for all earnings. Under the Deductions columns, list the federal and state income taxes withheld, the Social Security taxes withheld, the Medicare taxes withheld, and other deductions. The Social Security tax deduction equals the Social Security **taxable earnings** multiplied by an assumed rate of 6.2 percent. The Medicare tax deduction equals the Medicare taxable earnings multiplied by an assumed rate of 1.45 percent. The Net Amount column equals Total Earnings minus Total Deductions.

PRACTICE EXERCISE 4

Complete the payroll register on the following page. The employees are paid time-and-a-half for overtime.

	A	B	C	D	E	F	G	H
1				EARNINGS				
2			BEGINNING				ENDING	
3		TOTAL	CUMULATIVE				CUMULATIVE	
4	NAME	HOURS	EARNINGS	REGULAR	OVERTIME	TOTAL	EARNINGS	UNEMPLOYMENT
5	Abbott, Jack	40	55,820.00	1,487.20				0.00
6	Monohan, William	44	56,430.00	1,581.60				0.00
7	Romar, Sue	45	58,967.00	1,674.16				0.00
8	Williams, Emma	40	140,000.00	3,010.35				0.00
9			311,217.00	7,753.31				0.00
10								

SMITH COMPANY
PAYROLL REGISTER FOR WEEK ENDED December 8, 20—

I	J	K	L	M	N	O	P	Q
TAXABLE EARNINGS		DEDUCTIONS					PAYMENTS	
SOCIAL SECURITY	MEDICARE	FEDERAL INCOME TAX	STATE INCOME TAX	SOCIAL SECURITY TAX	MEDICARE TAX	TOTAL	NET AMOUNT	CK. NO.
		158.75	31.75					1520
		237.86	47.57					1521
		280.17	56.03					1522
		555.78	111.16					1523
		1,232.56	246.51					

PRACTICE EXERCISE 4 SOLUTION

	A	B	C	D	E	F	G	H
1				EARNINGS				
2			BEGINNING				ENDING	
3		TOTAL	CUMULATIVE				CUMULATIVE	
4	NAME	HOURS	EARNINGS	REGULAR	OVERTIME	TOTAL	EARNINGS	UNEMPLOYMENT
5	Abbott, Jack	40	55,820.00	1,487.20	0.00	1,487.20	57,307.20	0.00
6	Monohan, William	44	56,430.00	1,581.60	237.24	1,818.84	58,248.84	0.00
7	Romar, Sue	45	58,967.00	1,674.16	313.90	1,988.06	60,955.06	0.00
8	Williams, Emma	40	140,000.00	3,010.35	0.00	3,010.35	143,010.35	0.00
9			311,217.00	7,753.31	551.14	8,304.45	319,521.45	0.00
10								

SMITH COMPANY
PAYROLL REGISTER FOR WEEK ENDED December 8, 20—

I	J	K	L	M	N	O	P	Q
TAXABLE EARNINGS		DEDUCTIONS					PAYMENTS	
SOCIAL SECURITY	MEDICARE	FEDERAL INCOME TAX	STATE INCOME TAX	SOCIAL SECURITY TAX	MEDICARE TAX	TOTAL	NET AMOUNT	CK. NO.
1,487.20	1,487.20	158.75	31.75	92.21	21.56	304.27	1,182.93	1520
1,818.84	1,818.84	237.86	47.57	112.77	26.37	424.57	1,394.27	1521
1,988.06	1,988.06	280.17	56.03	123.26	28.83	488.29	1,499.77	1522
0.00	3,010.35	555.78	111.16	0.00	43.65	710.59	2,299.76	1523
5,294.10	8,304.45	1,232.56	246.51	328.24	120.41	1,927.72	6,376.73	

5 LEARNING OBJECTIVE

Journalize the payroll entry from a payroll register.

Totals are taken directly from the payroll register. Refer to the general journal illustrations on pages 268 and 269 for an example of the first payroll entry and examples of two ways to journalize the payment of the payroll—one from the company's regular checking account and one from a special **payroll bank account**.

PRACTICE EXERCISE 5

Based on the payroll register created in Practice Exercise 4, prepare the journal entry to record the payroll for the week of December 8, 20—.

PRACTICE EXERCISE 5 SOLUTION

GENERAL JOURNAL PAGE 31

Date		Description	Post. Ref.	Debit	Credit
20—					
Dec.	8	Wages Expense		8304 45	
		Employees' Federal Income			
		Tax Payable			1232 56
		FICA Taxes Payable			448 65
		Employees' State Income Tax			
		Payable			246 51
		Wages Payable			6376 73
		Payroll register for the			
		week ended December 8, 20—.			

$328.24 + $120.41 (FICA Taxes Payable)

LEARNING OBJECTIVE

Maintain employees' individual earnings records.

In the **employees' individual earnings records**, list the personal data for each employee. Based on the information contained in the payroll register, record the earnings and deductions for each payroll period.

PRACTICE EXERCISE 6

Update the following employee's individual earnings record for William Monohan for the December 8 payroll from the payroll register in Practice Exercise 4.

CHAPTER REVIEW

EMPLOYEE'S INDIVIDUAL EARNINGS RECORD

NAME	William Monohan			EMPLOYEE NO.	592
ADDRESS	17058 SE 97th Court			SOC. SEC. NO.	544-64-8240
	Miami, Florida 33158			PAY RATE	$39.54
MALE	X	FEMALE		OVERTIME PAY	1½x
MARRIED	X	SINGLE		DATE EMPLOYED	2/1/—
PHONE NO.	305-999-9001	DATE OF BIRTH	6/17/73	NO. OF EXEMPTIONS	1

PER HOUR X PER DAY ____ PER WEEK ____ PER MONTH ____

	A	B	C	D	E	F	G	H	I	J
1			HOURS WORKED		EARNINGS				DEDUCTIONS	
2								ENDING	FEDERAL	STATE
3	PERIOD	DATE						CUMULATIVE	INCOME	INCOME
4	ENDED	PAID	REGULAR	OVERTIME	REGULAR	OVERTIME	TOTAL	EARNINGS	TAX	TAX
5	11/17	11/18	40	8	1,581.60	474.48	2,056.08	53,029.56	297.17	59.43
6	11/24	11/25	40	2	1,581.60	118.62	1,700.22	54,729.78	208.21	41.64
7	12/1	12/2	40	2	1,581.60	118.62	1,700.22	56,430.00	208.21	41.64
8										
9										

K	L	M	N	O
DEDUCTIONS			PAYMENTS	
SOCIAL SECURITY TAX	MEDICARE TAX	TOTAL	NET AMOUNT	CK. NO.
127.48	29.81		1,542.19	920
105.41	24.65	513.89	1,320.31	1120
105.41	24.65	379.91	1,320.31	1325
		379.91		

PRACTICE EXERCISE 6 SOLUTION

EMPLOYEE'S INDIVIDUAL EARNINGS RECORD

NAME	William Monohan			EMPLOYEE NO.	592
ADDRESS	17058 SE 97th Court			SOC. SEC. NO.	544-64-8240
	Miami, Florida 33158			PAY RATE	$39.54
MALE	X	FEMALE		OVERTIME PAY	1½x
MARRIED	X	SINGLE		DATE EMPLOYED	2/1/—
PHONE NO.	305-999-9001	DATE OF BIRTH	6/17/73	NO. OF EXEMPTIONS	1

PER HOUR X PER DAY ____ PER WEEK ____ PER MONTH ____

	A	B	C	D	E	F	G	H	I	J
1			HOURS WORKED		EARNINGS				DEDUCTIONS	
2								ENDING	FEDERAL	STATE
3	PERIOD	DATE						CUMULATIVE	INCOME	INCOME
4	ENDED	PAID	REGULAR	OVERTIME	REGULAR	OVERTIME	TOTAL	EARNINGS	TAX	TAX
5	11/17	11/18	40	8	1,581.60	474.48	2,056.08	53,029.56	297.17	59.43
6	11/24	11/25	40	2	1,581.60	118.62	1,700.22	54,729.78	208.21	41.64
7	12/1	12/2	40	2	1,581.60	118.62	1,700.22	56,430.00	208.21	41.64
8	12/8	12/9	40	4	1,581.60	237.24	1,818.84	58,248.84	237.86	47.57
9										

K	L	M	N	O
DEDUCTIONS			PAYMENTS	
SOCIAL SECURITY TAX	MEDICARE TAX	TOTAL	NET AMOUNT	CK. NO.
127.48	29.81	513.89	1,542.19	920
105.41	24.65	379.91	1,320.31	1120
105.41	24.65	379.91	1,320.31	1325
112.77	26.37	424.57	1,394.27	1521

Glossary

Calendar year A twelve-month period beginning on January 1 and ending on December 31 of the same year. *(p. 263)*

Current Tax Payment Act (Income Tax Withholding) An act to require employers to withhold and pay to the U.S. Treasury employee funds. *(p. 256)*

Employee One who works for compensation under the direction and control of the employer. *(p. 255)*

Employee's individual earnings record A supplementary record for each employee showing personal payroll data and yearly cumulative earnings, deductions, and net pay. *(p. 270)*

Employee's Withholding Allowance Certificate (Form W-4) A form that specifies the number of allowances claimed by each employee and gives the employer the authority to withhold money for an employee's federal income taxes. *(p. 260)*

Exemption An amount of an employee's annual earnings not subject to income tax for the taxpayer, taxpayer's spouse, and dependents *(usually children). (p. 260)*

Fair Labor Standards Act The act of 1938 that provides for minimum standards for wages and overtime, including provisions related to child labor and equal pay for equal work. *(p. 255)*

FICA taxes Social Security taxes plus Medicare taxes, paid by both employee and employer under the provisions of the Federal Insurance Contributions Act. The proceeds are used to pay old-age and disability pensions and to fund the Medicare program. *(p. 261)*

Gross pay The total amount of an employee's pay before any deductions. *(p. 254)*

Independent contractor Someone who is engaged for a definite job or service, and who may choose his or her own means of doing the work. This person is not an employee of the firm for which the service is provided. *(p. 255)*

Medicare taxes Federal government taxes levied on employees and employers; proceeds are used for medical insurance for eligible people age 65 or over. *(p. 263)*

Net pay Gross pay minus deductions. Also called *take-home pay. (p. 254)*

Payroll bank account A special checking account used to pay a company's employees. *(p. 269)*

Payroll register A manual or computerized schedule prepared for each payroll period listing the earnings, deductions, and net pay for each employee. *(p. 264)*

Pre-tax deductions Employee deductions that are not subject to income tax. The deductions include medical insurance premiums and medical and dependent care expenses under a flexible spending plan. *(p. 259)*

Social Security Act of 1935 An act to provide for worker retirement funding through deductions from their wages and matching amounts from the employers. *(p. 256)*

Social Security taxes Federal government taxes levied on employees and employers; proceeds are used for old-age pensions and disability benefits. *(p. 263)*

Taxable earnings The amount of an employee's earnings subject to a tax. *(p. 260)*

Wage-bracket tax tables A chart providing the amounts to be deducted for income taxes based on amount of earnings, marital status, and number of allowances claimed. *(p. 261)*

Withholding allowance An amount of an employee's annual earnings not subject to income tax. *(p. 260)*

Workers' compensation laws Laws that protect employees and dependents against losses due to death or injury incurred on the job. *(p. 257)*

CHAPTER ASSIGNMENTS

Discussion Questions

1. Why must employers maintain employees' individual earnings records?
2. What information is included in an employee's individual earnings record?
3. What is the purpose of the payroll register?
4. Explain the difference between gross earnings and net earnings for a payroll period.
5. Describe how a special payroll bank account is useful in paying the wages and salaries of employees.
6. List three required deductions and four voluntary deductions from an employee's total earnings.

7. What is the difference between an employee and an independent contractor? List two examples of an independent contractor.
8. What information is needed to use the wage-bracket withholding table and where is it found?

Exercises

LO 1,2

PRACTICE EXERCISES 1,2

EXERCISE 7-1 Determine the gross pay for each employee listed below.

a. Gary Dale is paid time-and-a-half for all hours over 40. He worked 44 hours during the week. His regular pay rate is $21.60 per hour.
b. Moira Nole worked 50 hours during the week. She is entitled to time-and-a-half for all hours in excess of 40 per week. Her regular pay rate is $25.00 per hour.
c. Lora Mikel is paid a commission of 8 percent of her sales, which amounted to $20,885.
d. Margo Best's yearly salary is $81,600. During the week, Best worked 43 hours, and she is entitled to time-and-a-half for all hours over 40.

LO 1,2,3

PRACTICE EXERCISES 1,2,3

EXERCISE 7-2 Lisa Meilo works for Pacific Company, which pays its employees time-and-a-half for all hours worked in excess of 40 per week. Meilo's pay rate is $37.00 per hour. Her wages are subject to federal income tax, a Social Security tax deduction at the rate of 6.2 percent, and a Medicare tax deduction at the rate of 1.45 percent. She is married and claims three allowances. Meilo has an unpaid half-hour lunch break during an 8½-hour day. In the most recent pay period, she worked 50 hours. Meilo's beginning cumulative earnings are $73,654.

Complete the following.

a. _______ hours at straight time × $_______ per hour $ _______
b. _______ hours overtime × $_______ per hour _______
c. Total gross pay $ _______
d. Federal income tax withholding $256.81
e. Social Security tax withholding at 6.2 percent _______
f. Medicare tax withholding at 1.45 percent _______
g. Total withholding _______
h. Net pay $ _______

LO 1,2,3,4

PRACTICE EXERCISES 1,2,3,4

EXERCISE 7-3 Using the income tax withholding table in Figure 3, pages 262–263, for each employee of Miller Company, determine the net pay for the week ended January 21. Assume a Social Security tax of 6.2 percent and a Medicare tax of 1.45 percent. All employees have cumulative earnings, including this pay period, of less than $106,800. Assume all employees are married.

Employee	Allowances	Total Earnings	Federal Income Tax Withheld	Social Security Tax Withheld	Medicare Tax Withheld	Union Dues Withheld	United Way Contribution	Net Pay
a. Aston, F. B.	1	$ 900.00	$	$	$	$ 25.00	$ 35.00	$
b. Dwyer, S. J.	2	920.00				25.00	35.00	
c. Flynn, K. A.	3	1,110.00				25.00	40.00	
d. Harden, J. L.	0	1,025.00				25.00	40.00	
e. Nguyen, H.	2	925.00				25.00	35.00	
Totals		$4,880.00	$	$	$	$125.00	$185.00	$

	A	B	C	D	E	F	G	H
1			EARNINGS				TAXABLE EARNINGS	
2–4	NAME	BEGINNING CUMULATIVE EARNINGS	REGULAR	OVERTIME	TOTAL	ENDING CUMULATIVE EARNINGS	UNEMPLOYMENT	SOCIAL SECURITY
9		245,754.00	6,724.00	1,220.00	7,494.00	253,248.00	2,456.00	7,944.00
10								
11								

FIGURE 8
Payroll register for Benton, Inc.

1,4 LO

PRACTICE EXERCISES 1,4

EXERCISE 7-4 For the week ended September 7, the totals of the payroll register for Benton, Inc., are presented in Figure 8. The regular and overtime earnings are correct. List six errors that exist. None of the employees have earned more than $106,800, so all earnings are subject to Social Security and Medicare taxes. Assume that amounts for federal income tax, union dues, and charity are correct.

1,4 LO

PRACTICE EXERCISES 1,4

EXERCISE 7-5 For tax purposes, assume that the maximum taxable earnings are $106,800 for Social Security and $7,000 for the unemployment tax, and that all earnings are taxable for Medicare. For the payroll register for the month of November for Shelby, Inc., determine the taxable earnings for each employee.

	A	B	C	D	E	F	G
1					TAXABLE EARNINGS		
2–4	NAME	BEGINNING CUMULATIVE EARNINGS	TOTAL EARNINGS	ENDING CUMULATIVE EARNINGS	UNEMPLOYMENT	SOCIAL SECURITY	MEDICARE
5	Axton, C.	106,000.00	7,691.00	113,691.00			
6	Edgar, E.	145,465.00	10,900.00	156,365.00			
7	Gorman, L.	36,879.00	3,064.00	39,943.00			
8	Jolson, R.	24,634.00	2,325.00	26,959.00			
9	Nixel, P.	6,850.00	2,463.00	9,313.00			
10							

1,4,5 LO

PRACTICE EXERCISES 1,4,5

EXERCISE 7-6 On January 21, the column totals of the payroll register for Great Products Company showed that its sales employees had earned $14,960, its trucking employees had earned $10,692, and its office employees had earned $8,670. Social Security taxes were withheld at an assumed rate of 6.2 percent, and Medicare taxes were withheld at an assumed rate of 1.45 percent. Other deductions consisted of federal income tax, $3,975; and union dues, $560. Determine the amount of Social Security and Medicare taxes withheld, and record the general journal entry for the payroll, crediting Salaries Payable for the net pay. All earnings were taxable.

1,2,3 LO

PRACTICE EXERCISES 1,2,3

EXERCISE 7-7 Precision Labs has two employees. The following information was taken from its individual earnings records for the month of September. Determine the missing amounts, assuming that the Social Security tax is 6.2 percent and the

I	J	K	L	M	N	O	P	Q	R
	DEDUCTIONS						PAYMENTS		
MEDICARE	FEDERAL INCOME TAX	SOCIAL SECURITY TAX	MEDICARE TAX	UNION DUES	CHARITY	TOTAL	NET AMOUNT	CK. NO.	WAGES EXPENSE DEBIT
7,944.00	949.00	429.53	115.19	193.00	292.00	2,083.00	5,456.00		7,494.00

FIGURE 8
(Concluded)

Medicare tax is 1.45 percent. All earnings are subject to Social Security and Medicare taxes. Round amounts to the nearest penny.

	Brown	Ringness	Total
Regular earnings	$3,500.00	$?	$?
Overtime earnings	?	120.00	
Total earnings	$3,646.00	$?	$?
Federal income tax withheld	$ 268.07	$?	$?
State income tax withheld	?	26.37	?
Social Security tax withheld	226.05	169.76	?
Medicare tax withheld	52.87	39.70	?
Charity withheld	35.00	97.00	?
Total deductions	$ 635.60	$ 464.70	$?
Net pay	$?	$ 2,273.30	$?

LO 5

EXERCISE 7-8 Assume that the employees in Exercise 7-7 are paid from the company's regular bank account (check numbers 981 and 982). Prepare the entry to record and pay the payroll in general journal form, dated September 30.

PRACTICE EXERCISE 5

Problem Set A

For additional help, see the demonstration problem at the beginning of each chapter in your Working Papers.

LO 1,2,3

PROBLEM 7-1A Jennifer Ross, an employee of Hampton Company, worked 44 hours during the week of February 9 through 15. Her rate of pay is $30.00 per hour, and she receives time-and-a-half for work in excess of 40 hours per week. She is married and claims two allowances on her W-4 form. Her wages are subject to the following deductions:

a. Federal income tax (use the table in Figure 3, pages 262–263).
b. Social Security tax at 6.2 percent.
c. Medicare tax at 1.45 percent.
d. Union dues, $30.00.
e. Repay employee loan, $32.00.

Required
Compute Ross's regular pay, overtime pay, gross pay, and net pay.

Check Figure
Net pay, $1,079.43

CHAPTER ASSIGNMENTS

PROBLEM 7-2A Highridge Homes has the following payroll information for the week ended February 21:

Name	Earnings at End of Previous Week	Daily Time							Pay Rate	Federal Income Tax
		S	M	T	W	T	F	S		
Arthur, P.	7,800.00	8	8	8	8	8			45.00	233.15
Bills, D.	2,060.00			8	8	8	8	8	12.50	13.00
Carney, W.	2,085.00	8	8	8			8	8	12.95	14.00
Dorn, J.	748.00				8	8			22.00	0.00
Edgar, L.	2,687.00	8	8	8			8	8	15.00	26.00
Fitzwilson, G.	4,150.00	8	8		8	8	8	8	23.00	115.00

Taxable earnings for Social Security are based on the first $106,800. Taxable earnings for Medicare are based on all earnings. Taxable earnings for federal and state unemployment are based on the first $7,000. Employees are paid time-and-a-half for work in excess of 40 hours per week.

Check Figure
Net amount, $4,184.96

Required

1. Complete the payroll register. The Social Security tax rate is 6.2 percent, and the Medicare tax rate is 1.45 percent. Begin payroll checks with No. 2080.
2. Prepare a general journal entry to record the payroll. The firm's general ledger contains a Wages Expense account and a Wages Payable account.
3. Assuming that the firm has transferred funds from its regular bank account to its special payroll bank account, and that this entry has been made, prepare a general journal entry to record the payment of wages.

1,2,3,4,5 LO

PROBLEM 7-3A Alpine Company pays its employees time-and-a-half for hours worked in excess of 40 per week. The information available from time cards and employees' individual earnings records for the pay period ended October 14 is shown in the following chart.

Name	Earnings at End of Previous Week	Daily Time						Pay Rate	Income Tax Allowances
		M	T	W	T	F	S		
Bardin, J.	43,627.00	8	8	8	8	8	2	21.30	2
Caris, A.	44,340.00	8	8	8	8	8	8	21.60	1
Drew, W.	43,845.00	8	10	10	8	8	0	21.50	1
Garen, S.	105,900.00	8	8	8	8	8	0	49.00	3
North, O.	43,875.00	8	8	8	8	8	5	21.40	3
Ovid, N.	40,150.00	8	8	8	8	8	0	21.50	1
Ross, J.	6,430.00	8	8	8	8	8	4	20.50	1
Springer, O.	44,175.00	8	8	8	8	8	3	21.25	2

Taxable earnings for Social Security are based on the first $106,800. Taxable earnings for Medicare are based on all earnings. Taxable earnings for federal and state unemployment are based on the first $7,000.

Required

Check Figure
Net amount, $7,386.27

1. Complete the payroll register, using the wage-bracket income tax withholding table in Figure 3 (pages 262–263). The Social Security tax rate is 6.2 percent, and the Medicare tax rate is 1.45 percent. Assume that all employees are married. Garen's federal income tax is $238.06. In the payroll register, begin payroll checks with No. 3945.
2. Prepare a general journal entry to record the payroll. The firm's general ledger contains a Wages Expense account and a Wages Payable account.
3. Assuming that the firm has transferred funds from its regular bank account to its special payroll bank account, and that this entry has been made, prepare a general journal entry to record the payment of wages.

1,3,4,5

PROBLEM 7-4A The information for Titan Company, shown in the following chart, is available from Titan's time records and the employees' individual earnings records for the pay period ended December 22.

Name	Hours Worked	Earnings at End of Previous Week	Total Earnings	Class.	Federal Income Tax	Other Deductions	
Albee, C.	44	63,340.00	1,650.00	Sales	195.65	UW	25.00
Don, V.	40	136,410.00	2,841.00	Sales	508.37	AR	95.00
Fine, J.	40	76,860.00	1,507.00	Sales	161.72	UW	25.00
Ginny, N.	46	33,590.00	660.00	Office	35.00	UW	35.00
Johnson, J.	47	56,980.00	1,117.00	Office	103.00	UW	25.00
Lund, D.	43	104,900.00	2,100.00	Sales	308.15	UW	20.00
Maya, R.	42	66,860.00	1,310.00	Sales	133.00	AR	70.00
Nord, P.	41	36,750.00	720.00	Sales	44.00	UW	20.00
Oscar, T.	43	93,480.00	1,832.00	Sales	241.15	UW	25.00
Troy, B.	40	47,250.00	930.00	Sales	76.00	UW	20.00

Taxable earnings for Social Security are based on the first $106,800. Taxable earnings for Medicare are based on all earnings. Taxable earnings for federal and state unemployment are based on the first $7,000. The company does not pay for overtime hours.

Required

Check Figure
Net amount, $11,567.48

1. Complete the payroll register, using a Social Security tax rate of 6.2 percent and a Medicare tax rate of 1.45 percent. Concerning Other Deductions, AR refers to Accounts Receivable and UW refers to United Way. Begin payroll checks in the payroll register with No. 2914.
2. Prepare the general journal entry to record the payroll. The firm's general ledger contains a Salary Expense account and a Salaries Payable account.
3. Prepare the general journal entry to pay the payroll. Assume that funds for this payroll have been transferred to Cash—Payroll Bank Account and that this entry has been made.

Problem Set B

For additional help, see the demonstration problem at the beginning of each chapter in your Working Papers.

1,2,3 **LO**

PROBLEM 7-1B Erin Chang, an employee of Solutions Company, worked 48 hours during the week of October 11 through 17. Her rate of pay is $17.50 per hour, and she receives time-and-a-half for all work in excess of 40 hours per week. Chang is married and claims two allowances on her W-4 form. Her wages are subject to the following deductions:

a. Federal income tax (use the table in Figure 3, pages 262–263).
b. Social Security tax at 6.2 percent.
c. Medicare tax at 1.45 percent.
d. Union dues, $32.00.
e. Repay employee loan, $44.75.

Check Figure
Net pay, $701.63

Required

Compute Chang's regular pay, overtime pay, gross pay, and net pay.

1,2,3,4,5 **LO**

PROBLEM 7-2B Harvest Company has the following payroll information for the pay period ended April 14:

Name	Earnings at End of Previous Week	Daily Time						Pay Rate	Federal Income Tax
		M	T	W	T	F	S		
Grant, L.	7,536.00	8	8	8	8	8	0	18.00	44.00
Hamn, R.	6,496.00	8	8	8	8	8	0	18.10	44.00
Lisk, J.	6,798.00	0	8	8	8	8	8	17.80	43.00
Myre, G.	9,589.00	8	8	8	0	8	8	19.25	52.00
Segel, T.	6,585.00	8	8	8	8	8	6	17.95	67.00
Torgel, I.	7,501.00	0	8	8	8	8	8	18.70	47.00

Taxable earnings for Social Security are based on the first $106,800. Taxable earnings for Medicare are based on all earnings. Taxable earnings for federal and state unemployment are based on the first $7,000. Employees are paid time-and-a-half for work in excess of 40 hours per week.

Check Figure
Net amount, $3,908.23

Required

1. Complete the payroll register. The Social Security tax rate is 6.2 percent, and the Medicare tax rate is 1.45 percent. Begin payroll checks with No. 2944.
2. Prepare a general journal entry to record the payroll. The firm's general ledger contains a Wages Expense account and a Wages Payable account.
3. Assuming that the firm has transferred funds from its regular bank account to its special payroll bank account, and that this entry has been made, prepare a journal entry to record the payment of wages.

PROBLEM 7-3B Williams Company pays its employees time-and-a-half for hours worked in excess of 40 per week. The information available from time records and employees' individual earnings records for the pay period ended September 21 is shown in the following chart.

CHAPTER ASSIGNMENTS

Name	Earnings at End of Previous Week	Daily Time						Pay Rate	Income Tax Allowances
		M	T	W	T	F	S		
Bolt, D.	6,745.00	8	8	8	10	8	0	25.00	1
Dore, C.	136,240.00	8	8	8	8	8	0	49.50	2
Gayle, A.	32,730.00	8	10	8	8	8	0	24.50	2
Hale, R.	105,900.00	8	8	8	8	8	4	40.00	3
Jilly, B.	35,154.00	8	8	8	8	8	0	49.50	0
Karn, S.	29,938.00	8	8	9	8	8	0	20.50	2
Ober, N.	6,795.00	8	8	8	9	9	4	21.00	1
Wong, J.	27,252.00	8	8	10	8	8	0	20.00	2

Taxable earnings for Social Security are based on the first $106,800. Taxable earnings for Medicare are based on all earnings. Taxable earnings for federal and state unemployment are based on the first $7,000.

Required

Check Figure
Net amount, $8,891.78

1. Complete the payroll register, using the wage-bracket income tax withholding table in Figure 3 (pages 262–263). The Social Security tax rate is 6.2 percent, and the Medicare tax rate is 1.45 percent. Assume that all employees are married. The federal income tax deduction is $260.61 for Dore, $208.06 for Hale, and $295.70 for Jilly. In the payroll register, begin payroll checks with No. 1863.
2. Prepare a general journal entry to record the payroll. The firm's general ledger contains a Wages Expense account and a Wages Payable account.
3. Assuming that the firm has transferred funds from its regular bank account to its special payroll bank account, and that this entry has been made, prepare a general journal entry to record the payment of wages.

LO 1,3,4,5

PROBLEM 7-4B The information for Best Sports Company, shown in the following chart, is available from Best Sports' time records and employees' individual earnings records for the pay period ended December 29.

Name	Hours Worked	Earnings at End of Previous Week	Total Earnings	Class.	Federal Income Tax	Other Deductions	
Chang, C.	40	33,900.00	680.00	Sales	38.00	AR	80.00
Dugan, T.	42	38,270.00	2,841.00	Sales	508.37	UW	20.00
Fancher, K.	40	37,680.00	725.00	Sales	44.00	UW	25.00
Gannon, T.	40	33,245.00	660.00	Office	35.00		—
Jones, L.	40	37,789.00	750.00	Office	49.00	UW	25.00
Lange, M.	40	106,200.00	2,100.00	Office	308.15	UW	35.00
Milton, D.	40	37,684.00	1,310.00	Sales	133.00	UW	20.00
Naylor, B.	40	37,499.00	720.00	Sales	44.00		—
Orton, A.	44	94,338.00	1,780.00	Sales	228.15	AR	70.00
Tiosha, J.	42	48,120.00	1,065.00	Sales	95.00	UW	25.00

Taxable earnings for Social Security are based on the first $106,800. Taxable earnings for Medicare are based on all earnings. Taxable earnings for federal and state unemployment are based on the first $7,000. The company does not pay for overtime hours.

Check Figure
Net amount, $9,975.06

Required

1. Complete the payroll register, using a Social Security tax rate of 6.2 percent and a Medicare tax rate of 1.45 percent. Concerning Other Deductions, AR refers to Accounts Receivable and UW refers to United Way. Begin payroll checks in the payroll register with No. 2914.
2. Prepare the general journal entry to record the payroll. The firm's general ledger contains a Salary Expense account and a Salaries Payable account.
3. Prepare the general journal entry to pay the payroll. Assume that funds for this payroll have been transferred to Cash—Payroll Bank Account and that this entry has been made.

ACTIVITIES

CONSIDER AND COMMUNICATE

Southern Company pays its employees weekly by issuing checks on its regular bank account. The owner thinks it would be too much trouble to have a second checking account. Explain to the owner why this might be worth the additional effort.

A QUESTION OF ETHICS

An employee who is married and has three children submits a W-4 form to his employer. He checks the box that says "Single" and writes zero in the "Deductions Claimed" box. Is this action ethical, unethical, or illegal? Explain your reasoning.

Employer Taxes, Payments, and Reports

8

TRUGREEN, Memphis, Tennessee; PAWTUCKET RED SOX, Pawtucket, Rhode Island; HOCK IT TO ME, Albuquerque, New Mexico

WHY IT MATTERS

TruGreen is the world's largest lawn and landscape company, employing over 10,000 employees and serving more than 3.4 million customers through its 270 locations.

The Pawtucket Red Sox is a minor league baseball affiliate of the Boston Red Sox. The team's current roster consists of 24 active players, along with the team's manager, coaches, and mascots.

Hock It To Me is a privately owned pawn shop. The company has annual revenue of less than $500,000 and employs a staff of 1 to 4 people.

Even though each of these businesses has a unique payroll due to different amounts of salaries or wages, benefits, and withholdings, each business needs to accurately calculate the amount of payroll for each employee, determine the amount of payroll taxes for which the employer is liable, make the payroll tax deposits as required, and file the appropriate payroll tax returns on a timely basis.

LEARNING OBJECTIVES

After you have completed this chapter, you will be able to do the following:

1. *Calculate the amount of payroll tax expense and journalize the entry.*
2. *Journalize the entry for the deposit of employees' federal income taxes withheld and FICA taxes (both employees' withheld and employer's matching share) and prepare the deposit coupon.*
3. *Journalize the entries for the payment of employer's state and federal unemployment taxes.*
4. *Journalize the entry for the deposit of employees' state income taxes withheld.*
5. *Complete Employer's Quarterly Federal Tax Return, Form 941.*
6. *Prepare W-2 and W-3 forms and Form 940.*
7. *Calculate the premium for workers' compensation insurance, and prepare the entry for payment in advance.*
8. *Determine the amount of the end-of-the-year adjustments for (a) workers' compensation insurance and (b) accrued salaries and wages, and record the adjustments.*

ACCOUNTING LANGUAGE

Employer Identification Number (EIN) *(p. 286)*
Federal unemployment tax (FUTA) *(p. 289)*
Form 940 *(p. 300)*
Form 941 *(p. 295)*
Form W-2 *(p. 298)*
Form W-3 *(p. 299)*
Payroll Tax Expense *(p. 286)*
Quarter *(p. 291)*
State unemployment tax (SUTA) *(p. 289)*
Workers' compensation insurance *(p. 304)*

We have talked about how to compute and record such payroll data as gross pay, employees' income tax withheld, employees' FICA taxes withheld, and various deductions requested by employees. Now we will learn how to record the transactions to pay these withholding liabilities and the taxes levied on the employer.

EMPLOYER IDENTIFICATION NUMBER

Everyone must have a Social Security number or an Individual Taxpayer Identification Number (ITIN), a vital part of federal income tax returns. An employer's counterpart to the Social Security number is the **Employer Identification Number (EIN)** assigned by the Internal Revenue Service. Employers of one or more persons are required to have such a number, and it must be listed on all reports and payments of employees' federal income tax withholding and FICA taxes.

EMPLOYER'S PAYROLL TAXES

An employer's payroll taxes are based on the gross wages paid to employees. Payroll taxes—like property taxes—are an expense of doing business. Green Sales Company records these taxes in the **Payroll Tax Expense** account and debits the account for

The skyrocketing costs of Medicare have caused Congress and the president to try to make sweeping reforms. The issues are far-reaching. Medicare affects a large percentage of the population, who fear their benefits may be reduced.

the company's portion of FICA taxes and for state and federal unemployment taxes. In T account form, Payroll Tax Expense for Green Sales Company would look like the following example.

Payroll Tax Expense

+	−
FICA taxes (employer's matching portion)	Closed at the end of the year along with all other expense accounts
State unemployment tax	
Federal unemployment tax	

As you can see, **FICA taxes (employer's share of Social Security and Medicare taxes), state unemployment tax, and federal unemployment tax are included under the Payroll Tax Expense heading.** In most states, the unemployment taxes are levied on the employer only.

Employer's Matching Portion of FICA Taxes

FICA taxes (the combined Social Security and Medicare taxes) are imposed equally on both employer and employee. The employer's share is determined by multiplying the employer's tax rates (assumed to be 6.2 percent (0.062) for Social Security and 1.45 percent (0.0145) for Medicare) by the taxable earnings (assumed to be a

FIGURE 1

Partial payroll register for Green Sales Company

Amount of employees' earnings for the period that has not, as yet, been taxed as part of the $7,000 maximum liability

Amount of employees' earnings that are less than $106,800 per employee for the year

Amount of all employees' earnings

	A	B	F	G	H	I	J
1					(7) TAXABLE EARNINGS		
2				ENDING			
3		TOTAL		CUMULATIVE		SOCIAL	
4	NAME	HOURS	TOTAL	EARNINGS	UNEMPLOYMENT	SECURITY	MEDICARE
5	Anderson, Mark	46	1,124.58	46,084.58	0.00	1,124.58	1,124.58
6	Bodell, Anna	45	744.20	6,731.20	744.20	744.20	744.20
7	Dorn, David	49	916.00	7,702.00	214.00	916.00	916.00
8	Fields, Sarah	40	1,084.50	39,546.50	0.00	1,084.50	1,084.50
9	Graham, Jason	40	1,798.45	70,398.45	0.00	1,798.45	1,798.45
10	Lee, Jeremy	40	1,895.58	70,395.58	0.00	1,895.58	1,895.58
11	Mankowitz, Hanna	55	1,844.30	39,694.30	0.00	1,844.30	1,844.30
12	Olsen, Barbara	40	1,487.20	47,307.20	0.00	1,487.20	1,487.20
13	Parker, William	44	1,776.28	48,206.28	0.00	1,776.28	1,776.28
14	Raman, Soma	45	1,949.16	56,816.16	0.00	1,949.16	1,949.16
15	Tabor, Annette	40	1,168.83	43,908.83	0.00	1,168.83	1,168.83
16	Wallace, Grace	40	3,010.35	106,910.35	0.00	2,900.00	3,010.35
17			18,799.43	583,701.43	958.20	18,689.08	18,799.43
18		*(1)*	*(5)*	*(6)*	*(7A)*	*(7B)*	*(7C)*
19							

Employer's state unemployment tax $958.20 × 0.054 = **$51.74**

Employer's Social Security tax $18,689.08 × 0.062 = **$1,158.72**

Employer's Medicare tax $18,799.43 × 0.0145 = **$272.59**

Employer's federal unemployment tax $958.20 × 0.008 = **$7.67**

Combined Employer's FICA taxes (Social Security $1,158.72 + Medicare $272.59) = **$1,431.31**

maximum of $106,800 for Social Security and all earnings for Medicare). The same tax rates apply to both the employer and the employees.

The accountant obtains the Social Security and Medicare taxable earnings amounts from the payroll register. Figure 1 shows the Taxable Earnings columns taken from the payroll register for Green Sales Company as prepared in the previous chapter for the week ended October 7.

Before we look at the journal entry to record the employer's share of FICA taxes, let's look at the entry in T account form.

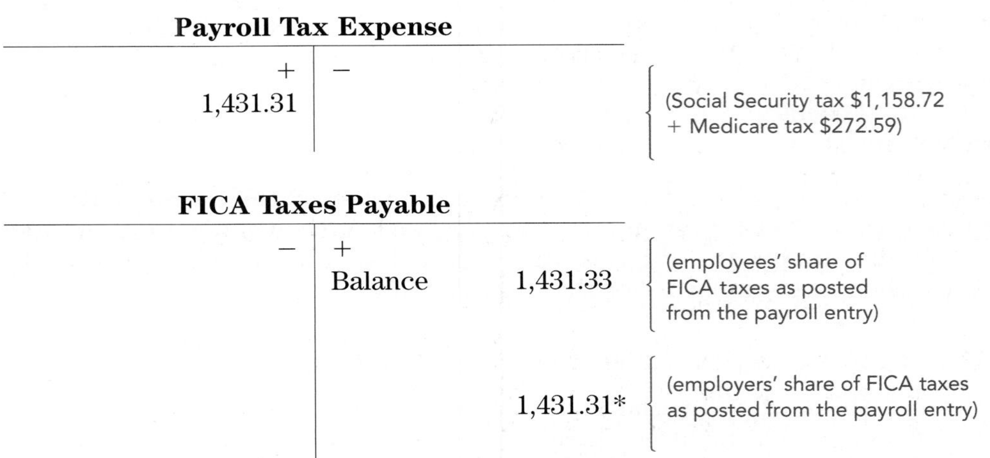

Payroll Tax Expense
+
−
1,431.31
(Social Security tax $1,158.72 + Medicare tax $272.59)
FICA Taxes Payable
−
+
Balance 1,431.33
(employees' share of FICA taxes as posted from the payroll entry)
1,431.31*
(employers' share of FICA taxes as posted from the payroll entry)

*$0.02 difference due to rounding.

Note particularly that the FICA Taxes Payable account is often used for both the tax liability of the employer and the amounts withheld from the employees. This is logical because both FICA taxes are paid at the same time and to the same place. There may be a slight difference (such as seen above) between the employer's and the employees' share of FICA taxes because of the rounding process. For the employees' share, the accountant uses the total of the employees' Social Security and Medicare tax deductions. For the employer's share, the accountant multiplies the total taxable earnings (Social Security and Medicare) by the tax rates.

Employer's State Unemployment Tax

The proceeds of the state unemployment tax (SUTA), which is levied only on the employer in most states, are used to pay subsistence benefits to unemployed workers. The rate of the state unemployment tax varies considerably among the states. Assume that Green Sales Company is subject to a rate of 5.4 percent (0.054) of the first $7,000 of each employee's earnings (the same base amount as for the federal unemployment tax). As shown in the portion of the payroll register illustrated in Figure 1, $958.20 of earnings are subject to the state unemployment tax. Accordingly, by T accounts, the state unemployment tax based on taxable earnings is as follows:

Payroll Tax Expense	
+	−
(958.20 × 0.054) 51.74	

State Unemployment Tax Payable	
−	+
	(958.20 × 0.054) 51.74

Employer's Federal Unemployment Tax

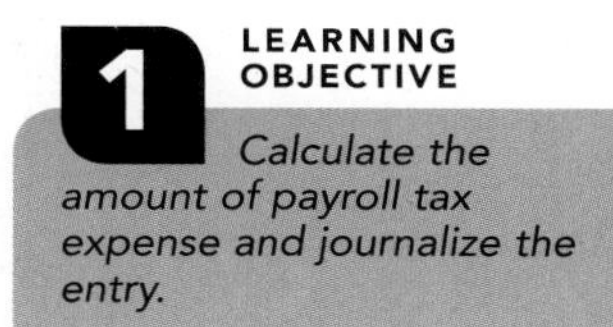

1
LEARNING OBJECTIVE
Calculate the amount of payroll tax expense and journalize the entry.

The federal unemployment tax (FUTA) is paid only by the employer. Congress may from time to time change the rate. Let's assume a rate of 0.8 percent (0.008) of the first $7,000 earned by each employee during the calendar year. For the weekly payroll period for Green Sales Company, the tax liability is $7.67 ($958.20 of unemployment taxable earnings, taken from the payroll register, multiplied by 0.008, the tax rate). The T account is as follows:

Payroll Tax Expense	
+	−
(958.20 × 0.008) 7.67	

Federal Unemployment Tax Payable	
−	+
	(958.20 × 0.008) 7.67

To make things clearer, figures for the employer's three payroll taxes have been presented separately. Now let's combine all of this information into one entry, which follows the regular payroll entry. Green Sales Company pays its employees weekly, so it also makes its Payroll Tax Expense entry weekly.

Date		Description	Post. Ref.	Debit	Credit
Oct.	7	Payroll Tax Expense		1,490.72	
		FICA Taxes Payable			1,431.31
		State Unemployment Tax Payable			51.74
		Federal Unemployment Tax Payable			7.67
		To record employer's share of FICA taxes and employer's state and federal unemployment taxes.			

JOURNAL ENTRIES FOR RECORDING PAYROLL

At this point, let's restate in general journal form the entries that have already been recorded. The sequence of steps for recording the payroll entries is:

STEP 1. Record the payroll for the present period in the payroll register.

STEP 2. Based on the payroll register, record the payroll entry in the journal.

STEP 3. Based on the Taxable Earnings columns of the payroll register, record Payroll Tax Expense in the journal.

STEP 4. Record a journal entry to pay the employees.

Once the payroll for the present period is recorded in the payroll register (see Chapter 7), the entry to record the payroll, which was also presented in Chapter 7, is journalized.

Date		Description	Post. Ref.	Debit	Credit
20—					
Oct.	7	Sales Wages Expense		11,321.80	
		Office Wages Expense		7,477.63	
		Employees' Federal Income Tax Payable			2,378.24
		FICA Taxes Payable			1,431.33
		Employees' State Income Tax Payable			475.65
		Employees' United Way Payable			195.00
		Accounts Receivable			50.00
		Wages Payable			14,269.21
		Payroll register for the week ended October 7, 20—.			

Next, the entry to record the employer's payroll taxes is journalized.

Date		Description	Post. Ref.	Debit	Credit
Oct.	7	Payroll Tax Expense		1,490.72	
		FICA Taxes Payable			1,431.31
		State Unemployment Tax Payable			51.74
		Federal Unemployment Tax Payable			7.67
		To record employer's share of FICA taxes and employer's state and federal unemployment taxes.			

Finally, the entry to pay the employees is journalized. Green Sales Company issues one check payable to a payroll bank account. To pay its employees, it will draw separate payroll checks on this payroll account. (The entry to transfer cash to the payroll bank account is not shown here.)

Date		Description	Post. Ref.	Debit	Credit
Oct.	8	Wages Payable		14 2 6 9 21	
		Cash—Payroll Bank Account			14 2 6 9 21
		Paid wages for week			
		ended October 7, 20—.			

As stated previously, in the first payroll entry, small employers will credit Cash directly instead of Wages Payable. These employers issue separate checks out of their regular bank accounts for each employee.

Next, we describe the entries for paying withholdings for employees' federal income tax and FICA taxes and the employer's matching share of FICA taxes. We also show the entries for paying the federal and state unemployment taxes and the withholdings for employees' state income taxes.

PAYMENTS OF FICA TAXES AND EMPLOYEES' FEDERAL INCOME TAX WITHHOLDING

2 LEARNING OBJECTIVE *Journalize the entry for the deposit of employees' federal income taxes withheld and FICA taxes (both employees' withheld and employer's matching share) and prepare the deposit coupon.*

After paying employees, the employer must make payments in the form of federal tax deposits. A deposit includes the combined total of three items:

1. Employees' federal income taxes withheld
2. Employees' FICA taxes (Social Security and Medicare) withheld
3. Employer's share of FICA taxes (Social Security and Medicare)

The timing for when the deposits are required to be made depends on the amount of payroll.

Deposits are made with a coupon to an authorized financial institution or electronically using the Electronic Federal Tax Payment System (EFTPS). The IRS requires some companies to make their deposits electronically because they have met certain criteria. Specifically, if total deposits during a calendar year exceed $200,000, the business is required to use EFTPS in the second succeeding calendar year. Once the business is required to use EFTPS, it will continue to be required to make its deposits electronically in subsequent years, even if its annual deposits fall below $200,000. See IRS Publication 15 (Circular E), Employer's Tax Guide, for more information on deposit requirements at www.irs.gov.

FYI There are substantial penalties applied for late deposits of federal taxes.

Employers submit a return, Form 941, every **quarter** (three consecutive months). The due dates for filing this return are as follows:

Quarter	Ending Date of Quarter	Due Date for Forms 941/941e
January–February–March	March 31	April 30
April–May–June	June 30	July 31
July–August–September	September 30	October 31
October–November–December	December 31	January 31

FYI We will show a Form 941 later in this chapter.

Federal Tax Deposit Coupon

Let's go back to Green Sales Company, where tax payments were up to date. From the payroll of October 7, the following federal taxes are owed:

Employees' federal income taxes withheld	$2,378.24
Employees' FICA taxes withheld ($1,158.73 + $272.60)	1,431.33
Employer's share of FICA taxes	1,431.31
Total federal undeposited taxes	$5,240.88

We continue on for the next payroll period, ended October 14. Assuming the payroll information for the week is the same as it was for the week ended October 7, the two periods would be:

	Oct. 7	Oct. 14	Total
Employees' federal income taxes withheld	$2,378.24	$2,378.24	$ 4,756.48
Employees' FICA taxes withheld	1,431.33	1,431.33	2,862.66
Employer's share of FICA taxes	1,431.31	1,431.31	2,862.62
Total federal undeposited taxes	$5,240.88	$5,240.88	$10,481.76

FYI

Because of rounding differences, the employee and employer amounts of FICA taxes may differ slightly. Line 7a of Form 941 accommodates this difference.

Green Sales Company, which deposits taxes semiweekly, receives a federal tax deposit card (printed with the company's name and employer identification number) from the Internal Revenue Service (Figure 2).

The accountant records the amount of the deposit, the employer identification number (unless preprinted), the type of tax, the tax period, and the name and address of the company. The entry in general journal form to record the deposit of two weeks' taxes looks like the following.

Date		Description	Post. Ref.	Debit	Credit
20—					
Oct.	15	Employees' Federal Income Tax			
		Payable		4 7 5 6 48	
		FICA Taxes Payable ($2,862.66 +			
		$2,862.62)		5 7 2 5 28	
		Cash			10 4 8 1 76
		Issued check for federal tax			
		deposit, Central National Bank.			

FIGURE 2

Federal Tax Deposit Coupon (Form 8109-B) for Green Sales Company

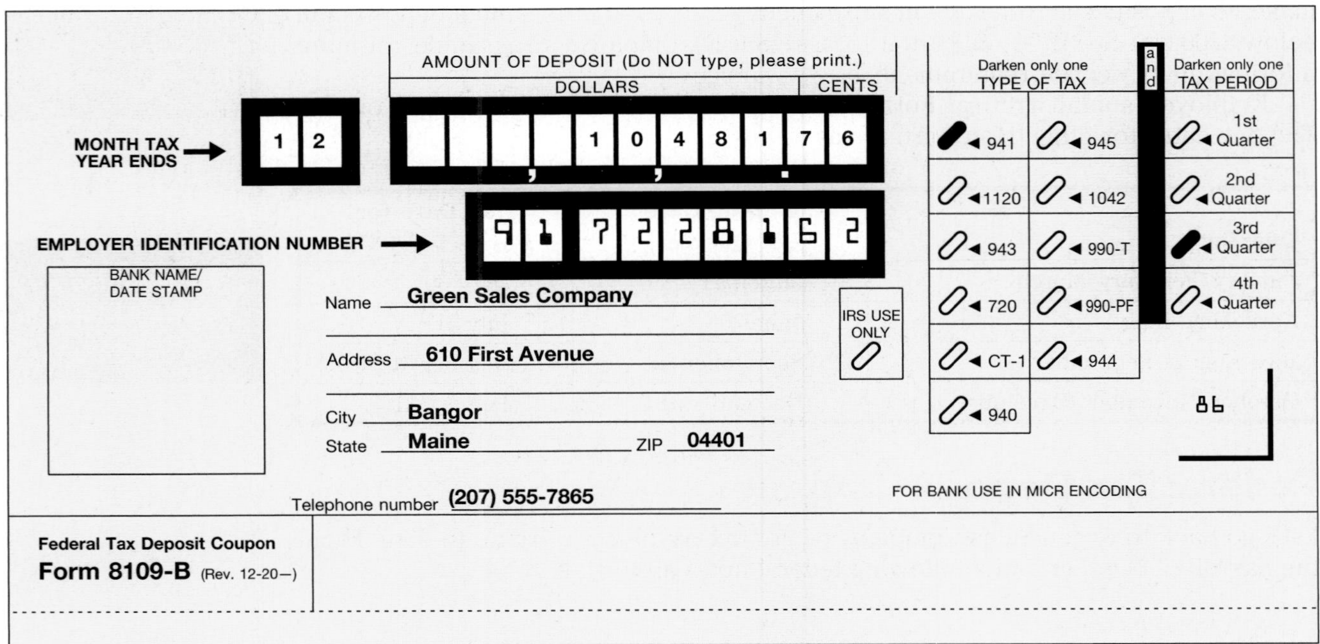

AMOUNT OF DEPOSIT (Do NOT type, please print.)

DOLLARS	CENTS
10,481	76

MONTH TAX YEAR ENDS: 1 2

EMPLOYER IDENTIFICATION NUMBER: 91 7228162

BANK NAME/ DATE STAMP

Name Green Sales Company

Address 610 First Avenue

City Bangor

State Maine ZIP 04401

Telephone number (207) 555-7865

IRS USE ONLY

Darken only one TYPE OF TAX: 941 (darkened), 945, 1120, 1042, 943, 990-T, 720, 990-PF, CT-1, 944, 940

Darken only one TAX PERIOD: 1st Quarter, 2nd Quarter, 3rd Quarter (darkened), 4th Quarter

86

FOR BANK USE IN MICR ENCODING

Federal Tax Deposit Coupon
Form 8109-B (Rev. 12-20—)

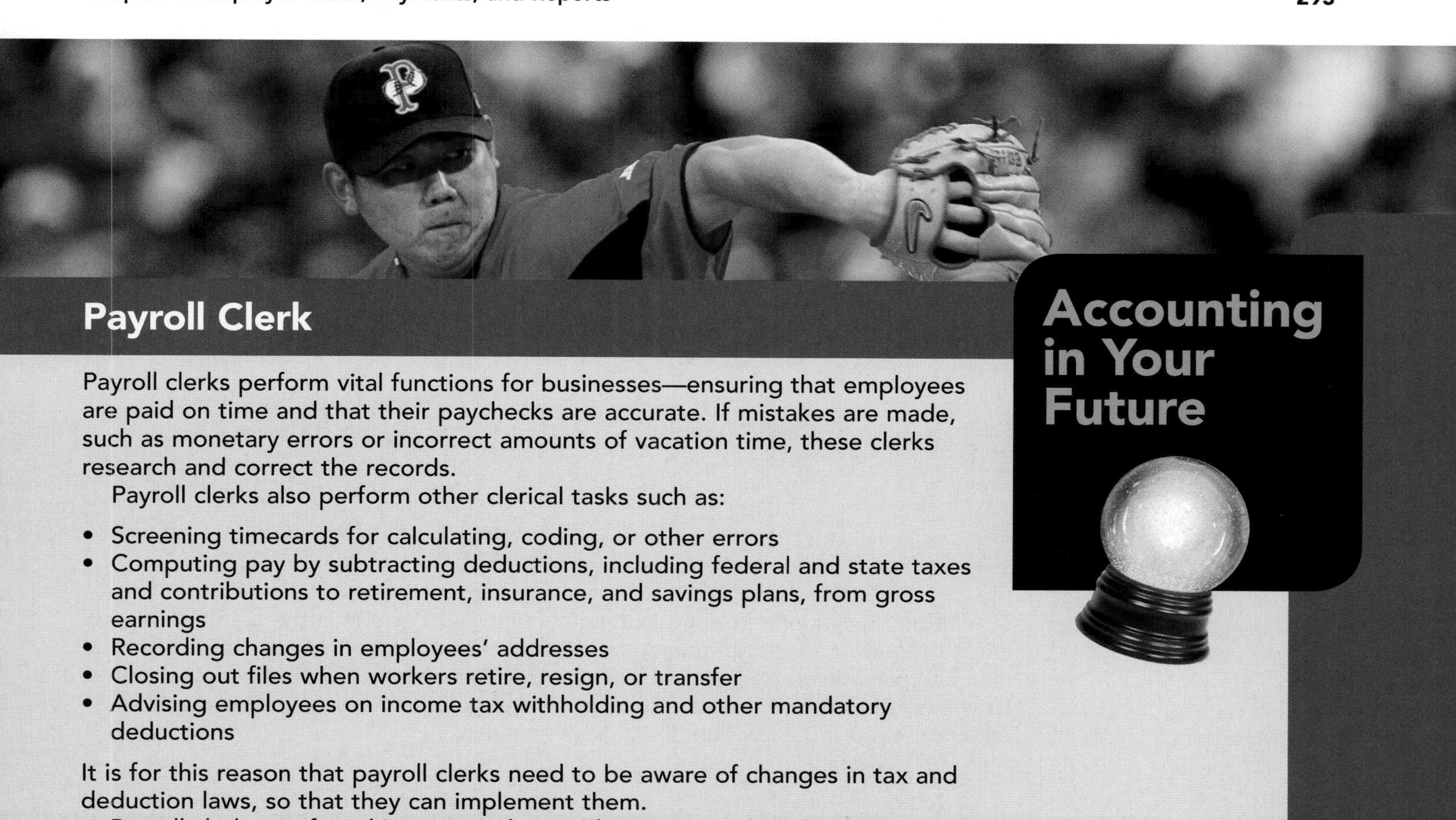

Accounting in Your Future

Payroll Clerk

Payroll clerks perform vital functions for businesses—ensuring that employees are paid on time and that their paychecks are accurate. If mistakes are made, such as monetary errors or incorrect amounts of vacation time, these clerks research and correct the records.

Payroll clerks also perform other clerical tasks such as:

- Screening timecards for calculating, coding, or other errors
- Computing pay by subtracting deductions, including federal and state taxes and contributions to retirement, insurance, and savings plans, from gross earnings
- Recording changes in employees' addresses
- Closing out files when workers retire, resign, or transfer
- Advising employees on income tax withholding and other mandatory deductions

It is for this reason that payroll clerks need to be aware of changes in tax and deduction laws, so that they can implement them.

Payroll clerks are found in every industry. They train on the job, gaining skills by watching and learning from other workers. Those who have completed a certification program will have an advantage in the job market.

As entering and recording payroll information becomes more simplified due to the increasing use of computers, the job itself is becoming more varied and complex. For example, companies now offer a greater variety of pension, 401(k), and other investment plans to their employees. These developments will contribute to job growth for payroll clerks in the years to come.

PAYMENTS OF STATE UNEMPLOYMENT INSURANCE

3 LEARNING OBJECTIVE *Journalize the entries for the payment of employer's state and federal unemployment taxes.*

As we stated before, states differ with regard to both the rate and the taxable base for unemployment insurance. In our example, we assume that the state tax is 5.4 percent (0.054) of the first $7,000 paid to each employee during the calendar year. **The state tax is usually paid quarterly and is due by the end of the month following the end of the quarter (the same as the due dates for Form 941).** Here is the entry in general journal form made by Green Sales Company for the first quarter (covering the months of January, February, and March). We assume that $70,325 was taxable for the quarter. The amount of the tax is $3,797.55 ($70,325 × 0.054).

Date		Description	Post. Ref.	Debit	Credit
20—					
Apr.	30	State Unemployment Tax Payable		3,797.55	
		Cash			3,797.55
		Issued check for payment of state unemployment tax.			

The T accounts are as follows:

Cash

+	–	
	Apr. 30	3,797.55

State Unemployment Tax Payable

–		+	
		Mar. 31	
Apr. 30	3,797.55	Balance	3,797.55

The March 31 balance in State Unemployment Tax Payable is the result of weekly entries recording the state unemployment portion of payroll tax expense. After the payment is made on April 30, the balance is shown as zero for illustrative purposes. However, throughout the month of April, the company would be making weekly entries to record the tax liability and tax expense.

PAYMENTS OF FEDERAL UNEMPLOYMENT TAX

The FUTA tax is calculated quarterly, during the month following the end of each calendar quarter. **If the accumulated tax liability is greater than $500, the tax is deposited in a financial institution, accompanied by a preprinted federal tax deposit card** like that used to deposit employees' federal income tax withholding and FICA taxes. The deposit may also be made electronically. The due date for this deposit is the last day of the month following the end of the quarter, the same as the due dates for the Employer's Quarterly Federal Tax Return and for state unemployment taxes.

Here is the entry in general journal form made by Green Sales Company for the first quarter. In our example, since the FUTA and state unemployment taxable earnings are the same (the first $7,000 for each employee), we assume that $70,325 was taxable for the quarter. The amount of the tax is $562.60 ($70,325 × 0.008).

Date		Description	Post. Ref.	Debit	Credit
20—					
Apr.	30	Federal Unemployment Tax Payable		562.60	
		Cash			562.60
		Issued check for payment of federal unemployment tax.			

The T accounts are as follows:

Cash			
+	–		
	Apr. 30	562.60	

Federal Unemployment Tax Payable			
	–	+	
		Mar. 31	
Apr. 30	562.60	Balance	562.60

The balance in Federal Unemployment Tax Payable is the result of weekly entries recording the federal unemployment portion of payroll tax expense.

DEPOSITS OF EMPLOYEES' STATE INCOME TAX WITHHOLDING

LEARNING OBJECTIVE 4 *Journalize the entry for the deposit of employees' state income taxes withheld.*

Assume that the withholdings for employees' state income taxes are deposited on a quarterly basis, payable at the same time as state unemployment tax. Also, as of March 31, the credit balance of Employees' State Income Tax Payable is $1,674.10. The entry in general journal form to record the payment for the first quarter takes the following form.

Date		Description	Post. Ref.	Debit	Credit
20—					
Apr.	30	Employees' State Income Tax Payable		1,674.10	
		Cash			1,674.10
		Issued check for state income tax deposit.			

The T accounts are as follows:

Cash			
+	–		
	Apr. 30	1,674.10	

Employees' State Income Tax Payable			
	–	+	
		Mar. 31	
Apr. 30	1,674.10	Balance	1,674.10

EMPLOYER'S QUARTERLY FEDERAL TAX RETURN (FORM 941)

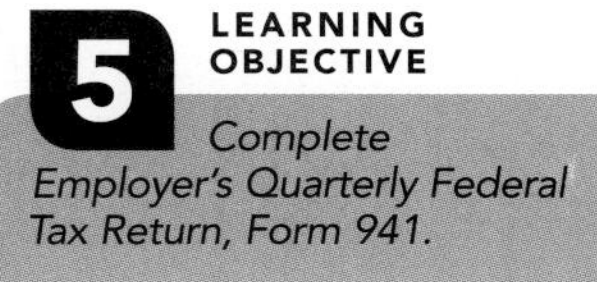

5
LEARNING OBJECTIVE
Complete Employer's Quarterly Federal Tax Return, Form 941.

If you are an employer, you must file a quarterly **Form 941**, Employer's Quarterly Federal Tax Return. The purpose of Form 941 is to report the tax liability for withholdings of employees' federal income tax and FICA taxes, and also the employer's share of FICA taxes. Total tax deposits made are also listed. As the title implies, the time period is three months. Remember that the due dates for the calendar year are: first quarter, April 30; second quarter, July 31; third quarter, October 31; fourth quarter, January 31.

A completed Form 941 for Green Sales Company is shown in Figure 3. There are five parts to this form. Figure 3 shows the information for Green Sales Company for Parts 1 and 2. Part 3 is used when you close your business and stop paying wages—this will also stop the IRS from automatically sending 941 forms. Part 4 is for you to give the IRS permission—or not—to speak with your third-party designee (employee, paid tax preparer for example). Part 5 is the signature, title, and date block for the paid preparer and/or employer. You can get instructions and can complete the form online at www.irs.gov, if you wish.

The top of the form contains basic information about the employer. Once an employer has secured an identification number and has filed the first return, the Internal Revenue Service automatically sends forms directly to the employer. These subsequent forms will have the employer's name, address, and identification number filled in.

Now let's look at completed Parts 1 and 2 of an Employer's Quarterly Federal Tax Return (Form 941) starting with its heading.

FIGURE 3

Employer's Quarterly Federal Tax Return (Form 941) for Green Sales Company

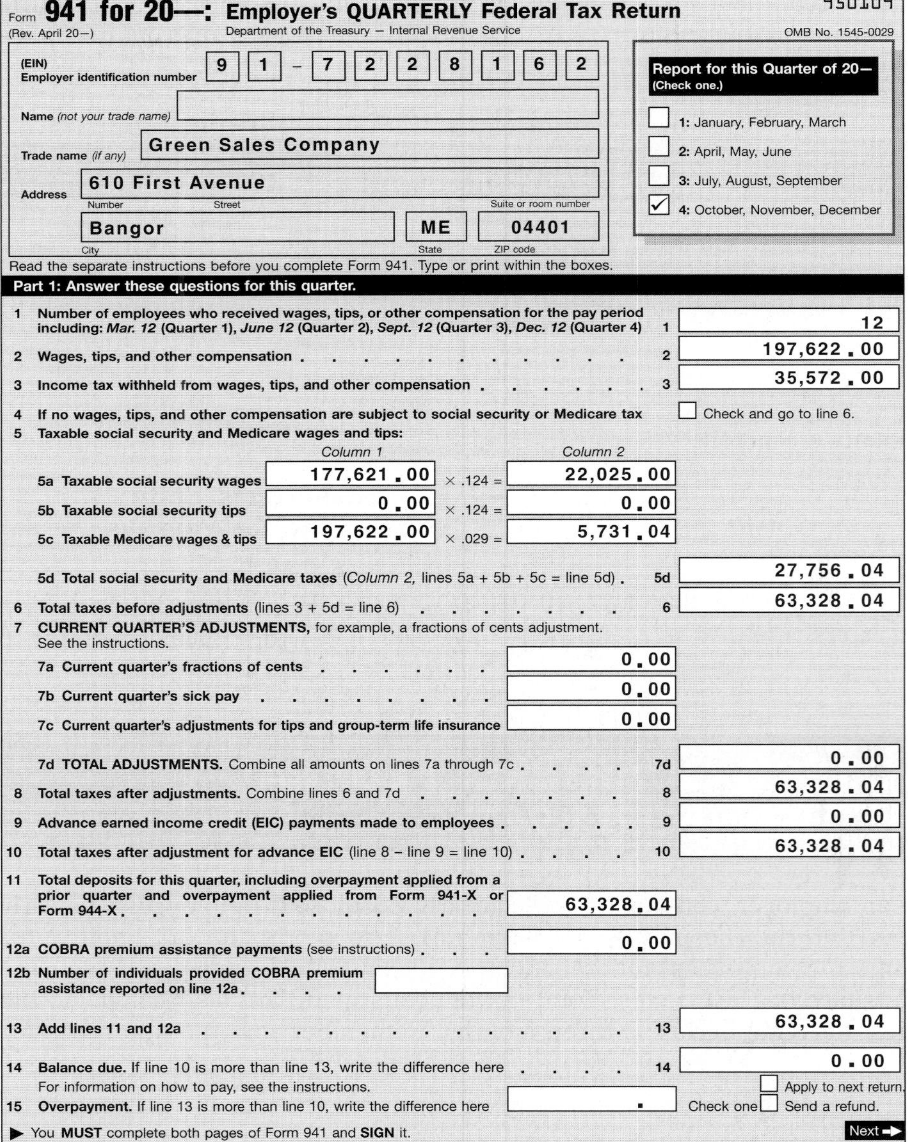

Form **941 for 20—: Employer's QUARTERLY Federal Tax Return** 950109
(Rev. April 20—) Department of the Treasury — Internal Revenue Service OMB No. 1545-0029

(EIN) Employer identification number 9 1 – 7 2 2 8 1 6 2

Name (not your trade name)

Trade name (if any) Green Sales Company

Address 610 First Avenue
Number Street Suite or room number

Bangor ME 04401
City State ZIP code

Report for this Quarter of 20— (Check one.)
☐ 1: January, February, March
☐ 2: April, May, June
☐ 3: July, August, September
☑ 4: October, November, December

Read the separate instructions before you complete Form 941. Type or print within the boxes.

Part 1: Answer these questions for this quarter.

Line	Description	Column 1		Column 2	Line	Amount
1	Number of employees who received wages, tips, or other compensation for the pay period including: *Mar. 12* (Quarter 1), *June 12* (Quarter 2), *Sept. 12* (Quarter 3), *Dec. 12* (Quarter 4)				1	12
2	Wages, tips, and other compensation				2	197,622.00
3	Income tax withheld from wages, tips, and other compensation				3	35,572.00
4	If no wages, tips, and other compensation are subject to social security or Medicare tax ☐ Check and go to line 6.					
5	Taxable social security and Medicare wages and tips:					
5a	Taxable social security wages	177,621.00	× .124 =	22,025.00		
5b	Taxable social security tips	0.00	× .124 =	0.00		
5c	Taxable Medicare wages & tips	197,622.00	× .029 =	5,731.04		
5d	Total social security and Medicare taxes (*Column 2,* lines 5a + 5b + 5c = line 5d)				5d	27,756.04
6	Total taxes before adjustments (lines 3 + 5d = line 6)				6	63,328.04
7	CURRENT QUARTER'S ADJUSTMENTS, for example, a fractions of cents adjustment. See the instructions.					
7a	Current quarter's fractions of cents			0.00		
7b	Current quarter's sick pay			0.00		
7c	Current quarter's adjustments for tips and group-term life insurance			0.00		
7d	TOTAL ADJUSTMENTS. Combine all amounts on lines 7a through 7c				7d	0.00
8	Total taxes after adjustments. Combine lines 6 and 7d				8	63,328.04
9	Advance earned income credit (EIC) payments made to employees				9	0.00
10	Total taxes after adjustment for advance EIC (line 8 – line 9 = line 10)				10	63,328.04
11	Total deposits for this quarter, including overpayment applied from a prior quarter and overpayment applied from Form 941-X or Form 944-X			63,328.04		
12a	COBRA premium assistance payments (see instructions)			0.00		
12b	Number of individuals provided COBRA premium assistance reported on line 12a					
13	Add lines 11 and 12a				13	63,328.04
14	Balance due. If line 10 is more than line 13, write the difference here. For information on how to pay, see the instructions.				14	0.00
15	Overpayment. If line 13 is more than line 10, write the difference here			.		Check one ☐ Apply to next return. ☐ Send a refund.

▶ You **MUST** complete both pages of Form 941 and **SIGN** it. Next ➔

Part 2: Tell us about your deposit schedule and tax liability for this quarter.

If you are unsure about whether you are a monthly schedule depositor or a semiweekly schedule depositor, see *Pub. 15 (Circular E)*, section 11.

16 | M | E | Write the state abbreviation for the state where you made your deposits OR write "MU" if you made your deposits in *multiple* states.

17 Check one: ☐ **Line 10 is less than $2,500.** Go to Part 3.

☐ **You were a monthly schedule depositor for the entire quarter. Enter your tax liability for each month.** Then go to Part 3.

Tax liability: Month 1 [.]

Month 2 [.]

Month 3 [.]

Total liability for quarter [.] Total must equal line 10.

☑ **You were a semiweekly schedule depositor for any part of this quarter.** Complete *Schedule B (Form 941): Report of Tax Liability for Semiweekly Schedule Depositors,* and attach it to Form 941.

FIGURE 3

(Concluded)

Questions Listed on Form 941 (Figure 3)

Tax forms can be somewhat intimidating. The best approach to completing a tax form is to have accurate and complete records, read and complete the form line by line, and don't look ahead. Green Sales Company's fourth quarter form, shown in Figure 3, has been completed as follows. Note that the employees at Green Sales Company earn only wages. Had they also earned tips or other compensation, such as bonuses, those would have been included in the form.

Part 1:

1. **Line 1** indicates the number of employees (12) who received wages.
2. **Line 2** shows the total of those wages for the quarter ($197,622.00).
3. **Line 3** shows the total income tax withheld from wages for the quarter ($35,572.00).
4. **Line 4** is not checked because all wages during the quarter are subject to Medicare tax.
5. **Lines 5a–d** provide information that indicates how the total of the Social Security and Medicare taxes ($22,025.00 + $5,731.04 = $27,756.04) is calculated. Note that the multipliers represent the combined FICA employee and employer contributions (for Social Security, 0.062 × 2 = 0.124; for Medicare, 0.0145 × 2 = 0.029).
6. **Line 6** ($63,328.04) is the total of the income taxes withheld (line 3) and the Social Security and Medicare taxes (line 5d), before adjustments.
7. **Lines 7a–d** indicate any tax adjustments that may be needed. Green Sales Company did not have any of those for the quarter. Note that these adjustments may be for fractions of cents due to rounding (line 7a) or corrections of errors in earlier filings of Form 941 (lines 7b and 7c).
8. **Line 8** shows the total taxes after adjustments (line 6 plus line 7d = $63,328.04).
9. **Line 9** discloses any payments of advanced earned income credit (EIC), a refundable federal income tax credit for low-income working individuals and families, that may have been made to employees. Green Sales Company did not have any this quarter.
10. **Line 10** is the total of lines 8 and 9 ($63,328.04).
11. **Line 11** shows the total deposits ($63,328.04) made by Green Sales Company for this quarter and includes any overpayments from prior quarters. As indicated, the company has made deposits equaling the total due for this quarter.
12. **Lines 12a and 12b** disclose any premium assistance payments of COBRA for eligible individuals and the number of individuals who were provided COBRA premium assistance. COBRA provides certain former employees, retirees, spouses, former spouses, and dependent children the right to temporary continuation of health coverage at group rates if their previous coverage is lost due to specific events such as a reduction in the number of hours of employment or a voluntary or

involuntary termination of employment for reasons other than gross misconduct. Green Sales Company did not have any COBRA payments this quarter.

13. **Line 13** is the total of lines 11 and 12a ($63,328.04).
14. **Lines 14** (underpayment) and 15 (overpayment), which indicate the difference between lines 10 and 13, show that the company's balance for the quarter is zero.

Part 2:

15. **Line 16** shows ME, the abbreviation for Maine, the state in which the deposits were made.
16. **Line 17** shows a checkmark in the third box because Green Sales Company was a semiweekly scheduled depositor for this quarter.

As stated earlier, the remaining parts of the 941 form require stating whether your business is closing, permission to allow third-party inquiries, signatures and titles of the preparer, and the date Form 941 is submitted. For thorough instructions to assist you in filling out any IRS form, go to www.irs.gov and enter the form or descriptive words into the search box.

Wage Withholding Statements for Employees (Form W-2)

LEARNING OBJECTIVE 6

Prepare W-2 and W-3 forms and Form 940.

After the end of a year (December 31) and by the following January 31, the employer must furnish for each employee a Wage and Tax Statement, known as **Form W-2.** This form contains information about the employee's earnings and tax deductions for the year. The source of the information used to complete Form W-2 is the employee's individual earnings record. The amounts used to complete Mark Anderson's W-2 form (in Figure 4) represent the amounts taken from his earnings record at the end of the calendar year, December 31.

Box 9 shows the total paid to the employee as advance earned income credit (EIC) payments. Box 13 is used for miscellaneous items, such as statutory employees

FIGURE 4

Wage and Tax Statement (Form W-2) for Mark Anderson

22222

a Employee's social security number: 543-24-1680

OMB No. 1545-0008

Safe, accurate, FAST! Use IRS e-file

Visit the IRS website at www.irs.gov/efile

b Employer identification number (EIN): 91-7228162

c Employer's name, address, and ZIP code:
Green Sales Company
610 First Avenue
Bangor, Maine 04401

d Control number

e Employee's first name and initial / Last name / Suff.
Mark E. Anderson
1104 Rosewood Street
Bangor, Maine 04401

f Employee's address and ZIP code

1 Wages, tips, other compensation	58,404.58	2 Federal income tax withheld	10,920.00
3 Social security wages	58,404.58	4 Social security tax withheld	3,621.08
5 Medicare wages and tips	58,404.58	6 Medicare tax withheld	846.87
7 Social security tips	0	8 Allocated tips	
9 Advance EIC payment	0	10 Dependent care benefits	0
11 Nonqualified plans	0	12a See instructions for box 12 (Code)	
13 Statutory employee / Retirement plan / Third-party sick pay	☐ ☐ ☐	12b (Code)	
14 Other		12c (Code)	
		12d (Code)	

15 State	Employer's state ID number	16 State wages, tips, etc.	17 State income tax	18 Local wages, tips, etc.	19 Local income tax	20 Locality name
ME	464-729	58,404.58	2,184.00	0	0	0

Form **W-2** Wage and Tax Statement 20—

Department of the Treasury—Internal Revenue Service

Copy B—To Be Filed With Employee's FEDERAL Tax Return.
This information is being furnished to the Internal Revenue Service.

(i.e., workers who are independent contractors under the common-law rules but are treated by statute as employees, such as full-time life insurance sales agents and traveling salespersons), 401(k) plan contributions, or sick pay that is not included in income because the employee contributed to the sick pay plan. Box 14 may include the value of noncash fringe benefits, such as providing a vehicle for the employee.

At least four copies of the W-2 form are required for each employee:

Copy A—Employer sends to the Social Security Administration.

Copy B—Employer gives to employee to be attached to the employee's individual federal income tax return.

Copy C—Employer gives to employee to be kept for his or her personal records.

Copy D—Employer keeps this copy as a record of payments made.

If state and local income taxes are withheld, the employer prepares additional copies to be sent to the appropriate tax agency.

FYI

A copy is also sent (if applicable) to the state and/or local tax department, and a copy is given to the employee to attach to the state/local tax return.

Employer's Annual Federal Income Tax Reports (Form W-3)

Accompanying Copy A of the employees' W-2 forms, Green Sales Company sends **Form W-3**, Transmittal of Wage and Tax Statements, to the Social Security Administration. This form is due on February 28, following the end of the calendar year.

For all employees, Form W-3 shows the total wages and tips, total federal income tax withheld, total Social Security and Medicare taxable wages, total Social Security and Medicare taxes withheld, and other information. These amounts must be the same as the grand totals of the W-2 forms and the four quarterly 941 forms for the year. Green Sales Company's completed Form W-3 is presented in Figure 5.

FIGURE 5

Transmittal of Wage and Tax Statements (Form W-3) for Green Sales Company

DO NOT STAPLE

33333	a Control number	For Official Use Only ▶ OMB No. 1545-0008	
b Kind of Payer ▶ 941 [X] Military [ ] 943 [ ] 944 [ ]; CT-1 [ ] Hshld. emp. [ ] Medicare govt. emp. [ ] Third-party sick pay [ ]		1 Wages, tips, other compensation 861,530.00	2 Federal income tax withheld 155,075.00
		3 Social security wages 775,358.00	4 Social security tax withheld 48,072.20
c Total number of Forms W-2 12	d Establishment number – – – – – –	5 Medicare wages and tips 861,530.00	6 Medicare tax withheld 12,492.19
e Employer identification number (EIN) 64-7228162		7 Social security tips 0	8 Allocated tips 0
f Employer's name Green Sales Company		9 Advance EIC payments 0	10 Dependent care benefits 0
610 First Avenue Bangor, Maine 04401		11 Nonqualified plans 0	12 Deferred compensation 0
		13 For third-party sick pay use only	
g Employer's address and ZIP code		14 Income tax withheld by payer of third-party sick pay 0	
h Other EIN used this year 0			
15 State ME	Employer's state ID number 464-729	16 State wages, tips, etc. 861,530.00	17 State income tax 31,015.00
		18 Local wages, tips, etc.	19 Local income tax
Contact person Eileen Green		Telephone number (207) 555-7865	For Official Use Only
Email address egreen@emailme.net		Fax number (207) 555-1477	

Under penalties of perjury, I declare that I have examined this return and accompanying documents, and, to the best of my knowledge and belief, they are true, correct, and complete.

Signature ▶ *Eileen Green* Title ▶ *Owner* Date ▶ *2/27/20–*

Form **W-3** Transmittal of Wage and Tax Statements 20—— Department of the Treasury Internal Revenue Service

Some boxes deserve an explanation. Box d, establishment number, may be used for a company that has separate establishments, with each establishment filing W-2 and W-3 forms separately. Box 9 is used for recording the amount of advance earned income credits shown on W-2 forms for qualified employees. Box h is used by a company that had more than one employer identification number (EIN) during the year.

To sum up thus far: The employer must submit the following at the end of the calendar year: Employer's Quarterly Federal Tax Return, Form 941, for the fourth quarter by January 31; Wage and Tax Statements, Form W-2, for all employees by January 31; Transmittal of Wage and Tax Statements, Form W-3, by February 28.

REPORTS AND PAYMENTS OF FEDERAL UNEMPLOYMENT TAX

Remember

If the accumulated FUTA tax liability at the end of a quarter is greater than $500, a deposit must be made.

As we stated previously, generally all employers are subject to the Federal Unemployment Tax Act. These employers must submit an Employer's Annual Federal Unemployment (FUTA) Tax Return, Form 940, no later than January 31 following the close of the calendar year. This deadline may be extended until February 10 if the employer has made deposits paying the FUTA tax liability in full. **Form 940** shows total wages paid to employees, total wages subject to federal unemployment tax, and other information.

Using Green Sales Company as our example, federal unemployment taxable earnings by quarter are as follows:

Federal Unemployment Tax	1st Quarter	2nd Quarter	3rd Quarter	4th Quarter	Cumulative Total
Taxable earnings	$70,325	$9,485	$10,316	$3,520	$93,646
Tax rate	× 0.008	× 0.008	× 0.008	× 0.008	× 0.008
Tax liability	$562.60	$75.88	$ 82.53	$28.16	$749.17

We now repeat the journal entry for the first quarter, in which $562.60 was deposited on April 30.

Date		Description	Post. Ref.	Debit	Credit
20—					
Apr.	30	Federal Unemployment Tax Payable		562.60	
		Cash			562.60
		Issued check for deposit of federal unemployment tax.			

During the second and third quarters, many employees' total earnings passed the $7,000 limit of taxable earnings, and the firm's tax liability was reduced accordingly. Because Green Sales Company's total accumulated liability of $158.41 ($75.88 + $82.53) was less than $500, deposits covering those quarters were not made.

By the end of the fourth quarter, each of the twelve employees' earnings passed the $7,000 mark. The total accumulated liability for the second, third, and fourth quarters is $186.57 ($75.88 + $82.53 + $28.16). This amount will be paid by January 31, accompanied by the completed Employer's Annual Federal Unemployment (FUTA) Tax Return, Form 940.

The T account for Federal Unemployment Tax Payable follows. The credits to the account were part of the entries to record the federal unemployment tax portion of Payroll Tax Expense for each payroll period.

Federal Unemployment Tax Payable

	−	+	
Apr. 30 deposit	562.60	1st quarter (liability)	562.60
		2nd quarter (liability)	75.88
		3rd quarter (liability)	82.53
Jan. 31 deposit	186.57	4th quarter (liability)	28.16

Employer's Annual Federal Unemployment (FUTA) Tax Return (Form 940)

Figure 6 shows a completed Form 940 for Green Sales Company. This form has seven parts. (Bear in mind that all forms change from time to time. Go to www.irs.gov for updates.)

Part 1:

1. **Line 1a** indicates the abbreviation for the state in which the business was required to pay taxes, while **line 1b** is for multi-state employers.
2. **Line 2** is for businesses that paid wages in a state that is subject to credit reduction. A credit reduction state is one that has not repaid money it borrowed from the federal government to pay unemployment benefits. Let's assume the U.S. Department of Labor announced that there are no credit reduction states for the current tax year, so Green Sales Company skips this line.

Part 2:

3. **Line 3** lists the total wages paid during the calendar year ($861,530.00).
4. **Line 4** lists the amount of wages exempt from FUTA tax—this includes such items as agricultural labor, family employment, and the value of meals and lodging. It is assumed that Green Sales Company had no such wages. If it had, the appropriate box or boxes on lines 4a–e would need to be checked to show the types of payments exempt from FUTA tax.
5. **Line 5** shows the exempt wages paid ($767,884.00)—wages paid to each employee over and above $7,000 for the calendar year.
6. **Line 6** is the total exempt payments ($767,884.00).
7. **Line 7** shows the total taxable FUTA wages ($93,646.00), which is computed by subtracting the total amount of exempt payments (line 6) from the total wages paid (line 3).
8. **Line 8** indicates the total amount of FUTA tax due before adjustments ($93,646.00 × 0.008 = $749.17).

Part 3:

9. **Lines 9 and 10** are to be completed if all or some of the FUTA wages paid were excluded from state unemployment tax. These lines do not apply to Green Sales Company, so they are left blank.
10. **Line 11** is also left blank due to the fact that the U.S. Department of Labor announced that there are no credit reduction states for the current tax year.

FIGURE 6 Employer's Annual Federal Unemployment (FUTA) Tax Return (Form 940) for Green Sales Company

Form **940 for 20—: Employer's Annual Federal Unemployment (FUTA) Tax Return**

850108

Department of the Treasury — Internal Revenue Service

OMB No. 1545-0028

(EIN) Employer identification number 9 1 – 7 2 2 8 1 6 2

Name *(not your trade name)*

Trade name *(if any)* Green Sales Company

Address 610 First Avenue
Number Street Suite or room number
Bangor ME 04401
City State ZIP code

Type of Return
(Check all that apply.)

☐ **a.** Amended
☐ **b.** Successor employer
☐ **c.** No payments to employees in 20--
☐ **d.** Final: Business closed or stopped paying wages

Read the separate instructions before you fill out this form. Please type or print within the boxes.

Part 1: Tell us about your return. If any line does NOT apply, leave it blank.

1 **If you were required to pay your state unemployment tax in ...**

1a **One state only,** write the state abbreviation . . . 1a ME

- OR -

1b **More than one state** (You are a multi-state employer) . . . . 1b ☐ Check here. Fill out Schedule A.

Skip line 2 for 20-- and go to line 3.

2 If you paid wages in a state that is subject to CREDIT REDUCTION . . . . 2 ☐ Check here. Fill out Schedule A (Form 940), Part 2.

Part 2: Determine your FUTA tax before adjustments for 20--. If any line does NOT apply, leave it blank.

3 **Total payments to all employees** 3 861,530.00

4 **Payments exempt from FUTA tax** 4 0.00

Check all that apply: 4a ☐ Fringe benefits 4c ☐ Retirement/Pension 4e ☐ Other
4b ☐ Group-term life insurance 4d ☐ Dependent care

5 **Total of payments made to each employee in excess of $7,000** 5 767,884.00

6 **Subtotal** (line 4 + line 5 = line 6) 6 767,884.00

7 **Total taxable FUTA wages** (line 3 – line 6 = line 7) 7 93,646.00

8 **FUTA tax before adjustments** (line 7 × .008 = line 8) 8 749.17

Part 3: Determine your adjustments. If any line does NOT apply, leave it blank.

9 **If ALL of the taxable FUTA wages you paid were excluded from state unemployment tax, multiply line 7 by .054** (line 7 × .054 = line 9). Then go to line 12 . . . . 9 0.00

10 **If SOME of the taxable FUTA wages you paid were excluded from state unemployment tax, OR you paid ANY state unemployment tax late** (after the due date for filing Form 940), fill out the worksheet in the instructions. Enter the amount from line 7 of the worksheet onto line 10 . 10 0.00

Skip line 11 for 20-- and go to line 12.

11 **If credit reduction applies,** enter the amount from line 3 of Schedule A (Form 940) . . . . 11 .

Part 4: Determine your FUTA tax and balance due or overpayment for 20--. If any line does NOT apply, leave it blank.

12 **Total FUTA tax after adjustments** (lines 8 + 9 + 10 + 11 = line 12) 12 749.17

13 **FUTA tax deposited for the year, including any payment applied from a prior year** . . . 13 562.60

14 **Balance due** (If line 12 is more than line 13, enter the difference on line 14.)
- If line 14 is more than $500, you must deposit your tax.
- If line 14 is $500 or less, you may pay with this return. For more information on how to pay, see the separate instructions 14 186.57

15 **Overpayment** (If line 13 is more than line 12, enter the difference on line 15 and check a box below.) . . . . 15 .

Check one: ☐ Apply to next return. ☐ Send a refund.

▶ You **MUST** fill out both pages of this form and **SIGN** it.

Next ➡

For Privacy Act and Paperwork Reduction Act Notice, see the back of Form 940-V, Payment Voucher. Cat. No. 11234O Form **940** (20--)

Part 5: Report your, FUTA tax liability by quarter only if line 12 is more than $500. If not, go to Part 6.

16 **Report the amount of your FUTA tax liability for each quarter; do NOT enter the amount you deposited. If you had no liability for a quarter, leave the line blank.**

16a	**1st quarter** (January 1 – March 31)	**16a**	562.60
16b	**2nd quarter** (April 1 – June 30)	**16b**	75.88
16c	**3rd quarter** (July 1 – September 30)	**16c**	82.53
16d	**4th quarter** (October 1 – December 31)	**16d**	28.16
17	**Total tax liability for the year** (lines 16a + 16b + 16c + 16d = line 17)	**17**	749.17 **Total must equal line 12.**

Part 6: May we speak with your third-party designee?

Do you want to allow an employee, a paid tax preparer, or another person to discuss this return with the IRS? See the instructions for details.

☐ **Yes.** Designee's name and phone number ( ) –

Select a 5-digit Personal Identification Number (PIN) to use when talking to IRS

☑ **No.**

Part 7: Sign here. You MUST fill out both pages of this form and SIGN it.

Under penalties of perjury, I declare that I have examined this return, including accompanying schedules and statements, and to the best of my knowledge and belief, it is true, correct, and complete, and that no part of any payment made to a state unemployment fund claimed as a credit was, or is to be, deducted from the payments made to employees. Declaration of preparer (other than taxpayer) is based on all information of which preparer has any knowledge.

✗ Sign your name here *Eileen Green*

Print your name here: Eileen Green

Print your title here: Owner

Date: 1 / 31 / 20—

Best daytime phone: (207) 555 – 7865

FIGURE 6

(Concluded)

Part 4:

11. **Line 12** indicates the amount of total FUTA tax after adjustments ($749.17), which is the sum of line 8 + lines 9–11.
12. **Line 13** shows the amount of total FUTA tax that was deposited for the year ($562.60).
13. **Line 14** is the difference between line 12 and line 13 ($749.17 – $562.60 = $186.57). This represents the balance due.
14. **Line 15** is completed if FUTA tax deposited for the year (line 13) is more than the total FUTA tax after adjustments (line 12). This indicates an overpayment.

Part 5:

15. **Lines 16a–d** ask for the amount of FUTA tax liability for each quarter.
16. **Line 17** discloses the total tax liability for the calendar year ($749.17). It should equal the amount given on line 12 and the total of lines 16a–d.

The remaining parts of the 940 form require whether or not you grant permission for third-party inquiries, signature and title of the preparer, and the date Form 940 is submitted.

WORKERS' COMPENSATION INSURANCE

LEARNING OBJECTIVE 7

Calculate the premium for workers' compensation insurance, and prepare the entry for payment in advance.

Most states require employers to provide **workers' compensation insurance** or industrial accident insurance for employees killed or injured on the job, either through plans administered by the state or through private insurance companies authorized by the state. The employer usually has to pay all the premiums. The premium rate varies with the amount of risk the job entails and the company's claims history. For example, handling molten steel ingots is much more dangerous than typing reports. Thus, it is important that employees be identified properly in terms of the insurance premium classifications. The rates as percentages of the payroll may be 0.15 percent for office work, 0.5 percent for sales work, and 3.5 percent for industrial labor in heavy manufacturing. These same rates may be expressed as $0.15 per $100 of the salaries or wages for office work, $0.50 per $100 for sales work, and $3.50 per $100 for industrial labor.

Generally, the employer pays a premium in advance, based on the estimated payroll for the year. After the year ends, the employer knows the exact amount of the payroll and can calculate the exact premium. At that time, depending on the difference between the estimated and exact premiums, the employer either pays an additional premium or gets a credit for having made an overpayment.

At Green Sales Company, there are two work classifications: office work and sales work. At the beginning of the year, the firm's accountant computed the estimated annual premium as follows:

Classification	Estimated Payroll	Rate per Hundred (Percent)	Estimated Premium	
Office work	$182,000	0.15	($182,000 ÷ 100) × 0.15 =	$ 273.00
Sales work	660,000	0.50	($660,000 ÷ 100) × 0.50 =	3,300.00
			Total estimated premium	$ 3,573.00

As shown by T accounts, the accountant made the following entry.

Prepaid Insurance, Workers' Compensation	
+	−
Jan. 10 3,573.00	

Cash	
+	−
	Jan. 10 3,573.00

Then, at the end of the calendar year, the accountant calculated the exact premium:

Classification	Actual Payroll	Rate per Hundred (Percent)	Exact Premium	
Office work	$188,990	0.15	($188,990 ÷ 100) × 0.15 =	$ 283.49
Sales work	672,540	0.50	($672,540 ÷ 100) × 0.50 =	3,362.70
			Total estimated premium	$3,646.19

Therefore, the amount of the unpaid premium is

$3,646.19	Total exact premium
3,573.00	Less total estimated premium paid
$ 73.19	Additional premium owed

Now the accountant makes an adjusting entry, similar to the adjusting entry for expired insurance. This entry appears on the work sheet. The accountant then makes an additional adjusting entry for the extra premium owed. By T accounts, the entries are as follows:

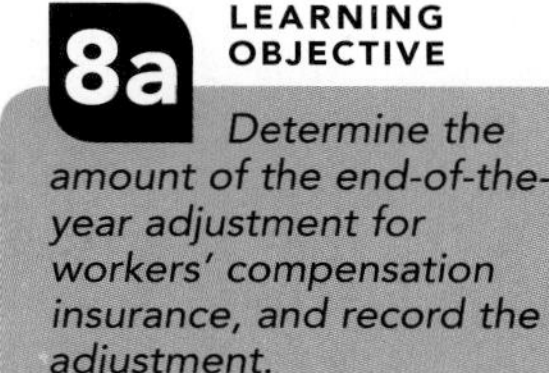
8a
LEARNING OBJECTIVE
Determine the amount of the end-of-the-year adjustment for workers' compensation insurance, and record the adjustment.

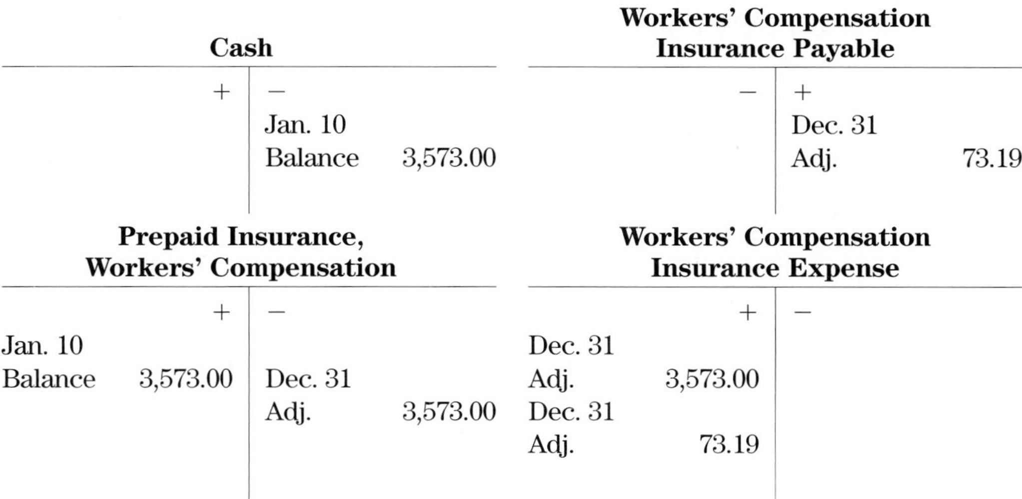

Cash

+	–
	Jan. 10 Balance 3,573.00

Workers' Compensation Insurance Payable

–	+
	Dec. 31 Adj. 73.19

Prepaid Insurance, Workers' Compensation

+	–
Jan. 10 Balance 3,573.00	Dec. 31 Adj. 3,573.00

Workers' Compensation Insurance Expense

+	–
Dec. 31 Adj. 3,573.00	
Dec. 31 Adj. 73.19	

Green Sales Company will pay $73.19, the amount of unpaid premium, in January, together with the estimated premium for the next year.

ADJUSTING FOR ACCRUED SALARIES AND WAGES

8b
LEARNING OBJECTIVE
Determine the amount of the end-of-the-year adjustment for accrued salaries and wages, and record the adjustment.

Assume that $2,400 of wages accrue for the time between the last payday and the end of the year. An adjusting entry is necessary.

Date		Description	Post. Ref.	Debit	Credit
20—		Adjusting Entry			
Dec.	31	Wages Expense		2 4 0 0 00	
		Wages Payable			2 4 0 0 00

For the accrual adjustment, gross salary and wages are recorded, not the net salary and wages. When the accrued salary and wages are paid, the amounts withheld for federal and state taxes, FICA taxes, and other deductions are then recorded.

Adjusting Entry for Accrual of Payroll Taxes

As you have seen, the following taxes come under the umbrella of the Payroll Tax Expense account: the employer's share of the FICA taxes, the state unemployment tax, and the federal unemployment tax. The employer becomes liable for these taxes only when the employees are actually paid, rather than at the time the liability to the employees is incurred. So there is no adjusting entry for Payroll Tax Expense until the wages are actually paid.

TAX CALENDAR

Now let's put it all together. To keep up with the task of paying and reporting the various taxes, the accountant compiles a chronological list of the due dates. We are including only the payroll taxes here, but any kind of taxes, such as sales taxes and property taxes, should also be listed. When you think about the penalties for nonpayment of taxes by the due dates, this chronological list seems to be well worth the effort. We assume for this purpose the employer is a monthly depositor for the federal tax deposit.

Jan.	10	Pay estimated annual premium for workers' compensation insurance. (This is an approximate date, as it varies among the states.)
	15	Make federal tax deposit for employees' income tax withholding, employees' FICA taxes withheld, and employer's FICA taxes for wages paid during the month of December.
	31	Complete Employer's Quarterly Federal Tax Return, Form 941, for the fourth quarter.
	31	Issue Copies B and C of Wage and Tax Statement, Form W-2, to employees.
	31	Pay state unemployment tax liability for the previous quarter, and submit state return, employer's tax report.
	31	Pay any remaining federal unemployment tax liability for the previous year, and submit Form 940, Employer's Annual Federal Unemployment (FUTA) Tax Return.
	31	Make state deposit for employees' state income tax withholding and submit any required state payroll reports. (Timing and required reports may differ from state to state.)
Feb.	15	Make federal tax deposit for employees' income tax withholding, employees' FICA taxes withholding, and employer's FICA taxes for wages paid during the month of January.
	28	Complete Transmittal of Wage and Tax Statements, Form W-3, and attach Copy A of W-2 forms for employees.
Mar.	15	Make federal tax deposit for employees' income tax withholding, employees' FICA taxes withholding, and employer's FICA taxes for wages paid during the month of February.
Apr.	15	Make federal tax deposit for employees' income tax withholding, employees' FICA taxes withholding, and employer's FICA taxes for wages paid during the month of March.
	30	Pay state unemployment tax liability for the previous quarter and submit state return, employer's tax report.
	30	Complete Employer's Quarterly Federal Tax Return, Form 941, for the first quarter.
	30	Make federal tax deposit for federal unemployment tax liability if it exceeds $500.
	30	Make state deposit for employees' state income tax withholding.

PAYROLL FRAUD

Payroll fraud can be a huge problem for a business in terms of both monies lost and time and frustration dealing with the problem. Payroll fraud can be categorized into three general areas:

1. *Ghost employee fraud*—Someone is recorded in the payroll system who does not work for the business.
2. *False wage claim fraud*—Extra hours or other relevant factors are added to wage information to increase the amount of pay.
3. *False expense reimbursement fraud*—Improper claims are made for the reimbursement of business expenses.

Internal controls should be in place to prevent and detect payroll fraud. Some of those controls would include the following:

1. Require mandatory vacations for those with payroll responsibilities, with other employees performing this function in their absence.
2. Use cash payments or checks minimally and increase the use of direct deposit of payroll checks.
3. Have employees physically sign and show proper identification to receive their paychecks.
4. Conduct periodic unannounced audits to ensure, for example, that all employees on the payroll actually work for the company.
5. Cross-reference the payroll roster for duplicate addresses or Social Security numbers.
6. Conduct a thorough pre-employment reference check for all payroll personnel.
7. Compare payroll expense per the payroll register to the actual amounts paid. Also, compare amounts to payroll deposits made.
8. Outsource payroll administration.

CHAPTER REVIEW

Study & Practice

LEARNING OBJECTIVE

Calculate the amount of payroll tax expense and journalize the entry.

Payroll tax expense consists of the employer's matching portion of FICA taxes, plus the **state unemployment tax (SUTA)**, plus the **federal unemployment tax (FUTA)**. *FICA taxes* consist of Social Security and Medicare taxes. *Social Security tax* equals total Social Security taxable earnings multiplied by 0.062 (6.2 percent assumed rate) on the taxable earnings. For this text, the maximum taxable is assumed to be $106,800. Total *Medicare tax* equals Medicare taxable earnings multiplied by 0.0145 (1.45 percent assumed rate). There is no maximum limit for Medicare—all earnings are taxable. *State unemployment tax* equals unemployment taxable earnings multiplied by 0.054 (5.4 percent assumed rate). *Federal unemployment tax* equals unemployment taxable earnings multiplied by 0.008 (0.8 percent assumed rate). Refer to the related journal entry on page 289.

PRACTICE EXERCISE 1

Quality Roofing has the following payroll information for the week ended May 31:

Total payroll	$56,000
Taxable earnings subject to Social Security	45,000
Taxable earnings subject to unemployment tax	2,000

Using the tax rates given above, prepare the journal entry to record the employer's payroll tax liability.

PRACTICE EXERCISE 1 SOLUTION

Date		Description	Post. Ref.	Debit	Credit
20—					
May	31	Payroll Tax Expense		3 7 2 6 00	
		FICA Taxes Payable			3 6 0 2 00
		State Unemployment Tax Payable			1 0 8 00
		Federal Unemployment Tax Payable			1 6 00
		To record employer's share of FICA			
		taxes and employer's state and			
		federal unemployment taxes.			

Computations:

FICA taxes payable:	Social Security	$45,000 × 0.062 =	$2,790.00
	Medicare	$56,000 × 0.0145 =	812.00
	Total		$3,602.00
State unemployment tax payable:		$2,000 × 0.054 =	$ 108.00
Federal unemployment tax payable:		$2,000 × 0.008 =	$ 16.00

LEARNING OBJECTIVE

2 *Journalize the entry for the deposit of employees' federal income taxes withheld and FICA taxes (both employees' withheld and employer's matching share) and prepare the deposit coupon.*

Refer to this journal entry on page 292.

PRACTICE EXERCISE 2

For the week ended May 31, Quality Roofing withheld the following taxes from its employees:

Federal income taxes withheld	$12,000
FICA taxes withheld	3,602

Prepare the journal entry to record the tax deposit to People's Bank. Include both the employees' and the employer's share of FICA taxes.

PRACTICE EXERCISE 2 SOLUTION

Date		Description	Post. Ref.	Debit	Credit
20—					
May	31	Employees' Federal Income Tax			
		Payable		12 0 0 0 00	
		FICA Taxes Payable*		7 2 0 4 00	
		Cash			19 2 0 4 00
		Issued check for federal tax			
		deposit, People's Bank.			

*FICA taxes payable include the employees' share of $3,602 plus the employer's share of $3,602, for a total of $7,204.

LEARNING OBJECTIVE 3

Journalize the entries for the payment of employer's state and federal unemployment taxes.

State unemployment tax is paid on a quarterly basis. Payment is due by the end of the next month following the end of the calendar **quarter**. Refer to this journal entry on the top of page 294.

If the amount of the accumulated federal unemployment tax liability exceeds $500 at the end of any quarter, the tax is due by the end of the next month following the end of the quarter. If the federal unemployment tax payable is less than $500 at the end of the year, it is due by January 31 of the next year. Refer to this journal entry on the bottom of page 294.

PRACTICE EXERCISE 3

Assume Best Computers had $90,325 taxable earnings for the first quarter (covering the months of January, February, and March). Assuming that the state tax is 5.4 percent (0.054) and the federal tax is 0.8 percent (0.008) of the first $7,000 paid to each employee during the calendar year, journalize the entries for the payment of Best Computers' state and federal unemployment taxes. Assume that no employee has surpassed the $7,000 limit.

PRACTICE EXERCISE 3 SOLUTION

Date		Description	Post. Ref.	Debit	Credit
20—					
Apr.	30	State Unemployment Tax Payable		4 8 7 7 55	
		Cash			4 8 7 7 55
		Issued check for payment of			
		state unemployment tax.			
	30	Federal Unemployment Tax Payable		7 2 2 60	
		Cash			7 2 2 60
		Issued check for payment of			
		federal unemployment tax.			

LEARNING OBJECTIVE

4 Journalize the entry for the deposit of employees' state income taxes withheld.

Employees' state income taxes withheld are paid on a quarterly basis or as required by the state. Payment may be due by the end of the next month following the end of the calendar quarter. Refer to this journal entry on page 295.

PRACTICE EXERCISE 4

For the quarter ended June 30, Quality Roofing has a credit balance of $28,000 for Employee's State Income Tax Payable. Assuming the withholdings are deposited on a quarterly basis, prepare the journal entry to record the payment.

PRACTICE EXERCISE 4 SOLUTION

Date		Description	Post. Ref.	Debit	Credit
20—					
July	31	Employees' State Income Tax			
		Payable		28 0 0 0 00	
		Cash			28 0 0 0 00
		Issued check for state income			
		tax deposit.			

LEARNING OBJECTIVE

5 Complete Employer's Quarterly Federal Tax Return, Form 941.

Form 941 is illustrated on page 296.

PRACTICE EXERCISE 5

Based on the Form 941 shown on page 296, what is the difference between Green Sales Company's taxable Social Security wages and taxable Medicare wages? How are the rates for each determined?

PRACTICE EXERCISE 5 SOLUTION

For taxable Medicare wages all wages are taxable, so the amount in Column 1 of $197,622 is the same amount as on line 2, Wages, tips and other compensation. For taxable Social Security wages of $177,621, only the first $106,800 of wages is taxable, so in this case some of the employees of Green Sales Company exceeded this limit. The rates of 0.124 and 0.029 represent both the employer's and employees' share of these taxes:

Social Security	6.2% + 6.2%	= 12.4% or 0.124
Medicare	1.45% + 1.45%	= 2.9% or 0.029

LEARNING OBJECTIVE

6 Prepare W-2 and W-3 forms and Form 940.

Form W-2 (Wage and Tax Statement) is illustrated on page 298. **Form W-3** (Transmittal of Wage and Tax Statements) is illustrated on page 299. **Form 940** (Employer's Annual Federal Unemployment (FUTA) Tax Return) is illustrated on pages 302 and 303.

PRACTICE EXERCISE 6

What do Form W-2, Form W-3, and Form 940 have in common?

PRACTICE EXERCISE 6 SOLUTION

Form W-2, Form W-3, and Form 940 all report the name, address, and Employer Identification Number of the company. (See Figures 4, 5, and 6 on pages 298, 299, and 302–303, respectively.) The total wages should be the same in Box 1 on Form W-3 and on Line 3 on Form 940. All three forms report state information, in this case for the State of Maine.

LEARNING OBJECTIVE

7 *Calculate the premium for workers' compensation insurance, and prepare the entry for payment in advance.*

Rates for **workers' compensation insurance** vary depending on the degree of physical risk involved in different occupations. The amount of the premium equals the predicted annual payroll multiplied by the premium rate. The entry is a debit to Prepaid Insurance, Workers' Compensation, and a credit to Cash.

PRACTICE EXERCISE 7

On January 15, Quality Roofing estimated the following payroll for the year:

Classification	Predicted Payroll	Rate (Percent)
Clerical/office work	$150,000	0.11
Project estimators	200,000	0.15
Roofer construction	670,000	2.20

Calculate the estimated premium and prepare the journal entry to record payment.

PRACTICE EXERCISE 7 SOLUTION

Classification	Predicted Payroll	Rate per Hundred (Percent)	Estimated Premium	
Clerical/office work	$150,000	0.11	($150,000 ÷ 100) × 0.11 =	$ 165.00
Project estimators	200,000	0.15	($200,000 ÷ 100) × 0.15 =	300.00
Roofer construction	670,000	2.20	($670,000 ÷ 100) × 2.20 =	14,740.00
			Total estimated premium	$15,205.00

Date		Description	Post. Ref.	Debit	Credit
20—					
Jan.	15	Prepaid Insurance, Workers'			
		Compensation		15 2 0 5 00	
		Cash			15 2 0 5 00
		To record payment of estimated			
		workers' compensation premium			
		for 20—.			

CHAPTER REVIEW

LEARNING OBJECTIVE

8

Determine the amount of the end-of-the-year adjustments for (a) workers' compensation insurance and (b) accrued salaries and wages, and record the adjustments.

When the total annual payroll is known, the exact cost of workers' compensation insurance can be determined by multiplying the total payroll by the premium rate. Two adjusting entries are required. The first adjusting entry records the expired insurance as a debit to Workers' Compensation Insurance Expense and a credit to Prepaid Insurance, Workers' Compensation. The second adjusting entry records the difference between the estimated and the actual premiums. If the actual premium is greater than the premium that was paid in advance, the entry is a debit to Workers' Compensation Insurance Expense and a credit to Workers' Compensation Insurance Payable. The adjustment for accrued salaries and wages accounts for the additional amount of salaries or wages paid in the next payroll that are incurred in the current fiscal period—a debit to Wages (or Salary) Expense. The credit to Wages (or Salaries) Payable accounts for the additional amount of liability incurred in the current period that will be paid with the next payroll that occurs in the following fiscal period.

PRACTICE EXERCISE 8

a. At the end of the year, Quality Roofing had the following payroll:

Classification	Actual Payroll	Rate (Percent)
Clerical/office work	$189,000	0.11
Project estimators	195,000	0.15
Roofer construction	695,000	2.20

Determine the amount of the end-of-the-year adjustment for workers' compensation insurance and prepare the journal entries to record the year-end adjustments for the insurance expired and for the additional premium.

b. Assume that Quality Roofing had $2,000 of salaries accrue for the time between the last payday and the end of the year. Record the adjusting entry for the accrued salaries.

PRACTICE EXERCISE 8 SOLUTION

a.

Classification	Actual Payroll	Rate per Hundred (Percent)	Exact Premium	
Clerical/office work	$189,000	0.11	($189,000 ÷ 100) × 0.11 =	$ 207.90
Project estimators	195,000	0.15	($195,000 ÷ 100) × 0.15 =	292.50
Roofer construction	695,000	2.20	($695,000 ÷ 100) × 2.20 =	15,290.00
			Total exact premium	$15,790.40

The amount of the unpaid premium is

$15,790.40	Total exact premium
15,205.00	Less total estimated premium paid (from PE 7)
$ 585.40	Additional premium owed

Date		Description	Post. Ref.	Debit	Credit
20—		Adjusting Entries			
Dec.	31	Workers' Compensation Insurance			
		Expense		15 2 0 5 00	
		Prepaid Insurance, Workers'			
		Compensation			15 2 0 5 00
	31	Workers' Compensation Insurance			
		Expense		5 8 5 40	
		Workers' Compensation			
		Insurance Payable			5 8 5 40

b.

Date		Description	Post. Ref.	Debit	Credit
20—		Adjusting Entry			
Dec.	31	Salary Expense		2 0 0 0 00	
		Salaries Payable			2 0 0 0 00

Before a Test Check: Chapters 6–8

PART I: COMPLETION

1. Checks issued by the depositor that have been paid or have cleared the bank are called __________ checks.
2. A deposit that is not recorded on the bank statement because it was made after the bank's closing date for preparation of bank statements is called a(n) __________.
3. The process by which the payee transfers ownership of the check to a bank or other party is called a(n) __________.
4. The person to whom a check is payable is called the __________.
5. A cash fund used to make small immediate cash payments is called a(n) __________.

PART II: APPLICATION

1. Cheryl Chang's salary is $3,550 per month. If she works more than 40 hours in one week, she is entitled to overtime pay at the rate of 1½ times her regular hourly rate. During the current week, she worked 45 hours. Calculate her gross pay.
2. On June 30, the column totals of Expert Training's payroll register showed that its training employees had earned $18,000 and its office employees had earned $6,000. Social Security taxes were withheld at 6.2 percent, and Medicare taxes were withheld at 1.45 percent. All earnings are taxable. Other deductions consisted of federal income tax, $3,600, and charitable contributions to the United Way, $500. Determine the amount of Social Security and Medicare taxes that should be withheld. Record the general journal entry to record the payroll, crediting Salaries Payable for the net pay.

3. Roxy Company's payroll for the week ended December 31 is as follows:

Gross earnings of employees	$155,000
Social Security taxable earnings	143,000
Medicare taxable earnings	155,000
Federal unemployment taxable earnings	22,000
State unemployment taxable earnings	22,000

Assume that the payroll is subject to Security tax of 6.2 percent (0.062), Medicare tax of 1.45 percent (0.0145), federal unemployment tax of 0.8 percent (0.008), and state unemployment tax of 5.4 percent (0.054). Write the entry in general journal form to record the employer's payroll tax expense.

PART III: TRUE/FALSE

T F **1.** There is no limit on the amount of taxable earnings for Medicare.

T F **2.** When journalizing the entry to reimburse the Petty Cash Fund, include a credit to Petty Cash Fund.

T F **3.** When journalizing the entry to account for a customer's NSF check, debit Accounts Payable.

T F **4.** An employee's net pay is the result of subtracting his or her deductions from gross pay.

T F **5.** The gross pay for an employee who works 45 hours, earns $8.50 per hour, and receives time and a half for hours worked over 40 hours is $402.75.

ANSWERS: PART I

1. canceled; **2.** deposit in transit or late deposit; **3.** endorsement; **4.** payee; **5.** petty cash fund

ANSWERS: PART II

1.

$3,550 per month × 12 months = $42,600 per year

$42,600 per year ÷ 52 weeks = $819.23 per week (rounded)

$819.23 per week ÷ 40 hours = $20.48 per regular hour (rounded)

$20.48 per regular hour × 1.5 = $30.72 per overtime hour

Earnings for 45 hours:

40 hours at straight time	(40 × $20.48) =	$819.20
5 hours overtime	(5 × $30.72) =	153.60
Total gross earnings		$972.80

CHAPTER REVIEW

2.

GENERAL JOURNAL PAGE ______

Date		Description	Post. Ref.	Debit	Credit
20—					
June	30	Training Salary Expense		18 0 0 0 00	
		Office Salary Expense		6 0 0 0 00	
		Employees' Federal Income Tax			
		Payable			3 6 0 0 00
		FICA Taxes Payable			
		($24,000 × 0.062) + ($24,000 × 0.0145)			1 8 3 6 00
		Employees' United Way Payable			5 0 0 00
		Salaries Payable			18 0 6 4 00
		Payroll register for the week ended,			
		June 30, 20—.			

3.

Date		Description	Post. Ref.	Debit	Credit
20—					
Dec.	31	Payroll Tax Expense		12 4 7 7 50	
		FICA Taxes Payable ($143,000 ×			
		0.062) + ($155,000 × 0.0145)			11 1 1 3 50
		State Unemployment Tax Payable			
		($22,000 × 0.054)			1 1 8 8 00
		Federal Unemployment Tax Payable			
		($22,000 × 0.008)			1 7 6 00
		To record employer's share of FICA			
		taxes and employer's state and			
		federal unemployment taxes.			

ANSWERS: PART III

1. T; **2.** F; **3.** F; **4.** T; **5.** F

Glossary

Employer Identification Number (EIN) The number assigned to each employer by the Internal Revenue Service for use in the submission of reports and payments for FICA taxes and federal income tax withheld. *(p. 286)*

Federal unemployment tax (FUTA) A tax levied only on the employer, equal to 0.8 percent of the first $7,000 of total earnings paid to each employee during the calendar year. This tax is used to administer the funds. *(p. 289)*

Form 940 An annual report filed by employers showing total wages paid to employees, total wages subject to federal unemployment tax, total federal unemployment tax, and other information. Also called the *Employer's Annual Federal Unemployment (FUTA) Tax Return. (p. 300)*

Form 941 A quarterly report showing the tax liability for withholdings of employees' federal income tax and FICA taxes and the employer's share of FICA taxes. Total tax deposits made in the quarter are also listed on this Employer's Quarterly Federal Tax Return. *(p. 295)*

Form W-2 A form containing information about employee earnings and tax deductions for the year. Also called *Wage and Tax Statement. (p. 298)*

Form W-3 An annual report sent to the Social Security Administration listing the total wages and tips, total federal income tax withheld, total Social Security and Medicare taxable wages, total Social Security and Medicare tax withheld, and other information for all employees of a firm. Also called the *Transmittal of Wage and Tax Statements. (p. 299)*

Payroll Tax Expense A general expense account used for recording the employer's matching portion of the FICA taxes, the federal unemployment tax, and the state unemployment tax. *(p. 286)*

Quarter Three consecutive months, also referred to as a *calendar quarter. (p. 291)*

State unemployment tax (SUTA) A tax levied only on the employer in most states. Rates differ among the various states; however, they are generally 5.4 percent or higher of the first $7,000 of total earnings paid to each employee during the calendar year. The proceeds are used to pay subsistence benefits to unemployed workers. *(p. 289)*

Workers' compensation insurance This insurance, primarily paid for by the employer, provides benefits for employees injured or killed on the job. The rates vary according to the degree of risk inherent in the job. The plans may be sponsored by states or by private firms. The employer generally pays the premium in advance at the beginning of the year, based on the estimated payroll. The rates are adjusted after the exact payroll is known. *(p. 304)*

CHAPTER ASSIGNMENTS

Discussion Questions

1. What taxes are employers accounting for that increase the debit to Payroll Tax Expense?
2. Describe the journal entry to
   a. record the payroll.
   b. record the employer's payroll tax contributions.
   c. pay the payroll.
3. Explain the deposit requirement for federal unemployment tax.
4. What is the purpose of Form 941? How often is it prepared, and what are the due dates?
5. How many copies are made of a Form W-2, and who uses the copies of the W-2 form?
6. What is the purpose of Form 940? How often is it prepared, and what is the due date?
7. Generally, what is the time schedule for payment of workers' compensation insurance premiums?
8. Explain the advantage of establishing a tax calendar.

Exercises

PRACTICE EXERCISE 1

EXERCISE 8-1 Signature Company's partial payroll register for the week ended January 7 is as follows.

CHAPTER ASSIGNMENTS

Name	Beginning Cumulative Earnings	Total Earnings	Ending Cumulative Earnings	Taxable Earnings: Unemployment	Taxable Earnings: Social Security	Taxable Earnings: Medicare
Barney, R. S.	———	1932 00	1932 00	1932 00	1932 00	1932 00
Fisk, M. C.	———	567 00	567 00	567 00	567 00	567 00
Hayes, W. O.	———	483 00	483 00	483 00	483 00	483 00
Lee, L. B.	———	679 00	679 00	679 00	679 00	679 00
Parks, S. J.	———	578 00	578 00	578 00	578 00	578 00
Tempy, E. B.	———	546 00	546 00	546 00	546 00	546 00
		4785 00	4785 00	4785 00	4785 00	4785 00

Assume that the payroll is subject to a Social Security tax of 6.2 percent of the first $106,800 and a Medicare tax of 1.45 percent on all earnings. Also assume that the federal unemployment tax is 0.8 percent of the first $7,000, and the state unemployment tax is 5.4 percent of the first $7,000. Give the entry in general journal form to record the payroll tax expense.

EXERCISE 8-2 On January 14, at the end of the second week of the year, the totals of Castle Company's payroll register showed that its store employees' wages amounted to $33,482 and its warehouse wages amounted to $13,560. Withholdings consisted of federal income taxes, $5,110; Social Security taxes at the rate of 6.2 percent of the first $106,800 and no employee has reached the limit; Medicare taxes at the rate of 1.45 percent on all earnings; charitable contributions withheld, $845.

PRACTICE EXERCISE 1

a. Calculate the amount of Social Security and Medicare taxes to be withheld, and write the general journal entry to record the payroll.
b. Write the general journal entry to record the employer's payroll taxes, assuming that the federal unemployment tax is 0.8 percent of the first $7,000, that the state unemployment tax is 5.4 percent of the same base, and that no employee has surpassed the $7,000 limit.

EXERCISE 8-3 Go Systems had the following payroll data for wages for the week ended February 5. The state income tax is assumed to be 20% of the federal income tax.

PRACTICE EXERCISE 1

Total Earnings	Ending Cumulative Earnings	Taxable Earnings: Unemployment	Taxable Earnings: Social Security	Taxable Earnings: Medicare	Deductions: Federal Income Tax	Deductions: State Income Tax	Deductions: Social Security Tax	Deductions: Medicare Tax
6770 00	27850 00	6770 00	6770 00	6770 00	1015 00	203 00	419 74	98 17

a. Write the general journal entry to record the payroll.
b. Write the general journal entry to record the employer's payroll taxes. Assume rates of 0.8 percent for federal unemployment tax and 5.4 percent for state unemployment tax based on the first $7,000 for each employee and that no employee has earned more than $7,000.

1 

PRACTICE EXERCISE 1

EXERCISE 8-4 The information on earnings and deductions for the pay period ended December 14 from King Company's payroll records is as follows.

Name	Gross Pay	Beginning Cumulative Earnings
Burgess, J. L.	$ 410	$ 6,750
Clayton, M. E.	785	40,200
Drugden, T. F.	860	38,500
Lui, L. W.	990	39,700
Sparks, C. R.	4,094	104,000
Stevers, D. H.	850	6,810

For each employee, the Social Security tax is 6.2 percent of the first $106,800 and the Medicare tax is 1.45 percent on all earnings. The federal unemployment tax is 0.8 percent of the first $7,000 of earnings of each employee. The state unemployment tax is 5.4 percent of the same base. Determine the total taxable earnings for unemployment, Social Security, and Medicare. Prepare a general journal entry to record the employer's payroll taxes.

2 

PRACTICE EXERCISE 2

EXERCISE 8-5 Selected columns of Lion Company's payroll register for the month of January are as follows. The employees' FICA taxes are matched by the employer.

Payment Date	Employees' Federal Income Tax	Employees' Social Security Tax	Employees' Medicare Tax
Jan. 7	1,192.00	475.00	112.25
14	1,135.00	518.14	122.31
21	1,245.00	572.62	124.24
28	1,452.00	561.27	143.26

Lion Company deposits taxes monthly. In general journal form, record the entry for the February 15 payment of FICA and federal income taxes for employees and employer.

2,3 

PRACTICE EXERCISES 2,3

EXERCISE 8-6 On September 30, Cody Company's selected account balances are as follows:

Employees' Federal Income Tax Payable	$4,738.00	
FICA Taxes Payable (employer and employee)	5,208.92	
State Unemployment Tax Payable	2,500.00	(Some employees have reached the limit.)
Federal Unemployment Tax Payable	570.00	

In general journal form, prepare the entries to record the following:

Oct. 15 Payment of liabilities for FICA taxes and the federal income tax.
31 Payment of liability for state unemployment tax.
31 Payment of liability for federal unemployment tax.

CHAPTER ASSIGNMENTS

LO 2,3

PRACTICE EXERCISES 2,3

EXERCISE 8-7 On September 30, Hilltop Company's selected payroll accounts are as follows:

FICA Taxes Payable

–	+	
	Sept. 30	2,314.84
	Sept. 30	2,314.84

State Unemployment Tax Payable

–	+	
	Sept. 30	1,183.40

Federal Unemployment Tax Payable

–	+	
	Sept. 30	575.32

Employees' Federal Income Tax Payable

–	+	
	Sept. 30	3,210.85

Prepare general journal entries to record the following:

Oct. 15 Payment of federal tax deposit of FICA taxes and the federal income tax.

31 Payment of state unemployment tax.

31 Payment of federal unemployment tax.

LO 7,8

PRACTICE EXERCISES 7,8

EXERCISE 8-8 Great Manufacturing Company received and paid a premium notice on January 2 for workers' compensation insurance stating the rates for the new year. Estimated employees' earnings for the year are as follows:

Classification	Estimated Wages and Salaries	Rate per Hundred (Percent)	Estimated Premium
Office clerical	$ 92,000	0.11	$ 101.20
Warehouse work	29,000	0.92	266.80
Manufacturing	264,000	2.20	5,808.00
			$6,176.00

At the end of the year, the exact figures for the payroll are as follows:

Classification	Actual Wages and Salaries	Rate per Hundred (Percent)	Exact Premium
Office clerical	$ 93,000	0.11	$ 102.30
Warehouse work	30,000	0.92	276.00
Manufacturing	267,000	2.20	5,874.00
			$6,252.30

a. Record the entry in general journal form for the payment on January 2 of the estimated premium.

b. Record the adjusting entries on December 31 for the insurance expired and for the additional premium.

Problem Set A

For additional help, see the demonstration problem at the beginning of each chapter in your Working Papers.

1 

PROBLEM 8-1A Mooney Labs had the following payroll for the week ended February 28:

Salaries		**Deductions**	
Technicians' salaries	$6,955.00	Federal income tax withheld	$1,145.00
Office salaries	2,260.00	Social Security tax withheld	571.33
Total	$9,215.00	Medicare tax withheld	133.62
		Charity withheld	165.00
		Total	$2,014.95

Assumed tax rates are as follows:

a. FICA: Social Security, 6.2 percent (0.062) on the first $106,800 for each employee, and Medicare, 1.45 percent (0.0145) on all earnings for each employee.
b. State unemployment tax, 5.4 percent (0.054) on the first $7,000 for each employee.
c. Federal unemployment tax, 0.8 percent (0.008) on the first $7,000 for each employee.

Check Figure
Payroll Tax Expense, $1,045.33

Required

Record the following entries in general journal form:

1. The payroll entry as of February 28.
2. The entry to record the employer's payroll taxes as of February 28, assuming that the total payroll is subject to the FICA taxes (combined Social Security and Medicare) and that $5,490 is subject to unemployment taxes.
3. The payment to the employees on March 2. (Assume that the company has transferred cash to Cash—Payroll Bank Account for this payroll.)

1 

PROBLEM 8-2A Complete Accounting Services has the following payroll information for the week ended December 7. State income tax is computed as 20 percent of federal income tax.

	A	B	C	D	E
1				DEDUCTIONS	
2		BEGINNING			
3		CUMULATIVE		FEDERAL	STATE
4	NAME	EARNINGS	TOTAL EARNINGS	INCOME TAX	INCOME TAX
5	Denato, T.	6,820.00	480.00	11.00	2.20
6	Herrera, M.	6,840.00	470.00	10.00	2.00
7	Joyner, J.	36,320.00	740.00	47.00	9.40
8	King, L.	26,200.00	540.00	17.00	3.40
9	Wilson, M.	104,360.00	2,720.00	474.49	94.90
10	Yee, N.	28,426.00	605.00	26.00	5.20

Assumed tax rates are as follows:

a. FICA: Social Security, 6.2 percent (0.062) on the first $106,800 for each employee, and Medicare, 1.45 percent (0.0145) on all earnings for each employee.

b. State unemployment tax, 5.4 percent (0.054) on the first $7,000 for each employee.
c. Federal unemployment tax, 0.8 percent (0.008) on the first $7,000 for each employee.

Required

Check Figure
Payroll Tax Expense, $428.68

1. Complete the payroll register. Payroll checks begin with Ck. No. 5714 in the payroll register.
2. Prepare a general journal entry to record the payroll as of December 7. The company's general ledger contains a Salary Expense account and a Salaries Payable account.
3. Prepare a general journal entry to record the payroll taxes as of December 7.
4. Journalize the entry to pay the payroll on December 9. (Assume that the company has transferred cash to the Cash—Payroll Bank Account for this payroll.)

LO 5

PROBLEM 8-3A For the third quarter of the year, Johnson Company, 415 Circle Avenue, Chicago, Illinois 60652, received Form 941 from the Internal Revenue Service. The identification number of Johnson Company is 91-4213171. Its payroll for the quarter ended September 30 is as follows.

	A	B	C	D	E	F	G
1			TAXABLE EARNINGS		DEDUCTIONS		
2							
3		TOTAL	SOCIAL		FEDERAL	SOCIAL	MEDICARE
4	NAME	EARNINGS	SECURITY	MEDICARE	INCOME TAX	SECURITY TAX	TAX
5	Brown, D. D.	16,629.00	16,629.00	16,629.00	2,494.00	1,031.00	241.12
6	Carey, L. R.	18,528.00	18,528.00	18,528.00	2,780.00	1,148.74	268.66
7	Domzalski, T. P.	14,665.00	14,665.00	14,665.00	2,100.00	909.23	212.64
8	Grisson, R. O.	13,721.00	13,721.00	13,721.00	2,058.00	850.70	198.95
9	Tyler, J. L.	17,406.00	17,406.00	17,406.00	2,510.00	1,079.17	252.39
10	Valdez, K. R.	15,287.00	15,287.00	15,287.00	2,295.00	947.79	221.66
11		96,236.00	96,236.00	96,236.00	14,237.00	5,966.63	1,395.42

The company has had six employees throughout the year. Assume that the Social Security tax is 6.2 percent of the first $106,800, and that the Medicare tax is 1.45 percent of all earnings. The employer matches the employees' FICA (Social Security and Medicare) taxes. There are no taxable tips, adjustments, backup withholding, or earned income credits. Johnson Company has submitted the following federal tax deposits and written the accompanying checks:

On August 15 for the July Payroll		**On September 15 for the August Payroll**		**On October 15 for the September Payroll**	
Employees' income tax withheld	$4,370.00	Employees' income tax withheld	$5,122.00	Employees' income tax withheld	$ 4,745.00
Employees' Social Security and Medicare tax withheld	2,259.76	Employees' Social Security and Medicare tax withheld	2,326.28	Employees' Social Security and Medicare tax withheld	2,776.01
Employer's Social Security and Medicare tax contributed	2,259.76	Employer's Social Security and Medicare tax contributed	2,326.28	Employer's Social Security and Medicare tax contributed	2,776.01
	$8,889.52		$9,774.56		$10,297.02

Required
Complete Part 1 of Form 941 for the third quarter for Johnson Company.

Check Figure
Total taxes, $28,961.10

CHAPTER ASSIGNMENTS

1,2,3 LO

PROBLEM 8-4A Lynden Company has the following balances in its general ledger as of June 1 of this year:

a. FICA Taxes Payable (liability for May), $1,719.40 (employee and employer).
b. Employees' Federal Income Tax Payable (liability for May), $995.00.
c. Federal Unemployment Tax Payable (liability for April and May), $380.00.
d. State Unemployment Tax Payable (liability for April and May), $1,205.75.

The company completed the following transactions involving the payroll during June and July:

June 13 Issued check for $2,714.40 payable to Security Bank, for the monthly deposit of May FICA taxes and employees' federal income tax withheld.

30 Recorded the payroll entry in the general journal from the payroll register for June. The payroll register has the following column totals:

Sales salaries	$11,490.00	
Office salaries	5,147.00	
Total earnings		$16,637.00
Employees' federal income tax deductions	$ 1,725.00	
Employees' Social Security tax deductions	1,031.49	
Employees' Medicare tax deductions	241.24	
Total deductions		2,997.73
Net pay		$13,639.27

30 Recorded payroll taxes. Employer matches the employees' FICA taxes. State unemployment tax is 5.4 percent, and federal unemployment tax is 0.8 percent. At this time, all employees' earnings are taxable for FICA and unemployment taxes.

30 Issued check for $13,639.27 from Cash—Payroll Bank Account to pay salaries for the month.

July 14 Issued check for $4,270.46, payable to Security Bank, for the monthly deposit of June FICA taxes (employee and employer matching) and employees' federal income tax withheld.

31 Issued check for $2,104.15, payable to the State Tax Commission, for state unemployment tax for April, May, and June. The check was accompanied by the quarterly tax return.

31 Issued check for $513.10, payable to Security Bank, for the deposit of federal unemployment tax for the months of April, May, and June.

Check Figure
Payroll Tax Expense, $2,304.23

Required

Record the transactions in the general journal, pages 77–78.

CHAPTER ASSIGNMENTS

Problem Set B

For additional help, see the demonstration problem at the beginning of each chapter in your Working Papers.

PROBLEM 8-1B Kovarik Company had the following payroll for the week ended March 21:

Salaries		**Deductions**	
Sales salaries	$7,620.00	Federal income tax withheld	$1,094.00
Office salaries	1,790.00	Social Security tax withheld	583.42
Total	$9,410.00	Medicare tax withheld	136.45
		Charity withheld	153.00
		Total	$1,966.87

Assumed tax rates are as follows:

a. FICA: Social Security, 6.2 percent (0.062) on the first $106,800 for each employee, and Medicare, 1.45 percent (0.0145) on all earnings for each employee.
b. State unemployment tax, 5.4 percent (0.054) on the first $7,000 for each employee.
c. Federal unemployment tax, 0.8 percent (0.008) on the first $7,000 for each employee.

Required
Record the following entries in general journal form:

Check Figure
Payroll Tax Expense, $1,027.70

1. The payroll entry as of March 21.
2. The entry to record the employer's payroll taxes as of March 21, assuming that the total payroll is subject to the FICA taxes (combined Social Security and Medicare) and that $4,965 is subject to unemployment taxes.
3. The payment of the employees on March 23. (Assume that the company has transferred cash to Cash—Payroll Bank Account for this payroll.)

PROBLEM 8-2B Kay's Agency has the following payroll information for the week ended December 14. State income tax is computed as 20 percent of federal income tax.

	A	B	C	D	E
1				DEDUCTIONS	
2		BEGINNING			
3		CUMULATIVE		FEDERAL	STATE
4	NAME	EARNINGS	TOTAL EARNINGS	INCOME TAX	INCOME TAX
5	Arivilo, R.	10,650.00	460.00	9.00	1.80
6	Baca, T.	38,820.00	970.00	82.00	16.40
7	Eubanks, E.	104,255.00	2790.00	494.09	98.82
8	Ling, D.	6,750.00	385.00	1.00	0.20
9	Metcalf, S.	31,670.00	694.00	40.00	8.00
10	Quinn, D.	48,961.00	1040.00	92.00	18.40

Assumed tax rates are as follows:

a. FICA: Social Security, 6.2 percent (0.062) on the first $106,800 for each employee, and Medicare, 1.45 percent (0.0145) on all earnings for each employee.
b. State unemployment tax, 5.4 percent (0.054) on the first $7,000 for each employee.

c. Federal unemployment tax, 0.8 percent (0.008) on the first $7,000 for each employee.

Check Figure
Payroll Tax Expense, $485.25

Required

1. Complete the payroll register. Payroll checks begin with Ck. No. 5923 in the payroll register.
2. Prepare a general journal entry to record the payroll as of December 14. The company's general ledger contains a Salary Expense account and a Salaries Payable account.
3. Prepare a general journal entry to record the payroll taxes as of December 14.
4. Journalize the entry to pay the payroll on December 16. (Assume that the company has transferred cash to the Cash—Payroll Bank Account for this payroll.)

PROBLEM 8-3B For the third quarter of the year, Barney Construction, 715 Red Rock Boulevard, San Francisco, California 94121, received Form 941 from the District Office of the Internal Revenue Service. The identification number for Barney Construction is 91-7382476. Its payroll for the quarter ended September 30 is as follows.

A	B	D		E	F	G
		TAXABLE EARNINGS		DEDUCTIONS		
NAME	TOTAL EARNINGS	SOCIAL SECURITY	MEDICARE	FEDERAL INCOME TAX	SOCIAL SECURITY TAX	MEDICARE TAX
Britton, D. L.	13,387.00	13,387.00	13,387.00	2,010.00	829.99	194.11
Finn, J. A.	16,753.00	16,753.00	16,753.00	2,510.00	1,038.69	242.92
Harrell, N. E.	17,780.00	17,780.00	17,780.00	2,767.00	1,102.36	257.81
Kelly, T. L.	16,243.00	16,243.00	16,243.00	2,430.00	1,007.07	235.52
Morton, S. M.	14,215.00	14,215.00	14,215.00	2,130.00	881.33	206.12
Rieck, A. J.	20,264.00	20,264.00	20,264.00	3,040.00	1,256.37	293.83
	98,642.00	98,642.00	98,642.00	14,887.00	6,115.81	1,430.31

The company has had six employees throughout the year. Assume that the Social Security tax is 6.2 percent of the first $106,800, and that the Medicare tax is 1.45 percent of all earnings. The employer matches the employees' FICA (Social Security and Medicare) taxes. There are no taxable tips, adjustments, backup withholding, or earned income credits. Barney Construction has submitted the following federal tax deposits and written the accompanying checks:

On August 15 for the July Payroll

Employees' income tax withheld	$ 5,226.00
Employees' Social Security and Medicare tax withheld	2,597.21
Employer's Social Security and Medicare tax contributed	2,597.21
	$10,420.42

On September 15 for the August Payroll

Employees' income tax withheld	$ 5,059.00
Employees' Social Security and Medicare tax withheld	2,591.58
Employer's Social Security and Medicare tax contributed	2,591.58
	$10,242.16

On October 15 for the September Payroll

Employees' income tax withheld	$4,602.00
Employees' Social Security and Medicare tax withheld	2,357.33
Employer's Social Security and Medicare tax contributed	2,357.32
	$9,316.65

Check Figure
Total taxes, $29,979.23

Required

Complete Part 1 of Form 941 for the third quarter for Barney Construction.

LO 1,2,3

GL

PROBLEM 8-4B Grande Company has the following balances in its general ledger as of March 1 of this year:

a. FICA Taxes Payable (liability for February), $9,180.00 (employee and employer).
b. Employees' Federal Income Tax Payable (liability for February), $9,000.00.
c. State Unemployment Tax Payable (liability for January and February), $3,442.50.
d. Federal Unemployment Tax Payable (liability for January and February), $510.00.

The company completed the following transactions involving the payroll during March and April:

Mar. 12 Issued check for $18,180.00 payable to Coast Bank, for the monthly deposit of February FICA taxes and employees' federal income tax withheld.

31 Recorded the payroll entry in the general journal from the payroll register for March. The payroll register had the following column totals:

Sales salaries	$47,654.00	
Office salaries	11,982.00	
Total earnings		$59,636.00
Employees' federal income tax deductions	$ 8,945.40	
Employees' Social Security tax deductions	3,697.43	
Employees' Medicare tax deductions	864.72	
Total deductions		13,507.55
Net pay		$46,128.45

31 Recorded payroll taxes. Employer matches the employees' FICA taxes. State unemployment tax is 5.4 percent. Federal unemployment tax is 0.8 percent. At this time, all employees' earnings are taxable for FICA and $1,000 of the earnings are taxable for unemployment taxes.

31 Issued check for $46,128.45 from Cash—Payroll Bank Account to pay salaries for the month.

Apr. 14 Issued check for $18,069.70, payable to Coast Bank, for the monthly deposit of March FICA taxes (employee and employer matching) and employees' federal income tax withheld.

30 Issued check for $3,496.50, payable to State Department of Revenue, for state unemployment tax for January, February, and March. The check was accompanied by the quarterly tax return.

30 Issued check for $518.00, payable to Coast Bank, for the deposit of federal unemployment tax for the months of January, February, and March.

Required

Record the transactions in the general journal, pages 77–78.

Check Figure
Payroll Tax Expense, $4,624.15

ACTIVITIES

A QUESTION OF ETHICS

Between the end of one month and the fifteenth day of the next month, the balance in the employer's business bank account has been getting smaller and smaller. An employee prepares the next payroll and correctly computes the necessary withholding taxes. The employer is supposed to pay accumulated employment taxes on the fifteenth of the next month. Payday is the last day of the month. However, the employer has used the funds withheld from employees to pay some of the business's bills. He hopes that enough of the customers who owe him money will pay their outstanding debts. If his assumption is true, the checking account will have enough in it to pay the federal deposit on the fifteenth of the month. Is the employer acting ethically? After all, he says he intends to have enough money in the account for the deposit.

Sales and Purchases

9

JAX MERCANTILE, Fort Collins, Colorado

WHY IT MATTERS

Jax Mercantile Co. has been Northern Colorado's premier outdoor gear source for over 50 years. Jax sells men's, women's, and children's clothing for any outdoor activity. You can also find camping and fishing gear, mountaineering tools, and hunting items. If you're not the outdoor type, Jax still has plenty of items for you, such as specialty kitchenware and household decorative items. Jax also carries a full line of optics and photography products, agricultural and automotive accessories, animal care products, and lawn and garden accessories.

Jax has succeeded in stocking a large inventory that meets customers' outdoor and indoor gear needs. When Jax purchases inventory for resale, it must have a way of recording these purchases. Jax also must have a way to record the sales of goods to customers and be able to handle returns and discounts. We will learn in this chapter how to record the sales and purchases of inventory for merchandising stores like Jax.

LEARNING OBJECTIVES

After you have completed this chapter, you will be able to do the following:

1. *Describe the specific accounts used by a merchandising firm.*
2. *Journalize sales transactions in a general journal, and post to the accounts receivable ledger and general ledger.*
3. *Prepare a schedule of accounts receivable.*
4. *Journalize sales returns and allowances, including credit memorandums and returns, in a general journal, and post to the accounts receivable ledger and general ledger.*
5. *Journalize sales transactions and returns involving sales tax.*
6. *Journalize purchase transactions in a general journal, and post to the accounts payable ledger and general ledger.*
7. *Prepare a schedule of accounts payable.*
8. *Journalize transactions involving purchases returns and allowances in a general journal, and post to the accounts payable ledger and general ledger.*
9. *Describe the procedures for handling freight charges on merchandise and other goods.*
10. *Journalize transactions in a sales journal, and post to the accounts receivable ledger and general ledger.*
11. *Journalize transactions in a three-column purchases journal, and post to the accounts payable ledger and general ledger.*

ACCOUNTING LANGUAGE

Accounts payable ledger *(p. 342)*
Accounts receivable ledger *(p. 333)*
Controlling account *(p. 334)*
Credit memorandum *(p. 335)*
FOB destination *(p. 346)*
FOB shipping point *(p. 346)*
Freight In account *(p. 329)*
Invoices *(p. 330)*
Merchandise inventory *(p. 329)*
Merchandising businesses *(p. 329)*
Periodic inventory system *(p. 329)*
Perpetual inventory system *(p. 329)*
Purchase order *(p. 339)*
Purchase requisition *(p. 339)*
Purchases account *(p. 329)*
Purchases Discounts account *(p. 329)*
Purchases journal *(p. 351)*
Purchases Returns and Allowances account *(p. 329)*
Retail business *(p. 329)*
Sales account *(p. 329)*
Sales Discounts account *(p. 329)*
Sales journal *(p. 348)*
Sales Returns and Allowances account *(p. 329)*
Sales Tax Payable account *(p. 329)*
Special journals *(p. 348)*
Subsidiary ledger *(p. 334)*
Summarizing entry *(p. 349)*
Wholesale business *(p. 329)*

In the previous chapters, we discussed companies that specialized in providing a service, such as Conner's Whitewater Adventures. Now, we will turn our focus to companies that buy and sell goods. These types of companies are known as **merchandising businesses**. A merchandising business can be a wholesale or a retail business. A **wholesale business**, which is sometimes called a "middleman" or a "distributor," buys goods from manufacturers and sells them to retailers. A **retail business** sells goods directly to consumers ("the public").

This chapter is divided into two parts. In part one, we discuss how to record sales and purchases transactions directly into the general journal. In part two, we explain the use of special journals in recording sales and purchases transactions. Before we begin analyzing transactions, let's take a moment to review the specific accounts for merchandising firms.

SPECIFIC ACCOUNTS FOR MERCHANDISING FIRMS

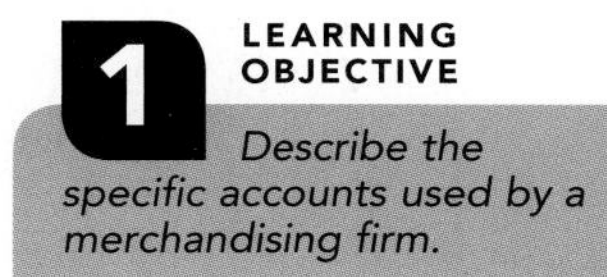
1
LEARNING OBJECTIVE
Describe the specific accounts used by a merchandising firm.

Merchandise inventory consists of a stock of goods that a company buys and intends to resell at a profit. Merchandise should be differentiated from other assets, such as furniture and equipment, that are acquired for use in the business and are not for resale.

Merchandise inventory can be recorded using either the periodic inventory system or the perpetual inventory system. The **periodic inventory system** requires that companies periodically take a physical count of merchandise on hand and then attach a value to it. Under the **perpetual inventory system,** companies keep continuous records of inventories by recording all transactions, so that at any given time they know what they should have on hand and the current cost of each item. In this chapter, we will assume that the company will record merchandise inventory using the periodic inventory system. We will demonstrate how to record the journal entries for merchandise inventory under the perpetual inventory system in the appendix to this chapter.

When merchandising firms record sales of merchandise, they use the **Sales account**.

The **Sales Returns and Allowances account** is a contra account that is used to record the physical return of merchandise by customers or a reduction in a bill because merchandise was damaged. Remember that a contra account is an account that is contrary to, or a deduction from, another account. Therefore, Sales Returns and Allowances is treated as a deduction from Sales.

The **Sales Tax Payable account** is used to record a tax levied by a state or city government on the retail sale of goods and services. The tax is paid by the consumer but collected by the retailer.

The **Purchases account** is used strictly to record the cost of merchandise bought for resale. The Purchases account is considered an expense because the accountant closes it along with the expense accounts at the end of the fiscal period. (This is explained more fully in Chapter 12.)

The **Purchases Returns and Allowances account** is a contra account that is used to record the company's returns of merchandise it had purchased from suppliers or reductions in bills because of damaged merchandise. It is treated as a deduction from Purchases.

The **Sales Discounts account** and **Purchases Discounts account** are also contra accounts that are used to record cash discounts granted for prompt payments, in accordance with the credit terms.

The **Freight In account** is used to record the transportation charges on incoming merchandise intended for resale. Debits to this account increase the cost of purchases.

Following is the fundamental accounting equation with the T accounts for merchandising businesses.

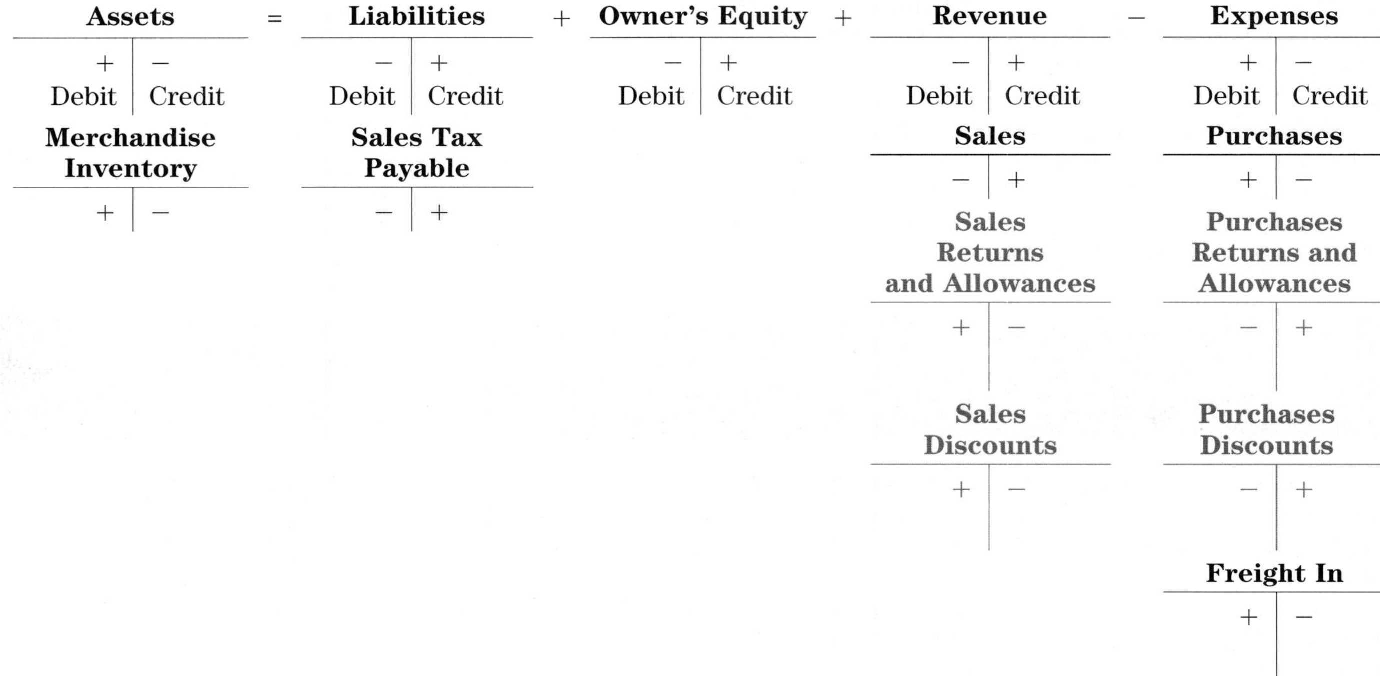

Notice that the T accounts for returns and allowances and for discounts (all contra accounts) are shown in red to emphasize that we are treating them as deductions from the related accounts placed above them. We list these accounts as deductions because they appear as deductions in the financial statements. Their relationship is similar to that between the Drawing account and the Capital account; remember that we deduct Drawing from Capital in the statement of owner's equity. These same types of accounts pertain to both retail and wholesale businesses.

PART ONE—RECORDING TRANSACTIONS INTO GENERAL JOURNAL

Source Documents Related to Sales

In a retail business, a salesperson usually prepares a sales ticket in either duplicate or triplicate for a sale on account. One copy goes to the customer and another to the accounting department, where it serves as the basis for an entry in the general journal (or the sales journal if the company is using special journals). A third copy may be used as a record of sales—to compute sales commissions or control inventory, for example.

In a wholesale business, the company usually receives a written order directly from a customer or through a salesperson who obtained the order from the customer. The credit department approves the order, and then sends it to the billing department, where the sales invoice is prepared.

Invoices are prepared in multiple copies. Figure 1 shows one possible distribution of sales invoice copies to various parties. The sales invoice for Whitewater Raft Supply's sale of merchandise to Mesa River Raft Company is shown in Figure 2.

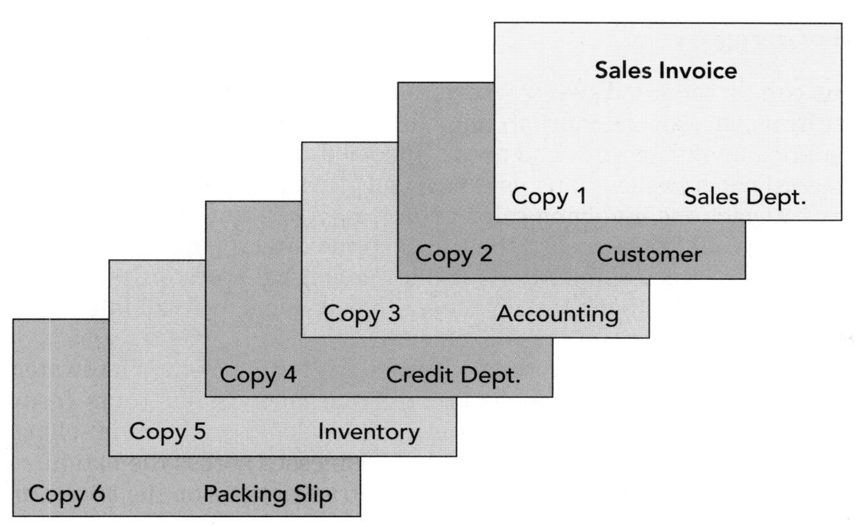

FIGURE 1
Possible distribution of sales invoice copies to various parties

Remember

The sales invoice is a source document and as such is evidence that serves as the basis for recording a transaction.

FIGURE 2
Sales invoice

Whitewater Raft Supply

Whitewater Raft Supply
1400 Front Street
Seattle, WA 98101
419-555-6123

Invoice

DATE	INVOICE #
08/01/20—	9384
TERMS	**DUE DATE**
2/10, n/30	08/31/20—

BILL TO

Mesa River Raft Company
5120 Gilman Avenue
Portland, OR 97202
503-555-6123

AMOUNT DUE	ENCLOSED
$1,933.50	

Please detach top portion and return with your payment.

Activity	Description	Quantity	Rate	Discount	Amount
15' Self Bailing Outfitter Raft #22B652		1	1,599.00		1,599.00
8" Outfitter Blades #37B411		2	63.00		126.00
Boat Bags #42B782		3	69.50		208.50
			Total Discount:	$0.00	
				Subtotal:	*$1,933.50*
				Sales Tax:	*$0.00*
				Total:	*$1,933.50*
				Payments:	*$0.00*
				Balance Due:	*$1,933.50*
			TOTAL		$1,933.50

Sales Transactions

2 LEARNING OBJECTIVE

Journalize sales transactions in a general journal, and post to the accounts receivable ledger and general ledger.

Sales transactions can be recorded two ways—either by recording directly into the general journal or by using a special journal called the sales journal. If a company has numerous transactions involving sales and uses a special journal, then the company would want to record sales transactions using special journals. If a company does not have as many transactions involving sales and/or does not want to use special journals, the company would then record the transactions directly into the general journal. We will introduce sales transactions using the general journal first. Then, because of the importance of understanding accounting systems, we will introduce the use of the sales journal in part two of this chapter.

In the previous chapters, we examined the transactions for Conner's Whitewater Adventures. Conner purchases the whitewater rafts she uses on her tours from Whitewater Raft Supply. Whitewater Raft Supply is a wholesaler specializing in selling rafts, kayaks, oars, paddles, and other accessories to businesses across the nation.

We will introduce recording sales by looking at five transactions on the books of Whitewater Raft Supply for the month of August.

Aug. 1 Sold merchandise on account to Mesa River Raft Company, invoice no. 9384, $1,933.50.

8 Sold merchandise on account to Green River Rafts, invoice no. 9385, $1,116.

14 Sold merchandise on account to Marty's Fly Fishing Adventures, invoice no. 9386, $1,594.

19 Sold merchandise on account to Hi-Flying Adventures, Inc., invoice no. 9387, $552.30.

25 Sold merchandise on account to Hi-Flying Adventures, Inc., invoice no. 9388, $1,674.

Whitewater Raft Supply will record the transactions into the general journal as follows:

GENERAL JOURNAL PAGE 26

Date		Description	Post. Ref.	Debit	Credit
20—					
Aug.	1	Accounts Receivable, Mesa River			
		Raft Company		1 9 3 3 50	
		Sales			1 9 3 3 50
		Sold merchandise to Mesa			
		River Raft Company,			
		invoice no. 9384.			
	8	Accounts Receivable, Green River			
		Rafts		1 1 1 6 00	
		Sales			1 1 1 6 00
		Sold merchandise to Green			
		River Rafts, invoice no. 9385.			
	14	Accounts Receivable, Marty's Fly			
		Fishing Adventures		1 5 9 4 00	
		Sales			1 5 9 4 00
		Sold merchandise to Marty's			
		Fly Fishing Adventures,			
		invoice no. 9386.			

19	Accounts Receivable, Hi-Flying Adventures, Inc.		5 5 2 30	
	Sales			5 5 2 30
	Sold merchandise to Hi-Flying Adventures, Inc., invoice no. 9387.			
25	Accounts Receivable, Hi-Flying Adventures, Inc.		1 6 7 4 00	
	Sales			1 6 7 4 00
	Sold merchandise to Hi-Flying Adventures, Inc., invoice no. 9388.			

Whitewater Raft Supply's accountant records a debit to Accounts Receivable to record the amount each customer owes the company and a credit to Sales for each transaction. The Sales account is credited because it is a revenue account that is used for recording sales of merchandise.

Here's how the accounts appear in the fundamental accounting equation:

Assets		=	Liabilities		+	Owner's Equity		+	Revenue		−	Expenses	
+ Debit	− Credit		− Debit	+ Credit		− Debit	+ Credit		− Debit	+ Credit		+ Debit	− Credit

Accounts Receivable		Sales	
+	−	−	+
1,933.50			1,933.50
1,116.00			1,116.00
1,594.00			1,594.00
552.30			552.30
1,674.00			1,674.00

Remember that the transactions are recorded assuming that Whitewater Raft Supply records merchandise inventory using the periodic inventory method. If Whitewater Raft Supply instead used the perpetual inventory method, an additional journal entry would be required. This additional journal entry will be discussed in the appendix to this chapter.

The Accounts Receivable Ledger

In the sales transactions for Whitewater Raft Supply, we recorded the receivable directly into the Accounts Receivable account. In order to know how much each credit customer owes a business, the firm also maintains an **accounts receivable ledger**. This ledger is a separate record containing a list of the credit customers with their respective balances, listed in either alphabetical order or by account number. It is important to maintain an accounts receivable ledger so that the company will know at any point in time the amount owed by the customer, if the amount is past due, and any payments made on the account. All computerized accounting systems post sales on account into an accounts receivable ledger. Figure 3 is an example of the accounts receivable ledger using a computerized accounting program, and Figure 4 is an example of a manual accounts receivable ledger. Note that either method includes much of the same information.

Remember

The balance of the Accounts Receivable controlling account at the end of the month must equal the total of the balances of the credit customer accounts in the accounts receivable ledger.

FIGURE 3
Accounts receivable ledger (computerized)

Whitewater Raft Supply
Customer Balance Detail
All Dates

Date	Type	Num	Due Date	Amount	Open Balance	Balance
Hi-Flying Adventures, Inc.						
08/19/20—	Invoice	9387	09/18/20—	552.30	552.30	552.30
08/25/20—	Invoice	9388	09/24/20—	1,674.00	1,674.00	2,226.30
Total for Hi-Flying Adventures, Inc.				**$2,226.30**	**$2,226.30**	
TOTAL				**$2,226.30**	**$2,226.30**	

FIGURE 4
Accounts receivable ledger (manual)

ACCOUNTS RECEIVABLE LEDGER

NAME Hi-Flying Adventures, Inc.
ADDRESS 3631 Crooked Tree Road
Seattle, WA 98101

Date		Item	Post. Ref.	Debit	Credit	Balance
20—						
Aug.	19		J26	552 30		552 30
	25		J26	1674 00		2226 30

Even though an accounts receivable ledger is maintained, the Accounts Receivable account in the general ledger should still be maintained. When all the postings are up to date, the balance of this account should equal the total of all the credit customers' individual account balances. The Accounts Receivable *account* in the general ledger is called a **controlling account**. The accounts receivable *ledger*, containing the accounts of all the credit customers, is really a special type of ledger, called a **subsidiary ledger**.

3 LEARNING OBJECTIVE
Prepare a schedule of accounts receivable.

Schedule of Accounts Receivable

From the information contained in the accounts receivable subsidiary ledger, the accountant can prepare a schedule of accounts receivable, like the one shown in Figure 5 listing each credit customer's account balance.

FIGURE 5
Schedule of accounts receivable

Whitewater Raft Supply
Schedule of Accounts Receivable
August 31, 20—

Green River Rafts	$1,116.00
Hi-Flying Adventures, Inc.	2,226.30
Marty's Fly Fishing Adventures	1,594.00
Mesa River Raft Company	1,933.50
Total Accounts Receivable	$6,869.80

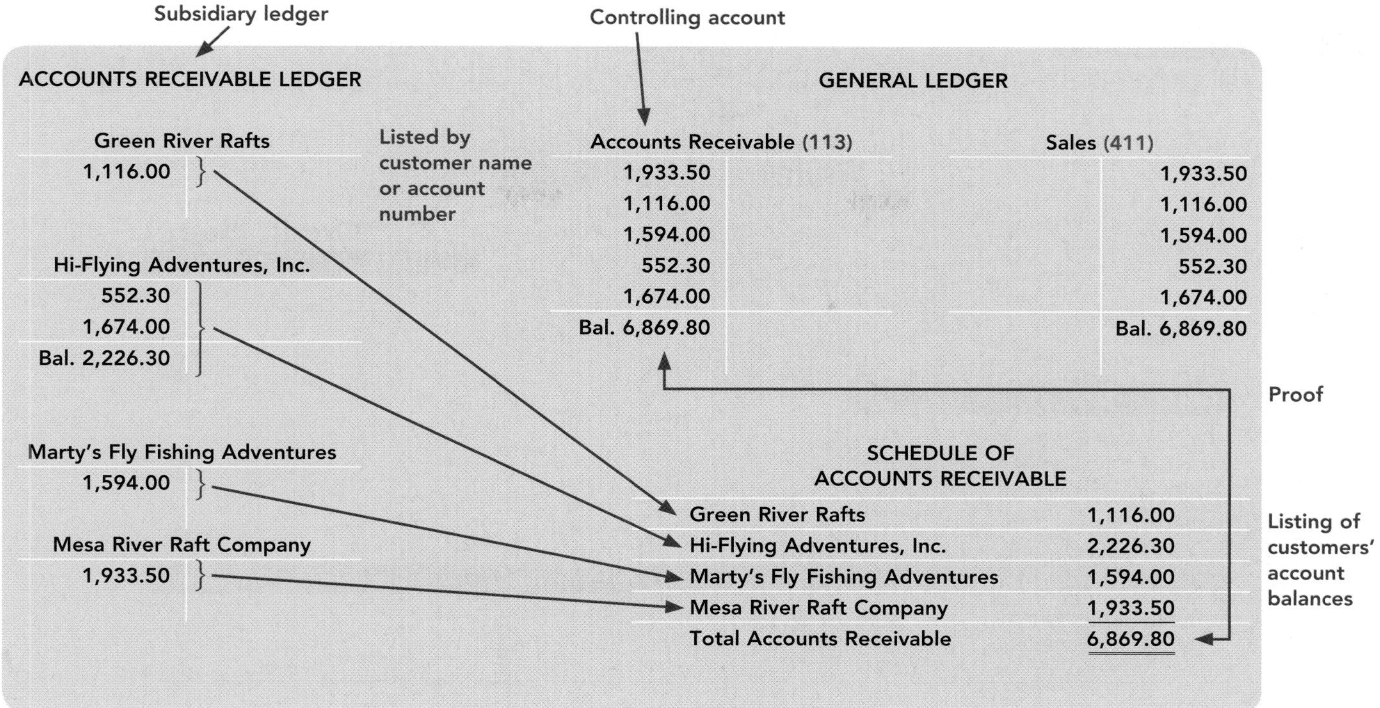

FIGURE 6
Interrelationship of the accounts receivable ledger, general ledger, and schedule of accounts receivable

Figure 6 diagrams the interrelationships of the subsidiary ledger, general ledger, and schedule of accounts receivable for Whitewater Raft Supply for the month of August. Notice that each entry is posted to Accounts Receivable and Sales in the general ledger. Also, the amount owed by the customer is posted to the subsidiary accounts receivable ledger to maintain a running balance of the amount each customer owes. If performing the posting manually, the accountant should post the individual amounts to the accounts receivable ledger every day, so that this ledger will have up-to-date information. Finally, since we assume that there were no previous balances in the customers' accounts, the Accounts Receivable controlling account in the general ledger will have the same balance, $6,869.80, as the schedule of accounts receivable.

In the simplified illustration in Figure 6, it just so happens that, since no payments were received from credit customers, the total of the Sales account equals the balance of Accounts Receivable. However, if $1,200 had been received from credit customers, both the balance of the Accounts Receivable controlling account and the total of the schedule of accounts receivable would be $5,669.80 ($6,869.80 – $1,200.00). The total of the Sales account would still be $6,869.80. Also, if some sales were cash only transactions, this would cause a difference between total Sales and the balance of Accounts Receivable.

Sales Returns and Allowances

4 LEARNING OBJECTIVE
Journalize sales returns and allowances, including credit memorandums and returns, in a general journal, and post to the accounts receivable ledger and general ledger.

The Sales Returns and Allowances account handles two types of transactions related to merchandise that has previously been sold. A *return* is a physical return of the goods. An *allowance* is a reduction from the original price because the goods were defective or damaged. It may not be economically worthwhile to have customers return the goods; each situation is a special case. To avoid writing a formal business letter each time to inform customers of their account adjustments, businesses use a special form called a **credit memorandum**. A credit memorandum (Figure 7) is a written statement indicating a seller's willingness to reduce the amount of a buyer's debt.

The Sales Returns and Allowances account is a contra account that is deducted from Sales. Using an account separate from Sales provides a better record of the total returns and allowances. Accountants deduct Sales Returns and Allowances from Sales on the income statement to determine net sales.

FIGURE 7
Credit memorandum

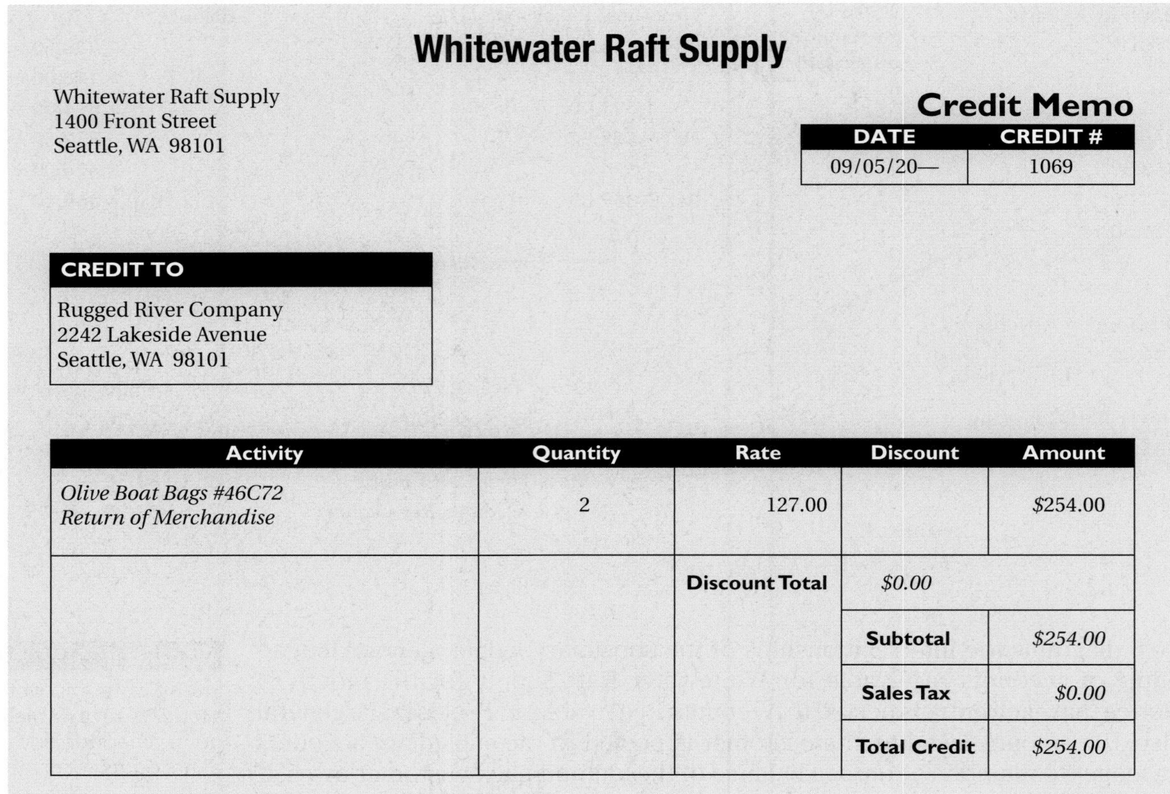

Whitewater Raft Supply

Whitewater Raft Supply
1400 Front Street
Seattle, WA 98101

Credit Memo

DATE	CREDIT #
09/05/20—	1069

CREDIT TO

Rugged River Company
2242 Lakeside Avenue
Seattle, WA 98101

Activity	Quantity	Rate	Discount	Amount
Olive Boat Bags #46C72 *Return of Merchandise*	2	127.00		*$254.00*
		Discount Total	*$0.00*	
			Subtotal	*$254.00*
			Sales Tax	*$0.00*
			Total Credit	*$254.00*

Using T accounts, here's an example of a return. The original sale is shown first, followed by the issuance of a credit memorandum.

Transaction (a). On September 1, Whitewater Raft Supply sold merchandise on account to Rugged River Company, $3,614, and recorded the sale in the general journal.

Transaction (b). On September 5, Rugged River Company returned $254 worth of the merchandise. Whitewater Raft Supply issued credit memorandum no. 1069 (see Figure 7).

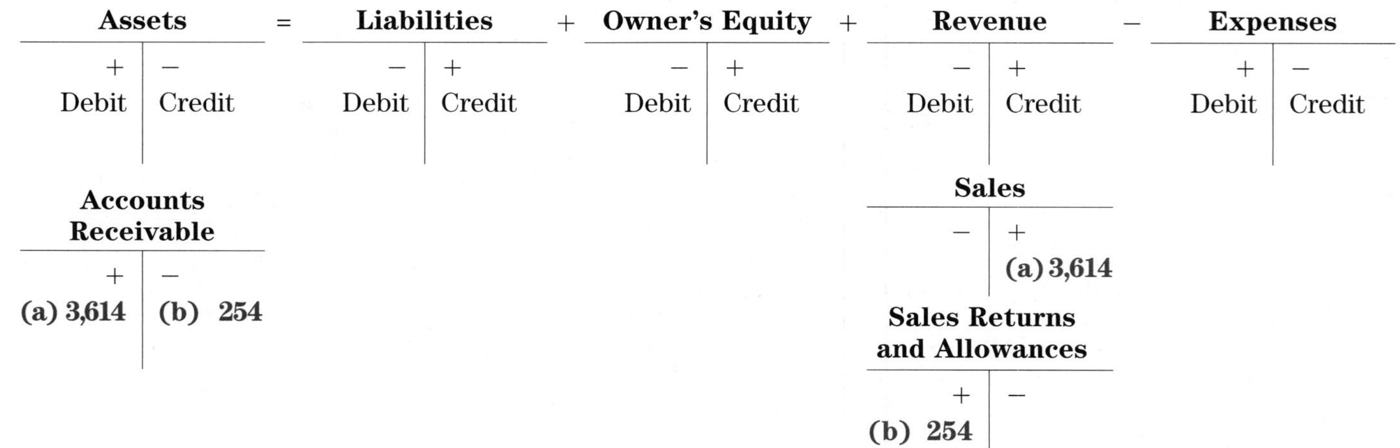

Whitewater Raft Supply's accountant debits Sales Returns and Allowances to increase it; then, the accountant credits Accounts Receivable to decrease it because the credit customer, Rugged River Company, owes less than before. If Whitewater Raft Supply was recording sales transactions using the perpetual system of inventory method, the accountant would be required to record another journal entry. This will be discussed in the appendix to this chapter.

The general journal entry serves as the posting source for crediting the Accounts Receivable controlling account in the general ledger. It also serves as the posting source for updating the accounts receivable ledger and therefore includes the name of the credit customer. If the balance of the Accounts Receivable controlling account is to equal the total of the individual account balances in the accounts receivable ledger, one must post to *both* the Accounts Receivable account in the general ledger *and* the account of Rugged River Company in the accounts receivable ledger.

If the accountant was using a computerized accounting system, the software would automatically post the credit memorandum to the Accounts Receivable controlling account and Rugged River Company's account in the accounts receivable ledger when the credit has been applied. In a manual system, to take care of this double posting, the accountant draws a slanted line in the Post. Ref. column. When the amount has been posted as a credit to the general ledger account, the accountant writes the account number of Accounts Receivable in the left part of the Post. Ref. column. After the credit has been posted to Rugged River Company's account in the subsidiary ledger, the accountant puts a check mark in the right portion of the Post. Ref. column. Sales Returns and Allowances is posted in the usual manner. The following entries in the general journal, general ledger, and accounts receivable ledger are shown after posting of the transaction is complete.

FYI

A company must manage its return policy carefully. Customers often take advantage of return privileges, creating significant handling costs for the merchant.

GENERAL JOURNAL PAGE 27

Date		Description	Post. Ref.	Debit	Credit
20—					
Sept.	5	Sales Returns and Allowances	412	254.00	
		Accounts Receivable, Rugged	113/✓		
		River Company			254.00
		Issued credit memo no. 1069.			

GENERAL LEDGER

ACCOUNT Sales Returns and Allowances ACCOUNT NO. 412

Date		Item	Post. Ref.	Debit	Credit	Balance Debit	Balance Credit
20—							
Sept.	5		J27	254.00		254.00	

ACCOUNTS RECEIVABLE LEDGER

NAME Rugged River Company
ADDRESS 2242 Lakeside Avenue
Seattle, WA 98101

Date		Item	Post. Ref.	Debit	Credit	Balance
20—						
Sept.	1		J26	3,614.00		3,614.00
	5		J27		254.00	3,360.00

Sales Transactions Involving Sales Tax

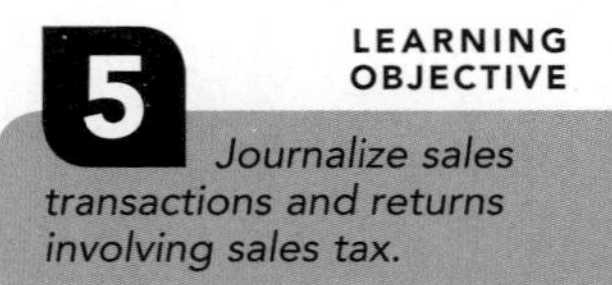

Journalize sales transactions and returns involving sales tax.

Most states and some cities levy a sales tax on retail sales of goods and services. The retailer collects the sales tax from customers and later pays it to the tax authorities.

When goods or services are sold on credit, the sales tax is charged to the customer and recorded at the time of the sale. It is necessary to compute and include the amount of the sales tax for each transaction. The customer owes the amount of the sale plus the applicable sales tax.

Assume that David Fly Fishing Outfitters, a retail store, had the following transaction that includes sales tax computed on the amount of the sale of merchandise:

Jan. 3 Sold merchandise on account to R. Martinez, invoice no. 101, $153.50 plus sales tax of $12.28.

The transaction would be recorded in T accounts and in the general journal as follows:

Assets		=	Liabilities		+	Owner's Equity		+	Revenue		−	Expenses	
+ Debit	− Credit		− Debit	+ Credit		− Debit	+ Credit		− Debit	+ Credit		+ Debit	− Credit

Accounts Receivable		Sales Tax Payable		Sales	
+	−	−	+	−	+
165.78			12.28		153.50

GENERAL JOURNAL PAGE 5

Date		Description	Post. Ref.	Debit	Credit
20—					
Jan.	3	Accounts Receivable, R. Martinez		165 78	
		Sales			153 50
		Sales Tax Payable			12 28
		Sold merchandise to			
		R. Martinez, invoice no. 101.			

At the end of the first quarter, the accountant for David Fly Fishing Outfitters determines that the total sales tax payable for the quarter is $124.50. When the sales tax is paid to the state, the accountant debits Sales Tax Payable and credits Cash for the total amount due.

GENERAL JOURNAL PAGE 8

Date		Description	Post. Ref.	Debit	Credit
20—					
Apr.	20	Sales Tax Payable		124 50	
		Cash			124 50
		Paid sales tax due for first			
		quarter.			

Sales Returns Involving Sales Tax

If a customer who returns merchandise to a retail store was originally charged a sales tax, the amount of the sale and the sales tax must be returned to the customer. Review the following two transactions for David Fly Fishing Outfitters.

Transaction (a). On May 1, David Fly Fishing Outfitters sold merchandise on account to B. Hill, $1,550, plus $124 sales tax.

Transaction (b). On May 5, B. Hill returned the merchandise and David Fly Fishing Outfitters issued credit memorandum no. 1152.

Following is the general journal entry required for this type of return:

GENERAL JOURNAL PAGE 5

Date		Description	Post. Ref.	Debit	Credit
20—					
May	5	Sales Returns and Allowances		1 5 5 0 00	
		Sales Tax Payable		1 2 4 00	
		Accounts Receivable, B. Hill			1 6 7 4 00
		Issued credit memo no. 1152.			

Notice that David Fly Fishing Outfitters credited B. Hill's account for the amount of the sale ($1,550) and the amount of the sales tax payable ($124).

Source Documents Related to Purchases

In a small retail store, the owner may do the buying. In large retail and wholesale businesses, department heads or division managers do the buying, after which the Purchasing Department goes into action: It places purchase orders, follows up on the orders, and sees that deliveries are made to the right departments. The Purchasing Department also acts as a source of information on current prices, price trends, quality of goods, prospective suppliers, and reliability of suppliers.

The Purchasing Department normally requires that any requests to buy merchandise be in writing, in the form of a **purchase requisition**. After the purchase requisition is approved, the Purchasing Department sends a purchase order to the supplier. A **purchase order** is the company's written offer to buy certain goods. The accountant does not make any entry at this point because the supplier has not yet indicated acceptance of the order. A purchase order has at least four copies. The original goes to the supplier; copies go to the Purchasing Department (as proof of what was ordered), the department that issued the requisition (telling it that the goods it wanted have been ordered), the Accounting Department, and a blind copy (with quantities omitted) goes to Receiving.

To continue with the accounts of Whitewater Raft Supply, the Boat Accessories Department submits a purchase requisition to the Purchasing Department, as shown in Figure 8.

The Purchasing Department completes the rest of the purchase requisition and then sends out the purchase order shown in Figure 9.

The seller then sends an invoice to the buyer as shown in Figure 10. This invoice should arrive in advance of the goods (or at least *with* the goods). Notice the line *Terms. Terms* means the terms of payment. For example, 2/10, n/30 means that if the buyer pays the amount due within 10 days, the buyer will receive a 2 percent discount; otherwise, the entire amount is due in 30 days.

Pataponia, Inc. (the seller) prepaid the freight cost and added the $85.50 to the bill, listing it separately. This is similar to buying something by mail order or online. Freight In is discussed in more detail later in the chapter.

FIGURE 8
Purchase requisition

NO. C–726

Whitewater Raft Supply
1400 Front Street
Seattle, WA 98101

PURCHASE REQUISITION

DEPARTMENT *Boat Accessories* DATE OF REQUEST *July 2, 20—*
ADVISE ON DELIVERY *C. Fenwick* DATE REQUIRED *Aug. 5, 20—*

QUANTITY	DESCRIPTION
12	*Rio Frio Personal Flotation Device (PFD) #772R*

APPROVED BY *D. M. Bruce* REQUESTED BY *J. C. Garcia*

FOR PURCHASING DEPT. USE ONLY

PURCHASE ORDER NO. *7918*
DATE *July 5, 20—*
ISSUED TO: *Pataponia, Inc.*
1614 Olivera Street
San Francisco, CA 94129

FIGURE 9
Purchase order

Whitewater Raft Supply
1400 Front Street
Seattle, WA 98101

PURCHASE ORDER

TO: *Pataponia, Inc.*
1614 Olivera Street
San Francisco, CA 94129

DATE: *July 5, 20—*
ORDER NO.: *7918*
SHIPPED BY:
TERMS: *2/10, n/30*

QUANTITY	DESCRIPTION	UNIT PRICE		TOTAL	
12	*Rio Frio Personal Flotation Device (PFD) #772R*	*142*	*50*	*1,710*	*00*
	Total			*1,710*	*00*

D. M. Bruce

FIGURE 10
Purchase invoice

No. 2706

Pataponia, Inc.
1614 Olivera Street
San Francisco, CA 94129

INVOICE

SOLD TO *Whitewater Raft Supply*
1400 Front Street
Seattle, WA 98101

DATE: *July 31, 20—*
CUSTOMER'S P.O. NO.: *7918*
SHIPPED BY: *Western Freight Line*
TERMS: *2/10, n/30*

YOUR ORDER NO.	SALESPERSON	TERMS
7918	*C.L.*	*2/10, n/30*
DATE SHIPPED	**SHIPPED BY**	**FOB**
July 31, 20—	*Western Freight Line*	*San Francisco*

QUANTITY	DESCRIPTION	UNIT PRICE		TOTAL	
12	*Rio Frio Personal Flotation Device (PFD) #772R*	*142*	*50*	*1,710*	*00*
	Freight			*85*	*50*
	Total			*1,795*	*50*

Purchase Transactions

LEARNING OBJECTIVE 6

Journalize purchase transactions in a general journal, and post to the accounts payable ledger and general ledger.

Now that we have reviewed the source documents for purchase transactions, let's move on to recording purchase transactions. Purchase transactions can be recorded in two ways—either by recording directly into the general journal or by using a special journal called the purchases journal. As with sales transactions, a company determines which method to use when recording purchase transactions based upon the occurrence of the transaction and the type of journals that are used in the company.

We will introduce purchase transactions using the general journal first. Then, we will discuss how to record the transactions into the purchases journal in part two of this chapter. As a reminder all transactions are recorded assuming a periodic inventory method. The perpetual inventory method will be demonstrated in the appendix to this chapter.

Let's look at four purchase transactions on the books of Whitewater Raft Supply for the month of August. Some of these transactions include the cost of delivering the merchandise, called Freight In, which will be discussed later in the chapter.

Aug. 2 Bought merchandise on account from Pataponia, Inc., invoice no. 2706, $1,710; terms 2/10, n/30; dated July 31; FOB San Francisco, freight prepaid and added to the invoice, $85.50 (total $1,795.50).

10 Bought merchandise on account from Langseth and Son, invoice no. 982, $2,772; terms net 30 days; dated August 8; FOB Cleveland, freight prepaid and added to the invoice, $157 (total $2,929).

17 Bought merchandise on account from Dana Manufacturing Company, invoice no. 10611, $564; terms 2/10, n/30; dated August 15; FOB Los Angeles.

26 Bought merchandise on account from Pataponia, Inc., invoice no. 2801, $2,503.70; terms 2/10, n/30; dated August 24; FOB San Francisco, freight prepaid and added to the invoice, $102.30 (total $2,606).

Whitewater Raft Supply will record the transactions into the general journal as follows:

GENERAL JOURNAL PAGE 26

Date		Description	Post. Ref.	Debit	Credit
20—					
Aug.	2	Purchases		1,710.00	
		Freight In		85.50	
		Accounts Payable, Pataponia, Inc.			1,795.50
		Purchased merchandise from Pataponia, Inc., invoice no. 2706, invoice dated 7/31, terms 2/10, n/30.			
	10	Purchases		2,772.00	
		Freight In		157.00	
		Accounts Payable, Langseth and Son			2,929.00
		Purchased merchandise from Langseth and Son, invoice no. 982, invoice dated 8/8, terms n/30.			

(continued)

Date		Description	Post. Ref.	Debit	Credit
Aug.	17	Purchases		5 6 4 00	
		Accounts Payable, Dana			
		Manufacturing Company			5 6 4 00
		Purchased merchandise from			
		Dana Manufacturing Company,			
		invoice no. 10611, invoice dated			
		8/15, terms 2/10, n/30.			
	26	Purchases		2 5 0 3 70	
		Freight In		1 0 2 30	
		Accounts Payable, Pataponia, Inc.			2 6 0 6 00
		Purchased merchandise from			
		Pataponia, Inc., invoice no.			
		2801, invoice dated 8/24,			
		terms 2/10, n/30.			

Whitewater Raft Supply's accountant records a debit to the Purchases account to record the cost of merchandise bought for resale. Remember that the Purchases account is similar to an expense account and, therefore, has a normal debit balance. Freight In (if applied) is also debited to record the increase to the cost of purchases for the transportation charges on incoming merchandise. The corresponding credit is to the Accounts Payable account. Note that the transactions are recorded on the day the merchandise is received.

Here's how the accounts appear in the fundamental accounting equation:

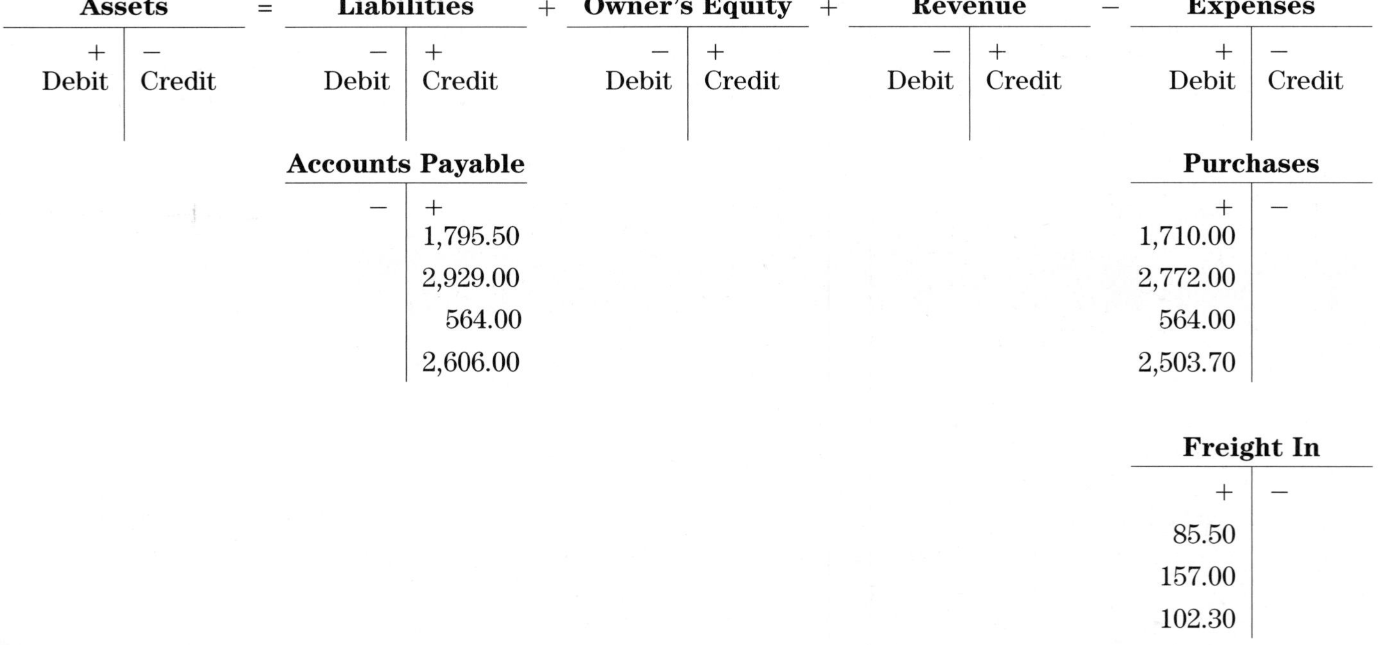

Assets = Liabilities + Owner's Equity + Revenue − Expenses
+ Debit | − Credit
− Debit | + Credit
− Debit | + Credit
− Debit | + Credit
+ Debit | − Credit
Accounts Payable
− | +
1,795.50
2,929.00
564.00
2,606.00
Purchases
+ | −
1,710.00
2,772.00
564.00
2,503.70
Freight In
+ | −
85.50
157.00
102.30

Remember

Creditors are companies or individuals to whom we owe money.

The Accounts Payable Ledger

Previously, we called the Accounts Receivable account in the general ledger a **controlling** account, and we saw that the accounts receivable ledger consists of an individual account for each credit customer.

Accounts Payable is a parallel case; it, too, is a controlling account in the general ledger. **The accounts payable ledger is a subsidiary ledger, and it consists of individual accounts for all the creditors listed in either alphabetical or**

numerical order. In a computerized accounting system, when the purchase is recorded, the software automatically posts to the appropriate accounts payable ledger. If posting manually, posting to the accounts payable ledger is usually done daily. Figure 11 is an example of the accounts payable ledger using a computerized system, while Figure 12 is an example of the manual version of the accounts payable ledger.

Even though an accounts payable ledger is maintained, the Accounts Payable account in the general ledger should still be maintained. When all the postings are up to date, the balance of this account should equal the total of all the creditors' individual account balances.

Remember

Increases in Accounts Payable are recorded in the Credit column. Decreases in Accounts Payable are recorded in the Debit column.

FIGURE 11
Accounts payable ledger (computerized)

Whitewater Raft Supply
Vendor Balance Detail
All Dates

Date	Type	Num	Due Date	Amount	Balance
Pataponia, Inc.					
08/02/20—	Bill	2706	09/01/20—	1,795.50	1,795.50
08/26/20—	Bill	2801	09/25/20—	2,606.00	4,401.50
Total for Pataponia, Inc.				**$4,401.50**	
TOTAL				**$4,401.50**	

FIGURE 12
Accounts payable ledger (manual)

ACCOUNTS PAYABLE LEDGER

NAME Pataponia, Inc.
ADDRESS 1614 Olivera Street
San Francisco, CA 94129

Date		Item	Post. Ref.	Debit	Credit	Balance
20—						
Aug.	2		J26		1 7 9 5 50	1 7 9 5 50
	26		J26		2 6 0 6 00	4 4 0 1 50

Schedule of Accounts Payable

7 LEARNING OBJECTIVE
Prepare a schedule of accounts payable.

Assuming there were no previous balances in the creditors' accounts and that no other transactions for Whitewater Raft Supply involved Accounts Payable, the schedule of accounts payable would appear as shown in Figure 13. Note that the schedule of accounts payable lists each creditor's account balance and that it equals the Accounts Payable account shown in the general ledger (Figure 14).

Purchases Returns and Allowances

8 LEARNING OBJECTIVE
Journalize transactions involving purchases returns and allowances in a general journal, and post to the accounts payable ledger and general ledger.

As its title implies, the Purchases Returns and Allowances account handles either a return of merchandise previously purchased or an allowance made for merchandise that arrived in damaged condition. In both cases, there is a reduction in the amount owed to the supplier. The buyer sends a letter or printed form to the supplier, who acknowledges the reduction by sending a credit memorandum. The buyer should wait for notice of the agreed deduction before making an entry.

FIGURE 13
Schedule of accounts payable

Whitewater Raft Supply
Schedule of Accounts Payable
August 31, 20—

Dana Manufacturing Company	$ 564.00
Langseth and Son	2,929.00
Pataponia, Inc.	4,401.50
Total Accounts Payable	$7,894.50

FIGURE 14
Accounts Payable controlling account

GENERAL LEDGER

ACCOUNT Accounts Payable ACCOUNT NO. 212

Date		Item	Post. Ref.	Debit	Credit	Balance Debit	Balance Credit
20—							
Aug.	2		J26		1 7 9 5 50		1 7 9 5 50
	10		J26		2 9 2 9 00		4 7 2 4 50
	17		J26		5 6 4 00		5 2 8 8 50
	26		J26		2 6 0 6 00		7 8 9 4 50

The Purchases Returns and Allowances account is a contra account to Purchases and is considered to be a deduction from Purchases. Using a separate account provides a better record of the total returns and allowances. Purchases Returns and Allowances is deducted from the Purchases account on the income statement. (We'll talk about this point later.) For now, let's look at an example consisting of a return on the books of Whitewater Raft Supply.

Transaction (a). On September 2, bought merchandise on account from Dana Manufacturing Company, $830.

Transaction (b). On September 8, received credit memorandum no. 1629 from Dana Manufacturing Company for $270.

First, here is how the transactions appear in the fundamental accounting equation:

Assets		=	Liabilities		+	Owner's Equity		+	Revenue		−	Expenses	
+	−		−	+		−	+		−	+		+	−
Debit	Credit		Debit	Credit		Debit	Credit		Debit	Credit		Debit	Credit

Accounts Payable

−	+
(b) 270	(a) 830

Purchases

+	−
(a) 830	

Purchases Returns and Allowances

−	+
	(b) 270

In the general journal, transaction (a) was journalized as a debit to Purchases and a credit to Accounts Payable. Transaction (b) is journalized as follows:

GENERAL JOURNAL PAGE 27

Date		Description	Post. Ref.	Debit	Credit
20—					
Sept.	8	Accounts Payable, Dana	212/✓		
		Manufacturing Company		2 7 0 00	
		Purchases Returns and			
		Allowances	512		2 7 0 00
		Credit memo no. 1629 for			
		return of merchandise.			

Purchases Returns and Allowances is credited because Whitewater Raft Supply has more returns and allowances than before. Accounts Payable is debited because Whitewater Raft Supply owes less than before.

The accountant must post the amount to both the Accounts Payable controlling account and the individual creditor's account in the accounts payable ledger. The account numbers in the Post. Ref. column indicate postings to the accounts in the general ledger, and the check marks indicate postings to the accounts in the accounts payable ledger.

GENERAL LEDGER

ACCOUNT Accounts Payable ACCOUNT NO. 212

Date		Item	Post. Ref.	Debit	Credit	Balance Debit	Balance Credit
20—							
Sept.	1	Balance	✓				7 8 9 4 50
	2		J27		8 3 0 00		8 7 2 4 50
	8		J27	2 7 0 00			8 4 5 4 50

ACCOUNT Purchases Returns and Allowances ACCOUNT NO. 512

Date		Item	Post. Ref.	Debit	Credit	Balance Debit	Balance Credit
20—							
Sept.	1	Balance	✓				1 6 4 0 00
	8		J27		2 7 0 00		1 9 1 0 00

ACCOUNTS PAYABLE LEDGER

NAME Dana Manufacturing Company

ADDRESS 254 Calle Mancha

Los Angeles, CA 90025

Date		Item	Post. Ref.	Debit	Credit	Balance
20—						
Sept.	1	Balance	✓			5 6 4 00
	2		J27		8 3 0 00	1 3 9 4 00
	8		J27	2 7 0 00		1 1 2 4 00

Freight Charges on Incoming Merchandise

LEARNING OBJECTIVE 9

Describe the procedures for handling freight charges on merchandise and other goods.

Companies use the Freight In account to keep a record of all separately charged delivery costs on incoming merchandise.

Freight costs are expressed as FOB (free on board) destination or shipping point. **(Destination is the buyer's location; shipping point is the seller's location.)** In both cases, the supplier loads the goods free on board the carrier. Beyond that point, there must be an understanding as to who is responsible for paying the freight charges. **If the seller assumes the entire cost of transportation, without any reimbursement from the buyer, the terms are FOB destination.** In this case, title or ownership changes hands when the buyer receives the goods. **If the buyer is responsible for paying the freight cost, the shipping terms are called FOB shipping point.** In this case, title or ownership changes hands when goods are transferred to a common carrier (freight company).

FYI

Unless the title to the goods is expressly reserved by the seller, whoever pays the freight charges customarily has title to the goods.

Briefly, when goods are shipped FOB destination, the freight charges are not stated, and the seller simply pays the amount of the freight. Suppose Whitewater Raft Supply, which is in Seattle, buys merchandise from a supplier in Chicago with shipping terms of FOB Seattle listed on the invoice. The total of the invoice is $1,740, and there is no separate listing of freight charges. In other words, the seller has included the transportation costs in the price.

When goods are shipped FOB shipping point, with the buyer responsible for paying the freight charges, transportation costs may be handled in two ways:

1. The buyer may pay the freight charges directly to the transportation company. For example, an automobile dealer in Houston buys cars FOB Detroit. In this case, the automobile dealer makes one check payable to the manufacturer and another check payable to the carrier for the freight charges. (FOB Detroit is the same as FOB shipping point.)
2. The transportation or shipping costs may be listed separately on the invoice. For example, suppose a person orders a computer from a company online. The company has prepaid (paid in advance) the freight charges as a favor or convenience for the buyer. However, the freight charges are listed on the bill or invoice, and the buyer is responsible for reimbursing the company for the freight charges. Similarly, when a business buys merchandise, the amount of the freight charges may be prepaid by the seller and listed separately on the invoice.

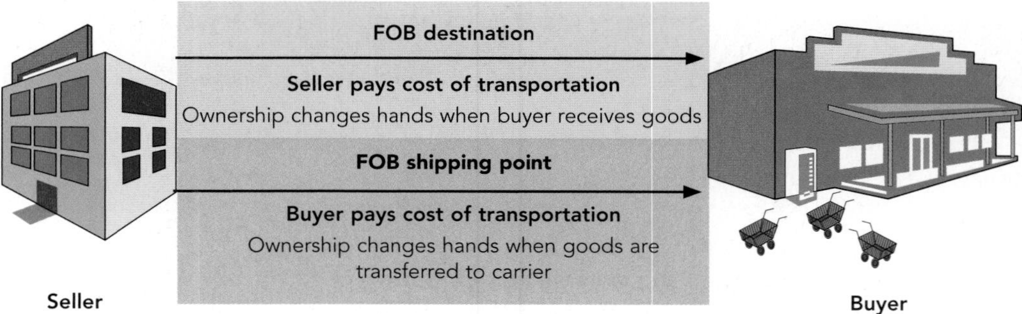

Look again at the invoice from Pataponia, Inc., on page 340. Note that the freight cost is listed separately, and the terms are FOB shipping point (San Francisco). Pataponia paid the transportation cost; Whitewater Raft Supply must reimburse Pataponia for this cost.

The transaction for the purchase from Pataponia, Inc., was recorded as follows:

GENERAL JOURNAL PAGE 26

Date		Description	Post. Ref.	Debit	Credit
20—					
Aug.	2	Purchases		1,710.00	
		Freight In		85.50	
		Accounts Payable, Pataponia, Inc.			1,795.50
		Purchased merchandise from			
		Pataponia, Inc., invoice no.			
		2706, invoice dated 7/31,			
		terms 2/10, n/30.			

Notice that the transportation cost is recorded separately as a debit to the Freight In account for $85.50. Also notice that because this purchase was FOB shipping point, the buyer (Whitewater Raft Supply) must reimburse the seller for the transportation costs by paying the total invoice cost of $1,795.50.

When the buyer pays for the cost of freight, the buyer records the cost as Freight In. Freight In is included in the cost of purchases and is reported on the income statement. If the seller pays for the cost of freight, the seller records the cost as Delivery Expense or Freight Out. Delivery Expense is recorded as a selling expense on the income statement.

Transportation Charges on the Buying of Goods and Services Other than Merchandise

Any freight charges incurred when buying any other assets, such as supplies or equipment, should be debited to the respective asset accounts. The Freight In account is used only to record the incoming transportation charges on merchandise intended for resale. For example, assume that Whitewater Raft Supply bought display cases on account from Carter Cabinet Shop, at a cost of $2,700 plus freight charges of $290. The seller of the display cases prepaid the transportation costs for Whitewater Raft Supply and then added the $290 to the invoice price of the cases. Let's visualize this with T accounts.

Store Equipment	
+	−
2,990	

Accounts Payable	
−	+
	2,990

Notice that Whitewater Raft Supply did not use the Freight In account to record the transportation costs. Instead, the company recorded the transportation costs directly into the Store Equipment account.

Internal Control of Purchases

Purchases is one of the areas in which internal control is essential. Efficiency and security require most companies to work out careful procedures for buying and paying for goods. This is understandable, as large sums of money are usually involved. The control aspect generally involves the following measures:

1. Purchases are made only after proper authorization is given. Purchase requisitions and purchase orders are all prenumbered, so that each form can be accounted for.

2. The receiving department carefully checks all goods upon receipt for count, damages, and description. Later, the report of the receiving department is verified against the purchase order and the purchase invoice.
3. The person who authorizes the payment is neither the person doing the ordering nor the person actually writing the check. Payment is authorized only after verifying the purchase invoice data against the receiving report and purchase order.
4. The person who actually writes the check has not been involved in any of the foregoing purchasing procedures.

PART TWO—RECORDING TRANSACTIONS INTO SALES JOURNAL AND PURCHASES JOURNAL

Special Journals

We have demonstrated sales and purchases by recording the transactions directly into the general journal. Companies can, however, also record sales and purchases into a special journal. **Special journals** are books of original entry used to simplify the recording process. One or more of these journals may be used in a manual accounting system, or they may be used in certain computerized systems designed to facilitate specialized types of repetitive transactions. The four most commonly used special journals are:

Sales journal (S) Used to record sales of merchandise sold on account *only*. For example, if Whitewater Raft Supply sells a kayak to a customer, on account, Whitewater Raft Supply could use this journal to record that sale. However, if the customer paid cash for the kayak, the sale would not be recorded in this journal. Also, if Whitewater Raft Supply sells some of its old computer equipment, on account, this journal would not be used because the equipment was not part of the business's merchandise sales.

Purchases journal (P) Used to record purchases of merchandise purchased on account for resale *only*. For example, this journal could be used by Whitewater Raft Supply for its purchase, on account, of whitewater rafts to resell to customers. However, this journal would not be used by Whitewater Raft Supply when buying a copy machine or supplies for the office, even though purchased on account, because those goods are not intended for resale to customers.

Cash receipts journal (CR) Used to record all transactions that include a debit to Cash, such as cash sales, checks received, or interest earned on a checking account.

Cash payments journal (CP) Used to record all transactions that include a credit to Cash, such as payments by check or bank service charges.

In part two of this chapter, we will demonstrate how Whitewater Raft Supply records sales and purchases transactions using the sales journal and purchases journal. In the next chapter, we will discuss the cash receipts journal and cash payments journal.

The Sales Journal

LEARNING OBJECTIVE 10

Journalize transactions in a sales journal, and post to the accounts receivable ledger and general ledger.

The **sales journal** records sales of merchandise **on account only.** This specialized type of transaction calls for debits to Accounts Receivable and credits to Sales.

Recall the sales transactions introduced for Whitewater Raft Supply for the month of August:

Aug. 1 Sold merchandise on account to Mesa River Raft Company, invoice no. 9384, $1,933.50.

Aug. 8 Sold merchandise on account to Green River Rafts, invoice no. 9385, $1,116.

14 Sold merchandise on account to Marty's Fly Fishing Adventures, invoice no. 9386, $1,594.

19 Sold merchandise on account to Hi-Flying Adventures, Inc., invoice no. 9387, $552.30.

25 Sold merchandise on account to Hi-Flying Adventures, Inc., invoice no. 9388, $1,674.

Let's assume that Whitewater Raft Supply uses the sales journal *instead of* the general journal to record the five transactions. The accountant will record each transaction into the sales journal only.

Remember

The sales journal is a book of original entry. Do not duplicate the transaction in the general journal.

SALES JOURNAL PAGE 38

Date		Inv. No.	Customer's Name	Post. Ref.	Accounts Receivable Dr. Sales Cr.
20—					
Aug.	1	9384	Mesa River Raft Company		1 9 3 3 50
	8	9385	Green River Rafts		1 1 1 6 00
	14	9386	Marty's Fly Fishing Adventures		1 5 9 4 00
	19	9387	Hi-Flying Adventures, Inc.		5 5 2 30
	25	9388	Hi-Flying Adventures, Inc.		1 6 7 4 00

Because *one* column is headed Accounts Receivable Dr./Sales Cr., each transaction requires only a single line. Repetition is avoided, and all entries for sales of merchandise on account are found in one place. Listing the invoice number makes it easier to check the details of a particular sale at a later date.

As with the general journal, the amount of each sale should be posted daily to the account of each credit customer in the accounts receivable ledger. After you post an amount from the sales journal to a credit customer's account in the accounts receivable ledger, put a check mark in the Post. Ref. column of the sales journal.

Posting from the Sales Journal

Using the sales journal also saves time and space in posting to the ledger accounts. Because every entry is a debit to Accounts Receivable and a credit to Sales, you can make a single posting to these accounts for the amount of the total as of the last day of the month. This entry is called a **summarizing entry** because it summarizes one month's transactions. Since Whitewater Raft Supply had no other sales transactions after August 25, the amounts in the Accounts Receivable Dr./Sales Cr. Column from the sales journal above are added up and totaled. The total ($6,869.80) is then posted to the Accounts Receivable and Sales accounts in the general ledger. In the Post. Ref. columns of the ledger accounts, the letter S designates the sales journal.

GENERAL LEDGER

ACCOUNT Accounts Receivable ACCOUNT NO. 113

Date		Item	Post. Ref.	Debit	Credit	Balance Debit	Balance Credit
20—							
Aug.	31		S38	6 8 6 9 80		6 8 6 9 80	

Remember

The purpose of posting reference numbers is to tell where in the ledger an amount was posted or the journal from which it came.

Remember

The T accounts look like this:

Accounts Receivable	
+	–
6,869.80	

Sales	
–	+
	6,869.80

GENERAL LEDGER

ACCOUNT Sales ACCOUNT NO. 411

Date		Item	Post. Ref.	Debit	Credit	Balance Debit	Balance Credit
20—							
Aug.	31		S38		6 8 6 9 80		6 8 6 9 80

After posting the total of the sales journal to the Accounts Receivable account in the general ledger, write the account number of Accounts Receivable at the left below the total of the sales journal. Repeat the process of posting for the total of the sales journal to the Sales account in the general ledger, placing the account number of Sales at the right below the total of the sales journal. **Don't record these account numbers until you have completed the postings.** Figure 15 shows the completed sales journal for Whitewater Raft Supply for the month of August. Notice that the ruling consists of a single line under the amount column and double lines extended through the Date, Post. Ref., and amount columns. The last day of the month is recorded on the same line as the total.

FIGURE 15
Sales journal

SALES JOURNAL PAGE 38

Date		Inv. No.	Customer's Name	Post. Ref.	Accounts Receivable Dr. Sales Cr.
20—					
Aug.	1	9384	Mesa River Raft Company	✓	1 9 3 3 50
	8	9385	Green River Rafts	✓	1 1 1 6 00
	14	9386	Marty's Fly Fishing Adventures	✓	1 5 9 4 00
	19	9387	Hi-Flying Adventures, Inc.	✓	5 5 2 30
	25	9388	Hi-Flying Adventures, Inc.	✓	1 6 7 4 00
	31		Total		6 8 6 9 80
					(113) (411)

Sales Journal with Sales Tax Payable

When recording sales transactions that involve sales tax, the sales journal will need to include three columns: Accounts Receivable Debit, Sales Tax Payable Credit, and Sales Credit.

Recall the transaction given for David Fly Fishing Outfitters earlier in the chapter:

Jan. 3 Sold merchandise on account to R. Martinez, invoice no. 101, $153.50 plus sales tax of $12.28.

As shown below, David Fly Fishing Outfitters would record the transaction in the sales journal as follows:

Remember

The sales journal is used to record only the sales of merchandise (goods) on account.

SALES JOURNAL PAGE 3

Date		Inv. No.	Customer's Name	Post. Ref.	Accounts Receivable Debit	Sales Tax Payable Credit	Sales Credit
20—							
Jan.	3	101	R. Martinez		1 6 5 78	1 2 28	1 5 3 50

At the end of the month, the accountant for David Fly Fishing Outfitters would total the columns and post them as a debit to Accounts Receivable, a credit to Sales Tax Payable, and a credit to Sales. However, with a journal that has more than one column, you should use the column totals to prove that the total debits equal the total credits before posting to the general ledger accounts. After posting, the respective account numbers are recorded in parentheses below the totals.

Purchases Journal (Three-Column)

11 LEARNING OBJECTIVE

Journalize transactions in a three-column purchases journal, and post to the accounts payable ledger and general ledger.

Following are the purchase transactions for Whitewater Raft Supply for the month of August. We will use these transactions to demonstrate the purchases journal.

Aug. 2 Bought merchandise on account from Pataponia, Inc., invoice no. 2706, $1,710; terms 2/10, n/30; dated July 31; FOB San Francisco, freight prepaid and added to the invoice, $85.50 (total $1,795.50).

10 Bought merchandise on account from Langseth and Son, invoice no. 982, $2,772; terms net 30 days; dated August 8; FOB Cleveland, freight prepaid and added to the invoice, $157 (total $2,929).

17 Bought merchandise on account from Dana Manufacturing Company, invoice no. 10611, $564; terms 2/10, n/30; dated August 15; FOB Los Angeles.

26 Bought merchandise on account from Pataponia, Inc., invoice no. 2801, $2,503.70; terms 2/10, n/30; dated August 24; FOB San Francisco, freight prepaid and added to the invoice, $102.30 (total $2,606).

As shown below, Whitewater Raft Supply's accountant will record each transaction into the **purchases journal**. Notice that by including a separate column for each account, Whitewater Raft Supply can record a typical purchase of merchandise on account on one line.

PURCHASES JOURNAL PAGE 29

Date		Supplier's Name	Inv. No.	Inv. Date	Terms	Post. Ref.	Accounts Payable Credit	Freight In Debit	Purchases Debit
20—									
Aug.	2	Pataponia, Inc.	2706	7/31	2/10, n/30		1 7 9 5 50	8 5 50	1 7 1 0 00
	10	Langseth and Son	982	8/8	n/30		2 9 2 9 00	1 5 7 00	2 7 7 2 00
	17	Dana Manufacturing Co.	10611	8/15	2/10, n/30		5 6 4 00		5 6 4 00
	26	Pataponia, Inc.	2801	8/24	2/10, n/30		2 6 0 6 00	1 0 2 30	2 5 0 3 70

Posting from the Purchases Journal to the General Ledger

If using a manual system, the accountant posts the totals of each column into the appropriate general ledger accounts. Figure 16 shows the journal entries in the purchases journal for Whitewater Raft Supply for all transactions involving the purchase of merchandise on account for August and the related ledger accounts for the same time period. In the Post. Ref. column of the ledger accounts, P designates the purchases journal. After posting the column totals for the month to the ledger accounts, the accountant goes back to the purchases journal and puts a check mark (✓) in the Post. Ref column and records the account numbers in parentheses directly below the total.

FIGURE 16
Purchases journal and general ledger accounts

PURCHASES JOURNAL PAGE 29

Date		Supplier's Name	Inv. No.	Inv. Date	Terms	Post. Ref.	Accounts Payable Credit	Freight In Debit	Purchases Debit
20—									
Aug.	2	Pataponia, Inc.	2706	7/31	2/10, n/30	✓	1,795.50	85.50	1,710.00
	10	Langseth and Son	982	8/8	n/30	✓	2,929.00	157.00	2,772.00
	17	Dana Manufacturing Co.	10611	8/15	2/10, n/30	✓	564.00		564.00
	26	Pataponia, Inc.	2801	8/24	2/10, n/30	✓	2,606.00	102.30	2,503.70
	31	Totals					7,894.50	344.80	7,549.70
							(212)	(514)	(511)

Remember

Transactions involving the buying of supplies or other assets should not be journalized in the three-column purchases journal, because this purchases journal may be used only for purchases of merchandise for resale.

GENERAL LEDGER

ACCOUNT Accounts Payable ACCOUNT NO. 212

Date		Item	Post. Ref.	Debit	Credit	Balance Debit	Balance Credit
20—							
Aug.	31		P29		7,894.50		7,894.50

ACCOUNT Purchases ACCOUNT NO. 511

Date		Item	Post. Ref.	Debit	Credit	Balance Debit	Balance Credit
20—							
Aug.	31		P29	7,549.70		7,549.70	

ACCOUNT Freight In ACCOUNT NO. 514

Date		Item	Post. Ref.	Debit	Credit	Balance Debit	Balance Credit
20—							
Aug.	31		P29	344.80		344.80	

CHAPTER REVIEW

Study & Practice

LEARNING OBJECTIVE

Describe the specific accounts used by a merchandising firm.

The **Merchandise Inventory** account is an asset account representing the cost of goods bought for resale.

The **Sales account** is a revenue account representing the total sales of merchandise.

The **Sales Returns and Allowances account** is a deduction from the Sales account, representing amounts allowed for returns of merchandise and damaged goods.

The **Sales Tax Payable account** is a liability account representing amounts owed to state or city governments.

The **Sales Discounts account** is a deduction from the Sales account, representing amounts deducted for prompt payments.

The **Purchases account** is a cost (expense) account representing the costs of goods bought for resale.

The **Purchases Returns and Allowances account** is a deduction from the Purchases account, representing amounts granted by suppliers for the return of merchandise or damaged goods.

The **Purchases Discounts account** is a deduction from the Purchases account, representing amounts suppliers allow for prompt payments.

The **Freight In account** is a cost (expense) representing the transportation charges on incoming merchandise.

2 LEARNING OBJECTIVE

Journalize sales transactions in a general journal, and post to the accounts receivable ledger and general ledger.

Sales transactions are recorded in the general journal by debiting Accounts Receivable and crediting Sales. The entry is posted to the Accounts Receivable and Sales accounts in the general ledger. The entries are also posted daily to the **accounts receivable ledger**.

PRACTICE EXERCISE 1

Record the following transaction for Rodgers Refrigerator Supply in general journal form.

Aug. 23 Sold merchandise on account to Robbins Hardware Store, invoice no. 3209, $1,340.

PRACTICE EXERCISE 1 SOLUTION

GENERAL JOURNAL PAGE ____

Date		Description	Post. Ref.	Debit	Credit
20—					
Aug.	23	Accounts Receivable, Robbins			
		Hardware Store		1 3 4 0 00	
		Sales			1 3 4 0 00
		Sold merchandise to Robbins			
		Hardware Store, invoice			
		no. 3209.			

3 LEARNING OBJECTIVE

Prepare a schedule of accounts receivable.

The schedule of accounts receivable consists of a listing of the individual account balances of the credit customers taken from the accounts receivable ledger.

PRACTICE EXERCISE 2

Fill in the missing amounts in the accounts receivable subsidiary ledgers for Willis Spas and Pools. Then, using the information from the ledgers, prepare a schedule of accounts receivable.

ACCOUNTS RECEIVABLE LEDGER

NAME J. Hersch
ADDRESS 3540 Key Avenue
Lampasas, TX 76550

Date		Item	Post. Ref.	Debit	Credit	Balance
20—						
May	2		J26	7 8 1 40		7 8 1 40
	8		J26	1 7 8 0 00		(a)
	22		J26		1 2 0 5 00	(b)

NAME M. Hill
ADDRESS 220 Lawrence Avenue
Copperas Cove, TX 76522

Date		Item	Post. Ref.	Debit	Credit	Balance
20—						
May	15		J26	4 8 1 40		4 8 1 40
	18		J26		2 0 4 80	(c)

NAME **R. D. Moen**
ADDRESS **416 Fifth Avenue**
Dallas, TX 75204

Date		Item	Post. Ref.	Debit	Credit	Balance
20—						
May	31		J26	312.60		312.60

PRACTICE EXERCISE 2 SOLUTION

(a) $2,561.40
(b) $1,356.40
(c) $276.60

Willis Spas and Pools
Schedule of Accounts Receivable
May 31, 20—

J. Hersch	$1,356.40
M. Hill	276.60
R. D. Moen	312.60
Total Accounts Receivable	$1,945.60

LEARNING OBJECTIVE 4

Journalize sales returns and allowances, including credit memorandums and returns, in a general journal, and post to the accounts receivable ledger and general ledger.

When a customer returns merchandise, or when his or her bill is reduced owing to an allowance for defective or damaged merchandise, the Sales Returns and Allowances account is debited and the Accounts Receivable account is credited. The entry is recorded in the general journal and posted to both the general ledger and the accounts receivable ledger.

PRACTICE EXERCISE 3

Refer to the transaction in Practice Exercise 1. Assume that on September 1, Robbins Hardware Store returned $81 of the merchandise. Rodgers Refrigerator Supply issued credit memo no. 114. Record the journal entry for the return.

PRACTICE EXERCISE 3 SOLUTION

GENERAL JOURNAL PAGE ______

Date		Description	Post. Ref.	Debit	Credit
20—					
Sept.	1	Sales Returns and Allowances		81.00	
		Accounts Receivable, Robbins			
		Hardware Store			81.00
		Issued credit memo no. 114.			

CHAPTER REVIEW

LEARNING OBJECTIVE

5 Journalize sales transactions and returns involving sales tax.

Sales tax is collected from customers by the retailer and then later paid to the appropriate tax authorities. When goods are sold, the sales tax is charged to the customer and recorded at the time of sale. The entry involves recording a debit to Accounts Receivable or Cash and credits to Sales and Sales Tax Payable.

PRACTICE EXERCISE 4

Record the following transaction for Powers Company in general journal form.

July 14 Sold merchandise on account to C. Heald, invoice no. D446, $560 plus $44.80 sales tax.

PRACTICE EXERCISE 4 SOLUTION

GENERAL JOURNAL PAGE ____

Date		Description	Post. Ref.	Debit	Credit
20—					
July	14	Accounts Receivable, C. Heald		604 80	
		Sales			560 00
		Sales Tax Payable			44 80
		Sold merchandise to C. Heald,			
		invoice no. D446.			

LEARNING OBJECTIVE

6 Journalize purchase transactions in a general journal, and post to the accounts payable ledger and general ledger.

Purchase transactions are recorded in the general journal by debiting the Purchases account and crediting Accounts Payable. If the company pays for freight, the company will also record a debit to Freight In. The purchase transactions are posted to the general ledger as a debit to Purchases, a debit to Freight In, and a credit to Accounts Payable. Each transaction must also be posted daily to the **accounts payable ledger**.

PRACTICE EXERCISE 5

Record the following transaction for Byrne Corporation in general journal form:

Apr. 14 Bought merchandise on account from Jabari, Inc., invoice no. C3009, $1,125; terms net 30 days; dated April 12; FOB shipping point, freight prepaid and added to the invoice, $72.50 (total $1,197.50).

PRACTICE EXERCISE 5 SOLUTION

GENERAL JOURNAL PAGE ____

Date		Description	Post. Ref.	Debit	Credit
20—					
Apr.	14	Purchases		1 1 2 5 00	
		Freight In		7 2 50	
		Accounts Payable, Jabari, Inc.			1 1 9 7 50
		Purchased merchandise from			
		Jabari, Inc., invoice no. C3009,			
		invoice dated 4/12, terms n/30.			

7 LEARNING OBJECTIVE

Prepare a schedule of accounts payable.

A schedule of accounts payable, listing the balance of each individual creditor's account, is prepared from the accounts payable ledger.

PRACTICE EXERCISE 6

Fill in the missing amounts in the accounts payable subsidiary ledgers for Updike Train Supply. Then, using the information from the ledgers, prepare a schedule of accounts payable.

ACCOUNTS PAYABLE LEDGER

NAME J. Fletcher and Sons
ADDRESS 326 Fairway Drive
Richmond, CA 94805

Date		Item	Post. Ref.	Debit	Credit	Balance
20—						
June	1		J73		1 7 5 1 55	1 7 5 1 55
	14		J73	1 5 7 6 15		(a)

NAME Rocky and Schlink
ADDRESS 542 Roselle Blvd.
Oakland, CA 94601

Date		Item	Post. Ref.	Debit	Credit	Balance
20—						
June	13		J73		2 1 8 00	2 1 8 00

NAME Tan Supplies
ADDRESS 120 Fish Road
Berkeley, CA 94720

Date		Item	Post. Ref.	Debit	Credit	Balance
20—						
June	5		J73		2,710.00	2,710.00
	23		J73		1,740.25	(b)
	29		J73	1,500.00		(c)

PRACTICE EXERCISE 6 SOLUTION

(a) $175.40
(b) $4,450.25
(c) $2,950.25

Updike Train Supply
Schedule of Accounts Payable
June 30, 20—

J. Fletcher and Sons	$ 175.40
Rocky and Schlink	218.00
Tan Supplies	2,950.25
Total Accounts Payable	$3,343.65

LEARNING OBJECTIVE 8

Journalize transactions involving purchases returns and allowances in a general journal, and post to the accounts payable ledger and general ledger.

When a credit memo is received for the return of merchandise or as an allowance for damaged goods, the buyer credits Purchase Returns and Allowances. If the merchandise was bought on account, the buyer debits Accounts Payable. The entry is recorded in the general journal and posted to both the general ledger and the accounts receivable ledger.

PRACTICE EXERCISE 7

Refer to the transaction in Practice Exercise 5. Assume that on April 24, Byrne Corporation received credit memo no. 117 from Jabari, Inc., for merchandise returned, $127. Record the transaction for the purchase return.

CHAPTER REVIEW

PRACTICE EXERCISE 7 SOLUTION

GENERAL JOURNAL PAGE ____

Date		Description	Post. Ref.	Debit	Credit
20—					
Apr.	24	Accounts Payable, Jabari, Inc.		127 00	
		Purchases Returns and			
		Allowances			127 00
		Credit memo no. 117 for			
		return of merchandise.			

9 LEARNING OBJECTIVE

Describe the procedures for handling freight charges on merchandise and other goods.

The Freight In account is debited for the cost of transportation charges on incoming merchandise intended for resale. Freight costs that apply to non-merchandise assets purchased are added to the asset account that applies.

PRACTICE EXERCISE 8

a. Who pays the freight when the terms of sale are FOB shipping point?
b. Who pays the freight when the terms of the sale are FOB destination?

PRACTICE EXERCISE 8 SOLUTION

a. Buyer
b. Seller

10 LEARNING OBJECTIVE

Journalize transactions in a sales journal, and post to the accounts receivable ledger and general ledger.

The **sales journal** is used to record only sales of merchandise on account. The entries are posted daily to the accounts receivable ledger. At the end of the month, the total is posted to the general ledger as a debit to the Accounts Receivable controlling account and a credit to the Sales account.

PRACTICE EXERCISE 9

Record the following sales of merchandise on account on page 25 of the sales journal and then post to the general ledger. (The company uses the same account numbers as Whitewater Raft Supply.)

Apr. 1 Sold merchandise on account to West Company, invoice no. 1054, $1,378.95.

15 Sold merchandise on account to Ruiz Company, invoice no. 1055, $578.15.

PRACTICE EXERCISE 9 SOLUTION

SALES JOURNAL — PAGE 25

Date		Inv. No.	Customer's Name	Post. Ref.	Accounts Receivable Dr. Sales Cr.
20—					
Apr.	1	1054	West Company		1 3 7 8 95
	15	1055	Ruiz Company		5 7 8 15
	30		Total		1 9 5 7 10
					(113) (411)

GENERAL LEDGER

ACCOUNT Accounts Receivable — ACCOUNT NO. 113

Date		Item	Post. Ref.	Debit	Credit	Balance Debit	Balance Credit
20—							
Apr.	30		S25	1 9 5 7 10		1 9 5 7 10	

ACCOUNT Sales — ACCOUNT NO. 411

Date		Item	Post. Ref.	Debit	Credit	Balance Debit	Balance Credit
20—							
Apr.	30		S25		1 9 5 7 10		1 9 5 7 10

11 LEARNING OBJECTIVE

Journalize transactions in a three-column purchases journal, and post to the accounts payable ledger and general ledger.

The three-column **purchases journal** handles the purchase of merchandise on account and freight charges that are prepaid by the seller and included in the invoice total. Amounts in the Accounts Payable credit column are posted daily to the accounts payable ledger. At the end of the month, the totals are posted to the general ledger as a debit to Purchases, a debit to Freight In, and a credit to Accounts Payable.

PRACTICE EXERCISE 10

Record the following purchases of merchandise on account on page 52 of the purchases journal and then post to the general ledger. (The company uses the same account numbers as Whitewater Raft Supply.)

Jan. 4 Bought merchandise on account from Switzer Corporation, invoice no. A459, $578; terms net 60 days; dated January 2; FOB destination.

24 Bought merchandise on account from Stevens Company, invoice no. 48512, $799.80; terms 2/10, n/30; dated January 22; FOB shipping point, freight prepaid and added to the invoice, $50 (total $849.80).

PRACTICE EXERCISE 10 SOLUTION

PURCHASES JOURNAL — PAGE 52

Date		Supplier's Name	Inv. No.	Inv. Date	Terms	Post. Ref.	Accounts Payable Credit	Freight In Debit	Purchases Debit
20—									
Jan.	4	Switzer Corporation	A459	1/2	n/60		578 00		578 00
	24	Stevens Company	48512	1/22	2/10, n/30		849 80	50 00	799 80
	31	Totals					1,427 80	50 00	1,377 80
							(212)	(514)	(511)

GENERAL LEDGER

ACCOUNT Accounts Payable — ACCOUNT NO. 212

Date		Item	Post. Ref.	Debit	Credit	Balance Debit	Balance Credit
20—							
Jan.	31		P52		1,427 80		1,427 80

ACCOUNT Purchases — ACCOUNT NO. 511

Date		Item	Post. Ref.	Debit	Credit	Balance Debit	Balance Credit
20—							
Jan.	31		P52	1,377 80		1,377 80	

ACCOUNT Freight In — ACCOUNT NO. 514

Date		Item	Post. Ref.	Debit	Credit	Balance Debit	Balance Credit
20—							
Jan.	31		P52	50 00		50 00	

Glossary

Accounts payable ledger A subsidiary ledger that lists the individual accounts of creditors in either alphabetical or numerical order with their respective balances. *(p. 342)*

Accounts receivable ledger A subsidiary ledger that lists the individual accounts of credit customers in either alphabetical or numerical order, with their respective transactions and balances. *(p. 333)*

Controlling account An account in the general ledger that summarizes the balances of a subsidiary ledger. *(p. 334)*

Credit memorandum A written statement indicating a seller's willingness to reduce the amount of a buyer's debt. The seller records the amount of the credit memorandum in the Sales Returns and Allowances account. *(p. 335)*

FOB destination Shipping terms under which the seller pays the freight charges and includes them in the selling price. Title or ownership changes hands when the buyer receives the goods. *(p. 346)*

FOB shipping point Shipping terms under which the buyer pays the freight charges between the point of shipment and the destination. Payment may be made directly to the carrier upon receiving the goods or to the supplier if the supplier prepaid the freight charges on behalf of the buyer. Title or ownership changes hands when goods are transferred to the freight company. *(p. 346)*

Freight In account The account used to record transportation charges on incoming merchandise intended for resale. *(p. 329)*

Invoices Business forms prepared by the seller that list the items shipped, their cost, the terms of the sale, and the mode of shipment. They may also state the freight charges. The buyer considers them purchase invoices; the seller considers them sales invoices. *(p. 330)*

Merchandise inventory Goods (an asset account) that a company buys and intends to resell at a profit. *(p. 329)*

Merchandising businesses Businesses that buy and sell goods. *(p. 329)*

Periodic inventory system A method of recording inventory that requires the company to determine the amount of goods on hand by periodically taking a physical count and then attaching a value to it. *(p. 329)*

Perpetual inventory system A method of recording inventory that provides the firm with a running balance of inventory. *(p. 329)*

Purchase order A written order from the buyer of goods to the supplier, listing the items wanted and the terms of the transaction. *(p. 339)*

Purchase requisition A form used to request that the Purchasing Department buy something. This form is intended for internal use within a company. *(p. 339)*

Purchases account An account for recording the cost of merchandise acquired for resale. *(p. 329)*

Purchases Discounts account An account that records cash discounts granted by suppliers in return for prompt payment; it is treated as a deduction from Purchases. *(p. 329)*

Purchases journal A special journal used to record only the buying of goods on account. It may be used to record the purchase of merchandise only. *(p. 351)*

Purchases Returns and Allowances account An account that records a company's return of merchandise it has purchased or a reduction in the bill because of damaged merchandise; it is treated as a deduction from Purchases. *(p. 329)*

Retail business A business that sells goods directly to consumers. *(p. 329)*

Sales account A revenue account for recording the sale of merchandise. *(p. 329)*

Sales Discounts account An account that records a deduction from the original price, granted by the seller to the buyer for the prompt payment of an invoice. *(p. 329)*

Sales journal A special journal for recording only the sale of merchandise on account. *(p. 348)*

Sales Returns and Allowances account The account a seller uses to record the physical return of merchandise by customers or a reduction in a bill because merchandise was damaged. Sales Returns and Allowances is treated as a deduction from Sales. This account is usually evidenced by a credit memorandum issued by the seller. *(p. 329)*

Sales Tax Payable account An account used to record a tax levied by a state or city government on the retail sale of goods and services. The tax is paid by the consumer but collected by the retailer. *(p. 329)*

Special journals Books of original entry in which specialized types of repetitive transactions are recorded. *(p. 348)*

Subsidiary ledger A group of accounts representing individual subdivisions showing the debits and credits of a controlling account. *(p. 334)*

Summarizing entry An entry made to post the column totals of a special journal to the appropriate accounts in the general ledger. *(p. 349)*

Wholesale business A business that buys goods from manufacturers and sells those goods (normally in large quantities) to retailers for resale. *(p. 329)*

CHAPTER ASSIGNMENTS

Discussion Questions

1. What is the difference between a wholesale business and a retail business?
2. For each of the following accounts, identify if the normal balance is a debit or credit. Also, specify if the account is a contra account.
   a. Sales Returns and Allowances
   b. Merchandise Inventory
   c. Sales

d. Freight In
e. Purchases Returns and Allowances
f. Sales Tax Payable
g. Sales Discounts
h. Purchases
i. Purchases Discounts

3. What is the purpose of a:
   a. Schedule of accounts receivable?
   b. Schedule of accounts payable?
4. Why is an accounts receivable ledger or an accounts payable ledger necessary for a business with large numbers of credit customers or large numbers of vendors/suppliers?
5. Why is it a good practice to post daily to the accounts receivable or accounts payable ledgers?
6. With regard to goods sold and purchased, explain how sales returns and allowances and purchases returns and allowances are different from each other.
7. Explain the meaning and importance of the shipping terms FOB destination and FOB shipping point. Who has title to the goods once they have been shipped?
8. Describe the four procedures that most companies follow to maintain internal control of purchases of merchandise.
9. Describe the posting procedures to the general ledger and the rules for totaling and ruling the:
   a. Sales journal.
   b. Purchases journal.
10. Describe the procedure for posting:
    a. From the sales journal to the accounts receivable ledger.
    b. From the purchases journal to the accounts payable ledger.

Exercises

LO 2,4

PRACTICE EXERCISES 1,3

EXERCISE 9-1 Record the following transactions in general journal form.

a. Sold merchandise on account to G. Frank, invoice no. 1230, $1,233.50.
b. Sold merchandise on account to Gregory Productions, invoice no. 1231, $950.00.
c. Gregory Productions returned $615.75 worth of the merchandise. Issued credit memo no. 93.

2,4

PRACTICE EXERCISES 1,3

EXERCISE 9-2 Post the following entry to the general ledger and subsidiary ledger.

GENERAL JOURNAL PAGE 52

Date		Description	Post. Ref.	Debit	Credit
20—					
June	16	Sales Returns and Allowances		241 27	
		Accounts Receivable, F. E. Dixon			241 27
		Issued credit memo no. 131.			

CHAPTER ASSIGNMENTS

GENERAL LEDGER

ACCOUNT Accounts Receivable ACCOUNT NO. 113

Date		Item	Post. Ref.	Debit	Credit	Balance Debit	Balance Credit
20—							
June	1	Balance	✓			6 5 1 1 19	

ACCOUNT Sales Returns and Allowances ACCOUNT NO. 412

Date		Item	Post. Ref.	Debit	Credit	Balance Debit	Balance Credit
20—							
June	1	Balance	✓			3 1 4 60	

ACCOUNTS RECEIVABLE LEDGER

NAME F. E. Dixon
ADDRESS 416 Fifth Avenue
Dallas, TX 75204

Date		Item	Post. Ref.	Debit	Credit	Balance
20—						
May	31		J51	3 1 2 60		3 1 2 60

5 

PRACTICE EXERCISE 4

EXERCISE 9-3 Describe the transactions recorded in the following T accounts.

Accounts Receivable			
(a)	967.50	(b)	53.70

Sales			
		(a)	900.00

Sales Tax Payable			
(b)	3.75	(a)	67.50

Sales Returns and Allowances			
(b)	49.95		

5 

PRACTICE EXERCISE 4

EXERCISE 9-4 Record the following transactions in general journal form.

a. Sold merchandise on account to A. Bauer, $680 plus $54.40 sales tax (invoice no. D446).

b. Bauer returned $105.50 of the merchandise. Issued credit memo no. 114 for $113.94 ($105.50 for the amount of the sale plus $8.44 for the amount of the sales tax).

LO 6,8

PRACTICE EXERCISES 5,7

EXERCISE 9-5 Describe the transactions recorded in the following T accounts.

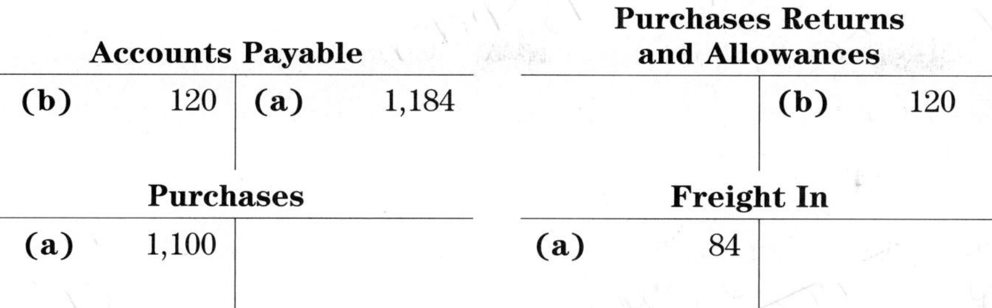

Accounts Payable			
(b)	120	(a)	1,184

Purchases Returns and Allowances			
		(b)	120

Purchases			
(a)	1,100		

Freight In			
(a)	84		

LO 6,8

PRACTICE EXERCISES 5,7

EXERCISE 9-6 Journalize the following transactions in general journal form.

a. Bought merchandise on account from Brewer, Inc., invoice no. B2997, $914; terms net 30 days; FOB destination.
b. Received credit memo no. 96 from Brewer, Inc., for merchandise returned, $238.

LO 6,8

PRACTICE EXERCISES 5,7

EXERCISE 9-7 Post the following entry to the general ledger and the subsidiary ledger.

GENERAL JOURNAL PAGE 92

Date		Description	Post. Ref.	Debit	Credit
20—					
July	14	Accounts Payable, Jensen and Silva		192 30	
		Purchases Returns and			
		Allowances			192 30
		Credit memo no. 942 for			
		return of merchandise.			

GENERAL LEDGER

ACCOUNT Accounts Payable ACCOUNT NO. 212

Date		Item	Post. Ref.	Debit	Credit	Balance Debit	Balance Credit
20—							
July	1	Balance	✓				2761 24

ACCOUNT Purchases Returns and Allowances ACCOUNT NO. 512

Date		Item	Post. Ref.	Debit	Credit	Balance Debit	Balance Credit
20—							
July	1	Balance	✓				230 16

CHAPTER ASSIGNMENTS

ACCOUNTS PAYABLE LEDGER

NAME Jensen and Silva
ADDRESS 542 Roselle Blvd.
Chicago, IL 60141

Date		Item	Post. Ref.	Debit	Credit	Balance
20—						
June	13		J92		2 1 8 00	2 1 8 00

2,4,6,8 LO

PRACTICE EXERCISES 1,3,5,7

EXERCISE 9-8 Record the following transactions in general journal form for Ford Education Outfitters and Romero Textbooks, Inc.

a. Ford Educational Outfitters bought merchandise on account from Romero Textbooks, Inc., invoice no. 10594, $1,875.34; terms net 30 days; FOB destination. Romero Textbooks, Inc., paid $93.80 for shipping.
b. Ford Education Outfitters received credit memo no. 513A from Romero Textbooks, Inc., for merchandise returned, $135.78.

4,8 

PRACTICE EXERCISES 3,7

EXERCISE 9-9 Using the following source document (credit memo issued by Chang Electronics), record the transaction in general journal form on the books of Chang Electronics, then on the books of The Merchandise Market.

Chang Electronics
4160 Broad Street
Chicago, Illinois 60627

CREDIT MEMORANDUM No. **121**

DATE: **November 6, 20—**

CREDIT TO:
The Merchandise Market
2241 Sullivan Street
Chicago, Illinois 60632

Your account has been credited for:

1 CPU tower $725.50

10 

PRACTICE EXERCISE 9

EXERCISE 9-10 Toby Company had the following sales transactions for the month of March:

Mar. 6 Sold merchandise on account to Osbourne, Inc., invoice no. 1128, $563.17.
14 Sold merchandise on account to Ortiz Company, invoice no. 1129, $823.50.
20 Sold merchandise on account to Bailey Corporation, invoice no. 1130, $2,350.98.
24 Sold merchandise on account to Shannon Corporation, invoice no. 1131, $1,547.07.

CHAPTER ASSIGNMENTS

Assume that Toby Company had beginning balances on March 1 of $3,569.80 (Sales 411) and $2,450.39 (Accounts Receivable 113). Record the sales of merchandise on account in the sales journal (page 24) and then post to the general ledger.

LO 11

PRACTICE EXERCISE 10

EXERCISE 9-11 Williams Corporation had the following purchases for the month of May:

May 3 Bought ten lawn rakes from Owens Company, invoice no. J34Y9, $250.25; terms net 15 days; dated May 1; FOB shipping point, freight prepaid and added to the invoice, $15 (total $265.25).

11 Bought one weedeater from Lionel's Lawn & Landscaping, invoice no. R7740, $219.72; terms 2/10, n/30; dated May 9; FOB shipping point, freight prepaid and added to the invoice, $35 (total $254.72).

15 Bought five bags of fertilizer from Wright's Farm Supplies, invoice no. 478, $210.97; terms net 30 days; dated May 13; FOB destination.

25 Bought one lawnmower from Gutierrez Corporation, invoice no. 2458, $425.39; terms net 30 days; dated May 22; FOB destination.

Assume that Williams Corporation had beginning balances on May 1 of $3,492.29 (Accounts Payable 212), $4,239.49 (Purchases 511), and $234.89 (Freight In 514). Record the purchases of merchandise on account in the purchases journal (page 13) and then post to the general ledger.

LO 3,7,10,11

PRACTICE EXERCISES 2,6,9,10

EXERCISE 9-12 Kelley Company has completed October's sales and purchases journals (see below and on the following page). Your job is to:

a. Total and post the journals to T accounts for the general ledger and the accounts receivable and accounts payable ledgers.
b. Complete a schedule of accounts receivable for October 31, 20—.
c. Complete a schedule of accounts payable for October 31, 20—.
d. Compare the balances of the schedules with their respective general ledger accounts. If they are not the same, find and correct the error(s).

SALES JOURNAL PAGE 18

Date		Inv. No.	Customer's Name	Post. Ref.	Accounts Receivable Dr. Sales Cr.
20—					
Oct.	3	414	Anderson Company		443 24
	4	415	R. T. Holcomb		1426 90
	7	416	Gray and Malo		1647 00
	11	417	Mercer Mobil		3112 16
	16	418	J. L. Anthony		2130 00
	22	419	C. A. Goldschmidt		1944 05
	31	420	F. A. Baumann		2791 00
	31		Total		
					( ) ( )

PURCHASES JOURNAL PAGE 10

Date		Supplier's Name	Inv. No.	Inv. Date	Terms	Post. Ref.	Accounts Payable Credit	Freight In Debit	Purchases Debit
20—									
Oct.	2	Colter, Inc.	2706	7/31	2/10, n/30		759 00	49 00	710 00
	3	Thomas and Son	982	8/2	n/30		829 00	57 00	772 00
	5	Archer Manufacturing Co.	10611	8/3	2/10, n/30		564 00		564 00
	9	Spence Products Co.	B643	8/6	1/10, n/30		165 00	10 00	155 00
	18	L. C. Walter	46812	8/17	n/60		228 00		228 00
	25	Delaney and Cox	1024	8/23	2/10, n/30		376 00	14 00	362 00
	26	Colter, Inc.	2801	8/25	2/10, n/30		406 00	22 00	384 00
	31	Totals							
							( )	( )	( )

Problem Set A

For additional help, see the demonstration problem at the beginning of each chapter in your Working Papers.

PROBLEM 9-1A Bell Florists sells flowers on a retail basis. Most of the sales are for cash; however, a few steady customers have credit accounts. Bell's sales staff fills out a sales slip for each sale. There is a state retail sales tax of 5 percent, which is collected by the retailer and submitted to the state. The following represent Bell Florists' charge sales for March:

Mar. 4 Sold potted plant on account to C. Morales, sales slip no. 242, \$27, plus sales tax of \$1.35, total \$28.35.

6 Sold floral arrangement on account to R. Dixon, sales slip no. 267, \$54, plus sales tax of \$2.70, total \$56.70.

12 Sold corsage on account to B. Cox, sales slip no. 279, \$16, plus sales tax of \$0.80, total \$16.80.

16 Sold wreath on account to All-Star Legion, sales slip no. 296, \$104, plus sales tax of \$5.20, total \$109.20.

18 Sold floral arrangements on account to Tucker Funeral Home, sales slip no. 314, \$260, plus sales tax of \$13, total \$273.00.

21 Tucker Funeral Home complained about a wrinkled ribbon on the floral arrangement. Bell Florists allowed a \$30 credit, plus the sales tax of \$1.50, credit memo no. 27.

23 Sold flower arrangements on account to Price Savings and Loan Association for their fifth anniversary, sales slip no. 337, \$180, plus sales tax of \$9, total \$189.

24 Allowed Price Savings and Loan Association credit, \$25, plus sales tax of \$1.25, because of a few withered blossoms in floral arrangements, credit memo no. 28.

Check Figure
Schedule of Accounts Receivable total, \$726.52

Required

1. Record these transactions in the general journal (pages 57 and 58).
2. Post the amounts from the general journal to the general ledger and accounts receivable ledger; Accounts Receivable 113, Sales Tax Payable 214, Sales 411, Sales Returns and Allowances 412.
3. Prepare a schedule of accounts receivable and compare its total with the balance of the Accounts Receivable controlling account.

LO 6,7,8

PROBLEM 9-2A Berry's Pet Store records purchase transactions in the general journal. The company is located in Boston, Massachusetts. In addition to a general ledger, Berry's Pet Store also uses an accounts payable ledger. Transactions for April related to the purchase of merchandise are as follows:

Apr. 2 Bought ten Carefree Pet Bedding bags from Blackburn Company, $399.90, invoice no. 4R48, dated April 1; terms net 30 days; FOB destination.

5 Bought seven Marine Betta Kits from Herrera Company, $83.93, invoice no. 4851, dated April 3; terms 2/10, n/30; FOB shipping point, freight prepaid and added to the invoice, $15 (total $98.93).

6 Bought fifteen Two Door Deluxe Kennels from Barrett, Inc., $719.85, invoice no. 1845R, dated April 5; terms 1/10, n/30; FOB destination.

8 Bought five Dome Top Bird Cages from Faulkner Company, $1,849.95, invoice no. 1485, dated April 7; terms 2/10, n/30; FOB shipping point, freight prepaid and added to the invoice, $76 (total $1,925.95).

13 Received credit memo no. 415 from Faulkner Company for merchandise returned, $589.13.

23 Bought three Five Tiered Cat Trees from Rhodes Manufacturing, $1,107, invoice no. 246J, dated April 21; terms net 60 days; FOB destination.

27 Bought thirty Glitter Collection Leashes from Solomon Products Company, $299.70, invoice no. 2675, dated April 25; terms net 30 days; FOB destination.

30 Received credit memo no. 861 from Solomon Products Company for merchandise returned, $76.25.

Required

Check Figure
Accounts Payable account balance, $7,048.50 credit

1. Open the following accounts in the accounts payable ledger and record the April 1 balances, if any, as given: Barrett, Inc., $185.25; Blackburn Company, $254.64; Faulkner Company, $485.12; Herrera Company; Rhodes Manufacturing, $452.31; Solomon Products Company, $1,785.23. For the accounts having balances, write "Balance" in the Item column and place a check mark in the Post. Ref. column.
2. Record the April 1 balances in the general ledger as given: Accounts Payable 212 controlling account, $3,162.55; Purchases 511, $559.06; Purchases Returns and Allowances 512, $123.50; Freight In 514, $15.20. Write "Balance" in the Item column and place a check mark in the Post. Ref. column.
3. Record the transactions in the general journal beginning on page 115.
4. Post to the general ledger and the accounts payable ledger.
5. Prepare a schedule of accounts payable, and compare the balance of the Accounts Payable controlling account with the total of the schedule of accounts payable.

LO 2,3,4,5,6,7,8

PROBLEM 9-3A Shirley's Beauty Store records sales and purchase transactions in the general journal. In addition to a general ledger, Shirley's Beauty Store also uses an accounts receivable ledger and an accounts payable ledger. Transactions for January related to the sales and purchase of merchandise are as follows:

Jan. 3 Bought thirty Mango Bath and Shower Gels from Madden, Inc., $660.00, invoice no. 3487, dated January 1; terms 2/10, n/30; FOB shipping point, freight prepaid and added to the invoice, $125.43 (total $785.43).

4 Bought ten Beauty Candle Travel Sets from Calhoun Candles, Inc., $420.00, invoice no. 4513, dated January 1; terms net 45; FOB destination.

12 Sold four Mango Bath and Shower Gels on account to R. Kielman, sales slip no. 1456, $120, plus sales tax of $9.60, total $129.60.

Jan. 13 Received credit memo no. 8715 from Calhoun Candles, Inc., for merchandise returned, $84.

21 Bought five Winter Skin Essentials Kits from Whitney and Waters, $197.50, invoice no. A875, dated January 18; terms 2/15, n/45; FOB destination.

25 Sold three Winter Skin Essentials on account to A. Benner, sales slip no. 1457, $135.75, plus sales tax of $10.86, total $146.61.

27 Issued credit memo no. 33 to A. Benner for merchandise returned, $45.25 plus $3.62 sales tax, total $48.87.

Check Figure
Schedule of Accounts Payable total, $2,297.56

Required

1. Open the following accounts in the accounts receivable ledger and record the balances as of January 1: A. Benner, $45.77; R. Kielman, $175.39. Write "Balance" in the Item column and place a check mark in the Post. Ref. column.
2. Open the following accounts in the accounts payable ledger and record the balances as of January 1: Calhoun Candles, Inc., $355.23; Madden, Inc., $573.15; Whitney and Waters, $50.25. Write "Balance" in the Item column and place a check mark in the Post. Ref. column.
3. Record the January 1 balances in the general ledger as given: Accounts Receivable 113 controlling account, $221.16; Accounts Payable 212 controlling account, $978.63; Sales Tax Payable 214, $128.45. Write "Balance" in the Item column and place a check mark in the Post. Ref. column.
4. Record the transactions in the general journal beginning on page 25.
5. Post the entries to the general journal and accounts receivable ledger or accounts payable ledger, as appropriate.
6. Prepare a schedule of accounts receivable.
7. Prepare a schedule of accounts payable.
8. Compare the totals of the schedules with the balances of the controlling accounts.

PROBLEM 9-4A Gomez Company sells electrical supplies on a wholesale basis. The following transactions took place during April of this year:

Apr. 1 Sold merchandise on account to Myers Company, invoice no. 761, $570.40.

5 Sold merchandise on account to L. R. Foster Company, invoice no. 762, $486.10.

6 Issued credit memo no. 50 to Myers Company for merchandise returned, $40.70.

10 Sold merchandise on account to Diaz Hardware, invoice no. 763, $293.35.

14 Sold merchandise on account to Brooks and Bennett, invoice no. 764, $640.16.

17 Sold merchandise on account to Powell and Reyes, invoice no. 765, $582.12.

21 Issued credit memo no. 51 to Brooks and Bennett for merchandise returned, $68.44.

24 Sold merchandise on account to Ortiz Company, invoice no. 766, $652.87.

26 Sold merchandise on account to Diaz Hardware, invoice no. 767, $832.19.

30 Issued credit memo no. 52 to Diaz Hardware for damage to merchandise, $98.50.

Check Figure
Accounts Receivable account balance, $5,018.97 debit

Required

1. Record these sales of merchandise on account in the sales journal (page 39). Record the sales returns and allowances in the general journal (page 74).

2. Immediately after recording each transaction, post to the accounts receivable ledger.
3. Post the amounts from the general journal daily. Post the sales journal amount as a total at the end of the month; Accounts Receivable 113, Sales 411, Sales Returns and Allowances 412.
4. Prepare a schedule of accounts receivable. Compare the balance of the Accounts Receivable controlling account with the total of the schedule of accounts receivable.

LO 7,11

PROBLEM 9-5A Patterson Appliance uses a three-column purchases journal. The company is located in Fresno, California. In addition to a general ledger, Patterson Appliance also uses an accounts payable ledger. Transactions for January related to the purchase of merchandise are as follows:

Jan.	2	Bought eighty 12-inch, 3-speed Brighton Oscillating Fans from Snyder and Jordan, $1,890, invoice no. 268J, dated January 2; terms net 60 days; FOB Fresno.
	4	Bought ten 35-pint-capacity Crystal Humidifiers from Simpson Company, $2,300, invoice no. 39426, dated January 2; terms 2/10, n/30; FOB Durango, freight prepaid and added to the invoice, $90 (total $2,390).
	7	Bought ten 16-inch Axel Window Fans from Tran, Inc., $360, invoice no. 452AD, dated January 6; terms 1/10, n/30; FOB Fresno.
	10	Bought twenty-four 4-blade Tiempo Ceiling Fans, Model 2760, from Ukele Company, $3,550, invoice no. D7742, dated January 7; terms 2/10, n/30; FOB Sacramento, freight prepaid and added to the invoice, $84 (total $3,634).
	14	Bought four Charger Electric Hedge Trimmers from Fernandez Products Company, $186, invoice no. 2542, dated January 13; terms net 30 days; FOB Fresno.
	22	Bought forty Lindon Electric Bug Killers from Snyder and Jordan, $2,265, invoice no. 392J, dated January 22; terms net 60 days; FOB Fresno.
	28	Bought ten Charger Electric Blowers from Fernandez Products Company, $830, invoice no. 2691, dated January 27; terms net 30 days; FOB Fresno.
	30	Bought ten Kole Powered Attic Ventilators from Porter Company, $446, invoice no. 664CC, dated January 27; terms 2/10, n/30; FOB Seattle, freight prepaid and added to the invoice, $48 (total $494).

Required

Check Figure
Accounts Payable account balance, $12,608.06 credit

1. Open the following accounts in the accounts payable ledger and record the January 1 balances, if any, as given: Fernandez Products Company; Porter Company, $163.17; Simpson Company, $167.19; Snyder and Jordan; Tran, Inc., $228.70; Ukele Company. For the accounts having balances, write "Balance" in the Item column and place a check mark in the Post. Ref. column.
2. Record the balance of $559.06 in the Accounts Payable 212 controlling account as of January 1. Write "Balance" in the Item column and place a check mark in the Post. Ref. column.
3. Record the transactions in the purchases journal beginning on page 81.
4. Post to the accounts payable ledger daily.
5. Post to the general ledger at the end of the month.
6. Prepare a schedule of accounts payable, and compare the balance of the Accounts Payable controlling account with the total of the schedule of accounts payable.

2,3,4,6,7,8,10,11 

PROBLEM 9-6A The following transactions relate to Reynolds Company during April of this year. Terms of sale are 2/10, n/30. The company is located in Atlanta.

Apr. 2 Sold merchandise on account to Shaw Company, invoice no. 1126, $1,746.

4 Bought merchandise on account from Payne Company, invoice no. 16521, $800; terms 1/10, n/30; dated April 2; FOB Atlanta.

9 Sold merchandise on account to Peterson and Black, invoice no. 1127, $860.

12 Bought merchandise on account from Vix Company, invoice no. L8552, $2,482; terms 2/10, n/30; dated April 11; FOB Rome, freight prepaid and added to the invoice, $49 (total $2,531).

15 Received credit memo no. 79 for merchandise returned to Knight and Company, for $120.

17 Sold merchandise on account to C. N. Hunt, invoice no. 1128, $1,015.

19 Issued credit memo no. 34 to Peterson and Black for merchandise returned, $86.

26 Bought merchandise on account from M. R. Palmer, Inc., invoice no. 7447, $1,482; terms 2/10, n/30; dated April 23; FOB Macon, freight prepaid and added to the invoice, $45 (total $1,527).

29 Bought office supplies on account from Thornton Stationery Company, invoice no. S336, $152; terms net 30 days; dated April 29.

30 Sold merchandise on account to Sampson and McDonald, invoice no. 1129, $2,601.

30 Issued credit memo no. 35 to Sampson and McDonald for merchandise returned, $153.

Check Figure
Accounts Payable account balance, $5,268 credit

Required

1. Open the following accounts in the accounts receivable ledger and record the balances as of April 1: C. N. Hunt; Peterson and Black, $426; Sampson and McDonald, $974; Shaw Company. For the accounts having balances, write "Balance" in the Item column and place a check mark in the Post. Ref. column.
2. Open the following accounts in the accounts payable ledger and record the balances as of April 1: Knight and Company, $262; M. R. Palmer, Inc., $116; Payne Company; Thornton Stationery Company; Vix Company. For the accounts having balances, write "Balance" in the Item column and place a check mark in the Post. Ref. column.
3. Record the transactions in the sales (page 24), purchases (page 18), or general journal (page 68), as appropriate.
4. Post the entries to the accounts receivable ledger daily.
5. Post the entries to the accounts payable ledger daily.
6. Post the entries in the general journal immediately after you make each journal entry.
7. Post the totals from the special journals at the end of the month.
8. Prepare a schedule of accounts receivable.
9. Prepare a schedule of accounts payable.
10. Compare the totals of the schedules with the balances of the controlling accounts.

Problem Set B

For additional help, see the demonstration problem at the beginning of each chapter in your Working Papers.

LO 2,3,4,5

PROBLEM 9-1B Abbott Florists sells flowers on a retail basis. Most of the sales are for cash; however, a few steady customers have credit accounts. Abbott's sales staff fills out a sales slip for each sale. There is a state retail tax of 5 percent, which is collected by the retailer and submitted to the state. Abbott Florists' charge sales for March are as follows:

Mar. 4 Sold floral arrangement on account to R. Duarte, sales slip no. 236, $45, plus sales tax of $2.25, total $47.25.

7 Sold potted plant on account to C. Meadows, sales slip no. 272, $61, plus sales tax of $3.05, total $64.05.

12 Sold wreath on account to Anthony Realty, sales slip no. 294, $63, plus sales tax of $3.15, total $66.15.

17 Sold floral arrangements on account to Travis Dress Shop, sales slip no. 299, $170, plus sales tax of $8.50, total $178.50.

20 Travis Dress Shop returned a flower spray, complaining that there were dead blooms. Abbott Florists allowed a credit of $36, plus the sales tax of $1.80, credit memo no. 27.

21 Sold flower arrangements on account to Porter Computers for their anniversary, sales slip no. 310, $236, plus sales tax of $11.80, total $247.80.

22 Allowed Porter Computers credit, $25, plus sales tax of $1.25, because of withered blossoms in floral arrangements, credit memo no. 28.

27 Sold corsage on account to B. Crosby, sales slip no. 332, $30, plus sales tax of $1.50, total $31.50.

Required

1. Record these transactions in the general journal (pages 57 and 58).
2. Post the amounts from the general journal to the general ledger and accounts receivable ledger; Accounts Receivable 113, Sales Tax Payable 214, Sales 411, Sales Returns and Allowances 412.
3. Prepare a schedule of accounts receivable and compare its total with the balance of the Accounts Receivable controlling account.

Check Figure
Schedule of Accounts Receivable total, $682.42

6,7,8

PROBLEM 9-2B Lowery's Pet Depot records purchase transactions in the general journal. The company is located in Cleveland, Ohio. In addition to a general ledger, Lowery's Pet Depot also uses an accounts payable ledger. Transactions for October related to the purchase of merchandise are as follows:

Oct. 3 Bought twelve Automatic Fish Feeders from Barrera Company, $959.88, invoice no. 5493, dated October 2; terms net 30 days; FOB shipping point, freight prepaid and added to the invoice, $79.45 (total $1,039.33).

4 Bought two 18 × 18 Terrarium Stands from Hickman Company, $259.98, invoice no. 2JYX, dated October 2; terms 2/10, n/30; FOB destination.

7 Bought four Chinchilla Bath Houses from Baldwin, Inc., $67.96, invoice no. 4183, dated October 6; terms 1/10, n/30; FOB destination.

Oct. 10 Received credit memo no. 123 from Baldwin, Inc., for merchandise returned, $13.94.

14 Bought twenty Zoo Slider Hoods from Douglas, Inc., $2,599.80, invoice no. X431, dated October 12; terms 2/10, n/30; FOB shipping point, freight prepaid and added to the invoice, $140.50 (total $2,740.30).

15 Bought four Hanging Bird Baths from Krause, Inc., $71.96, invoice no. A499, dated October 11; terms net 60 days; FOB destination.

24 Bought eight Automatic Cat Litter Boxes from Villa Manufacturing, $2,399.92, invoice no. 4429, dated October 21; terms net 30 days; FOB destination.

27 Received credit memo no. 452 from Villa Manufacturing for merchandise returned, $346.78.

Check Figure
Accounts Payable account balance, $8,372.74 credit

Required

1. Open the following accounts in the accounts payable ledger and record the October 1 balances, if any, as given: Baldwin, Inc., $46.57; Barrera Company, $743.15; Douglas, Inc., $615.20; Hickman Company; Krause, Inc., $23.45; Villa Manufacturing, $725.64. For the accounts having balances, write "Balance" in the Item column and place a check mark in the Post. Ref. column.
2. Record the October 1 balances in the general ledger as given: Accounts Payable 212 controlling account, $2,154.01; Purchases 511, $2,485.12; Purchases Returns and Allowances 512, $287.52; Freight In 514, $48.57. Write "Balance" in the Item column and place a check mark in the Post. Ref. column.
3. Record the transactions in the general journal beginning on page 95.
4. Post to the general ledger and the accounts payable ledger.
5. Prepare a schedule of accounts payable, and compare the balance of the Accounts Payable controlling account with the total of the schedule of accounts payable.

2,3,4,5,6,7,8 LO

PROBLEM 9-3B May's Beauty Store records sales and purchase transactions in the general journal. In addition to a general ledger, May's Beauty Store also uses an accounts receivable ledger and an accounts payable ledger. Transactions for January related to the sales and purchase of merchandise are as follows:

Jan. 2 Bought nine Matte Nail Color Kits from Mejia, Inc., $450, invoice no. 4521, dated January 1; terms 2/10, n/30; FOB shipping point, freight prepaid and added to the invoice, $87.50 (total $537.50).

5 Bought thirty Perfume Cocktail Rings from Braun, Inc., $1,200, invoice no. 37A, dated January 3; terms 2/10, n/30; FOB destination.

8 Sold two Matte Nail Color Kits on account to J. Herbert, sales slip no. 113, $110, plus sales tax of $8.80, total $118.80.

11 Received credit memo no. 455 from Braun, Inc., for merchandise returned, $315.25.

18 Bought fifteen Eye Palettes from Vargas, Inc., $660, invoice no. 910, dated January 14; terms net 30; FOB destination.

23 Sold four Eye Palettes on account to T. Cantrell, sales slip no. 114, $200, plus sales tax of $16, total $216.

26 Issued credit memo no. 12 to T. Cantrell for merchandise returned, $50 plus $4 sales tax, total $54.

Check Figure
Schedule of Accounts Payable balance, $2,776

Required

1. Open the following accounts in the accounts receivable ledger and record the balances as of January 1: T. Cantrell, $86.99; J. Hebert, $63.47. Write "Balance" in the Item column and place a check mark in the Post. Ref. column.
2. Open the following accounts in the accounts payable ledger and record the balances as of January 1: Braun, Inc., $513.20; Mejia, Inc., $113.40; Vargas, Inc.,

$67.15. Write "Balance" in the Item column and place a check mark in the Post. Ref. column.

3. Record the January 1 balances in the general ledger as given: Accounts Receivable 113 controlling account, $150.46; Accounts Payable 212 controlling account, $693.75; Sales Tax Payable 214, $237.89. Write "Balance" in the Item column and place a check mark in the Post. Ref. column.
4. Record the transactions in the general journal beginning on page 17.
5. Post the entries to the general journal and accounts receivable ledger or accounts payable ledger, as appropriate.
6. Prepare a schedule of accounts receivable.
7. Prepare a schedule of accounts payable.
8. Compare the totals of the schedules with the balances of the controlling accounts.

LO 2,3,4,10

PROBLEM 9-4B R. J. Hinton Company sells electrical supplies on a wholesale basis. The following transactions took place during April of this year.

Apr. 3 Sold merchandise on account to Maxwell Company, invoice no. 822, $652.80.

7 Sold merchandise on account to B. A. Fitzpatrick Company, invoice no. 823, $462.15.

8 Sold merchandise on account to Durham Hardware, invoice no. 824, $205.60.

13 Issued credit memo no. 61 to B. A. Fitzpatrick Company for merchandise returned, $136.50.

15 Sold merchandise on account to Briggs and Campos, invoice no. 825, $831.47.

21 Sold merchandise on account to Pena and Carr, invoice no. 826, $590.34.

24 Issued credit memo no. 62 to Briggs and Campos for merchandise returned, $80.45.

26 Sold merchandise on account to O'Neill Company, invoice no. 827, $569.90.

28 Issued credit memo no. 63 to Durham Hardware for damage to merchandise, $52.48.

30 Sold merchandise on account to Durham Hardware, invoice no. 828, $735.50.

Required

1. Record these sales of merchandise on account in the sales journal (page 39). Record the sales returns and allowances in the general journal (page 74).
2. Immediately after recording each transaction, post to the accounts receivable ledger.
3. Post the amounts from the general journal daily. Post the sales journal amount as a total at the end of the month; Accounts Receivable 113, Sales 411, Sales Returns and Allowances 412.
4. Prepare a schedule of accounts receivable. Compare the balance of the Accounts Receivable controlling account with the total of the schedule of accounts receivable.

Check Figure
Accounts Receivable account balance, $4,947.75 debit

7,11 LO

PROBLEM 9-5B West Bicycle Shop uses a three-column purchases journal. The company is located in Topeka, Kansas. In addition to a general ledger, the company also uses an accounts payable ledger. Transactions for January related to the purchase of merchandise are as follows:

Jan. 4 Bought fifty 10-speed bicycles from Nielsen Company, $4,775, invoice no. 26145, dated January 3; terms net 60 days; FOB Topeka.

7 Bought tires from Barton Tire Company, $792, invoice no. 9763, dated January 5; terms 2/10, n/30; FOB Topeka.

8 Bought bicycle lights and reflectors from Gross Products Company, $384, invoice no. 17317, dated January 6; terms net 30 days; FOB Topeka.

11 Bought hand brakes from Bray, Inc., $470, invoice no. 291GE, dated January 9; terms 1/10, n/30; FOB Kansas City, freight prepaid and added to the invoice, $36 (total $506).

19 Bought handle grips from Gross Products Company, $96.50, invoice no. 17520, dated January 17; terms net 30 days; FOB Topeka.

24 Bought thirty 5-speed bicycles from Nielsen Company, $1,487, invoice no. 26942, dated January 23; terms net 60 days; FOB Topeka.

29 Bought knapsacks from Davila Manufacturing Company, $304.80, invoice no. 762AC, dated January 26; terms 2/10, n/30; FOB Topeka.

31 Bought locks from Lamb Safety Net, $415.47, invoice no. 27712, dated January 26; terms 2/10, n/30; FOB Dodge City, freight prepaid and added to the invoice, $22 (total $437.47).

Check Figure
Accounts Payable account balance, $9,205.85 credit

Required

1. Open the following accounts in the accounts payable ledger and record the January 1 balances, if any, as given: Barton Tire Company, $156; Bray, Inc.; Davila Manufacturing Company, $82.88; Gross Products Company; Lamb Safety Net, $184.20; Nielsen Company. For the accounts having balances, write “Balance” in the Item column and place a check mark in the Post. Ref. column.
2. Record the balance of $423.08 in the Accounts Payable 212 controlling account as of January 1. Write “Balance” in the Item column and place a check mark in the Post. Ref. column.
3. Record the transactions in the purchases journal beginning with page 81.
4. Post to the accounts payable ledger daily.
5. Post to the general ledger at the end of the month.
6. Prepare a schedule of accounts payable, and compare the balance of the Accounts Payable controlling account with the total of the schedule of accounts payable.

4,6,7,8,10,11 LO

PROBLEM 9-6B The following transactions relate to Kaufman Metal Products during April of this year. Terms of sale are 2/10, n/30. The company is located in Los Angeles.

Apr. 1 Sold merchandise on account to Hubbard Hardware, invoice no. 5522, $607.40.

4 Bought merchandise on account from Roth Manufacturing Company, invoice no. C1142, $556; terms 1/10, n/30; dated April 2; FOB San Diego, freight prepaid and added to the invoice, $34 (total $590).

9 Sold merchandise on account to Booth Stores, invoice no. 5523, $1,025.30.

Apr. 11 Bought merchandise on account from Baird Products Company, invoice no. 8990, $1,756.80; terms 2/10, n/30; dated April 11; FOB San Francisco, freight prepaid and added to the invoice, $75 (total $1,831.80).

16 Sold merchandise on account J. A. Acevedo, invoice no. 5524, $921.56.

19 Issued credit memo no. 32 to Booth Stores for merchandise returned, $86.

24 Bought merchandise on account from Atkins Manufacturing Company, invoice no. P1981, $1,432.80; terms 2/10, n/30; dated April 22; FOB Santa Rosa, freight prepaid and added to the invoice, $76 (total $1,508.80).

27 Bought office supplies on account from Carson and Dyer, invoice no. E621A, $84.40; terms net 30 days; dated April 25.

28 Sold merchandise on account to Grimes Specialty Company, invoice no. 5525, $3,598.70.

29 Issued credit memo no. 33 to J. A. Acevedo for allowance on damaged merchandise, $80.

30 Received credit memo no. 79 for merchandise returned to Barajas, Inc., for $115.20.

Required

Check Figure
Accounts Payable account balance, $4,277.80 credit

1. Open the following accounts in the accounts receivable ledger and record the balances as of April 1: J. A. Acevedo; Booth Stores, $352.50; Grimes Specialty Company, $225.50; Hubbard Hardware, $822. For the accounts having balances, write "Balance" in the Item column and place a check mark in the Post. Ref. column.
2. Open the following accounts in the accounts payable ledger and record the balances as of April 1: Atkins Manufacturing Company; Baird Products Company, $122.46; Barajas, Inc., $255.54; Carson and Dyer; Roth Manufacturing Company. For the accounts having balances, write "Balance" in the Item column and place a check mark in the Post Ref. column.
3. Record the transactions in the sales (page 24), purchases (page 18), or general journal (page 68), as appropriate.
4. Post the entries to the accounts receivable ledger daily.
5. Post the entries to the accounts payable ledger daily.
6. Post the entries in the general journal immediately after you make each journal entry.
7. Post the totals from the special journals at the end of the month.
8. Prepare a schedule of accounts receivable.
9. Prepare a schedule of accounts payable.
10. Compare the totals of the schedules with the balances of the controlling accounts.

ACTIVITIES

CONSIDER AND COMMUNICATE

You are the bookkeeper at a small merchandising firm. You are comparing the income statements from the last three years. You notice that the Purchases Returns and Allowances account (as a percentage of net sales) has been increasing at an alarming rate. If you were a manager, who would you speak to in the organization to help you understand why so much merchandise is being returned? What types of questions would you ask?

CRITICAL THINKING

TO: Accounting Clerk SUBJECT: Errors in trial balance

FROM: Senior Accountant DATE: April 1, 20—

Following is a trial balance prepared just before you were hired. There are two accounts missing, and the amount for Sales is off. Here are a few facts to consider. Our business is in a state that collects sales tax. I ran some totals, and we collected $1,800 in sales tax. Customers returned $900 in goods, which would reduce the above sales tax by $70. Our books need to reflect these events. The former accounting clerk said she did record everything—somewhere. She said she may have credited the $1,800 sales tax to Sales and not to Sales Tax Payable. Plus, she looked confused when Sales Returns and Allowances was mentioned. She asked, "Why not just debit Sales?" Please determine the two missing accounts and correct the accounts that are off.

Pierce Retail Outlet
Trial Balance
March 31, 20—

Account Name	Debit	Credit
Cash	8,940	
Accounts Receivable	480	
Store Equipment	9,460	
Accounts Payable		958
D. Pierce, Capital		11,959
D. Pierce, Drawing	4,480	
Sales		18,000
Rent Expense	2,400	
Wages Expense	4,864	
Supplies Expense	175	
Miscellaneous Expense	118	
	30,917	30,917

1. Think about where these amounts might have been put, think about what accounts are missing, and use T accounts to solve the problems.
2. Prepare a corrected trial balance.

ACTIVITIES

All About You Spa

Sales and Purchases

Ms. Valli of All About You Spa has decided to expand her business by adding two lines of merchandise—a selection of products used in the salon for the body, the feet, and the face, as well as logo mugs, T-shirts, and baseball caps that can provide advertising benefits. She believes she will be able to increase her profits significantly. She has provided paper copies and computer files that report her revenues, operating expenses, and other accounting activity that occurred in June.

The first thing you want to do is to look at the post-closing trial balance as of June 30, 20— shown below. As you look at the post-closing trial balance for the spa, answer the question, "Why is the trial balance so short?"

Why is the trial balance so short?

All About You Spa
Post-Closing Trial Balance
June 30, 20—

Account Name	Debit	Credit
Cash	15,170.00	
Accounts Receivable	1,264.00	
Prepaid Insurance	800.00	
Spa Equipment	7,393.00	
Accumulated Depreciation, Spa Equipment		64.88
Office Equipment	1,150.00	
Accumulated Depreciation, Office Equipment		10.00
Accounts Payable		2,248.00
Wages Payable		369.50
A. Valli, Capital		23,084.62
	25,777.00	25,777.00

If you answered "There are no revenue, expense, or Drawing accounts," you are correct. But why are there no revenue, expense, or Drawing accounts? What happened to them?*

Directions for July Journal Entries

What do I do next?

1. Open the file entitled ***All_About_You_Spa_Ch09.IA7***. Enter your name when prompted and click ***OK***. Select "Yes" or "No" as desired when asked if you want to open on-screen instructions and check figures. As a reminder, these instructions may be opened at any time by clicking on the ***Info.*** toolbar button.
2. Click on the ***Save As*** toolbar button. When the Save As window appears, select the folder in which you wish to save your data files (if not already selected). In the File Name box, key ***All_About_You_Ch09_Your_Name.IA7*** (for example,

*Answer: There are no temporary owner's equity accounts (revenue, expense, or Drawing accounts) because they were closed; their balances were made zero to prepare the books for the next fiscal period. The only accounts remaining open (having a balance) are the real accounts—assets, liabilities, and owner's capital.

All_About_You_Spa_Ch09_John_Doe.IA7) to identify the file containing your work. Click on the ***Save*** button.

3. Make the following reversing entry, dated July 1, in the general journal. (The purpose of this entry is to reverse or undo the adjusting entry you made in Chapter 4. Reversing entries are explained in Chapter 12.)

Wages Payable		Wages Expense	
–	+	+	–
369.50			369.50

So that you can complete the journal entries for the month of July, Ms. Valli has also left the information you will need and directions on how to proceed.

4. Note that with the expansion of the business into merchandising, new accounts have been added to the chart of accounts. For example, an additional revenue account, Merchandise Sales, is needed. Since All About You Spa now needs a Purchases account, the chart of accounts needs to be modified as follows: All expense accounts need to be in the 600–699 range; for example, Wages Expense changes from 511 to 611. The 500–599 range is now used for the purchase-related accounts; for example, Purchases 511 and Freight In 515. Your new chart of accounts appears as follows.

CHART OF ACCOUNTS FOR ALL ABOUT YOU SPA

Assets
111 Cash
113 Accounts Receivable
117 Prepaid Insurance
124 Spa Equipment
125 Accum. Depr., Spa Equip.
128 Office Equipment
129 Accum. Depr., Office Eq.

Liabilities
211 Accounts Payable
212 Wages Payable
215 Sales Tax Payable

Owner's Equity
311 A. Valli, Capital
312 A. Valli, Drawing
313 Income Summary

Revenue
411 Income from Services
412 Merchandise Sales

Purchases
511 Purchases
515 Freight In

Expenses
611 Wages Expense
612 Rent Expense
613 Office Supplies Expense
614 Spa Supplies Expense
615 Laundry Expense
616 Advertising Expense
617 Utilities Expense
618 Insurance Expense
619 Depr. Expense, Spa Equip.
620 Depr. Expense, Office Eq.
630 Miscellaneous Expense

5. Note also that since you will be making purchases on account and sales on account, subsidiary ledgers will be needed to track what is due from individual customers and owed to individual vendors. A listing of customers and vendors with current balances are as follows.

ACCOUNTS RECEIVABLE LEDGER	
About Face Spa	$ 0.00
Jill Anson	325.00
Chaco's	0.00
Holmes Condos	0.00
Tory Ligman	344.00
Los Obrigados Lodge	0.00
Mini Spa	0.00
Jack Morgan	486.00
Pleasant Spa	0.00
Judy Wilcox	109.00

ACCOUNTS PAYABLE LEDGER	
Adco, Inc.	$ 397.00
Giftco	0.00
Golden Spa Supplies	492.00
Logo Products	0.00
Office Staples	120.00
Spa Equipment, Inc.	89.00
Spa Goods	0.00
Spa Magic	0.00
Superior Equipment	1,150.00

6. Click on the ***Journals*** toolbar button and key the journal entries for July. Use the information in the checkbook register and the transactions listings on the

CONTINUING CASE

following pages as the basis of your entries. Follow option a or b below, as directed by your instructor.

a. Key all transactions into the general journal, as you learned to do in previous chapters.

b. Key all transactions into the general journal, except sales on account and purchases on account transactions.

(1) For a sale on account, click on the ***Journals*** toolbar button and then the ***Sales*** tab. Enter the total amount of merchandise sold in the Merch. Sales Cr. column. Enter the amount of sales tax in the Sales Tax Pay. Cr. column. The software will automatically calculate the total and enter it into the Accounts Rec. Dr. column. Select a customer from the Customer drop-down list. Then click on the ***Post*** button (or press Enter).

(2) For a purchase on account, click on the ***Journals*** toolbar button and then the ***Purchases*** tab. Enter the total amount of merchandise purchased in the Purchases Dr. column. Enter the amount of freight charges in the Freight In Dr. column. The software will automatically calculate the total and enter it into the Accounts Pay. Cr. column. Select a vendor from the Vendor drop-down list. Then click on the ***Post*** button (or press Enter).

Remember to journalize a transaction in only one journal—either the sales journal *or* the purchases journal *or* the general journal.

7. Generate journal reports. Click on the ***Reports*** toolbar button. Click on ***Journals*** and ***General Journal*** to choose the report to display. Accept the ***Include All Journal Entries*** option and then click the ***OK*** button to display the General Journal report. To print the report, click on the ***Print*** button. If following option 6b above, also generate a Sales Journal report and a Purchases Journal report in the same manner by clicking on those options in the Report Selection window. Review the journal entries and make corrections as necessary.
8. Display a trial balance. Click on the ***Reports*** toolbar button. Click on ***Ledger Reports*** and ***Trial Balance*** to choose the report to display. To print the report, click on the ***Print*** button at the bottom of the report window.
9. Display a schedule of accounts receivable. Click on the ***Reports*** toolbar button. Click on ***Ledger Reports*** and ***Schedule of Accounts Receivable*** to choose the report to display. To print the report, click on the ***Print*** button at the bottom of the report window.
10. Display a schedule of accounts payable. Click on the ***Reports*** toolbar button. Click on ***Ledger Reports*** and ***Schedule of Accounts Payable*** to choose the report to display. To print the report, click on the ***Print*** button at the bottom of the report window.
11. Click on the ***Save*** toolbar button to save your data file.
12. Click on the ***Check*** toolbar button to check your solution against the answer key.

Check Figures
8. Trial balance total, July 31, $95,383.05
9. Schedule of accounts receivable total, July 31, $4,568.79
10. Schedule of accounts payable total, July 31, $20,720.00

Checkbook Register

Check No.	Date	Explanation	✓	Deposits	Check Amount
	7/1	Owner invested cash in business.		25,000.00	
1027	7/3	Bought additional spa equipment from Spa Equipment, Inc., for $8,235.00, paying $2,000.00 cash down, invoice no. 2731, dated 7/3; terms 2/10, n/60.			2,000.00
1028	7/3	Paid July's rent.			1,650.00

CONTINUING CASE

Check No.	Date	Explanation	✓	Deposits	Check Amount
1029	7/3	Paid on account to Spa Equipment, Inc., invoice no. 2013, dated June 3 (no discount). Paid in full.			89.00
1030	7/5	Paid on account to Golden Spa Supplies, invoice no. 804, dated June 3 (no discount). Paid in full.			492.00
1031	7/5	Paid on account to Office Staples, invoice no. 522, dated June 5 (no discount). Paid in full.			120.00
1032	7/5	Paid Celebrate, Inc., for flowers and balloons for lobby (Miscellaneous Expense).			98.00
1033	7/5	Paid on account to Adco, Inc., invoice no. 512, dated June 5 (no discount). Paid in full.			397.00
1034	7/5	Paid week's wages. *Note:* Payroll taxes related to wages will be ignored here for purposes of simplification.			1,845.50
	7/7	Deposited first week's cash sales: merchandise, $1,410.00; services, $3,110.00; sales tax collected, $361.60. (Use the new accounts Merchandise Sales 412 and Sales Tax Payable 215.)		4,881.60	
	7/7	Deposited check from Jill Anson, invoice no. 10, dated June 7 (balance due in August, $175.00).		150.00	
1035	7/12	Paid week's wages.			1,845.50
	7/14	Deposited check from Jack Morgan, invoice no. 11, dated June 14 (balance due in August, $286.00).		200.00	
	7/14	Deposited second week's cash sales: merchandise, $1,220.00; services, $2,630.00; sales tax collected, $308.00.		4,158.00	
1036	7/18	Paid on account to Superior Equipment, invoice no. 3140, dated June 5 (no discount). Paid in full.			1,150.00
1037	7/19	Paid week's wages.			1,840.50
	7/21	Deposited check from Tory Ligman, invoice no. 12, dated June 21 (balance due in August, $164.00).		180.00	
	7/21	Deposited third week's cash sales: merchandise, $1,940.00; services, $2,920.00; sales tax collected, $388.80.		5,248.80	
1038	7/25	Bought new nail cart for cash (debit Spa Equipment).			173.00
1039	7/26	Paid week's wages.			1,842.00

Check No.	Date	Explanation	✓	Deposits	Check Amount
1040	7/28	Paid month's laundry bill.			84.00
	7/28	Deposited check from Judy Wilcox, invoice no. 13, dated June 28 (paid in full).		109.00	
	7/31	Deposited end of month's cash sales: merchandise, $1,930.00; services, $4,062.00; sales tax collected, $479.36.		6,471.36	
1041	7/31	Owner withdrew cash for personal use.			2,500.00
1042	7/31	Paid July telephone bill.			225.00
1043	7/31	Paid July power and water bill.			248.00

Purchases Invoices for Merchandise Bought on Account During July

All About You Spa will pay all freight costs associated with purchases of merchandise to the supplier. Use the new accounts Purchases 511 and Freight In 515.

Date of Purchase	Transaction Information	Amount
July 1	Bought aromatherapy products from Spa Goods; invoice no. 312, dated 7/1; terms 2/10, n/60.	$5,300.00 plus $145.00 freight
1	Bought logo merchandise from Logo Products; invoice no. 1579, dated 7/1; terms 2/10, n/60.	$3,692.00 plus $104.00 freight
2	Bought bath and beauty products from Spa Magic; invoice no. 5033, dated 7/2; terms 2/10, n/30.	$2,623.00 plus $98.00 freight
5	Bought logo merchandise from Giftco; invoice no. 316, dated 7/5; terms 2/10, n/60.	$1,253.00 plus $56.00 freight

Sales Invoices for Gift Certificates Sold on Account During July

All About You Spa is responsible for collecting and paying the sales tax on merchandise that it sells. The sales tax rate where All About You Spa does business is 8 percent of each sale; for example, $\$325.00 \times 0.08 = \$26.00$.

Date of Sale	Transaction Information	Sales Amount (Before Tax)
July 2	Los Obrigados Lodge, invoice no. 14.	$ 325.00
4	Chaco's, invoice no. 15.	481.50
5	Pleasant Spa, invoice no. 16.	1,815.95
10	Holmes Condos, invoice no. 17.	340.25
10	Mini Spa, invoice no. 18.	206.00
12	About Face Spa, invoice no. 19.	482.95

Note: All gift certificates were redeemed for merchandise by the end of the month.

Other July Transactions

There were five other transactions in July. None involved cash.

Date	Transaction Information	Amount
July 1	Bought spa supplies on account from Golden Spa Supplies, invoice no. 1836, dated 7/1; terms n/45.	$ 490.00
5	Bought office equipment on account from Superior Equipment, invoice no. 3608, dated 7/5; terms 2/10, n/60.	420.00
5	Bought self-help books for the waiting room on account (Miscellaneous Expense) from Office Staples, invoice no. 1417, dated 7/5; terms n/30.	186.00
5	Bought office supplies on account from Office Staples, invoice no. 1418, dated 7/5; terms n/30.	118.00
31	Owner invested additional personal spa equipment (treadmill and bicycle) valued at $1,800.00.	1,800.00

Sales and Purchases— Perpetual Method

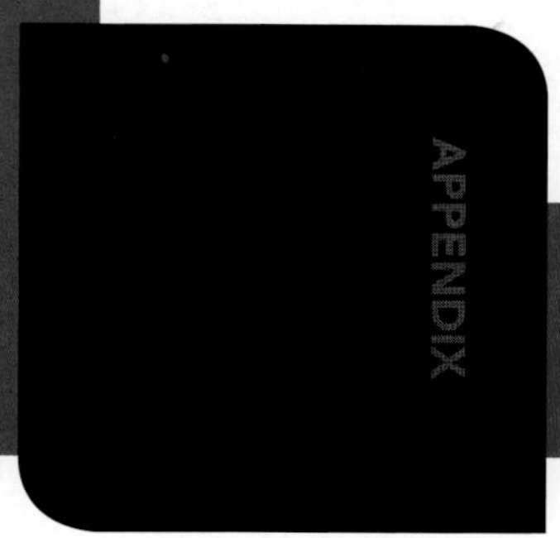

LEARNING OBJECTIVES

After you have completed this chapter, you will be able to do the following:

1 *Journalize sales transactions, including sales returns and allowances, in the general journal using the perpetual inventory system.*

2 *Journalize purchase transactions, including purchases returns and allowances, in the general journal using the perpetual inventory system.*

In Chapter 9, we discussed how to record sales and purchases transactions in the general journal using the periodic inventory system. The periodic inventory system requires that companies periodically take a physical count of inventory at the end of the period to determine the amount of inventory on hand.

The perpetual inventory system, on the other hand, keeps continuous records of inventories by recording all transactions, so that at any given time the companies knows the current amount of inventory. Under the perpetual inventory system, sales and purchases are recorded differently than the periodic inventory system.

SALES TRANSACTIONS

1 LEARNING OBJECTIVE

Journalize sales transactions, including sales returns and allowances, in the general journal using the perpetual inventory system.

Let's review the first two transactions on the books of Whitewater Raft Supply for the month of August:

Aug. 1 Sold merchandise on account to Mesa River Raft Company, invoice no. 9384, \$1,933.50. *Cost of inventory sold is \$1,643.48.*

8 Sold merchandise on account to Green River Rafts, invoice no. 9385, \$1,116. *Cost of inventory sold is \$948.60.*

Note the new information provided in italics. This information concerning the cost of the inventory sold is needed when sales transactions are recorded using the perpetual inventory system.

Whitewater Raft Supply's accountant would record the transactions in the general journal as follows:

GENERAL JOURNAL PAGE 26

Date		Description	Post. Ref.	Debit	Credit
20—					
Aug.	1	Accounts Receivable, Mesa River Raft Company		1 9 3 3 50	
		Sales			1 9 3 3 50
		Sold merchandise to Mesa River Raft Company, invoice no. 9384.			
		Cost of Goods Sold		1 6 4 3 48	
		Merchandise Inventory			1 6 4 3 48
		Cost of merchandise sold to Mesa River Raft Company, invoice no. 9384.			
	8	Accounts Receivable, Green River Rafts		1 1 1 6 00	
		Sales			1 1 1 6 00
		Sold merchandise to Green River Rafts, invoice no. 9385.			
		Cost of Goods Sold		9 4 8 60	
		Merchandise Inventory			9 4 8 60
		Cost of merchandise sold to Green River Rafts, invoice no. 9385.			

The sales portion of the transaction is recorded the same under either method. Whitewater Raft Supply's accountant records a debit to Accounts Receivable to record the amount each customer owes the company and a credit to Sales for each transaction. However, using the perpetual inventory system, the accountant must also record a debit to Cost of Goods Sold for the cost of the inventory sold and a credit to Merchandise Inventory. Cost of Goods Sold represents the cost of the inventory sold and is an expense account that is reported on the income statement. Cost of Goods Sold must increase and is therefore debited. The Merchandise Inventory account must decrease by the cost of the inventory sold, and so the accountant records a credit to Merchandise Inventory.

By recording sales transactions in this manner, the company can easily calculate the gross profit, or the profit on the sale of the inventory, by subtracting Cost of Goods Sold from Sales. Whitewater Raft Supply's gross profit is $290.02 ($1,933.50 – $1,643.48) on the August 1 sale.

SALES RETURNS AND ALLOWANCES

Sales returns and allowances must also be recorded differently under the perpetual inventory system. Let's look at Whitewater Raft Supply's return on September 5, with the original sale described first.

Transaction (a). On September 1, Whitewater Raft Supply sold merchandise on account to Rugged River Company, $3,614, and recorded the sale in the general journal. *Cost of inventory sold is $3,071.50.*

Transaction (b). On September 5, Rugged River Company returned $254 worth of the merchandise *having a cost of $215.90.* Whitewater Raft Supply issued credit memorandum no. 1069.

Again, note the additional information provided describing the cost of the inventory sold and returned. This information is necessary to record the transactions using the perpetual inventory system.

Whitewater Raft Supply's accountant would record the return on September 5 as follows:

GENERAL JOURNAL PAGE 27

Date		Description	Post. Ref.	Debit	Credit
20—					
Sept.	5	Sales Returns and Allowances		254 00	
		Accounts Receivable, Rugged			
		River Company			254 00
		Issued credit memo no. 1069.			
		Merchandise Inventory		215 90	
		Cost of Goods Sold			215 90
		Cost of merchandise returned,			
		credit memo no. 1069.			

The first part of the journal entry is the same as when using the periodic inventory system. The accountant debits Sales Returns and Allowances and credits Accounts Receivable to decrease it because the customer owes less than before. However, since Whitewater Raft Supply is using the perpetual inventory system, the company must also record the effect of this return on merchandise inventory by debiting Merchandise Inventory to increase it for the returned items and crediting Cost of Goods Sold to decrease the expense.

PURCHASE TRANSACTIONS

2 LEARNING OBJECTIVE

Journalize purchase transactions, including purchases returns and allowances, in the general journal using the perpetual inventory system.

As we learned in Chapter 9, when using the periodic inventory system, the accountant uses the Purchases and Freight In (if applied) accounts to record transactions involving purchases. Under the perpetual inventory system, all transactions related to the purchase of inventory are recorded in the Merchandise Inventory account. The accountant never uses the Purchases and Freight In accounts when recording purchase transactions under the perpetual inventory system because *all* costs of merchandise inventory (including freight) are included in the Merchandise Inventory account.

Let's look at two purchase transactions on the books of Whitewater Raft Supply for the month of August.

Aug. 2 Bought merchandise on account from Pataponia, Inc., invoice no. 2706, $1,710; terms 2/10, n/30; dated July 31; FOB San Francisco, freight prepaid and added to the invoice, $85.50 (total $1,795.50).

10 Bought merchandise on account from Langseth and Son, invoice no. 982, $2,772; terms net 30 days; dated August 8; FOB Cleveland, freight prepaid and added to the invoice, $157 (total $2,929).

Whitewater Raft Supply's accountant will record the transactions in the general journal as follows:

GENERAL JOURNAL PAGE 26

Date		Description	Post. Ref.	Debit	Credit
20—					
Aug.	2	Merchandise Inventory		1,795.50	
		Accounts Payable, Pataponia, Inc.			1,795.50
		Purchased merchandise from Pataponia, Inc., invoice no. 2706, invoice dated 7/31, terms 2/10, n/30.			
	10	Merchandise Inventory		2,929.00	
		Accounts Payable, Langseth and Son			2,929.00
		Purchased merchandise from Langseth and Son, invoice no. 982, invoice dated 8/8, terms n/30.			

Note that Whitewater Raft Supply records a debit to the Merchandise Inventory account (not Purchases and Freight In) to record the cost of merchandise, including freight, bought for resale.

PURCHASES RETURNS AND ALLOWANCES

Under the perpetual inventory system, purchases returns and allowances transactions are recorded directly into the Merchandise Inventory account. The Purchases Returns and Allowances account that is used to record returns and allowances under the periodic inventory system is not used.

Let's look at a return on September 8 for Whitewater Raft Supply, with the original purchase described first.

Transaction (a). On September 2, bought merchandise on account from Dana Manufacturing Company, $830.

Transaction (b). On September 8, received credit memorandum no. 1629 from Dana Manufacturing Company for $270.

Under the perpetual inventory system, the accountant would record the return on September 8 as follows:

GENERAL JOURNAL PAGE 27

Date		Description	Post. Ref.	Debit	Credit
20—					
Sept.	8	Accounts Payable, Dana Manufacturing Company		270.00	
		Merchandise Inventory			270.00
		Credit memo no. 1629 for return of merchandise.			

Whitewater Raft Supply's accountant debits the creditor's Accounts Payable account to decrease it and credits Merchandise Inventory (not Purchases Returns and Allowances) to decrease it. Recording the credit to the Merchandise Inventory account automatically decreases it for the cost of the inventory returned.

PERIODIC INVENTORY SYSTEM VS. PERPETUAL INVENTORY SYSTEM

Chart of Accounts

Following is an abbreviated version of the chart of accounts for both the periodic and perpetual inventory systems. Note that in the periodic inventory system, the company would use accounts such as Purchases, Purchases Returns and Allowances, and Freight In that are not used in the perpetual inventory system.

PERIODIC INVENTORY SYSTEM	PERPETUAL INVENTORY SYSTEM
Revenue (400–499)	**Revenue (400–499)**
411 Sales	411 Sales
412 Sales Returns and Allowances	412 Sales Returns and Allowances
Cost of Goods Sold (500–599)	**Cost of Goods Sold (500–599)**
511 Purchases	511 Cost of Goods Sold
512 Purchases Returns and Allowances	
514 Freight In	

Journal Entries

Now that we have reviewed the main differences between the periodic and perpetual inventory systems, let's take a moment to reflect on those differences. Figure A shows a comparison of the transactions that we have learned for both inventory systems. Make sure that you are familiar with each system and also how they differ.

FIGURE A Comparison of journal entries for periodic and perpetual inventory systems

Comparison: Periodic Versus Perpetual Inventory Systems

Transaction	Periodic Inventory System			Perpetual Inventory System		
Sold merchandise to customer on account, $1,933.50, having a cost of $1,643.48.	Accounts Receivable, Mesa River Raft Company	1,933.50		Accounts Receivable, Mesa River Raft Company	1,933.50	
	Sales		1,933.50	Sales		1,933.50
				Cost of Goods Sold	1,643.48	
				Merchandise Inventory		1,643.48
Customer returned merchandise, $254, having a cost of $215.90.	Sales Returns and Allowances	254.00		Sales Returns and Allowances	254.00	
	Accounts Receivable, Rugged River Company		254.00	Accounts Receivable, Rugged River Company		254.00
				Merchandise Inventory	215.90	
				Cost of Goods Sold		215.90
Purchased merchandise from supplier on account, $1,710, with prepaid freight of $85.50.	Purchases	1,710.00		Merchandise Inventory	1,795.50	
	Freight In	85.50		Accounts Payable, Pataponia, Inc.		1,795.50
	Accounts Payable, Pataponia, Inc.		1,795.50			
Returned merchandise to supplier, $270.	Accounts Payable, Dana Manufacturing Company	270.00		Accounts Payable, Dana Manufacturing Company	270.00	
	Purchases Returns and Allowances		270.00	Merchandise Inventory		270.00

Problems

1,2 LO

PROBLEM 9A-1 The following transactions relate to Hawkins, Inc., an office store wholesaler, during June of this year. Terms of sale are 2/10, n/30. The company is located in Los Angeles, California.

June 1 Sold merchandise on account to Hendrix Office Store, invoice no. 1001, $451.20. The cost of the merchandise was $397.06.

3 Bought merchandise on account from Krueger, Inc., invoice no. 845A, $485.15; terms 1/10, n/30; dated June 1; FOB San Diego, freight prepaid and added to the invoice, $15 (total $500.15).

10 Sold merchandise on account to Ballard Stores, invoice no. 1002, $2,483.65. The cost of the merchandise was $2,235.29.

13 Bought merchandise on account from Kennedy, Inc., invoice no. 4833, $2,450.13; terms 2/10, n/30; dated June 11; FOB San Francisco, freight prepaid and added to the invoice, $123 (total $2,573.13).

18 Sold merchandise on account to Lawson Office Store, invoice no. 1003, $754.99. The cost of the merchandise was $671.94.

20 Issued credit memo no. 33 to Lawson Office Store for merchandise returned, $103.25. The cost of the merchandise was $91.89.

25 Bought merchandise on account from Villarreal, Inc., invoice no. 4R32, $1,552.30; terms net 30; dated June 18; FOB Santa Rosa, freight prepaid and added to the invoice, $84 (total $1,636.30).

30 Received credit memo no. 44 for merchandise returned to Villarreal, Inc., for $224.50.

Check Figure
Net Merchandise Inventory, $1,272.68 debit

Required

Record the transactions in the general journal (pages 25 and 26) using the perpetual inventory system.

1,2 LO

PROBLEM 9A-2 The following transactions relate to Khan, Inc., a sporting goods wholesaler, during November of this year. Terms of sale are 2/10, n/30. The company is located in Denver, Colorado.

Nov. 3 Sold merchandise on account to Spence Tennis Shop, invoice no. 5420, $2,482.51. The cost of the merchandise was $1,961.18.

5 Issued credit memo no. 38 to Spence Tennis Shop for merchandise returned, $287.45. The cost of the merchandise was $227.09.

7 Bought merchandise on account from Maldonado Manufacturing, Inc., invoice no. 1548, $3,854.16; terms n/45; dated November 4; FOB Memphis, freight prepaid and added to the invoice, $135 (total $3,989.16).

9 Bought merchandise on account from Lozano, Inc., invoice no. 8755, $426.65; terms 1/15, n/30; dated November 5; FOB New York City, freight prepaid and added to the invoice, $67 (total $493.65).

12 Received credit memo no. 542 to Lozano, Inc., for merchandise returned, $102.20.

17 Sold merchandise on account to Jack's Golfing Shop, invoice no. 5421, $486.35. The cost of the merchandise was $432.85.

Nov. 23 Sold merchandise on account to Yates Sporting Goods, invoice no. 5422, $2,465.99. The cost of the merchandise was $1,972.79.

28 Bought merchandise on account from Fields, Inc., invoice no. 4599, $441.29; terms 2/10, n/30; dated November 25; FOB Austin, freight prepaid and added to the invoice, $102 (total $543.29).

Required

Record the transactions in the general journal (pages 84 and 85) using the perpetual inventory system.

Check Figure
Total Gross Sales, $5,434.85 credit

APPENDIX

10 Cash Receipts and Cash Payments

WHY IT MATTERS

BOOKSHOP SANTA CRUZ, Santa Cruz, California

If you're ever in Santa Cruz, California, take a few hours and step inside Bookshop Santa Cruz. Inside the doors you'll find books "that entertain, help solve problems, or, occasionally, change a life."

Since opening in 1966, Bookshop Santa Cruz has been a vital member of the Bay Area. It takes immense pride in being an independent bookseller, a rare commodity in today's world of large corporate booksellers such as Barnes & Noble and Borders.

The bookstore has several buyers who are responsible for spotting reading trends, reordering current books, and purchasing the newest and hottest books on the market. Each time a buyer makes a purchase and every time Bookshop Santa Cruz sells one of its books, a transaction must be recorded. In Chapter 9, we discussed how to record the purchase and sale of inventory. In this chapter, we will look at how a store, such as Bookshop Santa Cruz, records the receipt of cash from sales and the payment of cash for purchases.

LEARNING OBJECTIVES

After you have completed this chapter, you will be able to do the following:

1. *Determine cash discounts according to credit terms.*
2. *Journalize sales transactions in a general journal involving cash receipts from credit customers who are entitled to deduct the cash discount.*
3. *Journalize purchase transactions in a general journal involving cash payments when entitled to deduct the cash discount.*
4. *Journalize transactions involving trade discounts.*
5. *Journalize transactions for a merchandising business in a cash receipts journal and post from a cash receipts journal to a general ledger and an accounts receivable ledger.*
6. *Journalize transactions for a merchandising business in a cash payments journal and post from a cash payments journal to a general ledger and an accounts payable ledger.*

ACCOUNTING LANGUAGE

Cash discount *(p. 393)*
Cash payments journal *(p. 410)*
Cash receipts journal *(p. 405)*
Credit period *(p. 393)*
Notes Payable *(p. 408)*
Promissory note *(p. 408)*
Trade discounts *(p. 402)*

In the previous chapter, we discussed sales and purchases on account. Now we will learn how a company records cash receipts and cash payments for those transactions. We will begin by reviewing discounts and terms available to purchasers and sellers and then discuss recording the cash associated with merchandising transactions.

CREDIT TERMS

1 LEARNING OBJECTIVE *Determine cash discounts according to credit terms.*

When we discussed sales and purchases of merchandise in Chapter 9, we noted that each sale or purchase was associated with a *term*. The seller always stipulates the *terms*: How much credit can a customer be allowed? And, how much time should the customer be given to pay the full amount? The **credit period** is the time the seller allows the buyer before full payment has to be made. Retailers generally allow 25 to 30 days for payment.

Wholesalers and manufacturers often specify a **cash discount** in their credit terms. A cash discount is an amount that a customer can deduct if a bill is paid within a specified time. The discount is based on the *total amount of the invoice after any returns and allowances and freight charges billed on the invoice have been deducted.* Naturally, this discount acts as an incentive for credit customers to pay their bills promptly.

Let's say that a wholesaler offers customers credit terms of 2/10, n/30. These terms mean that the customer gets a 2 percent discount if the bill is paid within 10 days after the invoice date. The discount period begins the day after the invoice date. If the bill is not paid within the 10 days, the entire amount is due within 30 days after the invoice date. Other types of cash discounts that may be used are the following:

- **1/15, n/60** The seller offers a 1 percent discount if the bill is paid within 15 days after the invoice date, and the whole bill must be paid within 60 days after the invoice date.

- **2/10, EOM, n/60** The seller offers a 2 percent discount if the bill is paid within 10 days after the end of the month, and the whole bill must be paid within 60 days after the last day of the month.

A wholesaler or manufacturer that offers a cash discount adopts a single cash discount as a credit policy and makes this available to all its customers. The seller considers cash discounts as sales discounts; the buyer, on the other hand, considers cash discounts as purchases discounts.

PART ONE—RECORDING TRANSACTIONS INTO THE GENERAL JOURNAL

Occasionally, sales or purchases of merchandise will involve discounts. In this section, we will discuss discounts and how they are recorded in the general journal.

Sales Discounts

LEARNING OBJECTIVE 2

Journalize sales transactions in a general journal involving cash receipts from credit customers who are entitled to deduct the cash discount.

First we will concentrate on the sales discount. *The Sales Discounts account, like Sales Returns and Allowances, is a contra revenue account and is therefore deducted from Sales.*

To illustrate, we return to Whitewater Raft Supply. We will record the following transactions in the general journal and T accounts.

Transaction (a). On August 1, Whitewater Raft Supply sold merchandise on account to Mesa River Raft Company, invoice no. 9384, $1,933.50; terms 2/10, n/30. (Take a moment to review the source document on page 331 in Chapter 9 and identify the terms on the invoice.)

Transaction (b). On August 10, received check from Mesa River Raft Company for $1,894.83 in payment of invoice no. 9384, less cash discount ($1,933.50 × 0.02 = $38.67; $1,933.50 − $38.67 = $1,894.83).

GENERAL JOURNAL PAGE 26

Date		Description	Post. Ref.	Debit	Credit
20—					
Aug.	1	Accounts Receivable, Mesa River			
		Raft Company		1 9 3 3 50	
		Sales			1 9 3 3 50
		Sold merchandise to Mesa River Raft			
		Company, invoice no. 9384.			
	10	Cash		1 8 9 4 83	
		Sales Discounts		3 8 67	
		Accounts Receivable, Mesa River Raft			
		Company			1 9 3 3 50
		Collected cash on account,			
		invoice no. 9384.			

Remember

When journalizing a cash receipt involving a sales discount, be sure to credit Accounts Receivable for the total amount of the sales transaction.

To record the receipt of payment on August 10 from the customer, the accountant records a debit to Cash for the amount of cash received. The amount of discount granted is recorded as a debit to Sales Discounts. The Accounts Receivable account is credited so that the customer's account will decrease. Notice that the accountant records a credit to Accounts Receivable, Mesa River Raft Company for the total invoice amount, $1,933.50. This is important because if the receivable was credited for only the cash received, the customer's account would still show a balance owed.

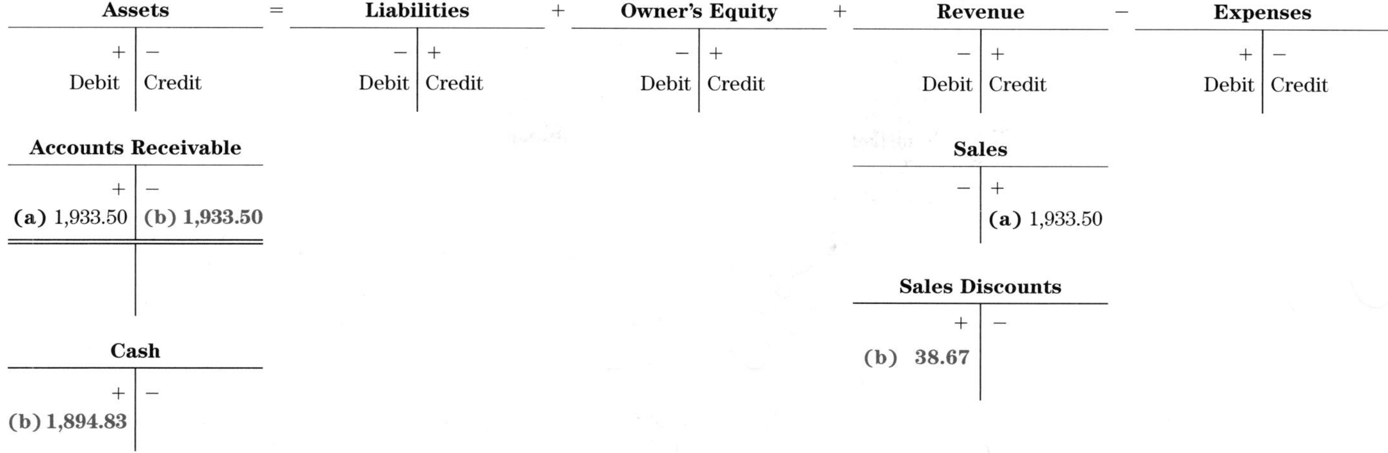

When a company receives a return of merchandise sold, the sales discount is calculated by excluding the amount of the returned items. Let's take a look at this example. The journal and T accounts for the following transactions are shown below and on the next page.

Transaction (a). On September 1, Whitewater Raft Supply sold merchandise on account to Rugged River Company, invoice no. 9391; $3,614, terms 2/10, n/30; and recorded the sale in the general journal.

Transaction (b). On September 5, Rugged River Company returned $254 worth of the merchandise. Whitewater Raft Supply issued credit memorandum no. 1069 and recorded the transaction. *Notice that after the return there is a balance in Accounts Receivable of $3,360, the amount of the original invoice less the return ($3,614 − $254).*

Transaction (c). On September 8, received check from Rugged River Company for $3,292.80 in payment of invoice no. 9391, less return and cash discount [($3,614 − $254) × 0.02 = $67.20; ($3,614 − $254) − $67.20 = $3,292.80].

GENERAL JOURNAL PAGE 27

Date		Description	Post. Ref.	Debit	Credit
20—					
Sept.	1	Accounts Receivable, Rugged River Company		3,614.00	
		Sales			3,614.00
		Sold merchandise to Rugged River Company, invoice no. 9391.			
	5	Sales Returns and Allowances		254.00	
		Accounts Receivable, Rugged River Company			254.00
		Issued credit memo no. 1069.			
	8	Cash		3,292.80	
		Sales Discounts		67.20	
		Accounts Receivable, Rugged River Company			3,360.00
		Collected cash on account, invoice no. 9391.			

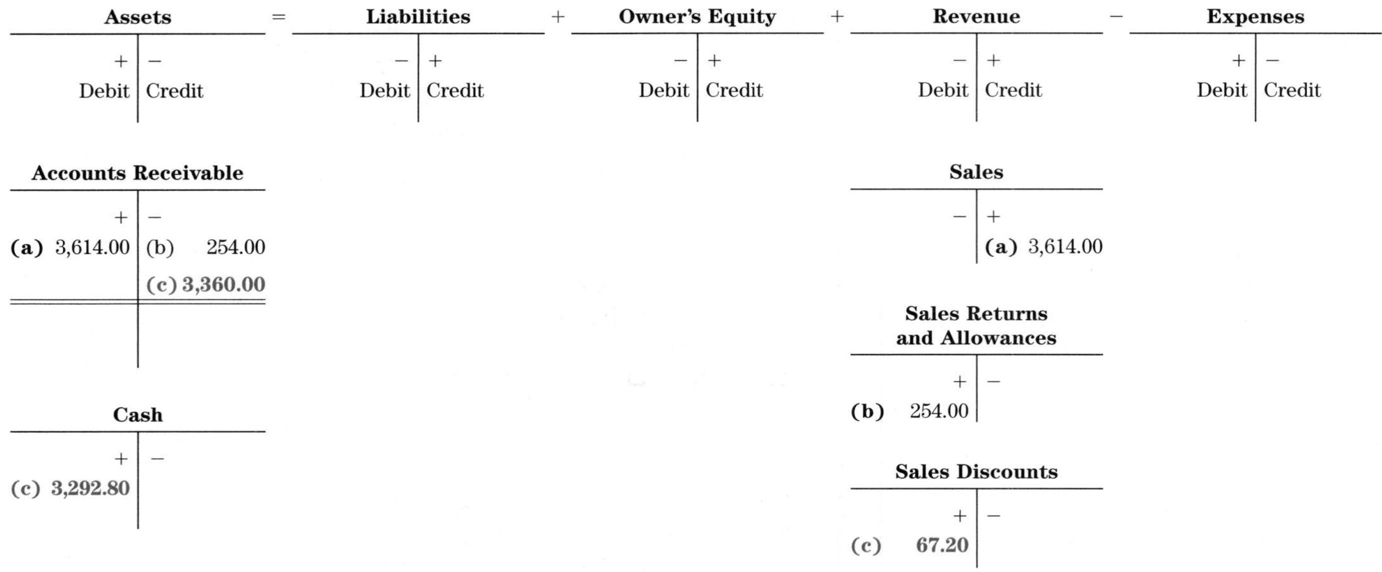

Notice that when the accountant records the receipt of cash, the discount is calculated less the sales return. This is because the company would grant a discount only on the remaining amount owed, not for the full sale amount.

No Sales Discounts Involved

When a transaction does not involve a sales discount or the discount has expired, the seller will record the receipt of payment on account by debiting Cash and crediting Accounts Receivable. Assume that Blue Merchandise Company recorded the following transactions:

Transaction (a). On April 1, Blue Merchandise Company sold merchandise on account to Yellow Company, invoice no. 1294, $9,450; terms 2/10, n/30; and recorded the sale in the general journal.

Transaction (b). On April 26, received check from Yellow Company for $9,450 in payment of invoice no. 1294.

Blue Merchandise Company's accountant would record the transactions in the general journal as:

GENERAL JOURNAL PAGE 65

Date		Description	Post. Ref.	Debit	Credit
20—					
Apr.	1	Accounts Receivable, Yellow			
		Company		9,450.00	
		Sales			9,450.00
		Sold merchandise to Yellow			
		Company, invoice no. 1294.			
	26	Cash		9,450.00	
		Accounts Receivable, Yellow			
		Company			9,450.00
		Collected cash on account,			
		invoice no. 1294.			

Notice that since Yellow Company did not make payment within 10 days, the discount was not applied to the invoice amount. Yellow Company paid the invoice in full.

Posting to the General Ledger and Subsidiary Ledger

To post cash receipts of sales, post each entry to Cash and any other accounts involved in the general ledger. Also, post the amounts paid by customers to the subsidiary accounts receivable ledger to maintain a running balance of the amount each customer owes.

Posting to the General Ledger and Subsidiary Ledger—A Computerized Approach

Most computer accounting software allows businesses to post cash receipts for sales and apply discounts. In Figure 1, the cash receipt of $1,894.83 in payment of invoice no. 9384 is being recorded into the accounting software.

Notice that this software system allows the accountant to apply a discount. Look in the lower right corner to see the discount application button. In Figure 2, the accountant is recording the discount into the system.

After the discount has been applied, the invoice is now showing as paid (Figure 3) and the balance due is $0.00. Using a computerized accounting system is an excellent way for businesses to keep track of cash receipts and discounts. Most computerized accounting software can also handle returns and allowances of merchandise that has been sold.

Sales Returns and Allowances and Sales Discounts on an Income Statement

In the fundamental accounting equation, to be consistent with the income statement, we placed Sales Returns and Allowances and Sales Discounts under Sales with the plus and minus signs reversed. Both accounts are contra accounts, so we subtract their totals from Sales on the income statement. The Revenue from Sales section of the annual income statement of Whitewater Raft Supply is shown in Figure 4.

FIGURE 1

Recording a cash receipt using accounting software

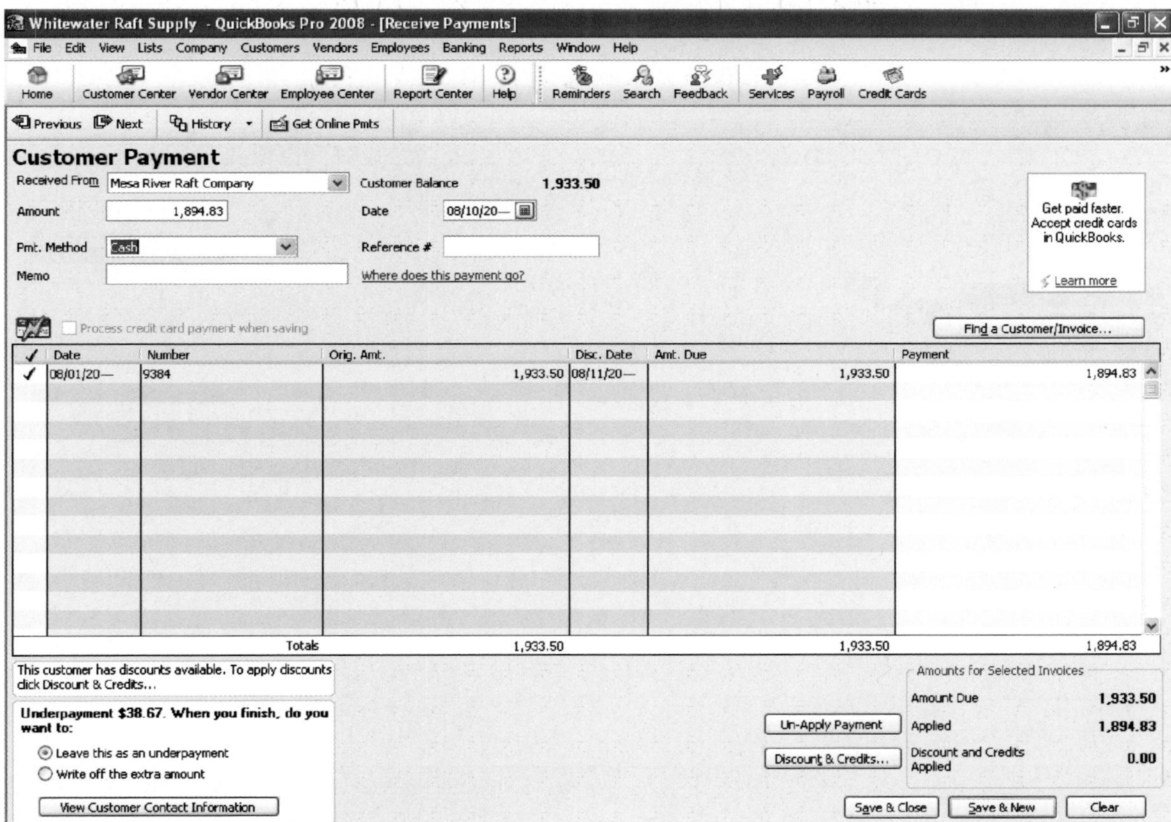

FIGURE 2

Recording a cash discount using accounting software

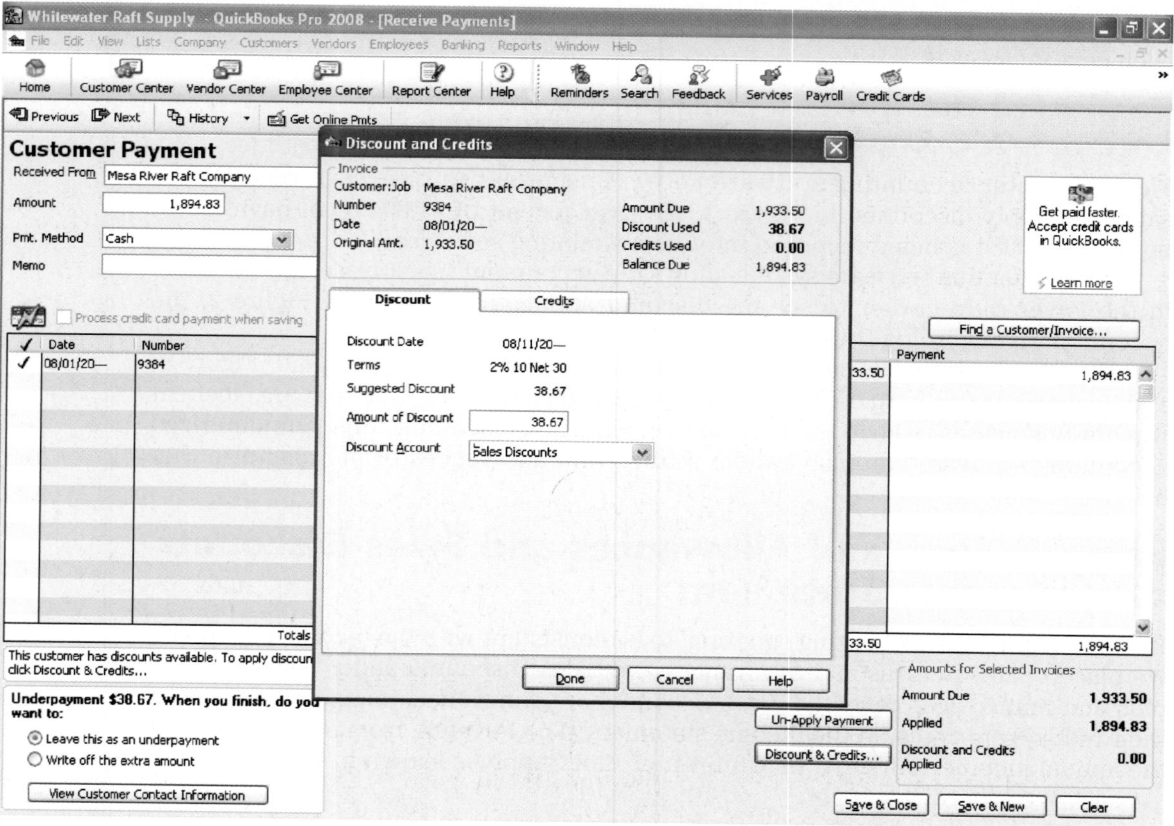

FIGURE 3

Paid invoice

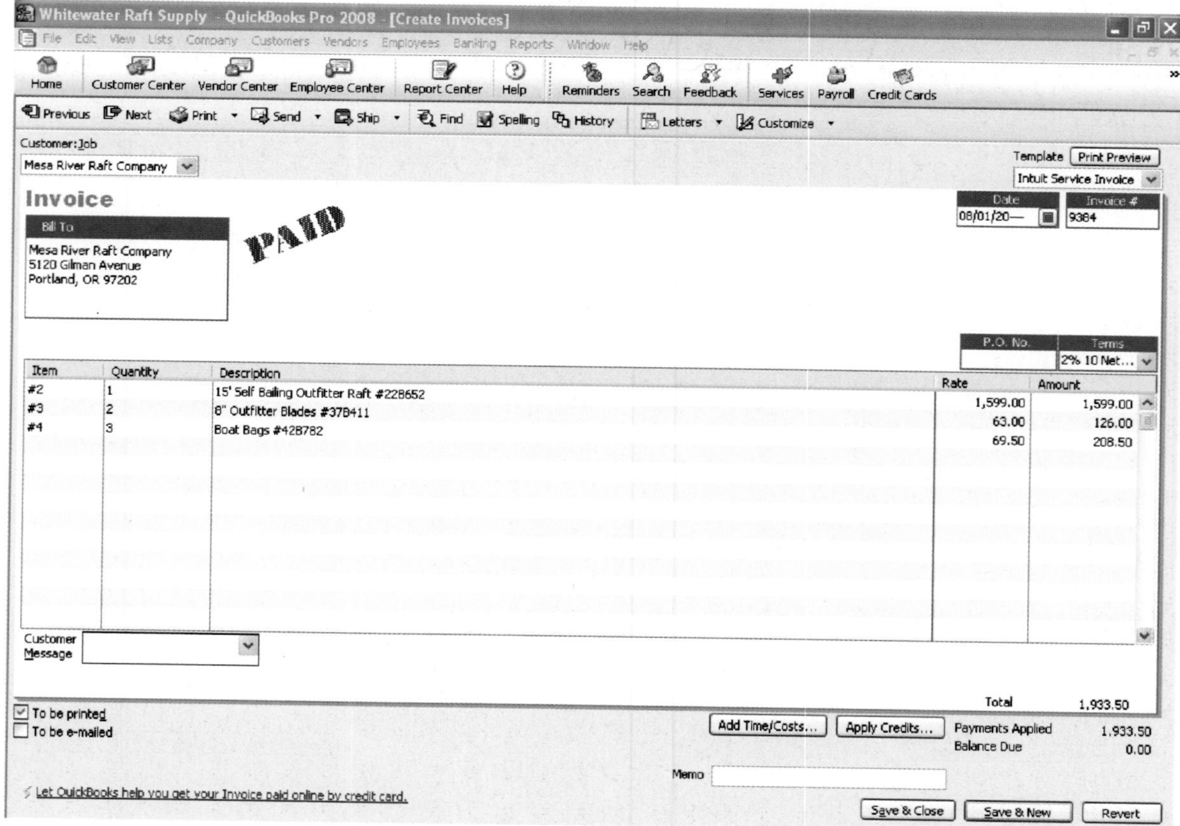

Whitewater Raft Supply
Income Statement
For the Year Ended December 31, 20—

Revenue from Sales:			
Sales		$257,180	
Less: Sales Returns and Allowances	$ 940		
Sales Discounts	1,980	2,920	
Net Sales			$254,260

FIGURE 4
Revenue from sales section of income statement

Purchase Discounts

LEARNING OBJECTIVE 3
Journalize purchase transactions in a general journal involving cash payments when entitled to deduct the cash discount.

Recall that a cash discount is the amount that the buyer may deduct from the bill; this acts as an incentive to get the buyer to pay the bill promptly. The buyer considers the cash discount to be a purchases discount, because it relates to the buyer's purchase of merchandise. *The Purchases Discounts account, like Purchases Returns and Allowances, is a contra account and is treated as a deduction from Purchases on the buyer's income statement.*

Let's return to Whitewater Raft Supply and assume that the following transactions take place.

Transaction (a). On August 2, Whitewater Raft Supply bought merchandise on account from Pataponia, Inc., invoice no. 2706, $1,710; terms 2/10, n/30; dated July 31; FOB San Francisco, freight prepaid and added to the invoice, $85.50 (total $1,795.50).

Transaction (b). On August 8, issued Ck. No. 2076 to Pataponia, Inc., in payment of invoice no. 2706, less cash discount of $34.20, $1,761.30 ($1,795.50 − $34.20).

Remember
The cash discount does not apply to freight charges billed separately on an invoice.

Notice that when calculating the discount, the discount applies only to the amount billed for the merchandise ($1,710 × 0.02 = $34.20). **You do not include the freight cost when determining the discount**.

GENERAL JOURNAL PAGE 26

Date		Description	Post. Ref.	Debit	Credit
20—					
Aug.	2	Purchases		1 7 1 0 00	
		Freight In		8 5 50	
		Accounts Payable, Pataponia, Inc.			1 7 9 5 50
		Purchased merchandise from			
		Pataponia, Inc., invoice no. 2706,			
		invoice dated 7/31, terms			
		2/10, n/30.			
	8	Accounts Payable, Pataponia, Inc.		1 7 9 5 50	
		Cash			1 7 6 1 30
		Purchases Discounts			3 4 20
		Paid Pataponia, Inc., for			
		invoice no. 2706, Ck. No. 2076.			

To record the payment to Pataponia, Inc., the accountant records a debit to Accounts Payable and a credit to Cash for the amount of cash paid. The amount of discount received is recorded as a credit to Purchases Discounts. Notice that the accountant records a debit to Accounts Payable, Pataponia, Inc., for the total invoice amount, $1,795.50. This is important because if the payable was debited for only the cash paid, the account would still show a balance due.

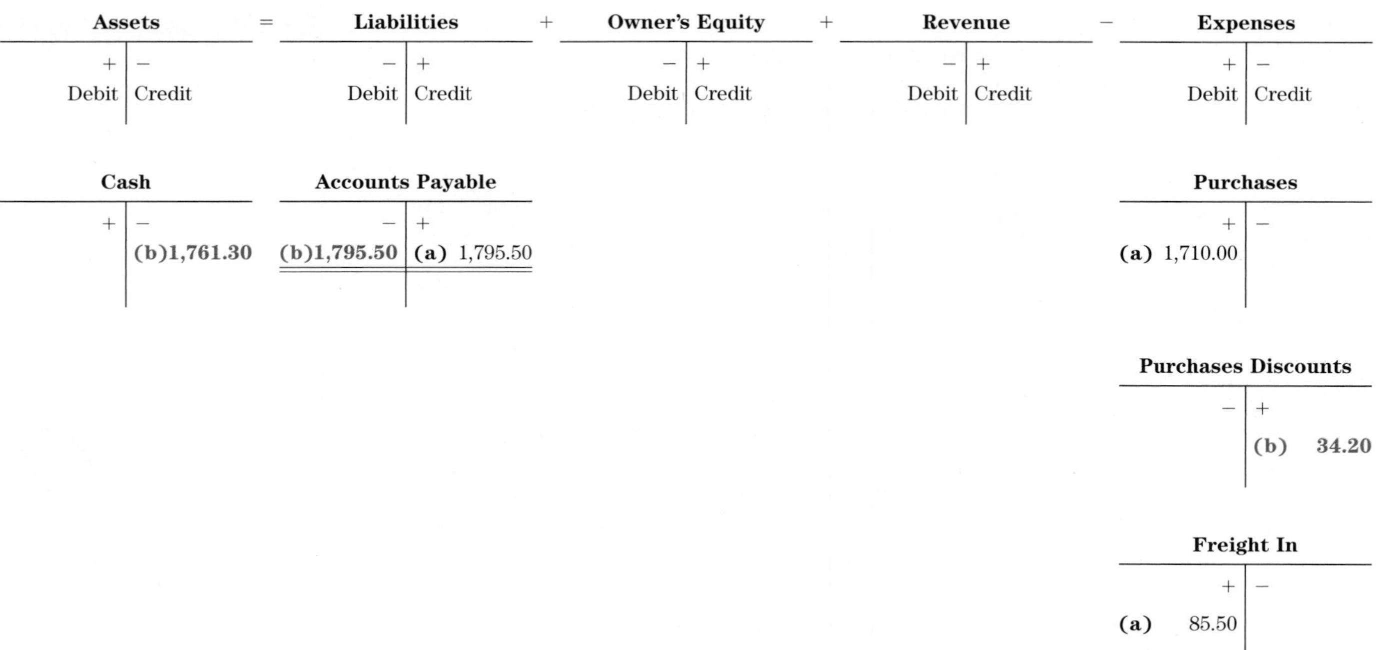

Similar to sales returns, purchase returns and allowances are also not included when calculating the discount. Remember to always leave out any prepaid freight and returns and allowances when determining the amount of the discount.

No Purchase Discounts Involved

When a transaction does not involve a purchase discount or the discount has expired, the buyer will record the payment by debiting Accounts Payable and crediting Cash. Assume that Blue Merchandise Company recorded the following transactions:

Transaction (a). On November 1, Blue Merchandise Company bought merchandise on account from Grey, Inc., invoice no. 3901, $4,600; terms 2/10, n/30; dated October 31.

Transaction (b). On November 28, issued Ck. No. 1151 to Grey, Inc., in payment of invoice no. 3901, $4,600.

Blue Merchandise Company's accountant would record the transactions in the general journal as:

GENERAL JOURNAL PAGE 81

Date		Description	Post. Ref.	Debit	Credit
20—					
Nov.	1	Purchases		4 6 0 0 00	
		Accounts Payable, Grey, Inc.			4 6 0 0 00
		Purchased merchandise from			
		Grey, Inc., invoice no. 3901,			
		invoice dated 10/31, terms			
		2/10, n/30.			
	28	Accounts Payable, Grey, Inc.		4 6 0 0 00	
		Cash			4 6 0 0 00
		Paid Grey, Inc., for invoice			
		no. 3901, Ck. No. 1151.			

Notice that since Blue Merchandise Company did not make payment within 10 days, the discount was not applied to the invoice amount. Blue Merchandise Company paid the invoice in full.

Posting to the General Ledger and Subsidiary Ledger

To post cash payments of purchases, post each entry to Cash, Accounts Payable, and any other accounts involved in the general ledger. Also, post the amounts owed to vendors to the subsidiary accounts payable ledger to maintain a running balance of the amount owed to each vendor.

Posting to the General Ledger and Subsidiary Ledger—A Computerized Approach

Businesses can use a computerized accounting program to enter cash payments to vendors. Cash payments are applied to vendor invoices that are created by the accountant in the software program. In Figure 5, the accountant is beginning to record the payment of the invoice by selecting the correct invoice due.

After the accountant has selected the bill on which to make payment, the accountant can then apply any discount granted and process the payment. Figure 6 shows the bill payment check screen that shows payment has been applied to the invoice.

Purchases Returns and Allowances, Purchases Discounts, and Freight In on an Income Statement

In the fundamental accounting equation, to be consistent with the income statement, we placed Purchases Returns and Allowances and Purchases Discounts under Purchases with the plus and minus signs reversed. Both accounts are contra accounts, so we subtract their totals from Purchases on the income statement. Since Freight In increases the cost of purchases, it must be added. A portion of the Cost of Goods Sold section of the annual income statement of Whitewater Raft Supply, as well as the Revenue from Sales section (taken from Figure 4 on page 399), is shown in Figure 7.

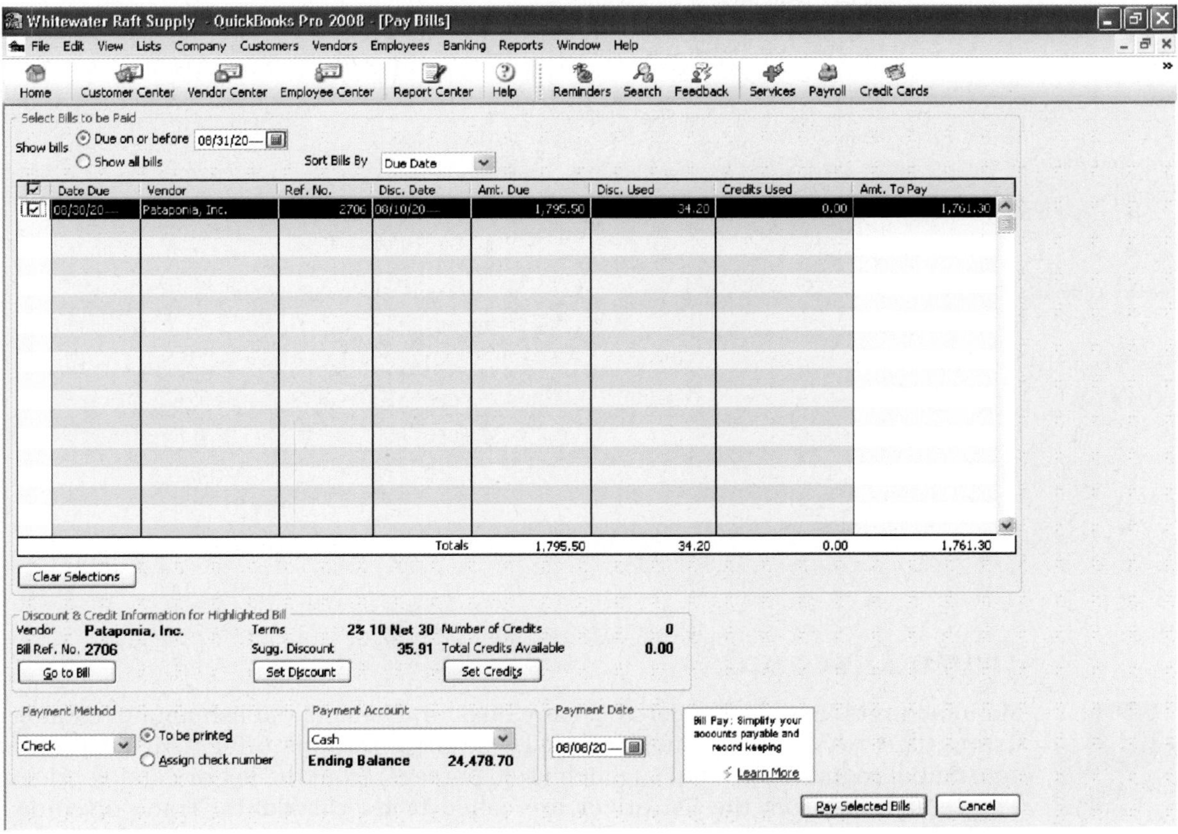

FIGURE 5
Recording a cash payment using accounting software

FIGURE 6
Bill payment

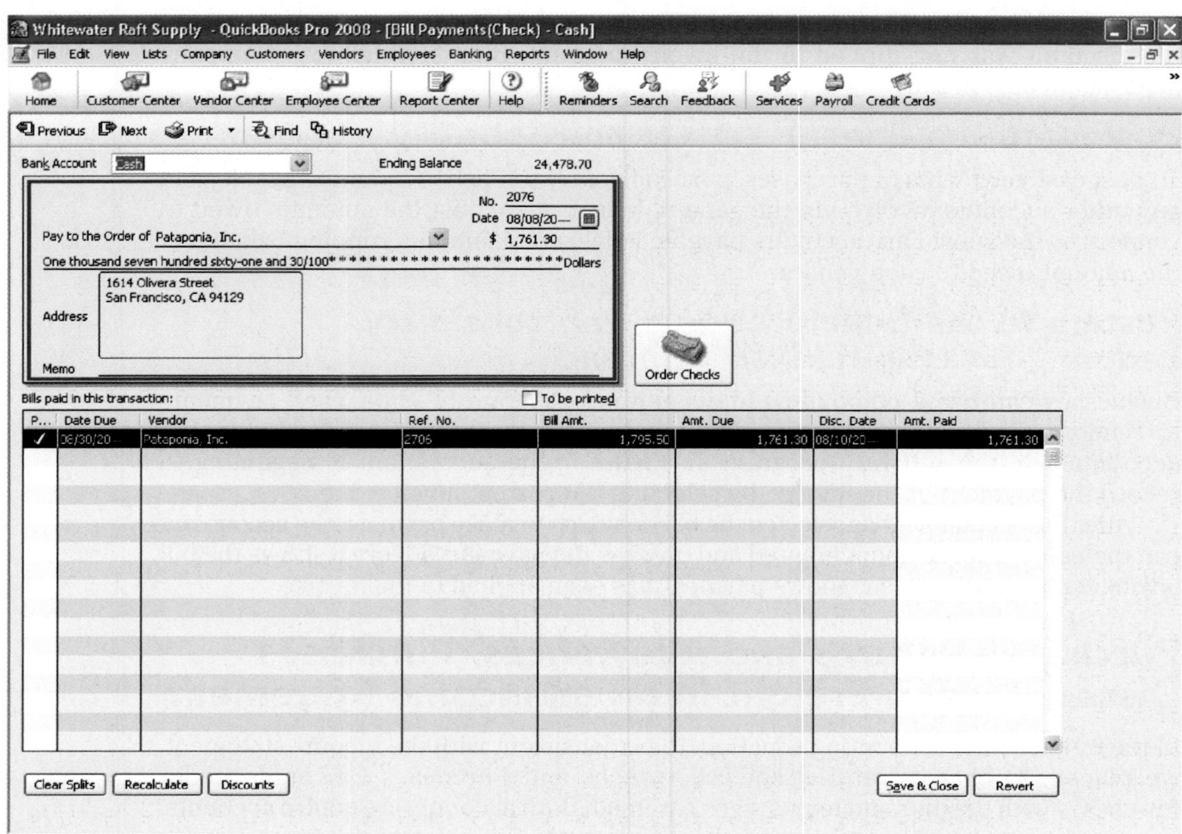

FIGURE 7
Partial income statement for Whitewater Raft Supply

Whitewater Raft Supply Income Statement For the Year Ended December 31, 20—				
Revenue from Sales:				
Sales			$257,180	
Less: Sales Returns and Allowances		$ 940		
Sales Discounts		1,980	2,920	
Net Sales				$254,260
Cost of Goods Sold:				
Merchandise Inventory, January 1, 20—			$ 67,000	
Purchases		$87,840		
Less: Purchases Returns and Allowances	$ 932			
Purchases Discounts	1,348	2,280		
Net Purchases		$85,560		
Add Freight In		2,360		
Delivered Cost of Purchases			87,920	
Cost of Goods Available for Sale			$154,920	

Trade Discounts

Manufacturers and wholesalers of many lines of products publish annual catalogs listing their products at retail prices. These organizations offer their customers substantial reductions (often as much as 40 percent) from the list or catalog prices. The reductions from the list prices are called **trade discounts**. Trade discounts are not journalized. Remember, firms grant cash discounts for prompt payment of invoices. Trade discounts are *not related* to cash payments. Manufacturers and wholesalers use trade discounts to avoid the high cost of reprinting catalogs when selling prices change. To change prices, the manufacturer or wholesaler simply issues a sheet or online posting that shows a new list of trade discounts to be applied to the catalog prices. Trade discounts can also be used to differentiate between classes of customers. For example, a manufacturer may use one schedule of trade discounts for wholesalers and another schedule for retailers.

Firms may quote trade discounts as a single percentage. *Example:* A distributor of furnaces grants a single discount of 40 percent off the listed catalog price of $8,000. In this case, the selling price is calculated as follows:

List or catalog price	$8,000
Less trade discount of 40% ($8,000 × 0.40)	3,200
Selling price	$4,800

Neither the seller nor the buyer records trade discounts in the accounts; they enter only the selling price. Using T accounts, the furnace distributor records the sale like this:

Accounts Receivable	
+	−
4,800	

Sales	
−	+
	4,800

The buyer records the purchase as follows:

Purchases	
+	−
4,800	

Accounts Payable	
−	+
	4,800

Firms may also quote trade discounts as a chain, or series, of percentages. For example, a distributor of automobile parts grants discounts of 30 percent, 10 percent, and 10 percent off the listed catalog price of $900. In this case, the selling price is calculated as follows:

List or catalog price	$900.00
Less first trade discount of 30% ($900 × 0.30)	270.00
Remainder after first discount	$630.00
Less second trade discount of 10% ($630 × 0.10)	63.00
Remainder after second discount	$567.00
Less third discount of 10% ($567 × 0.10)	56.70
Selling price	$510.30

Using T accounts, the automobile parts distributor records the sale as follows:

Accounts Receivable	
+	−
510.30	

Sales	
−	+
	510.30

The buyer records the purchase as follows:

Purchases	
+	−
510.30	

Accounts Payable	
−	+
	510.30

In the situation involving a chain of discounts, the additional discounts are granted for large-volume transactions, either in dollar amount or in size of shipment, such as carload lots.

Cash discounts could also apply in situations involving trade discounts. *Example:* Suppose that the credit terms of the preceding sale include a cash discount of 2/10, n/30, and that the buyer pays the invoice within 10 days. The seller applies the cash discount to the selling price. The seller records the transaction as shown in the following T accounts:

Cash		Sales Discounts		Accounts Receivable	
+	–	+	–	+	–
500.09		10.21			510.30

The buyer records the transaction as follows:

Cash		Purchases Discounts		Accounts Payable	
+	–	+	–	+	–
	500.09		10.21	510.30	

Remember

To the seller, a cash discount is a sales discount, and to the purchaser, a cash discount is a purchases discount.

A Review of Purchases and Sales Transactions

Now that we have covered all of the transactions involving purchases and sales, let's take a moment to review. Remember that each transaction affects a purchaser and a seller. In Figure 8, we show how each transaction would be recorded by a purchaser (Able Company) and a seller (Baker Company).

FIGURE 8

Transactions for two companies' purchases and sales

Purchaser's Books—Able Company			Seller's Books—Baker Company		
Bought merchandise from Baker Company, $500; terms 2/10, n/30.			Sold merchandise to Able Company, $500; terms 2/10, n/30.		
Purchases	500		Accounts Receivable	500	
Accounts Payable		500	Sales		500
Received credit memo from Baker Company for return of merchandise, $100.			Issued credit memo to Able Company for return of merchandise, $100.		
Accounts Payable	100		Sales Returns and Allowances	100	
Purchases Returns and Allowances		100	Accounts Receivable		100
Paid Baker Company within the discount period, $392 ($500 − $100 = $400; $400 × .02 = $8; $400 − $8 = $392).			Received cash from Able Company within the discount period, $392.		
Accounts Payable	400		Cash	392	
Cash		392	Sales Discounts	8	
Purchases Discounts		8	Accounts Receivable		400

PART TWO—RECORDING TRANSACTIONS INTO THE CASH RECEIPTS JOURNAL AND CASH PAYMENTS JOURNAL

In Chapter 9, we saw that using a sales journal and a purchases journal enables an accountant to carry out the journalizing and posting processes much more efficiently. These special journals make it possible to post column totals rather than individual figures. They also make the division of labor more efficient because the journalizing functions can be delegated to different persons. The *cash receipts journal* and the *cash payments journal* further extend these advantages.

The Cash Receipts Journal

The **cash receipts journal** contains all transactions in which cash is received, or increased. When a cash receipts journal is used, all transactions in which cash is debited *must* be recorded in it. It may be used for a service as well as a merchandising business. Let's list some typical transactions of a merchandising business, Whitewater Raft Supply, that result in an increase in cash. To get a better picture of the transactions, let's first record them in T accounts and then in the general journal.

5 LEARNING OBJECTIVE

Journalize transactions for a merchandising business in a cash receipts journal and post from a cash receipts journal to a general ledger and an accounts receivable ledger.

Oct. 1 Sold merchandise on account to Green River Rafts, invoice no. 10050, $3,500; terms 2/10, n/30.

Accounts Receivable	
+	−
3,500	

Sales	
−	+
	3,500

Oct. 4 Sold merchandise, $500, and the customer used a credit card.

The bank issuing the card bills the customer directly each month. The business, on the other hand, deposits the bank credit card receipts every day. The bank *deducts a discount* and credits the firm's account with cash. We will assume that the discount is 4 percent. The firm therefore records the amount of the discount under Credit Card Expense: $500.00 × 0.04 = $20.00 credit card expense; $500.00 − $20.00 = $480.00.

Cash	
+	−
480	

Credit Card Expense	
+	−
20	

Sales	
−	+
	500

As an alternative, many businesses postpone recording the amount of bank credit card expense until they actually receive notification from their bank on their bank statement. For example, total credit card sales for a restaurant for a time period amount to $10,600 plus 8 percent sales tax. The entry is as follows:

Cash	
+	−
11,448	

Sales Tax Payable	
−	+
	848

Sales	
−	+
	10,600

The restaurant's next bank statement includes a debit memorandum for credit card charges of $457.92, using an assumed 4 percent discount rate ($11,448 × 0.04). The business handles this in a similar manner to a check service charge:

Credit Card Expense	
+	−
457.92	

Cash	
+	−
	457.92

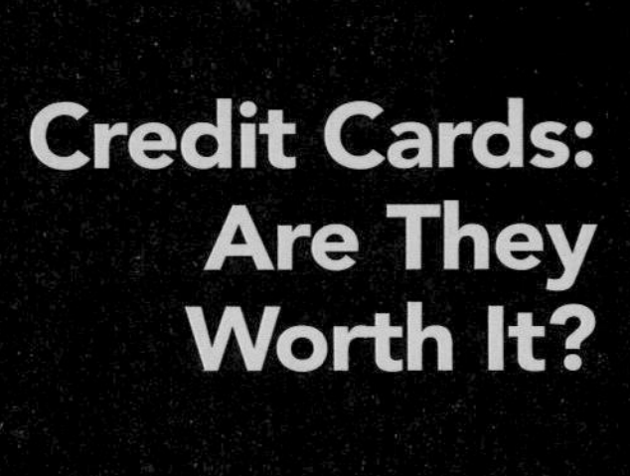

Credit Cards: Are They Worth It?

SMALL BUSINESS SUCCESS

Accepting credit cards for sales of merchandise or services has become a natural part of business for most companies. However, some small businesses still don't accept credit cards and rely only on cash sales. The decision to accept credit cards comes at a cost to the business, in the form of a fee. The bank that processes your credit card sales will charge your company a fee for any credit card sales. The amount of the fee will vary, based on the bank that you are using and the amount of transactions your company processes. In addition to banks, there are specific companies, often called merchant service companies, that offer credit card processing services.

Why would a company choose to accept credit cards in the form of payment? There are many reasons. One is that it will possibly increase sales by allowing customers more flexibility in payment methods. Also, the bank or processing company assumes all risk associated with non-paying customers. Unlike uncollectible accounts receivables, the company will always get paid when a transaction involves a credit card sale.

How does a company begin accepting credit cards? The first step is to apply for merchant status. Applying for merchant status is similar to applying for a loan. Your company must fill out an application and have its financial records reviewed. Once merchant status is approved for your company, you will be able to accept most common credit cards. The bank or merchant services company that you partner with will transfer the cash proceeds, less the fee, for each credit card sale to your bank account. The transaction fee or service charge usually ranges from 1.5 to 5 percent of the sale. In addition, there may be monthly or other fees associated with credit card transactions.

Oct. 5 Collected cash on account from L. R. Ray, a charge customer, $416.

Cash		Accounts Receivable	
+	−	+	−
416			416

Oct. 7 The owner, D. M. Bruce, invested cash in the business, $9,000.

Cash		D. M. Bruce, Capital	
+	−	−	+
9,000			9,000

Oct. 8 Sold equipment for cash at cost, $500.

Cash		Equipment	
+	−	+	−
500			500

Oct. 10 Received check from Green River Rafts for $3,430 in payment of invoice no. 10050, less cash discount ($3,500 × 0.02 = $70; $3,500 − $70 = $3,430).

Cash		Sales Discounts		Accounts Receivable	
+	−	+	−	+	−
3,430		70			3,500

Oct 15. Cash sales for first half of the month, $2,460.

Cash	
+	−
2,460	

Sales	
−	+
	2,460

The same transactions are shown in general journal form as follows:

GENERAL JOURNAL PAGE 29

Date		Description	Post. Ref.	Debit	Credit
20—					
Oct.	1	Accounts Receivable, Green River Rafts		3 5 0 0 00	
		Sales			3 5 0 0 00
		Sold merchandise to Green			
		River Rafts, invoice no. 10050.			
	4	Cash		4 8 0 00	
		Credit Card Expense		2 0 00	
		Sales			5 0 0 00
		Sold merchandise involving a credit			
		card.			
	5	Cash		4 1 6 00	
		Accounts Receivable, L. R. Ray			4 1 6 00
		Collected cash on account.			
	7	Cash		9 0 0 0 00	
		D. M. Bruce, Capital			9 0 0 0 00
		Owner invested cash.			
	8	Cash		5 0 0 00	
		Equipment			5 0 0 00
		Sold equipment at cost.			
	10	Cash		3 4 3 0 00	
		Sales Discounts		7 0 00	
		Accounts Receivable, Green River Rafts			3 5 0 0 00
		Received a check in payment of			
		invoice no. 10050, less cash			
		discount.			
	15	Cash		2 4 6 0 00	
		Sales			2 4 6 0 00
		Cash sales for the first half			
		of the month.			

Now let's analyze these seven transactions: The transaction on October 1 does not involve cash; therefore, it would not be recorded in the cash receipts journal. Instead, this transaction would be recorded in either the general journal or the sales journal. The transactions occurring on October 4, 5, 10, and 15 would occur frequently; the transactions on October 7 and 8 would occur less frequently. When designing a cash receipts journal, it is logical to include a Cash Debit column because all the transactions involve an increase in cash. If a business regularly collects cash from credit customers, there should be an Accounts Receivable Credit column and Sales Discounts Debit column. If a firm often sells merchandise for cash and collects a sales tax, there should be a Sales Credit column and a Sales Tax Payable Credit column. If the business accepts credit cards and wants to record the amount of the discount at the time of each transaction, there should be a Credit Card Expense Debit column for the amount deducted by the bank.

However, the credit to D. M. Bruce, Capital, and the credit to Equipment do not occur very often, so it would not be practical to set up special columns for these credits. They can be handled adequately by an Other Accounts Credit column, which can be used for credits to all accounts that have no special column.

The accountant would record these transactions in a cash receipts journal (see Figure 9). Notice that there are columns for each of the most common cash transactions. The accountant would record each transaction directly into the cash receipts journal by placing each amount into the appropriate column.

FIGURE 9
Cash receipts journal

CASH RECEIPTS JOURNAL — PAGE 41

Date		Account Credited	Post. Ref.	Cash Debit	Credit Card Expense Debit	Sales Discounts Debit	Accounts Receivable Credit	Sales Credit	Other Accounts Credit
20—									
Oct.	4	———		480 00	20 00			500 00	
	5	L. R. Ray		416 00			416 00		
	7	D.M. Bruce,							
		Capital		9000 00					9000 00
	8	Equipment		500 00					500 00
	10	Green							
		River Rafts		3430 00		70 00	3500 00		
	15	———		2460 00				2460 00	

Remember

Special journals include a sales journal (S), a purchases journal (P), a cash receipts journal (CR), and a cash payments journal (CP). They are used to save time by posting totals of the special columns rather than individual amounts to the general ledger.

Posting from the Cash Receipts Journal

Here are some other transactions made during the month that involve increases in cash.

Oct. 16 Received check from Floyd Mercantile for $1,366.12 in payment of invoice no. 10052, less cash discount ($1,394.00 − $27.88 = $1,366.12).
17 Borrowed $9,000 from the bank, receiving cash and giving the bank a promissory note.
21 Received check from Hartman Guides for $3,696.80 in payment of invoice no. 10055, less cash discount ($3,772.24 − $75.44 = $3,696.80).
30 Received check from Bowers River Co. for $1,710.00 in payment of invoice no. 10054. (This is longer than the 10-day period, so the cash discount is not allowed.)
31 Cash sales for second half of the month, $2,620.

In the transaction of October 17, in which $9,000 was borrowed from the bank, the bank was given a **promissory note** (a written promise to pay a specified amount at a specified time) as evidence of the debt. The account **Notes Payable**, instead of Accounts Payable, is used to represent the amount owed on the promissory note. The Accounts Payable account is reserved for charge accounts with creditors, which are normally paid on a 30-day basis.

Let's assume that all the month's transactions involving debits to Cash have now been recorded in the cash receipts journal. The cash receipts journal (see Figure 10) and the T accounts following it illustrate the postings to the general ledger and the accounts receivable ledger.

Individual amounts in the Accounts Receivable Credit column of the cash receipts journal are usually posted daily to the accounts receivable ledger. Individual amounts in the Other Accounts Credit column are usually posted daily.

At the end of the month, we can post the special column totals in the cash receipts journal to the general ledger accounts. These columns include Cash Debit, Credit Card Expense Debit, Sales Discounts Debit, Accounts Receivable Credit, and Sales Credit.

FIGURE 10

Posting from the cash receipts journal to the general ledger and accounts receivable ledger

CASH RECEIPTS JOURNAL PAGE 41

Date		Account Credited	Post. Ref.	Cash Debit	Credit Card Expense Debit	Sales Discounts Debit	Accounts Receivable Credit	Sales Credit	Other Accounts Credit
20—									
Oct.	4	————	—	480.00	20.00			500.00	
	5	L. R. Ray	✓	416.00			416.00		
	7	D. M. Bruce, Capital	311	9,000.00					9,000.00
	8	Equipment	124	500.00					500.00
	10	Green River Rafts	✓	3,430.00		70.00	3,500.00		
	15	————	—	2,460.00				2,460.00	
	16	Floyd Mercantile	✓	1,366.12		27.88	1,394.00		
	17	Notes Payable	211	9,000.00					9,000.00
	21	Hartman Guides	✓	3,696.80		75.44	3,772.24		
	30	Bowers River Co.	✓	1,710.00			1,710.00		
	31	————	—	2,620.00				2,620.00	
	31	Total		34,678.92	20.00	173.32	10,792.24	5,580.00	18,500.00
				(111)	(615)	(413)	(113)	(411)	(X)

Accounts Receivable Ledger

Bowers River Co.

+		−	
Beg. Bal.	2,500.00	Oct. 30	1,710.00
End. Bal.	790.00		

Floyd Mercantile

+		−	
Beg. Bal.	1,394.00	Oct. 16	1,394.00

Green River Rafts

+		−	
Beg. Bal.	5,000.00	Oct. 10	3,500.00
End Bal.	1,500.00		

Hartman Guides

+		−	
Beg. Bal.	3,772.24	Oct. 21	3,772.24

L. R. Ray

+		−	
Beg. Bal.	416.00	Oct. 5	416.00

General Ledger

Cash 111

+		−	
Oct. 31	34,678.92		

D. M. Bruce, Capital 311

−		+	
		Oct. 7	9,000.00

Accounts Receivable 113

+		−	
		Oct. 31	10,792.24

Sales 411

−		+	
		Oct. 31	5,580.00

Equipment 124

+		−	
		Oct. 8	500.00

Sales Discounts 413

+		−	
Oct. 31	173.32		

Notes Payable 211

−		+	
		Oct. 17	9,000.00

Credit Card Expense 615

+		−	
Oct. 31	20.00		

In the Post. Ref. column, the check marks (✓) indicate that the amounts in the Accounts Receivable Credit column have been posted to the individual credit customers' accounts as credits. The account numbers show that the amounts in the Other Accounts Credit column have been posted separately to the accounts described in the Account Credited column. An (X) goes under the total of the Other Accounts Credit column; it means "do not post—the figures have already been posted separately." This column is totaled to make it easier to prove that the debits equal the credits.

Debit Totals		Credit Totals	
Cash	$34,678.92	Accounts Receivable	$10,792.24
Credit Card Expense	20.00	Sales	5,580.00
Sales Discounts	173.32	Other Accounts	18,500.00
	$34,872.24		$34,872.24

Advantages of a Cash Receipts Journal

The advantages of using a cash receipts journal include:

1. Transactions generally can be recorded on one line.
2. All transactions involving debits to Cash are recorded in one place.
3. It eliminates much repetition in posting when there are numerous transactions involving Cash debits. The Cash Debit side can be posted as one total.
4. Special columns can be used for specialized transactions and posted as one total.

The Cash Payments Journal

LEARNING OBJECTIVE 6

Journalize transactions for a merchandising business in a cash payments journal and post from a cash payments journal to a general ledger and an accounts payable ledger.

The **cash payments journal**, as the name implies, is a special journal used to record all transactions in which cash goes out, or decreases. When the cash payments journal is used, all transactions in which cash is credited *must* be recorded in it. This journal may be used for either a service or a merchandising business.

To get acquainted with the cash payments journal, let's list some typical transactions of a merchandising business that result in a decrease in cash. To illustrate, we record the following transactions in T accounts:

Oct. 2 Bought merchandise on account from Pataponia, Inc., invoice no. 2746, $2,500; terms 2/10, n/30; dated September 30; FOB San Francisco, freight prepaid and added to the invoice, $100.25 (total $2,600.25).

Accounts Payable		Purchases		Freight In	
−	+	+	−	+	−
	2,600.25	2,500.00		100.25	

Oct. 8 Issued Ck. No. 2226 to Pataponia, Inc., in payment of invoice no. 2730, less cash discount of $50.00, $2,550.25 ($2,600.25 − $50.00). (Notice that the discount applies only to the amount billed for the merchandise (2 percent of $2,500).

Cash		Accounts Payable		Purchases Discounts	
+	−	−	+	−	+
	2,550.25	2,600.25			50.00

Oct. 10 Paid cash for liability insurance, Ck. No. 2227 $4,890.

Prepaid Insurance		Cash	
+	−	+	−
4,890			4,890

Oct. 12 Paid wages for two weeks, Ck. No. 2228, $6,220 (previously recorded in the payroll entry).

Wages Payable		Cash	
−	+	+	−
6,220			6,220

Oct. 14 Paid rent for the month, Ck. No. 2229, $2,950.

Rent Expense		Cash	
+	−	+	−
2,950			2,950

The same transactions are now shown in general journal form as follows:

GENERAL JOURNAL PAGE 29

Date		Description	Post. Ref.	Debit	Credit
20—					
Oct.	2	Purchases		2,500.00	
		Freight In		100.25	
		Accounts Payable, Pataponia, Inc.			2,600.25
		Purchased merchandise			
		from Pataponia, Inc., invoice			
		no. 2746, invoice dated 9/30,			
		terms 2/10, n/30.			
	8	Accounts Payable, Pataponia, Inc.		2,600.25	
		Cash			2,550.25
		Purchases Discounts			50.00
		Paid on account, Ck. No. 2226.			
	10	Prepaid Insurance		4,890.00	
		Cash			4,890.00
		Paid liability insurance,			
		Ck. No. 2227.			
	12	Wages Payable		6,220.00	
		Cash			6,220.00
		Paid wages for two weeks,			
		Ck. No. 2228.			
	14	Rent Expense		2,950.00	
		Cash			2,950.00
		Paid rent for month, Ck. No. 2229.			

Now let's analyze these five transactions. The transaction on October 2 does not involve cash; therefore, it would not be recorded in the cash payments journal. Instead, this transaction would be recorded in either the general journal or the purchases journal. The transaction on October 8 would occur frequently, as payments to creditors are made several times a month. Of the other transactions, the debit to Wages Payable might occur twice a month, the debit to Rent Expense once a month, and the debit to Prepaid Insurance only occasionally.

It is logical to include a Cash Credit column in a cash payments journal because all transactions recorded in this journal involve a decrease in cash. Since payments to creditors are made often, there should also be an Accounts Payable Debit column and a Purchases Discounts Credit column. You can set up any other column that is used often enough to warrant it. Otherwise, an Other Accounts Debit column takes care of all the other transactions.

Now let's record these same transactions in a cash payments journal and include a column titled Ck. No. (see Figure 11). If you think for a moment, you will see that this is consistent with good management of cash. All expenditures except Petty Cash expenditures should be paid for by check.

FIGURE 11
Cash payments journal

CASH PAYMENTS JOURNAL PAGE 62

Date		Ck. No.	Account Debited	Post. Ref.	Other Accounts Debit	Accounts Payable Debit	Purchases Discounts Credit	Cash Credit
20—								
Oct.	8	2226	Pataponia, Inc.			2,600.25	50.00	2,550.25
	10	2227	Prepaid Insurance		4,890.00			4,890.00
	12	2228	Wages Payable		6,220.00			6,220.00
	14	2229	Rent Expense		2,950.00			2,950.00

Here are some other transactions of Whitewater Raft Supply involving decreases in cash during October. Note that credit terms vary among the different creditors.

Oct. 15 Issued Ck. No. 2230 to Gibbs Company in payment of invoice no. 10611 ($564), less return ($270); less cash discount, terms 2/10, n/30; $288.12 ($564 − $270 = $294; $294.00 × 0.02 = $5.88; $294.00 − $5.88 = $288.12).

16 Issued Ck. No. 2231 to Gardner Products Company in payment of invoice no. B643 ($1,245), less return ($315); less cash discount, terms 1/10, n/30; $921.60 [$1,245 − $315 = $930; freight charges totaled $90 ($930 − $90 = $840); $840.00 × 0.01 = $8.40; $930.00 − $8.40 = $921.60].

17 Bought merchandise for cash, Ck. No. 2232, payable to Jones and Son, $200.

19 Received bill and issued Ck. No. 2233 to Monroe Express for freight charges on merchandise purchased earlier from Gibbs Company, $60.

23 Voided Ck. No. 2234.

25 Paid wages for two-week period, Ck. No. 2235, $1,750 (previously recorded in the payroll entry).

27 Paid F. P. Franz for merchandise returned on a cash sale, Ck. No. 2236, $51.

27 Issued Ck. No. 2237 to Langseth and Son in payment of invoice no. 902, $1,180; terms net 30 days.

The transaction of October 19 paying the freight bill to Monroe Express increases the Freight In account, as the transportation charges are for merchandise purchased.

You should list all checks in consecutive order, even those checks that must be voided. In this way, *every* check is accounted for, which is necessary for internal control.

These transactions are recorded in the cash payments journal illustrated in Figure 12. Notice that an (X) is placed under the Other Accounts column. That means "do not post—the figures have already been posted separately."

The posting process for the cash payments journal is similar to the posting process for the cash receipts journal. Individual amounts in the Accounts Payable Debit column are usually posted daily to the subsidiary ledger. After posting, put a check mark (✓) in the Post. Ref. column. Individual amounts in the Other Accounts Debit column are usually posted daily to the general ledger. Post these figures individually, then place the account number in the Post. Ref. column. Totals of the Cash Credit column, Purchases Discounts Credit column, and Accounts Payable Debit column are posted to the general ledger accounts at the end of the month. Write the appropriate general ledger account number in parentheses below the column totals. Put an (X) below the total of the Other Accounts Debit column to indicate that the total amount is not posted.

At the end of the month, after totaling the columns, check the accuracy of the footings by proving that the sum of the debit totals equals the sum of the credit totals. Since you have posted the individual amounts in the Other Accounts Debit column to the general ledger, the only posting that remains is the credit to the Cash account for $21,060.97, the credit to Purchases Discounts account for $64.28 and the debit to the Accounts Payable (controlling) account for $5,004.25.

Remember

The (X) below the total of the Other Accounts Debit column means "do not post total."

Debit Totals		**Credit Totals**	
Accounts Payable	$ 5,004.25	Cash	$21,060.97
Other Accounts	16,121.00	Purchases Discounts	64.28
	$21,125.25		$21,125.25

FIGURE 12
Cash payments journal

CASH PAYMENTS JOURNAL PAGE 62

Date		Ck. No.	Account Debited	Post. Ref.	Other Accounts Debit	Accounts Payable Debit	Purchases Discounts Credit	Cash Credit
20—								
Oct.	8	2226	Pataponia, Inc.	✓		2 6 0 0 25	5 0 00	2 5 5 0 25
	10	2227	Prepaid Insurance	116	4 8 9 0 00			4 8 9 0 00
	12	2228	Wages Payable	213	6 2 2 0 00			6 2 2 0 00
	14	2229	Rent Expense	612	2 9 5 0 00			2 9 5 0 00
	15	2230	Gibbs Company	✓		2 9 4 00	5 88	2 8 8 12
	16	2231	Gardner Products Company	✓		9 3 0 00	8 40	9 2 1 60
	17	2232	Purchases	511	2 0 0 00			2 0 0 00
	19	2233	Freight In	514	6 0 00			6 0 00
	23	2234	Void	—				
	25	2235	Wages Payable	213	1 7 5 0 00			1 7 5 0 00
	27	2236	Sales Returns and Allowances	412	5 1 00			5 1 00
	27	2237	Langseth and Son	✓		1 1 8 0 00		1 1 8 0 00
	31		Totals		16 1 2 1 00	5 0 0 4 25	6 4 28	21 0 6 0 97
					(X)	(2 1 2)	(5 1 3)	(1 1 1)

Advantages of a Cash Payments Journal

The advantages of the cash payments journal are similar to the advantages of the cash receipts journal:

1. Transactions generally can be recorded on one line.
2. All transactions involving credits to Cash are recorded in one place.
3. For numerous transactions involving Cash credits, the Cash Credit side can be posted as one total.
4. Special columns can be used for specialized transactions and posted as one total.

COMPARISON OF THE FIVE TYPES OF JOURNALS

We have now looked at four special journals and the general journal. It is important for a business to select and use the journals that provide the most efficient accounting system possible. Figure 13 summarizes the applications of the journals we have discussed and the correct procedures for using them.

FIGURE 13
Using special journals

Types of Transactions				
Sale of merchandise on account	Purchase of merchandise on account	Receipt of cash	Payment of cash	All other
Evidenced by Source Documents				
Sales invoice	Purchase invoice	Credit card receipts Cash Checks Electronic funds transfers	Check stub Electronic funds transfers	Miscellaneous
Types of Journals				
Sales journal	Purchases journal	Cash receipts journal	Cash payments journal	General journal
Posting to Ledger Accounts				
Individual amounts posted daily to the accounts receivable ledger and the total posted monthly to the general ledger.	*Individual amounts posted daily to the accounts payable ledger and the totals of the special columns posted monthly to the general ledger.*	*Individual amounts in the Accounts Receivable Credit column posted daily to the accounts receivable ledger.* *Individual amounts in the Other Accounts columns posted daily to the general ledger.* *Totals of special columns posted monthly to the general ledger.*	*Individual amounts in the Accounts Payable Debit column posted daily to the accounts payable ledger.* *Individual amounts in the Other Accounts columns posted daily to the general ledger.* *Totals of special columns posted monthly to the general ledger.*	*Entries posted daily to the subsidiary ledgers and the general ledger.*

Recommended Order of Posting to the Subsidiary Ledgers and the General Ledger

To avoid errors and negative balances in accounts, post from the special journals in this order:

1. Sales journal
2. Purchases journal
3. Cash receipts journal
4. Cash payments journal

CHAPTER REVIEW

Study & Practice

LEARNING OBJECTIVE

Determine cash discounts according to credit terms.

The amount of the discount is determined by multiplying the invoice total (excluding freight charges and any returns and allowances) by the **cash discount** rate.

PRACTICE EXERCISE 1

For the following purchases of merchandise, determine the amount of cash to be paid:

Purchase	Invoice Date	Credit Terms	FOB	Amount of Purchase	Freight Charges	Total Invoice Amount	Returns and Allowances	Date Paid
a.	June 12	1/10, n/30	Destination	$700	—	$ 700	$100	June 21
b.	June 14	2/10, n/30	Shipping point	940	$60	1,000	—	June 20
c.	June 18	n/30	Shipping point	820	40	860	30	July 17

PRACTICE EXERCISE 1 SOLUTION

a. $594 ($700 − $100) − ($600 × 0.01) = $600 − $6 = $594
b. $981.20 ($940 + $60) − ($940 × 0.02) = $1,000 − $18.80 = $981.20
c. $830 ($820 + $40) − $30 = $830

2 LEARNING OBJECTIVE

Journalize sales transactions in a general journal involving cash receipts from credit customers who are entitled to deduct the cash discount.

When recording a cash receipt from a customer within the discount period, the business records a debit to Cash for the amount received, a debit to Sales Discounts for the amount of the discount, and a credit to Accounts Receivable for the full amount of the invoice less any returns and allowances.

PRACTICE EXERCISE 2

Record the following sales transactions in general journal form on the books of Fry Company (the seller).

a. Sold merchandise on account to Lee Company, invoice no. 8765, $1,500; terms 2/10, n/30.

b. Issued credit memo no. 967 to Lee Company for damaged merchandise, $100.

c. Lee Company paid the account in full within the discount period.

PRACTICE EXERCISE 2 SOLUTION

GENERAL JOURNAL PAGE ____

Date		Description	Post. Ref.	Debit	Credit
	a.	Accounts Receivable, Lee Company		1 5 0 0 00	
		Sales			1 5 0 0 00
		Sold merchandise to Lee			
		Company, invoice no. 8765.			
	b.	Sales Returns and Allowances		1 0 0 00	
		Accounts Receivable, Lee Company			1 0 0 00
		Issued credit memo no. 967.			
	c.	Cash		1 3 7 2 00	
		Sales Discounts		2 8 00	
		Accounts Receivable, Lee Company			1 4 0 0 00
		Received payment in full.			

3 LEARNING OBJECTIVE

Journalize purchase transactions in a general journal involving cash payments when entitled to deduct the cash discount.

When recording a payment to a vendor within the discount period, the business records a debit to Accounts Payable for the full amount of the invoice less any returns and allowances, a credit to Purchase Discounts for the amount of the discount, and a credit to Cash for the amount paid.

PRACTICE EXERCISE 3

Record the following purchase transactions in general journal form on the books of Lee Company (the buyer).

a. Purchased merchandise on account from Fry Company, invoice no. 8765, $1,500; terms 2/10, n/30.

b. Received credit memo no. 967 from Fry Company for damaged merchandise, $100.

c. Paid Fry Company in full within the discount period.

PRACTICE EXERCISE 3 SOLUTION

GENERAL JOURNAL PAGE ____

Date		Description	Post. Ref.	Debit	Credit
	a.	Purchases		1,500.00	
		Accounts Payable, Fry Company			1,500.00
		Purchased merchandise from			
		Fry Company, invoice no. 8765.			
	b.	Accounts Payable, Fry Company		100.00	
		Purchases Returns and Allowances			100.00
		Received credit memo no. 967.			
	c.	Accounts Payable, Fry Company		1,400.00	
		Purchases Discounts			
		(($1,500 − $100) × .02)			28.00
		Cash			1,372.00
		Paid invoice no. 8675 in full.			

LEARNING OBJECTIVE **4**

Journalize transactions involving trade discounts.

In transactions involving **trade discounts**, the trade discounts are deducted from the list prices to arrive at the selling prices. Both sellers and buyers record the transactions at the selling prices.

PRACTICE EXERCISE 4

Record the following transaction involving a trade discount.

Feb. 2 Bought merchandise on account from Coffee Company, $3,500, received a 40% trade discount, invoice no. 234C, dated Jan. 31; terms 2/10, n/EOM.

PRACTICE EXERCISE 4 SOLUTION

GENERAL JOURNAL PAGE ____

Date		Description	Post. Ref.	Debit	Credit
20—					
Feb.	2	Purchases		2,100.00	
		Accounts Payable, Coffee Company			2,100.00
		Purchased merchandise from			
		Coffee Company, invoice no. 234C.			
		($3,500 − ($3,500 × .40))			

LEARNING OBJECTIVE **5**

Journalize transactions for a merchandising business in a cash receipts journal and post from a cash receipts journal to a general ledger and an accounts receivable ledger.

A transaction for a merchandising business can be recorded on one line in a **cash receipts journal.** The cash receipts journal usually contains the following columns: Date, Account Credited, Post. Ref., Cash Debit, Credit Card Expense Debit, Sales Discounts Debit, Accounts Receivable Credit, Sales Credit, Sales Tax Payable Credit, and Other Accounts Credit.

The accountant posts daily from the Accounts Receivable Credit column to the individual credit customers' accounts in the accounts receivable ledger. After posting, the accountant puts a check mark (✓) in the Post. Ref. column. The accountant also posts the amounts in the Other Accounts Credit column daily and records the account numbers in the Post. Ref. column. The special columns are posted as totals at the end of the month. The accountant then writes the account numbers in parentheses under the totals. An (X) below the total of the Other Accounts Credit column shows that amounts are posted individually and the total is not posted.

PRACTICE EXERCISE 5

Indicate the appropriate columns in which each of the following transactions would be recorded in the cash receipts journal.

Transaction	Cash Debit	Credit Card Expense Debit	Sales Discounts Debit	Accounts Receivable Credit	Sales Credit	Other Accounts Credit
a. Collected cash on account from a charge customer.						
b. Received check from a charge customer in payment of an invoice within the discount period.						
c. Borrowed money from the bank, receiving cash and giving the bank a promissory note.						
d. Received check from a charge customer in payment of an invoice past the discount period.						
e. Recorded cash sales for the month.						

PRACTICE EXERCISE 5 SOLUTION

Transaction	Cash Debit	Credit Card Expense Debit	Sales Discounts Debit	Accounts Receivable Credit	Sales Credit	Other Accounts Credit
a. Collected cash on account from a charge customer.	✓			✓		
b. Received check from a charge customer in payment of an invoice within the discount period.	✓		✓	✓		
c. Borrowed money from the bank, receiving cash and giving the bank a promissory note.	✓					✓
d. Received check from a charge customer in payment of an invoice past the discount period.	✓			✓		
e. Recorded cash sales for the month.	✓				✓	

LEARNING OBJECTIVE

6

Journalize transactions for a merchandising business in a cash payments journal and post from a cash payments journal to a general ledger and an accounts payable ledger.

A cash payment by a merchandising business that includes a purchase discount can be recorded on one line in a **cash payments journal**. The cash payments journal usually contains the following columns: Date, Ck. No., Account Debited, Post. Ref., Other Accounts Debit, Accounts Payable Debit, Purchases Discounts Credit, and Cash Credit.

The accountant posts daily from the Accounts Payable Debit column to the individual suppliers' accounts in the accounts payable ledger. After posting, the accountant puts a check mark (✓) in the Post. Ref. column. The accountant also posts the amounts in the Other Accounts Debit column daily and records the account numbers in the Post. Ref. column. The special columns are posted as totals at the end of the month. The accountant then writes the account numbers in parentheses under the totals. An (X) below the total of the Other Accounts Debit column shows that amounts are posted individually and the total is not posted.

PRACTICE EXERCISE 6

Indicate the appropriate columns in which each of the following transactions would be recorded in the cash payments journal.

Transaction	Other Accounts Debit	Accounts Payable Debit	Purchases Discounts Credit	Cash Credit
a. Issued check to vendor in payment of an invoice within the discount period.				
b. Paid customer for merchandise returned on a cash sale.				
c. Paid wages for two weeks.				
d. Issued check to vendor in payment of an invoice past the discount period.				
e. Paid rent for the month.				

PRACTICE EXERCISE 6 SOLUTION

Transaction	Other Accounts Debit	Accounts Payable Debit	Purchases Discounts Credit	Cash Credit
a. Issued check to vendor in payment of an invoice within the discount period.		✓	✓	✓
b. Paid customer for merchandise returned on a cash sale.	✓			✓
c. Paid wages for two weeks.	✓			✓
d. Issued check to vendor in payment of an invoice past the discount period.		✓		✓
e. Paid rent for the month.	✓			✓

Before a Test Check: Chapters 9–10

PART I: COMPLETION

Complete each of the following statements by writing the appropriate word(s) in the spaces provided.

1. The normal balance of the Purchases Discounts account is on the __________ side.
2. Entries in the Accounts Payable Debit column of a cash payments journal are posted daily to the __________.
3. A(n) __________ is the amount a customer may deduct for paying a bill within a specified period of time.
4. The form sent to the supplier of merchandise is called a(n) __________.
5. The __________ account is used to record the buying of merchandise only.
6. If the freight charges are FOB shipping point, the __________ pays the transportation charges.
7. The time the seller allows the buyer before full payment has to be made is the __________.
8. Increases in Sales Returns and Allowances are recorded on the __________ side.
9. The sales journal is used to record all __________.
10. The schedule of accounts receivable lists the balances of all the __________ accounts at the end of the month.

PART II: MATCHING

For each numbered item, choose the appropriate journal, and write the identifying letter.

_____ **1.** Paid freight bill on merchandise purchased.
_____ **2.** Bought office equipment on account.
_____ **3.** Received a credit memo for merchandise returned.
_____ **4.** Bought office equipment for cash.
_____ **5.** Sold merchandise on account.
_____ **6.** Journalized the closing entries.
_____ **7.** Paid state sales tax to the state revenue department.
_____ **8.** Bought merchandise on account.
_____ **9.** Sold merchandise for cash.
_____ **10.** Bought merchandise for cash.

S Sales journal
P Purchases journal (3 columns)
CR Cash receipts journal
CP Cash payments journal
J General journal

PART III: TRUE/FALSE

For each statement circle T if it is True or circle F if it is False.

T F **1.** The Purchases Discounts account is classified as a revenue account.
T F **2.** The normal balance of the Sales Discounts account is on the debit side.
T F **3.** Check marks in the Posting Reference column of the sales journal indicate that the amounts are not to be posted.
T F **4.** The purchases journal is used for the buying of merchandise for cash and on account.
T F **5.** On the income statement, Freight In is subtracted from Purchases.

ANSWERS: PART I

1. credit; **2.** accounts payable ledger; **3.** cash discount; **4.** purchase order; **5.** Purchases; **6.** buyer; **7.** credit period; **8.** debit; **9.** sales of merchandise on account; **10.** credit customers

ANSWERS: PART II

1. CP; **2.** J; **3.** J; **4.** CP; **5.** S; **6.** J; **7.** CP; **8.** P; **9.** CR; **10.** CP

ANSWERS: PART III

1. F; **2.** T; **3.** F; **4.** F; **5.** F

Glossary

Cash discount The amount a customer can deduct for paying a bill within a specified period of time; used to encourage prompt payment. Not all sellers offer cash discounts. *(p. 393)*

Cash payments journal A special journal used to record all transactions involving cash payments or decreases. *(p. 410)*

Cash receipts journal A special journal used to record all transactions involving cash receipts or increases. *(p. 405)*

Credit period The time the seller allows the buyer before full payment on a charge sale has to be made. *(p. 393)*

Notes Payable The account containing the balance of promissory notes. *(p. 408)*

Promissory note A written promise to pay a specified amount at a specified time. *(p. 408)*

Trade discounts Substantial discounts from the list or catalog prices of goods, granted by the seller; not recorded by the buyer or the seller. *(p. 402)*

CHAPTER ASSIGNMENTS

Discussion Questions

1. What are the normal balances of (a) Purchases? (b) Sales Discounts? (c) Purchases Returns and Allowances? (d) Sales? (e) Purchases Discounts? (f) Sales Returns and Allowances?
2. What does an X under the total of a special journal's Other Accounts column signify?
3. Explain the following credit terms: (a) n/30; (b) 2/10, n/60; (c) 1/15, EOM, n/30.
4. In a cash receipts journal, both the Accounts Receivable Credit column and the Cash Debit column were mistakenly underadded by $700. How will this error be discovered?
5. If a cash payments journal is supposed to save writing, why are there so many entries in the Other Accounts Debit column?
6. Describe the posting procedure for a cash payments journal with an Other Accounts Debit column and several special columns, including an Accounts Payable Debit column.
7. An electronics business purchased speakers for resale. The total of the invoice is $2,580, and it is subject to trade discounts of 15 percent, 10 percent, and 5 percent. Compute the amount the dealer will pay for the speakers.
8. What is the difference between a cash discount and a trade discount?

Exercises

LO 1,3

PRACTICE EXERCISES 1,3

EXERCISE 10-1 For the following purchases of merchandise, determine the amount of cash to be paid:

Purchase	Invoice Date	Credit Terms	FOB	Amount of Purchase	Freight Charges	Total Invoice Amount	Returns and Allowances	Date Paid
a.	June 1	2/10, n/30	Destination	$550	—	$ 550	—	June 30
b.	June 12	1/10, n/30	Destination	700	—	700	$100	June 21
c.	June 14	2/10, n/30	Shipping point	940	$60	1,000	—	June 23
d.	June 21	n/30	Shipping point	830	70	900	130	July 20
e.	June 24	1/10, n/30	Shipping point	760	50	810	90	July 3

2 LO

EXERCISE 10-2 Describe the transactions recorded in the following T accounts:

PRACTICE EXERCISE 2

Cash

Debit	Credit
(c) 5,042.10	

Accounts Receivable

Debit	Credit
(a) 5,320	(b) 175
	(c) 5,145

Sales

Debit	Credit
	(a) 5,320

Sales Returns and Allowances

Debit	Credit
(b) 175	

Sales Discounts

Debit	Credit
(c) 102.90	

3 LO

EXERCISE 10-3 Describe the transactions recorded in the following T accounts:

PRACTICE EXERCISE 3

Cash

Debit	Credit
	(c) 1,176

Accounts Payable

Debit	Credit
(b) 150	(a) 1,350
(c) 1,200	

Purchases

Debit	Credit
(a) 1,350	

Purchases Returns and Allowances

Debit	Credit
	(b) 150

Purchases Discounts

Debit	Credit
	(c) 24

2,3 LO

EXERCISE 10-4 Record the following transactions in general journal form:

PRACTICE EXERCISES 2,3

May 4 Sold merchandise on account to Singh, Inc., $640; terms 2/10, n/30.

10 Bought merchandise on account from Mack Company, $750; terms 1/10, n/60; FOB shipping point.

11 Paid Gaines Freight Lines for freight charges on merchandise purchased from Mack Company, $22.

13 Received full payment from Singh, Inc.

14 Received a credit memo from Mack Company for defective merchandise returned, $104.

19 Paid Mack Company in full within the discount period.

28 Bought merchandise on account from Baldwin Company, $900; terms 2/10, n/30; freight prepaid and added to the invoice, $47 (total $947).

PRACTICE EXERCISES 2,3

EXERCISE 10-5 Record the following transactions in general journal form, first on the books of the seller (Fuentes Company) and then on the books of the buyer (Lowe Company).

Fuentes Company

a. Sold merchandise on account to Lowe Company, $1,500; terms 2/10, n/30.
b. Issued a credit memo to Lowe Company for damaged merchandise, $100.
c. Lowe Company paid the account in full within the discount period.

Lowe Company

a. Purchased merchandise on account from Fuentes Company, $1,500; terms 2/10, n/30.
b. Received a credit memo from Fuentes Company for damaged merchandise, $100.
c. Paid Fuentes Company in full within the discount period.

PRACTICE EXERCISES 2,3,4

EXERCISE 10-6 Record general journal entries to correct the errors described below. Assume that the incorrect entries were posted in the same period in which the errors occurred.

a. A freight cost of $57 incurred on equipment purchased for use in the business was debited to Freight In.
b. The issuance of a credit memo to Marks Company for $126 for merchandise returned was recorded as a debit to Purchases Returns and Allowances and a credit to Accounts Receivable, Marks Company.
c. A cash sale of $92 to M. A. Manning was recorded as a sale on account.
d. A purchase of merchandise from Avila Company in the amount of $1,000 with a 30 percent trade discount was recorded as a debit to Purchases and a credit to Accounts Payable of $1,000 each.

PRACTICE EXERCISE 5

EXERCISE 10-7 Label the blanks in the column heads as either debit or credit.

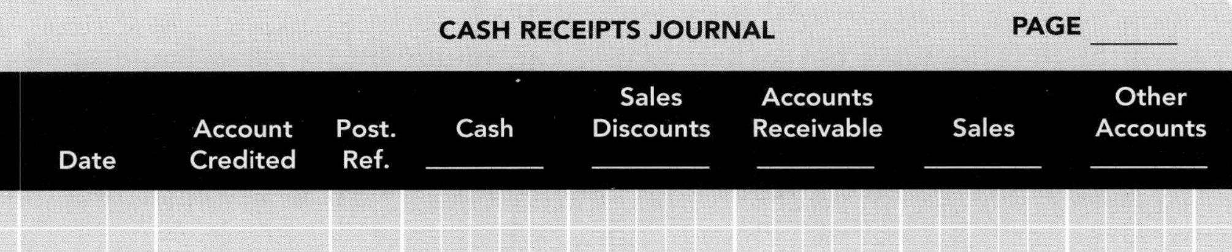
CASH RECEIPTS JOURNAL PAGE ____

Date	Account Credited	Post. Ref.	Cash ____	Sales Discounts ____	Accounts Receivable ____	Sales ____	Other Accounts ____

PRACTICE EXERCISE 5

EXERCISE 10-8 Describe the transaction recorded.

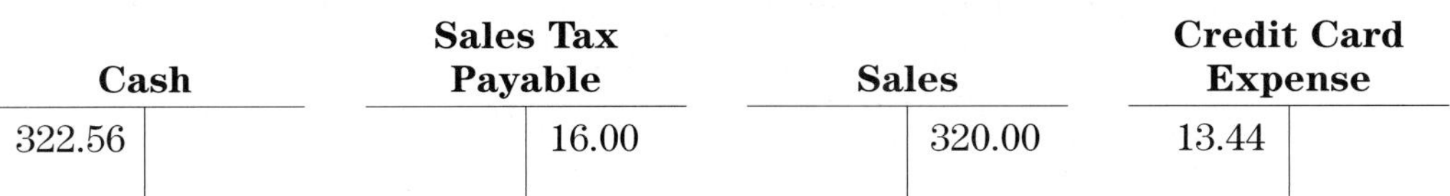

Cash		Sales Tax Payable		Sales		Credit Card Expense	
322.56			16.00		320.00	13.44	

PRACTICE EXERCISE 6

EXERCISE 10-9 Label the blanks in the column heads as either debit or credit.

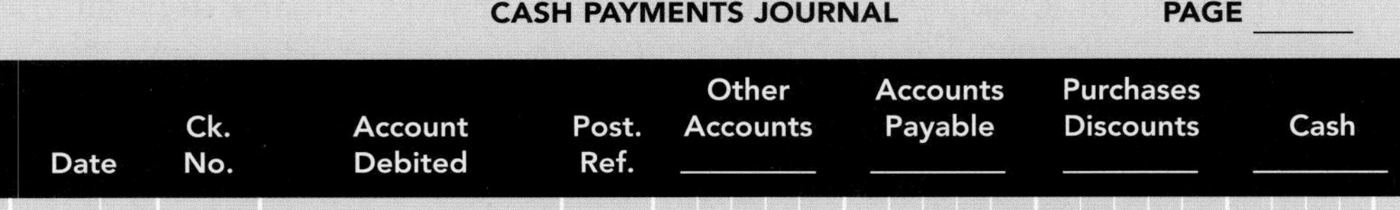
CASH PAYMENTS JOURNAL PAGE ____

Date	Ck. No.	Account Debited	Post. Ref.	Other Accounts ____	Accounts Payable ____	Purchases Discounts ____	Cash ____

CHAPTER ASSIGNMENTS

PRACTICE EXERCISES 5,6

EXERCISE 10-10 Indicate the journal in which each of the following transactions should be recorded. Assume a three-column purchases journal.

Transaction	Journal				
	S	P	CR	CP	J
a. Paid a creditor on account.					
b. Bought merchandise on account.					
c. Sold merchandise for cash.					
d. Adjusted for insurance expired.					
e. Received payment on account from a charge customer.					
f. Received a credit memo for merchandise returned.					
g. Bought equipment on credit.					
h. Sold merchandise on account.					
i. Recorded a customer's NSF check.					
j. Invested personal noncash assets in the business.					
k. Withdrew cash for personal use.					

Problem Set A

For additional help, see the demonstration problem at the beginning of each chapter in your Working Papers.

GL

PROBLEM 10-1A The following transactions were completed by Hammond Auto Supply during January, which is the first month of this fiscal year. Terms of sale are 2/10, n/30.

Jan.	2	Issued Ck. No. 6981 for monthly rent, $775.
	2	J. Hammond, the owner, invested an additional $3,500 in the business.
	4	Bought merchandise on account from Valencia and Company, invoice no. A691, $2,930; terms 2/10, n/30; dated January 2.
	4	Received check from Vega Appliance for $980 in payment of $1,000 invoice less discount.
	4	Sold merchandise on account to L. Paul, invoice no. 6483, $850.
	6	Received check from Petty, Inc., $637, in payment of $650 invoice less discount.
	7	Issued Ck. No. 6982, $588, to Fischer and Son, in payment of invoice no. C1272 for $600 less discount.
	7	Bought supplies on account from Doyle Office Supply, invoice no. 1906B, $108; terms net 30 days.
	7	Sold merchandise on account to Ellison and Clay, invoice no. 6484, $787.
	9	Issued credit memo no. 43 to L. Paul, $54, for merchandise returned.
	11	Cash sales for January 1 through January 10, $4,863.20.
	11	Issued Ck. No. 6983, $2,871.40, to Valencia and Company, in payment of $2,930 invoice less discount.
	14	Sold merchandise on account to Vega Appliance, invoice no. 6485, $2,050.

CHAPTER ASSIGNMENTS

Jan. 18 Bought merchandise on account from Costa Products, invoice no. 7281D, $4,854; terms 2/10, n/60; dated January 16; FOB shipping point, freight prepaid and added to the invoice, $147 (total $5,001).

21 Issued Ck. No. 6984, $194, to M. Miller for miscellaneous expenses not recorded previously.

21 Cash sales for January 11 through January 20, $4,591.

23 Issued Ck. No. 6985 to Forbes Freight, $96, for freight charges on merchandise purchased on January 4.

23 Received credit memo no. 163, $376, from Costa Products for merchandise returned.

29 Sold merchandise on account to Bruce Supply, invoice no. 6486, $1,835.

31 Cash sales for January 21 through January 31, $4,428.

31 Issued Ck. No. 6986, $53, to M. Miller for miscellaneous expenses not recorded previously.

31 Recorded payroll entry from the payroll register: total salaries, $6,200; employees' federal income tax withheld, $872; FICA taxes withheld, $474.30.

31 Recorded the payroll taxes: FICA taxes, $474.30; state unemployment tax, $334.80; federal unemployment tax, $49.60.

31 Issued Ck. No. 6987, $4,853.70, for salaries for the month.

31 J. Hammond, the owner, withdrew $1,000 for personal use, Ck. No. 6988.

Required

Check Figure
Trial balance totals, $65,288.80

1. Record the transactions for January, using a general journal, page 1. The chart of accounts is as follows:

111 Cash
113 Accounts Receivable
114 Merchandise Inventory
116 Prepaid Insurance
121 Equipment

212 Accounts Payable
215 Salaries Payable
216 Employees' Federal Income Tax Payable
217 FICA Taxes Payable
218 State Unemployment Tax Payable
219 Federal Unemployment Tax Payable

311 J. Hammond, Capital
312 J. Hammond, Drawing

411 Sales
412 Sales Returns and Allowances
413 Sales Discounts

511 Purchases
512 Purchases Returns and Allowances
513 Purchases Discounts
514 Freight In

621 Salary Expense
622 Payroll Tax Expense
625 Supplies Expense
627 Rent Expense
631 Miscellaneous Expense

2. Post daily all entries involving customer accounts to the accounts receivable ledger.
3. Post daily all entries involving creditor accounts to the accounts payable ledger.
4. Post daily the general journal entries to the general ledger. Write the owner's name in the Capital and Drawing accounts.
5. Prepare a trial balance.
6. Prepare a schedule of accounts receivable and a schedule of accounts payable. Do the totals equal the balances of the related controlling accounts?

PROBLEM 10-2A Preston Company sells candy wholesale, primarily to vending machine operators. Terms of sales on account are 2/10, n/30, FOB shipping point. The following transactions involving cash receipts and sales of merchandise took place in May of this year:

May	1	Received $2,156 cash from L. Reilly in payment of April 22 invoice of $2,200, less cash discount.
	4	Received $1,096 cash in payment of $1,000 note receivable and interest of $96.
	7	Received $588 cash from K. L. Shannon in payment of April 29 invoice of $600, less cash discount.
	8	Sold merchandise on account to D. Padilla, invoice no. 272, $489.
	16	Cash sales for first half of May, $2,265.
	17	Received cash from D. Padilla in payment of invoice no. 272, less cash discount.
	20	Received $325 cash from L. N. Salas in payment of April 16 invoice, no discount.
	21	Sold merchandise on account to R. O. Wilcox, invoice no. 273, $935.
	24	Received $220 cash refund for return of defective equipment that was originally bought for cash.
	27	Sold merchandise on account to R. Jarvis, invoice no. 274, $450.
	31	Cash sales for second half of May, $2,845.

Check Figure
Total Cash Debit, $9,974.22

Required

1. Journalize the transactions for May in the cash receipts journal and the sales journal.
2. Total and rule the journals.
3. Prove the equality of debit and credit totals.

1,6 **LO**

PROBLEM 10-3A MacDonald Bookshop had the following transactions that occurred during February of this year:

Feb.	3	Issued Ck. No. 4312, $892, to Kent Company for invoice no. 68172, recorded previously for $910.20, less 2 percent cash discount.
	4	Issued Ck. No. 4313 to Kirby Express Company for freight charges, $35, for books purchased.
	6	Issued Ck. No. 4314 to Morse Land Company for monthly rent, $590.
	11	Received and paid bill for advertising in the *Ballard News*, $105.79, Ck. No. 4315.
	11	Issued Ck. No. 4316, $1,078.11, to Contreras Book Company for invoice no. A3322, recorded previously for $1,089, less 1 percent cash discount.
	17	Paid wages recorded previously for first half of February, $487; Ck. No. 4317.
	21	R. D. MacDonald, the owner, withdrew $1,200 for personal use; Ck. No. 4318.
	26	Issued Ck. No. 4319 to First National Bank for payment on bank loan, $560, consisting of $500 on the principal and $60 interest.
	27	Issued Ck. No. 4320, $645, to Graham Publishing Company for invoice no. 7768, recorded previously (no discount).

Feb. 28 Voided Ck. No. 4321.

28 Paid wages recorded previously for second half of February, $641; Ck. No. 4322.

Required

1. Journalize the transactions for February in the cash payments journal.
2. Total and rule the journal.
3. Prove the equality of the debit and credit totals.

Check Figure
Total Cash Credit, $6,233.90

1,2,3,5,6

PROBLEM 10-4A Refer to the information for Problem 10-1A on pages 424–425.

Required

1. Record the transactions for January, using a sales journal, page 73; a purchases journal, page 56; a cash receipts journal, page 38; a cash payments journal, page 45; and a general journal, page 100.

Check Figure
Schedule of Accounts Receivable total, $5,468.00

111 Cash
113 Accounts Receivable
114 Merchandise Inventory
116 Prepaid Insurance
121 Equipment

212 Accounts Payable
215 Salaries Payable
216 Employees' Federal Income Tax Payable
217 FICA Taxes Payable
218 State Unemployment Tax Payable
219 Federal Unemployment Tax Payable

311 J. Hammond, Capital
312 J. Hammond, Drawing

411 Sales
412 Sales Returns and Allowances
413 Sales Discounts

511 Purchases
512 Purchases Returns and Allowances
513 Purchases Discounts
514 Freight In

621 Salary Expense
622 Payroll Tax Expense
625 Supplies Expense
627 Rent Expense
631 Miscellaneous Expense

2. Post daily all entries involving customer accounts to the accounts receivable ledger.
3. Post daily all entries involving creditor accounts to the accounts payable ledger.
4. Post daily those entries involving the Other Accounts columns and the general journal to the general ledger. Write the owner's name in the Capital and Drawing accounts.
5. Add the columns of the special journals, and prove the equality of debit and credit totals on scratch paper.
6. Post the appropriate totals of the special journals to the general ledger.
7. Prepare a trial balance.
8. Prepare a schedule of accounts receivable and a schedule of accounts payable. Do the totals equal the balances of the related controlling accounts?

Problem Set B

For additional help, see the demonstration problem at the beginning of each chapter in your Working Papers.

1,2,3 LO

PROBLEM 10-1B The following transactions were completed by Yang Restaurant Equipment during January, the first month of this fiscal year. Terms of sale are 2/10, n/30.

Jan.	2	Issued Ck. No. 6981 for monthly rent, $850.
	2	L. Yang, the owner, invested an additional $4,500 in the business.
	4	Bought merchandise on account from Valentine and Company, invoice no. A694, $2,830; terms 2/10, n/30; dated January 2.
	4	Received check from Velez Appliance for $980 in payment of invoice for $1,000 less discount.
	4	Sold merchandise on account to L. Parrish, invoice no. 6483, $755.
	6	Received check from Peck, Inc., $637, in payment of $650 invoice less discount.
	7	Issued Ck. No. 6982, $588, to Frost and Son, in payment of invoice no. C127 for $600 less discount.
	7	Bought supplies on account from Dudley Office Supply, invoice no. 190B, $93.54; terms net 30 days.
	7	Sold merchandise on account to Ewing and Charles, invoice no. 6484, $1,115.
	9	Issued credit memo no. 43 to L. Parrish, $47, for merchandise returned.
	11	Cash sales for January 1 through January 10, $4,454.87.
	11	Issued Ck. No. 6983, $2,773.40, to Valentine and Company, in payment of $2,830 invoice less discount.
	14	Sold merchandise on account to Velez Appliance, invoice no. 6485, $2,100.
	14	Received check from L. Parrish, $693.84, in payment of $755 invoice, less return of $47 and less discount.
	19	Bought merchandise on account from Crawford Products, invoice no. 7281, $3,700; terms 2/10, n/60; dated January 16; FOB shipping point, freight prepaid and added to invoice, $142 (total $3,842).
	21	Issued Ck. No. 6984, $245, to A. Bautista for miscellaneous expenses not recorded previously.
	21	Cash sales for January 11 through January 20, $3,689.
	23	Received credit memo no. 163, $87, from Crawford Products for merchandise returned.
	29	Sold merchandise on account to Bradford Supply, invoice no. 6486, $1,697.20.
	29	Issued Ck. No. 6985 to Western Freight, $64, for freight charges on merchandise purchased January 4.
	31	Cash sales for January 21 through January 31, $3,862.
	31	Issued Ck. No. 6986, $65, to M. Pineda for miscellaneous expenses not recorded previously.

Jan. 31 Recorded payroll entry from the payroll register: total salaries, $5,900; employees' federal income tax withheld, $795; FICA taxes withheld, $451.35.

31 Recorded the payroll taxes: FICA taxes, $451.35; state unemployment tax, $265.50; federal unemployment tax, $47.20.

31 Issued Ck. No. 6987, $4,653.65, for salaries for the month.

31 L. Yang, the owner, withdrew $1,000 for personal use, Ck. No. 6988.

Required

Check Figure
Trial balance totals, $63,187.61

1. Record the transactions for January, using a general journal, page 1. The chart of accounts is as follows:

111 Cash
113 Accounts Receivable
114 Merchandise Inventory
116 Prepaid Insurance
121 Equipment

212 Accounts Payable
215 Salaries Payable
216 Employees' Federal Income Tax Payable
217 FICA Taxes Payable
218 State Unemployment Tax Payable
219 Federal Unemployment Tax Payable

311 L. Yang, Capital
312 L. Yang, Drawing

411 Sales
412 Sales Returns and Allowances
413 Sales Discounts

511 Purchases
512 Purchases Returns and Allowances
513 Purchases Discounts
514 Freight In

621 Salary Expense
622 Payroll Tax Expense
625 Supplies Expense
627 Rent Expense
631 Miscellaneous Expense

2. Post daily all entries involving customer accounts to the accounts receivable ledger.
3. Post daily all entries involving creditor accounts to the accounts payable ledger.
4. Post daily the general journal entries to the general ledger. Write the owner's name in the Capital and Drawing accounts.
5. Prepare a trial balance.
6. Prepare a schedule of accounts receivable and a schedule of accounts payable. Do the totals equal the balances of the related controlling accounts?

LO 1,5

PROBLEM 10-2B C. R. McIntyre Company sells candy wholesale, primarily to vending machine operators. Terms of sales on account are 2/10, n/30, FOB shipping point. The following transactions involving cash receipts and sales of merchandise took place in May of this year:

May 2 Received $411.60 cash from N. Rojas in payment of April 23 invoice of $420, less cash discount.

5 Received $2,085 cash in payment of $2,000 note receivable and interest of $85.

8 Sold merchandise on account to G. Soto, invoice no. 862, $830.

9 Received $11,838.40 cash from D. Maddox in payment of April 30 invoice of $12,080, less cash discount.

May 15 Received cash from G. Soto in payment of invoice no. 862, less cash discount.

16 Cash sales for first half of May, $3,259.

19 Received $296 cash from R. O. Higgins in payment of April 14 invoice, no discount.

22 Sold merchandise on account to N. T. Jennings, invoice no. 863 $753.

25 Received $239 cash refund for return of defective equipment bought in April for cash.

28 Sold merchandise on account to M. E. Mueller, invoice no. 864 $964.

31 Cash sales for second half of May, $4,728.

Check Figure
Total Cash Debit, $23,670.40

Required

1. Journalize the transactions for May in the cash receipts journal and the sales journal.
2. Total and rule the journals.
3. Prove the equality of debit and credit totals.

PROBLEM 10-3B Jacobs Company had the following transactions that occurred during February of this year:

Feb. 1 Issued Ck. No. 4311, $637, to Barker Company for invoice no. 3113E, recorded previously for $650, less cash discount of $13.

2 Issued Ck. No. 4312 to Bonilla Express Company for freight charges, $48, for merchandise purchased.

4 Issued Ck. No. 4313 to Dillon Realty for monthly rent, $560.

9 Received and paid bill for advertising in *The Nickel News*, $84, Ck. No. 4314.

10 Issued Ck. No. 4315, $990, to Dorsey Company for invoice no. D642, recorded previously for $1,000, less 1 percent cash discount.

15 Paid wages recorded previously for first half of month, $1,678; Ck. No. 4316.

19 R. Jacobs, the owner, withdrew $900 for personal use; Ck. No. 4317.

25 Issued Ck. No. 4318 to First National Bank for payment on bank loan, $896, consisting of $800 on principal and $96 interest.

27 Issued Ck. No. 4319, $430, to Long Company for invoice no. 6317, recorded previously (no discount).

28 Voided Ck. No. 4320.

28 Paid wages recorded previously for second half of month, $1,648; Ck. No. 4321.

28 Received and paid telephone bill, $86; Ck. No. 4322, payable to Southwestern Telephone Company.

Check Figure
Total Cash Credit, $7,957

Required

1. Journalize the transactions for February in the cash payments journal.
2. Total and rule the journal.
3. Prove the equality of the debit and credit totals.

1,2,3,5,6

PROBLEM 10-4B Refer to the information for Problem 10-1B on pages 428–429.

Check Figure
Schedule of Accounts Receivable total, $4,912.20

Required

1. Record the transactions for January, using a sales journal, page 91; a purchases journal, page 74; a cash receipts journal, page 56; a cash payments journal, page 63; and a general journal, page 119.

111 Cash
113 Accounts Receivable
114 Merchandise Inventory
116 Prepaid Insurance
121 Equipment

212 Accounts Payable
215 Salaries Payable
216 Employees' Federal Income Tax Payable
217 FICA Taxes Payable
218 State Unemployment Tax Payable
219 Federal Unemployment Tax Payable

311 L. Yang, Capital
312 L. Yang, Drawing

411 Sales
412 Sales Returns and Allowances
413 Sales Discounts

511 Purchases
512 Purchases Returns and Allowances
513 Purchases Discounts
514 Freight In

621 Salary Expense
622 Payroll Tax Expense
625 Supplies Expense
627 Rent Expense
631 Miscellaneous Expense

2. Post daily all entries involving customer accounts to the accounts receivable ledger.
3. Post daily all entries involving creditor accounts to the accounts payable ledger.
4. Post daily those entries involving the Other Accounts columns and the general journal to the general ledger. Write the owner's name in the Capital and Drawing accounts.
5. Add the columns of the special journals, and prove the equality of debit and credit totals on scratch paper.
6. Post the appropriate totals of the special journals to the general ledger.
7. Prepare a trial balance.
8. Prepare a schedule of accounts receivable and a schedule of accounts payable. Do the totals equal the balances of the related controlling accounts?

ACTIVITIES

CONSIDER AND COMMUNICATE

You are the manager of the Accounts Receivable Department for a merchandising business. Your billing clerk sent a bill for $2 to a customer who had charged $100 in goods (including sales tax) with terms 2/10, n/30. The customer has called and indicated his displeasure; he can't understand an error like this, since he paid on time. Explain to your billing clerk why Accounts Receivable is credited for $100 and not $98. How was permission given to send less than the full amount?

WHAT'S WRONG WITH THIS PICTURE?

Suppose we collected cash from a charge customer, and our debit was to Cash and the credit to Sales. How and when would this error be discovered?

CRITICAL THINKING

You work for Gregory Plumbing Supply. You are responsible for training a new accounting clerk. He has the following questions for you to answer about this invoice:

Gregory Plumbing Supply
14 Indiana Avenue
Chicago, Illinois 60612

No. 320

INVOICE

SOLD TO: *C. P. Lund Company*
5210 Gilman Avenue
San Diego, CA 92102

DATE: *August 1, 20—*
CUSTOMER'S P.O. NO.: *5384*
SHIPPED BY: *Faster Freight*
TERMS: *2/10, n/30*
SALESPERSON: *H. T.*

QUANTITY	DESCRIPTION	UNIT PRICE		TOTAL	
6	*Olin single-control tub shower faucet #44B652*	51	50	309	00
6	*Olin dual-control washerless lavatory faucet #59B641*	22	20	133	20
12	*Olin massage shower head, antique brass #37B411*	11	56	138	72
	Subtotal			580	92
	Freight			63	80
	Total			644	72

1. Who is the buyer?
2. Who is paying the freight?
3. What is the customer's order number?
4. What percentage of the goods bought is the cost of the freight?
5. What are the credit terms and what do they mean?
6. How much will the buyer actually have to pay if the money is received within 10 days?
7. What is the dollar amount of the discount?
8. Who receives the discount?
9. What is the due date for payment to get the discount?
10. Why would a seller give a buyer a discount?

ACTIVITIES

All About You Spa

Cash Receipts and Cash Payments

All About You Spa decided to expand into merchandising. Because of instances where goods received or sold may prove less than satisfactory, new accounts for purchases returns and allowances and sales returns and allowances need to be added to the chart of accounts. Although not applicable to this period, sales discounts may be granted to customers in the future and purchases discounts may be taken based on terms from vendors in the future, so accounts for these are being added as well. A revised chart of accounts for All About You Spa is as follows:

CHART OF ACCOUNTS FOR ALL ABOUT YOU SPA

Assets
111 Cash
113 Accounts Receivable
117 Prepaid Insurance
124 Spa Equipment
125 Accum. Depr., Spa Equip.
128 Office Equipment
129 Accum. Depr., Office Eq.

Liabilities
211 Accounts Payable
212 Wages Payable
215 Sales Tax Payable

Owner's Equity
311 A. Valli, Capital
312 A. Valli, Drawing
313 Income Summary

Revenue
411 Income from Services
412 Merchandise Sales
413 Sales Discounts
414 Sales Returns & Allow.

Purchases
511 Purchases
512 Purchases Discounts
513 Purch. Ret. & Allow.
515 Freight In

Expenses
611 Wages Expense
612 Rent Expense
613 Office Supplies Expense
614 Spa Supplies Expense
615 Laundry Expense
616 Advertising Expense
617 Utilities Expense
618 Insurance Expense
619 Depr. Expense, Spa Equip.
620 Depr. Expense, Office Eq.
630 Miscellaneous Expense

Ms. Valli has provided the trial balance as of July 31, schedules of accounts receivable and payable, as well as transactions for the month of August to be entered into the system.

Directions for August Journal Entries

1. Open the file entitled ***All_About_You_Spa_Ch10.IA7***. Enter your name when prompted and click ***OK***. Select "Yes" or "No" as desired when asked if you want to open on-screen instructions and check figures. As a reminder, these instructions may be opened at any time by clicking on the ***Info.*** toolbar button.

All About You Spa
Trial Balance
July 31, 20—

Account Name	Debit	Credit
Cash	44,969.26	
Accounts Receivable	4,568.79	
Prepaid Insurance	800.00	
Spa Equipment	17,601.00	
Accumulated Depreciation, Spa Equipment		64.88
Office Equipment	1,570.00	
Accumulated Depreciation, Office Equipment		10.00
Accounts Payable		20,720.00
Sales Tax Payable		1,829.90
A. Valli, Capital		49,884.62
A. Valli, Drawing	2,500.00	
Income from Services		12,722.00
Merchandise Sales		10,151.65
Purchases	12,868.00	
Freight In	403.00	
Wages Expense	7,004.00	
Rent Expense	1,650.00	
Office Supplies Expense	118.00	
Spa Supplies Expense	490.00	
Laundry Expense	84.00	
Utilities Expense	473.00	
Miscellaneous Expense	284.00	
	95,383.05	95,383.05

All About You Spa
Schedule of Accounts Receivable
July 31, 20—

About Face Spa	$ 521.59
Jill Anson	175.00
Chaco's	520.02
Holmes Condos	367.47
Tory Ligman	164.00
Los Obrigados Lodge	351.00
Mini Spa	222.48
Jack Morgan	286.00
Pleasant Spa	1,961.23
Total Accounts Receivable	$4,568.79

All About You Spa
Schedule of Accounts Payable
July 31, 20—

Giftco	$ 1,309.00
Golden Spa Supplies	490.00
Logo Products	3,796.00
Office Staples	304.00
Spa Equipment, Inc.	6,235.00
Spa Goods	5,445.00
Spa Magic	2,721.00
Superior Equipment	420.00
Total Accounts Payable	$20,720.00

2. Click on the ***Save As*** toolbar button. When the Save As window appears, select the folder in which you wish to save your data files (if not already selected). In the File Name box, key ***All_About_You_Spa_Ch10_Your_Name.IA7*** (for example, All_About_You_Spa_Ch10_John_Doe.IA7) to identify the file containing your work. Click on the ***Save*** button.
3. Click on the ***Journals*** toolbar button and key the journal entries for August. Use the information in the checkbook register and the transactions listings on the following pages as the basis of your entries. Follow option a or b below, as directed by your instructor.
   a. Key all August transactions into the General Journal.
   b. Key August transactions into special journals and the General Journal. Key sales on account and purchases on account transactions as you learned to do in Chapter 9. Key credit memo transactions into the General Journal. Key cash receipts and cash payments transactions as follows:
      (1) For a cash receipt, click on the ***Journals*** toolbar button and then the ***Cash Receipts*** tab.

      For a receipt of a payment on account, enter the amount of the payment in the Accounts Rec. Cr. column. The debit to Cash will automatically be entered for you by the software. Tab to the Customer column and select from the drop-down list. Then click on the ***Post*** button (or press Enter).

      For weekly cash sales, enter the amount received for services in the Services Inc., Cr. column, enter the amount received for merchandise in the Merch. Sales Cr. column, and enter the amount of sales tax in the Sales Tax Pay. Cr. column. The debit to Cash will automatically be calculated and entered for you by the software. Then click on the ***Post*** button (or press Enter).

      (2) For a cash payment, click on the ***Journals*** toolbar button and then the ***Cash Payments*** tab.

      For a payment on account, enter the check number in the Refer. column (abbreviate as "Ck.1044" for fit). Enter the amount of the payment in the Accounts Pay. Dr. column. The credit to Cash will automatically be entered for you in the Cash Cr. column. Tab to the Customer column and select from the drop-down list. Then click on the ***Post*** button (or press Enter).

      For all other payments, enter the check number in the Refer. column. Enter the account number of the account to be debited in the Acct. No. column (or select from the Chart of Accounts while the Acct. No. column has the focus). Enter the amount to be debited in the Debit column. The credit to Cash will automatically be entered for you in the Cash Cr. column. Then click on the ***Post*** button (or press Enter).
4. Generate journal reports. Click on the ***Reports*** toolbar button. Click on ***Journals*** and ***General Journal*** to choose the report to display. Accept the ***Include All Journal Entries*** option and then click the ***OK*** button to display the General Journal report. To print the report, click on the ***Print*** button. If following option 2b above, also generate a Sales Journal report, a Purchases Journal report, a Cash Payments Journal report, and a Cash Receipts Journal report in the same manner by clicking on those options in Report Selection window. Review the journal entries and make corrections as necessary.
5. Display a trial balance. Click on the ***Reports*** toolbar button. Click on ***Ledger Reports*** and ***Trial Balance*** to choose the report to display. To print the report, click on the ***Print*** button at the bottom of the report window.

6. Display a schedule of accounts receivable. Click on the ***Reports*** toolbar button. Click on ***Ledger Reports*** and ***Schedule of Accounts Receivable*** to choose the report to display. To print the report, click on the ***Print*** button at the bottom of the report window.

Check Figures
5. Trial balance total, August 31, $120,364.27
6. Schedule of accounts receivable total, August 31, $7,196.63
7. Schedule of accounts payable total, August 31, $20,393.00

7. Display a schedule of accounts payable. Click on the ***Reports*** toolbar button. Click on ***Ledger Reports*** and ***Schedule of Accounts Payable*** to choose the report to display. To print the report, click on the ***Print*** button at the bottom of the report window.
8. Click on the ***Save*** toolbar button to save your data file.
9. Click on the ***Check*** toolbar button to check your solution against the answer key.

Checkbook Register

Check No.	Date	Explanation	✓	Deposits	Check Amount
1044	8/1	Paid August's rent.			1,650.00
	8/1	Deposited Chaco's payment received on account, invoice no. 15.		400.00	
	8/1	Deposited Mini Spa's payment received on account, invoice no. 18. Paid in full.		222.48	
1045	8/1	Paid accumulated sales tax payable to State Revenue Dept.			1,829.90
1046	8/2	Paid advertising expense for August photo ad.			455.00
1047	8/2	Paid week's wages.			1,845.50
1048	8/2	Paid Spa Magic for invoice no. 5033, dated June 2. Paid in full.			2,721.00
1049	8/3	Bought silk flower arrangement for the salon (Miscellaneous Expense).			87.90
	8/3	Deposited Tory Ligman's payment received on account. Paid in full.		164.00	
1050	8/4	Bought spa supplies—5 cases of bottled water for clients (debit Spa Supplies Expense).			45.00
	8/4	Deposited Jill Anson's payment received on account.		87.50	
1051	8/5	Bought a digital camera for confidential before-and-after pictures (debit Spa Equipment).			482.00
1052	8/5	Paid Office Staples for invoice 1417, dated July 5. Paid in full.			186.00
1053	8/5	Paid on account to Giftco, invoice no. 316, dated July 5.			709.00
	8/6	Deposited Pleasant Spa's payment received on account, invoice no. 16.		997.42	
1054	8/6	Paid Golden Spa Supplies for invoice no. 1836, dated July 1. Paid in full.			490.00
	8/7	Deposited first week's cash sales: merchandise $1,630.00; services $3,350.00; sales tax collected $398.40.		5,378.40	

Check No.	Date	Explanation	✓	Deposits	Check Amount
	8/8	Deposited Los Obrigados Lodge's payment received on account, invoice no. 14.		200.00	
	8/9	Deposited Holmes Condo's payment received on account, invoice no. 17.		200.00	
1055	8/9	Paid week's wages.			1,850.00
	8/14	Deposited second week's cash sales: merchandise $1,330.00; services $2,340.00; sales tax collected $293.60.		3,963.60	
	8/15	Deposited About Face Spa's payment received on account, invoice no. 19.		265.00	
1056	8/16	Paid week's wages.			1,853.00
1057	8/18	Paid Superior Equipment for invoice no. 3608, dated July 5. Paid in full.			420.00
	8/19	Deposited Jack Morgan's payment received on account. Paid in full.		286.00	
	8/21	Deposited third week's cash sales: merchandise $2,220.00; services $2,810.00; sales tax collected $402.40.		5,432.40	
1058	8/22	Paid on account to Logo Products, invoice no. 1579, dated July 1.			2,500.00
1059	8/23	Paid on account to Spa Goods, invoice no. 312, dated July 1.			2,000.00
1060	8/23	Paid week's wages.			1,847.50
1061	8/28	Paid month's laundry bill.			95.00
1062	8/28	Owner withdrew cash for personal use.			2,500.00
1063	8/30	Paid week's wages.			1,850.00
	8/31	Deposited end of month's cash sales: merchandise $2,030.00; services $4,176.00; $496.48 sales tax.		6,702.48	
1064	8/31	Paid August telephone bill.			235.00
1065	8/31	Paid on account to Spa Equipment, Inc., invoice no. 2731, dated July 3.			3,000.00
1066	8/31	Paid August power and water bill.			255.00

Purchases Invoices for Merchandise Bought on Account During August

All About You Spa will pay all freight costs associated with purchases of merchandise to the supplier.

Date of Purchase	Transaction Information	Amount
Aug. 1	Bought logo merchandise from Giftco; invoice no. 416, dated 8/1; terms 2/10, n/30.	$4,100.00 plus $180.00 freight
1	Bought bath and beauty products from Spa Magic; invoice no. 5235, dated 8/1; terms 2/10, n/30.	$3,562.00 plus $155.00 freight
2	Bought logo merchandise from Logo Products; invoice no. 1680, dated 8/2; terms 2/10, n/30.	$2,451.00 plus $144.00 freight
5	Bought spa accessories from Spa Goods; invoice no. 387, dated 8/5; terms 2/10, n/30.	$1,120.00 plus $110.00 freight

Sales Invoices for Gift Certificates Sold on Account During August

All About You Spa is responsible for collecting and paying the sales tax on merchandise that it sells. The sales tax rate where All About You Spa does business is 8 percent of each sale; for example, $650.00 × 0.08 = $52.00.

Date of Sale	Transaction Information	Sales Amount (Before Tax)
Aug. 1	About Face Spa, invoice no. 20.	$ 650.00
5	Chaco's, invoice no. 21.	395.00
8	Holmes Condos, invoice no. 22.	1,294.00
9	Pleasant Spa, invoice no. 23.	1,560.00
11	Los Obrigados Lodge, invoice no. 24.	356.00
14	Mini Spa, invoice no. 25.	873.00

Note: All gift certificates were redeemed for merchandise by the end of the month.

Other August Transactions

There were two other transactions in August. Neither involved cash.

Date	Transaction Information	Amount
Aug. 9	Issued credit memorandum no. 1 to About Face Spa for an allowance for damaged goods. (Debit the new account Sales Returns and Allowances 414.)	$ 88.00
29	Received a credit memorandum for damaged spa accessories from Spa Magic. (Credit the new account Purchases Returns and Allowances 513.)	123.00

APPENDIX

The Voucher System of Accounting

LEARNING OBJECTIVES

After you have completed this chapter, you will be able to do the following:

1. *Prepare vouchers.*
2. *Record vouchers in a voucher register.*
3. *Record payment of vouchers in a check register.*
4. *Record transactions involving canceling or altering an original voucher.*

ACCOUNTING LANGUAGE

Voucher *(p. 439)*

Voucher register *(p. 443)*

The voucher system is a means of achieving internal control and enabling the owner or manager to maintain contact with day-to-day transactions. This system promotes the delegation of duties and responsibilities.

OBJECTIVE OF THE VOUCHER SYSTEM

The objective of the voucher system is to control the incurrence of all liabilities and the payment of all expenditures—in other words, to control the purchase of (1) merchandise or materials, (2) other assets, and (3) services. The voucher system is suitable for companies of varying sizes that require a clear separation of duties. The voucher system has the following components: vouchers, voucher register, check register, unpaid voucher file, paid voucher file, and general journal.

VOUCHERS

A **voucher** is a document that serves as proof of a transaction and, from a business point of view, also serves as a full description of the transaction. **When a business is using the voucher system, a voucher must be filled out for every invoice**

FIGURE 1 Steps for processing a voucher for a purchase of merchandise

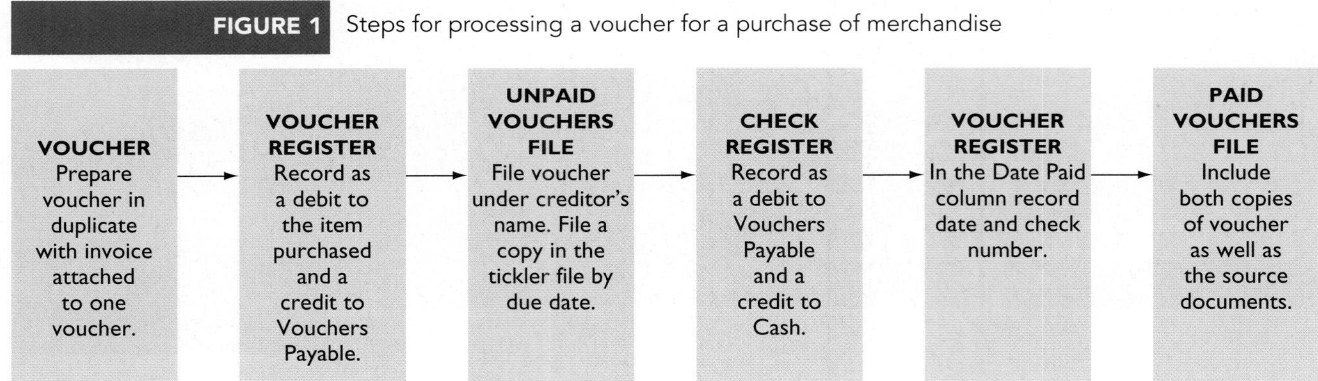
VOUCHER
Prepare voucher in duplicate with invoice attached to one voucher.
VOUCHER REGISTER
Record as a debit to the item purchased and a credit to Vouchers Payable.
UNPAID VOUCHERS FILE
File voucher under creditor's name. File a copy in the tickler file by due date.
CHECK REGISTER
Record as a debit to Vouchers Payable and a credit to Cash.
VOUCHER REGISTER
In the Date Paid column record date and check number.
PAID VOUCHERS FILE
Include both copies of voucher as well as the source documents.

or bill received, whether it is to be paid immediately or in the future. The invoice or bill is usually stapled to the voucher.

Characteristics of Vouchers

Just as the form of invoices varies from one company to another, so too the form of vouchers varies from one company to another. However, the following characteristics are usually present.

- Vouchers are numbered consecutively.
- The name and address of the payee or creditor appear on the voucher.
- The amount and credit terms of the invoice appear on the voucher.
- Vouchers state due dates so that firms can take advantage of possible cash discounts.
- For internal control, vouchers require signatures approving payment.
- Vouchers record payment: date paid and check number.

A completed voucher, with the invoice or bill stapled to it, describes an entire transaction as well as the procedure for processing the voucher. First, so that you can see the big picture, Figure 1 presents the steps involved in processing a voucher for a purchase of merchandise.

Preparation and Approval of Vouchers

1 LEARNING OBJECTIVE *Prepare vouchers.*

To cite a familiar example, let's assume that Whitewater Raft Supply has now achieved such a volume of business that it is using a voucher system. Let's also assume that Whitewater Raft Supply has received from its supplier, Pataponia, Inc., the invoice shown here.

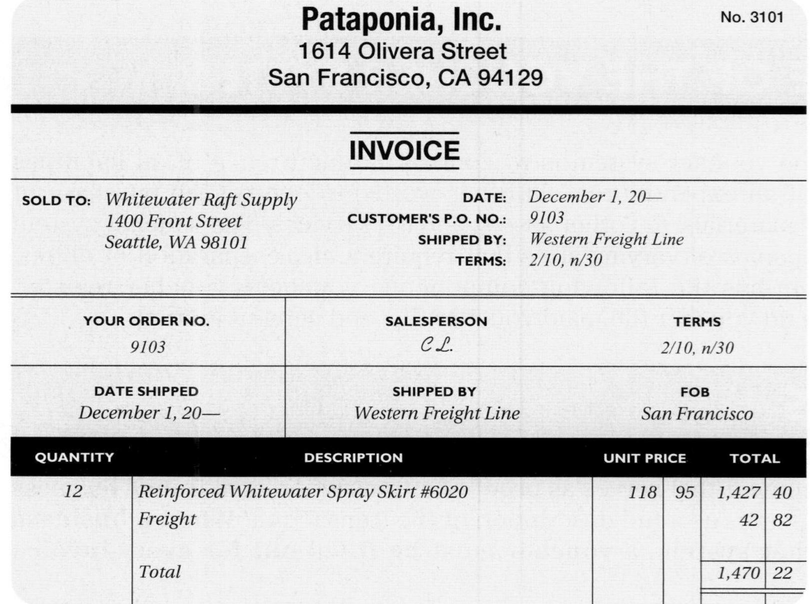

Pataponia, Inc.
1614 Olivera Street
San Francisco, CA 94129

No. 3101

INVOICE

SOLD TO: *Whitewater Raft Supply*
1400 Front Street
Seattle, WA 98101

DATE: *December 1, 20—*
CUSTOMER'S P.O. NO.: *9103*
SHIPPED BY: *Western Freight Line*
TERMS: *2/10, n/30*

YOUR ORDER NO.	SALESPERSON	TERMS
9103	*C.L.*	*2/10, n/30*
DATE SHIPPED	**SHIPPED BY**	**FOB**
December 1, 20—	*Western Freight Line*	*San Francisco*

QUANTITY	DESCRIPTION	UNIT PRICE	TOTAL
12	*Reinforced Whitewater Spray Skirt #6020*	*118 95*	*1,427 40*
	Freight		*42 82*
	Total		*1,470 22*

Whitewater Raft Supply's accountant, using the invoice as the source of information, fills out the following voucher. The face of the voucher lists the details of the transaction.

WHITEWATER RAFT SUPPLY No. 118
1400 Front Street
Seattle, WA 98101

VOUCHER

PAY TO: *Pataponia, Inc.*
1614 Olivera St.
San Francisco, CA 94129

DATE *12/1/20—*

DATE OF INVOICE	TERMS	DESCRIPTION	AMOUNT
12/1	*2/10, n/30*	*Invoice No. 3101*	*1,427 40*
		Less discount	*28 55*
		Freight	*42 82*
		Net amount payable	*1,441 67*

APPROVAL	DATES	APPROVED BY
Extensions and footings verified	*12/2*	*M. C. L.*
Prices in agreement with purchase order	*12/2*	*S. T.*
Credit terms in agreement with purchase order	*12/2*	*S. T.*
Quantities in agreement with receiving report	*12/2*	*J. D. S.*
Approved for payment	*12/7*	*R. L. R.*

ACCOUNT DISTRIBUTION

VOUCHER NO. *118*

ACCOUNT DEBITED	AMOUNT
Purchases	*1,427.40*
Freight In	*42.82*
Wages Payable	
Supplies Expense	
Miscellaneous Expense	
Total Vouchers Payable Cr.	*1,470.22*

DUE DATE: *12/8*

PAY TO: *Pataponia, Inc.*
1614 Olivera Street
San Francisco, CA 94129

SUMMARY OF CHARGES

Amount of invoice	*1,470.22*
Less cash discount	*28.55*
Net amount	*1,441.67*

RECORD OF PAYMENT

Paid by check no.	*2815*
Date of check	*12/8*
Amount of check	*1,441.67*

ACCOUNT DISTRIBUTION by *R. R. H.*

ENTERED IN VOUCHER REG. by *M. C. L.*

The *due date* represents the last day on which one can take advantage of the cash discount. For example, the invoice of Pataponia, Inc., was dated December 1, with terms of 2/10, n/30. The discount period ends on December 11. Therefore, at the latest, send the check on December 8 to receive the discount.

Remember

Since the check register replaces the cash payments journal and the voucher register replaces the purchases journal, the special-column totals from the voucher register must be posted before those from the check register.

The Account Distribution section is used to record the account titles and amounts to be debited, the total amount to be credited to Vouchers Payable, and the initials of the person authorized to determine the distribution.

THE VOUCHERS PAYABLE ACCOUNT

When you use a voucher system, you substitute the Vouchers Payable account for Accounts Payable. For example, when a firm buys merchandise on account, the accountant enters it as a debit to Purchases and a credit to Vouchers Payable. Similarly, when a firm buys store equipment on account, the accountant records it as a debit to Store Equipment and a credit to Vouchers Payable. Also, if a company incurs an expense on account, such as Advertising, the entry is a debit to Advertising Expense and a credit to Vouchers Payable.

When a check is issued in payment of a voucher, record the entry in the check register as a debit to Vouchers Payable and a credit to Cash. Again, we emphasize that *all* liabilities are recorded in the Vouchers Payable account.

Date		Vou. No.	Creditor	Payment Date		Payment Ck. No.	Vouchers Payable Credit	Purchases Debit
20—								
Dec.	1	117	Fast-Way Freight	12	1	2808	63.00	
	1	118	Pataponia, Inc.	12	8	2815	1,470.22	1,427.40
	3	119	Dell Office Supply	12	3	2809	48.72	
	5	120	Stable Ins. Company	12	5	2812	174.00	
	9	121	Langseth and Son	12	18	2829	328.00	306.00
	10	122	Payroll Bank Account	12	10	2818	1,690.00	
	12	123	Southland Journal				176.00	
	12	124	Bradley Construction	12	12	2820	116.00	
	15	125	D. M. Bruce	12	15	2824	500.00	
	15	126	C. A. Waters, Inc.	12	18	Note	421.00	421.00
	29	149	Dana Mfg. Company				714.00	714.00
	30	150	Safety National Bank	12	30	2837	1,507.50	
	31		Totals				11,674.90	5,095.10
							(212)	(511)

	Debits		Credit
Purchases	*$ 5,095.10*	*Vouchers Payable*	*$11,674.90*
Freight In	*234.32*		
Wages Payable	*3,314.00*		
Supplies Expense	*121.79*		
Miscellaneous Expense	*83.69*		
Other Accounts	*2,826.00*		
	$11,674.90		

THE VOUCHER REGISTER

2 LEARNING OBJECTIVE

Record vouchers in a voucher register.

The **voucher register** has the status of a journal; it is a book of original entry. All vouchers must be recorded in it, in numerical order. Think of it as a multicolumn purchases journal. The voucher register has only one credit column, Vouchers Payable Credit, but a number of debit columns. Headings for the debit columns are selected on the basis of their frequency of use. In addition to the special columns, the voucher register also has space for recording the voucher number, the name of the creditor, the date of payment, and the check number. The voucher register for Whitewater Raft Supply appears below.

When you first record the voucher, leave the Payment Date and Ck. No. columns blank. After you have recorded the payment in the check register, go back to the voucher register and enter the date of payment and the number of the check.

Remember

A voucher is prepared for every invoice or bill the company receives.

Posting from the Voucher Register

The entries in the Other Accounts columns are posted *daily* to the general ledger, just as the Other Accounts columns of the other special journals are posted daily.

VOUCHER REGISTER PAGE 3

Freight In Debit	Wages Payable Debit	Supplies Expense Debit	Miscellaneous Expense Debit	Other Accounts Debit: Account	Post. Ref.	Amount
63 00						
42 82						
		48 72				
				Prepaid Insurance	116	174 00
22 00						
	1690 00					
				Advertising Expense	618	176 00
				Sales Returns and Allowances	412	116 00
				D. M. Bruce, Drawing	312	500 00
				Notes Payable	211	1500 00
				Interest Expense	634	7 50
234 32	3314 00	121 79	83 69			2826 00
(514)	(213)	(622)	(619)			(X)

APPENDIX

The (X) under the column total means "do not post." At the end of the month, total all the columns, and prove the equality of the debit and credit entries by comparing the combined total of the debit columns with the total of the Vouchers Payable Credit column.

THE CHECK REGISTER

3 LEARNING OBJECTIVE

Record payment of vouchers in a check register.

Any company or organization using a voucher system uses both the voucher register and the check register as books of original entry. Now let's look at the procedure for the check register. Since checks are issued only in payment of approved and recorded vouchers, the entry in the check register is always a debit to Vouchers Payable and a credit to Cash. A Vouchers Payable Debit column in the check register offsets the Vouchers Payable Credit column in the voucher register. Recall that after you record the entry in the check register, you enter the date and check number on the appropriate line in the voucher register and on the outside of the voucher in the Record of Payment section.

CHECK REGISTER PAGE 11

Date		Ck. No.	Payee	Vou. No.	Vouchers Payable Debit	Purchases Discounts Credit	Cash Credit
20—							
Dec.	1	2808	Fast-Way Freight	117	63 00		63 00
	3	2809	Dell Office Supply	119	48 72		48 72
	3	2810	Gardner Products Company	114	206 00	2 06	203 94
	4	2811	Dana Manufacturing Company	115	540 00	10 80	529 20
	5	2812	Stable Insurance Company	120	174 00		174 00
	6	2813	Void				
	6	2814	Langseth and Son	116	464 00	9 28	454 72
	8	2815	Pataponia, Inc.	118	1470 22	28 55	1441 67
	30	2837	Safety National Bank	150	1507 50		1507 50
	31		Totals		7281 20	90 09	7191 11
					(212)	(513)	(111)

Debit	Credit
$7,281.20	$ 90.09
	7,191.11
	$7,281.20

HANDLING OF UNPAID VOUCHERS

Firms usually prepare vouchers in duplicate. In the system used by Whitewater Raft Supply, the invoice is attached to the original copy of the voucher. Then the voucher is circulated within the company for the necessary signatures. After a voucher is recorded in the voucher register, it is filed under the name of the creditor. (Other companies may prepare only one copy of the voucher and file it only under the date on which it is supposed to be paid.)

At Whitewater Raft Supply, the Unpaid Vouchers file contains all outstanding vouchers or credit memos. This file, organized by names of creditors, now acts as a subsidiary ledger. In fact, at Whitewater Raft Supply, this file substitutes for the accounts payable ledger.

The *second* copy of the voucher goes to the treasurer, who files it chronologically by due date. This tickler file (a file of unpaid vouchers filed by due date) helps the treasurer forecast the amount of cash that will be needed to pay outstanding bills and take advantage of cash discounts.

At the end of the month, the accountant lists all the vouchers payable, taking the information directly from the Unpaid Vouchers file.

Remember

The Vouchers Payable account is a controlling account, similar to Accounts Payable being a controlling account.

Whitewater Raft Supply
Schedule of Vouchers Payable
December 31, 20—

Vou. No.	Name of Creditor	Amount
123	Southland Journal	$176
149	Dana Manufacturing Company	714
	Total Vouchers Payable	$890

FILING PAID VOUCHERS

Now let's assume that the firm has paid its bill. The payment is recorded in the check register and in the Payment columns of the voucher register. Then the voucher is stapled to the copy in the tickler file, marked paid, and filed in numerical order in a Paid Vouchers file.

SITUATIONS REQUIRING SPECIAL TREATMENT

When a firm is using the voucher system, it inevitably runs into an occasional nonroutine transaction that does not fit into the fixed channels of the voucher system and therefore may require an entry in the general journal. You can consider such treatment as an adjustment to the voucher system.

4 LEARNING OBJECTIVE

Record transactions involving canceling or altering an original voucher.

Return of a Purchase Before Original Voucher Has Been Recorded

Normally, if a business with an efficient purchasing department is going to return any merchandise, it returns the merchandise before the vouchers are recorded in the voucher register. The accountant records the deduction right on the invoice and records the invoice in the voucher register for the net amount.

Return of a Purchase After Original Voucher Has Been Recorded

Assume that a business purchased merchandise for $566. The transaction was recorded in the voucher register as a debit to Purchases and a credit to Vouchers Payable. Later, the company returns $26 worth of defective merchandise. The return is recorded in the general journal as a debit to Vouchers Payable and a credit to Purchases Returns and Allowances. A notation "Return" is entered in the Payment column of the voucher register.

Installment Payments Planned at Time of Original Purchase

In a voucher system, invoices not subject to cash discounts are generally paid in full. Sometimes, however, management prefers to pay for an item in installments. When this happens, the company's accountant prepares a separate voucher for each installment and records each of these vouchers in the voucher register. Each voucher's due date corresponds to the date on which that installment is to be paid.

Installment Payments After Original Voucher Has Been Recorded

However, suppose that the buyer records the entire amount of the invoice on one voucher and *later* decides to pay the invoice in installments. The accountant must now cancel the original voucher by means of a general journal entry and issue a new voucher for each installment. A notation listing the new voucher numbers is made in the Payment column of the voucher register.

Correcting an Amount After Original Voucher Has Been Recorded

If an error in the purchase of merchandise is discovered after the voucher has been recorded in the voucher register, the original voucher must be canceled by means of a general journal entry debiting Vouchers Payable and crediting Purchases. Next, a new entry is made in the voucher register for the correct amount, debiting Purchases and crediting Vouchers Payable. A notation listing the new voucher number is made in the Payment column of the voucher register.

Issuing a Note Payable After Original Voucher Has Been Recorded

If a note is issued for the amount of an unpaid invoice after the voucher has been recorded, an entry must be made in the general journal to cancel the original voucher. The entry is a debit to Vouchers Payable and a credit to Notes Payable. A notation, "Note," is made in the Date Paid column of the voucher register. When the note is to be paid, a new voucher is issued for the amount of the principal and interest, debiting Notes Payable and Interest Expense and crediting Vouchers Payable.

Glossary

Voucher A document that serves as proof of a transaction and, from a business point of view, also serves as a full description of the transaction. *(p. 439)*

Voucher register A book of original entry in which all vouchers are recorded in numerical order. *(p. 443)*

Problems

2,3 

PROBLEM 10A-1 Saenz Company uses a voucher system in which it records invoices at the **gross amount**. The following vouchers were issued during February and were unpaid on March 1:

Voucher Number	Company	For	Date of Voucher	Amount
1729	Kipley Company	Merchandise, FOB destination	Feb. 26	$3,436
1732	J. R. Steven	Merchandise, FOB destination	Feb. 28	4,710

The following transactions were completed during March:

Mar. 3 Issued voucher no. 1734 in favor of Larry Company for March rent, $1,220.

3 Issued Ck. No. 1829 in payment of voucher no. 1734, $1,220.

5 Bought merchandise on account from Lorenzo, Inc., $3,890; terms 2/10, n/30; FOB shipping point; freight prepaid and added to the invoice, $72 (total, $3,962). Issued voucher no. 1735.

5 Issued Ck. No. 1830 in payment of voucher no. 1729, $3,401.64 ($3,436 less 1 percent cash discount).

9 Issued voucher no. 1736 in favor of Mario Electric Company for electric bill, $216.

9 Issued Ck. No. 1831 in payment of voucher no. 1736, $216.

9 Issued Ck. No. 1832 in payment of voucher no. 1732, $4,615.80 ($4,710 less 2 percent cash discount).

13 Issued Ck. No. 1833 in payment of voucher no. 1735, less the cash discount, $3,884.20. Recall that the freight portion is not eligible for discount.

16 Bought merchandise on account from McGinnis Manufacturing Company, $6,260; terms 2/10 EOM; FOB destination. Issued voucher no. 1737.

25 Issued voucher no. 1738 for note payable previously recorded in the general journal: principal, $4,000, plus $30 interest. The note is payable to the Keller State Bank.

25 Issued Ck. No. 1834 in payment of voucher no. 1737, $6,134.80 ($6,260 less 2 percent cash discount).

31 Issued voucher no. 1739 for wages payable, $4,985, in favor of the payroll bank account. (Assume that the payroll entry was previously recorded in the general journal.)

31 Paid voucher no. 1739 by issuing Ck. No. 1835, $4,985, payable to Payroll Bank Account.

Required

1. Using the voucher issue date, enter the unpaid invoices in the voucher register (page 65), beginning with voucher no. 1729. Then draw double lines across all columns to separate the vouchers of February from those of March.
2. Record the transactions for March in the voucher register. Also record the appropriate transactions in the check register (page 71).
3. Total and rule the voucher register and the check register.
4. Prove the equality of the debits and credits in the voucher register and the check register.

Check Figure
Voucher Register, Vouchers Payable Credit total, $20,673

LO 2,3,4

PROBLEM 10A-2 Hartman Company, which uses a voucher system, has the following unpaid vouchers on July 1. The firm follows the practice of recording vouchers at the **gross amount**.

Voucher Number	Company	For	Date of Voucher	Amount
4789	Garrison and Son	Store equipment	June 15	$ 4,996
4795	Fenner and Company	Merchandise, FOB destination	June 28	8,571
4797	J. R. Paige Company	Merchandise, FOB destination	June 28	10,710

The company completed the following transactions during July:

July 1 Issued voucher no. 4800 in favor of Mortenson Insurance Company for a premium on a 12-month fire insurance policy, $890.

2 Paid voucher no. 4789 by issuing Ck. No. 8219, $4,996.

2 Issued Ck. No. 8220 in payment of voucher no. 4800, $890.

3 Issued voucher no. 4801 in favor of Quinn Quick Freight for transportation charges on merchandise purchases, $223.

5 Paid voucher no. 4801 by issuing Ck. No. 8221, $223.

7 Issued Ck. No. 8222 in payment of voucher no. 4795, $8,485.29 ($8,571 less 1 percent cash discount).

8 Issued Ck. No. 8223 in payment of voucher no. 4797, $10,602.90 ($10,710 less 1 percent cash discount).

11 Established a petty cash fund of $250. Issued voucher no. 4802.

11 Paid voucher no. 4802 by issuing Ck. No. 8224, $250.

13 Issued voucher no. 4803 in favor of Mohammad Company for merchandise, $14,708; terms 2/10, n/30; FOB shipping point; freight prepaid and added to the invoice, $384 (total, $15,092).

15 Received bill for advertising in the *Weekly Ads*. Issued voucher no. 4804 in the amount of $410.

17 Received a credit memo for $764 from Mohammad Company for merchandise returned to them, credit memo no. 540 (pertaining to voucher no. 4803).

20 Issued voucher no. 4805 in favor of Vinson County for six months' property tax (Prepaid Property Taxes), $2,272.

20 Paid voucher no. 4805 by issuing Ck. No. 8225, $2,272.

21 Issued Ck. No. 8226 in payment of voucher no. 4803, $14,049.12 ($14,708 less $764 return, less cash discount, plus freight).

23 Bought merchandise on account from Summers and Company, $6,039; terms 1/10, n/30; FOB destination. Issued voucher no. 4806.

27 Received a credit memo for $984 from Summers and Company for damaged merchandise, credit memo no. 437 (pertaining to voucher no. 4806).

31 Issued voucher no. 4807 to reimburse petty cash fund. The charges were:

Supplies Expense	$110.43
H. Hartman, Drawing	75.00
Miscellaneous Expense	39.67

31 Issued Ck. No. 8227 in payment of voucher no. 4807, $225.10.

31 Issued voucher no. 4808 for wages payable, $8,448, in favor of the payroll bank account. (Assume that the payroll entry was recorded previously in the general journal.)

31 Paid voucher no. 4808 by issuing Ck. No. 8228, payable to Payroll Bank Account.

Check Figure
Check Register, Cash Credit total $50,441.41

Required

1. Using the voucher issue date, enter the unpaid invoices in the voucher register (page 75), beginning with voucher no. 4789. Then draw double lines across all columns to separate the vouchers of June from those of July.

APPENDIX

2. Enter the transactions for July in the voucher register at the **gross amount**. Also record the appropriate transactions in the check register (page 86) and the general journal (page 41).
3. Total and rule the voucher register and the check register for the transactions recorded during July.
4. Prove the equality of the debits and credits on the voucher register and the check register.

PROBLEM 10A-3 Nathan Systems uses a voucher system in which it records invoices at the **gross amount**. During October, it completed the following transactions:

Oct. 2 Issued voucher no. 2632 in favor of Myers and Horn for the purchase of merchandise with an invoice price of $5,831; terms n/30; FOB shipping point; freight prepaid and added to the invoice, $192 (total, $6,023). Leave an extra line after this entry.

3 Issued vouchers no. 2633 for $1,010, 2634 for $1,010, and 2635 for $1,010. The debt arose because Nathan Systems bought a laptop and printer from Fitzpatrick, Inc., The terms are $1,010 cash on delivery, $1,010 in 30 days, and $1,010 in 60 days. (Use three lines.)

5 Issued Ck. No. 2725 in payment of voucher no. 2633, $1,010.

9 Issued voucher no. 2636 in favor of Cordero Company for the purchase of supplies, $360.50; terms n/30.

12 Issued voucher no. 2637 in favor of Goode Realty for rent for the month, $1,650.

12 Issued Ck. No. 2726 in payment of voucher no. 2637, $1,650.

16 Issued voucher no. 2638 in favor of French Cargo for freight charges on merchandise purchased, $104.

16 Issued voucher no. 2639 in favor of Holley Company for the purchase of merchandise having a list price of $6,512 with a 25 percent trade discount (record voucher for $4,884); terms 2/10, n/30; FOB shipping point. Leave an extra line after this entry.

16 Issued Ck. No. 2727 in payment of voucher no. 2638, $104.00.

16 Canceled voucher no. 2632 because the invoice will be paid in two installments as follows: voucher no. 2640, payable November 1, $3,011.50; voucher no. 2641, payable November 15, $3,011.50. Issued vouchers no. 2640 and 2641.

17 Received a credit memo from Holley Company for merchandise returned, $352, credit memo no. 580, voucher no. 2639.

22 Issued voucher no. 2642 in favor of Pardo Telephone Company for telephone bill, $164.90.

22 Issued Ck. No. 2728 in payment of voucher no. 2642, $164.90.

23 Issued Ck. No. 2729 in payment of voucher no. 2639, $4,441.36. ($4,884 less $352 return, less cash discount.)

31 Issued voucher no. 2643 for wages payable, $4,550, in favor of Payroll Bank Account. (Assume that the payroll entry was recorded previously in the general journal.)

31 Issued Ck. No. 2730 in payment of voucher no. 2643, $4,550.

31 Issued voucher no. 2644 in favor of N. S. Nathan, the owner, for personal withdrawal, $1,400.

31 Issued Ck. No. 2731 in payment of voucher no. 2644, $1,400.

APPENDIX

Check Figure
Schedule of Vouchers Payable total, $8,403.50

Required

1. Record the transactions for October in the voucher register (page 32), the check register (page 34), and the general journal (page 18).
2. Total and rule the voucher register and the check register.
3. Prove the equality of the debits and credits on the voucher register and the check register.
4. Post the amounts from the registers and the general journal to the Vouchers Payable account, No. 212. Assume no previous balance in the account. (Posting from the voucher register should be marked as VR32. Posting from the check register should be marked as CkR34.)
5. Prepare a schedule of vouchers payable. Compare this total with the balance of the Vouchers Payable account.

Work Sheet and Adjusting Entries

11

BURT'S BEES, Durham, North Carolina

WHY IT MATTERS

Burt's Bees describes itself as an "Earth Friendly, Natural Personal Care Company" making products for health, beauty, and personal hygiene. The company manufactures over 150 products distributed in nearly 30,000 retail outlets worldwide.

As a merchandising company, Burt's Bees closely follows its inventory. This requires monitoring the receipt, production, purchasing, and planning of inventory. At the end of each time period, Burt's Bees must make necessary adjusting entries in order to prepare its financial statements accurately. Many of the adjustments are entries that you have already learned, such as depreciation, expiration of prepaid expenses, and recording accrued expenses. However, merchandising companies also require adjusting entries related to merchandise inventory. In this chapter, you will learn how companies such as Burt's Bees monitor inventory, prepare a work sheet, and record adjusting entries using either the perpetual or periodic inventory system.

LEARNING OBJECTIVES

After you have completed this chapter, you will be able to do the following:

1. *Prepare an adjustment for supplies.*
2. *Prepare an adjustment for unearned revenue.*
3. *Prepare an adjustment for merchandise inventory under the periodic inventory system.*
4. *Record the adjustment data in a work sheet (including merchandise inventory, unearned revenue, supplies remaining, expired insurance, depreciation, and accrued wages or salaries).*
5. *Complete the work sheet.*
6. *Journalize the adjusting entries for a merchandising business under the periodic inventory system.*
7. *Prepare and journalize the adjusting entry for merchandise inventory under the perpetual inventory system.*

ACCOUNTING LANGUAGE

Inventory shrinkage *(p. 464)*
Physical inventory *(p. 455)*
Unearned revenue *(p. 453)*

We have talked about the journals and accounts kept by a merchandising business. Now we take another step toward completing the accounting cycle by presenting the related adjustments and the work sheet. First, let's briefly review the adjusting entries that you have learned so far. To begin, look over the following accounts. Here are the data for the adjustments, along with the related adjusting entries:

Insurance expired, $3,600. (The amount expired is the amount used.)

Prepaid Insurance

	+	–	
Bal.	4,000	Adj.	3,600
Bal.	**400**		

Insurance Expense

	+	–	
Adj.	3,600		

Additional depreciation, $1,800. (Add to both accounts.)

Depreciation Expense, Equipment

	+	–	
Adj.	1,800		

Accumulated Depreciation, Equipment

	–	+	
		Bal.	11,000
		Adj.	1,800
		Bal.	**12,800**

Accrued wages (owed but not yet paid), $2,900. (Add to both accounts.)

Wages Expense

	+	–	
Bal.	25,000		
Adj.	2,900		
Bal.	**27,900**		

Wages Payable

	–	+	
		Adj.	2,900

In this chapter, we introduce three more adjusting entries:

1. **Supplies.** This adjustment can be used for merchandising and manufacturing businesses.
2. **Unearned revenue.** This adjustment could apply to either a merchandising, manufacturing, or a service business.
3. **Merchandise inventory.** This adjustment is used exclusively for a merchandising business. We will show adjusting entries for both the periodic inventory and perpetual inventory methods.

ADJUSTMENT FOR SUPPLIES

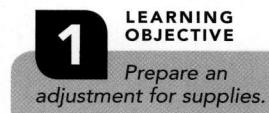

1 LEARNING OBJECTIVE

Prepare an adjustment for supplies.

Previously, when we were talking about the buying of supplies for a service business, we debited Supplies Expense and credited Cash or Accounts Payable.

When a merchandising business buys supplies for cash or on credit, the accounting would generally be the same as for a service business. However, if the amount of supplies held at the end of the accounting period is substantial, then an adjustment should be made to capitalize the supplies that were not consumed during the accounting period. The adjustment would be to debit Supplies (an asset account) and credit Supplies Expense. The amount is determined by a physical count of the supplies left over. For a retail business, supplies would consist of everything from paper or plastic bags to paper forms.

As an illustration, let's say that Marlin & Co. has a balance of $12,000 in the Supplies Expense account as a result of buying supplies during the fiscal period. Now, by taking a count of the supplies on hand, it is determined that $9,052 of supplies are left.

To record the amount of the supplies used, Marlin & Co. has to make an adjusting entry. The purpose of an adjusting entry is to bring the books up to date at the end of the accounting period.

Let's look at this in T account form. We need to add to the balance sheet the supplies still on hand at the end of the accounting period (debit Supplies, an asset account) and reduce the amount of supplies expensed during the accounting period (credit Supplies Expense).

Remember

For the adjustment of supplies, first find the amount of the adjustment by determining the amount of the supplies that remain. In the adjusting entry, deduct the amount of the remaining supplies from Supplies Expense and add it to the asset account Supplies.

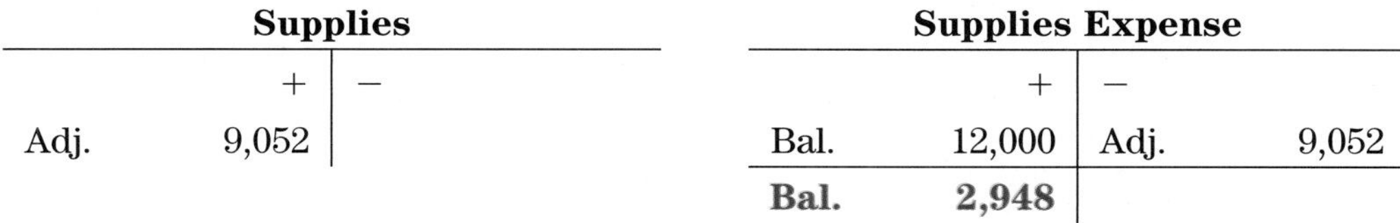

Supplies

	+	−	
Adj.	9,052		

Supplies Expense

	+	−	
Bal.	12,000	Adj.	9,052
Bal.	**2,948**		

ADJUSTMENT FOR UNEARNED REVENUE

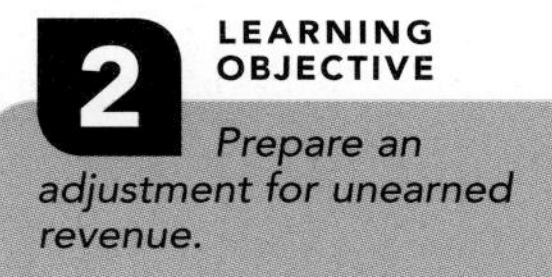
2
LEARNING OBJECTIVE
Prepare an adjustment for unearned revenue.

Now let's introduce another adjusting entry, **unearned revenue**, which is cash received in advance for goods or services to be delivered or performed later. This entry could pertain to a service business as well as to a merchandising or manufacturing business. Frequently, cash is received in advance for services to be performed in the future. For example, a professional sports team sells tickets in advance, a concert association sells season tickets in advance, a magazine publisher sells subscriptions in advance, and an insurance company receives premiums in advance. If the cash

College students pay in advance to participate in a meal plan. Until all those meals are consumed, this money represents unearned revenue for the college or university dining hall services.

amounts received by each of these organizations will be earned during the present fiscal period, the amounts should be credited to revenue accounts. On the other hand, if the amounts received will *not* be earned during the current fiscal period, the amounts should be credited to unearned revenue accounts. **An unearned revenue account is classified as a liability,** because an organization is liable for (owes) the amount received in advance until it is earned.

To illustrate, assume that on April 1, Ressor Publishing Company receives $73,000 in cash for subscriptions paid in advance and records them originally as debits to Cash and credits to Unearned Subscriptions. At the end of the year, Ressor finds that $32,400 of the subscriptions has been earned. Accordingly, Ressor's accountant makes an adjusting entry, debiting Unearned Subscriptions and crediting Subscriptions Income. In other words, the accountant takes the earned portion out of Unearned Subscriptions and adds it to Subscriptions Income. T accounts show the situation as follows:

Cash

	+	−	
Apr. 1	73,000		

Unearned Subscriptions

	−	+	
Dec. 31 Adj.	32,400	Apr. 1	73,000
		Bal.	**40,600**

Subscriptions Income

	−	+	
		Dec. 31 Adj.	32,400

To look at another example, suppose that Trey's Landscape Supply offers a how-to course in landscape maintenance. On November 1, Trey's Landscape Supply receives $2,400 in fees for a three-month course. Because Trey's Landscape Supply's fiscal period ends on December 31, the three months' worth of fees received in advance will not all be earned during this fiscal period. Therefore, Trey's Landscape Supply's accountant records the transaction as a debit to Cash of $2,400 and a credit to Unearned Course Fees of $2,400. Unearned Course Fees is a liability account, because Trey's Landscape Supply must complete the how-to course or refund a portion of the money it collected. **Any account beginning with the word *Unearned* is always a liability.**

On December 31, because two months' worth of course fees have now been earned, Trey's Landscape Supply's accountant makes an adjusting entry to transfer $1,600 (⅔ of $2,400) from Unearned Course Fees to Course Fees Income. T accounts for the entries look like this:

Cash

	+	−	
Nov. 1	2,400		

Unearned Course Fees

	−	+	
Dec. 31 Adj.	1,600	Nov. 1	2,400
		Bal.	**800**

Course Fees Income

	−	+	
		Dec. 31 Adj.	1,600

ADJUSTMENT FOR MERCHANDISE INVENTORY USING THE PERIODIC INVENTORY SYSTEM

3 LEARNING OBJECTIVE

Prepare an adjustment for merchandise inventory under the periodic inventory system.

Under the periodic inventory system, we do not make an entry in the Merchandise Inventory account until an actual **physical inventory** or count of the stock of goods on hand has been taken. Instead, we record the purchase of merchandise as a debit to Purchases for the amount of the cost and the sale of the merchandise as a credit to Sales for the amount of the selling price. Finally, after a physical count of merchandise has been taken, one method of adjusting inventory is to make two adjusting entries to record the dollar amount of the inventory. The first adjusting entry is to remove the beginning inventory. The second entry is to enter the ending inventory.

Consider this example. A firm has a Merchandise Inventory balance of $183,000, which represents the cost of the inventory at the beginning of the fiscal period. At the end of the fiscal period, the firm takes an actual count of the stock on hand and determines the cost of the ending inventory to be $186,000. Naturally, in any business, goods are constantly being bought, sold, and replaced. The cost of the ending inventory is larger than the cost of the beginning inventory because the firm bought more than it sold. When we adjust the Merchandise Inventory account, we place the new figure of $186,000 in the account. This method requires two steps.

Remember

The Income Summary account is the same Income Summary account that we used to record closing entries for service businesses. Income Summary now has the extra function of being the balancing or offsetting account in the adjustment of Merchandise Inventory.

STEP 1. Eliminate the amount of the beginning inventory from the Merchandise Inventory account by transferring the amount into Income Summary. (Remove the beginning inventory.)

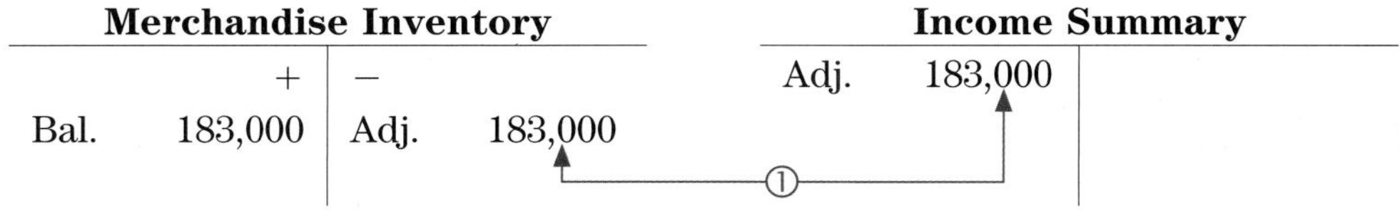

We debit Income Summary and then credit Merchandise Inventory.

STEP 2. Enter the ending or latest physical count of Merchandise Inventory, because you must record on the books the cost of the asset remaining on hand. (Enter the ending inventory.)

Let's repeat the T accounts, showing step 1 and adding step 2.

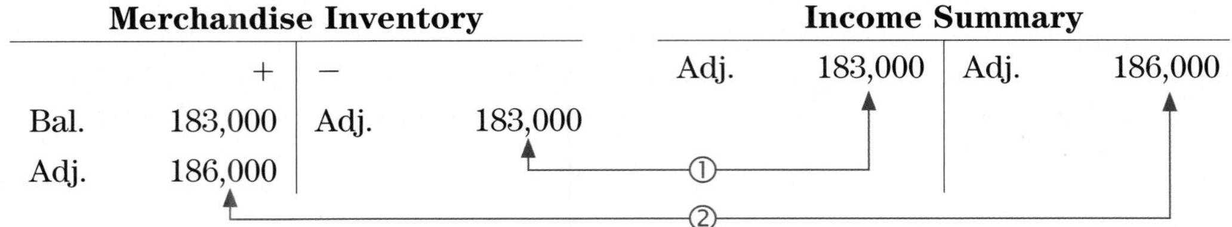

In step 2, we debit Merchandise Inventory (recording the asset on the plus side of the account) and credit Income Summary.

The reason for adjusting the Merchandise Inventory account in these two steps is that both the beginning and the ending amounts appear as distinct figures in the Income Statement columns of a work sheet, and these columns are used as the basis for preparing the income statement.

Whitewater Raft Supply's chart of accounts follows. Notice that Whitewater Raft Supply has an account titled Unearned Course Fees. In addition to selling rafting supplies, Whitewater Raft Supply also provides courses to small business owners on how to start and run a successful rafting company. If the small business owner pays in advance for the course before it is offered, the receipt of cash is recorded as Unearned Course Fees. The account number arrangement will be discussed in Chapter 12.

Assets (100–199)

111 Cash
112 Notes Receivable
113 Accounts Receivable
114 Merchandise Inventory
115 Supplies
116 Prepaid Insurance
121 Land
122 Building
123 Accumulated Depreciation, Building
124 Equipment
125 Accumulated Depreciation, Equipment

Liabilities (200–299)

211 Notes Payable
212 Accounts Payable
213 Wages Payable
217 Unearned Course Fees
221 Mortgage Payable

Owner's Equity (300–399)

311 D. M. Bruce, Capital
312 D. M. Bruce, Drawing
313 Income Summary

Revenue (400–499)

411 Sales
412 Sales Returns and Allowances
413 Sales Discounts
421 Course Fees Income
422 Interest Income

Cost of Goods Sold (500–599)

511 Purchases
512 Purchases Returns and Allowances
513 Purchases Discounts
514 Freight In

Expenses (600–699)

611 Wages Expense
622 Supplies Expense
623 Insurance Expense
624 Depreciation Expense, Building
625 Depreciation Expense, Equipment
626 Property Tax Expense
634 Interest Expense

Before we demonstrate how to record adjustments, let's first look at the trial balance section of Whitewater Raft Supply's work sheet (Figure 1).

FIGURE 1 Trial balance section of Whitewater Raft Supply's work sheet

Whitewater Raft Supply
Work Sheet
For Year Ended December 31, 20—

Account Name	Trial Balance		Adjustments	
	Debit	Credit	Debit	Credit
Cash	24,154.00			
Notes Receivable	4,000.00			
Accounts Receivable	29,546.00			
Merchandise Inventory	67,000.00			
Prepaid Insurance	960.00			
Land	122,100.00			
Building	129,000.00			
Accumulated Depreciation, Building		51,000.00		
Equipment	33,100.00			
Accumulated Depreciation, Equipment		16,400.00		
Notes Payable		36,600.00		
Accounts Payable		3,300.00		
Unearned Course Fees		1,200.00		
Mortgage Payable		7,800.00		
D. M. Bruce, Capital		253,774.00		
D. M. Bruce, Drawing	77,000.00			
Sales		257,180.00		
Sales Returns and Allowances	940.00			
Sales Discounts	1,980.00			
Interest Income		220.00		
Purchases	87,840.00			
Purchases Returns and Allowances		932.00		
Purchases Discounts		1,348.00		
Freight In	2,360.00			
Wages Expense	45,900.00			
Supplies Expense	1,540.00			
Property Tax Expense	1,860.00			
Interest Expense	474.00			
	629,754.00	629,754.00		

DATA FOR THE ADJUSTMENTS

Listing the adjustment data appears to be a relatively minor task. In a business situation, however, one must take actual physical counts of the inventories and match them up with costs. One must check insurance policies to determine the amount of insurance that has expired. Finally, one must systematically write off, or depreciate, the cost of buildings and equipment.

Record the adjustment data in a work sheet (including merchandise inventory, unearned revenue, supplies remaining, expired insurance, depreciation, and accrued wages or salaries).

Here are the adjustment data for Whitewater Raft Supply. We will show the adjustments recorded in T accounts.

a–b. Ending merchandise inventory, $64,800. The adjustments for inventory are generally placed first.

Merchandise Inventory

+		−	
Bal.	67,000	**(a)** Adj.	67,000
(b) Adj.	64,800		

Income Summary

(a) Adj.	67,000	**(b)** Adj.	64,800

c. Course fees earned, $800.

Unearned Course Fees

−		+	
(c) Adj.	800	Bal.	1,200

Course Fees Income

−		+	
		(c) Adj.	800

Remember

The amount of the adjusting entry for supplies equals the amount of the ending inventory of supplies.

d. Ending supplies inventory, $415.

Supplies

+		−	
(d) Adj.	415		

Supplies Expense

+		−	
Bal.	1,540	**(d)** Adj.	415

e. Insurance expired, $520.

Prepaid Insurance

+		−	
Bal.	960	**(e)** Adj.	520

Insurance Expense

+		−	
(e) Adj.	520		

f. Additional year's depreciation of building, $3,500.

Accumulated Depreciation, Building

−		+	
		Bal.	51,000
		(f) Adj.	3,500

Depreciation Expense, Building

+		−	
(f) Adj.	3,500		

g. Additional year's depreciation of equipment, $4,900.

Accumulated Depreciation, Equipment

−		+	
		Bal.	16,400
		(g) Adj.	4,900

Depreciation Expense, Equipment

+		−	
(g) Adj.	4,900		

h. Wages owed but not paid to employees at end of year, $1,030.

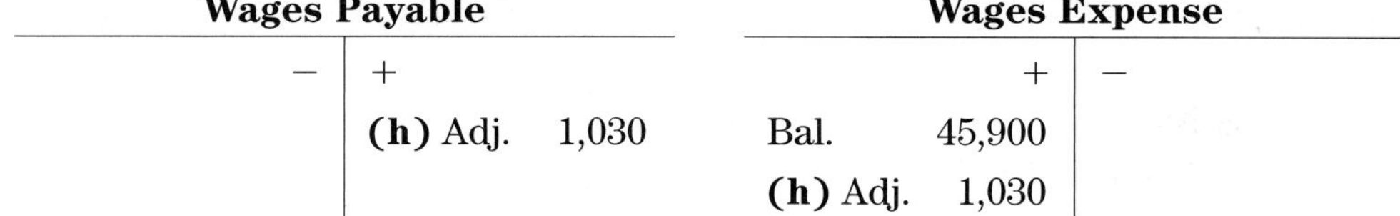

Wages Payable
–
+
(h) Adj. 1,030
Wages Expense
+
–
Bal. 45,900
(h) Adj. 1,030

We now record these in the Adjustments columns of the work sheet, using the same letters to identify the adjustments (see Figure 2).

FIGURE 2 Trial balance and adjustments sections of Whitewater Raft Supply's work sheet

Whitewater Raft Supply
Work Sheet
For Year Ended December 31, 20—

Account Name	Trial Balance Debit	Trial Balance Credit	Adjustments Debit	Adjustments Credit
Cash	24,154.00			
Notes Receivable	4,000.00			
Accounts Receivable	29,546.00			
Merchandise Inventory	67,000.00		(b) 64,800.00	(a) 67,000.00
Prepaid Insurance	960.00			(e) 520.00
Land	122,100.00			
Building	129,000.00			
Accumulated Depreciation, Building		51,000.00		(f) 3,500.00
Equipment	33,100.00			
Accumulated Depreciation, Equipment		16,400.00		(g) 4,900.00
Notes Payable		36,600.00		
Accounts Payable		3,300.00		
Unearned Course Fees		1,200.00	(c) 800.00	
Mortgage Payable		7,800.00		
D. M. Bruce, Capital		253,774.00		
D. M. Bruce, Drawing	77,000.00			
Sales		257,180.00		
Sales Returns and Allowances	940.00			
Sales Discounts	1,980.00			
Interest Income		220.00		
Purchases	87,840.00			
Purchases Returns and Allowances		932.00		
Purchases Discounts		1,348.00		
Freight In	2,360.00			
Wages Expense	45,900.00		(h) 1,030.00	
Supplies Expense	1,540.00			(d) 415.00
Property Tax Expense	1,860.00			
Interest Expense	474.00			
	629,754.00	629,754.00		
Income Summary			(a) 67,000.00	(b) 64,800.00
Course Fees Income				(c) 800.00
Supplies			(d) 415.00	
Insurance Expense			(e) 520.00	
Depreciation Expense, Building			(f) 3,500.00	
Depreciation Expense, Equipment			(g) 4,900.00	
Wages Payable				(h) 1,030.00
			142,965.00	142,965.00

COMPLETION OF THE WORK SHEET

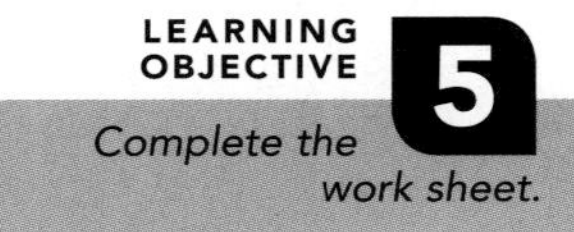

Previously, in introducing work sheets, we included the Adjusted Trial Balance columns as a means of verifying that the accounts were in balance after recording the adjusting entries. At this time, to reduce the number of columns in the work sheet, we will eliminate the Adjusted Trial Balance columns. The account balances after the adjusting entries will be carried directly into the Income Statement and Balance Sheet columns.

The completed work sheet looks like Figure 3 below.

FIGURE 3 Completed work sheet for Whitewater Raft Supply

Whitewater Raft Supply
Work Sheet
For Year Ended December 31, 20—

Account Name	Trial Balance Debit	Trial Balance Credit	Adjustments Debit	Adjustments Credit
Cash	24,154.00			
Notes Receivable	4,000.00			
Accounts Receivable	29,546.00			
Merchandise Inventory	67,000.00		(b) 64,800.00	(a) 67,000.00
Prepaid Insurance	960.00			(e) 520.00
Land	122,100.00			
Building	129,000.00			
Accumulated Depreciation, Building		51,000.00		(f) 3,500.00
Equipment	33,100.00			
Accumulated Depreciation, Equipment		16,400.00		(g) 4,900.00
Notes Payable		36,600.00		
Accounts Payable		3,300.00		
Unearned Course Fees		1,200.00	(c) 800.00	
Mortgage Payable		7,800.00		
D. M. Bruce, Capital		253,774.00		
D. M. Bruce, Drawing	77,000.00			
Sales		257,180.00		
Sales Returns and Allowances	940.00			
Sales Discounts	1,980.00			
Interest Income		220.00		
Purchases	87,840.00			
Purchases Returns and Allowances		932.00		
Purchases Discounts		1,348.00		
Freight In	2,360.00			
Wages Expense	45,900.00		(h) 1,030.00	
Supplies Expense	1,540.00			(d) 415.00
Property Tax Expense	1,860.00			
Interest Expense	474.00			
	629,754.00	629,754.00		
Income Summary			(a) 67,000.00	(b) 64,800.00
Course Fees Income				(c) 800.00
Supplies			(d) 415.00	
Insurance Expense			(e) 520.00	
Depreciation Expense, Building			(f) 3,500.00	
Depreciation Expense, Equipment			(g) 4,900.00	
Wages Payable				(h) 1,030.00
Net Income			142,965.00	142,965.00

Observe in particular the way we carry forward the figures for Merchandise Inventory and Income Summary. **Income Summary is the only account in which we don't combine the debit and credit figures. Instead, we carry them into the Income Statement columns in Figure 3 as two distinct figures—move the two figures as a pair to the Income Statement columns.** The reason for moving them as a pair is that both figures are needed for completion of the income statement. The debit amount in Income Summary in the Income Statement Debit column is the *beginning* merchandise inventory. The credit amount in Income Summary in the Income Statement Credit column is the *ending* merchandise inventory. We will talk about this topic in greater detail in Chapter 12 when we formulate the income statement for a merchandising entity.

Income Statement		Balance Sheet	
Debit	Credit	Debit	Credit
		24,154.00	
		4,000.00	
		29,546.00	
		64,800.00	
		440.00	
		122,100.00	
		129,000.00	
			54,500.00
		33,100.00	
			21,300.00
			36,600.00
			3,300.00
			400.00
			7,800.00
			253,774.00
		77,000.00	
	257,180.00		
940.00			
1,980.00			
	220.00		
87,840.00			
	932.00		
	1,348.00		
2,360.00			
46,930.00			
1,125.00			
1,860.00			
474.00			
67,000.00	64,800.00		
	800.00		
		415.00	
520.00			
3,500.00			
4,900.00			
			1,030.00
219,429.00	325,280.00	484,555.00	378,704.00
105,851.00			105,851.00
325,280.00	325,280.00	484,555.00	484,555.00

Using an electronic spreadsheet, such as Excel, can be an efficient way of preparing a work sheet. When completing a work sheet, complete one stage at a time before moving to the next stage:

STEP 1. Record the trial balance, and make sure that the total of the Debit column equals the total of the Credit column before going to the adjustments.

STEP 2. Record the adjustments in the Adjustments columns, and make sure that the totals are equal before extending the new totals into the Income Statement and Balance Sheet columns.

STEP 3. Complete the Income Statement and Balance Sheet columns by recording the adjusted balance of each account. The accounts and classifications pertaining to a merchandising business using the periodic inventory system appear in these columns:

Income Statement		Balance Sheet	
Debit	**Credit**	**Debit**	**Credit**
Expenses + Sales Returns and Allowances + Sales Discounts + Purchases + Freight In + Income Summary	Revenues + Purchases Returns and Allowances + Purchases Discounts + Income Summary	Assets + Drawing	Accumulated Depreciation + Liabilities + Capital

Study the following example of a work sheet, noting especially the way we treat these accounts for a merchandising business using the periodic inventory system:

	Location on Work Sheet			
	Income Statement		Balance Sheet	
Account Name	**Debit**	**Credit**	**Debit**	**Credit**
Merchandise Inventory			64,800.00	
Sales		257,180.00		
Sales Returns and Allowances	940.00			
Sales Discounts	1,980.00			
Purchases	87,840.00			
Purchases Returns and Allowances		932.00		
Purchases Discounts		1,348.00		
Freight In	2,360.00			
Income Summary	67,000.00	64,800.00		

ADJUSTING ENTRIES USING THE PERIODIC INVENTORY SYSTEM

LEARNING OBJECTIVE 6

Journalize the adjusting entries for a merchandising business under the periodic inventory system.

Figure 4 shows the adjusting entries as taken from the Adjustments columns of the work sheet and recorded in the general journal.

FIGURE 4
Adjusting entries for Whitewater Raft Supply

GENERAL JOURNAL PAGE 96

Date		Description	Post. Ref.	Debit	Credit
20—		Adjusting Entries			
Dec.	31	Income Summary		67 0 0 0 00	
(a)		Merchandise Inventory			67 0 0 0 00
(b)	31	Merchandise Inventory		64 8 0 0 00	
		Income Summary			64 8 0 0 00
(c)	31	Unearned Course Fees		8 0 0 00	
		Course Fees Income			8 0 0 00
(d)	31	Supplies		4 1 5 00	
		Supplies Expense			4 1 5 00
(e)	31	Insurance Expense		5 2 0 00	
		Prepaid Insurance			5 2 0 00
(f)	31	Depreciation Expense, Building		3 5 0 0 00	
		Accumulated Depreciation, Building			3 5 0 0 00
(g)	31	Depreciation Expense, Equipment		4 9 0 0 00	
		Accumulated Depreciation, Equipment			4 9 0 0 00
(h)	31	Wages Expense		1 0 3 0 00	
		Wages Payable			1 0 3 0 00

ADJUSTMENT FOR MERCHANDISE INVENTORY UNDER THE PERPETUAL INVENTORY SYSTEM

7 LEARNING OBJECTIVE
Prepare and journalize the adjusting entry for merchandise inventory under the perpetual inventory system.

Before we demonstrate how to record the adjustment for the perpetual inventory system, let's first look at a portion of the trial balance section of Whitewater Raft Supply's work sheet (Figure 5) assuming they were using the perpetual inventory system.

Under the perpetual inventory system, a business continually maintains a record of each item in stock. **When merchandise is purchased, the Merchandise**

FIGURE 5
A portion of the trial balance section of Whitewater Raft Supply's work sheet (perpetual inventory system)

Account	Debit	Credit
Sales		25 7 1 8 0 00
Sales Returns and Allowances	9 4 0 00	
Sales Discounts	1 9 8 0 00	
Interest Income		2 2 0 00
Cost of Goods Sold	90 1 2 0 00	
Wages Expense	46 9 3 0 00	
Supplies Expense	1 1 2 5 00	

Inventory account (not the Purchases account) is debited for the cost of the merchandise and Accounts Payable or Cash is credited. When merchandise is sold, there are two journal entries. First, debit Accounts Receivable or Cash and credit Sales. Second, the Cost of Goods Sold account is debited for the cost of merchandise and the Merchandise Inventory account is credited for the cost of merchandise.

Many firms use electronic devices to keep track of stock items under the perpetual inventory system. For example, when a sale is made at a supermarket checkout counter, as the bar code on each item is scanned, the price and stock number are recorded. The cash register is connected to a computer that updates the inventory record and records the cost of the item. So the business perpetually (always) knows how much inventory it should have on hand.

However, to verify the inventory record, a physical count should be taken from time to time. The amount shown by the physical count may be less than the computer record as a result of errors, shrinkage, or shoplifting. This difference is called **inventory shrinkage**, and an adjusting entry must be. This entry is a debit to the Cost of Goods Sold account (an expense account) and a credit to the Merchandise Inventory account. The opposite is true if the physical count is more than the computer record; the adjusting entry would then be a debit to Merchandise Inventory and a credit to Cost of Goods Sold.

ADJUSTING ENTRY UNDER THE PERPETUAL INVENTORY SYSTEM

Here are examples of entries under the perpetual inventory system when the physical count does not agree with the computer record of merchandise inventory. Assume a beginning inventory of $75,000.

1. Bought merchandise on account, $50,000.

Merchandise Inventory

	+	−	
Bal.	75,000		
(1)	50,000		

Accounts Payable

	−	+	
		(1)	50,000

2. Sold merchandise for $84,000 having a cost of $60,300.

Accounts Receivable

	+	−	
(2)	84,000		

Sales

	−	+	
		(2)	84,000

Cost of Goods Sold

	+	−	
(2)	60,300		

Merchandise Inventory

	+	−	
Bal.	75,000	**(2)**	60,300
(1)	50,000		
Bal.	**64,700**		

3a. The adjusting entry for the perpetual inventory system is computed by determining the difference between the computer record and the physical count for ending inventory, \$63,200. The recorded balance of the perpetual inventory is \$64,700 (\$75,000 + \$50,000 − \$60,300).

Cost of Goods Sold			Merchandise Inventory			
	+	−		+	−	
(2)	60,300		Bal.	75,000	**(2)**	60,300
(3) Adj.	1,500		**(1)**	50,000	**(3)** Adj.	1,500
Bal.	**61,800**		**Bal.**	**63,200**		

Remember

The ending inventory of one period becomes the beginning inventory of the next period.

The difference of \$1,500 (\$64,700 − \$63,200) is the adjustment amount under the perpetual inventory system. The adjusting entry required to record the \$1,500 loss is shown in Figure 6.

3b. Suppose, on the other hand, that the physical count of the stock of merchandise (\$65,200) were more than the recorded amount (\$64,700). The adjusting entry is to debit Merchandise Inventory and credit Cost of Goods Sold (account) for the difference (\$65,200 − \$64,700 = \$500). (See Figure 6.)

Additional adjusting entries would follow, such as those for supplies remaining, insurance expired, accrued wages, and other such expenses.

On the income statement, under the perpetual inventory system, the Cost of Goods Sold account is listed under one line, rather than there being a Cost of Goods Sold section. The following is a comparison of income statements under the periodic and perpetual inventory systems assuming scenario 3a from above.

Periodic

Sales (net)		\$84,000
Cost of Goods Sold:		
Merchandise Inventory (beginning)	\$ 75,000	
Purchases (net)	50,000	
Cost of Goods Available for Sale	\$125,000	
Less Merchandise Inventory (ending)	63,200	
Cost of Goods Sold		61,800
Gross Profit		\$22,200

Perpetual

Sales (net)	\$84,000
Cost of Goods Sold	61,800
Gross Profit	\$22,200

GENERAL JOURNAL PAGE 96

	Date		Description	Post. Ref.	Debit	Credit
	20—		Adjusting Entries			
3a.	Dec.	31	Cost of Goods Sold		1 5 0 0 00	
			Merchandise Inventory			1 5 0 0 00
3b.		31	Merchandise Inventory		5 0 0 00	
			Cost of Goods Sold			5 0 0 00

FIGURE 6
Adjusting entry for ending inventory under the perpetual inventory system

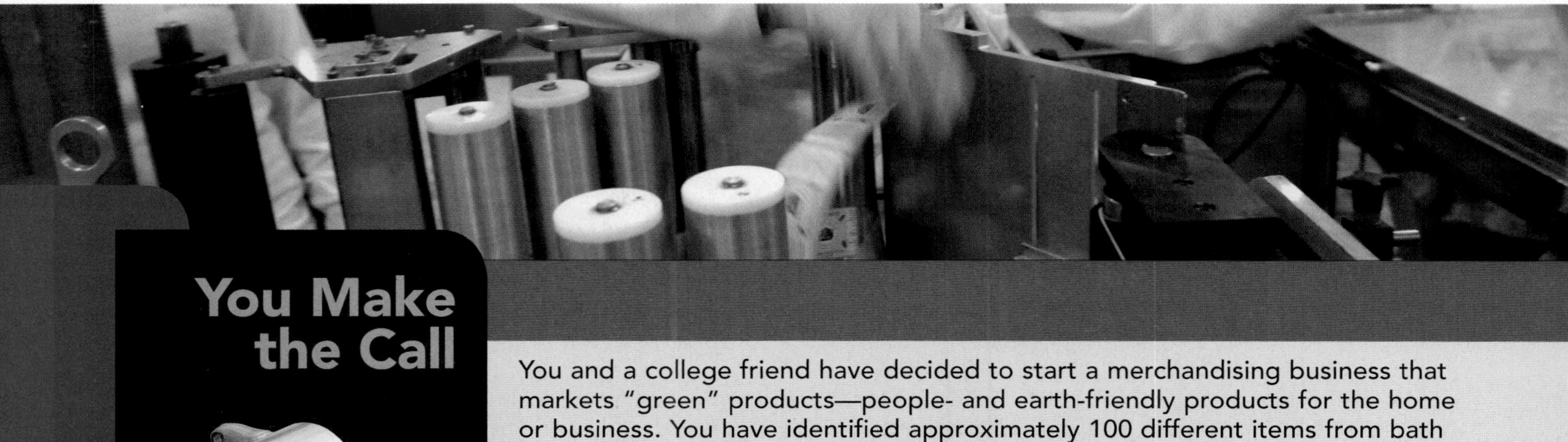

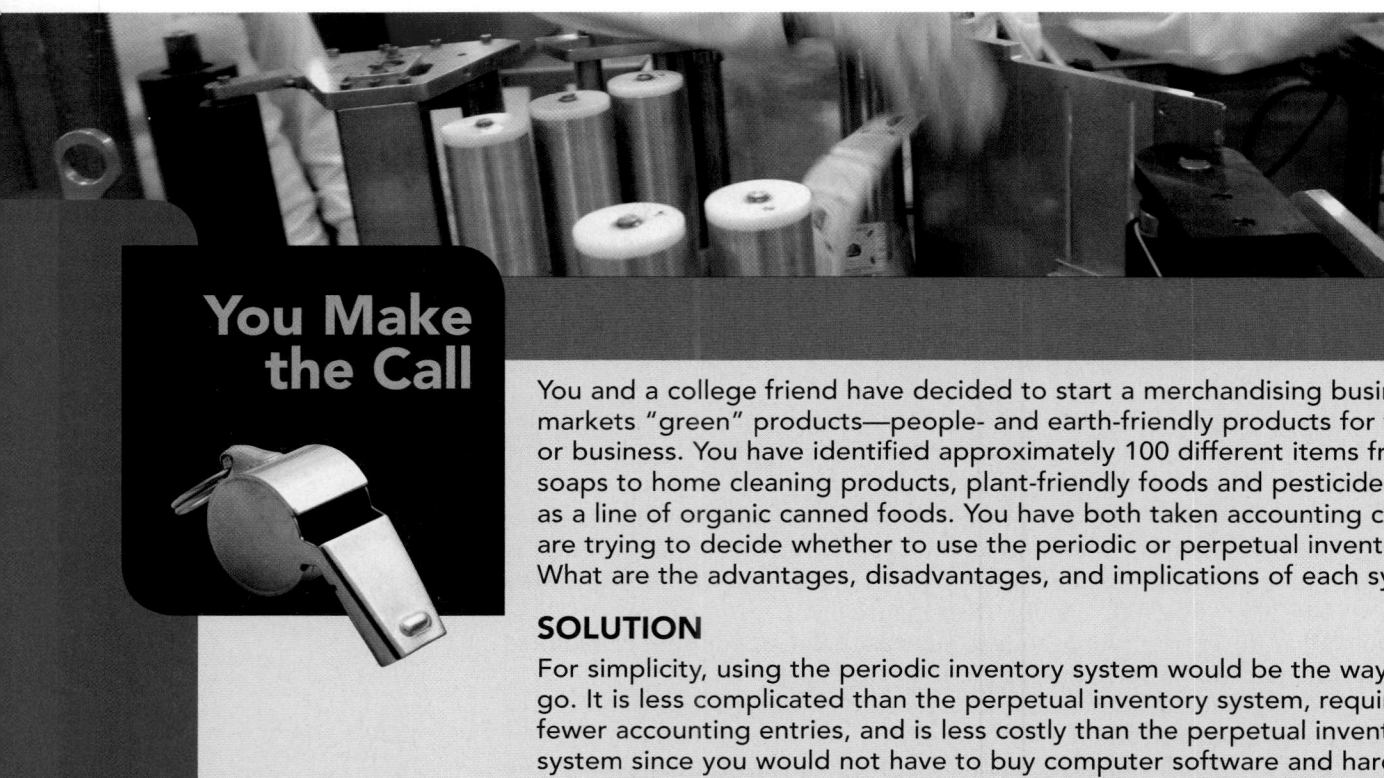

You Make the Call

You and a college friend have decided to start a merchandising business that markets "green" products—people- and earth-friendly products for the home or business. You have identified approximately 100 different items from bath soaps to home cleaning products, plant-friendly foods and pesticides, as well as a line of organic canned foods. You have both taken accounting courses and are trying to decide whether to use the periodic or perpetual inventory system. What are the advantages, disadvantages, and implications of each system?

SOLUTION

For simplicity, using the periodic inventory system would be the way to go. It is less complicated than the perpetual inventory system, requires fewer accounting entries, and is less costly than the perpetual inventory system since you would not have to buy computer software and hardware and various electronic devices to keep track of the inventory. However, the perpetual inventory system offers a higher degree of control and is better for management of proper inventory levels since it allows for up-to-the-minute data for your purchasing needs—two advantages that might very well outweigh the disadvantages of using a perpetual inventory system.

CHAPTER REVIEW

Study & Practice

LEARNING OBJECTIVE 1

Prepare an adjustment for supplies.

When supplies are bought during the year, they are recorded by debiting (increasing) Supplies Expense. At the end of the year, an inventory is taken to determine the amount of supplies on hand. If the ending inventory of supplies is significant, then an adjusting entry is made for the amount remaining, debiting Supplies (an asset account) and crediting Supplies Expense.

PRACTICE EXERCISE 1

Assume that Bowie Corporation has a balance of $9,340 in the Supplies Expense account as a result of buying supplies throughout the year. However, after taking a count of the supplies on hand, it is determined that $2,599 of supplies are left. Journalize the year-end adjusting entry for Bowie Corporation.

CHAPTER REVIEW

PRACTICE EXERCISE 1 SOLUTION

GENERAL JOURNAL PAGE ____

Date		Description	Post. Ref.	Debit	Credit
20—		Adjusting Entries			
Dec.	31	Supplies		2 5 9 9 00	
		Supplies Expense			2 5 9 9 00

LEARNING OBJECTIVE

2 *Prepare an adjustment for unearned revenue.*

For revenue received in advance, an adjustment is required to separate the portion that has been earned from the portion that is unearned. We assume that the amount of cash received in advance was originally recorded as **unearned revenue**, which is a liability. In the adjusting entry for the amount actually earned, debit the unearned revenue account (Unearned Course Fees) and credit the revenue account (Course Fees Income).

PRACTICE EXERCISE 2

On June 1, Thompson Company receives $148,540 in cash for subscriptions covering two years. At the end of the year, December 31, Thompson finds that $94,302 of the subscriptions have been earned. Record in general journal form (a) the original receipt of cash on June 1 and (b) the year-end adjusting entry for Thompson Company.

PRACTICE EXERCISE 2 SOLUTION

GENERAL JOURNAL PAGE ____

Date		Description	Post. Ref.	Debit	Credit
20—					
June	1	Cash		148 5 4 0 00	
(a)		Unearned Subscriptions			148 5 4 0 00
		Adjusting Entries			
Dec.	31	Unearned Subscriptions		94 3 0 2 00	
(b)		Subscriptions Income			94 3 0 2 00

LEARNING OBJECTIVE

3 *Prepare an adjustment for merchandise inventory under the periodic inventory system.*

The adjustment for merchandise inventory under the periodic inventory system requires two adjusting entries. In the first adjusting entry (to remove the beginning inventory), debit Income Summary and credit Merchandise Inventory. In the second adjusting entry (to enter the ending inventory), debit Merchandise Inventory and credit Income Summary.

PRACTICE EXERCISE 3

Morkin Company's beginning inventory amounted to $264,072. A physical count at the end of the year reveals that the ending inventory amount is $267,322. Record the necessary adjustments in the T accounts.

PRACTICE EXERCISE 3 SOLUTION

Merchandise Inventory

	+	−	
Bal.	264,072	**(a)** Adj.	264,072
(b) Adj.	267,322		

Income Summary

(a) Adj.	264,072	**(b)** Adj.	267,322

LEARNING OBJECTIVE 4

Record the adjustment data in a work sheet (including merchandise inventory, unearned revenue, supplies remaining, expired insurance, depreciation, and accrued wages or salaries).

In the Adjustments columns of the work sheet, record the following adjusting entries:

For merchandise inventory: First, debit Income Summary and credit Merchandise Inventory (to remove the beginning inventory); next, debit Merchandise Inventory and credit Income Summary (to enter the ending inventory).

For unearned revenue: Debit the unearned revenue account and credit the revenue account (to record revenue earned).

For supplies remaining: Debit Supplies and credit Supplies Expense.

For expired insurance: Debit Insurance Expense and credit Prepaid Insurance.

For depreciation: Debit Depreciation Expense and credit Accumulated Depreciation.

For accrued wages or salaries: Debit Wages Expense or Salaries Expense and credit Wages Payable or Salaries Payable.

PRACTICE EXERCISE 4

Following are the adjustment data for Majors Company:

a–b. Merchandise inventory, $64,800.
c. Course fees earned, $1,800.
d. Supplies inventory, $2,415.
e. Insurance expired, $1,520.
f. Depreciation of building, $13,500.
g. Depreciation of equipment, $5,900.
h. Wages accrued, $2,030.

Record these data in the Adjustments column of the following work sheet.

Majors Company
Work Sheet
For Year Ended December 31, 20—

Account Name	Trial Balance Debit	Trial Balance Credit	Adjustments Debit	Adjustments Credit
Cash	23,010.00			
Notes Receivable	6,000.00			
Accounts Receivable	28,540.00			
Merchandise Inventory	68,000.00			
Prepaid Insurance	2,110.00			
Land	120,100.00			
Building	128,000.00			
Accumulated Depreciation, Building		50,000.00		
Equipment	34,100.00			
Accumulated Depreciation, Equipment		19,600.00		
Notes Payable		34,600.00		
Accounts Payable		4,300.00		
Unearned Course Fees		2,200.00		
Mortgage Payable		8,800.00		
R. L. Majors, Capital		252,774.00		
R. L. Majors, Drawing	65,000.00			
Sales		253,980.00		
Sales Returns and Allowances	940.00			
Sales Discounts	1,880.00			
Interest Income		1,220.00		
Purchases	88,840.00			
Purchases Returns and Allowances		832.00		
Purchases Discounts		1,448.00		
Freight In	2,460.00			
Wages Expense	44,900.00			
Supplies Expense	12,440.00			
Property Tax Expense	2,860.00			
Interest Expense	574.00			
	629,754.00	629,754.00		
Income Summary				
Course Fees Income				
Supplies				
Insurance Expense				
Depreciation Expense, Building				
Depreciation Expense, Equipment				
Wages Payable				

PRACTICE EXERCISE 4 SOLUTION

Majors Company
Work Sheet
For Year Ended December 31, 20—

	Trial Balance		Adjustments	
Account Name	Debit	Credit	Debit	Credit
Cash	23,010 00			
Notes Receivable	6,000 00			
Accounts Receivable	28,540 00			
Merchandise Inventory	68,000 00		*(b)* 64,800 00	*(a)* 68,000 00
Prepaid Insurance	2,110 00			*(e)* 1,520 00
Land	120,100 00			
Building	128,000 00			
Accumulated Depreciation, Building		50,000 00		*(f)* 13,500 00
Equipment	34,100 00			
Accumulated Depreciation, Equipment		19,600 00		*(g)* 5,900 00
Notes Payable		34,600 00		
Accounts Payable		4,300 00		
Unearned Course Fees		2,200 00	*(c)* 1,800 00	
Mortgage Payable		8,800 00		
R. L. Majors, Capital		252,774 00		
R. L. Majors, Drawing	65,000 00			
Sales		253,980 00		
Sales Returns and Allowances	940 00			
Sales Discounts	1,880 00			
Interest Income		1,220 00		
Purchases	88,840 00			
Purchases Returns and Allowances		832 00		
Purchases Discounts		1,448 00		
Freight In	2,460 00			
Wages Expense	44,900 00		*(h)* 2,030 00	
Supplies Expense	12,440 00			*(d)* 2,415 00
Property Tax Expense	2,860 00			
Interest Expense	574 00			
	629,754 00	629,754 00		
Income Summary			*(a)* 68,000 00	*(b)* 64,800 00
Course Fees Income				*(c)* 1,800 00
Supplies			*(d)* 2,415 00	
Insurance Expense			*(e)* 1,520 00	
Depreciation Expense, Building			*(f)* 13,500 00	
Depreciation Expense, Equipment			*(g)* 5,900 00	
Wages Payable				*(h)* 2,030 00
			159,965 00	159,965 00

LEARNING OBJECTIVE

5 Complete the work sheet.

Carry the Income Summary account from the Adjustments columns into the Income Statement columns as two separate figures. For merchandise inventory, record the amount of the ending inventory in the Balance Sheet Debit column. For unearned revenue, record the unearned revenue account in the Balance Sheet Credit column and the revenue account in the Income Statement Credit column.

PRACTICE EXERCISE 5

Complete the Income Statement and Balance Sheet columns of the work sheet for Majors Company from Practice Exercise 4.

PRACTICE EXERCISE 5 SOLUTION

Majors Company
Work Sheet
For Year Ended December 31, 20—

Account Name	Trial Balance Debit	Trial Balance Credit	Adjustments Debit	Adjustments Credit
Cash	23 0 1 0 00			
Notes Receivable	6 0 0 0 00			
Accounts Receivable	28 5 4 0 00			
Merchandise Inventory	68 0 0 0 00		(b) 64 8 0 0 00	(a) 68 0 0 0 00
Prepaid Insurance	2 1 1 0 00			(e) 1 5 2 0 00
Land	120 1 0 0 00			
Building	128 0 0 0 00			
Accumulated Depreciation, Building		50 0 0 0 00		(f) 13 5 0 0 00
Equipment	34 1 0 0 00			
Accumulated Depreciation, Equipment		19 6 0 0 00		(g) 5 9 0 0 00
Notes Payable		34 6 0 0 00		
Accounts Payable		4 3 0 0 00		
Unearned Course Fees		2 2 0 0 00	(c) 1 8 0 0 00	
Mortgage Payable		8 8 0 0 00		
R. L. Majors, Capital		252 7 7 4 00		
R. L. Majors, Drawing	65 0 0 0 00			
Sales		253 9 8 0 00		
Sales Returns and Allowances	9 4 0 00			
Sales Discounts	1 8 8 0 00			
Interest Income		1 2 2 0 00		
Purchases	88 8 4 0 00			
Purchases Returns and Allowances		8 3 2 00		
Purchases Discounts		1 4 4 8 00		
Freight In	2 4 6 0 00			
Wages Expense	44 9 0 0 00		(h) 2 0 3 0 00	
Supplies Expense	12 4 4 0 00			(d) 2 4 1 5 00
Property Tax Expense	2 8 6 0 00			
Interest Expense	5 7 4 00			
	629 7 5 4 00	629 7 5 4 00		
Income Summary			(a) 68 0 0 0 00	(b) 64 8 0 0 00
Course Fees Income				(c) 1 8 0 0 00
Supplies			(d) 2 4 1 5 00	
Insurance Expense			(e) 1 5 2 0 00	
Depreciation Expense, Building			(f) 13 5 0 0 00	
Depreciation Expense, Equipment			(g) 5 9 0 0 00	
Wages Payable				(h) 2 0 3 0 00
Net Income			159 9 6 5 00	159 9 6 5 00

Income Statement		Balance Sheet	
Debit	Credit	Debit	Credit
		23,010.00	
		6,000.00	
		28,540.00	
		64,800.00	
		590.00	
		120,100.00	
		128,000.00	
			63,500.00
		34,100.00	
			25,500.00
			34,600.00
			4,300.00
			400.00
			8,800.00
			252,774.00
		65,000.00	
	253,980.00		
940.00			
1,880.00			
	1,220.00		
88,840.00			
	832.00		
	1,448.00		
2,460.00			
46,930.00			
10,025.00			
2,860.00			
574.00			
68,000.00	64,800.00		
	1,800.00		
		2,415.00	
1,520.00			
13,500.00			
5,900.00			
			2,030.00
243,429.00	324,080.00	472,555.00	391,904.00
80,651.00			80,651.00
324,080.00	324,080.00	472,555.00	472,555.00

CHAPTER REVIEW

LEARNING OBJECTIVE

6 *Journalize the adjusting entries for a merchandising business under the periodic inventory system.*

Take the adjusting entries recorded in the journal directly from the Adjustments columns of the work sheet.

PRACTICE EXERCISE 6

Prepare the year-end adjusting entries from the Adjustments column of Major Company's work sheet from Practice Exercise 4.

PRACTICE EXERCISE 6 SOLUTION

GENERAL JOURNAL PAGE ____

Date		Description	Post. Ref.	Debit	Credit
20—		Adjusting Entries			
Dec.	31	Income Summary		68,000.00	
(a)		Merchandise Inventory			68,000.00
(b)	31	Merchandise Inventory		64,800.00	
		Income Summary			64,800.00
(c)	31	Unearned Course Fees		1,800.00	
		Course Fees Income			1,800.00
(d)	31	Supplies		2,415.00	
		Supplies Expense			2,415.00
(e)	31	Insurance Expense		1,520.00	
		Prepaid Insurance			1,520.00
(f)	31	Depreciation Expense, Building		13,500.00	
		Accumulated Depreciation,			
		Building			13,500.00
(g)	31	Depreciation Expense, Equipment		5,900.00	
		Accumulated Depreciation,			
		Equipment			5,900.00
(h)	31	Wages Expense		2,030.00	
		Wages Payable			2,030.00

LEARNING OBJECTIVE

7 *Prepare and journalize the adjusting entry for merchandise inventory under the perpetual inventory system.*

Assuming that the amount of the physical count of the stock of merchandise is less than the recorded amount, the adjusting entry is a debit to Cost of Goods Sold and a credit to Merchandise Inventory for the amount of the difference. On the other hand, if the physical count of the stock of merchandise is more than the recorded amount, the adjusting entry is to debit Merchandise Inventory and credit Cost of Goods Sold for the amount of the difference.

PRACTICE EXERCISE 7

Larkin Company employs the perpetual inventory system. Cost of Goods Sold for the year before any adjustment is $553,250. The computer record shows the amount of ending inventory to be $369,583, while the physical count shows ending inventory to be $362,720. Record the adjustment into T accounts and then journalize the adjusting entry.

PRACTICE EXERCISE 7 SOLUTION

Cost of Goods Sold

	+		–
Bal.	553,250		
Adj.	6,863		

Merchandise Inventory

	+		–
Bal.	369,583	Adj.	6,863*

*Adjustment = $362,720 – $369,583 = $(6,863)

GENERAL JOURNAL PAGE ____

Date		Description	Post. Ref.	Debit	Credit
20—		Adjusting Entries			
Dec.	31	Cost of Goods Sold		6 8 6 3 00	
		Merchandise Inventory			6 8 6 3 00

Glossary

Inventory shrinkage The amount by which inventory diminishes due to theft, misplacement, loss, or mismarking. *(p. 464)*

Physical inventory An actual count of the stock of goods on hand. *(p. 455)*

Unearned revenue Cash received in advance for goods or services to be delivered later; considered to be a liability until the revenue is earned. *(p. 453)*

CHAPTER ASSIGNMENTS

Discussion Questions

1. What is a physical inventory? What does the word *periodic* mean in the term *periodic inventory*?
2. On the Income Summary line of a work sheet, $126,220 appears in the Income Statement Debit column, and $123,300 appears in the Income Statement Credit column. Which figure represents the beginning inventory?
3. Using the perpetual inventory system, what account is debited when a business finds its physical count of inventory is greater than the recorded amount?
4. On a work sheet, where will the amount of the ending merchandise inventory be recorded?

5. Explain what is meant by unearned revenue, and why it is treated as a liability.
6. Why is it necessary to adjust the Merchandise Inventory account under a periodic inventory system?
7. A merchandising company shows $8,842 in the Supplies Expense account on the preadjusted trial balance. After taking inventory of the actual supplies, it still owns $3,638.
   a. Write the adjusting entry.
   b. How much was used or expired?
8. Assume that a college receives $84,000 for one semester's dormitory rent in advance and an entry is made debiting Cash and crediting Unearned Rent. At the end of the year, $68,000 of the rent has been earned. What adjusting entry would be made?

Exercises

1 

PRACTICE EXERCISE 1

EXERCISE 11-1 For the following Supplies Expense ledger account, determine the debits and credits for each amount posted to the account and briefly describe each transaction. The entry of December 16 involved the return of defective goods.

ACCOUNT Supplies Expense ACCOUNT NO. 615

Date		Item	Post. Ref.	Debit	Credit	Balance Debit	Balance Credit
20—							
Jan.	1	Balance	✓			740 00	
Apr.	7		J25	290 00		1,030 00	
May	30		J82	420 00		1,450 00	
Nov.	19		J104	315 00		1,765 00	
Dec.	16		J115		186 00	1,579 00	
	18		J127	571 00		2,150 00	
	31	Adj.	J141		1,470 00	680 00	

2 

PRACTICE EXERCISE 2

EXERCISE 11-2 For the university football program's Unearned Season Tickets account, list the debits and credits for each amount posted to the account and briefly describe each transaction.

ACCOUNT Unearned Season Tickets ACCOUNT NO. 214

Date		Item	Post. Ref.	Debit	Credit	Balance Debit	Balance Credit
20—							
Jan.	1	Balance	✓				12,900 00
Oct.	15		J42		36,780 00		49,680 00
Nov.	1		J43		42,600 00		92,280 00
Dec.	31	Adj.	J52	43,125 00			49,155 00

2

PRACTICE EXERCISE 2

EXERCISE 11-3 On October 31, the Vermillion Igloos Hockey Club received $800,000 in cash in advance for season tickets for eight home games. The transaction was recorded as a debit to Cash and a credit to Unearned Admissions. By December 31, the end of the fiscal year, the team had played three home games and received an additional $450,000 cash admissions income at the gate.

a. Journalize the adjusting entry as of December 31.
b. List the title of the account and the related balance that will appear on the income statement.
c. List the title of the account and the related balance that will appear on the balance sheet.

3

PRACTICE EXERCISE 3

EXERCISE 11-4 Basga Company uses the periodic inventory system. Beginning inventory amounted to $241,072. A physical count reveals that the latest inventory amount is $256,339. Record the adjusting entries using T accounts.

5

PRACTICE EXERCISE 5

EXERCISE 11-5 Indicate the work sheet columns (Income Statement Debit, Income Statement Credit, Balance Sheet Debit, Balance Sheet Credit) in which the balances of the following accounts should appear:

a. F. Dexter, Drawing
b. Advertising Expense
c. Merchandise Inventory (ending)
d. Purchases Discounts
e. Unearned Fees
f. Sales Returns and Allowances
g. Accumulated Depreciation, Building
h. Income Summary
i. Fees Income
j. Prepaid Rent

6

PRACTICE EXERCISE 6

EXERCISE 11-6 Journalize the required adjusting entries for the year ended December 31 for Morgan Yoga Accessories. Morgan Yoga Accessories uses the periodic inventory system.

a–b. On December 31, a physical count of inventory was taken. The physical count amounted to $19,342. The Merchandise Inventory account shows a balance of $18,368.
c. On June 1 of this year, $1,200 was paid for a one-year insurance policy.
d. On October 1 of this year, $360 was paid for four months of advertising.
e. As of December 31, the balance of the Unearned Membership Fees account is $12,800. Of this amount, $7,800 has now been earned.
f. Equipment purchased on April 1 of this year for $6,500 is expected to have a useful life of five years, with a trade-in value of $1,000. All other equipment has been fully depreciated. The straight-line method is used.
g. As of December 31, two days' wages at $230 per day had accrued.

6

PRACTICE EXERCISE 6

EXERCISE 11-7 On December 31, the end of the year, the accountant for *Fireside Magazine* was called away suddenly because of an emergency. However, before leaving, the accountant jotted down a few notes pertaining to the adjustments. Journalize the necessary adjusting entries. Assume that *Fireside Magazine* uses the periodic inventory system.

a–b. A physical count of inventory revealed a balance of $199,830. The Merchandise Inventory account shows a balance of $202,839.

c. Subscriptions received in advance amounting to $156,200 were recorded as Unearned Subscriptions. At year end, $103,120 has been earned.
d. Depreciation of equipment for the year is $12,300.
e. The amount of expired insurance for the year is $1,612.
f. The balance of Prepaid Rent is $2,400, representing four months' rent. Three months' rent has now expired.
g. Three days' salaries will be unpaid at the end of the year; total weekly (five days') salaries are $4,000.

7 

EXERCISE 11-8 On December 31, Marchant Company took a physical count of its merchandise inventory. It operates under the perpetual inventory system. The physical count amounted to $185,294. The Merchandise Inventory account shows a balance of $187,936. Journalize the adjusting entry.

Problem Set A

For additional help, see the demonstration problem at the beginning of each chapter in your Working Papers.

4,5 LO

PROBLEM 11-1A The trial balance of Hadden Company as of December 31, the end of its current fiscal year, is as follows:

Hadden Company
Trial Balance
December 31, 20—

Account Name	Debit	Credit
Cash	9,246.52	
Merchandise Inventory	63,674.80	
Prepaid Insurance	1,420.00	
Store Equipment	36,230.00	
Accumulated Depreciation, Store Equipment		22,726.00
Accounts Payable		13,196.96
Sales Tax Payable		1,236.98
R. M. Hadden, Capital		56,339.32
R. M. Hadden, Drawing	28,000.00	
Sales		175,864.31
Sales Returns and Allowances	1,573.72	
Purchases	77,300.04	
Purchases Returns and Allowances		1,744.32
Purchases Discounts		1,413.62
Freight In	2,427.00	
Salary Expense	35,458.85	
Rent Expense	14,600.00	
Store Supplies Expense	1,466.34	
Miscellaneous Expense	1,124.24	
	272,521.51	272,521.51

Here are the data for the adjustments:

a–b. Merchandise Inventory at December 31, $64,742.80.
c. Store supplies inventory, $420.20.

CHAPTER ASSIGNMENTS

d. Insurance expired, $738.
e. Salaries accrued, $684.50.
f. Depreciation of store equipment, $3,620.

Required

Complete the work sheet after entering the account names and balances onto the work sheet.

Check Figure
Net income, $41,517.76

LO 4,5,6

PROBLEM 11-2A The balances of the ledger accounts of Beldren Home Center as of December 31, the end of its fiscal year, are as follows:

Cash	$ 10,592
Accounts Receivable	43,962
Merchandise Inventory	120,838
Prepaid Insurance	2,628
Store Equipment	35,924
Accumulated Depreciation, Store Equipment	29,420
Office Equipment	10,436
Accumulated Depreciation, Office Equipment	1,720
Notes Payable	5,000
Accounts Payable	29,822
Unearned Rent	3,200
A. P. Beldren, Capital	120,532
A. P. Beldren, Drawing	29,000
Sales	653,000
Sales Returns and Allowances	9,748
Purchases	519,374
Purchases Returns and Allowances	12,440
Purchases Discounts	8,634
Freight In	24,724
Wages Expense	54,200
Supplies Expense	1,570
Interest Expense	772

Data for the adjustments are as follows:

a–b. Merchandise Inventory at December 31, $102,765.
c. Wages accrued at December 31, $1,834.
d. Supplies inventory at December 31, $645.
e. Depreciation of store equipment, $5,782.
f. Depreciation of office equipment, $1,791.
g. Insurance expired during the year, $845.
h. Rent earned, $2,500.

Required

1. Complete the work sheet after entering the account names and balances onto the work sheet.
2. Journalize the adjusting entries on journal page 16.

Check Figure
Net income, $38,506

4,5,6

PROBLEM 11-3A A portion of the work sheet of Sadie's Flowers for the year ended December 31 is as follows:

Account Name	Income Statement Debit	Income Statement Credit	Balance Sheet Debit	Balance Sheet Credit
Cash			9,340.00	
Merchandise Inventory			76,940.00	
Prepaid Insurance			240.00	
Store Equipment			39,280.00	
Accumulated Depreciation, Store Equipment				26,220.00
Accounts Payable				14,600.00
S. R. Rodriguez, Capital				68,940.00
S. R. Rodriguez, Drawing			27,600.00	
Sales		173,420.00		
Sales Returns and Allowances	1,520.00			
Purchases	82,312.00			
Purchases Returns and Allowances		940.00		
Purchases Discounts		1,600.00		
Freight In	1,948.00			
Salary Expense	37,560.00			
Rent Expense	14,800.00			
Supplies Expense	944.00			
Income Summary	65,680.00	76,940.00		
Depreciation Expense, Store Equipment	4,040.00			
Insurance Expense	760.00			
Supplies			256.00	
Salaries Payable				560.00
	209,564.00	252,900.00	153,656.00	110,320.00

Check Figure
Salaries accrued, $560

Required

1. Determine the entries that appeared in the Adjustments columns and present them in general journal form on page 41.
2. Determine the net income for the year.
3. What is the amount of the ending capital?

PROBLEM 11-4A Here are the accounts in the ledger of Misha's Jewel Box, with the balances as of December 31, the end of its fiscal year.

Cash	$ 13,242
Accounts Receivable	3,984
Merchandise Inventory	126,540
Prepaid Insurance	2,655
Land	18,000
Building	97,000
Accumulated Depreciation, Building	38,240
Store Equipment	46,170
Accumulated Depreciation, Store Equipment	16,250
Accounts Payable	8,270
Sales Tax Payable	2,371
Mortgage Payable	77,871
M. Beloit, Capital	185,000
M. Beloit, Drawing	48,000
Sales	379,354
Sales Returns and Allowances	3,892
Cost of Goods Sold	279,198
Salary Expense	54,400

Advertising Expense	$ 3,526
Store Supplies Expense	2,484
Utilities Expense	2,538
Property Tax Expense	1,162
Miscellaneous Expense	1,613
Interest Expense	2,952

Here are the data for the adjustments. Assume that Misha's Jewel Box uses the perpetual inventory system.

a. Merchandise Inventory at December 31, $124,630.
b. Insurance expired during the year, $1,294.
c. Depreciation of building, $3,300.
d. Depreciation of store equipment, $6,470.
e. Salaries accrued at December 31, $2,470.
f. Store supplies inventory at December 31, $1,959.

Required

Check Figure
Net income, $14,104

1. Complete the work sheet after entering the account names and balances onto the work sheet.
2. Journalize the adjusting entries on journal page 63.

Problem Set B

For additional help, see the demonstration problem at the beginning of each chapter in your Working Papers.

4,5

PROBLEM 11-1B The trial balance of Jillson Company as of December 31, the end of its current fiscal year, is as follows:

Jillson Company
Trial Balance
December 31, 20—

Account Name	Debit	Credit
Cash	18,463.92	
Merchandise Inventory	47,356.00	
Prepaid Insurance	1,660.00	
Store Equipment	26,580.00	
Accumulated Depreciation, Store Equipment		15,320.00
Accounts Payable		25,578.80
Sales Tax Payable		1,243.36
G. L. Jillson, Capital		75,630.00
G. L. Jillson, Drawing	28,440.00	
Sales		92,026.74
Sales Returns and Allowances	1,542.04	
Purchases	43,348.45	
Purchases Returns and Allowances		1,748.09
Purchases Discounts		1,987.90
Freight In	2,775.00	
Salary Expense	25,758.80	
Rent Expense	15,300.00	
Store Supplies Expense	1,321.12	
Miscellaneous Expense	989.56	
	213,534.89	213,534.89

Here are the data for the adjustments.

a–b. Merchandise Inventory at December 31, $54,845.00.
c. Store supplies inventory, $488.50.
d. Insurance expired, $680.
e. Salaries accrued, $692.
f. Depreciation of store equipment, $3,760.

Check Figure
Net income, $7,573.26

Required

Complete the work sheet after entering the account names and balances onto the work sheet.

PROBLEM 11-2B The balances of the ledger accounts of Pelango Furniture as of December 31, the end of its fiscal year, are as follows:

Cash	$ 12,482
Accounts Receivable	38,962
Merchandise Inventory	118,628
Prepaid Insurance	2,488
Store Equipment	32,824
Accumulated Depreciation, Store Equipment	26,420
Office Equipment	11,236
Accumulated Depreciation, Office Equipment	3,410
Notes Payable	6,000
Accounts Payable	23,420
Unearned Rent	3,150
L. Pelango, Capital	120,532
L. Pelango, Drawing	28,000
Sales	647,090
Sales Returns and Allowances	8,848
Purchases	519,374
Purchases Returns and Allowances	12,440
Purchases Discounts	8,634
Freight In	22,824
Wages Expense	52,800
Supplies Expense	1,850
Interest Expense	780

Data for the adjustments are as follows:

a–b. Merchandise Inventory at December 31, $104,565.
c. Wages accrued at December 31, $934.
d. Supplies inventory at December 31, $755.
e. Depreciation of store equipment, $4,982.
f. Depreciation of office equipment, $1,531.
g. Insurance expired during the year, $935.
h. Rent earned, $2,450.

Check Figure
Net income, $42,448

Required

1. Complete the work sheet after entering the account names and balances onto the work sheet.
2. Journalize the adjusting entries on journal page 16.

PROBLEM 11-3B A portion of the work sheet of Habib Company for the year ended December 31 follows.

CHAPTER ASSIGNMENTS

Account Name	Income Statement Debit	Income Statement Credit	Balance Sheet Debit	Balance Sheet Credit
Cash			7,736.00	
Merchandise Inventory			74,298.00	
Prepaid Insurance			250.00	
Store Equipment			37,960.00	
Accumulated Depreciation, Store Equipment				29,440.00
Accounts Payable				13,760.00
O. B. Habib, Capital				75,142.00
O. B. Habib, Drawing			30,800.00	
Sales		171,816.00		
Sales Returns and Allowances	1,434.00			
Purchases	85,934.00			
Purchases Returns and Allowances		964.00		
Purchases Discounts		1,636.00		
Freight In	2,658.00			
Salary Expense	37,852.00			
Rent Expense	14,400.00			
Supplies Expense	884.00			
Income Summary	68,228.00	74,298.00		
Depreciation Expense, Store Equipment	4,360.00			
Insurance Expense	552.00			
Supplies			298.00	
Salaries Payable				588.00
	216,302.00	248,714.00	151,342.00	118,930.00

Required

1. Determine the entries that appeared in the Adjustments columns and present them in general journal form on page 41.
2. Determine the net income for the year.
3. What is the amount of the ending capital?

Check Figure
Salaries accrued, $588

LO 4,5,7

PROBLEM 11-4B The accounts in the ledger of Markey's Mountain Shop, with the balances as of December 31, the end of its fiscal year, are as follows:

Cash	$ 12,840
Accounts Receivable	3,242
Merchandise Inventory	137,757
Prepaid Insurance	2,845
Land	22,000
Building	86,000
Accumulated Depreciation, Building	36,940
Store Equipment	54,952
Accumulated Depreciation, Store Equipment	13,348
Notes Payable	10,500
Accounts Payable	18,540
Sales Tax Payable	5,706
B. Markey, Capital	171,000
B. Markey, Drawing	52,000
Sales	458,905
Sales Returns and Allowances	7,590
Cost of Goods Sold	265,315
Salary Expense	52,973
Advertising Expense	6,288
Utilities Expense	7,355

(Continued)

Store Supplies Expense	$ 1,530
Property Tax Expense	800
Miscellaneous Expense	775
Interest Expense	677

Data for the adjustments are as follows. Assume that Markey's Mountain Shop uses the perpetual inventory system.

a. Merchandise Inventory at December 31, $140,357.
b. Store supplies inventory at December 31, $540.
c. Depreciation of building, $3,400.
d. Depreciation of store equipment, $3,800.
e. Salaries accrued at December 31, $1,250.
f. Insurance expired during the year, $1,480.

Check Figure
Net income, $108,812

Required

1. Complete the work sheet after entering the account names and balances onto the work sheet.
2. Journalize the adjusting entries on journal page 63.

ACTIVITIES

CONSIDER AND COMMUNICATE

You have a friend who is a seamstress specializing in *Star Wars* ensembles. She receives cash well in advance of the required date, often in the fiscal period prior to the date of delivery of the ensemble, not only to enable her to purchase material, but to cover her labor. She always debits Cash and credits Ensemble Income. First, explain to her why this entry violates the matching principle. Second, identify the classification of Unearned Revenue. Third, explain when the Unearned Revenue account is used.

WHAT'S WRONG WITH THIS PICTURE?

What could happen if a business spent the cash it had received in advance for services it promised to perform at a later date?

CRITICAL THINKING

On November 1, an exterior painting company received $5,310 for a paint job that will not be finished for a few months. As of December 31, which is the end of the fiscal period, $2,400 worth of painting will not have been completed. The bookkeeper completed the following entries prior to leaving on vacation:

Cash			
11/1	5,310		

Painting Income			
12/31	2,400	11/1	5,310

Unearned Painting Income			
		12/31	2,400

The owner wants to get a bank loan by December 1. The bank requires interim financial statements to be submitted as of December 1. How will the bookkeeper's entries affect the accuracy of the interim balance sheet and income statements? What difference will the bookkeeper's methods make in the December 31 balance sheet and income statement?

A QUESTION OF ETHICS

The owner of a motorcycle shop allows his two sons to take motorcycles home to try them out on different types of surfaces because he believes that they need to be familiar with the products they sell. Sometimes the motorcycles are not returned to the store by the time the physical count of inventory takes place. Respond to this practice.

All About You Spa

Adjusting Entries

Two months (July and August) have passed since Ms. Valli has seen the financial statements for All About You Spa. It is time to begin their preparation. Several accounts need adjusting. These include the accounts you adjusted in Chapter 4 as well as any accounts involved with merchandising.

What additional accounts need to be adjusted?

Directions for Adjusting Entries

1. If desired, or as instructed, prepare a work sheet on paper or with a spreadsheet program. Then enter the adjustments shown on the work sheet into your software program. Adjustment information is provided on the following pages.
2. Open the file entitled ***All_About_You_Spa_Ch11.IA7***. Enter your name when prompted and click ***OK***. Select "Yes" or "No" as desired when asked if you want to open on-screen instructions and check figures. As a reminder, these instructions may be opened at any time by clicking on the ***Info.*** toolbar button.
3. Click on the ***Save As*** toolbar button. When the Save As window appears, select the folder in which you wish to save your data files (if not already selected). In the File Name box, key ***All_About_You_Ch11_Your_Name.IA7*** (for example, All_About_You_Spa_Ch11_John_Doe.IA7) to identify the file containing your work. Click on the ***Save*** button.
4. Click on the ***Journals*** toolbar button and key the adjusting journal entries in the General Journal. Follow these steps for each entry: (a) Key the date, Aug. 31, in the Date column. (b) Enter a reference of "Adj.Ent." in the Refer. column (this is required for generating the Adjusting Journal Entries report later). (c) Enter the debit and credit parts of the entry as you learned to do in Chapter 3.
5. Display the adjusting journal entries. Click on the ***Reports*** toolbar button. Click on ***Journals*** and ***General Journal*** to choose a report to display. Click on ***Customize Journal Report***. In the Reference drop-down list, choose "Adj. Ent." and then click the ***OK*** button to display the Adjusting Journal Entries report. To print the report, click on the ***Print*** button.
6. Review your entries and make corrections to them, if necessary. In the General Journal window, click on the entry to correct, key the correction(s), and click on the ***Post*** button (or press Enter).
7. Display the adjusted Trial Balance report. Click on the ***Reports*** toolbar button. Click on ***Ledger Reports*** and ***Trial Balance*** to choose the report to display. Be sure the run date is set to Aug. 31. To print the report, click on the ***Print*** button at the bottom of the report window.
8. Click on the ***Save*** toolbar button to save your data file.
9. Click on the ***Check*** toolbar button to check your solution against the answer key.

Check Figures

5. Adjusting Entries General Journal report total, $13,961.43
7. Adjusted trial balance total, $133,624.03

Adjusting Entry Information

The pre-adjusted trial balance for August 31 is as follows:

All About You Spa
Trial Balance
August 31, 20—

Account Name	Debit	Credit
Cash	40,361.74	
Accounts Receivable	7,196.63	
Prepaid Insurance	800.00	
Spa Equipment	18,083.00	
Accumulated Depreciation, Spa Equipment		64.88
Office Equipment	1,570.00	
Accumulated Depreciation, Office Equipment		10.00
Accounts Payable		20,393.00
Sales Tax Payable		2,001.12
A. Valli, Capital		49,884.62
A. Valli, Drawing	5,000.00	
Income from Services		25,398.00
Merchandise Sales		22,489.65
Sales Returns and Allowances	88.00	
Purchases	24,101.00	
Purchases Returns and Allowances		123.00
Freight In	992.00	
Wages Expense	16,250.00	
Rent Expense	3,300.00	
Office Supplies Expense	118.00	
Spa Supplies Expense	535.00	
Laundry Expense	179.00	
Advertising Expense	455.00	
Utilities Expense	963.00	
Miscellaneous Expense	371.90	
	120,364.27	120,364.27

Merchandise Inventory Adjustment (a)

A new account, Merchandise Inventory 116, has been added to the Chart of Accounts. The August 31 pre-adjustment balance in that account is zero. But you know that merchandise has been purchased for resale and that you have sold merchandise. In addition, there is possible inventory shrinkage for several reasons: breakage, theft, misplacement, use as samples, etc. A physical count was taken, and the inventory was valued at $13,110. Enter the correct inventory count by debiting Merchandise Inventory and crediting Income Summary.

Supplies Adjustments (b) and (c)

A physical count has been taken of the two supplies accounts. The values of the remaining inventories of supplies are:

Office Supplies	$ 75.00
Spa Supplies	345.00

All About You Spa has been entering all purchases of supplies directly into the expense accounts, but the inventories of supplies remaining should appear as

CONTINUING CASE

assets. Therefore, two asset accounts have been added to the Chart of Accounts: Spa Supplies 114 and Office Supplies 115. You will need to make two adjusting entries removing (crediting) the above amounts from the expense accounts and debiting the asset accounts.

Prepaid Insurance Adjustment (d)

A review of the insurance records determined that $281.67 in liability insurance coverage had been used during the last two months.

Depreciation Adjustments (e) and (f)

Estimated depreciation amounts for the two equipment accounts are:

Spa Equipment	$129.76
Office Equipment	20.00

Remember to credit the accumulated depreciation (contra asset) accounts, *not* the equipment accounts.

Wages Expense/Wages Payable Adjustment

There is no need for a Wages Expense/Wages Payable adjustment because the end of the fiscal period did not come in the middle of a pay period. (The spa was closed on August 31.)

12 Financial Statements, Closing Entries, and Reversing Entries

WHY IT MATTERS

COSTCO WHOLESALE CORPORATION, Issaquah, Washington

Costco is the largest membership warehouse club chain in the world based on sales volume and is the fifth largest general retailer in the United States. Costco focuses on selling products at low prices, often at very high volume. These goods are usually bulk-packaged and marketed primarily to large families and businesses. Costco became the first company ever to grow from zero to $3 billion in sales in less than six years.

For fiscal year 2008, Costco's sales totaled $70.9 billion, a 12.5 percent increase from 2007, and its net income reached $1.28 billion in 2008, an 18.5 percent increase from 2007. This information, and much more, can be derived from the financial statements that merchandising firms such as Costco must prepare on a regular basis to provide shareholders and other interested parties information about the company's activities and financial performance. These various financial statements and the information contained in them are the focus of this chapter.

LEARNING OBJECTIVES

After you have completed this chapter, you will be able to do the following:

1. *Prepare a classified income statement for a merchandising firm.*
2. *Prepare a classified balance sheet for any type of business.*
3. *Compute working capital and current ratio.*
4. *Journalize the closing entries for a merchandising firm.*
5. *Determine which adjusting entries can be reversed, and journalize the reversing entries.*

ACCOUNTING LANGUAGE

Cost of Goods Sold *(p. 494)*
Current Assets *(p. 499)*
Current Liabilities *(p. 499)*
Current ratio *(p. 500)*
Delivered Cost of Purchases *(p. 495)*
General Expenses *(p. 495)*
Gross Profit *(p. 492)*
Liquidity *(p. 499)*
Long-Term Liabilities *(p. 499)*
Net Income or **Net Profit** *(p. 492)*
Net Purchases *(p. 495)*
Net Sales *(p. 493)*
Notes Receivable (current) *(p. 499)*
Property and Equipment *(p. 499)*
Reversing entries *(p. 505)*
Selling Expenses *(p. 495)*
Temporary-equity accounts *(p. 502)*
Working capital *(p. 500)*

In this chapter, we review how to prepare financial statements directly from a work sheet. We also explain the functions of closing entries and reversing entries as means of completing the accounting cycle. Finally, we look at the financial statements in their entirety and explain their various subdivisions.

First, here is the chart of accounts for Whitewater Raft Supply.

PERIODIC INVENTORY CHART OF ACCOUNTS	PERPETUAL INVENTORY CHART OF ACCOUNTS
Assets (100–199)	**Assets (100–199)**
111 Cash	111 Cash
112 Notes Receivable	112 Notes Receivable
113 Accounts Receivable	113 Accounts Receivable
114 Merchandise Inventory	114 Merchandise Inventory
115 Supplies	115 Supplies
116 Prepaid Insurance	116 Prepaid Insurance
121 Land	121 Land
122 Building	122 Building
123 Accumulated Depreciation, Building	123 Accumulated Depreciation, Building
124 Equipment	124 Equipment
125 Accumulated Depreciation, Equipment	125 Accumulated Depreciation, Equipment
Liabilities (200–299)	**Liabilities (200–299)**
211 Notes Payable	211 Notes Payable
212 Accounts Payable	212 Accounts Payable

FYI

Accountants sometimes number contra accounts as subaccounts. For example, Accumulated Depreciation, Building, is 122.1, Sales Returns and Allowances is 411.1, Sales Discounts is 411.2, Purchases Returns and Allowances is 511.1, and so on.

213 Wages Payable
217 Unearned Course Fees
221 Mortgage Payable

Owner's Equity (300–399)
311 D. M. Bruce, Capital
312 D. M. Bruce, Drawing
313 Income Summary

Revenue (400–499)
411 Sales
412 Sales Returns and Allowances
413 Sales Discounts
421 Course Fees Income
422 Interest Income

Cost of Goods Sold (500–599)
511 Purchases
512 Purchases Returns and Allowances
513 Purchases Discounts
514 Freight In

Expenses (600–699)
611 Wages Expense
622 Supplies Expense
623 Insurance Expense
624 Depreciation Expense, Building
625 Depreciation Expense, Equipment
626 Property Tax Expense
634 Interest Expense

213 Wages Payable
217 Unearned Course Fees
221 Mortgage Payable

Owner's Equity (300–399)
311 D. M. Bruce, Capital
312 D. M. Bruce, Drawing
313 Income Summary

Revenue (400–499)
411 Sales
412 Sales Returns and Allowances
413 Sales Discounts
421 Course Fees Income
422 Interest Income

Cost of Goods Sold (500–599)
511 Cost of Goods Sold

Expenses (600–699)
611 Wages Expense
622 Supplies Expense
623 Insurance Expense
624 Depreciation Expense, Building
625 Depreciation Expense, Equipment
626 Property Tax Expense
634 Interest Expense

THE INCOME STATEMENT

LEARNING OBJECTIVE 1

Prepare a classified income statement for a merchandising firm.

As you know, the work sheet is merely a tool used by accountants to prepare the financial statements. In Figure 1, we present the part of the work sheet for Whitewater Raft Supply that includes the Income Statement columns. Of course, **each of the amounts that appear in the Income Statement columns of the work sheet will be used in the income statement**. Notice that the amounts for the beginning and ending merchandise inventory appear separately on the Income Summary line. Recall that you were asked to pick up the two figures and move them—not to take the difference between the two. Figure 2 shows the entire income statement. Take your time to look it over carefully; then we will break it down into its components.

The income statement follows a logical pattern that is much the same for any type of merchandising business. The ability to interpret the income statement and extract parts from it is very useful when gathering information for decision making. To realize the full value of an income statement, however, you need to know the basic format of an income statement. Let's look at the statement section by section.

Net Sales	$254,260
− Cost of Goods Sold	90,120
Gross Profit	$164,140
− Operating Expenses	58,835
Income from Operations	$105,305

FIGURE 1 Partial work sheet for Whitewater Raft Supply

Whitewater Raft Supply
Work Sheet
For Year Ended December 31, 20—

Account Name	Trial Balance Debit	Trial Balance Credit	Adjustments Debit	Adjustments Credit	Income Statement Debit	Income Statement Credit
Cash	24,154.00					
Notes Receivable	4,000.00					
Accounts Receivable	29,546.00					
Merchandise Inventory	67,000.00		(b) 64,800.00	(a) 67,000.00		
Prepaid Insurance	960.00			(e) 520.00		
Land	122,100.00					
Building	129,000.00					
Accumulated Depr., Building		51,000.00		(f) 3,500.00		
Equipment	33,100.00					
Accumulated Depr., Equipment		16,400.00		(g) 4,900.00		
Notes Payable		36,600.00				
Accounts Payable		3,300.00				
Unearned Course Fees		1,200.00	(c) 800.00			
Mortgage Payable		7,800.00				
D. M. Bruce, Capital		253,774.00				
D. M. Bruce, Drawing	77,000.00					
Sales		257,180.00				257,180.00
Sales Returns and Allowances	940.00				940.00	
Sales Discounts	1,980.00				1,980.00	
Interest Income		220.00				220.00
Purchases	87,840.00				87,840.00	
Purchases Returns and Allowances		932.00				932.00
Purchases Discounts		1,348.00				1,348.00
Freight In	2,360.00				2,360.00	
Wages Expense	45,900.00		(h) 1,030.00		46,930.00	
Supplies Expense	1,540.00			(d) 415.00	1,125.00	
Property Tax Expense	1,860.00				1,860.00	
Interest Expense	474.00				474.00	
	629,754.00	629,754.00				
Income Summary			(a) 67,000.00	(b) 64,800.00	67,000.00	64,800.00
Course Fees Income				(c) 800.00		800.00
Supplies			(d) 415.00			
Insurance Expense			(e) 520.00		520.00	
Depreciation Expense, Building			(f) 3,500.00		3,500.00	
Depreciation Expense, Equipment			(g) 4,900.00		4,900.00	
Wages Payable				(h) 1,030.00		
			142,965.00	142,965.00	219,429.00	325,280.00
Net Income					105,851.00	
					325,280.00	325,280.00

FIGURE 2
Income statement for Whitewater Raft Supply

Whitewater Raft Supply Income Statement For Year Ended December 31, 20—				
Revenue from Sales:				
Sales			$257,180	
Less: Sales Returns and Allowances		$ 940		
Sales Discounts		1,980	2,920	
Net Sales				$254,260
Cost of Goods Sold:				
Merchandise Inventory, January 1, 20—			$ 67,000	
Purchases		$87,840		
Less: Purchases Returns and Allowances	$ 932			
Purchases Discounts	1,348	2,280		
Net Purchases		$85,560		
Add Freight In		2,360		
Delivered Cost of Purchases			87,920	
Cost of Goods Available for Sale			$154,920	
Less Merchandise Inventory, December 31, 20—			64,800	
Cost of Goods Sold				90,120
Gross Profit				$164,140
Operating Expenses:				
Wages Expense			$ 46,930	
Supplies Expense			1,125	
Insurance Expense			520	
Depreciation Expense, Building			3,500	
Depreciation Expense, Equipment			4,900	
Property Tax Expense			1,860	
Total Operating Expenses				58,835
Income from Operations				$105,305
Other Income:				
Course Fees Income			$ 800	
Interest Income			220	
Total Other Income			$ 1,020	
Other Expenses:				
Interest Expense			474	546
Net Income				$105,851

To illustrate the concepts of **gross** and **net**, here is an example of a simple single-sale transaction.

Several years ago, Della Reyes bought an antique table at a second-hand store for $800. She sold the table for $1,850. She advertised it in the daily newspaper at a cost of $73. How much did she make as clear profit?

Sale of Table	$1,850
Less Cost of Table	800
Gross Profit	$1,050
Less Advertising Expense	73
Net Income or Net Profit (gain on the sale)	$ 977

Gross Profit is the profit on the sale of the table before any expenses have been deducted; in this case, it is $1,050. **Net Income,** or **Net Profit,** is the final or clear profit after all expenses have been deducted. In a single-sale situation such as this, we refer to the final outcome as the net profit. But for a business that has many sales and expenses, most accountants prefer the term *net income.* Regardless of which word you use, *net* refers to clear profit—after all expenses have been deducted.

Revenue from Sales

Now let's look at the Revenue from Sales section of the income statement for Whitewater Raft Supply:

Revenue from Sales:			
Sales		$257,180	
Less: Sales Returns and Allowances	$ 940		
Sales Discounts	1,980	2,920	
Net Sales			$254,260

When we introduced Sales Returns and Allowances and Sales Discounts, we treated them as deductions from Sales. You can see that on the income statement, they are deducted from Sales to give us **Net Sales**. Note that we record these items in the same order in which they appear in the ledger.

Remember

Returns and Allowances (Sales or Purchases) is listed on one line, and Discounts (Sales or Purchases) is listed below.

Ratio Analysis

Gross Profit Percentage

An important function of accounting is to provide tools for interpreting the financial statements or the results of operations. One ratio that is frequently used to analyze financial statements is *gross profit percentage*.

Southern Office Furniture will serve as our example (see the comparative income statement below).

Southern Office Furniture
Comparative Income Statement
For Years Ended January 31, 2011, and January 31, 2010

	2011		2010	
	Amount	Percent	Amount	Percent
Revenue from Sales:				
Sales	$533,600	101%	$510,000	102%
Less Sales Returns and Allowances	5,600	1	10,000	2
Net Sales	$528,000	100%	$500,000	100%
Cost of Goods Sold:				
Merchandise Inventory, February 1	$ 46,000	9%	$ 64,000	13%
Delivered Cost of Purchases	290,000	55	230,000	46
Cost of Goods Available for Sale	$336,000	64%	$294,000	59%
Less Merchandise Inventory, January 31	58,000	11	46,000	9
Cost of Goods Sold	$278,000	53%	$248,000	50%
Gross Profit	$250,000	47%	$252,000	50%
Operating Expenses:				
Sales Salary Expense	$ 63,600	12%	$ 58,000	12%
Rent Expense	24,000	5	24,000	5
Advertising Expense	21,400	4	16,000	3
Depreciation Expense, Equipment	20,000	4	18,000	4
Insurance Expense	2,000	—	2,000	—
Store Supplies Expense	1,000	—	1,000	—
Miscellaneous Expense	1,000	—	1,000	—
Total Operating Expenses	$133,000	25%	$120,000	24%
Net Income	$117,000	22%	$132,000	26%

For each year, net sales is the base (100 percent). All other items on the income statement can be expressed as a percentage of net sales for the particular year involved. For example, let's look at the following percentages:

$$\text{Gross Profit \% (2011)} = \frac{\text{Gross Profit for 2011}}{\text{Net Sales for 2011}} = \frac{\$250{,}000}{\$528{,}000} = 0.473 = 47\%$$

$$\text{Gross Profit \% (2010)} = \frac{\text{Gross Profit for 2010}}{\text{Net Sales for 2010}} = \frac{\$252{,}000}{\$500{,}000} = 0.504 = 50\%$$

$$\text{Sales Salary Expense \% (2011)} = \frac{\text{Sales Salary Expense for 2011}}{\text{Net Sales for 2011}}$$

$$= \frac{\$63{,}600}{\$528{,}000} = 0.120 = 12\%$$

$$\text{Sales Salary Expense \% (2010)} = \frac{\text{Sales Salary Expense for 2010}}{\text{Net Sales for 2010}}$$

$$= \frac{\$58{,}000}{\$500{,}000} = 0.116 = 12\%$$

Here's how you might interpret a few of the percentages:

2011

- For every $100 in net sales, gross profit amounted to $47.
- For every $100 in net sales, sales salary expense amounted to $12.
- For every $100 in net sales, net income amounted to $22.

2010

- For every $100 in net sales, gross profit amounted to $50.
- For every $100 in net sales, sales salary expense amounted to $12.
- For every $100 in net sales, net income amounted to $26.

The gross profit percentage declined from 50% in 2010 to 47% in 2011 because the Cost of Goods Sold percentage increased from 50% in 2010 to 53% in 2011.

Cost of Goods Sold

The section of the income statement that requires the greatest amount of concentration is the **Cost of Goods Sold** section, where the cost of the goods we sold is computed. Let's repeat it in its entirety:

Cost of Goods Sold:				
Merchandise Inventory, January 1, 20—			$ 67,000	
Purchases		$87,840		
Less: Purchases Returns and Allowances	$ 932			
Purchases Discounts	1,348	2,280		
Net Purchases		$85,560		
Add Freight In		2,360		
Delivered Cost of Purchases			87,920	
Cost of Goods Available for Sale			$154,920	
Less Merchandise Inventory, December 31, 20—			64,800	
Cost of Goods Sold				90,120

First, let's look closely at the Purchases section.

Purchases		$87,840	
Less: Purchases Returns and Allowances	$ 932		
Purchases Discounts	1,348	2,280	
Net Purchases		$85,560	
Add Freight In		2,360	
Delivered Cost of Purchases			87,920

Note the parallel to the Revenue from Sales section. To arrive at **Net Purchases**, we deduct the sum of Purchases Returns and Allowances and Purchases Discounts from Purchases. To complete the Purchases section we add Freight In to Net Purchases to get **Delivered Cost of Purchases**.

Now let's look at the full Cost of Goods Sold section. You might think of Cost of Goods Sold like this:

Amount we started with (beginning inventory)	$ 67,000
+ Net amount we purchased, including freight charges	87,920
Total amount that could have been sold (available)	$154,920
− Amount left over (ending inventory)	64,800
Cost of the goods that were actually sold	$ 90,120

Here's the Cost of Goods Sold expressed in proper wording.

Merchandise Inventory, January 1, 20—	$ 67,000
+ Delivered Cost of Purchases	87,920
Cost of Goods Available for Sale	$154,920
− Merchandise Inventory, December 31, 20—	64,800
Cost of Goods Sold	$ 90,120

Operating Expenses

Operating expenses, as the name implies, are the regular expenses of doing business. We list the accounts and their respective balances in the order in which they appear in the ledger.

Many firms use subclassifications of operating expenses, such as the following:

1. **Selling Expenses** Any expenses directly connected with the selling activity, such as
   - Sales Salary Expense
   - Sales Commissions Expense
   - Advertising Expense
   - Store Supplies Expense
   - Delivery Expense
   - Depreciation Expense, Store Equipment
2. **General Expenses** Any expenses related to the office or administration, or any expense that cannot be directly connected with a selling activity:
   - Office Salary Expense
   - Property Tax Expense
   - Depreciation Expense, Office Equipment
   - Rent Expense
   - Insurance Expense

FYI

In preparing the income statement, classifying expense accounts as selling expenses or general expenses is a matter of judgment. The only reason we're not using this breakdown here is that we're trying to keep the number of accounts to a basic few.

- Office Supplies Expense
- Miscellaneous General Expense*

Income from Operations

Now let's repeat the skeleton outline:

Net Sales
− Cost of Goods Sold

Gross Profit
− Operating Expenses

Income from Operations

If Operating Expenses are the regular, recurring expenses of doing business, then Income from Operations should be the regular or recurring income from normal business operations. When you compare the results of operations over a number of years, Income from Operations is the figure to use as a basis for comparison.

Other Income and Other Expenses

The Other Income classification, as the name implies, includes any revenue account other than Revenue from Sales. What we are trying to do is to isolate Sales at the top of the income statement as the major revenue account, so that the Gross Profit figure represents the profit made on the sale of merchandise *only*. Additional accounts that may appear under the heading of Other Income are Rent Income (the firm is subletting part of its premises), Interest Income (the firm holds an interest-bearing note or contract), Gain on Disposal of Property and Equipment (the firm makes a profit on the sale of property and equipment), and Miscellaneous Income (the firm has an overage recorded in the Cash Short and Over account).

The classification Other Expenses records various nonoperating expenses, such as Interest Expense or Loss on Disposal of Property and Equipment.

THE STATEMENT OF OWNER'S EQUITY AND THE BALANCE SHEET

Remember

Net income appears on both the income statement and the statement of owner's equity.

Figure 3 is a partial work sheet for Whitewater Raft Supply. Here again we find that **every figure in the Balance Sheet columns of the work sheet is used in either the statement of owner's equity or the balance sheet.**

Preparation of the financial statements follows the same order we presented before: first, the income statement; second, the statement of owner's equity; third, the balance sheet. The statement of owner's equity shows why the balance of the Capital account has changed from the beginning of the fiscal period to the end of it. In preparing the statement of owner's equity, always look into the ledger for the owner's Capital account to find any changes, such as additional investments, made during the year.

In Figure 4 we observe the balance of D. M. Bruce, Capital, listed on the work sheet as $253,774. We note from the ledger account a credit of $9,000 representing an additional investment. Therefore, the beginning balance of D. M. Bruce, Capital, was $244,774 ($253,774 – $9,000).

Remember

The columns on the financial statements *do not* represent debit or credit columns. The columns are for making computations and listing totals.

*If the Cash Short and Over account has a debit balance (net shortage), the balance is added to and reported as Miscellaneous General Expense. Conversely, if the Cash Short and Over account has a credit balance (net overage), the balance is added to and reported as Miscellaneous Income, which is classified as Other Income.

FIGURE 3 Partial work sheet for Whitewater Raft Supply

Whitewater Raft Supply
Work Sheet
For Year Ended December 31, 20—

Account Name	Trial Balance Debit	Trial Balance Credit	Adjustments Debit	Adjustments Credit	Balance Sheet Debit	Balance Sheet Credit
Cash	24 1 5 4 00				24 1 5 4 00	
Notes Receivable	4 0 0 0 00				4 0 0 0 00	
Accounts Receivable	29 5 4 6 00				29 5 4 6 00	
Merchandise Inven.	67 0 0 0 00		(b) 64 8 0 0 00	(a) 67 0 0 0 00	64 8 0 0 00	
Prepaid Insurance	9 6 0 00			(e) 5 2 0 00	4 4 0 00	
Land	122 1 0 0 00				122 1 0 0 00	
Building	129 0 0 0 00				129 0 0 0 00	
Accum. Depr., Building		51 0 0 0 00		(f) 3 5 0 0 00		54 5 0 0 00
Equipment	33 1 0 0 00				33 1 0 0 00	
Accum. Depr., Equipment		16 4 0 0 00		(g) 4 9 0 0 00		21 3 0 0 00
Notes Payable		36 6 0 0 00				36 6 0 0 00
Accounts Payable		3 3 0 0 00				3 3 0 0 00
Unearn. Course Fees		1 2 0 0 00	(c) 8 0 0 00			4 0 0 00
Mortgage Payable		7 8 0 0 00				7 8 0 0 00
D. M. Bruce, Capital		253 7 7 4 00				253 7 7 4 00
D. M. Bruce, Draw.	77 0 0 0 00				77 0 0 0 00	
Sales		257 1 8 0 00				
Sales Returns and Allowances	9 4 0 00					
Sales Discounts	1 9 8 0 00					
Interest Income		2 2 0 00				
Purchases	87 8 4 0 00					
Purchases Returns and Allowances		9 3 2 00				
Purchases Discounts		1 3 4 8 00				
Freight In	2 3 6 0 00					
Wages Expense	45 9 0 0 00		(h) 1 0 3 0 00			
Supplies Expense	1 5 4 0 00			(d) 4 1 5 00		
Property Tax Expense	1 8 6 0 00					
Interest Expense	4 7 4 00					
	629 7 5 4 00	629 7 5 4 00				
Income Summary			(a) 67 0 0 0 00	(b) 64 8 0 0 00		
Course Fees Income				(c) 8 0 0 00		
Supplies			(d) 4 1 5 00		4 1 5 00	
Insurance Expense			(e) 5 2 0 00			
Depr. Expense, Building			(f) 3 5 0 0 00			
Depr. Expense, Equipment			(g) 4 9 0 0 00			
Wages Payable				(h) 1 0 3 0 00		1 0 3 0 00
			142 9 6 5 00	142 9 6 5 00	484 5 5 5 00	378 7 0 4 00
Net Income						105 8 5 1 00
					484 5 5 5 00	484 5 5 5 00

FIGURE 4
Statement of owner's equity for Whitewater Raft Supply

Whitewater Raft Supply Statement of Owner's Equity For Year Ended December 31, 20—		
D. M. Bruce, Capital, January 1, 20—		$244,774
Investment during the Year	$ 9,000	
Net Income for the Year	$105,851	
Subtotal	$114,851	
Less Withdrawals for the Year	77,000	
Increase in Capital		37,851
D. M. Bruce, Capital, December 31, 20—		$282,625

BALANCE SHEET CLASSIFICATIONS

LEARNING OBJECTIVE 2
Prepare a classified balance sheet for any type of business.

Balance sheet classifications are generally uniform for all types of business enterprises. You are strongly urged to take the time to learn the following definitions of the classifications and the order of accounts within them. As you read, refer to Figure 5.

FIGURE 5
Balance sheet for Whitewater Raft Supply

Whitewater Raft Supply Balance Sheet December 31, 20—			
Assets			
Current Assets:			
Cash		$ 24,154	
Notes Receivable		4,000	
Accounts Receivable		29,546	
Merchandise Inventory		64,800	
Prepaid Insurance		440	
Supplies		415	
Total Current Assets			$123,355
Property and Equipment:			
Land		$122,100	
Building	$129,000		
Less Accumulated Depreciation	54,500	74,500	
Equipment	$ 33,100		
Less Accumulated Depreciation	21,300	11,800	
Total Property and Equipment			208,400
Total Assets			$331,755
Liabilities			
Current Liabilities:			
Notes Payable		$ 36,600	
Mortgage Payable (current portion)		2,000	
Accounts Payable		3,300	
Wages Payable		1,030	
Unearned Course Fees		400	
Total Current Liabilities			$ 43,330
Long-Term Liabilities:			
Mortgage Payable			5,800
Total Liabilities			$ 49,130
Owner's Equity			
D. M. Bruce, Capital			282,625
Total Liabilities and Owner's Equity			$331,755

Current Assets

Current Assets consist of cash and any other assets or resources that are expected to be realized in cash or to be sold or consumed during the normal operating cycle of the business (or one year, if the normal operating cycle is less than twelve months).

Accountants list current assets in the order of their convertibility into cash—in other words, their **liquidity**. (If you have an asset such as a car or a stereo and you sell it quickly and turn it into cash, you are said to be turning it into a *liquid* state.) If the first four accounts shown under Current Assets in Figure 5 are present, they are always recorded in the same order: (1) Cash, (2) Notes Receivable, (3) Accounts Receivable, and (4) Merchandise Inventory.

Notes Receivable (current) are short-term (one year or less) promissory notes (promise-to-pay notes) held by the firm. A note is generally received from a customer as a substitute for a charge account.

Prepaid Insurance and Supplies are considered prepaid items that will be used up or will expire within the following operating cycle or year. Generally, these prepaid items are not converted into cash and that's why they appear at the bottom of the Current Assets section.

FYI

Some companies are so successful that they accumulate cash from earnings that is not needed to pay current obligations. Rather than leaving the cash in a bank account, companies may prefer to invest it in short-term government or corporate notes or bonds. These are called marketable securities. On the balance sheet, Marketable Securities is a separate account listed just below Cash.

Property and Equipment

Property and Equipment are relatively long-lived assets that are held for use in the production or sale of other assets or services; some accountants refer to them as *fixed assets*. The three types of accounts that usually appear in this category are Land, Building, and Equipment (refer to Figure 5). Note that the Building and Equipment accounts are followed by their respective Accumulated Depreciation accounts. We list these assets in order of their length of life, with the longest-lived asset placed first.

Remember

Since Accumulated Depreciation is a contra account, it is deducted from the appropriate asset.

Current Liabilities

Current Liabilities are debts that will become due within the normal operating cycle of the business, usually within one year; they normally will be paid, when due, from current assets. List current liabilities in the order of their expected payment. Notes Payable represents the amount owed on promissory notes. Mortgage Payable is the payment one makes to reduce the principal of the mortgage in a given year. Accounts Payable are debts owed to creditors. Wages Payable and any other accrued liabilities, such as Commissions Payable and the current portion of unearned revenue accounts, usually fall at the bottom of the list of current liabilities.

Long-Term Liabilities

Long-Term Liabilities are debts that are payable over a comparatively long period, usually longer than one year. The current portion of notes, contracts, and loans (the amount of principal due within the next year) is shown as a current liability. The remaining amount is shown as a long-term liability. Note that for Whitewater Raft Supply, $2,000 of the Mortgage Payable represents the current portion and is shown as a current liability. The remaining $5,800 is shown as a long-term liability. (Refer to Figure 5.)

Working Capital and Current Ratio

3 LEARNING OBJECTIVE

Compute working capital and current ratio.

Both the management and the short-term creditors of a firm are vitally interested in two questions:

1. Does the firm have a sufficient amount of capital to operate?
2. Does the firm have the ability to pay its debts?

Two measures used to answer these questions are a firm's working capital and its current ratio; the necessary data are taken from a classified balance sheet.

© GEORGE ROBINSON/PHOTOLIBRARY

The barn, the tractor, and the land this man is working are all classified as fixed assets in the Property and Equipment section. Only the barn and tractor, however, are subject to depreciation.

Working capital is determined by subtracting current liabilities from current assets; thus,

$$\text{Working Capital} = \text{Current Assets} - \text{Current Liabilities}$$

The normal operating cycle for most firms is less than one year. Because current assets equal cash—or items that can be converted into cash or used up within one year—and current liabilities equal the total amount that the company must pay out within one year, working capital is appropriately named. It is the amount of capital the company has available to use or to work with. The working capital for Whitewater Raft Supply is as follows:

$$\text{Working Capital} = \$123{,}355 - \$43{,}330 = \$80{,}025$$

The **current ratio** is useful in revealing a firm's ability to pay its bills. It is determined by dividing current assets by current liabilities:

$$\text{Current Ratio} = \frac{\text{Current Assets (amount coming in within one year)}}{\text{Current Liabilities (amount going out within one year)}}$$

The current ratio for Whitewater Raft Supply is calculated like this:

$$\text{Current Ratio} = \frac{\$123{,}355}{\$43{,}330} = 2.85$$

In the case of Whitewater Raft Supply, \$2.85 in current assets is available to pay every dollar currently due on December 31.

FYI

The current ratio has a weakness. It favors companies with many current assets. However, the current ratio does not attempt to measure the overall strength of a company.

You Make the Call

J. J. Marston owns Woodland Toys, a small business selling handmade wooden toys. Sales have been a bit slow, so he has come up with some strategies to increase sales as well as to begin exporting his specialty toys. The problem is that he needs cash to hire assistants and to purchase several woodworking tools to increase production. He has tried to figure out how he can manage the investment. He has no idea how to analyze his financial statements to provide valuable decision-making information. How would you recommend that he use his most recent balance sheet (shown below) and the two formulas discussed in the chapter to help in making the decision to expand his operation?

Woodland Toys
Balance Sheet
December 31, 20—

Assets		
Current Assets:		
Cash	$22,751	
Accounts Receivable	7,692	
Merchandise Inventory	45,018	
Prepaid Insurance	1,265	
Total Current Assets		$76,726
Property and Equipment:		
Shop Equipment	$18,357	
Less Accumulated Depreciation	6,020	
Total Property and Equipment		12,337
Total Assets		$89,063
Liabilities		
Current Liabilities:		
Accounts Payable	$10,340	
Total Current Liabilities		$10,340
Long-Term Liabilities:		
Mortgage Payable		3,500
Total Liabilities		$13,840
Owner's Equity		
J. J. Marston, Capital		75,223
Total Liabilities and Owner's Equity		$89,063

SOLUTION

While there are many more tools for analyzing financial statements than we have introduced, you have learned two formulas in this chapter that can assist your friend in determining his ability to expand his business—working capital and current ratio.

Working capital is the amount of capital the company has available to use or to work with. To compute Woodland Toys' working capital, subtract its current liabilities from its current assets:

$$\text{Working Capital} = \$76{,}726 - \$10{,}340 = \$66{,}386$$

While J. J. Marston does not want to liquidate all his assets, he can see that there is adequate capital to begin planning his business expansion.

A second formula that can help in making the decision to expand is the current ratio. It is useful in revealing a firm's ability to pay its bills. To compute Woodland Toys' current ratio, divide its current assets by its current liabilities.

$$\text{Current Ratio} = \frac{\$76{,}726}{\$10{,}340} = 7.42$$

This means that $7.42 in current assets is available to pay every dollar of debt currently due on December 31. The higher the current ratio the better position the company is in to pay short-term debt. A current ratio of 7.42 shows that Woodland Toys is in a very favorable position.

Chart of Accounts

When we introduced the chart of accounts and the account number arrangement, we said that the first digit represents the classification of an account. Since you are now acquainted with classified income statements and balance sheets, we can introduce the second digit. The second digit stands for the subclassification.

Assets	1– –	Revenue	4– –
Current Assets	11–	Revenue from Sales	41–
Property and Equipment	12–	Other Income	42–
Liabilities	2– –	Cost of Goods Sold	5– –
Current Liabilities	21–	Purchases	51–
Long-Term Liabilities	22–	Expenses	6– –
Owner's Equity	3– –	Selling Expenses	61–
Capital	31–	General Expenses	62–
		Other Expenses	63–

Remember

A common organization for the chart of accounts is

Assets	1– –
Liabilities	2– –
Owner's Equity	3– –
Revenue	4– –
Cost of Goods Sold	5– –
Expenses	6– –

The third digit indicates the placement of the account within the subclassification. For example, account number 411 represents Sales, which is the first account listed under Revenue. Account number 512 represents Purchases Returns and Allowances, which is the second account listed under Cost of Goods Sold. Account number 312 represents Drawing, which is the second account listed under Owner's Equity.

CLOSING ENTRIES

LEARNING OBJECTIVE 4

Journalize the closing entries for a merchandising firm.

Now let's look at closing entries for a merchandising business. You follow the same four steps to close or zero out the revenue, expense, and Drawing accounts as you do for a service business.

At the end of a fiscal period, you close the revenue and expense accounts so that you can start the next fiscal period with zero balances. You close the Drawing account because it, too, applies to one fiscal period. Recall that these accounts are called **temporary-equity accounts**, or *nominal accounts*.

Figure 6 shows the isolated Income Statement columns. After you have looked them over, let's look at the four steps of the closing procedure.

FIGURE 6 Partial work sheet for Whitewater Raft Supply

Account Name	Trial Balance Debit	Trial Balance Credit	Income Statement Debit	Income Statement Credit
Cash	24,154.00			
Notes Receivable	4,000.00			
Accounts Receivable	29,546.00			
Merchandise Inventory	67,000.00			
Prepaid Insurance	960.00			
Land	122,100.00			
Building	129,000.00			
Accumulated Depreciation, Building		51,000.00		
Equipment	33,100.00			
Accumulated Depreciation, Equipment		16,400.00		
Notes Payable		36,600.00		
Accounts Payable		3,300.00		
Unearned Course Fees		1,200.00		
Mortgage Payable		7,800.00		
D. M. Bruce, Capital		253,774.00		
D. M. Bruce, Drawing	77,000.00			
Sales		257,180.00		257,180.00
Sales Returns and Allowances	940.00		940.00	
Sales Discounts	1,980.00		1,980.00	
Interest Income		220.00		220.00
Purchases	87,840.00		87,840.00	
Purchases Returns and Allowances		932.00		932.00
Purchases Discounts		1,348.00		1,348.00
Freight In	2,360.00		2,360.00	
Wages Expense	45,900.00		46,930.00	
Supplies Expense	1,540.00		1,125.00	
Property Tax Expense	1,860.00		1,860.00	
Interest Expense	474.00		474.00	
	629,754.00	629,754.00		
Income Summary			67,000.00	64,800.00
Course Fees Income				800.00
Supplies				
Insurance Expense			520.00	
Depreciation Expense, Building			3,500.00	
Depreciation Expense, Equipment			4,900.00	
Wages Payable				
			219,429.00	325,280.00
Net Income			105,851.00	
			325,280.00	325,280.00

Four Steps in the Closing Procedure

These four steps should be followed when closing:

STEP 1. Close the revenue accounts and the other accounts that appear on the income statement and have credit balances (all temporary or nominal accounts with credit balances) into Income Summary. **(Debit the figures that are credited in the Income Statement columns of the work sheet, except the figure on the Income Summary line.)** This entry is illustrated for Whitewater Raft Supply as follows:

GENERAL JOURNAL PAGE 97

Date		Description	Post. Ref.	Debit	Credit
20—		Closing Entries			
Dec.	31	Sales		257,180.00	
		Interest Income		220.00	
		Purchases Returns and Allowances		932.00	
		Purchases Discounts		1,348.00	
		Course Fees Income		800.00	
		Income Summary			260,480.00

STEP 2. Close the expense accounts and the other accounts appearing on the income statement that have debit balances (all temporary or nominal accounts with debit balances) into Income Summary. **(Credit the figures that are debited in the Income Statement columns of the work sheet, except the figure on the Income Summary line.)**

Note that you close Purchases Discounts and Purchases Returns and Allowances in step 1 along with the revenue accounts. Note also that in step 2 you close Sales Discounts and Sales Returns and Allowances along with the expense accounts.

GENERAL JOURNAL PAGE 97

Date		Description	Post. Ref.	Debit	Credit
Dec.	31	Income Summary		152,429.00	
		Sales Returns and Allowances			940.00
		Sales Discounts			1,980.00
		Purchases			87,840.00
		Freight In			2,360.00
		Wages Expense			46,930.00
		Supplies Expense			1,125.00
		Property Tax Expense			1,860.00
		Interest Expense			474.00
		Insurance Expense			520.00
		Depreciation Expense, Building			3,500.00
		Depreciation Expense, Equipment			4,900.00

STEP 3. Close the Income Summary account into the Capital account, transferring the net income or loss to the Capital account.

GENERAL JOURNAL PAGE 97

Date		Description	Post. Ref.	Debit	Credit
Dec.	31	Income Summary		105,851.00	
		D. M. Bruce, Capital			105,851.00

Here is what the T accounts look like. Note that the Income Summary account already contains adjusting entries for merchandise inventory.

Income Summary

Adj. (Beginning Merchandise Inventory)	67,000	Adj. (Ending Merchandise Inventory)	64,800
Closing (Expenses and other debit balance accounts)	152,429	Closing (Revenue and other credit balance accounts)	260,480
Closing (Net Income)	105,851		

D. M. Bruce, Capital

	−	+	
		Bal.	253,774
		Closing (Net Income)	105,851

STEP 4. Close the Drawing account into the Capital account.

GENERAL JOURNAL — PAGE 97

Date		Description	Post. Ref.	Debit	Credit
Dec.	31	D. M. Bruce, Capital		77 0 0 0 00	
		D. M. Bruce, Drawing			77 0 0 0 00

Here is what the T accounts would look like:

D. M. Bruce, Drawing

	+	−	
Bal.	77,000	Closing	77,000

D. M. Bruce, Capital

	−	+	
Closing (Drawing)	77,000	Bal.	253,774
		Closing (Net Income)	105,851
		Bal.	282,625

REVERSING ENTRIES

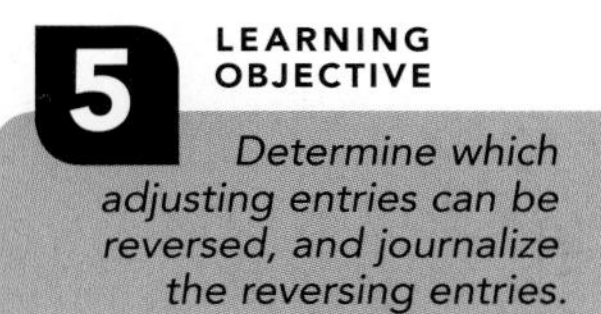

5
LEARNING OBJECTIVE
Determine which adjusting entries can be reversed, and journalize the reversing entries.

Reversing entries are general journal entries that are the exact reverse of certain adjusting entries. A reversing entry enables the accountant to record routine transactions in the usual manner, *even though* an adjusting entry affecting one of the accounts involved in the transaction has intervened. We can understand this concept best by looking at an example.

Suppose there is an adjusting entry for accrued wages owed to employees at the end of the fiscal year. Assume that all the employees of Mason Company earn, altogether, $400 per day for a five-day week and that payday occurs every Friday throughout the year. When the employees get their checks at 5:00 P.M. on Friday, the checks include their wages for that day and for the preceding four days. And

FYI

The use of reversing entries is optional.

assume that, one year, the last day of the fiscal year happens to fall on Wednesday, December 31. A diagram of this situation would look like this:

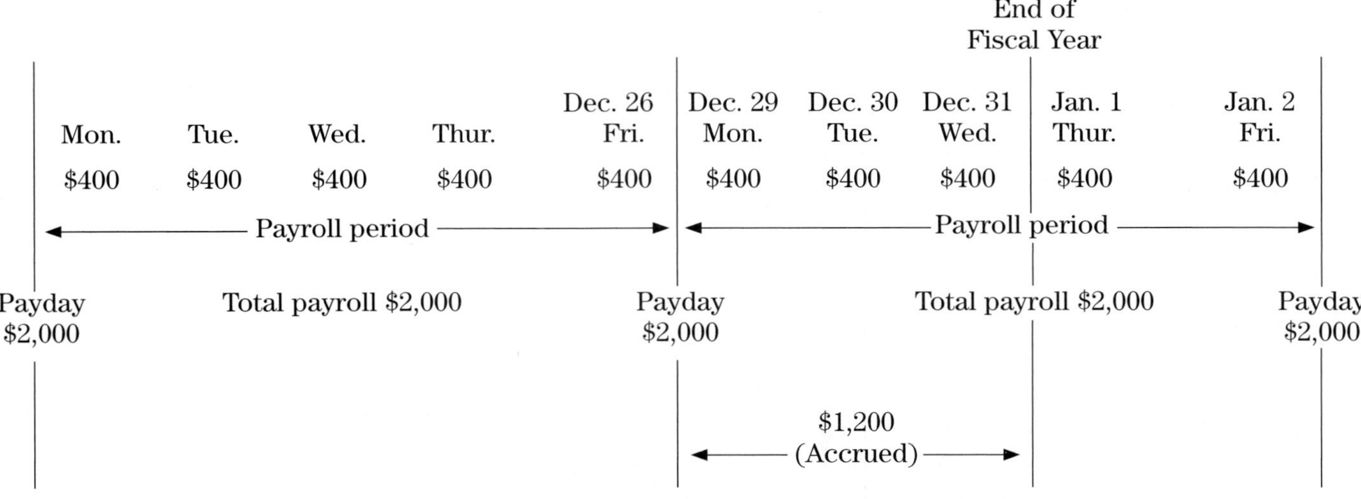

Each Friday during the year, the payroll has been debited to the Wages Expense account and credited to the Cash account. As a result, Wages Expense has a debit balance of $102,000. Here is the adjusting entry in T account form:

Wages Expense

	+	−
Bal.	102,000	
Dec. 31 Adj.	1,200	

Wages Payable

−	+	
	Dec. 31 Adj.	1,200

Next, when all the expense accounts are closed, Wages Expense is closed by crediting it for $103,200. However, Wages Payable continues to have a credit balance of $1,200. The $2,000 payroll on January 2 must be split up by debiting Wages Payable $1,200, debiting Wages Expense $800, and crediting Cash $2,000.

The employee who records the payroll not only has to record this particular payroll differently from all other weekly payrolls for the year but also has to refer back to the adjusting entry to determine what portion of the $2,000 is debited to Wages Payable and what portion is debited to Wages Expense. In many companies, however, the employee who records the payroll does not have access to the adjusting entries.

There is a solution to this problem. The need to refer to the earlier entry and divide the debit total between the two accounts is eliminated *if a reversing entry is made on the first day of the following fiscal period*. You make an entry that is the exact reverse of the adjusting entry, as follows:

GENERAL JOURNAL PAGE 118

Date		Description	Post. Ref.	Debit	Credit
20—		Reversing Entries			
Jan.	1	Wages Payable		1 2 0 0 00	
		Wages Expense			1 2 0 0 00

Now let's bring the T accounts up to date.

Wages Expense

	+	−	
Bal.	102,000	Dec. 31 Closing	103,200
Dec. 31 Adjusting	1,200		
Bal.	——	Jan. 1 Reversing	1,200

Wages Payable

	+	−	
Jan. 1 Reversing	1,200	Dec. 31 Adj.	1,200

The reversing entry has the effect of transferring the $1,200 liability from Wages Payable to the credit side of Wages Expense. Wages Expense will temporarily have a credit balance until the next payroll is recorded in the routine manner. In our example, this occurs on January 2 as follows:

Wages Expense

	+	−	
Bal.	102,000	Dec. 31 Closing	103,200
Dec. 31 Adj.	1,200		
Bal.	——		
Jan. 2	2,000	Jan. 1 Reversing	1,200
Bal.	800		

Wages Payable

	−	+	
Jan. 1 Reversing	1,200	Dec. 31 Adj.	1,200

Cash

	+	−	
		Jan. 2	2,000

There is now a *net debit balance* of $800 in Wages Expense, which is the correct amount ($400 for January 1 and $400 for January 2). To see this, look at the following ledger accounts. December 26 was the last payday of one year, and January 2 is the first payday of the next year.

GENERAL LEDGER

ACCOUNT Wages Expense — ACCOUNT NO. 611

Date		Item	Post. Ref.	Debit	Credit	Balance Debit	Balance Credit
20—							
Dec.	26		CP16	2 000 00		102 000 00	
	31	Adjusting	J116	1 200 00		103 200 00	
	31	Closing	J117		103 200 00	—	—
20—							
Jan.	1	Reversing	J118		1 200 00		1 200 00
	2		CP17	2 000 00		800 00	

ACCOUNT Wages Payable — ACCOUNT NO. 213

Date		Item	Post. Ref.	Debit	Credit	Balance Debit	Balance Credit
20—							
Dec.	31	Adjusting	J116		1 200 00		1 200 00
20—							
Jan.	1	Reversing	J118	1 200 00		—	—

The reversing entry for accrued salaries or wages applies to service as well as merchandising companies. You can see that a reversing entry simply switches around an adjusting entry. The question is: Which adjusting entries should be reversed? Here are two handy rules for reversing. **If an adjusting entry is to be reversed, it must meet both of the following qualifications:**

1. **The adjusting entry increases an asset or liability account.**
2. **The asset or liability account did not have a previous balance.**

With the exception of the first year of operations, Merchandise Inventory and contra accounts—such as Accumulated Depreciation—always have previous balances. Consequently, adjusting entries involving these accounts should never be reversed.

Let's apply these rules to the adjusting entries for Whitewater Raft Supply.

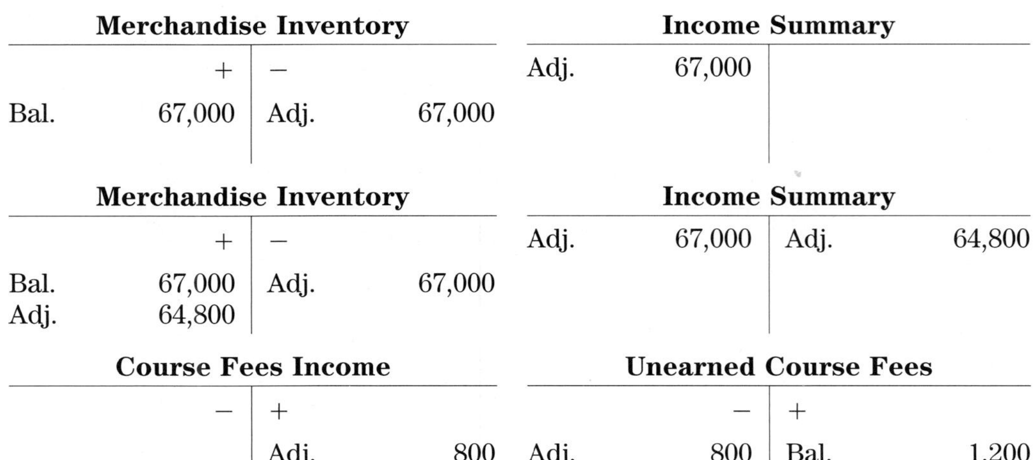

(Do not reverse; Merchandise Inventory is an asset, but it was decreased. Also, it has a previous balance.)

Merchandise Inventory

	+	−	
Bal.	67,000	Adj.	67,000

Income Summary

Adj.	67,000		

(Do not reverse; Merchandise Inventory is an asset, but it has a previous balance.)

Merchandise Inventory

	+	−	
Bal.	67,000	Adj.	67,000
Adj.	64,800		

Income Summary

Adj.	67,000	Adj.	64,800

(Do not reverse; Unearned Course Fees is a liability, but it was decreased. Also, it has a previous balance.)

Course Fees Income

	−	+	
		Adj.	800

Unearned Course Fees

	−	+	
Adj.	800	Bal.	1,200

Supplies

	+	−
Adj.	415	

Supplies Expense

	+	−	
Bal.	1,540	Adj.	415

(Reverse; Supplies is an asset account. It was increased, and it had no previous balance.)

Insurance Expense

	+	−
Adj.	520	

Prepaid Insurance

	+	−	
Bal.	960	Adj.	520

(Do not reverse; Prepaid Insurance is an asset account, but it was decreased. Also, it has a previous balance.)

Depreciation Expense, Building

	+	−
Adj.	3,500	

Accumulated Depreciation, Building

−	+	
	Bal.	51,000
	Adj.	3,500

(Do not reverse; Accumulated Depreciation is a contra asset, and it always has a previous balance after the first year.)

Depreciation Expense, Equipment

	+	−
Adj.	4,900	

Accumulated Depreciation, Equipment

−	+	
	Bal.	16,400
	Adj.	4,900

(Do not reverse; Accumulated Depreciation is a contra asset, and it always has a previous balance after the first year.)

Wages Expense

	+	−
Bal.	45,900	
Adj.	1,030	

Wages Payable

−	+	
	Adj.	1,030

(Reverse; Wages Payable is a liability account. It was increased, and it had no previous balance.)

Whenever we introduce additional adjusting entries, we will make it a point to state whether they can be reversed.

Remember

- Reversing entries are optional.

CHAPTER REVIEW

Study & Practice

LEARNING OBJECTIVE

Prepare a classified income statement for a merchandising firm.

The outline of the income statement looks like this:

Revenue from Sales

	Gross Sales
−	Sales Returns and Allowances
−	Sales Discounts
=	**Net Sales**

(Continued)

− **Cost of Goods Sold**			Beginning Merchandise Inventory
	+ **Delivered Cost of Purchases**		Gross Purchases
		−	Purchases Returns and Allowances
		−	Purchases Discounts
		+	Freight In
		=	Delivered Cost of Purchases
	=		Cost of Goods Available for Sale
	−		Ending Merchandise Inventory
	=		Cost of Goods Sold
= **Gross Profit**			
− **Operating Expenses**	**Selling Expenses** **General Expenses**		
= **Income from Operations**			
+ **Other Income**	Interest Income Rent Income Gain on Disposal of Property and Equipment		
− **Other Expenses**	Interest Expense Loss on Disposal of Property and Equipment		
= **Net Income**			

PRACTICE EXERCISE 1

Using the following information, prepare the Cost of Goods Sold section of an income statement.

Purchases Discounts	$ 9,000
Merchandise Inventory, December 31	192,000
Purchases	480,000
Merchandise Inventory, January 1	188,000
Purchases Returns and Allowances	16,000
Freight In	27,000

PRACTICE EXERCISE 1 SOLUTION

Cost of Goods Sold:				
Merchandise Inventory, January 1, 20—			$188,000	
Purchases		$480,000		
Less: Purchases Returns and Allowances	$16,000			
Purchases Discounts	9,000	25,000		
Net Purchases		$455,000		
Add Freight In		27,000		
Delivered Cost of Purchases			482,000	
Cost of Goods Available for Sale			$670,000	
Less Merchandise Inventory, December 31, 20—			192,000	
Cost of Goods Sold				478,000

2 LEARNING OBJECTIVE

Prepare a classified balance sheet for any type of business.

The outline of the balance sheet looks like this:

Assets Current Assets (listed in the order of their convertibility into cash)

1. Cash
2. Notes Receivable
3. Accounts Receivable
4. Merchandise Inventory
5. Prepaid items (Supplies; Prepaid Insurance)

Property and Equipment (listed in the order of their length of life; the asset with the longest life is placed first)

1. Land
2. Buildings
3. Equipment

Liabilities Current Liabilities (listed in the order of their urgency of payment; the most pressing obligation is placed first)

1. Notes Payable
2. Mortgage Payable or Contracts Payable (current portion)
3. Accounts Payable
4. Accrued liabilities (Wages Payable; Commissions Payable)
5. Unearned Revenue

Long-Term Liabilities (Contracts Payable; Mortgage Payable)

Owner's Equity Capital balance at end of the fiscal year

PRACTICE EXERCISE 2

Identify each of the following items relating to sections of a balance sheet as Current Assets (CA), Property and Equipment (PE), Current Liabilities (CL), Long-Term Liabilities (LTL), or Owner's Equity (OE).

a. Land
b. Unearned Course Fees
c. Merchandise Inventory
d. Cash
e. Salaries Payable
f. Accumulated Depreciation, Building
g. Note Payable (current)
h. Note Payable (due in 10 years)
i. F. R. Fred, Capital

PRACTICE EXERCISE 2 SOLUTION

a. Land, PE
b. Unearned Course Fees, CL
c. Merchandise Inventory, CA
d. Cash, CA
e. Salaries Payable, CL
f. Accumulated Depreciation, Building, PE
g. Note Payable (current), CL
h. Note Payable (due in 10 years), LTL
i. F. R. Fred, Capital, OE

LEARNING OBJECTIVE

3 *Compute working capital and current ratio.*

These two measures help analysts determine whether a firm has enough capital to operate and whether it can pay its debts.

$$\textbf{Working capital} = \text{Current assets} - \text{Current liabilities}$$

$$\textbf{Current ratio} = \frac{\text{Current assets}}{\text{Current liablities}}$$

PRACTICE EXERCISE 3

On December 31, 20—, Laredo Company's balance sheet shows that total current assets equal \$450,784, and total current liabilities equal \$435,209. Determine the amount of Laredo Company's working capital and current ratio, and explain what these measures mean.

PRACTICE EXERCISE 3 SOLUTION

$$\text{Working capital} = \$450{,}784 - \$435{,}209 = \$15{,}575$$

$$\text{Current ratio} = \frac{\$450{,}784}{\$435{,}209} = 1.04$$

Laredo Company's working capital shows that it has $15,575 to use or to work with; for example, for expansion or other improvements. Its current ratio shows that the company has $1.04 available to pay for every dollar currently due.

LEARNING OBJECTIVE

Journalize the closing entries for a merchandising firm.

There are four steps in making closing entries for a merchandising business:

STEP 1. Close the revenue accounts and the other accounts that appear on the income statement and have credit balances (all temporary or nominal accounts with credit balances) into Income Summary.

STEP 2. Close the expense accounts and the other accounts appearing on the income statement that have debit balances (all temporary or nominal accounts with debit balances) into Income Summary.

STEP 3. Close the Income Summary account into the Capital account, transferring the net income or loss to the Capital account.

STEP 4. Close the Drawing account into the Capital account.

PRACTICE EXERCISE 4

From the following partial work sheet for Glasco Company, journalize the closing entries dated December 31:

Account Name	Trial Balance Debit	Trial Balance Credit	Income Statement Debit	Income Statement Credit
O. E. Glasco, Capital		250 800 00		
O. E. Glasco, Drawing	77 000 00			
Sales		256 150 00		256 150 00
Sales Returns and Allowances	960 00		960 00	
Sales Discounts	1 860 00		1 860 00	
Interest Income		1 230 00		1 230 00
Purchases	87 840 00		87 840 00	
Purchases Returns and Allowances		922 00		922 00
Purchases Discounts		1 348 00		1 348 00
Freight In	2 460 00		2 460 00	
Wages Expense	45 900 00		46 930 00	
Supplies Expense	1 540 00		1 125 00	
Property Tax Expense	1 960 00		1 960 00	
Interest Expense	374 00		344 00	
	630 631 00	630 631 00		
Income Summary			65 740 00	62 700 00
Course Fees Income				730 00
Supplies				
Insurance Expense			550 00	
Depreciation Expense, Building			5 000 00	
Depreciation Expense, Equipment			3 400 00	
Wages Payable				
			218 169 00	323 080 00
Net Income			104 911 00	
			323 080 00	323 080 00

CHAPTER REVIEW

PRACTICE EXERCISE 4 SOLUTION

GENERAL JOURNAL PAGE ____

Date		Description	Post. Ref.	Debit	Credit
20—		Closing Entries			
Dec.	31	Sales		256,150.00	
		Interest Income		1,230.00	
		Purchases Returns and Allowances		922.00	
		Purchases Discounts		1,348.00	
		Course Fees Income		730.00	
		Income Summary			260,380.00
	31	Income Summary		152,429.00	
		Sales Returns and Allowances			960.00
		Sales Discounts			1,860.00
		Purchases			87,840.00
		Freight In			2,460.00
		Wages Expense			46,930.00
		Supplies Expense			1,125.00
		Property Tax Expense			1,960.00
		Interest Expense			344.00
		Insurance Expense			550.00
		Depreciation Expense, Building			5,000.00
		Depreciation Expense, Equipment			3,400.00
	31	Income Summary*		104,911.00	
		O. E. Glasco, Capital			104,911.00
		*($62,700 + $260,380) − ($65,740 + $152,429)			
	31	O. E. Glasco, Capital		77,000.00	
		O. E. Glasco, Drawing			77,000.00

LEARNING OBJECTIVE 5

Determine which adjusting entries can be reversed, and journalize the reversing entries.

The use of **reversing entries** is optional. Reverse the adjusting entries that increase either asset or liability accounts that do not have previous balances. A contra account like Accumulated Depreciation should not be reversed. Reversing entries are dated as of the first day of the next fiscal period.

PRACTICE EXERCISE 5

From the following T accounts, determine which adjusting entries can be reversed, and journalize the reversing entries.

Merchandise Inventory

	+	−	
Bal.	68,500	Adj.	68,500

Income Summary

Adj.	68,500		

Merchandise Inventory

	+	−	
Bal.	68,500	Adj.	68,500
Adj.	70,320		

Income Summary

Adj.	68,500	Adj.	70,320

Course Fees Income

	−	+	
		Adj.	800

Unearned Course Fees

	−	+	
Adj.	800	Bal.	850

Supplies

	+	−	
Adj.	735		

Supplies Expense

	+	−	
Bal.	1,620	Adj.	735

Insurance Expense

	+	−	
Adj.	1,620		

Prepaid Insurance

	+	−	
Bal.	2,110	Adj.	1,620

Depreciation Expense, Building

	+	−	
Adj.	3,200		

Accumulated Depreciation, Building

	−	+	
		Bal.	46,000
		Adj.	3,200

Depreciation Expense, Equipment

	+	−	
Adj.	4,300		

Accumulated Depreciation, Equipment

	−	+	
		Bal.	21,400
		Adj.	4,300

Wages Expense

	+	−	
Bal.	32,560		
Adj.	2,230		

Wages Payable

	−	+	
		Adj.	2,230

PRACTICE EXERCISE 5 SOLUTION

GENERAL JOURNAL PAGE ____

Date		Description	Post. Ref.	Debit	Credit
20—		Reversing Entries			
Jan.	1	Supplies Expense		735 00	
		Supplies			735 00
	1	Wages Payable		2,230 00	
		Wages Expense			2,230 00

CHAPTER REVIEW

Before a Test Check: Chapters 11–12

PART I: COMPLETION

Complete each of the following statements by writing the appropriate word(s) in the spaces provided.

1. An actual count of a stock of goods is called a(n) __________.
2. Under the __________ system, entries to record the purchase of merchandise are recorded in the Merchandise Inventory account.
3. Unearned revenue is classified as a(n) __________.
4. Under the periodic inventory system, the first adjustment is to debit __________ for the amount of the beginning inventory.
5. Under the perpetual inventory system, after recording the sale of the goods, the accountant debits __________ and credits __________.
6. An increase in Rent Expense results in a(n) __________ to net income.
7. Gross Profit is calculated by subtracting __________ from Net Sales.
8. Current Assets minus Current Liabilities equals __________.
9. Gross Profit minus Total Operating Expenses equals __________.
10. Net Purchases plus __________ equals Delivered Cost of Purchases.

PART II: TRUE/FALSE

For each statement, circle T if it is True or circle F if it is false.

T F **1.** The second adjustment for Merchandise Inventory under the periodic inventory system is to debit Cost of Goods Sold and credit Merchandise Inventory.

T F **2.** Unearned Rent Income is classified as a revenue.

T F **3.** The perpetual inventory system requires that each sale of goods has two entries: one to reduce inventory and affix the cost of the goods sold and one to record the sale.

T F **4.** The periodic inventory system requires two adjusting entries: one to remove the old inventory amount and one to enter the latest inventory amount.

T F **5.** The adjustment to unearned revenue allows the correct amount of liability and revenue to be applied to each fiscal period involved.

T F **6.** Freight In is classified in the Operating Expenses section of an income statement.

T F **7.** Under the perpetual inventory system, the cost of goods sold is calculated by subtracting ending inventory from the cost of goods available for sale.

T F **8.** Reversing entries are optional, and only some adjusting entries are reversed.

T F **9.** Delivery Expense is added to Net Purchases to arrive at Delivered Cost of Purchases.

T F **10.** Purchases Returns and Allowances increases Income from Operations.

PART III: APPLICATION

1. Alphonse Company uses the periodic inventory system. Employees have just taken a physical count of its inventory. This ending inventory has been valued at $136,000. The company's accounting records show the Merchandise Inventory account with a debit balance of $132,000. Journalize the entries on December 31 to adjust the records for this situation.

2. Regletto Company uses the perpetual inventory system. Employees have just taken a physical count of its inventory. This ending inventory has been valued at $146,000. The company's accounting records show the Merchandise Inventory account with a debit balance of $148,000. Journalize the entry on December 31 to adjust the records for this situation.
3. On December 1, Wesley Company collected $20,000 for a remodeling job that will be completed on March 31 of the following year. The revenue will be earned evenly over four months. Wesley Company's fiscal period ends December 31. Make the entries to record the collection of the cash and the year-end adjustment to reflect the amount of revenue earned in December.
4. Yorkland Company has total assets of $250,000, of which noncurrent assets amount to $140,000. The company also has total liabilities of $130,000, of which $80,000 are long-term liabilities. Calculate (a) working capital and (b) current ratio.

ANSWERS: PART I

1. physical inventory; **2.** perpetual inventory; **3.** current liability; **4.** Income Summary; **5.** Cost of Goods Sold; Merchandise Inventory; **6.** decrease; **7.** Cost of Goods Sold; **8.** working capital; **9.** Income from Operations; **10.** Freight In

ANSWERS: PART II

1. F; **2.** F; **3.** T; **4.** T; **5.** T; **6.** F; **7.** F; **8.** T; **9.** F; **10.** T

ANSWERS: PART III

1.

GENERAL JOURNAL PAGE ____

Date		Description	Post. Ref.	Debit	Credit
20—		Adjusting Entries			
Dec.	31	Income Summary		132 0 0 0 00	
		Merchandise Inventory			132 0 0 0 00
	31	Merchandise Inventory		136 0 0 0 00	
		Income Summary			136 0 0 0 00

2.

GENERAL JOURNAL PAGE ____

Date		Description	Post. Ref.	Debit	Credit
20—		Adjusting Entries			
Dec.	31	Cost of Goods Sold		2 0 0 0 00	
		Merchandise Inventory			2 0 0 0 00

3.

GENERAL JOURNAL PAGE ______

Date		Description	Post. Ref.	Debit	Credit
20—					
Dec.	1	Cash		20 0 0 0 00	
		Unearned Revenue			20 0 0 0 00
		To record collection of cash for a four-month job.			
		Adjusting Entry			
	31	Unearned Revenue		5 0 0 0 00	
		Remodeling Revenue			5 0 0 0 00
		To record one month's revenue earned.			

4. a. \$250,000 total assets – \$140,000 noncurrent assets = \$110,000 current assets
\$130,000 total liabilities – \$80,000 long-term liabilities = \$50,000 current liabilities
\$110,000 current assets – \$50,000 current liabilities = \$60,000 working capital

b. $\frac{\$110{,}000 \text{ current assets}}{\$50{,}000 \text{ current liabilities}} = 2.20$ current ratio

Glossary

Cost of Goods Sold A section of the income statement in which the amount of the cost of the goods the business sold is calculated. Terms often used to describe the same thing are *cost of merchandise sold* and *cost of sales.*

	Merchandise Inventory (beginning)
+	Delivered Cost of Purchases
	Cost of Goods Available for Sale
−	Merchandise Inventory (ending)
	Cost of Goods Sold *(p. 494)*

Current Assets Cash and any other assets or resources that are expected to be realized in cash or to be sold or consumed during the normal operating cycle of the business (or one year, if the normal operating cycle is less than twelve months). *(p. 499)*

Current Liabilities Debts that will become due within the normal operating cycle of a business, usually within one year, and that are normally paid from current assets. *(p. 499)*

Current ratio A firm's current assets divided by its current liabilities. Portrays a firm's short-term debt-paying ability. *(p. 500)*

Delivered Cost of Purchases Net Purchases plus Freight In:

	Net Purchases
+	Freight In
	Delivered Cost of Purchases *(p. 495)*

General Expenses Expenses incurred in the administration of a business, including office expenses and any expenses that are not completely classified as Selling Expenses or Other Expenses. *(p. 495)*

Gross Profit Net Sales minus Cost of Goods Sold, or profit before deducting expenses:

	Net Sales
−	Cost of Goods Sold
	Gross Profit *(p. 492)*

Liquidity The ability of an asset to be quickly turned into cash, either by selling it or by putting it up as security for a loan. *(p. 499)*

Long-Term Liabilities Debts payable over a comparatively long period, usually more than one year. *(p. 499)*

Net Income or **Net Profit** The final figure on an income statement after all expenses have been deducted from revenues. *(p. 492)*

Net Purchases Purchases minus Purchases Returns and Allowances and minus Purchases Discounts:

Purchases
– Purchases Returns and Allowances
– Purchases Discounts

Net Purchases *(p. 495)*

Net Sales Sales minus Sales Returns and Allowances and minus Sales Discounts:

Sales
– Sales Returns and Allowances
– Sales Discounts

Net Sales *(p. 493)*

Notes Receivable (current) Written promises to pay the seller/lender the amount due in a period of less than one year. *(p. 499)*

Property and Equipment Long-lived assets that are held for use in the production or sale of other assets or services; also called *fixed assets. (p. 499)*

Reversing entries The reverse of certain adjusting entries, recorded as of the first day of the following fiscal period. The use of reversing entries is optional. *(p. 505)*

Selling Expenses Expenses directly connected with the selling activity, such as salaries of sales staff, advertising expenses, and delivery expenses. *(p. 495)*

Temporary-equity accounts Accounts whose balances apply to one fiscal period only, such as revenues, expenses, and the Drawing account. Temporary-equity accounts are also called *nominal accounts. (p. 502)*

Working capital A firm's current assets less its current liabilities. The amount of capital a firm has available to use or to work with during a normal operating cycle. *(p. 500)*

CHAPTER ASSIGNMENTS

Discussion Questions

1. What is the order for listing accounts in the Current Assets section of the balance sheet?
2. What is the difference between the cost of goods available for sale and the cost of goods sold?
3. What are the basic classifications found on an income statement for a merchandising business as compared to a service business?
4. On a balance sheet, what is the difference between Current Liabilities and Long-Term Liabilities? Give an example of an account in each classification.
5. On an income statement, what is the difference between income from operations and net income? Which is more useful in comparing the results of operations over a number of years?
6. Explain the calculation of net sales and net purchases.
7. In the closing procedure, what happens to (a) Purchases Discounts, (b) Sales Returns and Allowances, (c) Freight In, (d) Gain on Disposal of Property and Equipment?
8. What are the rules for recognizing whether or not an adjusting entry should be reversed?

Exercises

LO 1

EXERCISE 12-1 Calculate the missing items in the following:

PRACTICE EXERCISE 1

Sales	Sales Returns and Allowances	Net Sales	Beginning Merchandise Inventory	Net Purchases	Cost of Goods Available for Sale	Ending Merchandise Inventory	Cost of Goods Sold	Gross Profit
a. $242,000	$ 6,000	———	$152,000	$170,000	———	$136,000	$186,000	———
b. 304,000	———	$297,000	134,000	———	$404,000	176,000	228,000	———
c. ———	10,000	628,000	———	416,000	486,000	89,000	———	———

EXERCISE 12-2 Using the following information, prepare the Cost of Goods Sold section of an income statement.

PRACTICE EXERCISE 1

Purchases Discounts	$ 8,500
Merchandise Inventory, December 31	189,000
Purchases	476,000
Merchandise Inventory, January 1	185,000
Purchases Returns and Allowances	9,000
Freight In	12,000

EXERCISE 12-3 Identify each of the following items relating to sections of an income statement as Revenue from Sales (S), Cost of Goods Sold (CGS), Selling Expenses (SE), General Expenses (GE), Other Income (OI), or Other Expenses (OE).

PRACTICE EXERCISE 1

a. Advertising Expense
b. Rent Expense
c. Purchases Discounts
d. Sales Returns and Allowances
e. Interest Income
f. Freight In
g. Depreciation Expense, Building
h. Interest Expense
i. Insurance Expense
j. Delivery Expense

EXERCISE 12-4 The Income Statement columns of the June 30 (year-end) work sheet for Bajia Company are shown here. From the information given, prepare an income statement for the company. To save time and space, the expenses have been grouped together into two categories.

PRACTICE EXERCISE 1

Account Name	Income Statement Debit	Income Statement Credit
Income Summary	26 0 0 0 00	22 0 0 0 00
Sales		292 9 0 0 00
Sales Returns and Allowances	12 1 0 0 00	
Sales Discounts	6 1 0 0 00	
Purchases	115 0 0 0 00	
Purchases Returns and Allowances		1 1 0 0 00
Purchases Discounts		1 2 0 0 00
Freight In	6 5 0 0 00	
Selling Expenses	57 0 0 0 00	
General Expenses	46 0 0 0 00	
	268 7 0 0 00	317 2 0 0 00
Net Income	48 5 0 0 00	
	317 2 0 0 00	317 2 0 0 00

EXERCISE 12-5 Identify each of the following items relating to sections of a balance sheet as Current Assets (CA), Property and Equipment (PE), Current Liabilities (CL), Long-Term Liabilities (LTL), or Owner's Equity (OE).

PRACTICE EXERCISE 2

CHAPTER ASSIGNMENTS

a. Accounts Receivable
b. Building
c. Wages Payable
d. Prepaid Property Taxes
e. Mortgage Payable (current)
f. Supplies
g. Mortgage Payable (due in 3 years)
h. Unearned Fees
i. D. Marlor, Capital
j. Notes Payable (due in 3 months)

PRACTICE EXERCISE 3

EXERCISE 12-6 On December 31, 20—, the following selected accounts and amounts appeared on the balance sheet for Delo Company. Determine the amount of the working capital and the current ratio.

Building	$170,000
Prepaid Insurance	1,600
Merchandise Inventory	72,000
Store Equipment	14,000
Unearned Fees	800
Notes Payable (due in 6 months)	5,000
Accumulated Depreciation, Building	72,000
Accounts Payable	23,000
Land	40,000
Cash	19,000
Store Supplies	1,200
Accumulated Depreciation, Store Equipment	6,000
Notes Receivable (due in 4 months)	3,000
Mortgage Payable (current portion)	3,500
Salaries Payable	2,700
D. Delo, Capital	101,500
Mortgage Payable (due in 4 years)	85,000

PRACTICE EXERCISE 4

EXERCISE 12-7 From the following T accounts, journalize the closing entries dated December 31 for Baylor Company:

Salary Expense

+	–
65,000	

H. Baylor, Drawing

+	–
55,000	

Purchases Returns and Allowances

–	+
	8,600

Purchases

+	–
235,600	

Miscellaneous Expense

+	–
12,200	

Rent Expense

+	–
22,000	

Sales Returns and Allowances

+	–
7,400	

Freight In

+	–
11,200	

Sales

–	+
	502,000

Income Summary

87,000	103,000

H. Baylor, Capital

–	+
	335,000

Purchases Discounts

–	+
	4,300

EXERCISE 12-8 From the following information, journalize the last two closing entries, and present a statement of owner's equity for Nishimoto Company:

PRACTICE EXERCISE 4

H. Nishimoto, Capital

–		+	
		Jan. 1 Bal.	450,000
		Apr. 7	18,000

Income Summary

Dec. 31 Adj.	190,000	Dec. 31 Adj.	206,000
Dec. 31 Closing	415,000	Dec. 31 Closing	492,000

H. Nishimoto, Drawing

+		–	
Mar. 1	35,000		
Dec. 9	40,000		

Problem Set A

For additional help, see the demonstration problem at the beginning of each chapter in your Working Papers.

PROBLEM 12-1A A partial work sheet for The Fan Shop is presented here. The merchandise inventory at the beginning of the year was $52,300. P. G. Ochoa, the owner, withdrew $30,500 during the year.

The Fan Shop
Work Sheet
For Year Ended December 31, 20—

Account Name	Income Statement Debit	Income Statement Credit
Sales		324 0 0 0 00
Sales Returns and Allowances	3 4 0 0 00	
Sales Discounts	2 7 0 7 00	
Interest Income		1 8 3 0 00
Purchases	201 4 9 0 00	
Purchases Returns and Allowances		2 8 8 0 00
Freight In	9 7 9 0 00	
Wages Expense	46 2 4 0 00	
Rent Expense	12 6 1 0 00	
Commissions Expense	8 3 1 0 00	
Supplies Expense	1 8 4 2 00	
Interest Expense	8 5 4 00	
Income Summary	52 3 0 0 00	54 5 8 0 00
Insurance Expense	1 2 4 0 00	
Depreciation Expense, Building	4 6 0 0 00	
Depreciation Expense, Equipment	2 6 0 0 00	
	347 9 8 3 00	383 2 9 0 00
Net Income	35 3 0 7 00	
	383 2 9 0 00	383 2 9 0 00

CHAPTER ASSIGNMENTS

Check Figure
Cost of Goods Sold, $206,120

Required

1. Prepare an income statement.
2. Journalize the closing entries.

PROBLEM 12-2A Here is the partial work sheet for Eckland Stereo.

Eckland Stereo
Work Sheet
For Year Ended December 31, 20—

Account Name	Balance Sheet Debit	Balance Sheet Credit
Cash	14,815.00	
Notes Receivable	7,500.00	
Accounts Receivable	30,170.00	
Merchandise Inventory	50,244.00	
Prepaid Property Taxes	2,115.00	
Prepaid Insurance	1,640.00	
Land	16,700.00	
Building	50,000.00	
Accumulated Depreciation, Building		15,900.00
Computer Equipment	6,892.00	
Accumulated Depreciation, Computer Equipment		5,674.00
Store Equipment	7,230.00	
Accumulated Depreciation, Store Equipment		4,424.00
Delivery Equipment	4,300.00	
Accumulated Depreciation, Delivery Equipment		3,470.00
Notes Payable		5,215.00
Accounts Payable		27,140.00
Mortgage Payable (current portion)		2,800.00
Mortgage Payable		65,200.00
M. J. Eckland, Capital		57,314.00
M. J. Eckland, Drawing	23,000.00	
Wages Payable		1,984.00
	214,606.00	189,121.00
Net Income		25,485.00
	214,606.00	214,606.00

Check Figure
Working capital, $69,345

Required

1. Prepare a statement of owner's equity (no additional investment).
2. Prepare a balance sheet.
3. Determine the amount of the working capital.
4. Determine the current ratio (carry to two decimal places).

PROBLEM 12-3A The following partial work sheet covers the affairs of Masanto and Company for the year ended June 30:

CHAPTER ASSIGNMENTS

Masanto and Company
Work Sheet
For Year Ended June 30, 20—

Account Name	Income Statement Debit	Income Statement Credit	Balance Sheet Debit	Balance Sheet Credit
Cash			21,034.00	
Accounts Receivable			89,016.00	
Merchandise Inventory			116,400.00	
Prepaid Insurance			3,210.00	
Delivery Equipment			12,400.00	
Accumulated Depreciation, Delivery Equipment				4,600.00
Store Equipment			30,400.00	
Accumulated Depreciation, Store Equipment				8,700.00
Accounts Payable				55,300.00
P. R. Masanto, Capital				172,720.00
P. R. Masanto, Drawing			26,000.00	
Sales		516,000.00		
Purchases	399,101.00			
Purchases Returns and Allowances		9,600.00		
Purchases Discounts		6,800.00		
Freight In	14,000.00			
Salary Expense	46,000.00			
Truck Expense	10,600.00			
Supplies Expense	2,700.00			
Miscellaneous Expense	1,459.00			
Income Summary	112,200.00	116,400.00		
Salaries Payable				1,240.00
Insurance Expense	2,840.00			
Depreciation Expense, Delivery Equipment	1,400.00			
Depreciation Expense, Store Equipment	2,600.00			
	592,900.00	648,800.00	298,460.00	242,560.00
Net Income	55,900.00			55,900.00
	648,800.00	648,800.00	298,460.00	298,460.00

Required

1. Journalize the six adjusting entries.
2. Journalize the closing entries.
3. Journalize the reversing entry.

Check Figure
Reversing entry amount, $1,240

LO 1,2,4,5

PROBLEM 12-4A The following accounts appear in the ledger of Celso and Company as of June 30, the end of this fiscal year:

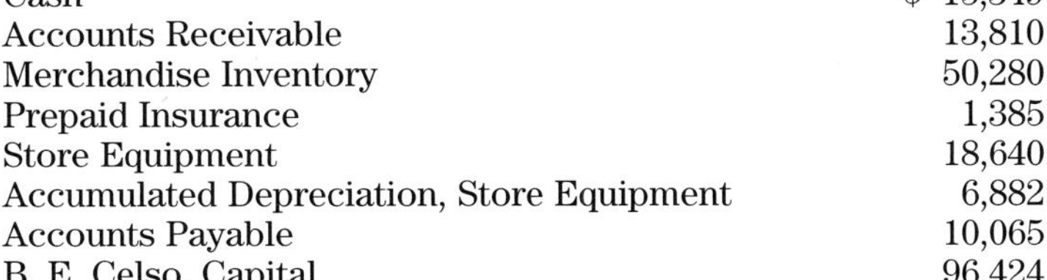

Cash	$ 15,349
Accounts Receivable	13,810
Merchandise Inventory	50,280
Prepaid Insurance	1,385
Store Equipment	18,640
Accumulated Depreciation, Store Equipment	6,882
Accounts Payable	10,065
B. E. Celso, Capital	96,424
B. E. Celso, Drawing	30,000
Sales	208,030

(Continued)

Sales Returns and Allowances	$ 1,740
Purchases	133,050
Purchases Returns and Allowances	4,295
Purchases Discounts	3,853
Freight In	8,350
Wages Expense	35,400
Advertising Expense	7,710
Rent Expense	12,000
Store Supplies Expense	1,835

The data needed for the adjustments on June 30 are as follows:

a–b. Merchandise inventory, June 30, $54,600.
c. Insurance expired for the year, $475.
d. Depreciation for the year, $4,380.
e. Accrued wages on June 30, $1,492.

Check Figure
Net income, $14,066

Required

1. Prepare a work sheet for the fiscal year ended June 30.
2. Prepare an income statement.
3. Prepare a statement of owner's equity. No additional investments were made during the year.
4. Prepare a balance sheet.
5. Journalize the adjusting entries.
6. Journalize the closing entries.
7. Journalize the reversing entry.

Problem Set B

For additional help, see the demonstration problem at the beginning of each chapter in your Working Papers.

1,4 

PROBLEM 12-1B A partial work sheet for McKnight Music Store is presented here. The merchandise inventory at the beginning of the fiscal period was $48,473. W. J. McKnight, the owner, withdrew $40,000 during the year.

McKnight Music Store
Work Sheet
For Year Ended December 31, 20—

Account Name	Income Statement Debit	Income Statement Credit
Sales		315,483.00
Sales Returns and Allowances	4,348.00	
Sales Discounts	1,817.00	
Interest Income		925.00
Purchases	185,272.00	
Purchases Returns and Allowances		1,547.00
Freight In	9,173.00	
Wages Expense	40,615.00	
Rent Expense	10,840.00	
Commissions Expense	8,220.00	
Supplies Expense	1,826.00	
Interest Expense	1,258.00	
Income Summary	48,473.00	48,850.00
Insurance Expense	2,624.00	
Depreciation Expense, Building	4,220.00	
Depreciation Expense, Equipment	4,500.00	
	323,186.00	366,805.00
Net Income	43,619.00	
	366,805.00	366,805.00

Required

1. Prepare an income statement.
2. Journalize the closing entries.

Check Figure
Cost of Goods Sold, $192,521

CHAPTER ASSIGNMENTS

PROBLEM 12-2B Here is the partial work sheet for Meyer Mountain Shop.

Meyer Mountain Shop
Work Sheet
For Year Ended December 31, 20—

	Balance Sheet	
Account Name	Debit	Credit
Cash	18,525.00	
Notes Receivable	4,500.00	
Accounts Receivable	22,680.00	
Merchandise Inventory	53,542.00	
Prepaid Property Taxes	1,820.00	
Prepaid Insurance	2,450.00	
Land	18,600.00	
Building	42,000.00	
Accumulated Depreciation, Building		22,500.00
Computer Equipment	4,424.00	
Accumulated Depreciation, Computer Equipment		2,250.00
Store Equipment	7,480.00	
Accumulated Depreciation, Store Equipment		5,085.00
Delivery Equipment	5,740.00	
Accumulated Depreciation, Delivery Equipment		3,225.00
Notes Payable		6,500.00
Accounts Payable		19,455.00
Mortgage Payable (current portion)		2,500.00
Mortgage Payable		54,600.00
M. E. Meyer, Capital		75,085.00
M. E. Meyer, Drawing	35,250.00	
Wages Payable		1,460.00
	217,011.00	192,660.00
Net Income		24,351.00
	217,011.00	217,011.00

Check Figure
Working capital, $73,602

Required

1. Prepare a statement of owner's equity (no additional investment).
2. Prepare a balance sheet.
3. Determine the amount of the working capital.
4. Determine the current ratio (carry to two decimal places).

PROBLEM 12-3B The following partial work sheet covers the affairs of Ketcher and Company for the year ended June 30:

Ketcher and Company
Work Sheet
For Year Ended June 30, 20—

Account Name	Income Statement Debit	Income Statement Credit	Balance Sheet Debit	Balance Sheet Credit
Cash			37,302.00	
Accounts Receivable			97,557.00	
Merchandise Inventory			117,274.00	
Prepaid Insurance			2,410.00	
Delivery Equipment			12,700.00	
Accumulated Depreciation, Delivery Equipment				6,240.00
Store Equipment			35,900.00	
Accumulated Depreciation, Store Equipment				10,480.00
Accounts Payable				77,328.00
J. Ketcher, Capital				193,810.00
J. Ketcher, Drawing			40,350.00	
Sales		532,262.00		
Purchases	397,830.00			
Purchases Returns and Allowances		8,817.00		
Purchases Discounts		6,935.00		
Freight In	23,400.00			
Salary Expense	54,700.00			
Truck Expense	9,492.00			
Supplies Expense	2,416.00			
Miscellaneous Expense	1,800.00			
Income Summary	113,202.00	117,274.00		
Salaries Payable				1,645.00
Insurance Expense	2,940.00			
Depreciation Expense, Delivery Equipment	2,800.00			
Depreciation Expense, Store Equipment	2,718.00			
	611,298.00	665,288.00	343,493.00	289,503.00
Net Income	53,990.00			53,990.00
	665,288.00	665,288.00	343,493.00	343,493.00

Required

1. Journalize the six adjusting entries.
2. Journalize the closing entries.
3. Journalize the reversing entry.

Check Figure
Reversing entry amount, $1,645

PROBLEM 12-4B The following accounts appear in the ledger of Sheldon Company on January 31, the end of this fiscal year:

Cash	$ 16,400
Accounts Receivable	15,100
Merchandise Inventory	55,500
Prepaid Insurance	3,080
Store Equipment	24,900
Accumulated Depreciation, Store Equipment	3,860
Accounts Payable	14,400
M. E. Sheldon, Capital	126,384

(Continued)

M. E. Sheldon, Drawing	$ 36,000
Sales	227,000
Sales Returns and Allowances	2,000
Purchases	172,000
Purchases Returns and Allowances	2,375
Purchases Discounts	3,567
Freight In	7,491
Wages Expense	24,800
Advertising Expense	5,912
Rent Expense	12,900
Store Supplies Expense	1,503

The data needed for adjustments on January 31 are as follows:

a–b. Merchandise inventory, January 31, $55,750.
c. Insurance expired for the year, $1,285.
d. Depreciation for the year, $5,482.
e. Accrued wages on January 31, $1,503.

Check Figure
Net loss, $1,684

Required

1. Prepare a work sheet for the fiscal year ended January 31.
2. Prepare an income statement.
3. Prepare a statement of owner's equity. No additional investments were made during the year.
4. Prepare a balance sheet.
5. Journalize the adjusting entries.
6. Journalize the closing entries.
7. Journalize the reversing entry.

Comprehensive Review Problem

You are to record transactions completed by Fabulous Furnishings during the month of February of this year. Beginning balances for the accounts listed below have been provided in your Working Papers. This company is located in Dallas. To gain practice in completing the steps in the accounting cycle, assume that the fiscal period consists of one month.

CHART OF ACCOUNTS

Assets (100–199)
111 Cash
112 Petty Cash Fund
113 Accounts Receivable
114 Merchandise Inventory
118 Prepaid Insurance
122 Equipment
123 Accumulated Depreciation, Equipment

Liabilities (200–299)
221 Accounts Payable
226 Employees' Income Tax Payable
227 FICA Tax Payable
228 State Unemployment Tax Payable
229 Federal Unemployment Tax Payable
230 Salaries Payable

Owner's Equity (300–399)
311 M. L. Langdon, Capital
312 M. L. Langdon, Drawing
313 Income Summary

Revenue (400–499)
411 Sales
412 Sales Returns and Allowances

Cost of Goods Sold (500–599)
511 Purchases
512 Purchases Returns and Allowances
513 Purchases Discounts
514 Freight In

Expenses (600–699)
611 Salary Expense
612 Payroll Tax Expense
613 Rent Expense
614 Utilities Expense
616 Supplies Expense
617 Insurance Expense
618 Depreciation Expense, Equipment
619 Miscellaneous Expense

JOURNALS
Sales Journal, page 56
Purchases Journal, page 62
Cash Receipts Journal, page 69
Cash Payments Journal, page 75
General Journal, pages 89–95

ACCOUNTS RECEIVABLE
Fashion Decor
Hotel Beritz
Jason and Waldon

ACCOUNTS PAYABLE
Brandon, Inc.
Kingston Fabrics
Magnuson Textiles
Tyson Manufacturing Company

TRANSACTIONS
The following transactions were completed during February of this year.

Feb. 1 Reversed the adjusting entry for accrued salaries, $620.

1 Sold merchandise on account to Hotel Beritz, $12,520.86, invoice no. 5221.

2 Issued Ck. No. 7216, $16,593.46, to Kingston Fabrics, in payment of its invoice no. D1739 for $16,932.10 less 2 percent discount.

5 Bought merchandise on account from Magnuson Textiles, $4,874.80, invoice no. RE275, dated February 2; terms 1/10, n/30; FOB Louisville; freight prepaid and added to the invoice, $158 (total, $5,032.80).

5 Received an electric bill and paid Countywide Power, Ck. No. 7217, $358.

6 Received check from Jason and Waldon, $10,780.51, in payment of account.

7 Issued Ck. No. 7218, $9,684.18, to Magnuson Textiles, in payment of its invoice no. RE64 for $9,782 less 1 percent discount.

9 Cash sales for February 1 through February 9, $9,745.40.

12 Recorded the payroll in the payroll register for regular semimonthly salaries for period ended February 12. Salaries: R. W. Harris, $2,840; T. L. Newkirk, $2,374. Income tax withholdings are $287 for Harris and $216 for Newkirk. Assume the following tax rates and taxable earnings limits (see the payroll register in your Working Papers for beginning cumulative earnings):

- Social Security taxable earnings, $106,800, with a rate of 6.2 percent.
- Medicare taxable earnings, all earnings, with a rate of 1.45 percent.

12 Recorded the payroll entry, crediting Salaries Payable.

12 Issued Ck. No. 7219, $2,335.74, to R. W. Harris. Issued Ck. No. 7220, $1,976.39, to T. L. Newkirk. Use two lines and debit Salaries Payable. (Verify these amounts.)

12 Recorded payroll taxes. Assume the following tax rates and taxable earnings:

- Federal unemployment taxable earnings, $7,000, with a rate of 0.8 percent.
- State unemployment taxable earnings, $7,000, with a rate of 5.4 percent.

Note: Harris's taxable earnings for unemployment amount to $1,535 and Newkirk's amount to $2,374.

12 Received a credit memo from Magnuson Textiles for defective merchandise, $692, credit memo no. 916.

14 Issued Ck. No. 7221, $2,900.80, to Mid-State Bank for monthly deposit of January employees' federal income tax withheld, $1,285, and FICA taxes, $1,615.80.

CHAPTER ASSIGNMENTS

Feb. 14 Sold merchandise on account to Jason and Waldon, $15,781.30, invoice no. 5222.

14 Issued Ck. No. 7222, $4,298.97, to Magnuson Textiles, in payment of its invoice no. RE275 less the credit memo for defective merchandise and less the discount ($41.83). *Note*: Debit Accounts Payable, $4,340.80, and credit Purchases Discounts, $41.83. Verify these amounts: $5,032.80, less $158 freight, less $692 return, less 1 percent cash discount (cash discounts can't be taken on freight). Remember to add $158 freight back to compute the cash credit.

18 Bought merchandise on account from Brandon, Inc., $21,375.20, invoice no. 164M, dated February 14; terms 2/10, n/30; FOB Miami; freight prepaid and added to the invoice, $1,242 (total, $22,617.20).

18 Cash sales for February 10 through February 18, $7,889.24.

19 Issued Ck. No. 7223 payable to Quicker Printing for invoice forms, $336 (not previously recorded). (Debit Supplies Expense.)

19 Received check from Fashion Decor, $4,830.65, in payment of account.

22 Issued Ck. No. 7224, $12,540, to Tyson Manufacturing Company, in payment of its invoice no. 9264D.

22 Sold merchandise on account to Fashion Decor, $17,435.32, invoice no. 5223.

24 Issued credit memo no. 214 to Fashion Decor, $185, for merchandise returned.

24 Bought merchandise on account from Kingston Fabrics, $16,536.90, invoice no. D1797, dated February 22; terms 2/10, n/30; FOB Dallas.

26 Recorded the payroll in the payroll register for regular semimonthly salaries for period ended February 26. Salaries: R. W. Harris, $2,840; T. L. Newkirk, $2,374. Income tax withholdings are $287 for Harris and $216 for Newkirk. *Note*: See the entry of February 12 for taxable earnings limits and tax rates. See the payroll register this payroll's beginning cumulative earnings.

26 Recorded the payroll entry, crediting Salaries Payable.

26 Issued Ck. No. 7225, $2,335.74, to R. W. Harris. Issued Ck. No. 7226, $1,976.39, to T. L. Newkirk. Use two lines and debit Salaries Payable.

26 Ck. No. 7227 voided.

26 Recorded payroll taxes. Assume the following tax rates and taxable earnings:
- Federal unemployment taxable earnings, $7,000, with a rate of 0.8 percent.
- State unemployment taxable earnings, $7,000, with a rate of 0.8 percent.

Note: Harris's taxable earnings for unemployment are zero because earnings exceeded $7,000 in the prior pay period. Newkirk's taxable earnings for unemployment amount to $46.

27 Issued Ck. No. 7228, $1,035, to JIT Freight Line for transportation charge on merchandise purchased from Kingston Fabrics.

28 Issued Ck. No. 7229, $55.60, payable to Cash to reimburse the petty cash fund. Petty cash payments consist of Supplies Expense, $30.24, and Miscellaneous Expense, $25.36.

28 Cash sales for February 19 through February 28, $8,986.60.

28 Issued Ck. No. 7230, $2,290, to Global Rental Agency for monthly rent.

28 M. L. Langdon (owner) withdrew $5,000 for personal use, Ck. No. 7231.

Required

1. Journalize and post the transactions completed during February using either a general journal or special journals or both. (Your instructor will assign you which one(s) to use.)

General Journal

a. Post daily all entries involving customer accounts to the accounts receivable ledger.

b. Post daily all entries involving creditor accounts to the accounts payable ledger.

c. Post daily the general journal entries to the general ledger.

Special Journals

a. Post daily the amounts in the Other Accounts columns of the special journals.
b. Post daily the general journal.
c. Post the totals of the special columns of the special journals at the end of the month.

2. Prepare a schedule of accounts receivable and a schedule of accounts payable.
3. Complete the work sheet for February.
   Data for the month-end adjustments are as follows:

   a–b. Merchandise inventory at February 28, $45,484.
   c. Salaries accrued at February 28, $2,084.
   d. Insurance expired during February, $210.
   e. Depreciation of equipment during February, $1,885.

4. Journalize and post the adjusting entries.
5. Prepare an income statement.
6. Prepare a statement of owner's equity. (No additional investment was made during the month.)
7. Prepare a balance sheet.
8. Journalize and post the closing entries.
9. Prepare a post-closing trial balance.

ACTIVITIES

CONSIDER AND COMMUNICATE

A music store sells new instruments. The store also sells used instruments for people who are willing to give the store part of the sales price. The sales of used instruments, called commissions, amount to about one-fourth of total sales. On the firm's classified income statement under the Revenue heading are both New Instrument Sales and Sales Commissions. Comment on this practice.

WHAT'S WRONG WITH THIS PICTURE?

What if the freight charges on a new desk for the owner were journalized and posted to the Freight In account? Would this affect the Cost of Goods Sold section? If so, how?

CRITICAL THINKING

You are an owner/bookkeeper in a country whose economy has been nearly destroyed. Goods are scarce; in fact, you have no goods to sell at the start of each day. You go out early each morning to purchase goods and haul them back to sell. At the end of the day, you have sold everything. Prepare a Cost of Goods Sold section for a day when you purchased $400 in goods. What conclusion can you draw?

A QUESTION OF ETHICS

Marty is an accountant. Sometimes printouts of financial statements have errors and are not usable. Marty doesn't like to waste anything, so he takes the unusable financial statements to his son's day care center to use for drawing paper. Explain why you think this is or is not unethical behavior.

All About You Spa

Closing Entries and Financial Statements

It is now August 31. You have journalized and posted the adjustments in the All About You Spa accounting records, and Ms. Valli wants to see financial statements for the last two months (July and August).

Why is it essential that you generate and print your income statement and statement of owner's equity *before* zeroing out or closing the temporary owner's equity accounts?

In many cases (although not required for this problem), you may wish to save a data file before closing with "BC" (before closing) included in the name so that you can go back to it later and review Income Statement and Statement of Owner's Equity reports if desired. Then save the data file with "PC" (post-closing) included in the name after generating closing entries.

Directions for Closing Entries

1. Open the file entitled ***All_About_You_Spa_Ch12.IA7***. Enter your name when prompted and click ***OK***. Select "Yes" or "No" as desired when asked if you want to open on-screen instructions and check figures. As a reminder, these instructions may be opened at any time by clicking on the ***Info.*** toolbar button.
2. Click on the ***Save As*** toolbar button. When the Save As window appears, select the folder in which you wish to save your data files (if not already selected). In the File Name box, key ***All_About_You_Ch12_Your_Name.IA7*** (for example, All_About_You_Spa_Ch12_John_Doe.IA7) to identify the file containing your work. Click on the ***Save*** button.
3. Display an income statement and a statement of owner's equity. Click on the ***Reports*** toolbar button, then in turn click on ***Income Statement*** and ***Statement of Owner's Equity*** to generate each of these financial statements. To print these reports, click on the ***Print*** button at the bottom of each report window.
4. Generate closing entries. Select ***Generate Closing Journal Entries*** from the ***Options*** menu. When the dialog box appears, click ***Yes*** to confirm that you wish the computer to generate the closing journal entries. The entries will display in a preview window. Click on the ***Post*** button to post the closing journal entries to the general journal.
5. Display the closing journal entries. Click on the ***Reports*** toolbar button. Click on ***Journals*** and ***General Journal*** to choose the report to display. Click on ***Customize Journal Report***. In the Reference drop-down list, choose "Clo. Ent." and then click the ***OK*** button to display the Closing Journal Entries report. To print the report, click on the ***Print*** button.
6. Display a post-closing trial balance. Click on the ***Reports*** toolbar button. Click on ***Ledger Reports*** and ***Trial Balance*** to choose the report to display. To print the report, click on the ***Print*** button at the bottom of the report window.
7. Display a balance sheet. Click on the ***Reports*** toolbar button, then click on ***Balance Sheet*** to generate this financial statement. To print the report, click on the ***Print*** button at the bottom of the report window.
8. Click on the ***Save*** toolbar button to save your data file.
9. Click on the ***Check*** toolbar button to check your solution against the answer key.

Generate the Balance Sheet report *after* the closing entries so that it shows the final balance of the capital account after the income statement and drawing accounts have been closed to it.

Congratulations! You have completed your work with All About You Spa.

Check Figures

3. Net income, $13,756.32
3. A. Valli, Capital (end of period), $58,640.94
5. Closing Journal Entries report total, $114,131.30
6. Post-closing trial balance total, $81,259.70
7. Balance Sheet report total assets, $81,035.06

Methods of Depreciation

A
APPENDIX

LEARNING OBJECTIVES

After you have completed this appendix, you will be able to do the following:

1. *Prepare a schedule of depreciation using the straight-line method.*
2. *Prepare a schedule of depreciation using the double-declining-balance method.*
3. *Prepare a schedule of depreciation for five-year property under the Modified Accelerated Cost Recovery System.*

As you have learned, depreciation is the the process of allocating the cost of an asset to an expense over its useful life. In this appendix, we will illustrate three methods of depreciation (straight-line, double-declining-balance, and Modified Accelerated Cost Recovery System) using the example of a delivery truck. Assume that the truck was bought at the beginning of Year 1 and at a cost of \$24,000. The truck is estimated to have a useful life of five years and a trade-in value of \$6,000 at the end of the five-year period.

STRAIGHT-LINE METHOD

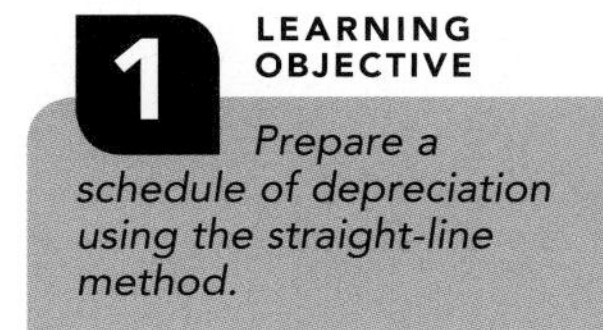
1 LEARNING OBJECTIVE
Prepare a schedule of depreciation using the straight-line method.

The straight-line method was demonstrated in Chapter 4. This method provides an equal amount of depreciation each year.

$$\text{Yearly depreciation} = \frac{\text{Cost of asset} - \text{Trade-in value}}{\text{Years of life}} = \frac{\$24{,}000 - \$6{,}000}{5 \text{ years}}$$

$$= \frac{\$18{,}000}{5 \text{ years}} = \$3{,}600 \text{ per year}$$

Year	Depreciation for the Year	Accumulated Depreciation	Book Value (Cost Less Accumulated Depreciation)
1	\$18,000 ÷ 5 years = \$ 3,600	\$ 3,600	\$24,000 − \$ 3,600 = \$20,400
2	18,000 ÷ 5 years = 3,600	\$ 3,600 + \$3,600 = 7,200	24,000 − 7,200 = 16,800
3	18,000 ÷ 5 years = 3,600	7,200 + 3,600 = 10,800	24,000 − 10,800 = 13,200
4	18,000 ÷ 5 years = 3,600	10,800 + 3,600 = 14,400	24,000 − 14,400 = 9,600
5	18,000 ÷ 5 years = 3,600	14,400 + 3,600 = 18,000	24,000 − 18,000 = 6,000
	\$18,000		

DOUBLE-DECLINING-BALANCE METHOD

LEARNING OBJECTIVE 2

Prepare a schedule of depreciation using the double-declining-balance method.

The double-declining-balance method calculates depreciation at double the straight-line rate. With an estimated useful life of five years, the straight-line rate is 1/5, or 0.20. Twice, or double, the straight-line rate is 2/5 (1/5 × 2) or 0.40. The trade-in value is not taken into account until the end of the schedule. Multiply *book value* at beginning of year by twice the straight-line rate.

Year	Depreciation for the Year	Accumulated Depreciation	Book Value (Cost Less Accumulated Depreciation)
1	$24,000 × 0.40 = $ 9,600	$ 9,600	$24,000 – $ 9,600 = $14,400
2	$14,400 × 0.40 = 5,760	$ 9,600 + $5,760 = 15,360	24,000 – 15,360 = 8,640
3	$8,640 – $6,000 = 2,640	15,360 + 2,640 = 18,000	24,000 – 18,000 = 6,000
4	0	18,000	24,000 – 18,000 = 6,000
5	0	18,000	24,000 – 18,000 = 6,000
	$18,000		

If the schedule is continued for Year 3, depreciation expense would be $3,456 ($8,640 × 0.40), accumulated depreciation would be $18,816 ($15,360 + $3,456), and book value would be $5,184 ($24,000 – $18,816). However, the book value cannot drop below the established trade-in value of $6,000. So for Year 3 an adjustment must be made limiting the depreciation for the year to $2,640, which will bring the accumulated depreciation up to $18,000. Consequently, the book value at the end of the year will be $6,000 ($24,000 cost – $18,000 accumulated depreciation) and no further depreciation will be taken.

TAX REQUIREMENT—MACRS

LEARNING OBJECTIVE 3

Prepare a schedule of depreciation for five-year property under the Modified Accelerated Cost Recovery System.

Modified Accelerated Cost Recovery System (MACRS) is the title given by the Internal Revenue Service for a variety of tax rate schedules. The term *recovery* is used because MACRS is a means of recovering or deducting the cost of an asset. Most small businesses use MACRS for financial statement reporting and tax reporting. MACRS is a combination of the declining-balance and straight-line depreciation methods. For more information, see IRS Publication 946, available at www.irs.gov.

According to MACRS, property is divided into eight classes, as follows:

3-year property—certain horses and tractor units for use over the road

5-year property—autos, light and heavy duty general purpose trucks, computers, and office equipment (copiers, etc.); also, furniture, appliances, window treatments, and carpeting in residential rental buildings

7-year property—office furniture and fixtures and any property that does not have a class life and that is not, by law, in any other class

10-year property—vessels, barges, tugs, and similar water transportation equipment

15-year property—wharves, roads, fences, and any municipal wastewater treatment plant

20-year property—certain farm buildings and municipal sewers

27.5-year residential rental property—rental houses and apartments

39-year real property—office buildings, store buildings, and warehouses

Under MACRS, trade-in value is ignored. The following table lists the depreciation rates that a business typically may use for tax purposes.

	Depreciation for Recovery Period			
Year	**3-Year**	**5-Year**	**7-Year**	**10-Year**
1	33.33%	20.00%	14.29%	10.00%
2	44.45	32.00	24.49	18.00
3	14.81	19.20	17.49	14.40
4	7.41	11.52	12.49	11.52
5		11.52	8.93	9.22
6		5.76	8.92	7.37
7			8.93	6.55
8			4.46	6.55
9				6.56
10				6.55
11				3.28

Our delivery truck qualifies as 5-year property.

Year	Depreciation for the Year	Accumulated Depreciation	Book Value (Cost Less Accumulated Depreciation)
1	\$24,000 × 0.20 = \$ 4,800.00	\$ 4,800.00	\$24,000.00 – \$ 4,800.00 = \$19,200.00
2	24,000 × 0.32 = 7,680.00	\$ 4,800.00 + \$7,680.00 = 12,480.00	24,000.00 – 12,480.00 = 11,520.00
3	24,000 × 0.192 = 4,608.00	12,480.00 + 4,608.00 = 17,088.00	24,000.00 – 17,088.00 = 6,912.00
4	24,000 × 0.1152 = 2,764.80	17,088.00 + 2.764.80 = 19,852.80	24,000.00 – 19,852.80 = 4,147.20
5	24,000 × 0.1152 = 2,764.80	19,852.80 + 2,764.80 = 22,617.60	24,000.00 – 22,617.60 = 1,382.40
6	24,000 × 0.0576 = 1,382.40	22,617.60 + 1,382.40 = 24,000.00	24,000.00 – 24,000.00 = 0
	\$24,000.00		

Problems

PROBLEM A-1 A delivery van was bought for \$18,000. The estimated life of the van is four years. The trade-in value at the end of four years is estimated to be \$2,000.

Required
Prepare a depreciation schedule for the four-year period using the straight-line method.

Check Figure
Year 1 depreciation, \$4,000

PROBLEM A-2 Use the information in Problem A-1 to solve this problem.

Required
Prepare a schedule of depreciation using the double-declining-balance method.

Check Figure
Year 2 depreciation, \$4,500

PROBLEM A-3 Use the information in Problem A-1 to solve this problem. Assume the van is 5-year property for tax purposes.

Required
Prepare a schedule of depreciation under MACRS. Round figures to the nearest whole dollar.

Check Figure
Year 3 depreciation, \$3,456

Bad Debts

LEARNING OBJECTIVES

After you have completed this appendix, you will be able to do the following:

1. *Prepare the adjusting entry for bad debts using the allowance method, based on a percentage of credit sales.*
2. *Prepare the entry to write off an account as uncollectible when the allowance method is used.*
3. *Prepare the entry to write off an account as uncollectible when the specific charge-off method is used.*

As you know, not all credit customers pay their bills. In this appendix, we turn our attention to the accounts receivable that will not be collected. There are two basic methods of providing for writing or charging off credit customers' accounts that are considered uncollectible. They are the allowance method and the specific charge-off method.

ALLOWANCE METHOD

The allowance method provides for bad debt losses in advance, by estimating them. Though there are a number of ways to estimate the amount of future losses from open accounts, we will base our estimate on a percentage of credit sales.

For example, based on its experience with bad debt losses, Miami Printing estimates that 1 percent of its revenue from services on account for the year will be uncollectible. Obviously, Miami Printing does not know which credit customers will not pay their bills. If the company were certain that a particular customer would not pay his or her bill, then it wouldn't perform services without requiring cash in advance.

Adjusting Entry and Writing Off an Account

1 LEARNING OBJECTIVE *Prepare the adjusting entry for bad debts using the allowance method, based on a percentage of credit sales.*

Miami Printing's total income from services on account for last year was $500,000. One percent of $500,000 is $5,000. On its work sheet, Miami Printing makes an adjusting entry. We show this in T account form assuming a credit balance of $170 in the Allowance for Doubtful Accounts account.

Bad Debts Expense	
+	−
Dec. 31 Adj. 5,000	

Allowance for Doubtful Accounts	
−	+
	Bal. 170
	Dec. 31 Adj. 5,000

Allowance for Doubtful Accounts is treated as a deduction from Accounts Receivable. Consequently, Allowance for Doubtful Accounts is a contra account. The adjusting entry is similar to the entry for depreciation in that there is a debit to an expense account and a credit to a contra-asset account. In T account form, assuming a balance of $7,000 in the accumulated depreciation, equipment account, the adjustment for depreciation looks like this:

Depreciation Expense, Equipment

+		−
Adj.	2,800	

Accumulated Depreciation, Equipment

−	+	
	Bal.	7,000
	Adj.	2,800

Assume that Miami Printing's Accounts Receivable balance is $90,000 and its Equipment balance is $75,000. Let's show the accounts and the adjusting entries in T account form.

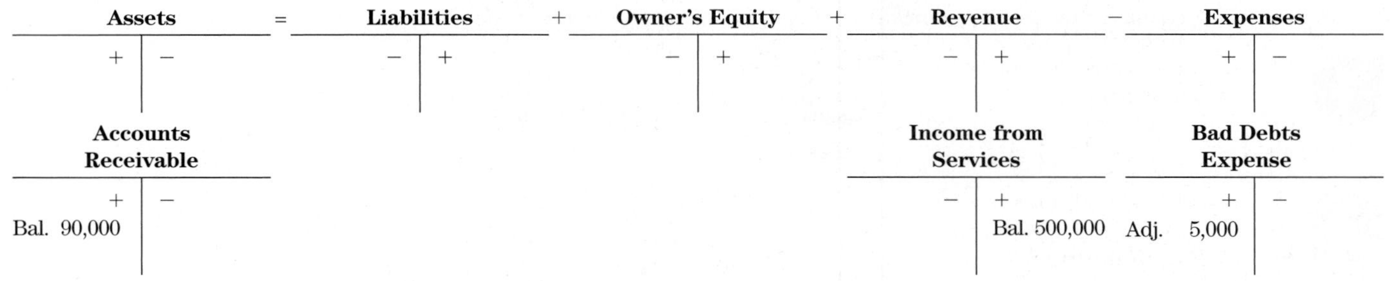

Allowance for Doubtful Accounts

−	+	
	Bal.	170
	Adj.	5,000
	Bal.	**5,170**

Depreciation Expense, Equipment

+		−
Adj.	2,800	

Equipment

+		−
Bal.	75,000	

Accumulated Depreciation, Equipment

−	+	
	Bal.	7,000
	Adj.	2,800
	Bal.	**9,800**

APPENDIX B

The Depreciation Expense, Equipment, account comes into existence as an adjusting entry at the end of the year. It is closed immediately after being brought into existence. The same thing happens to Bad Debts Expense; it comes into existence as an adjusting entry, and it is immediately closed during the closing process.

As certain credit customers' accounts are determined to be uncollectible and are written off, the losses are taken out of Allowance for Doubtful Accounts. Think of the Allowance for Doubtful Accounts as a reservoir. By means of the adjusting entry, the account is filled up at the end of the year and is gradually drained off (reduced) during the next year by write-offs of credit customer accounts. The $170 balance in Allowance for Doubtful Accounts at the end of the year (prior to the adjusting entry of $5,000) indicates that less accounts receivable were actually written off as uncollectible during the year than previously estimated. As a result, Bad Debts Expense in the period was overstated and therefore net income understated.

FYI

Companies generally have a credit balance left in the Allowance account.

Let's go on to the next year. On January 2, Miami Printing finally gives up on its attempts to collect $720 from its credit customer Ace Computer, which is included in Accounts Receivable. Miami Printing now writes off the account in the amount of $720, shown in T account form.

2 LEARNING OBJECTIVE

Prepare the entry to write off an account as uncollectible when the allowance method is used.

Accounts Receivable

	+	−	
Bal.	90,000	Jan. 2 (write-off)	720
Bal.	**89,280**		

Allowance for Doubtful Accounts

	−	+	
Jan. 2 (write-off)	720	Bal.	5,170
		Bal.	**4,450**

As you can see, the write-off has reduced both the balance of Accounts Receivable and the balance of Allowance for Doubtful Accounts but has not changed the net realizable value of accounts receivable. The general journal entry is shown below.

GENERAL JOURNAL PAGE ____

Date		Description	Post. Ref.	Debit	Credit
20—					
Jan.	2	Allowance for Doubtful Accounts		720 00	
		Accounts Receivable			720 00
		Wrote off the account of Ace			
		Computer as uncollectible.			

An Advantage and a Disadvantage of the Allowance Method

The allowance method is consistent with the accrual basis of accounting in that it matches revenues of one year with expenses of the same year. The bad-debt loss potential is provided in the same year in which the revenue is earned. The conformity with the matching principle places the allowance method in compliance with generally accepted accounting principles as recognized by the FASB. However, the allowance method cannot be used for federal income tax purposes.

SPECIFIC CHARGE-OFF METHOD

LEARNING OBJECTIVE 3

Prepare the entry to write off an account as uncollectible when the specific charge-off method is used.

Under the specific charge-off method, when a credit customer's account is determined to be uncollectible, the account is simply written off. The terms *write-off* and *charge-off* mean the same thing. No allowance account is used with the specific charge-off method because no estimate of uncollectible accounts receivable is calculated. As an illustration, Walter Company uses the specific charge-off method. On May 5, Walter Company writes off the account of Garber Construction, $1,220. For the purpose of this example, we will use a separate Accounts Receivable account for Garber Construction. T accounts pertaining to Garber's account look like this:

Accounts Receivable, Garber Construction

	+	−	
Bal.	1,220	May 5 (write-off)	1,220

Bad Debts Expense

	+	−
May 5 (write-off)	1,220	

The general journal entry is shown below.

GENERAL JOURNAL PAGE ____

Date		Description	Post. Ref.	Debit	Credit
20—					
May	5	Bad Debts Expense		1 2 2 0 00	
		Accounts Receivable			1 2 2 0 00
		Wrote off the account of			
		Garber Construction as			
		uncollectible.			

Under this method, entries will be made directly into the Bad Debts Expense account during the year. No adjusting entry is needed, and Allowance for Doubtful Accounts is not used.

Advantages of the Specific Charge-off Method

The main advantage is that the method may be used for federal income tax purposes. It is not necessary to make an adjusting entry. Also, one less account (Allowance for Doubtful Accounts) is required.

A Disadvantage of the Specific Charge-off Method

This method is not consistent with the accrual basis of accounting (recognizing revenue when it is earned and expenses when they are incurred). The method does not match up the revenues of one year with the expenses of the same year. This lack of conformity with the matching principle places the specific charge-off method in violation of generally accepted accounting principles. For example, the sale of services on account to Garber Construction could have been made two years ago. Since the account receivable will never be collected, the revenue for that year was too high (overstated). Consequently, net income is also overstated during that year. Now, two years later, $1,220 is written off as an expense. So net income for this year is too low (understated) because of the added expense.

Problems

 1,2

PROBLEM B-1 Rogan Company's total sales on account for the year amounted to $327,000. The company, which uses the allowance method, estimated bad debts at 1 percent of its credit sales.

Check Figure
Adjusting entry amount, $3,270

Required
Journalize the following selected entries:

2010

Dec.	31	Record the adjusting entry.

2011

Mar.	2	Write off the account of A. M. Billson as uncollectible, $584.
June	6	Write off the account of W. H. Gilders as uncollectible, $492.

LO 1,2

PROBLEM B-2 Hardy's Landscape Service's total revenue on account for 2010 amounted to $273,205. The company, which uses the allowance method, estimates bad debts at ½ percent of total revenue on account.

Check Figure
Adjusting entry amount, $1,366.03

Required
Journalize the following selected entries:

2010

Dec.	12	Record services performed on account for E. E. Morton, $245.
	31	Record the adjusting entry for Bad Debts Expense.
	31	Record the closing entry for Bad Debts Expense.

2011

Feb.	18	Write off the account of E. E. Morton as uncollectible, $245.

LO 5

PROBLEM B-3 Nillson's Nursery uses the specific charge-off method for recording bad debts.

Check Figure
Total amount debited to Bad Debts Expense in 2010, $677

Required
Journalize the following selected entries:

2010

Apr.	10	Write off the account of P. A. Seldon as uncollectible, $286.
July	27	Write off the account of J. M. Weller as uncollectible, $391.

Inventory Methods

LEARNING OBJECTIVES

After you have completed this appendix, you will be able to do the following:

1. *Determine the amount of the ending merchandise inventory by the weighted-average-cost method.*
2. *Determine the amount of the ending merchandise inventory by the first-in, first-out method (FIFO).*
3. *Determine the amount of the ending merchandise inventory by the last-in, first-out method (LIFO).*

To determine the dollar amount of the ending merchandise inventory, it is necessary under the periodic inventory system to take a physical count of the various items in stock and match them up with their costs. In other words, the ending inventory consists of the number of units of each type of item on hand multiplied by the cost of each unit.

If each unit were purchased at exactly the same price, the job of determining the total cost of the inventory would be simple. For example, if there are 100 units of Product A on hand, and all 100 units were bought at $15, the total cost of the ending inventory is $1,500 (100 × $15). However, over a period of time, costs of individual purchases of units may differ. Changes in costs of individual units make the different methods of inventory valuation necessary.

We will use Bruce Medical Supply, a distributor of medical supplies, to illustrate the three methods of inventory valuation. Bruce records inventory on a periodic inventory system. Bruce's ending inventory consists of 176 Standard 2.5v diagnostic sets acquired through various purchases, as follows:

Specific Purchase	Number of Units	Cost per Unit	Total Cost
Beginning inventory	34	$145	$ 4,930
First purchase	60	152	9,120
Second purchase	256	156	39,936
Third purchase	164	162	26,568
Total units available	514		$80,554

Of the 514 units available for sale, 176 units are still on hand and 338 have been sold (514 – 176).

Bruce Medical Supply may choose any one of the following three methods of recording the total cost of the 176 units in the ending inventory of medical supplies.

WEIGHTED-AVERAGE-COST METHOD

LEARNING OBJECTIVE 1

Determine the amount of the ending merchandise inventory by the weighted-average-cost method.

$$\text{Average Cost per Unit} = \frac{\text{Total Cost}}{\text{Total Units Available}} = \frac{\$80{,}554}{514} = \$156.72 \text{ (rounded)}$$

Cost of Ending Inventory (176 units) = $156.72 × 176 units = $27,582.72

FIRST-IN, FIRST-OUT METHOD

LEARNING OBJECTIVE 2

Determine the amount of the ending merchandise inventory by the first-in, first-out method (FIFO).

This method is based on the assumption that the first units of diagnostic sets purchased will be sold first. The costs of the units left will be those of the most recently purchased units. You may think of this as the way a grocery store sells milk. Because milk will sour, the oldest milk is moved to the front of the display shelf and is sold first. Consequently, the cartons of milk remaining on the shelf are the freshest milk.

Relating to our illustration of diagnostic sets:

Specific Purchase	Number of Units	Cost per Unit	Total Cost
Beginning inventory	34	$145	$ 4,930
First purchase	60	152	9,120
Second purchase	256	156	39,936
Third purchase	164	162	26,568
Total units available	514		$80,554

The cost of ending merchandise inventory or the 176 diagnostic sets on hand (most recently purchased) is as follows:

164	units (third purchase)	@ $162 each =	$26,568
12	units (second purchase)	@ $156 each =	1,872
176	units		$28,440

LAST-IN, FIRST-OUT METHOD

LEARNING OBJECTIVE 3

Determine the amount of the ending merchandise inventory by the last-in, first-out method (LIFO).

This method is based on the assumption that the last units of diagnostic sets purchased will be sold first. The costs of the units left over will be those of the earliest purchased units. You may think of this as the way a coal yard sells coal. When the coal yard sells coal to its customers, it takes coal off the top of the pile. Consequently, the tons of coal in the ending inventory consist of those first few tons at the bottom of the pile.

Relating to our illustration of diagnostic sets shown above, the cost of the ending merchandise inventory or the 176 diagnostic sets on hand (earliest purchased) is as follows:

34	units (beginning inventory)	@ $145 each =	$ 4,930
60	units (first purchase)	@ $152 each =	9,120
82	units (second purchase)	@ $156 each =	12,792
176	units		$26,842

APPENDIX C

Comparison of Three Methods		
Method	Ending Inventory (176 units)	Cost of Goods Sold (Goods Available for Sale – Ending Inventory) (338 units = 514 – 176)
Weighted-average-cost	$27,582.72	$52,971.28 ($80,554.00 – $27,582.72)
First-in, first-out	28,440.00	52,114.00 ($80,554.00 – $28,440.00)
Last-in, first-out	26,842.00	53,712.00 ($80,554.00 – $26,842.00)

Assume that the diagnostic sets were sold for $245 each.

	Weighted-Average-Cost	First-in, First-out	Last-in, First-out
Sales (338 units × $245 each)	$82,810.00	$82,810.00	$82,810.00
Less: Cost of Goods Sold	52,971.28	52,114.00	53,712.00
Gross Profit	$29,838.72	$30,696.00	$29,098.00

As you can see, the inventory method used can have an effect on the gross profit of a business. Once an inventory method is adopted by a business, the method must be consistently used. If a company wants to change its inventory method for tax purposes, the company must request permission from the Internal Revenue Service.

Problems

LO 1

PROBLEM C-1 Bean Nursery sells bark to its customers at retail. Bean buys bark from a plywood mill in bulk and transports the bark in its own trucks. Information relating to the beginning inventory and purchases of bark is as follows:

Beginning inventory	1,500 cubic yards @ $0.40 per cubic yard
First purchase	2,100 cubic yards @ $0.42 per cubic yard
Second purchase	1,400 cubic yards @ $0.46 per cubic yard
Third purchase	1,000 cubic yards @ $0.47 per cubic yard

Required

Find the cost of 1,200 cubic yards in the ending inventory by the weighted-average-cost method. Carry average cost per cubic yard to four decimals.

Check Figure
Cost of ending inventory, $519.24

LO 2

PROBLEM C-2 Use the information presented in Problem C-1 to solve this problem.

Required

Find the cost of the ending inventory by the first-in, first-out method.

Check Figure
Cost of ending inventory, $562

 3

PROBLEM C-3 Use the information presented in Problem C-1 to solve this problem.

Required

Find the cost of the ending inventory by the last-in, first-out method.

Check Figure
Cost of ending inventory, $480

The Statement of Cash Flows

LEARNING OBJECTIVES

After you have completed this appendix, you will be able to do the following:

 *Classify cash flows as Operating Activities, Investing Activities, and Financing Activities.*

 *Prepare a statement of cash flows.*

ACCOUNTING LANGUAGE

Cash equivalents *(p. D-2)*
Financing Activities *(p. D-1)*
Investing Activities *(p. D-1)*
Operating Activities *(p. D-1)*
Statement of cash flows *(p. D-1)*

The fourth major financial statement is the **statement of cash flows**. This statement explains in detail how the balance of Cash has changed between the beginning and the end of the fiscal period.

SECTIONS OF THE STATEMENT OF CASH FLOWS

1 LEARNING OBJECTIVE
Classify cash flows as Operating Activities, Investing Activities, and Financing Activities.

The statement has three main sections: **Operating Activities**, **Investing Activities**, and **Financing Activities**. Cash flows are subdivided as cash inflows and cash outflows.

Operating Activities	
Cash Inflows (Receipts):	*Cash Outflows (Payments):*
• From customers for the sales of merchandise and services	• For merchandise purchases • For operating expenses • For interest paid

Investing Activities	
Cash Inflows (Receipts):	*Cash Outflows (Payments):*
• From the sale of property and equipment • From the sale of investments or bonds in another corporation • From the collection of loan principal from borrowers	• To purchase property and equipment • To purchase investments or bonds in another corporation • For loans made to borrowers
Financing Activities	
Cash Inflows (Receipts):	*Cash Outflows (Payments):*
• From short- or long-term borrowings • From investment of cash by owner	• For repayments of loans • For payments to owner (drawings)

Cash, for purposes of the cash flow statement, includes checking and savings accounts and also **cash equivalents**. A company that has idle cash temporarily during the year may prefer to invest in short-term interest-bearing notes or money market funds. These short-term funds are considered to be cash equivalents.

FINANCIAL STATEMENTS NEEDED FOR PREPARING THE STATEMENT OF CASH FLOWS

The financial statements required for preparing the statement of cash flows consist of the income statement and the statement of owner's equity for the fiscal period, the balance sheet at the end of the fiscal period, and the balance sheet at the end of the previous fiscal period. Using the two balance sheets, we can prepare a comparative balance sheet for the two fiscal periods, showing the increases and decreases in the various accounts.

ILLUSTRATION OF THE STATEMENT OF CASH FLOWS

LEARNING OBJECTIVE 2

Prepare a statement of cash flows.

The financial statements for Perkins Company are shown here. Based on the comparative balance sheet, the first step is to record the increases and decreases in the accounts.

Perkins Company
Income Statement
For Year Ended December 31, 2011

Revenue from Sales:		
Net Sales	$645,000	
Less Cost of Goods Sold	400,000	
Gross Profit		$245,000
Operating Expenses:		
Salary Expense	$ 70,000	
Rent Expense	8,000	
Depreciation Expense, Equipment	6,000	
Supplies Expense	2,000	
Total Operating Expenses		86,000
Net Income		$159,000

Perkins Company
Statement of Owner's Equity
For Year Ended December 31, 2011

K. Perkins, Capital, January 1, 2011		$ 80,000
Investments during the Year	$ 15,000	
Net Income for the Year	159,000	
Subtotal	$174,000	
Less Withdrawals for the Year	65,000	
Increase in Capital		109,000
K. Perkins, Capital, December 31, 2011		$189,000

Perkins Company
Comparative Balance Sheet
December 31, 2011 and December 31, 2010

	2011		2010		Increase (Decrease)
Assets					
Cash		$ 12,000		$ 7,000	$ 5,000
Accounts Receivable		60,000		56,000	4,000
Merchandise Inventory		183,000		77,000	106,000
Supplies		3,000		4,000	(1,000)
Equipment	$ 72,000		$ 60,000		12,000
Less Accumulated Depreciation	(62,000)	10,000	(56,000)	4,000	(6,000)
Total Assets		$268,000		$148,000	$120,000
Liabilities					
Accounts Payable	$ 75,000		$ 63,000		$ 12,000
Salaries Payable	4,000		5,000		(1,000)
Total Liabilities		$ 79,000		$ 68,000	$ 11,000
Owner's Equity					
K. Perkins, Capital		189,000		80,000	109,000
Total Liabilities and Owner's Equity		$268,000		$148,000	$120,000

Note the $5,000 increase in Cash. First let's see how this increase comes about.

- Cash flows related to operating activities involve changes in current asset and current liability accounts.
- Cash flows related to investing activities involve changes in property and equipment (long-term asset) accounts (with the exception of Accumulated Depreciation).
- Cash flows related to financing activities involve changes in owner's equity accounts and long-term liabilities accounts.

Now let's present the statement of cash flows.

Perkins Company
Statement of Cash Flows
For Year Ended December 31, 2011

Cash Flows from (Used by) Operating Activities		
Net Income	$ 159,000	
Add (Deduct) Items to Convert Net Income		
from Accrual Basis to Cash Basis:		
Depreciation Expense	6,000	
Increase in Accounts Receivable	(4,000)	
Increase in Merchandise Inventory	(106,000)	
Decrease in Supplies	1,000	
Increase in Accounts Payable	12,000	
Decrease in Salaries Payable	(1,000)	
Net Cash Flows from Operating Activities		$ 67,000
Cash Flows from (Used by) Investing Activities		
Purchase of Equipment	$ (12,000)	
Net Cash Flows Used by Investing Activities		(12,000)
Cash Flows from (Used by) Financing Activities		
Cash Investment by Owner	$ 15,000	
Cash Withdrawals by Owner	(65,000)	
Net Cash Flows Used by Financing Activities		(50,000)
Net Increase (Decrease) in Cash		$ 5,000
Cash Balance, January 1, 2011		7,000
Cash Balance, December 31, 2011		$ 12,000

EXPLANATION OF ITEMS IN THE STATEMENT OF CASH FLOWS

Cash Flows from Operating Activities

- Net income of $159,000, from the income statement, included such items as sale of services or merchandise, miscellaneous income, and payment of expenses such as salaries or wages, utilities, and interest.
- Depreciation of $6,000 was included as an expense on the income statement, but it did not result in the payment of cash to anyone. Since depreciation expense was deducted on the income statement, we now add $6,000 back in. Depreciation expense is always an addition under Cash Flows from Operating Activities.
- Accounts Receivable increased by $4,000. Of the amount shown as Sales on the income statement, $4,000 was in the form of additional charge account balances and therefore were not cash inflows. So we deduct $4,000 from Cash Flows from Operating Activities.
- Merchandise Inventory increased by $106,000. Because the inventory increased by $106,000 during the year (more merchandise was bought than was sold), we can assume that the change resulted in a $106,000 decrease in Cash Flows from Operating Activities.
- Decrease in Supplies of $1,000 means that the company used up supplies bought in a previous fiscal period and included the entire amount of supplies used as Supplies Expense on the income statement. In other words, the $1,000 of Supplies Expense shown on the income statement did not result in a payment of cash in

the current period. For this appendix, Supplies is considered a significant asset of the business, so the ending inventory is recorded as an asset.

- Increase in Accounts Payable of $12,000 in this case means that $12,000 of the amount listed as Purchases on the income statement (not shown because we included Purchases in Cost of Goods Sold) did not result in the payment of cash. So we add $12,000 to Cash Flows from Operating Activities.
- Decrease in Salaries Payable of $1,000 means that the amount listed as Salary Expense on the income statement is $1,000 less than the amount of cash spent by the company. So we deduct $1,000 from Cash Flows from Operating Activities.

Cash Flows from Investing Activities

Equipment increased by $12,000. We would have to look at the journal entry to determine how much cash was involved. In this case, we assume that the purchase of equipment resulted in a payment of $12,000 cash. So we deduct $12,000 from Cash Flows from Investing Activities.

Cash Flows from Financing Activities

- The owner's Capital account increased by $15,000 as a result of an additional investment. We would have to look at the journal entry to determine how much cash was involved. In this case, we assume that the investment was in the form of cash. So we add $15,000 to Cash Flows from Financing Activities.
- The owner's Drawing account increased by $65,000. We would have to look at the journal entries to determine how much cash was involved. In this case, we assume that the withdrawals were in the form of cash. So we deduct $65,000 from Cash Flows from Financing Activities.

Here are some handy guidelines for preparing a statement of cash flows.

Item	Effect on Net Income
Depreciation Expense	+
Increase in Current Assets	−
Decrease in Current Assets	+
Increase in Current Liabilities	+
Decrease in Current Liabilities	−

Glossary

Cash equivalents Items included in the broad definition of cash. Included are short-term, highly liquid investments, such as money market accounts, U.S. Treasury bills, and commercial paper, having maturities with a maximum of 90 days from the date acquired. *(p. D-2)*

Financing Activities A category on the statement of cash flows *(involving inflows and outflows)* that includes borrowing money or repaying loans and additional cash investments or reductions of owner's investments through personal withdrawals. *(p. D-1)*

Investing Activities A category on the statement of cash flows *(involving inflows and outflows)* that includes the buying and selling of property and equipment and the making and collecting of loans. *(p. D-1)*

Operating Activities A category on the statement of cash flows *(involving inflows and outflows)* that includes cash receipts from customers for the sale of merchandise and services, cash payments for merchandise purchases, cash payments for operating expenses, and cash payments for interest. *(p. D-1)*

Statement of cash flows A financial statement that explains in detail how the balance of cash and cash equivalents has changed between the beginning and the end of a fiscal period. *(p. D-1)*

Problems

1,2 

PROBLEM D-1 Mahoney Company has the following financial statements for 2010 and 2011. Assume that the withdrawals were in the form of cash.

Mahoney Company
Income Statement
For Year Ended December 31, 2011

Revenue:		
Income from Services		$154,000
Expenses:		
Wages Expense	$67,000	
Rent Expense	8,000	
Depreciation Expense, Equipment	5,000	
Supplies Expense	2,000	
Total Expenses		82,000
Net Income		$ 72,000

Mahoney Company
Statement of Owner's Equity
For Year Ended December 31, 2011

A. M. Mahoney, Capital, January 1, 2011		$ 85,000
Net Income for the Year	$72,000	
Less Withdrawals for the Year	60,000	
Increase in Capital		12,000
A. M. Mahoney, Capital, December 31, 2011		$ 97,000

Mahoney Company Comparative Balance Sheet December 31, 2011 and December 31, 2010					
	2011		2010		Increase (Decrease)
Assets					
Cash		$ 18,800		$ 9,000	$ 9,800
Supplies		10,000		4,500	5,500
Equipment	$105,000		$98,000		7,000
Less Accumulated Depreciation	(18,000)	87,000	(13,000)	85,000	(5,000)
Total Assets		$115,800		$98,500	$17,300
Liabilities					
Accounts Payable	$ 13,000		$ 7,000		$ 6,000
Rent Payable	5,800		6,500		(700)
Total Liabilities		$ 18,800		$13,500	$ 5,300
Owner's Equity					
A. M. Mahoney, Capital		97,000		85,000	12,000
Total Liabilities and Owner's Equity		$115,800		$98,500	$17,300

Required

Prepare a statement of cash flows for the year ended December 31, 2011.

Check Figure
Net cash flows from operating activities, $76,800

LO 1,2

PROBLEM D-2 The financial statements for Rosario and Company follow. Assume that the additional investment and the withdrawals were in the form of cash.

Rosario and Company Income Statement For Year Ended December 31, 2011		
Revenue:		
Income from Services		$270,000
Expenses:		
Wages Expense	$161,000	
Rent Expense	18,000	
Depreciation Expense, Equipment	12,000	
Supplies Expense	4,000	
Insurance Expense	1,000	
Total Expenses		196,000
Net Income		$ 74,000

Rosario and Company
Statement of Owner's Equity
For Year Ended December 31, 2011

R. U. Rosario, Capital, January 1, 2011		$150,000
Investment during the Year	$ 2,000	
Net Income for the Year	74,000	
Subtotal	$76,000	
Less Withdrawals for the Year	70,000	
Increase in Capital		6,000
R. U. Rosario, Capital, December 31, 2011		$156,000

Rosario and Company
Comparative Balance Sheet
December 31, 2011 and December 31, 2010

	2011		2010		Increase (Decrease)
Assets					
Cash		$ 11,800		$ 2,800	$ 9,000
Accounts Receivable		32,000		26,000	6,000
Supplies		10,000		9,400	600
Prepaid Insurance		3,200		600	2,600
Equipment	$145,400		$145,400		—
Less Accumulated Depreciation	(36,000)	109,400	(24,000)	121,400	(12,000)
Total Assets		$166,400		$160,200	$ 6,200
Liabilities					
Accounts Payable		$ 10,400		$ 10,200	$ 200
Owner's Equity					
R. U. Rosario, Capital		156,000		150,000	6,000
Total Liabilities and Owner's Equity		$166,400		$160,200	$ 6,200

Check Figure
Net cash flows from operating activities, $77,000

Required

Prepare a statement of cash flows for the year ended December 31, 2011.

1,2

PROBLEM D-3 The financial statements for Zhang Company follow. Assume that the withdrawals were in the form of cash.

Zhang Company
Income Statement
For Year Ended December 31, 2011

Revenue from Sales:		
Net Sales	$1,042,000	
Less Cost of Goods Sold	853,600	
Gross Profit		$188,400
Operating Expenses:		
Salary Expense	$ 66,900	
Rent Expense	18,000	
Depreciation Expense, Equipment	10,000	
Supplies Expense	4,700	
Insurance Expense	2,800	
Total Operating Expenses		102,400
Net Income		$ 86,000

Zhang Company
Statement of Owner's Equity
For Year Ended December 31, 2011

C. L. Zhang, Capital, January 1, 2011		$196,000
Net Income for the Year	$86,000	
Less Withdrawals for the Year	90,000	
Decrease in Capital		(4,000)
C. L. Zhang, Capital, December 31, 2011		$192,000

Zhang Company
Comparative Balance Sheet
December 31, 2011 and December 31, 2010

	2011		2010		Increase (Decrease)
Assets					
Cash		$ 9,400		$ 10,900	$ (1,500)
Accounts Receivable		56,000		48,600	7,400
Merchandise Inventory		104,600		104,400	200
Supplies		8,200		6,000	2,200
Prepaid Insurance		1,600		1,800	(200)
Equipment	$156,000		$156,000		—
Less Accumulated Depreciation	(76,400)	79,600	(66,400)	89,600	(10,000)
Total Assets		$259,400		$261,300	$ (1,900)
Liabilities					
Accounts Payable	$ 62,700		$ 60,400		$ 2,300
Salaries Payable	4,700		4,900		(200)
Total Liabilities		$ 67,400		$ 65,300	$ 2,100
Owner's Equity					
C. L. Zhang, Capital		192,000		196,000	(4,000)
Total Liabilities and Owner's Equity		$259,400		$261,300	$ (1,900)

Check Figure
Net cash flows used by financing activities, $(90,000)

Required
Prepare a statement of cash flows for the year ended December 31, 2011.

Departmental Accounting

LEARNING OBJECTIVES

After you have completed this appendix, you will be able to do the following:

 *Compile a departmental income statement.*

 *Understand departmental margin.*

ACCOUNTING LANGUAGE

Apportionment of expenses *(p. E-3)*
Departmental margin *(p. E-5)*
Direct expenses *(p. E-5)*
Indirect expenses *(p. E-6)*

A company that carries on several different business activities should be divided into a number of subdivisions or departments. This enables the company's management to delegate authority to departmental managers, who are responsible for their respective departments, and to measure the profitability of each department. It is the element of profitability that we discuss in this appendix. The companies shown in this appendix are corporations. If your instructor covered only Chapters 1–12, some of the accounts, terms, and financial statements might look new to you. You should, however, be able to obtain a general sense of how a departmental income statement is compiled.

GROSS PROFIT BY DEPARTMENTS

A department's gross profit depends on its sales volume and its markup on the goods sold:

Net Sales – Cost of Goods Sold = Gross Profit

To determine the gross profit of a given department, you need a separate set of figures for the department for each element entering into the gross profit. There are two ways to obtain these figures:

1. Keep separate general ledger accounts for each item affecting gross profit, such as a Sales account for each department, a Sales Returns and Allowances account for each department, and so on. Then record the balances of these accounts on the income statement, OR

2. Keep only one general ledger account for each item affecting gross profit, and apportion the balance to the various departments. For example, maintain one Sales account and one Sales Returns and Allowances account for the company, and in addition keep a breakdown of sales and sales returns for each department. Then record the figures for each department on the income statement.

Keeping Separate Accounts by Department

Keeping separate accounts by department yields the most accurate accounting data. You need separate accounts for each department for Sales, Sales Returns and Allowances, Sales Discounts, Purchases, Purchases Returns and Allowances, Purchases Discounts, Freight In, and Merchandise Inventory. For example, Boag Hardware has five departments and uses five Sales accounts, five Sales Returns and Allowances accounts, five Sales Discounts accounts, five Merchandise Inventory accounts, and so forth. The accountant posts each total to a separate account, as indicated by the ledger account numbers.

Maintaining One General Ledger Account

When a company keeps only one general ledger account for each item involved in gross profit, the accountant has to distribute the total amount among the various departments at the end of the accounting period. To do so, the accountant has to accumulate departmental information on supplementary records. Sales, sales returns, purchases, purchases returns and allowances, purchases discounts, and so forth are recorded in a journal and are also recorded on a departmental analysis sheet. At the end of the accounting period, these analysis sheets give departmental breakdowns for each item.

Preparing a Departmental Income Statement

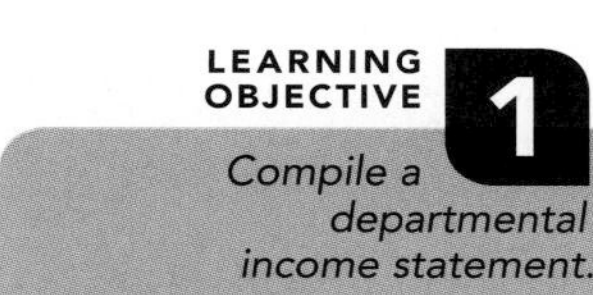

Joyce & Co., Inc., has two departments, A and B, and keeps separate accounts for each. The company keeps separate accounts for each item that enters into gross profit and apportions the operating expenses between Gross Profit and Income from Operations to Department A or Department B on a logical basis.

An outline of this process is as follows:

From Sales Through Income from Operations

Departmentalized

Revenue from Sales Less Cost of Goods Sold	} Separate departmental accounts or supplementary analysis sheets
Gross Profit Less Selling Expenses Less General Expenses	} Account balances are apportioned
Income from Operations	

Nondepartmentalized

Add Other Income
Less Other Expenses

Income Before Income Taxes
Less Income Tax Expense

Net Income

Joyce & Co., Inc.'s, income statement for the fiscal year ended December 31 appears in Figure 1 on pages E-4–E-5.

Gross Profit

Since each department keeps separate accounts for gross profit items, such as sales and cost of goods sold, these items are reported separately on the income statements.

Apportionment of Operating Expenses

Joyce & Co., Inc., combines operating expenses such as Advertising Expense and Utilities Expense. Therefore, each department must assume its share of overhead expenses. **Apportionment of expenses** is a crucial element of departmental accounting. It consists of allocating operating expenses among operating departments. You can readily identify some operating expenses as belonging to a given department. For example, if a salesperson makes sales in one department only, the accountant assigns that salesperson's salary or commission directly to that department. However, other operating expenses, such as Utilities Expense, cannot be restricted to one department and must be divided on some equitable basis. Let's look at the operating expenses of Joyce & Co. and see how they are apportioned.

Sales Salary Expense

Joyce & Co. allocates the salespersons' salaries to Department A or Department B according to the payroll register, which lists each employee by department. Department A's share is $88,625; Department B's is $52,200.

Advertising Expense

Joyce & Co. advertises only on the radio and allocates the cost of radio advertising to the two departments according to the amount of air time each department uses. In a year, Joyce & Co. buys 1,250 minutes of radio time, divided according to departments as shown here:

Advertising for Dept. A: 675 minutes or $\frac{675}{1{,}250} = \underline{\underline{54\%}}$

Advertising for Dept. B: 575 minutes or $\frac{575}{1{,}250} = \underline{\underline{46\%}}$

Dept. A's share of cost of radio advertising: 54% of $17,600 = $\underline{\underline{\$9{,}504}}$

Dept. B's share of cost of radio advertising: 46% of $17,600 = $\underline{\underline{\$8{,}096}}$

Depreciation Expense, Store Equipment

Joyce & Co. keeps a property and equipment ledger that notes the department in which each piece of equipment is located. The total year's depreciation of the equipment used in Department A is $1,840; the total year's depreciation of the equipment used in Department B is $1,460.

Rent Expense and Utilities Expense

Joyce & Co. rents 40,000 square feet of floor space and allocates the expenses of rent and utilities on the basis of floor space occupied by each department, as follows. (Yearly expense for rent is $16,400; yearly expense for utilities is $4,840.)

Dept. A occupies 25,000 square feet or $\frac{25{,}000}{40{,}000} = \underline{\underline{62.5\%}}$

Dept. B occupies 15,000 square feet or $\frac{15{,}000}{40{,}000} = \underline{\underline{37.5\%}}$

Remember

To apportion or to allocate means to divide up.

FIGURE 1
Income statement for Joyce & Co., Inc.

Joyce & Co., Inc.
Income Statement
For Year Ended December 31, 20—

	Department A		
Revenue from Sales:		$560,000	
Sales		14,200	
Less: Sales Returns and Allowances			$545,800
Net Sales			
Cost of Goods Sold:			
Merchandise Inventory, Jan. 1, 20—		$ 96,400	
Purchases	$312,115		
Less: Purchases Returns and Allowances	9,580		
Purchases Discounts	5,740		
Net Purchases	$296,795		
Add Freight In	13,005		
Delivered Cost of Purchases		309,800	
Cost of Goods Available for Sale		$406,200	
Less Merchandise Inventory, Dec. 31, 20—		110,000	
Cost of Goods Sold			296,200
Gross Profit			$249,600
Operating Expenses:			
Selling Expenses:			
Sales Salary Expense	$ 88,625		
Advertising Expense	9,504		
Depreciation Expense, Store Equipment	1,840		
Total Selling Expenses		$ 99,969	
General Expenses:			
Rent Expense	$ 10,250		
Utilities Expense	3,025		
Total General Expenses		13,275	
Total Operating Expenses			113,244
Income from Operations			$136,356
Other Income:			
Interest Income			
Other Expenses:			
Interest Expense			
Income Before Income Taxes			
Income Tax Expense			
Net Income			

Dept. A's share of rent: 62.5% of \$16,400 = \$10,250

Dept. B's share of rent: 37.5% of \$16,400 = \$6,150

Dept. A's share of utilities: 62.5% of \$4,840 = \$3,025

Dept. B's share of utilities: 37.5% of \$4,840 = \$1,815

Nonapportioned Expenses

Other Income and Expense Items, such as Interest Income, Interest Expense, and Income Tax Expense, are not apportioned among the departments. Instead, these items are only included in total on the income statement.

Department B			Total		
	$240,000			$800,000	
	5,800			20,000	
		$234,200			$780,000
	$ 82,740			$179,140	
$161,175			$473,290		
4,756			14,336		
3,274			9,014		
$153,145			$449,940		
6,715			19,720		
	159,860			469,660	
	$242,600			$648,800	
	90,000			200,000	
		152,600			448,800
		$ 81,600			$331,200
$ 52,200			$140,825		
8,096			17,600		
1,460			3,300		
	$ 61,756			$161,725	
$ 6,150			$ 16,400		
1,815			4,840		
	7,965			21,240	
		69,721			182,965
		$ 11,879			$148,235
				$ 3,624	
				2,400	1,224
					$149,459
					24,278
					$125,181

DEPARTMENTAL MARGIN

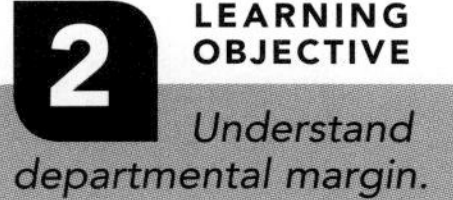
2
LEARNING OBJECTIVE
Understand departmental margin.

Departmental margin is a measurement of the contribution that a given department makes to the income of the firm—gross profit of a department minus the department's direct expenses. When a company breaks down its expense figures on a departmental-margin basis, its income statement indicates the contribution each department makes toward the overhead expenses incurred on behalf of the business as a whole. You can divide operating expenses into two classes: (1) **direct expenses**, which are incurred for the sole benefit of a given department and are under the control of the department head but not necessarily under the department being considered; and

(2) **indirect expenses**, which are incurred as overhead expenses of the entire business and thus are not under the control of one department head. For example, Sales Salary Expense is a direct expense because it is incurred purely for the benefit of one department. Officers' Salary Expense, on the other hand, is an overhead expense incurred for the business as a whole; it is not directly chargeable to one department.

Some operating expenses may be partially direct and partially indirect. For example, suppose that Rivera Company has five departments. Rivera Company's Advertising Expense consisted partially of billboard advertising, which stresses the name and location of the company, and partially of newspaper and radio advertising, which directly benefits separate departments of the company. So the part of the advertising budget that went to billboard advertising is an indirect expense, and the part that went to newspaper and radio advertising is a direct expense. When you classify an expense as direct or indirect, use this rule of thumb to identify direct expenses: **The expense would not have been incurred if the department were not in existence.** The expense must be directly related to the department.

Here is an outline of an income statement that emphasizes departmental margin:

From Sales Through Departmental Margin

Revenue from Sales Less Cost of Goods Sold	} Based on separate departmental accounts or supplementary analysis sheets
Gross Profit Less Direct Departmental Expenses	} Expenses that are directly related to the department
Departmental Margin Less Indirect Expenses	
Income from Operations Add Other Income Less Other Expenses	
Income Before Income Taxes Less Income Tax Expense	
Net Income	

The Meaning of Departmental Margin

Departmental margin is the most realistic portrayal of the profitability of a department. **If the company closes the department, the company's income before income taxes will decrease or increase by the amount of the departmental margin.** For example, assume that Rivera Company's income from operations for last year was $120,000, which is about the same as it has been for the past four years. Rivera's partial income statement, in which all operating expenses are apportioned to the various departments, shows that Department E has a loss from operations of $9,000. In an abbreviated departmental-margin format, the results of the fiscal year are shown in the following table:

Item	Department E (only)	Departments A to D (only)	Total, Departments A to E	Total, Departments A to D (with E eliminated)
Sales	$120,000	$1,480,000	$1,600,000	$1,480,000
Cost of Goods Sold	72,000	880,000	952,000	880,000
Gross Profit	$ 48,000	$ 600,000	$ 648,000	$ 600,000
Direct Departmental Expenses	32,000	336,000	368,000	336,000
Departmental Margin	$ 16,000	$ 264,000	$ 280,000	$ 264,000
Indirect Expenses	25,000	135,000	160,000	160,000
Income (Loss) from Operations	$ (9,000)	$ 129,000	$ 120,000	$ 104,000

Now suppose that Rivera Company eliminates Department E. Because Department E's departmental margin amounts to $16,000, the Income from Operations of the entire firm will decrease by $16,000 ($120,000 − $104,000 = $16,000). Another factor Rivera Company has to consider is possible "spillover sales" of Department E; that is, customers of Department E may buy things in other departments. Also, any change in income will cause a change in the amount of income taxes paid by Rivera Company. However, to simplify our analysis, we have omitted income taxes from our discussion.

The Usefulness of Departmental Margin

Income statements that show departmental margin are extremely useful when it comes to controlling a company's direct expenses, because the company can hold the head of a given department accountable for expenses directly chargeable to that department. If a department head reduces direct expenses, this action will have a favorable effect on the departmental margin.

A company that manufactures a number of different products can also use the concept of departmental margin to determine the profitability of a particular product. This is clearly one of the most important uses of departmental margin.

Management can use an income statement showing departmental margin as a tool for making future plans and analyzing future operations. Sometimes such an income statement may even lead to the elimination of a department, as we saw with Rivera Company.

Remember

Direct expenses are those incurred for the sole benefit of a department. If the department did not exist, the expense would not have been incurred.

Glossary

Apportionment of expenses Allocating operating expenses among operating departments. *(p. E-3)*

Departmental margin The contribution that a given department makes to the income of the firm—gross profit of a department minus the department's direct expenses. *(p. E-5)*

Direct expenses Expenses that benefit only one department and are controlled by the head of the department. *(p. E-5)*

Indirect expenses Overhead expenses that benefit several departments or the business as a whole and are not under the control of any one department head. *(p. E-6)*

Problems

LO 1

PROBLEM E-1 Bay Book and Software has two sales departments: Book and Software. After recording and posting all adjustments, including the adjustments for merchandise inventory, the accountant prepared the adjusted trial balance (shown on the next page) at the end of the fiscal year.

Merchandise inventories at the beginning of the year were as follows: Book Department, $53,410; Software Department, $23,839. The bases (and sources of figures) for apportioning expenses to the two departments are as follows (rounded to the nearest dollar):

- Sales Salary Expense (payroll register): Book Department, $45,559; Software Department, $35,629
- Advertising Expense (newspaper column inches): Book Department, 550 inches; Software Department, 450 inches
- Depreciation Expense, Store Equipment (property and equipment ledger): Book Department, $7,851; Software Department, $2,682

Bay Book and Software
Adjusted Trial Balance
December 31, 20—

Account Name	Debit	Credit
Cash	31,924	
Accounts Receivable	34,880	
Allowance for Doubtful Accounts		1,893
Merchandise Inventory, Book Department	53,557	
Merchandise Inventory, Software Department	24,987	
Store Supplies	532	
Store Equipment	42,332	
Accumulated Depreciation, Store Equipment		32,619
Accounts Payable		32,280
Sales Tax Payable		895
Income Tax Payable		1,166
Common Stock		74,630
Retained Earnings		18,300
Income Summary	53,410	53,557
	23,839	24,987
Sales, Book Department		317,400
Sales, Software Department		136,000
Sales Returns and Allowances, Book Department	8,161	
Sales Returns and Allowances, Software Department	551	
Purchases, Book Department	199,895	
Purchases, Software Department	96,273	
Purchases Returns and Allowances, Book Department		2,817
Purchases Returns and Allowances, Software Department		864
Purchases Discounts, Book Department		3,923
Purchases Discounts, Software Department		2,853
Freight In, Book Department	7,250	
Freight In, Software Department	2,875	
Sales Salary Expense	81,188	
Advertising Expense	10,670	
Depreciation Expense, Store Equipment	10,533	
Store Supplies Expense	404	
Miscellaneous Selling Expense	350	
Rent Expense	6,400	
Utilities Expense	2,960	
Bad Debts Expense	1,470	
Miscellaneous General Expense	520	
Interest Expense	1,208	
Income Tax Expense	8,015	
	704,184	704,184

- Store Supplies Expense (requisitions): Book Department, $205; Software Department, $199
- Miscellaneous Selling Expense (volume of gross sales): Book Department, $240; Software Department, $110
- Rent Expense and Utilities Expense (floor space): Book Department, 9,000 square feet; Software Department, 7,000 square feet
- Bad Debts Expense (volume of gross sales): Book Department, $1,029; Software Department, $441

APPENDIX E

- Miscellaneous General Expense (volume of gross sales): Book Department, $364; Software Department, $156

Required

Prepare an income statement by department to show income from operations, as well as a nondepartmentalized income statement (using the Total columns) to show net income for the entire company.

Check Figure
Net Income, $26,429

 1

PROBLEM E-2 La Hacienda, Inc., has two departments: Furniture and Lighting. La Hacienda's accountant prepares an adjusted trial balance (shown below) at the end of the fiscal year.

La Hacienda, Inc.
Adjusted Trial Balance
January 31, 20—

Account Name	Debit	Credit
Cash	5,666	
Accounts Receivable	68,890	
Allowance for Doubtful Accounts		2,620
Merchandise Inventory, Furniture Department	84,142	
Merchandise Inventory, Lighting Department	41,138	
Store Supplies	762	
Store Equipment	50,682	
Accumulated Depreciation, Store Equipment		41,810
Accounts Payable		38,680
Sales Tax Payable		1,284
Income Tax Payable		1,733
Common Stock		69,444
Retained Earnings		41,875
Income Summary	83,850	84,142
	42,630	41,138
Sales, Furniture Department		409,800
Sales, Lighting Department		273,200
Sales Returns and Allowances, Furniture Department	11,685	
Sales Returns and Allowances, Lighting Department	1,716	
Purchases, Furniture Department	251,847	
Purchases, Lighting Department	165,242	
Purchases Returns and Allowances, Furniture Department		4,618
Purchases Returns and Allowances, Lighting Department		1,792
Purchases Discounts, Furniture Department		5,496
Purchases Discounts, Lighting Department		2,964
Freight In, Furniture Department	13,255	
Freight In, Lighting Department	6,885	
Sales Salary Expense	123,220	
Advertising Expense	14,000	
Depreciation Expense, Store Equipment	13,436	
Store Supplies Expense	742	
Miscellaneous Selling Expense	680	
Rent Expense	8,000	
Utilities Expense	4,100	
Bad Debts Expense	1,800	
Miscellaneous General Expense	820	
Interest Expense	2,800	
Income Tax Expense	22,608	
	1,020,596	1,020,596

The trial balance is prepared after all adjustments, including the adjustments for merchandise inventory, have been recorded and posted.

Merchandise inventories at the beginning of the year were as follows: Furniture Department, $83,850; Lighting Department, $42,630. The bases (and sources of figures) for apportioning expenses to the two departments are as follows (rounded to the nearest dollar):

- Sales Salary Expense (payroll register): Furniture Department, $74,800; Lighting Department, $48,420
- Advertising Expense (newspaper column inches): Furniture Department, 600 inches; Lighting Department, 400 inches
- Depreciation Expense, Store Equipment (property and equipment ledger): Furniture Department, $9,616; Lighting Department, $3,820
- Store Supplies Expense (requisitions): Furniture Department, $418; Lighting Department, $324
- Miscellaneous Selling Expense (volume of gross sales): Furniture Department, $408; Lighting Department, $272
- Rent Expense and Utilities Expense (floor space): Furniture Department, 2,500 square feet; Lighting Department, 1,500 square feet
- Bad Debts Expense (volume of gross sales): Furniture Department, $1,080; Lighting Department, $720
- Miscellaneous General Expense (volume of gross sales): Furniture Department, $492; Lighting Department, $328

Check Figure
Net Income, $53,834

Required

Prepare an income statement by department to show income from operations, as well as a nondepartmentalized income statement (using the Total columns) to show net income for the entire company.

PROBLEM E-3 Moon, Inc., is considering eliminating its Drapery Department. Management does not believe that the indirect expenses and the level of operations in the other departments will be affected if the Drapery Department closes. Information from Moon's income statement for the fiscal year ended December 31, which is considered a typical year, is as follows:

	Drapery Department	All Other Departments	Total of All Departments (including Drapery)
Sales	$75,000	$563,000	$638,000
Cost of Goods Sold	49,000	395,000	444,000
Gross Profit	26,000	$168,000	$194,000
Operating Expenses	32,000	112,000	144,000
Income (Loss) from Operations	$(6,000)	$ 56,000	$ 50,000

Moon considers that $19,000 of the operating expenses of the Drapery Department are direct expenses.

Check Figure
Gross Profit, $26,000

Required

Calculate the departmental margin of the Drapery Department.

Index

A

B

C

Steps in the Closing Process

STEP 1. Close the revenue account(s) into Income Summary.

STEP 2. Close the expense accounts into Income Summary.

STEP 3. Close the Income Summary account into the Capital account, transferring the net income or net loss to the Capital account.

STEP 4. Close the Drawing account into the Capital account.

The Accounting Cycle

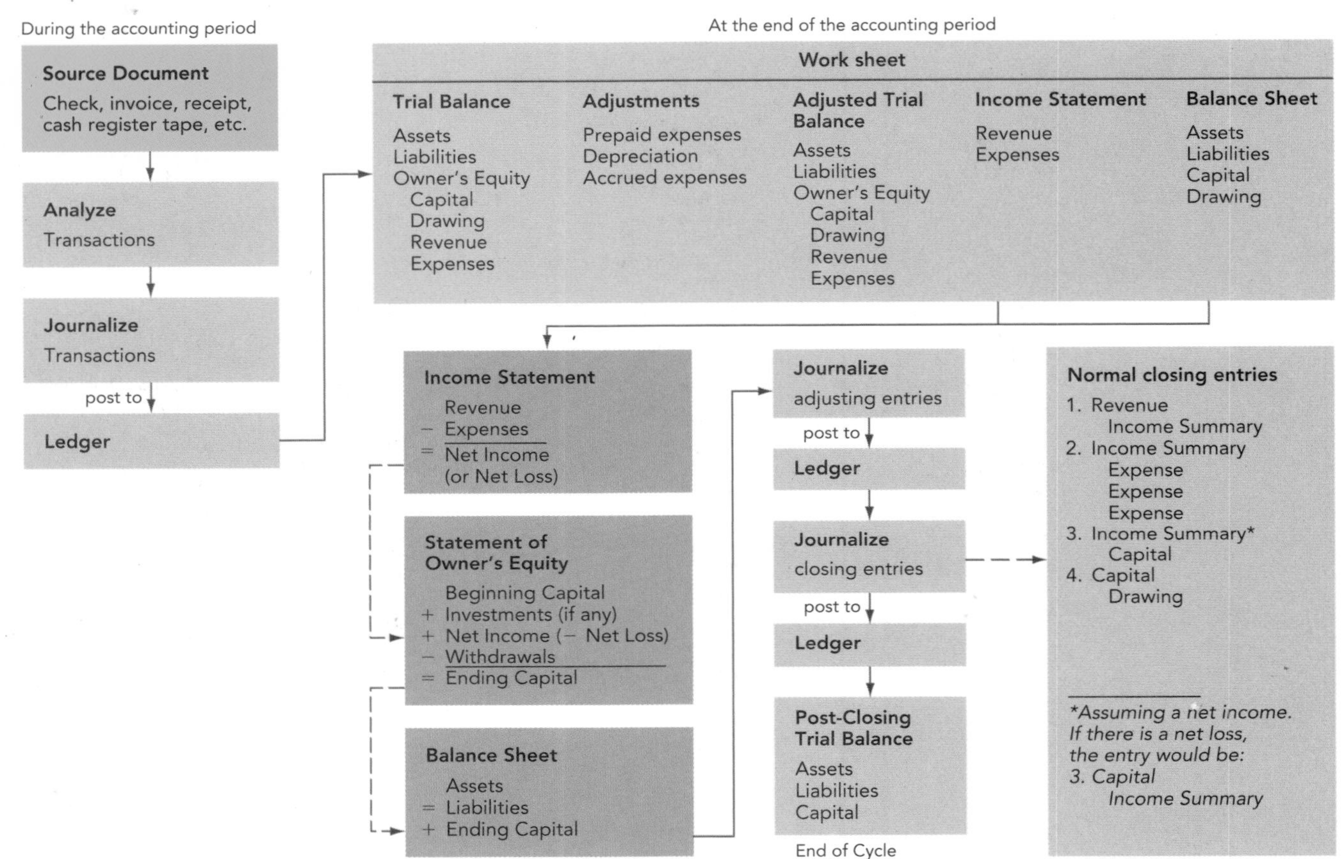